Prepared for
NEW YORK STATE ENERGY RESEARCH AND DEVELOPMENT AUTHORITY
Project Manager: David R. Wolcott
&
UNITED STATES DEPARTMENT OF ENERGY

ENVIRONMENTAL COSTS *of* ELECTRICITY

Prepared by

PACE UNIVERSITY CENTER FOR ENVIRONMENTAL LEGAL STUDIES

RICHARD L. OTTINGER • DAVID R. WOOLEY
NICHOLAS A. ROBINSON • DAVID R. HODAS • SUSAN E. BABB

Policy Analysts:
Shepard C. Buchanan: *Environmental Economics Consultant*
Paul L. Chernick • Emily Caverhill: *PLC, Inc.*
Alan Krupnick • Winston Harrington • Seri Radin: *Resources for the Future*
Uwe Fritsche: *OKO-Institut*

1990
OCEANA PUBLICATIONS, INC.
NEW YORK • LONDON • ROME

NOTICE FROM THE AUTHORS

This is a study of existing literature valuing environmental costs of electric utility operations. No original valuation research was performed. The figures cited are illustrative of those in the literature. Some of the studies reviewed were inadequately documented or substantively deficient. THE VALUATION FIGURES CITED DO NOT PURPORT TO BE DEFINITIVE COSTING ESTIMATES.

Printed in the United States of America

SUMMARY TABLE OF CONTENTS

DETAILED TABLE OF CONTENTS

INDEX OF TABLES

CHAPTER II - EXECUTIVE SUMMARY

CHAPTER III - ANALYTICAL FRAMEWORK

CHAPTER IV - FOSSIL FUEL EMISSIONS

CHAPTER V.A. - EXTERNALITY COSTS BY EMISSION GLOBAL WARMING

Chapter V.B. - EXTERNALITY COSTS BY EMISSION SULPHUR DIOXIDE (EXCLUDING ACID RAIN EFFECTS)

Chapter V.C. - EXTERNALITY COSTS BY EMISSION NITROGEN OXIDES AND OZONE (EXCLUDING ACID RAIN EFFECTS)

Chapter V.D. - EXTERNALITY COSTS BY EMISSION ACID DEPOSITON

Chapter V.E. - EXTERNALITY COSTS BY EMISSION PARTICULATES

Chapter V.F. - EXTERNALITY COSTS BY EMISSION LAND USE AND WATER POLLUTION IMPACTS

CHAPTER VI.A. - EXTERNALITY COSTS BY RESOURCE COAL PLANT OPERATIONS

CHAPTER VI.B. - EXTERNALITY COSTS BY RESOURCE OIL PLANT OPERATIONS

CHAPTER VI.C. - EXTERNALITY COSTS BY RESOURCE NATURAL GAS PLANT OPERATIONS

CHAPTER VI.D. - EXTERNALITY COSTS BY RESOURCE NUCLEAR PLANT OPERATIONS

CHAPTER VI.E. - EXTERNALITY COSTS BY RESOURCE RENEWABLE GENERATION RESOURCES

INDEX OF FIGURES

I. INTRODUCTION

I. INTRODUCTION

A. BACKGROUND

This report[1] reviews studies that quantify the externality costs[2] of environmental damage caused by electric power services. It surveys how state regulatory commissions have required or encouraged incorporation of these environmental externality costs in electric utility planning, bid evaluation and other resource selection procedures.

B. ORGANIZATION OF THE REPORT

After Chapters I, Introduction and II, Executive Summary, extensive treatment is given in Chapter III, Analytical Framework, to the often controversial questions of how environmental externality costs should be derived and measured. Various methods of measuring damages are discussed such as revealed preference, hedonic pricing, and contingent valuation. The definitions of benefits and costs are covered, as well as risk and uncertainty, utilization of market prices and published values, direct, indirect and transfer costs, discount rates (on which there is substantial difference among the experts), real value escalation, and generic vs. site-specific analyses. Allocating costs to joint projects, zero and infinite costs and non-priced effects are discussed. A separate subsection deals with health risk valuation.

Fossil fuel emissions are addressed in Chapter IV. The starting point for costing fossil fuels is the emissions from power plants using different technologies and fuels. Tables showing these emissions are given together with a brief explanation of their significance.

Chapter V describes global warming and acid rain costs as well as costs by type of emission: the various air pollutants (CO_2, SO_2, NOx, particulates) and land and water pollution.

Chapter VI treats environmental costs by resource type (coal, oil, natural gas, nuclear and waste-to-energy plants, along with renewable and demand side management resources). For fossil fuels, it is essentially a summary chapter

---

[1] This report is undertaken pursuant to NYSERDA Agreement No. 1182-EEED-AEP-89 dated October 14, 1988, approved by NYSERDA, together with the authorized subcontract of Pace with Shepard Buchanan, effective December 2, 1988. The contract was supplemented by Modification No. 1 effective August 24, 1989, adding funds for the purposes stated therein. The funding for the contract was subsequently supplemented by Subcontract No. 274391-S of September 14, 1989, between Pace and Brookhaven National Laboratory [to Prime Contract No. DE-AC02-76CH00016 between the U.S. Department of Energy (DOE) and Associated Universities, Inc. ("Brookhaven")].

[2] The term, "externality costs" is used in this report to mean what economists refer to as unpaid "values", "benefits" or "damages" because that is the term that has been adopted by state regulatory commissions. It is recognized that usages such as the above, "externality costs of environmental damages," may thus involve technical redundancy.

combining the emissions described in Chapter IV with the cost data from the literature reviewed in Chapter V.

Chapter VII evaluates existing models that could be adapted for calculating environmental externality costs, together with the elements and requirements for an ideal model.

Chapter VIII provides a spreadsheet available on computer software (Lotus 1-2-3). Typical spreadsheet runs are provided demonstrating environmental costing at a typical power plant, showing how changes in variables such as fuel changes, pollution controls, populations exposed, discount rates and other factors affect environmental costs.

Research needs are addressed, in Chapter IX. Many areas where little or no research has been done are important when determining environmental costs. These include, for example, valuing the risks of nuclear proliferation and the psychological effects of living near a nuclear plant or coal facility. There are also areas where existing studies are inadequate. The report seeks to identify, in many of the sections, the areas in which research is most needed, and to pull these findings together in Chapter IX.

State and federal actions to incorporate externality costs in utility planning and resource acquisition procedures are described in Chapter X. Section G of this Chapter gives a "State-by-State Survey of Environmental Cost Treatment." The different methodologies, used and proposed, that are available to utilities and regulatory commissions for incorporation of environmental costs are described. In-depth coverage is given to treatment by the states that have been most active in incorporating environmental costs.

Chapter X analyzes alternatives for treatment of environmental externalities. Pollution fees or taxes, subsidies and combinations of state statutory and regulatory methodologies are analyzed and discussed. Tables at the end of Section D of this chapter graphically portray the methodologies that have been used by each state.

Chapter XI provides an overall conclusion to the entire report.

Chapter XII provides a glossary of the technical terms used in the report, and in Chapter XIII provides a partially annotated bibliography of the sources reviewed is presented. There are also bibliographic references given at the end of individual chapters.

Appendix A contains sample runs on TEMIS computer software for computing environmental damages, developed by Uwe Fritsche of OKO-Institut in Darmstadt, Federal Republic of Germany.

C. REPORT RESPONSIBILITIES

Pace University's Center for Environmental Legal Studies is ultimately responsible for the contents of the report. We could not have done it without the hard work of our students who did initial research for most sections of the report. Their lack of economic or utility regulation backgrounds was compensated for by expert consultant help from PLC, Inc., Shepard Buchanan, an environmental economics consultant, and Alan Krupnick and his associates at Resources for the Future (RFF).

Pace University Law School students did the initial research and drafts of the following sections: Brian T. Henderberg and Stephen C. Hughes, the Nuclear Costing section; Michelle L. Fields and Todd Masterman, Particulates; Berkeley Johnson and David Prior, Emissions; Carol Conyers, Acid Rain & SO_2; David R. Everett, Ozone & NO_x; Dina Berger, Solar; Rosalie Rusinko, Carol Padron and Elizabeth Barbanes, Bibliography. Fred Koelsch did editorial work on a number of sections including Hydro costs; Michael E. Waller, was clean-up batter.

The following students helped in revising the report: Karl R. Rabago contributed an able LL.M. thesis on environmental impacts on aquatic ecosystems of cooling water intake systems and drafted the water impacts and fish impingement subsections of the Land and Water section. Terzah N. Lewis, Paul Schmidt, Christopher King, Melanie Fund-Pien, Kevin Desharnais, Eric Blaha and Rosemarie Bria did follow-up research and provided editorial assistance in preparation of the final report.

David R. Hodas, currently a professor at Widener University School of Law and Senior Fellow of the Pace University Center for Environmental Legal Studies, wrote and edited the global warming section as his Pace LL.M. thesis, and then helped edit the entire report. Judy Oken Hodas provided extremely valuable editorial assistance on crucial portions of the Report. Dean Anthony J. Santoro's very generous support of their work is appreciated. Mary Spinelli did the reams of retyping.

A former Pace Center staff member, Susan E. Babb, drafted the fossil fuel emissions tables, the solid waste discussion in the land and water costing section (V.F.), the initial renewable energy draft and parts of the incorporation section. She also organized and wrote much of the bibliography, and supervised the students during the first year of the study.

David R. Wooley, appointed Executive Director of the Center in January, 1990, authored the waste to energy and DSM sections, wrote large parts of the renewables, land and water, research needs and emissions portions of the report. He also edited the final draft and supervised the students during the final seven months of the study.

Richard L. Ottinger, director of the study, edited all contributions, wrote this introduction, the executive summary, except for the resource costing section, and with Babb, the incorporation section.

Shepard Buchanan, the subcontractor was designated in our NYSERDA and DOE contracts, was responsible for the Analytical Framework, Evaluation of Models, Spreadsheet and Glossary sections of the report.

Paul Chernick, President of PLC, Inc. and PLC Research Associate, Emily Caverhill, took on the enormous task of rewriting and revising all the other pollution costing sections. Without their invaluable contributions, this report would not have been produced with anything like the quality presented.

PLC wrote the coal, oil and natural gas costing sections of the report and the executive summary section on resource costing, took the lead on Research Needs, rewrote the SO_2, NO_x/Ozone, Particulates and Nuclear sections, and edited the Global Warming section.

Alan Krupnick and Winston Harrington of Resources for the Future (RFF), with Sari Radin, rewrote the Acid Rain chapter.

Uwe Fritsche of the OKO Institut, Darmstadt, FRG, contributed Appendix A, giving a sample run of his TEMIS software for calculating environmental externalities for a typical U.S. coal-fired electric utility generating plant.

Buchanan, Chernick and Krupnick; Professor Nicholas A. Robinson, Co-Director of the Pace Center and a member of the Pace Law School faculty; David Hodas; and Uwe Fritsche all participated in editing and gave helpful comments on sections for which they were not directly responsible. As mentioned, Judy Oken Hodas did the over-all editing of the report. Pace did the final editing on all contributions.

* * * * *

As can be seen from the above, this report has many authors, and it is not surprising, given such a controversial subject, they sometimes represented quite different points of view. Buchanan and Krupnick are economists, Chernick is a utility specialist, Ottinger is an energy and utility expert, Wooley an attorney and air pollution specialist and Hodas an environmental professor.

These differences are sometimes reflected in this report. Thus, with respect to discount rates, Chernick prefers a utility discount rate, Buchanan a social rate of time preference, while Ottinger, Wooley and Hodas would opt for a zero discount rate in valuing environmental externalities. Chernick is much more inclined to use control or mitigation costs than the other authors, particularly Krupnick who feels they should not be used at all. The other authors agree, however, that control costs should be used where damage values are not ascertainable. Krupnick is far more cautious about using past pollution damages to value marginal damages than are the other authors and is less willing to use studies from one part of the country or the world to extrapolate estimates of future damages generically. The acid rain section, authored by Krupnick and his associates, reflects this conservatism about both the scientific ability to predict damages and the ability to value damages, which makes this section quite different from the other sections of the report. For example, note the different treatment of material damages from acid deposition in Chapter V.D. and from SO_2 in Chapter V.B.

All the authors agree, however, that seeking to value damages is vitally important and that this report presents valuable data that can be used to make more definitive damage determinations in the future.

D. ACKNOWLEDGMENTS

We are very grateful to NYSERDA and DOE for giving us the opportunity to do this work, and particularly to our Contract Manager, David R. Wolcott, of NYSERDA for his invaluable help, advice, and patience; and Laurence B. DeWitt, formerly Director of Conservation and Renewables at NYSERDA, and now staff director in those areas for the PSC, who proposed the project and ushered it through NYSERDA. At the U.S. Department of Energy we wish to thank John Millhone, Director and John

Beldock of the Conservation and Renewables staff, as well as Jerome Lamontagne and Barbara Pierce at Brookhaven National Laboratory, all of whom are responsible for the DOE contributions to our work.

A task force review team of interested New York State agencies assembled by NYSERDA also gave us invaluable comments and assistance. The review team included David Wolcott, Gunnar Walmet, the Director of Conservation and Renewables at NYSERDA; John Smolinsky and Surry Putta of the PSC staff; John Smith and Dr. Ajay Sanghi of the N.Y. State Energy Office; and Ronald Miller and Ron Harvey of the N.Y. State Department of Environmental Conservation.

Our international contacts have been invaluable to us, most notably Olav Hohmeyer of Fraunhofer Institut, Karlsruhe, FRG, who has done the only recent comprehensive study of the environmental externality costs of electric power production, Social Costs of Energy Consumption, Springer-Verlag 1988, and Uwe Fritsche of OKO-Institut, Darmstadt, FRG. They helped us edit the document. There are a number of other German researchers who have made outstanding contributions to the costing field: consequently, we have arranged a German-American conference to be held October 23-25, 1990 in Heidelberg, FRG between the leading people in the field in both countries. The conference is sponsored by The German Marshall Fund of the United States and the Daimler-Stiftung Foundation.

The only previous comprehensive study in the United States of environmental externality costs of electricity was done by Michael Shuman and Ralph Cavanagh, A Model Conservation and Electric Power Plan for the Pacific Northwest, Appendix A, Northwest Conservation Act Coalition, Seattle, Washington, November 1982. This report draws heavily on their pioneering efforts.

Eighteen states have started to incorporate environmental externality costs in their resource planning and selection procedures since this report was commenced. The state commission staff members, too many to mention, have been of help to us.

The National Association of Regulatory Utility Commissioners (NARUC) started a major effort in environmental costing under the leadership of Commissioner Mary Lou Munts of the Wisconsin Commission who chairs NARUC's Conservation Committee and is holding a national conference on environmental costing in October 1990. Cheryl Harrington of the Maine Commission, who chairs the New England Conference of Public Utility Commissioners, hosted an environmental costing conference in January, 1990. Both have been helpful in focusing attention on the issue and by gathering the key national costing experts and key utility and regulatory commission personnel to exchange information.

Several people working on NARUC's environmental costing initiatives deserve special thanks, including Steve Brick, Vice President of MSB Associates, Madison, WI, formerly of the Wisconsin Commission staff, and Geoffrey Crandall, formerly of the Michigan Commission and NARUC staffs and now also with MSB Associates. Crandall, together with S. Cohen, J. Eto, and C. Goldman of Lawrence Berkeley Laboratory (LBL) and J. Beldock of DOE prepared a very useful state-by-state survey of state costing efforts on which we drew heavily in Chapter X.

John Beldock of DOE, who participated in the above survey, also hosted a very useful costing forum in Washington and was instrumental in obtaining DOE participation. Florentin Krause, an LBL expert in the field, was an invaluable help, as was Jonathan Koomey of LBL who did a very useful comparative analysis of environmental externality costing studies.

We also wish to thank Governor Mario Cuomo and his excellent energy and environmental staff for their support. Governor Cuomo hosted The National Governors' Association's very significant national global warming conference with Cornell University.

The New York State Energy Office also produced an excellent study of control costs of electric power plant pollutants while this report was under way and issued a State Energy Plan that includes a mandate for considering environmental externality costs in electric utility resource selection.

Our appreciation extends to many experts in this field who reviewed our work, though responsibility for the contents of the report is solely ours:

Dr. Stephen S. Bernow	Tellus, Inc.
Dr. Jan Beyea	National Audubon Society
Peter D. Blair	U.S. Office of Technology Assessment
Steve Brick	MSB Associates
Stephen H. Burrington	Conservation Law Foundation
Dr. John Beldock	U.S. Department of Energy
Ralph Cavanagh	Natural Resources Defense Council
Craig Conley	Sierra Energy Research Assessment
Rob Coppock	National Academy of Sciences
J William Currie	Battelle Pacific N.W. Laboratory
Dr. Joseph Diamond	California Energy Commission
Dieter Deumling	Environmental Forestry Consultant
Dr. Timothy P. Duane	Energy & Environment Consultant
Dan Dudek	Environmental Defense Fund
Dr. Joseph Eto	Lawrence Berkeley Laboratory
Dr. Uwe Fritsche	OKO-Institut, FRG
Susan Hedman	Center for Global Change
Robert Hill	Newcastle-on-Tyne Photovoltaic Research Center, U.K.
Dr. Olav Hohmeyer	Fraunhofer Institut, FRG
Dr. Jonathan Koomey	Lawrence Berkeley Laboratory
Charles Komanoff	Komanoff Energy Associates
Dr. Florentin Krause	Lawrence Berkeley Laboratory
Warren Liebold	Environmental Planning Lobby, NY
Dr. Frederick W. Lipfert	Brookhaven National Laboratory; National Acid Precipitation Program
G. Blair Martin	U.S. Environmental Protection Agency
Dr. Irving Mintzer	Center for Global Change
Steven A. Mitnick	Putnam, Hayes & Bartlett
Dr. Joseph Morreale	Pace University, Professor, Economics
Dr. Donald C. Peterson, Jr.	RCG/Hagler, Bailly, Inc.
Edward Radle	N.Y. Department of Environmental Conservation
Michael J. Scott	Battelle Pacific N.W. Laboratory
John Smolinsky	N.Y. Department of Public Service
Thomas J. Spitznas	Economic Consultant
Anita C. Springer	Wisconsin Public Service Commission

Allan M. Teplitzky	Chairman, N.Y. Power Pool Task Force on Environmental Externalities
Stephen Wiel	Commissioner, Nevada PSC
William Wechsler	U.S. Environmental Protection Agency
Ronald H. White	American Lung Association

In addition, the following contributed materials and references that were useful in completing the Study:

Dorene Bolze	National Audubon Society
Dr. William J. Currie	Battelle Pacific N.W. Laboratory
Kathleen J. Daniel	National Resource Council of Maine
Maarten de Kadt	Inform Inc.
Juanita M. Haydel	ICF Resources, Inc.
Kathleen B. Hogan	U.S. Environmental Planning Agency
Mary Jo Kealy	U.S. Environmental Planning Agency
John Kleefeld	Ontario Hydro
Alice Le Blanc	Environmental Defense Fund
Timothy Mount	Cornell University
Gillian Mulvale	Ontario Hydro
Dr. Ronald J. Nesse	NPAP
Dr. Roland B. Parker	Maine Public Utilities Commission
Dr. Donald C. Peterson, Jr.	RCG/Hagler, Bailly, Inc.
Surry Putta	New York Public Service Commission
Samuel Raskin, R.A.	California Energy Commission
Robert L. San Martin	Department of Energy
Rick Sellers	Solar Energy Industries Association
Walt Westman	Lawrence Berkeley Laboratory

Our thanks, too, to the Pace University Provost, Joseph Pastore, former Pace Law School Dean Janet Johnson and present Dean Steven Goldberg for their steadfast support of our work, along with Professors Jeffrey Miller, Nancy Long and William Slye, Co-Directors with Professors Ottinger and Robinson of the Pace Center. Many thanks, too, to the Pace Law School Library staff: David Williams, Library computer services; Susan Noessir, Interlibrary Loan Librarian and Ann Sauter, Government Documents Librarian. Superb secretaries helped us, with their incredible patience and much unpaid overtime, to put the documents together. They are Loretta Musial, Theresa Clark (who undertook all of the formatting and most of the word processing of the report), Gloria Pagonico, Delores Vohnout and Jennifer Chin.

II. EXECUTIVE SUMMARY

II. EXECUTIVE SUMMARY

A. INTRODUCTION

This is a report on studies that value the environmental impacts resulting from generation and conservation of electric power. The purpose is to review the literature on the methodologies used to assign monetary costs to environmental externalities[1] and to present the results of studies which have applied these methodologies. For those environmental damages for which the literature has not established a value, the report identifies the indicated ranges of adverse effects and provides a road map of issues that require research.

The report is intended to assist utilities, government regulators, legislators, policy analysts and public interest groups in estimating the costs of the environmental impacts of electricity. It should be useful, as well, to assist in valuing the environmental impacts of pollutants from other industries, for setting environmental control standards, and in establishing pollution taxes or fees.

1. Electric Utility Operations and Environmental Costs

United States electric utilities are a major contributor to global environmental damages. They cause about two-thirds of United States sulphur dioxide emissions and one-third of United States nitrogen oxide emissions, both of which cause acid deposition.[2] United States electric utilities cause one-third of the national emissions and 11% of the global emissions of carbon dioxide, the principal greenhouse gas.[3] Thus, United States electric power production has a significant environmental impact on the United States and the world, the cost of which is not included in the price of electric power.

---

[1] "Environmental externality costs," as used here, are costs to society (human health and other environmental damages) resulting from provision of electric services, which costs are not already incorporated in the price of electric services. They are those costs which occur after all government-imposed environmental standards and regulations are met. Economists generally refer to these costs simply as environmental costs or damages. Wherever the terms, "environmental costs" or environmental damages" are used, they are used to mean environmental externality costs.

[2] In 1985 electric utilities contributed 68% of the national SO_2 emissions (16,204,000tons of 23,699,000 tons nationally), and 33% of the national NO_x emissions (6,989,000tons of 21,054,000tons nationally). National Acid Precipitation Assessment Program (NAPAP), Interim Assessment, Vol. I (1987).

[3] U.S. electric utilities accounted for 33% of U.S. CO_2 emissions in 1988. CO_2 accounted for 66% of the global warming from 1880 to 1980. U.S. E.P.A., Office of Policy, Planning and Evaluation, Policy Options for Stabilizing Global Change, Draft Report to Congress, February, 1989 [Hereafter cited as EPA Report]. It has been predicted that CO_2 will account for 80% of future warming because of its long duration in the atmosphere. Lashof and Ahuja, "Relative Contributions Of Greenhouse Gas Emissions To Global Warming", 344 Nature 529, April 5, 1990. The remaining greenhouse gases, CH_4, CFC 11 & 12, N_2O, and others, accounted for the gases contributing to the balance of global warming. EPA Report, id.

Until recently, New York utilities and regulators, along with most others throughout the country, have determined the cost of electric services and selecting supply and demand side resources on a least economic cost basis, ignoring the social costs of environmental effects that occur despite compliance with federal and state environmental laws and regulations. However, government-imposed standards and regulations do not purport to eliminate pollution. Rather, they merely limit emissions to levels established by a combination of legislative compromise and regulatory feasibility.[4] The environmental impacts that remain after regulation are significant, as shown in the literature reviewed for this report. Not all emissions are regulated, and even those emissions that are regulated are not eliminated. To the extent that power producers price and select resources solely on the basis of complying with government standards, the effect is that residual environmental impacts are ignored.

To determine what is truly "least cost" in the selection of resources, one must consider the environmental externality costs imposed on society by use of those resources. To ignore these environmental costs in planning, pricing and resource selection, values them at zero.[5] Quantifying the cost in dollars of utility environmental externalities will give utilities and governmental regulators the tools by which to reflect these costs in planning and resource selection and to minimize health and other pollution damages. In practical terms, the result will be to encourage utilities to invest in less polluting resources.

The need to quantify environmental externality costs and include them in utility resource selection decisions was well expressed by F. Paul Bland, in his article, Problems of Price and Transportation: Two Proposals to Encourage Competition from Alternative Energy Resources, 10 Harv. Env. L. Rev. 345, 386 -87 (1986):

> While it is difficult to quantify externalized costs, one cannot escape setting some value. A decision not to consider external costs in itself quantifies them by setting their value at zero. This is unreasonable, given both the strong evidence that the costs are massive, and the significant difference between the externalized costs of traditional central station plants and alternative energy facilities. A crude approximation, made as exact as possible and changed over time to reflect new information, would be preferable to the manifestly unjust approximation caused by ignoring these costs.

As difficult as it is to fix exact dollar figures on environmental damages, as demonstrated by the review of the relevant studies which follows, one always has to come back to the basic tenet that "a crude approximation" of these damage costs is closer to an accurate accounting for resource costs than is a value of zero.

---

[4] The political nature of standards is well demonstrated by the political compromises now being made in Congress over the extent of additional air pollution regulation in the Clean Air Act.

[5] Full costing of electric power externalities should eliminate the value of the various government subsidies to oil, coal, gas, uranium, etc., discussed in Chapter X.D.

2. Why Utilities Should Incorporate Environmental Costs

It could be argued that consideration of environmental externalities should be addressed solely by pollution controls and taxes or fees enacted by Congress and state legislatures rather than by utility actions and regulatory commission orders affecting resource selection. Indeed, currently, environmental costs for other industries such as automobile and chemical manufacturing, smelting, etc. are addressed only through legislated controls.

National pollution fees could internalize environmental externality costs for all polluting sources, thus sending universally improved price signals to the marketplace.[6] Of course, complete regulation, eliminating all pollution that poses a threat to human health and the environment would also internalize environmental externality costs universally. Neither solution appears to be politically feasible at present, however.

In the absence of legislative internalization, utilities nevertheless will continue selecting resources which, after regulation, will still impose significant environmental costs on society. If utilities and their regulatory commissions continue to assign only traditional direct costs to these resources as a principal basis for their selection, these environmental costs still will be ignored. For a full accounting of costs in this continuing resource selection process it is important that the environmental costs be counted.

There are two principal reasons why utilities and regulatory commissions should consider environmental externalities in their resource selection processes: (1) utilities are franchised monopolies vested with a duty to serve the public interest, a responsibility that includes environmental protection[7]; and (2) foreseeable international, federal and state environmental laws and regulations are likely to impose stringent environmental controls over the thirty to forty-year life span of electric power plants, making it imprudent for utilities to invest in resources which will have to be abandoned or which will require expensive environmentally-required retrofits.[8] It is

---

[6] Another way to place pollution values in the marketplace is by setting stricter standards and allocating emission trading rights to facilitate pollution reduction at least cost. This method does not give an incentive for reducing pollution below the standards, however, as do taxes or fees. Emission trading rights have been proposed legislatively for the first time on a large scale in the Administration's submission for Clean Air Act amendments now pending before Congress; these provisions have recently been adopted by both the House of Representatives and Senate.

[7] See, for example, the New York Environmental Quality Review Act (SEQRA), New York Environmental Conservation Law, Section 8-0107 and its implementing regulation, 6 NYCRR, Part 617.9(c)(3), which require all state agencies to assess and minimize or avoid environmental impacts "to the maximum extent practicable." As noted above, however, these regulations do not eliminate substantial environmental impacts and costs to society.

[8] Tighter national controls are already in prospect. Among these are the revision being considered in Congress of the law which governs disposal of solid wastes. Resource Conservation and Recovery Act, 42 U.S.C.6901 et. seq. International negotiations for accords that would affect electric utilities are also in progress such as those before the Intergovernmental Panel on Climate Change, Working Group III, considering a 20% reduction in carbon dioxide by 2020 and 50% thereafter. If and when these national laws and treaties are enacted, however, there will still be large residual environmental impacts and damages requiring valuation.

within the traditional role of utility regulatory commissions to oversee utility public interest obligations and to prevent imprudent investments.[9]

It should be noted that when commissions require consideration of environmental externalities in utility planning and resource selection, they are not internalizing these costs in the existing rate structure, but are using them as a means of making prudent selection of new resources. Accounting for environmental externalities in utility decision making will not only help to avoid the economic costs of future environmental controls, it will also reduce the level of uncertainty associated with utility resource plans and increase system reliability.

B. SCOPE OF REPORT

This report generally reviews studies of the value of environmental damage costs (rather than control costs) resulting from electricity services. With respect to utility electricity resources, it deals only with costs from utility operations through waste disposal at the end of the fuel cycle. It reviews studies of costing methodologies and how federal and state legislatures and regulatory authorities have incorporated or might incorporate environmental costs.

The scope of this report is limited in several respects. First, from its inception and by agreement with its principal sponsor, The New York State Energy Research & Development Authority (NYSERDA), this report was limited to a review and analysis of existing studies. No original research was contemplated or undertaken.[10]

Second, the costs from the front end of the fuel cycle (mining, oil drilling, fuel processing, equipment manufacturing, transport to the site, etc.) were excluded by the contract for reasons of limited resources, not because the authors or NYSERDA believed they were insignificant.[11]

---

[9] Many utility regulatory commissions still do not require least cost planning or rule in advance on the prudence of utility investments. However, utilities in these jurisdictions are still subject to prudency reviews after they have invested, in their next rate-setting proceedings.

[10] There were additional constraints placed on the study by the NYSERDA contract. As interpreted by David R. Wolcott, the NYSERDA Contract Manager, in a letter to Richard Ottinger of June 21, 1990, the following limits were set:

"Relevant to the Statement of Work, nowhere are you asked to make recommendations. There was no intent for you to provide prescriptive guidance as a result of your analysis...However, you can certainly present various policy options in the context of 'alternative approaches.'...any advocacy positions in the report are inappropriate. The work must be rigorously objective with no unsupported opinions of the authors expressed...Conclusions must flow directly from the data presented...It is essential that conflicting points of view be fully ventilated in the report without prejudice to one side or the other in the debate...However, you do have the responsibility to acknowledge the different points of view and fully present both perspectives."

The report strives to meet this rigorous standard of objectivity.

[11] The studies reviewed indicate that the front-end costs excluded from this study are significant, however, and that they are essential to a complete assessment of the environmental costs of electricity.

Third, with few exceptions, the costs of controlling or mitigating damages were also excluded by the contract because these control and mitigation costs were felt to be generally well defined. The exceptions, where control costs are used, include global warming and certain water pollution impacts where damage costs were found to be too difficult to determine.

Fourth, non-environmental externalities of electricity were excluded.[12] It should be recognized, however, that non-environmental externalities of electricity can be large. Examples of such large externalities are the balance of payments and national security costs associated with oil imports. The most thorough study of externality costs, completed recently for the European Economic Community, seeks to value impacts on production, employment and trade balance; depletion of non-renewable resources; public subsidies and R&D expenditures; and "induced public expenditures" such as defense costs; as well as traditional environmental costs.[13] Although these non-environmental externalities are beyond the scope of this study, they merit research and consideration for incorporation into utility planning and resource selection procedures.

Other limitations of this report are attributable to the limitations of the studies reviewed. Some of the studies reviewed are inadequately documented, making it difficult to assess their accuracy. Other studies, while documented, have varying degrees of adequacy in their thoroughness and assumptions. Many of the studies are site or area-specific. Most costing work has been done in the Northwest, for example, where the population is relatively sparse and the human population composition (age, health, etc.), flora and fauna differ substantially from those found in other regions of the country. It is difficult to apply these studies to other regions of the country, particularly the highly populated and urbanized Northeast.

There are also effects for which no valuation studies could be found. These effects include the costs to taxpayers resulting from increased health care costs, infrastructure repairs to public facilities, damage to artistic and historic properties, the psychological effects of fear of cancer and nuclear power plant accidents, the risk of nuclear proliferation emanating from civilian power plants, the environmental effects of changes in the energy and nutrient cycles associated with ambient air pollution, and the environmental effects of the loss of ecosystem and habitat diversity. The links between ecological considerations and economic values are not well understood, but are important. Exposures for which there are thresholds are poorly distinguished from those for which there are no thresholds. Distinctions are also inadequate between irreversible and reversible damages.

Some damages are inappropriate for economic valuation at all and must be dealt with strictly on a political basis. For example the value of destruction of the Grand

---

12 This report deals only with the externality costs of electricity. There are other environmental externality costs associated with emissions from direct use of fuels, automobiles, manufacturing and commercial activities that are beyond the scope of this study.

13 Hohmeyer, O., Social Costs of Energy Consumption, Springer-Verlag, 1989. For a viewpoint on non-environmental externalities that may be contrary to Hohmeyer's, see Sanghi, A. The Role of Externalities in Utility Bidding Programs, New York State Energy Office, presented at the Ninth Annual Conference of the Advance Workshop in Regulation and Public Utility Economics, Rutgers University, May 31, 1990.

Canyon could not conceivably be measured in dollars; measurement of the cost of diminished tourist trade there would be a ludicrous valuation of the loss.

These limitations mean that the costing figures in this report must be used with great caution. They are a starting point for valuing damages. They do not purport to be a complete estimate of damage values. The reported figures do show that the environmental externality costs of producing electricity clearly are significant and worth pursuing through more definitive research.

C. ANALYTICAL FRAMEWORK

1. The Valuation Process

A five-step process describes the economic valuation of environmental effects.[14] The first step ascertains the pollution sources, the quantity of their harmful emissions and the constituents of the emissions that can cause environmental damages. The second step determines the dispersal of the emissions. The third step determines the populations[15] exposed to the pollutants. The fourth step determines the exposed populations' responses to the pollutant.[16] The fifth step determines the cost of that statistically expected outcome.[17] This process is demonstrated graphically in Figure 1.[18]

[14] For discussion of all the externalities methodologies, their applications, advantages and disadvantages, see Chapter III of this report and Myrick, F., The Benefits of Environmental Improvement: Theory and Practice, Johns Hopkins press, 1979; The Appropriateness and Feasibility of Various Methods of Calculating Avoided Costs, (National Regulatory Research Institute), 1982; and EPRI, Benefits of Environmental Controls: Measures, Methods and Applications, EA-6030, Project 2661-10, October 1988.

[15] "Populations" includes people (including subsets of human populations by age, health and vulnerability, of ethnic background or otherwise), flora, fauna and materials impacted by utility emissions.

[16] In the studies reviewed, this dose-response relationship was found to need the greatest amount of research.

[17] It should be noted that there are some considerations other than the five-step valuation of emissions that must be considered, including the size of populations exposed, the background pollution level, the synergistic effects of the mix of pollutants involved, and the durations of exposure.

[18] This figure was created and furnished by Donald C. Peterson, Jr., Senior Associate, RCG/Hagler, Bailly, Inc., Boulder, Colorado, a reviewer of this report.

FIGURE 1

Schematic of Overall Methodology to Assess Air Pollution Externality Costs Associated with Electricity Generation

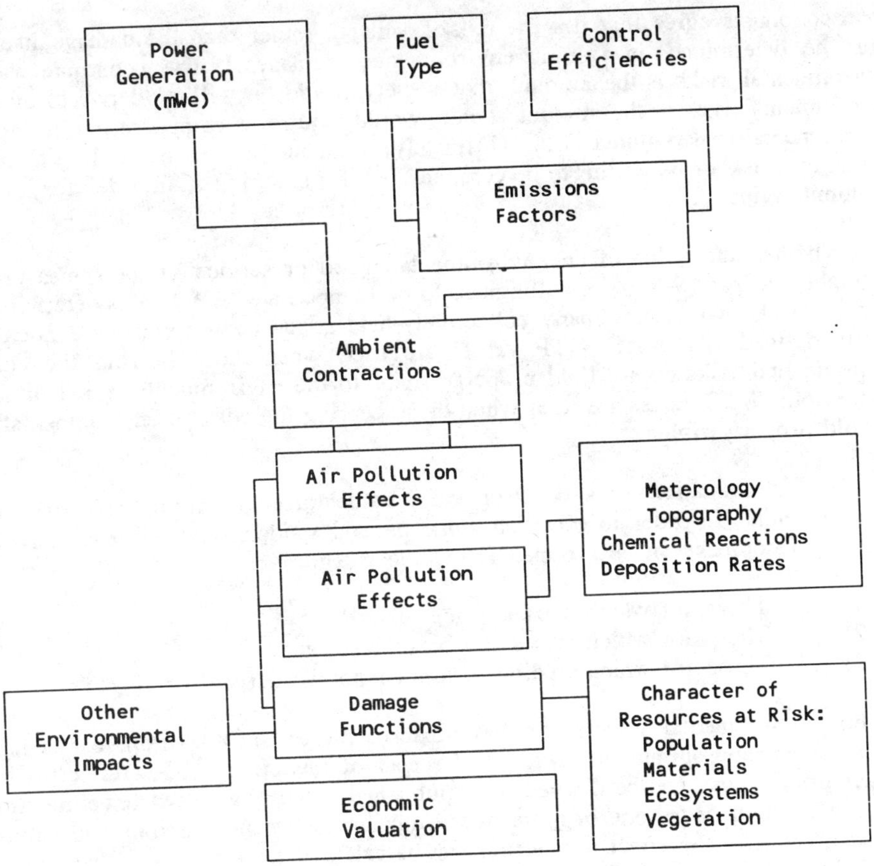

Because utility resource planning is prospective, the environmental costs and benefits of energy resources must be estimated before the environmental effects actually occur. The five-step linkages process previously described above can help predict which populations will be harmed by an emission and, within a range of certainty, what proportion of the population is expected to be harmed.

Economists agree that it is the risk of damage, rather than the damage itself, that must be determined in valuing environmental damages. The economic value of environmental risks is the amount that society would be willing to pay to avoid the environmental risk, or the amount society would require as compensation to incur the environmental risk voluntarily.[19] Ultimately, someone has to be willing to pay for assuming a risk, or be willing to be compensated for enduring it, in order for it to have economic value.

Whether the value of an environmental good or service[20] is best measured by willingness to pay (WTP) or willingness to be compensated (WTC) is determined by property rights which, for many collectively-held goods and services, are not always clearly defined. In brief, WTP values are used when those bearing the costs of environmental risks do not hold property rights to the environmental good or service in question; WTC values are used when those bearing the costs of environmental risks do hold property rights.[21]

The determination of a WTP or WTC value for an environmental risk has no single formula. In order to establish some general guidelines, environmental effects of energy resources can be grouped into three categories:

1) Those for which market prices exist;
2) Those for which prices can be derived; and,
3) Those for which credible prices cannot be derived.

For environmental effects that have market prices, such as crop losses, market prices are an appropriate measure of the cost of the effect.[22] For effects without market prices, costs can be derived from published values that may exist either for the effect in question or for one or more of the linkages between emissions and valuation, so that a value for the effect in question can be calculated. For effects that cannot be valued by reference to published values, value may be derived by one of the following valuation techniques:

---

[19] The economic value of environmental risks can be based either on the costs of avoiding the risk, the "control costs," or the costs of the damage imposed on society by the risk, the "damage costs." Which measure to use is the subject of debate, which is discussed in Chapter III D.2. and summarized in Section G., "Major Valuation Issues," below.

[20] Although the term, "environmental goods and services," is sometimes used synonymously with "natural resources," it refers more precisely to the dimensions of natural resources that have, or may have economic value.

[21] Carson, R. and P. Navarro, "Natural Resources Damage Assessment", Natural Resources Journal, Fall, 1988 at p. 815. How and why WTP and WTC may differ, how they can be measured, which measure is preferable for the good or service under consideration, and their relation to property rights are discussed in Chapter III.

[22] Minor exceptions are discussed in Chapter III.

* accounting method which bases value on an accounting of expenditures required to cope with or mitigate the damages caused by an environmental effect;

* revealed preference method (including hedonic pricing method) which is based on observed consumer behavior;

* contingent valuation method, that uses survey techniques to elicit values from a sample population; and,

* awards method, that derives damage costs from jury awards.

Some environmental risks seem to defy economic valuation. Consideration of non-priced environmental risks in the comparison of energy resource values requires subjective judgment. That judgment is no more severe or difficult than the subjective judgment required where there is no consideration of non-priced environmental risks. Regardless, non-priceable effects are not non-cost effects. The environmental risks imposed by energy resources result in costs paid by someone, regardless of whether analysts are willing or able to derive estimates of those costs.

Once values for environmental effects have been obtained, they must be adjusted for certain characteristics of risk. Risk is determined by actuarial analysis of scientific evidence, to varying degrees of reliability.[23] Actuarial values and the perceptions of risk held by members of the public who will bear the risk may be quite different. Actuarial values may mask low probability, high cost ("catastrophic") outcomes, which the public may find to be unacceptable. At the other extreme, aggregation and rounding errors may lead to false estimates of zero cost in a situation where a small amount of damage is experienced by each of a large number of people.

Public perception of risk can be affected by a number of factors, the most notable of which is the phenomenon of risk aversion[24]; that people tend to be risk averse does not mean simply that people do not like bad outcomes, but that bad outcomes are sometimes perceived as "worse" than equivalent good outcomes are perceived as "better". While actuarial values are objective measures and the appropriate measure of risk in most instances, decision makers must be aware of and account for circumstances in which people's perceived risks diverge significantly from actuarial risks.

Selection of the appropriate discount rate to apply to environmental damage costs, particularly for damage to human health, is a subject of debate, discussed in Chapter III and summarized in Section G. of this chapter under, "Major Valuation Issues."

The environmental costs of electricity products from a resource like cogeneration cannot be determined until a decision has been made as to how to allocate costs between the products. One method of allocating joint costs is by the value of the product. For example, if 60% of the total value produced is from electricity sales, then

---

23 Gregory, R., R. Mendelsohn, and P. Slovic, Review of Uncertainty and Risk in BPA-Sponsored Analyses of Energy Resources, Bonneville Power Administration, Portland, OR, November 18, 1987.

24 Kahneman, D. and A. Tversky, "Prospect Theory: An Analysis of Decision Under Risk," Econometrica, Vol. 47, No. 2, March, 1979.

60% of the costs would be allocated to electricity. Another method is to allocate by the purpose of the plant -- for example, to allocate to electricity only the costs from the incremental decision to produce electricity. Allocation by plant heat rate is another method; the heat rate for the thermal process alone is subtracted from total heat used to generate each kilowatt hour.

Treatment of other major valuations issues, such as valuation of human health risks, transboundary issues, site-specific issues, treatment of uncertainty and impacts on competition and customer rates is treated in Chapter III and summarized in Section G of this chapter under "Major Valuation Issues."

D. ENVIRONMENTAL COSTS COVERED

The report first reviews costing studies by emissions, covering air, land and water pollution. It then reviews studies assessing damages for: coal, oil and natural gas-fired power plants utilizing low and high sulphur fuels and various combustion technologies; nuclear power plants;[25] renewable supply technologies (including solar, biomass, geothermal and hydroelectric resources); waste-to-energy plants; and demand-side management resources.

The studies reviewed consider the impacts of electric power plant operations on the following populations:

* human individuals;
* flora and fauna, particularly crops, forests and fisheries;
* materials, such as buildings, structural metals, textiles and art works;
* social assets, particularly climate, recreation, and visibility.

The largest reported environmental costs electric utilities impose on society are from the risks to human health[26] and to the environment from air pollutants emitted by fossil fuel-fired generation and from the radiation risks of nuclear plant operations.

1. Externality Costs by Emission

a. Air Pollution

The principal pollutant damages covered in this report are from carbon dioxide (CO_2) emissions, the principal "greenhouse" gas; emissions (other than from acid

---

[25] Fish impingement and impaction from nuclear plant operations is treated in Land and Water Pollution Impacts, Section V.F., rather than in Nuclear Plant Operations, Chapter VI.D.

[26] The effects on human populations are primarily health effects that include increased risk of mortality and morbidity, including acute effects, exacerbation of chronic illness and increased risk of developing chronic disease.

deposition) of sulphur dioxide (SO_2), nitrogen oxides (NO_x) and tropospheric ozone[27]; acid deposition; and particulate pollution.[28]

Carbon Dioxide (CO_2) emissions from electric utility operations are caused principally by burning fossil fuels and from the nuclear fuel cycle.[29] The possibility of global climate change is increasingly recognized as a major environmental problem. To date, the predicted agricultural losses, rising sea levels and resulting coastline inundation, etc., from CO_2-caused global warming are too uncertain for their damage costs to be measured. This report uses control costs, primarily tree planting costs, as a proxy for greenhouse damage costs since no adequate CO_2 damage studies could be found.[30]

Sulphur dioxide (SO_2) is a gas with effects in its own right, apart from its role as a precursor of acid aerosols that result in acid deposition. This report discusses direct effects of SO_2 separately from its indirect acid deposition effects.[31] SO_2 and its transformation products, sulfates (discussed primarily in the Particulates section, V.E.), are found by the studies reviewed to cause significant environmental effects, particularly on human health.

NO_x and Ozone are major electric power plant pollutants.[32] Ozone pollution has been found by the studies reviewed to cause damage to human health, agriculture, to other species of flora and fauna and to structural and artistic materials.[33] The links between ambient ozone and a variety of health and other environmental effects are among the most studied and best understood of all pollutants. However, the studies nearly always view hydrocarbons,[34] rather than NO_x, as the beginning of the causal chain. The literature is sparse on how to allocate an appropriate proportion of the damages to NO_x emissions.

Acid deposition is found by the studies reviewed to cause damage to water quality, fish, wildlife, forests and materials, and it may also cause damage to human health. These deleterious effects are being experienced in many places throughout the country and the world. The report summarizes and evaluates the few published acid rain

---

27 Tropospheric ozone results from complex interactions between NO_x, carbon monoxide, oxygen and volatile organic compounds in the presence of sunlight.

28 Sulphate particulates that are derived from SO_2 emissions are the primary impacts described.

29 See infra, note 39.

30 Chapter V.A. The possibility of using energy efficiency and low-polluting supply costs are also discussed as alternative proxies.

31 Chapter V.B.

32 They are discussed in Chapter V.C.

33 The harmful ozone discussed here is ground level, tropospheric ozone. Stratospheric ozone is beneficial, protecting the earth from harmful ultra-violet rays.

34 Utilities account for only a small fraction of total hydrocarbon emissions.

damage-costing studies available, but concludes that they are too flawed to use as generic cost assessments for the incremental damage effects of utility emissions.[35]

Particulates can be either solid particles or liquid droplets, ranging in diameter from 1 micron to 100 microns or more. The smallest, including acid aerosols, are said to be responsible for health effects because they can penetrate deep into the lung. They are also the primary cause of visibility impairment due to regional haze conditions. The most serious damage is said to be caused by sulfates emanating from SO_2 emissions. The coarser particulates have been linked to soiling. Particulate pollution has also been linked to serious health and visibility effects in urban areas such as the Los Angeles Basin and London, England. Particulate pollution cost studies are evaluated.[36]

Many air pollutants have a synergistic environmental effect, inflicting damage greater than the sum of their separate damages. Synergistic effects are incompletely understood, and no studies valuing their effects are available.

b. Water Pollution & Land Use

In addition to air pollution and radiation damages, the studies reviewed indicate that electric power generation affects on water quality and land use.[37] While these reported effects are generally smaller than the effects of air pollution and radiation damages, they nonetheless merit consideration.

i. Water Pollution

Fossil fuel generating plants have environmental effects on water quality through thermal discharges of their cooling systems and, if their wastes are disposed of in landfills, through leachate contamination of ground water. Nuclear generating plants also have thermal discharge impacts on water ecology. Both may cause fish impingement and entrainment through water intake into their cooling systems. Hydroelectric generating stations cause major water impacts both from damming of reservoirs and releasing of water through the spillways. The hydroelectric studies, while not giving reliable generic costs, do indicate the range and severity of externality costs.

---

[35] See Chapter V.D.

[36] See Chapter V.E.

[37] Electromagnetic field damage has also been identified as potentially damaging to the environment but no studies were found valuing it.

ii. Land Use

All electric generating plants affect land values by occupying land; sometimes contaminating it with pollutants and creating pubic fear of contamination and, in the case of coal plants, by disposal of combustion wastes. Nuclear facilities have unique radioactive waste disposal problems which are dealt with in Nuclear Plant Operations, Chapter VI.D. For solar and wind generating stations, land impacts constitute a major portion of their low environmental costs. Hydroelectric generating stations have major land impacts primarily through upstream flooding that often inundates large amounts of valuable land, but the costs are too site-specific to derive generic values. No literature was found that establishes a value for land and water effects. Land and water damages are discussed in Chapter V.F.

2. Externality Costs by Resource

a. Fossil Fuel Plant Damages

The damages from coal, oil and natural gas-fired plants are summarized in tables in Chapter VI.A.- C. reproduced in Section E below. These tables combine the fossil fuel plant emissions set forth in Chapter IV with the fossil fuel pollutant damage costs reviewed in Chapter V. Coal-fired generation damages for high and low sulphur coals and for a variety of commonly used and experimental combustion technologies are included.

b. Nuclear Power Damages

Environmental externality costs from nuclear power plants arise from routine radiation emissions from plant operations, from the risk of catastrophic accidents such as occurred at Chernobyl and Three Mile Island, and from disposal of mill tailings and of high and low level nuclear waste.[38] Nuclear plant cooling water systems can cause damage to fish populations. The nuclear fuel cycle causes carbon dioxide emissions during uranium mining, fuel enrichment, fabrication and power plant construction. These emissions, currently are a small fraction of CO_2 emissions from fossil fuel plants, but appear to exceed CO_2 emissions from renewables.[39] All of these impacts

---

[38] Considerable uninternalized damages are reported from the front-end of the nuclear fuel cycle, excluded from this report, including uranium mining, milling, fuel processing and transport to the plant site, as well as the costs of importing uranium.

[39] Meridian Corporation, Energy System Emissions and Material Requirements, prepared for the Deputy Assistant Secretary for Renewable Energy, U.S. DOE, Washington, DC, February, 1989 (showing nuclear CO_2 emissions at 8.590 tons/GWh). One recent report, however, asserts that nuclear fuel cycle CO_2 emissions could become comparable to CO_2 emissions from fossil fuel plants if nuclear plant construction were greatly accelerated.Hill, R., The Impact of Energy on Environment and Development, IVth Nobel Prizewinners Meeting, December 1989, Man - Environment and Development - Towards a Global Approach, prepared for the Nova Spes Meeting Proceedings, February 1990. This is a peer-reviewed paper citing "Proof of Evidence to Public Enquiry on Proposed Nuclear Power Station, Hinkley Point C", Aspects of the Green House Effect, Nigel Mortimer, FoEG, HM Stationery Office, 1989.

are reported to impose significant costs on society that are largely unaccounted for under current regulation.[40]

c. Renewable Generation Resource Plant Damages

Renewable energy technologies reviewed in this report include photovoltaics, solar-thermal, wind, geothermal, hydropower and biomass. With the exception of hydropower and geothermal, the studies identify externality costs. The costs are low compared to fossil and nuclear power plant costs. Renewable energy technology externalities are discussed in Chapter VI.E.

Photovoltaic damages are found to be primarily caused by toxic materials that may be used to manufacture solar cells (e.g., gallium arsenide and cadmium),[41] and through disposal of obsolete systems using these materials. Currently, however, most cells are manufactured from silicone which has much lower risks.[42] Dispersed photovoltaics would avoid the considerable line losses that occur in transmission[43] as well as the environmental costs of fossil emissions and nuclear plant risks. Photovoltaic and solar-thermal technologies are found to require substantial amounts of land and, for the latter, water.

Wind energy externalities are found to derive primarily from noise pollution. Geothermal energy is found to have noise impacts and to emit various forms of air pollutants, but the overall environmental impacts are small.

For hydroelectric power, the literature does not reveal a generally applicable externality value. The externalities of hydropower can, depending on site conditions, be severe on fish, wildlife, water quality and affected ecological systems. Hydroelectric damages are found to be caused by flooding of land upstream of dams, disturbance of

---

Hill says at p. 14: "Over the lifetime of a typical 1 GW PWR, about 6.7 Mt of CO_2 are produced during fuel enrichment and fabrication, 0.69 Mt during uranium mining and 0.84 Mt during power station construction. The high concentration uranium ores mined at present are quite limited and the CO_2 emissions from nuclear power rise considerably as lower concentration ore grades need to be used, as shown in Figure 13. A programme of replacement of coal-fired power stations by nuclear power stations would use up the higher grade ores within 30 years or so, after which nuclear stations would emit CO_2 at the same or greater rates than coal-fired stations."

Among the disputed assumptions in this report are whether it is proper to assume that fossil fuel plants would continue to supply the energy for uranium mining and processing, whether alternative ore processing methods will emerge that require less energy, and how long reserves of high grade ore will sustain expansion of nuclear power generation.

[40] Nuclear costs are discussed in Chapter VI.D.

[41] While these are front-end costs excluded from this report, the impacts are briefly discussed.

[42] Hohmeyer, O., Social Costs of Energy Consumption, Springer-Verlag, 1988, at pp. 54, 55; Kolb, P., Use of GeH4 and Germanium Fluoride in Amorphous Silicone Photovoltaic Manufacturing, Brookhaven National Laboratory, 1989, at pp. 261-269.

[43] A new EPRI study indicates large line losses for peak (12.9%), intermediate (12%) and base load (6.1%) transmission. Strategic Assessment of Storage Plants, Economic Studies, EPRI GS-6646, January, 1990.

water ecology below dams and damages to fish, particularly through blocking migration of spawning stock.

Biomass energy facilities emit a variety of conventional air pollutants, and may have adverse land use impacts.

Costing studies were found only for the direct solar technologies, hydro, wind and wood used for power generation. For the other renewable energy technologies, the report reviews studies describing the range and impacts of environmental damages.

d. Waste-to-Energy Plant Damages

Waste-to-energy plants (commonly referred to as incinerators or resource recovery plants) reportedly have significant environmental impacts. They are found to emit conventional and toxic air pollutants at a rate per kWh that generally exceed emissions from New Source Performance Standard (NSPS) coal-fired power plants. Incinerator ash is found to have larger concentrations of soluble heavy metals than combustion waste from coal-fired power plants. These externality costs present allocation problems between the waste disposal and energy production functions of the plants.

Although additional research is needed to arrive at reliable social cost figures, the studies indicate that waste-to-energy plants have externality values similar to or greater than coal-fired plants meeting NSPS standards.

e. Demand Side Management Damages

Demand side management resources are also found to have few and insignificant environmental impacts, although no studies valuing those impacts were found. Weatherization may effect indoor air quality, although the literature indicates that economic mitigation measures are available. Some weatherization materials and efficient light bulbs may have potential impacts, again generally subject to low cost prevention or remediation.

Load-shifting measures may have a significant impact if they involve shifting the load from gas-fired peaking turbines to base-load coal or oil plants. Demand side management impacts are discussed in Chapter VI.G.

E. SUMMARY OF COST ESTIMATES FROM REPORTS REVIEWED

The externalities from electric power supply options, expressed in \$/kWh,[44] depend on two factors: 1) the amounts and types of externalities from each option, which are specific to the resource type or to the plant; and 2) the value of avoiding each externality, which must be consistent across all options. In this report, the value

---

[44] All costs reported are converted into 1989 dollars unless otherwise specified. Tables 1, 2 & 3, referred to in this section, are included at the end of the section.

of avoiding most externalities has been estimated by reviewing studies that estimate the direct costs of externalities. The uncertainties of the environmental externality values in the studies reviewed fully are discussed in the body of the report.

1. Power Plants Using Fossil Fuels

To evaluate the externalities from fossil fuel-fired plants, air emissions data have been provided in Chapter IV. Pollutant-specific studies of the environmental costs of fossil plant emissions are reviewed in Chapter V. Chapter VI (A.- C.) combines this information in tables providing "starting point" values for the environmental externality costs of coal, oil and natural gas-fired plants, using various technologies and sulphur-content of fuels.

"Starting point" values, as used in this report, are those that seem to most reasonably represent the range of values in the studies reviewed, considering the locations at which the studies were performed, their documentation and thoroughness. The term, "starting point," is used because the figures do not pretend to be cost estimates -- too many relevant costs were excluded from this study and the studies reviewed are often of too uneven quality and documentation -- but the "starting point" figures do give the order-of-magnitude of the studies reviewed and they should provide a good starting point for further research.

Emissions from electric power plants are generally available on a plant specific basis. However, it is difficult to estimate a "typical"set of emissions for any resource type. Emissions depend on several factors other than simply the plant type, including: the age and type of the plant; fuel type, grade and sulfur content; installed emissions control technology; plant operations, including heat rate, combustion temperature, and steam or limestone injection. Finally, the estimate of emissions per unit of energy output can be further complicated by the allocation of emissions to joint products, such as steam and electricity. In the examples presented, all of the externalities have been allocated to electricity output.[45]

In Chapter VI, Sections A.- C. the externality values are estimated for three coal-fired technologies, two oil-fired technologies with three different sulfur content assumptions, and two natural gas-fired technologies with differing control equipment. These examples are illustrative of the relative externalities of different fossil-fired resource options, both existing and new, but are not meant to represent average externalities of these technologies.

The reports reviewed estimate the following "starting point" values, in dollars per pound of emissions: \$2.03/lb SO_2, influenced primarily by the estimated health effects; \$0.82/lb NO_x, also dominated by health effects; and \$1.19/lb particulates, based primarily on visibilityeffects (\$0.83/lb.), with a strong contribution from health effects

---

[45] Emissions data for SO_2, NO_x, Particulates, CO_2, air toxics and radionuclides are provided in Chapter IV.

($0.36/lb.).[46] The value of reducing CO_2 emissions was estimated to be 2.5 cents/lb carbon (or 0.68 cents/lb CO_2) using a mitigation cost estimate for tree planting from the middle of the range found in the studies described in Chapter V A. These ranges vary from $17.08/T of carbon to $80/T, depending on fixation rates, discount rates and other assumptions.

For coal-fired facilities, dollar per pound figures are converted into a cent per kilowatt hour cost. See Table 1. No pollution control equipment is used for any of the example plants for SO_2, NO_x or CO_2. This assumption applies for many older coal-fired boilers in most of the country, and it provides a base-line for comparing plants with control technologies. The absence of control could also apply to newer facilities built in the 1970's because they may be able to meet the standards by controlling emissions through improved operating procedures.[47] For particulates, some pollution control equipment (e.g. a bag-house) is assumed to be installed on each plant. The "starting point" externalities from the older coal-fired boiler burning 1.2% sulfur coal are on the order of 5.7 cents/kWh generated, or 6.7 cents/kWh delivered. For an Atmospheric Fluidized Bed Combustion (AFBC) plant with the same heat rate and burning 1.1% sulfur coal, these externalities are on the order of 2.8 cents/kWh (generated). For an Integrated Gas Combined Cycle (IGCC) plant with the same heat rate and sulfur content of 0.45% sulfur these externalities are on the order of 2.5 cents/kWh (generated).

The results for oil-fired facilities are shown in, Table 2. Again, and for the same reasons as for coal-fired plants, no pollution control equipment is used on any of the example plants for SO_2, NO_x or CO_2. This is typical for many older residual oil-fired boilers, and controls are not generally necessary for a distillate oil-fired combustion turbine to meet NSPS standards. The SO_2 and particulate emissions are strongly dependent on the sulfur content of the oil. Table 2 shows "starting point" estimates of the externalities from two different oil-fired technologies: boilers burning residual oil with three different sulfur contents and a combustion turbine burning distillate oil. The "starting point" externalities from a residual oil-fired boiler burning 0.5% sulfur oil are about 2.7 cents/kWh (generated). For the same boiler burning 1% sulfur oil these externalities are 3.8 cents/kWh (generated), and for the same boiler burning 2.2% sulfur oil these externalities are 6.7 cents/kWh (generated). The "starting point" externalities of a combustion turbine burning distillate oil, and having lower efficiency than boilers, are on the order of 2.5 cents/kWh (generated).

For natural gas-fired facilities, the results are shown in, Table 3. No special NO_x-control equipment is assumed to be used on the gas-fired boiler or the combined cycle unit. However, selective catalytic reduction (SCR) and steam water injection (SWI) are applied on the BACT unit, which is a combined cycle unit fitted with best available

---

46 Sulfates (SO_4), which are very small particulates, are believed to contribute significantly to particulate-related health effects. Sulfates can be emitted from a power plant either as particulates or as SO_2, which is then converted to SO_4 in the atmosphere. This report includes estimates of the health effects of SO_2 emissions and the health effects of particulate emissions, both of which probably include health damages caused by SO_4. This is not believed to cause the double-counting of health effects.

47 This would not be true for coal-fired plants built after promulgation of the most recent New Source Performance Standards, however. These plants are required to have scrubbers regardless of sulphur content of fuels. The Clean Air Act Amendments of 1990, presently being considered by Congress, may modify the requirement for scrubbers on some newly constructed plants. A cost figure for an NSPS-controlled plant is provided in Table 1.

control technology. SO_2 emissions from natural gas combustion are shown to be negligible. The "starting point" externalities from the natural gas-fired steam plant are on the order of 1.0 cent/kWh (generated). For a combined cycle unit these externalities are estimated to be on the order of 1.0 cent/kWh (generated) also. For a combined cycle unit fitted with SCR and SWI, these externalities drop to 0.7 cents/kWh (generated).

These results show that the externalities of older coal- and oil-fired boilers are dominated by SO_2 and NO_x emissions. For newer coal and oil-fired technologies, and for gas-fired plants, the externalities are largely dominated by CO_2 emissions. This shift in the emphasis of the externalities is shown by the studies reviewed to be largely due to improved boiler design and efficiency, improved control equipment efficiency, and increasing use of control equipment and emissions-reducing operating procedures in response to ever-tightening emissions regulations.

Finally, these externality estimates leave out so many potential external effects that they are likely to be conservative rather than overstated. To derive more complete cost estimates, other externalities should be incorporated into future environmental cost estimates for fossil fuel-fired power plants, including: air emissions from combustion not included in the studies reviewed, such as the greenhouse gases methane and N_2O; air toxics including heavy metals, ozone precursors, and VOCs; and other externalities related to fossil-fuel combustion for which valuation studies could not be found, such as water use, land use, and solid waste disposal;[48] and externalities related to the front end of the fuel cycle, such as extraction, transportation and processing, which were excluded from this report.

Tables 1-3 below summarize the environmental costs of fossil-fuel plants from the studies reviewed and "starting point" cost for these plants. The figures in the these tables should be viewed with caution, and in connection with the caveats noted in the substantive chapters below.

[48] Water, land use and waste disposal impacts are discussed at length in the report, but cost studies based on damages were not reported in the literature. A mitigation cost for fish entrainment effects is discussed under Land and Water Pollution Impacts, Section V.F.

TABLE 1

EXTERNALITY COSTS FOR COAL-FIRED UNITS
(Emissions - lbs/MMBTU)

Externality	$/lb	Existing Boiler (1.2% S)	AFBC (1.1% S)	IGCC (.45% S)	NSPS (N/A)
	[A]	[B]	[C]	[D]	[E]
[1] SO_2	$ 2.03	1.80	0.55	0.48	1.2
[2] NO_x	$ 0.82	0.607	0.3	0.06	0.006
[3] Particulates	$ 1.19	0.15	0.01	0.01	0.03
[4] CO_2	$ 0.0068	209	209	209	209
Totals:					
[5] $/MMBTU Input		$ 5.76	$ 2.80	$ 2.46	$ 3.90
[6] Heat Rate (BTU/kWh)		10,000	10,000	10,000	10,000
[7] $/kWh Generated		$ 0.058	$ 0.028	$ 0.025	$ 0.039
[8] $kWh Delivered		$ 0.068	$ 0.033	$ 0.028	$ 0.045

Notes:

[A]: Unit Values derived in Chapter V.
[B][C][D][E]: Emissions are from PLC (1989); SO_2 and CO_2 emissions have been restated as lbs SO_2 and lbs CO_2. All emissions are expressed as lbs/MMBTU fuel input.
[E]: NSPS regulations require 1.2 lbs/MMBTU and 90% reduction for plants with emissions greater than 0.6 lb/MMBTU; for plants with emissions less than 0.6 lb/MMBTU; NSPS requires 70% reduction in emissions.
[1]: No SO_2 scrubbers are installed on the first three plants.
[2]: NO_x emissions are uncontrolled in each case.
[3]: Particulates emissions vary widely and are extremely dependent on the ash content and sulfur content and sulfur content of the coal. NSPS requries 0.03 lbs/MMBTU and 90% reduction.
[4]: CO_2 emissions are derived in PLC (1989).
[5]: Sum of (value x emissions for each externality) for each plant.
[6]: Assumed heat rates for each plant.
[7]: [5] x [6]/1,000,000.
[8]: Assumes 15% marginal energy losses.

TABLE 2

EXTERNALITY COSTS FOR OIL-FIRED UNITS
(Emissions - lbs/MMBTU)

Externality	$/lb	Boiler # 6 Oil (.5% S)	Boiler # 6 Oil (1% S)	Boiler # 6 Oil (2.2% S)	Combustion Turbine # 2 Oil (1% S)
	[A]	[B]	[C]	[D]	[E]
[1] SO_2	$ 2.03	0.54	1.08	2.38	0.16
[2] NO_x	$ 0.82	0.357	0.287	0.357	0.498
[3] Particulates	$ 1.19	0.055	0.09	0.174	0.036
[4] CO_2	$ 0.0068	169	169	169	161
Totals:					
[5] $/MMBTU Input		$ 2.60	$ 3.68	$ 6.48	$ 1.87
[6] Heat Rate (BTU/kWh)		10,400	10,400	10,400	13,600
[7] $/kWh Generated		$ 0.027	$ 0.038	$ 0.067	$ 0.025
[8] $kWh Delivered		$ 0.032	$ 0.045	$ 0.079	$ 0.030

Notes:

[A]: Unit Values derived in Chapter V.
[B][C][D][E]: Emissions are from PLC (1989); SO_2 and CO_2 emissions have been restated as lbs SO_2 and lbs CO_2. All emissions are expressed as lbs/MMBTU fuel input.
[1]: SO_2 emissions are uncontrolled in each case.
[2]: NO_x emissions are uncontrolled in each case.
[3]: Particulates emissions are calculated from EPA Ap-42 using the formula: 0.02 + 0.07 x S, where S ia the sulfur content in percent.
[4]: CO_2 emissions are derived in PLC (1989).
[5]: Sum of (value x emissions for each externality) for each plant.
[6]: Assumed heat rates for each plant.
[7]: [5]*[6]/1,000,000.
[8]: Assumes 15% marginal energy losses.

TABLE 3

EXTERNALITY COSTS FOR NATURAL GAS-FIRED UNITS
(Emissions - lbs/MMBTU)

Externality	$/lb	Existing Steam Plant	Combined Cycle	BACT (SCR, SWI)
	[A]	[B]	[C]	[D]
[1] SO_2	$ 2.03	0	0	0
[2] NO_x	$ 0.82	0.248	0.42	0.042
[3] Particulates	$ 1.19	0.003	0.003	0.0002
[4] CO_2	$ 0.0068	110	110	110
Totals:				
[5] $/MMBTU Input		$ 0.95	$ 1.10	$ 0.78
[6] Heat Rate (BTU/kWh)		10,400	9,000	9,000
[7] $/kWh Generated		$ 0.010	$ 0.010	$ 0.007
[8] $kWh Delivered		$ 0.012	$ 0.011	$ 0.008

Notes:

[A]: Unit Values derived in Chapter V.
[B][C][D]: Emissions are from PLC (1989); SO_2 and CO_2 emissions have been restated as lbs SO_2 and lbs CO_2. All emissions are expressed as lbs/MMBTU fuel input.
[1]: SO_2 emissions are zero from gas combustion.
[2]: NO_x emissions are uncontrolled in the first two cases; For the BACT case, Selective Catalytic Reduction and Steam Water injection are assumed.
[3]: Particulates emissions are estimated for CEC (1989). BACT assumes fabric filter control.
[4]: CO_2 emissions are derived in PLC (1989).
[5]: Sum of (value x emissions for each externality) for each plant.
[6]: Assumed heat rates for each plant.
[7]: [5]*[6]/1,000,000.
[8]: Assumes 15% marginal energy losses.

2. Nuclear Plants

The external costs of nuclear power have been evaluated in Chapter VI.D. by division into the following categories: (1) the health, property value and wildlife costs caused by routine emissions; (2) the costs caused by non-routine emissions (for which no studies were found); (3) the health and property damage costs associated with accidental emissions; and (4) decommissioning costs that are not internalized.[49]

The "starting point" environmental costs from nuclear operations are estimated to be 2.91 cents/kWh, which is the sum of: 1) 0.11 cents/kWh for routine operations; 2) 2.3 cents/kWh for accidents; and, 3) 0.5 cents/kWh for decommissioning costs. This analysis omits all front-end costs from extraction and transportation of uranium.

Table 4 below represents the nuclear plant's "starting point" values.

TABLE 4

STARTING POINT VALUES FOR NUCLEAR POWER EXTERNALITY COSTS

Area	Cents/kWh
Routine Operations	0.11
Accidents	2.30
Decommissioning	0.50
TOTAL	2.91

3. Waste-to-Energy Plants

The one study located which values externalities estimated the costs of waste-to-energy plant emissions at 11.14 cents/kWh. If half of this value were allocated to the energy production function of the plant, then the environmental externality costs would be approximately 5.5 cents/kWh. The study apparently did not consider the risks from exposure to toxic substances in the incinerator ash and may have undervalued the risks from toxic emissions.

Since the types of emissions from garbage incinerators are similar to those from coal-fired plants, one costing approach is to apply the dollar-per-pound values for coal plant emissions to incinerators. This provides a lower value of approximately 4

---

[49] In addition, fish impingement/entrainment damages at nuclear facilities are discussed under Land and Water Pollution Impacts, Chapter V.F.

cents/kWh solely for SO_2, NO_x, HCL and particulate emissions, not including a value for human health effects from HCL, for which no value was found.

Table 5 describes the environmental externality costs of waste-to-energy plants as derived by the latter approach.

TABLE 5

CALCULATION OF CONVENTIONAL WASTE-TO-ENERGY PLANT EMISSION EXTERNALITY COSTS

Pollutant	Cost Per Pound[1]	Pounds Per Kilowatt Hour[2]	Externality Cost in Cents/Kilowatt Hour[3]
SO_2	\$2.03	.014	2.89
NO_x	.82	.002	.164
HCL	.12	.077	.924
Particulate	\$1.19	.00075	.089
Carbon Monoxide	-	.00085	-
Volatile Organic Hydrocarbons	-	.00015	-
CO2	-	-	-
		TOTAL	4.019

(1) Derived from Table 2, Chapter V.C. "Sulfur Oxides", Table 1, Chapter V.D. "Nitrogen Oxides" and Table 3 Chapter V.E. "Particulates" of this report. These figures do not include acid rain effects.

(2) This figure is derived from the projected annual SO_2, HCL and NO_x emissions for the 3000 ton per day Brooklyn Navy Yard Plant. It is based on 60% capacity divided by three to estimate the emissions from a typical 1000 ton per day plant, and is then further divided by the typical annual kilowatt hour production for a 1000 megawatt plant (138 million kWh/yr.). Kilowatt hour production figures for the Brooklyn plant were unavailable as that plant will produce exclusively steam. The Brooklyn plant emission rates were chosen because of similarity between proposed emission controls and proposed EPA new source performance standards.

(3) The externality cost for Hydrogen Chloride (HCL) is assumed to be the same as the materials damage cost for SO_2. No externality value was found for the HCL human health effects. See Table 2, Chapter V.C. "Sulfur Oxides" of this report.

4. Solar, Wind and Biomass

"Starting point" costs are given in Table 6 below for the environmental externalities of solar, wind, and biomass power generating systems. These costs cannot be directly compared, however, because the figures were developed using different methodologies for each technology.

TABLE 6

SUMMARY OF ENVIRONMENTAL COSTS FOR VARIOUS RENEWABLE ENERGY TECHNOLOGIES

Technology Type	Cents/kWh
Solar	0 to 0.4
Wind	0 to 0.1
Biomass	0 to 0.7

F. INCORPORATION OF ENVIRONMENTAL EXTERNALITIES

1. Incorporation by Utilities and Regulatory Commissions

A surprising number of states, twenty-nine, have required or are actively considering requiring, their utilities to include environmental externality costs in some manner in planning, bidding or other resource acquisition procedures.[50] Nine states plus the Bonneville Power Administration and the Northwest Power Planning Council have sought to quantify environmental costs or have quantification measures pending;

---

[50] Orders: AZ, CA, CO, ID, KA, MA, MICH, MN, NJ, NY, OH, OR, PA, TX, VA, VT, WI.
Statutes: ALSK, NV.
Pending: CT, IA, MN.
Consideration: DC, HW, ME, MD, MONT, RI, VT.
None: ALA, ARK, DE, FL, GA, IL, IND, KY, LA, MISS, MO, NB, NH, NM, ND, NC, OK, SG, SD, TN, WA, WVA, WYO.

Chapter X discusses these incorporation issues and Chapter X.G. summarizes state-by-state, with citations, the treatment of environmental externalities. At the end of this section, Table 7 shows the status of state actions incorporating environmental externality costs and Table 8 shows the type of action taken by states that have acted to incorporate environmental externality costs.

three other states are actually considering such measures.[51] Those entities are approaching incorporation in several ways:

Quantitative. Some utility commissions either increase the cost of a proposed new resource by a specific amount/kWh, reflecting the environmental consequences of using the resources (e.g. New York) or allow a credit to reduce the effective kWh cost of less-polluting resources (e.g. Wisconsin). The adder or credit is based on quantified costs.

Qualitative. Several utility commissions require utilities to consider environmental impacts without specifying how the costs are to be calculated or incorporated (e.g. Arizona).

Rate of return. A number of utility commissions award an increased rate of return on specific non-polluting resource investments (e.g. demand side management in Washington) or an increased rate of return based on over all performance in utilizing non-polluting resources (e.g. Idaho).[52]

Avoided cost. Some utility commissions increase avoided costs to take into account environmental costs (e.g. Virginia).

Ranking. A few utility commissions permit a utility to be guided in selecting resources by a commission-imposed or commission-approved ranking system that weights resources by their environmental impacts or by other criteria, not their environmental costs, e.g. New England Electric System (NEES) in Massachusetts was allowed to use a ranking based on a customer survey[53].

Collaborative. Several utility commissions authorize utilities to determine environmental costs and their treatment through a collaborative negotiating process involving regulators, state agencies and public interest intervenors. Outside experts are usually hired to design programs, evaluation procedures and incentives rates for utilities, and to determine how environmental costs will be calculated and incorporated. The process is approved by and subject to oversight by the commission.

Several innovative incorporation methodologies have not yet been applied in any state. These include **"Environmental LCUP,"** in which pollution reduction targets are set for particular pollutants and the utilities are required to meet these targets at least cost; **environmental dispatch**, in which utilities or a power pool are required to include environmental costs in least cost dispatch of existing resources; **cost-charging**,

---

51 Orders: CA, CO, NJ, NY, OR, WI, VT;
Pending: CT, MA, CA;
Consideration: DC, MA, MICH.

52 The New York PSC was recently upheld in providing utility rate incentives for engaging in DSM programs. Multiple Intervenors v. New York State Public Service Commission, No. 249-90 (N.Y. Sup. Ct.), June 7, 1990. The Pace Center for Environmental Legal Studies filed a brief in the case in support of the PSC.

53 Comments by Massachusetts Electric Co. (a NEES subsidiary) at pp. 17-21 and Attachment 2, Investigation by the Department of Public Utilities on Its Own Motion Into Proposed Rules to Implement Integrated Resource Management Practices for Electric Companies in the Commonwealth, Mass. D.P.U. No. 89-239, February 23, 1990.

in which quantified environmental costs are charged to the resource-owner and the proceeds used to establish a pollution mitigation fund; and **set-asides**, in which utilities are required to set aside a specified portion of their capacity needs for designated resources considered to be relatively environmentally benign.

Table 7, below, shows graphically the status of state actions incorporating environmental externality costs, and Table 8 shows the type of action taken by states that have acted to incorporate these costs.[54]

[54] These tables are based largely on a 50-state survey of state regulatory commissions on state treatment of environmental externalities done in November, 1989 and recently updated. The survey was done for the National Association of Regulatory Utility Commissioners (NARUC) by Lawrence Berkeley Laboratory (LBL), to be published shortly. Cohen, S.D., J.H. Eto, J. Beldock, and G. Crandall, A Survey of State Regulatory Commission Activities to Incorporate Environmental Externalities into Electric Utility Planning and Regulation, draft of May, 1990. For the other sources, see the State-by-State Survey Sources at the end of Chapter X.G.

TABLE 7

STATUS OF STATE ACTIONS INCORPORATING ENVIRONMENTAL EXTERNALITY COSTS

Legend

O - Incorporation Ordered
P - Incorporation Order Pending
U - Under Consideration
N - No Action

STATE	O	P	U	N		STATE	O	P	U	N	
ALABAMA				X		NEBRASKA				X	
ALASKA	X				1	NEVADA	X				1
ARIZONA	X					NEW HAMPSHIRE				X	
ARKANSAS				X		NEW JERSEY	X				
CALIFORNIA	X				2	NEW MEXICO				X	
COLORADO	X					NEW YORK	X				
CONNECTICUT		X				NORTH CAROLINA			X		
DELAWARE				X		NORTH DAKOTA				X	
DISTRICT OF COLUMBIA			X			OHIO	X				
FLORIDA				X		OKLAHOMA				X	
GEORGIA				X		OREGON	X				
HAWAII			X			PENNSYLVANIA	X				
IDAHO	X					RHODE ISLAND			X		
ILLINOIS				X		SOUTH CAROLINA				X	
INDIANA				X		SOUTH DAKOTA				X	
IOWA		X				TENNESSEE				X	
KANSAS	X					TEXAS	X				
KENTUCKY				X		UTAH			X		
LOUISIANA				X		VERMONT	X				
MAINE			X			VIRGINIA	X				
MARYLAND			X			WASHINGTON				X	
MASSACHUSETTS	X				2	WEST VIRGINIA				X	
MICHIGAN	X				2	WISCONSIN	X				
MINNESOTA	X				2	WYOMING				X	
MISSISSIPPI				X							
MISSOURI				X	3	BPA	X				1
MONTANA			X			NWPPC	X				1

This table is derived from the references at the end of Chapter X.G.

(1) Established by legislation.

(2) Order issued to consider externalities; implementation pending.

(3) Commission has stated that it may consider externalities.

TABLE 8

TYPE OF ACTION BY STATES ACTING TO INCORPORATE ENVIRONMENTAL EXTERNALITY COSTS

Legend

O - Incorp. Ordered
P - Incorp. Order Pending
U - Under Consideration
QN- Quantitative Consid.
QL- Qualitative Consid.
ROR- Rate Consideration
AC - Avoided Cost Consid.
ED - Environmental Dispatch
C - Collaborative Action
PL - Planning Consideration
B - Bidding Consideration
L - Legislative Action

State	QN	QL	ROR	AC	ED	C	PL	B	Comment
ALSK				O			L		
AZ		O					O		
CA	OP				U	C*	O		*Collab. ended
CO	O*							O*	*by fuel type
CT	P		L*			C	P	P	*5% ROR adder
DC							U		
HW							U		
ID			O	O					
IA				P		C			
KA	P		O						
ME		U					U		
MD	U					C		U	
MA	P*					C	P	P	*DSM Evaluations
MICH	U			O			U		
MN*		O					P		*Law caps SO2
MT		U	L*				U		*2% adder for DSM
NV		L					L		
NH							L*		*Law under consid.
NJ	O			O				O	
NY	O		O	L		C	O	O	
OH		O					O		
OK			O*						*ROR, trash only
OR*	O	O					O		*Law caps CO_2
PA		O*					O*		*Not implemented
RI							U		
UT							U		
TX		L					L		
VT	O*					C	O*	O*	*15% on DSM
VA				O*					*15% DSM adder to AC
WA			L*						*2% ROR law for DSM
WI	O		O		U		O		
BPA	L						L	U	
NWPPC	L						L		

This table is derived from the references at the end of Chapter X.G.

2. Other Means of Incorporation

The studies reviewed indicate that FERC has taken no action to incorporate environmental externalities in the wholesale and interstate markets that it regulates. The recent Notices of Proposed Rulemaking it issued on PURPA bidding guidelines do not even address DSM options or environmental costs.

Federal consideration of environmental costs has been primarily through environmental regulation which, by reducing pollutants, internalizes some of the environmental costs. Federal subsidies and tax credits, on the other hand, are found to benefit fossil and nuclear electricity which bear high environmental costs much more than less polluting electricity options such as renewables and DSM. All subsidies are found to distort marketplace pricing of energy resources.

Pollution taxes or fees imposed by international, federal or state authorities, are found to put environmental costs into the marketplace and internalize these costs most equitably and efficiently. Section X.D. contains a discussion of federal and state tax and subsidy measures which address environmental externality costs.

G. MAJOR VALUATION ISSUES

1. Use of Damage vs. Control Costs

The studies reviewed differ as to whether to use the costs of the damages inflicted on society by pollutants, or the costs of controlling or mitigating pollution damages, in valuing environmental externalities.[55]

a. Damage Costs

The main advantage of using damage costs is that they are the most relevant. It is the damages to society that are sought to be addressed and alleviated by incorporating environmental externality costs into utility resource selection. Most economists (but not necessarily utility experts) believe that adequate studies exist for valuing damages, damage costs should be used.[56] While damage costs are difficult to determine, they may be ascertained by methods that could withstand the scrutiny of the methods used by the EPA to determine health and safety standards. The EPA's standards are based on scientific and economic studies similar to those used by economists.[57]

The main disadvantage of using damage costs is the difficulty of calculating them. Some experts feel that utility regulatory commissions (as opposed to agencies with environmental expertise like EPA) would have difficulty dealing with technical matters

---

55 See discussion, Chapter III. D.2.

56 Damage costs are useful as well for determining how much to spend on additional controls.

57 Courts tend to defer to administrative agencies on matters within their delegated authority. For PSCs to value environmental damages is no more complex than determining rate structures and conducting prudency reviews.

like valuation of human life and non-monetized costs like valuation of recreational facilities. It should be recognized, however, that utilities regularly estimate values that are difficult to quantify, such as demand forecasts and rate impacts, and state regulatory commissions routinely deal with these estimates.

If damage cost studies are inadequate, as with global warming, use of control costs or an estimated adder can serve as a proxy. This is found to be far superior to ignoring environmental externality costs and thus valuing them at zero.[58]

b. Control Costs

The main advantage to use of control costs is that they are easier to determine than damage costs because data on the costs of control is more readily available. As a result of the relative ease of determining control costs, all state commissions that have ordered consideration of environmental externality costs to date have used control costs both as the basis for quantification of such costs and in the calculation of adders to the cost of polluting resources.[59]

An argument has been made that since legislative standards controlling emissions of a pollutant have been determined by a legislative body, these standards must represent the value society has placed on environmental damages from the pollutant controlled. On the other hand it is argued that legislated standards tend to be determined politically, rather than based on scientific or economic evidence. Standards are sometimes used in damage valuation as revealed preference costs.

The disadvantages of using control costs are that they may bear little or no relationship to the cost of the damages imposed on society by the relevant pollutants. Statutory controls usually fall substantially short of marginal damage costs, since Western societies tend to enact controls well below marginal damage costs for political reasons.

Furthermore, control standards like the National Ambient Air Quality Standards of the Clean Air Act (NAAQS)[60] are addressed to impacts. NAAQS are adopted at a level to protect the public health and welfare with "an adequate margin of safety,"[61] for example, without reference to the costs to society of health and welfare damages. In fact, as demonstrated by the pollution problems of acid rain, urban smog, etc. that persist after application of legislated standards, NAAQS standards are not sufficiently stringent to protect public health and the environment. And there are many power plant pollutants, such as CO_2, for which no standards have been set.

---

[58] Bland (1986), supra at p. 2. When legislative controls are adopted (e.g. the currently pending Clean Air Act amendments), the effects of the new controls on damage costs must be taken into account, since enactment will internalize the costs of the pollutants subject to the controls.

[59] The Oregon Commission, however, has ordered its utilities to seek to quantify damage costs in evaluating resource selections, Re Least Cost Planning, UM 180, OR PSC Order No. 89-507 (April 20, 1989), and the New York Commission has ordered a pooled study by its utilities of their environmental externality damage costs, NY PSC Case 28223, Electric Utility Conservation Programs, Opinion and Order 89-15 (May 23, 1989).

[60] 41 U.S.C. Sec. 7409.

[61] 41 U.S.C. Sec. 7409(b)(2).

2. Discount Rates

Among economists, scientists and utility experts, there is much controversy as to what discount rate, if any, should be applied to environmental externalities.[62] Discount rates are used to assess the value today of economic benefits and costs that may occur in the future. Low discount rates give more weight to the future than high discount rates do. The question is, what discount rate should be used in the economic analysis of environmental externalities?

Some experts believe that the discount rate applied by utilities to their capital investments should be used as a matter of consistency and because use of lower discount rates will overvalue future environmental costs from a utility planning perspective. They assert that all utility resource selection decisions should be made on the same financial basis.[63]

Others maintain that a zero discount rate should be used, particularly with respect to human life and health risks, for moral reasons, because a life in the future is as valuable as a present life.[64] They maintain that sound environmental stewardship mandates that the value placed on future lives and other environmental assets should be weighted the same as the value placed on present lives and environmental assets.

They maintain that discounting (at rates higher than zero) double-discounts future risks since, in the calculation of economic values, risk is already diminished by the probability the risk may not be realized. The calculation of the value of risk to a statistical life is, by the means it is calculated, already reduced to present value. They assert that it is inappropriate to discount such catastrophic risks as those from nuclear proliferation or long-lasting risks, such as those from high level nuclear wastes which pose risks for millennia.

The reasons for rejecting a zero discount rate for risks to human life and health are first, the assertion that the value of risks decrease over time, and second that a zero discount rate places the present value of future environmental damages too high. They assert, for example, that few would be willing to pay anything substantial for the risk of human fatality 10,000 years from now, and therefore that the damages are too remote to value. Also they state that it is likely that, long before that distant time, technology will resolve the environmental threat (or the world will be destroyed). Use of discount rates higher than zero takes into account the lesser values that may be put on future risks.

Advocates of a discount rate higher than zero also assert that the moral issue is moot once it is determined to put dollar values on human life and health risks. Then

---

[62] See discussion, Chapter III. J.4.

[63] Chernick, P. and E. Caverhill, The Valuation of Externalities from Energy Production, Delivery and Use, PLC, Inc., Boston, Massachusetts 1989.

[64] Shuman, M. and R. Cavanagh, A Model Electric Power and Conservation Plan for the Pacific Northwest, Environmental Costs, Appendix 2, Northwest Conservation Act Coalition, Seattle, WA, November 1982.

the question is how to determine those values.[65] Placing lower values on future lives than on present ones, they assert, takes into account the lesser willingness of the public to pay for damages far into the future and the likelihood that the risks will be alleviated during long time periods.

However, there are serious intergenerational problems that must be considered with respect to future risks that cannot be remedied by new technology, such as loss of unique habitat and species. Some actions taken today could prevent future generations from acting. A zero discount rate better accounts for such irreversible effects.

Other economists apply a social rate of time preference discount,[66] usually about 3%, which is lower than utility investment rates, which approximate 6.5%, but higher than a zero discount rate. They calculate the present value from the time an environmental risk is created.[67] The main reason asserted for using a social discount rate rather than the utility discount rate is that it is the value of environmental costs and benefits to the public that is being evaluated (and discounted), not the investments of the utility.

Most of the studies reviewed in this report did not disclose the discount rate used, if any. The report uses externality figures as they are presented in the studies reviewed, unaltered to reflect a discount rate different from that used in the studies (if any).[68]

3. Valuation of Human Health Risks

It must be reiterated that economists value the risk to, not the value of, human health.[69] The preferred methodology measures what the public is willing to pay to avoid the risk or to be compensated for it. Loss of earnings is generally rejected as a measure of the value of a risk to life because it values the risk to life of non-earners at zero. Health care costs, are considered not to be an adequate measure of the value of a risk to life because the benefit of avoiding health care costs is far exceeded by the value people place on risk of loss of their lives. Medical costs and lost earnings are

---

65 It is asserted that risk to life must be given a dollar value does not mean that loss of life is treated as a strictly economic commodity, any more than jury awards for pain and suffering mean that suffering is a purely economic commodity. The inadequacy of current macroeconomic theory to analyze risks to human life and the environment, and the need for a new vision of ecological economics, was described by Herman Daly at a conference of the International Society for Ecological Economists, The Ecological Economics of Sustainability, The World Bank, Washington, DC, May 21-23, 1990.

66 The social rate of time preference (social discount rate) is the rate at which society is willing to exchange consumption now for consumption in the future. It reflects the ability of society to remedy environmental hazards over time.

67 Evaluation of Generic Cost and Benefit Studies, BPA, Portland, Oregon 1986b, at p. 22. This position is discussed in Chapter III of this report.

68 All cost figures in this report are converted to 1989 dollars. In the one case where discount rates were used in this report, valuing the costs of tree planting as a proxy for global warming damages, the figures are given for both a social rate of time preference rate (3%) and a utility discount rate (6.5%).

69 Valuation of human health risks is discussed in Chapter III. It bears reiteration that health-related damages depend on the number of people exposed and the composition of the populations exposed. These damages are therefore likely to vary considerably according to specific sites.

subsumed in the amounts people would be willing to pay to avoid, or be willing to accept as compensation, to incur voluntarily risks to their health and safety.

The range of values in the studies reviewed varies from $440,000to $12,800,000. The value used in this report of $4 million (in 1989 dollars) was arrived at by taking the median of the middle group of valuations. The range for sensitivity analyses was found to be from $1 million to $10 million, encompassing most of the studies reviewed. For morbidity risks, a value of $400,000per statistical injury or illness was selected on a similar basis.

4. Transboundary Issues

Environmental costs from electric utility-generated pollution emissions are often not restricted to the state or country in which the plant is located. Thus, much of the acid rain damage to the Northeastern United States and Canada is found to derive from midwestern power plant emissions. Water pollution in rivers often crosses state and national borders, and CO_2 emissions have global warming effects.

The costs accounted for in this report are not site-specific or limited by any political boundaries. As with most state jurisdictions that have addressed environmental impact costs, this report assumes that all costs to society should be accounted for, not just those affecting the jurisdiction in which a plant is located. Indeed, if a state or utility sought to exclude exported pollution from its costs then, logically, it should include the costs of pollution imported into its jurisdiction from outside sources, a much more complicated calculation.[70]

5. Site-Specific Issues

There are site-specific considerations that must be taken into account in valuing environmental externality costs.[71] Clearly, a plant's polluting emissions affecting a heavily populated metropolis will create vastly greater human health risk costs than a plant located where the emissions affect unpopulated areas or the oceans. Similarly, agricultural damage risk costs will be more significant when emissions are deposited on farming communities than when they fall on urban areas.

Human exposure to air pollution from a specific source depends on many factors: the location of the source relative to population, the area's meteorology and topography which influence dispersion, and the vegetation and water bodies in the areas which may absorb the pollutants. These factors vary not only from urban to rural areas, but from one city to another. Extrapolating estimates for one location to another requires careful examination of differences between the two locations for all these factors and calls for adjustment of the damage estimates based on the differences.

---

[70] Other transboundary considerations, beyond the scope of this report, include the increased use of electricity imported from Canada to the Northeast and Northwest regions of the United States, which result in a transfer to Canada of the environmental externality costs of power production.

[71] Generic vs. site-specific considerations are discussed in Chapter III.

In this report, an attempt is made to differentiate the pollution costs in urban and rural settings; where possible, health costs are stated in terms of tons of pollutant per unit of population. To determine costs for any particular resource, these site-specific considerations must be addressed.

6. Treatment of Uncertainty

Valuation of all environmental externality costs must deal with a considerable margin of uncertainty.[72] Often wide ranges of costs are advanced in different studies, for example the enormous range of nuclear accident probability figures.

There are alternative ways to deal with such uncertainties. One can take the average of each possible outcome multiplied by its average likelihood of occurrence - - its "expected value". Or one can choose either the outcome or the probabilities that fit with one's assumptions -- for example, one could chose to make a best case or a worst case assumption. Uncertainty is dealt with in this report by reviewing studies showing the full range of costs and their bases, including sensitivity analysis. A reasonable point within the ranges of the studies is selected and the rationale given for the selection.

7. Competitive and Rate Impacts

Requiring incorporation of environmental costs could have a significant impact on rates and the competitive position of electric utilities, though none of the studies reviewed documents this.[73] So far, rate impacts have not been a significant problem because the environmental adders (or credits to non-combustion sources) have not been large enough to have a significant effect on rates, and the costs have been applied only to selection of new resources, rather than to more highly polluting existing resources. If, however, the full environmental damage costs are ascertained and used, and particularly if application is made to existing resources, the impact on rates could be considerable. On the other hand, if consideration of environmental costs causes utilities to invest more in energy efficiency resources, which generally have economic and social costs lower than traditional supply alternatives, then the electric bills of participating customers may be reduced (even though utility rates charged to consumers will increase).

Another equitable issue that must be addressed is whether these rate impacts should be borne by all ratepayers or only the class of customers eligible to participate in the utility DSM investment. All customers will benefit by environmental enhancement, and to the extent that DSM is undertaken, all will benefit from avoidance of more expensive supply resource costs. However, if all ratepayers are required to pay for DSM investments, the ineligible classes of customers will pay for DSM without being able to enjoy any of its direct benefits. New York has permitted utilities to experiment with both treatments with respect to allocation of DSM rate impacts.

---

[72] Treatment of uncertainty is discussed in Chapter III. J.2.a.

[73] The comments of Steven A. Mitnick, Senior Consultant, Putnam, Hayes & Bartlett, Inc. in a letter dated 24 April 1990 to Professor Richard L. Ottinger, of the Pace Center emphasize these considerations strongly.

There also may be competitive problems arising from rate impacts. If the impact of consideration of environmental costs is sufficiently great, it may overprice electricity in relationship to resources that are not incorporating environmental costs. Thus, it may promote more direct use of polluting fuels (such as oil or gas heating rather than electric heating, for example), or self-generation of electricity by major customers who do not have to consider environmental costs.

Fuel-switching may take place as a result of utilizing environmental externality costs. This may cause rate impacts even though it may result in environmental improvements. If significant environmental costs are incorporated, natural gas, which is cleaner than oil and coal, may be preferred to an extent that will drive up gas prices. Also, there are many who feel that natural gas is too valuable a finite resource to be used as a boiler fuel. The much-debated role of nuclear fuels as an environmentally preferable substitute for fossil fuels will probably not be affected because the studies reviewed show that nuclear plants bear large environmental externality costs in addition to their heavy capital costs and long lead times. Solar electricity, wind generation, biomass and DSM measures, however, should be considerably advantaged by incorporation of externalities, because the studies reviewed find their environmental costs are small.

H. RESEARCH NEEDS

Valuation of environmental externalities is a discipline still in its infancy. For each externality reviewed there remain significant uncertainties. For some effects, no valuation studies could be found, and with respect to many others information was scarce. A principal contribution of this study may be to point out, in some individual chapters then in Chapter IX, the principal research needs that exist. To increase confident use of environmental externality values, a major research effort is found to be needed, one that must uniquely combine the expertise of scientists, economists and utility experts.

I. CONCLUSION

Despite the uncertainties, the studies reviewed in this report demonstrate that the environmental externality costs of most electricity-related environmental impacts can be valued. The studies also show the means of valuing them. The report reviews the studies of these values for all supply and demand-related resources. It shows the various means by which environmental costs have been and might be incorporated into utility planning and resource selection procedures.

Electricity is found to have substantial environmental costs, not presently included in most utility resource selection. While many of the cost studies found are incomplete and of varying adequacy, they do indicate the order of magnitude of these costs.

If environmental costs are to be internalized universally in the future through pollution taxes or fees, reliable damage figures are as important to their accurate determination as they are to the incorporation of accurate externality costs in utility resource selections.

That more than half of the utility commissions have started to consider environmental externality costs is encouraging, although only a handful (nine) have actually attempted to quantify those costs and use quantified environmental costs in utility resource selection procedures.

The studies reviewed indicate that many utilities are reluctant to incorporate environmental externality costs. Progress has been most pronounced when commissions have required quantification of environmental costs and when rate of return consideration is given for investment in less polluting resources.

Despite the reluctance of many utilities, the electric utility industry (including independent power producers and demand-side energy service companies) is pioneering in consideration of environmental costs in resource selection. The results for improvement of the environment could be of great significance.

III. ANALYTICAL FRAMEWORK

III. ANALYTICAL FRAMEWORK

A. INTRODUCTION

The purpose of this analytical framework is to outline significant issues in estimating the economic value of environmental impacts from operating electric energy resources and to alert decision makers to valuation issues that can be resolved only at the management or regulatory level.

One goal of utility planning and regulation is to develop energy resources having the lowest social cost among many possible resource choices.[1] The social cost of a resource consists of both its internal costs--i.e., the utility's revenue requirements that are paid by ratepayers--and its external costs--i.e., the costs associated with the resource which are not paid by the ratepayers, but by other economic agents.[2] A significant and largely external cost of power production is the environmental cost. Thus, environmental costs and benefits estimates occur within the context of resource cost effectiveness evaluations. The general problem is portrayed in Figure 1, Hypothetical Resource Cost Comparisons. As Figure 1 shows, one resource providing the same amount of power as another may have lower internal costs but external costs so much greater that the overall cost of the first resource is actually higher than the overall cost of the other. The lighter shaded area in Figure 1 is the subject of this report: which costs are included as environmental costs, whose costs are counted, how costs are measured, and how costs are weighed in the analysis. The task is to measure and aggregate the environmental costs of constructing,[3] operating, and decommissioning an energy resource.[4] Although this report deals almost solely with economic efficiency, it would be remiss if it did not mention the subject of equity or

---

[1] Buchanan, S., Accounting for External Costs of Energy Resources in Least-Cost Utility Planning, for Executive Office of Energy Resources, Commonwealth of Massachusetts, March 1988. These are not the only factors considered by utilities when selecting resources. This report, focuses on the economic valuation of potential power resources, [hereafter cited as "Buchanan".]

[2] Turvey, R., "On Divergence Between Social Cost and Private Cost", Economics, Vol. 30, August, 1963. Most external costs can be grouped under the heading of "environmental costs," although other external costs and benefits may be associated with the resource, for example, balance of trade. This report addresses environmental externalities, explicitly, although many of the concepts and issues discussed here also would apply to non-environmental externalities. For an introduction to externalities see, Bator, F., "The Anatomy of Market Failure," Quarterly Journal of Economics. Vol. 72, 1958, at p. 351. For a more in depth review see Mishan, E., "The Postwar Literature on Externalities: An Interpretive Essay," Journal of Economic Literature, Vol. 9, 1971, pp. 1-28.

[3] The environmental costs of plant construction are excluded from the costs analyzed in the following chapters, as one of the limitations of the contract with NYSERDA; although, based on economic theory, they should be included to arrive at a complete social cost of electricity.

[4] Because some resources--such as hydroelectric resources, which are operated for peak rather than base-load conditions--may have different effects on the environment, the environmental costs and benefits associated with an energy resource are measured with the resource built and operating in the utility's system and are compared to the costs measured in the same system without the resource. Bonneville Power Administration, (BPA), Cost Effectiveness Methodology, [hereafter cited as BPA, 1986a]. Bonneville Power Administration, DOE/BP-751, Portland, Oregon, 1986a. The difference in the value of environmental costs between the two cases is the marginal or incremental environmental cost of the energy resource in question.

fairness. Benefit/cost analysis, and all its derivatives, has the objective of maximizing net economic benefits.[5] Often overlooked is how benefits and costs are distributed, and the perceived fairness of the distributions. When economists address the question of the optimal allocation of resources, it is nearly always one of optimizing efficiency and it is the alternative yielding the greatest amount of net benefits that would be the efficient alternative. Equity considerations have typically been assigned a minor role. Explicit analyses and recommendations regarding pricing policies to effect distributional incomes are rare. This focus on efficiency, however, ignores who will be the recipients of the benefits or the payers of the costs. If all benefits accrue to a single, wealthy individual but the costs are paid by the poorest members of society, the new allocation would not be fair and desirable, regardless of the amount of the net benefits.

Fairness, like beauty, may be in the eyes of the beholder. It is beyond the scope of this work to derive a theory of equity, or to evaluate the equity of, say, a given level of nitrogen oxides emissions. Nevertheless, several equity issues are discussed with respect to significant valuation issues. How are costs borne by future generations to be discounted? When are willingness to be compensated measures appropriate? What perspective should be adopted for analyses and whose costs should be counted? These and other questions are addressed in this report primarily because they have implications for the kinds of costs to be evaluated and for the methods by which they will be evaluated.

Therefore, although environmental costs and benefits are intended to be measures of gains and losses of economic efficiency, the equally important issues of equity are acknowledged. While valuation issues that have equity overtones are discussed, no claim is made to have adequately addressed the full array of equity issues. Fairness is a factor that should be considered, however, in resolving environmental costing issues.

B. ESTABLISHING LINKAGES BETWEEN PLANT OPERATION AND ENVIRONMENTAL COSTS

A five-step process may be applied to environmental effects created by each of the three stages of a power plant's life and used for almost any economic valuation of environmental risks:[6] 1) emission; 2) transport and disposal; 3) exposure; 4) response; and 5) valuation. The five step sequence is straightforward, although each step may be technically complex and subject to uncertainty.

The first step is to identify **what is emitted** by the plant, and to determine which emissions create environmental risks. Each pollutant that potentially could cause an environmental risk must be identified and the amount of pollutant emitted by the plant over some period of time, or during the production of a unit of energy--e.g., a kilowatt-hour--measured or estimated by an engineering calculation. Emissions include not only what goes up the smokestack or out the discharge pipes, but also other by-products of

---

[5] Prest, A. and R. Turvey, "Cost-Benefit Analysis: A Survey", Surveys of Economic Theory, Vol. I., St. Martin's Press, New York, 1967.

[6] Bonneville Power Administration, Issue Backgrounder: Counting the Costs -- How BPA Performs Environmental Cost Analysis, BPA, DOE/BP-405, June 1985, [hereafter cited as BPA, 1985].

operation--such as sludge, ash, heat, or radioactivity--that leave the plant and affect air, water, or land.

Step two determines the **dispersal of the pollutant**, taking into account climatic factors, geographical features, and wind and water currents. During dispersal, the chemistry of pollutants may change; for example, sulfur oxides may be transformed into sulfates. These transformations and the paths taken by the pollutants must be measured or estimated. Using models that engineers have developed to portray the dispersal of pollutants after emission from the plant, a "map" is produced of how the pollutants change and where they travel after they are emitted from the plant.

As the pollutant disperses, people, materials, wildlife, and vegetation are exposed. Step three estimates the size and type of **population exposed** to the environmental risks associated with the pollutant. "Population" here means population of people, plants, animals, buildings, or anything that could be affected by exposure. Relevant characteristics of the population are also identified, including the size of the population, its age, its vulnerability to the pollutant, its proximity to the pollutant, and other factors for use in step four.

Step four estimates the **response of each population exposed** to the pollutant. The response is any change in the affected population, such as slower plant growth, degraded scenery, corrosion, respiratory ailments, death, injury, or loss of habitat. Typically, these changes are estimated by close-response functions that relate the severity or probability of a response to the amount of pollutant to which an individual is exposed.[7] This step, like the previous three, has only a physical, not an economic, dimension.[8]

Finally, in step five, the change in the affected population is valued as a change in an environmental good or service. This **valuation** is the subject of the remainder of this chapter.

C. DEFINING BENEFITS AND COSTS

1. Value and Environmental Goods and Services

A term frequently used in this report is "value." Unfortunately, this useful term is, well, value-laden. "Value" in this report means the net benefit (or net cost) of an

---

[7] ECO Northwest, Estimating Environmental Costs and Benefits for Five Generating Resources, for Bonneville Power Administration, DOE/BP-11551-1, Portland, Oregon, April, 1986,[hereater cited as ECO Northwest, 1986].

[8] Economic agents may, as a result of environmental costs, alter their behavior, thus altering the response associated with exposure to a pollutant. For simplicity of exposition, that feedback is not considered.

economic good or service. While lacking precision, for economists the in exactterm "value" is meaningful.[9]

Natural resources produce many kinds of value, including moral or intrinsic value, ecological value, and economic value,[10] which has meaning only in the context of human action.[11] Changes in the ecosystem that do not eventually affect the availability of opportunities to humans have no economic value. The economic value of a thing--whether the thing is a manufactured good, a tree, a plant, or a bug--is defined by the benefits provided, not by any intrinsic moral value. Intrinsic or moral value may be included in economic value only if the services a natural resource provides to humans include its intrinsic or moral dimensions. Ultimately, someone has to be willing to pay for a service or be willing to sell it for it to have economic value.

Although the term "environmental goods and services" sometimes is used synonymously with "natural resources", it refers more precisely to the dimensions of natural resources that have, or potentially have, economic value. A resource may provide multiple environmental goods and services--for example, the multiple benefits of clean water, which include better recreation, healthier drinking water, and thriving fisheries, among others.[12]

Something has economic value if someone would be willing to buy it or sell it.[13] This willingness to pay or to sell might exist only under hypothetical circumstances, and might be constrained by geographic, temporal, or other considerations, but implies some right to partial or temporary ownership, or yielding of ownership. For example, in a hypothetical market one may speak of willingness to "buy" wilderness, even though no one may actually do so. Willingness to pay indicates the value of wilderness to an individual. Conversely, one may be willing to "sell" the wilderness, even if one is only a member of the public-at-large who owns the wilderness.

2. Benefits and Costs

An environmental good or service's value is the benefit it confers less its cost. A benefit is any improvement in one's well-being. Benefits may accrue in several ways:

---

[9] As with many other topics covered in this report, theoretical precision may be sacrificed to avoid obscuring the message in a tangle of qualifiers. More elegant descriptions of the theory appear in the referenced studies. See Freeman, A., The Benefits of Environmental Improvement, Johns Hopkins Press, Baltimore, Md., 1979.

[10] An emerging branch of philosophy known as environmental ethics considers such questions of moral value as whether animals and plants have rights, feelings, or souls. Varner, G. "Do Species Have Standing?", Environmental Ethics, Vol. 9, No. 1, Spring, 1987. Ecologists who study the complex web of interrelationships among plants and animals in a region are likely to define the value of a species in terms of its value to other species coexisting in the biosystem: in other words, in terms of ecological value.

[11] von Mises, L., Human Action, Yale Univ. Press, New Haven, CT, 1949.

[12] Krutilla, J. and A. Fisher, The Economics of Natural Environments, Resources for the Future, Johns Hopkins University Press, Baltimore, MD, 1975, p. 7; Bower, B. and A. Kneese, Managing Water Quality, Johns Hopkins Press, Baltimore, MD, 1968.

[13] Samuelson, P., Economics, McGraw-Hill, New York, 1973 [hereafter cited as Samuelson].

increases in the quantity available, increases in the quality available, or decreases in damages or threat of damages. Costs are reductions in well-being or the value of forgone opportunities.[14] Costs accrue in ways opposite to benefits: decreases in quality or quantity, or increases in damage, or the threat of damage. Costs are, therefore, the inverse of benefits; a negative cost is a benefit, a negative benefit is a cost. Moreover, in economic discussions, costs are typically cast in terms of forgone benefits. In this report, the term "costs" is more widely used, reflecting the view that most of the environmental effects associated with energy resources result in costs,[15] although environmental benefits also may be created.

D. DEFINING MEASURES OF ENVIRONMENTAL COSTS

1. The Value of Risk as a Measure of Environmental Costs

A central theme of this report concerns defining and estimating environmental costs. A major tenet of economics is that environmental costs are the total value of the risk imposed on society by the environmental effects of an energy resource.

Risk is the set of all possible responses to an environmental intrusion and their probability distributions. The term, "risk" often refers to the variability of an estimate.[16] A broader view is used here. Risk includes the expected value of the effect, or its mean, as well as the variability of all possible outcomes and their associated probabilities. The expected value of a probability distribution is typically used as a single estimate of the value of the variable because it is an unbiased estimate.[17] In utility resource planning models, for example, expected values are typically used for variables, such as construction lead time, plant life, size of plant, and even fuel costs, construction costs, and load growth rates.[18]

Because utility resource planning is prospective, the environmental costs and benefits of energy resources must be estimated before the environmental effects actually occur--just as other economic variables, such as load forecasts, fuel prices, and hydro conditions, are forecast subject to uncertainty. Because environmental effects are complex, and because there may be a long lag between emissions and response, and because it is unlikely that all the actual victims of an energy resource's environmental effects can be identified, the environmental effects caused by an energy

---

14 Alchian, A. and W. Allen, Exchange and Production: Theory in Use, Wadsworth, Belmont, Calif., 1969, Ch. 14.

15 Georgescu-Roegen, N., The Entropy Law and the Economic Process, Harvard University Press, Cambridge, 1971.

16 Rescher, N., Risk: A Philosophical Introduction to the Theory of Risk Evaluation and Management, University Press of America, Lanham, Md., 1983, p. 5 [hereafter cited as Rescher].

17 Id. p. 50.

18 BPA, 1986a, supra note 4 at p. 14.

resource may never be known precisely.[19] Yet we can predict from the five step linkages process described above, which population includes the individuals who will be harmed by an emission and, within a range of certainty, what proportion of the population is expected to be harmed.

Therefore, the risk is held collectively by all members of the exposed population because everyone exposed to the pollutant is at some risk, however small, of being harmed. The cost of the environmental risks associated with a pollutant, or some other environmental effect, is the amount that the average member of society would pay to avoid the risk, or, conversely, the amount of compensation that would be required to induce someone to bear the risk voluntarily.[20] It is that risk, borne by all members of the population, that is valued.

In the case of health effects, for example, it is not the value of a specific human life that is at issue. Rather, it is the risk of mortality or morbidity which is shared by all members of the exposed population that is relevant for economic valuation purposes.[21] The same holds true for virtually all environmental costs. While we seldom know exactly which crops will be damaged, which forests will be denuded, or whose recreation opportunities will be diminished, but we do know which crops, which forests and which recreation opportunities are at risk.[22]

Using risk as the basis for valuation may be clarified by referring to an insurance analogy. The actuarial value of insurance is its expected value, determined by integrating the economic costs of all consequences over the probability distribution of those consequences.[23] In the simplest case one multiplies the probability of an event (or consequence) by its cost, to get an expected value of the cost of the event. Thus, if one of every 10,000 people could be expected to die following exposure to a pollutant, and if the average value of that risk--that is, the average amount each individual would pay to avoid the risk--is $100, then the total value of the risk is $1,000,000. Therefore, society should be willing to pay $1,000,000 to insure that none of its members were exposed to the risk.

The most common way to determine the value of risks is to determine the expected value of the cost of damage for different outcomes and their probability distributions,[24] which can be estimated without identifying who will be affected. An

---

19 ECO Northwest, Generic Coal Study, for Bonneville Power Administration, DE-AM79-86BP62884, Portland, OR, 1987 at p. 3-2 [hereafter cited as ECO Northwest, 1987]. If specific victims can be identified, we assume that costs will be determined by the judicial system.

20 Viscusi, W., "Toward a Diminished Role for Tort Liability: Social Insurance, Government Regulation, and Contemporary Risks to Health and Safety", Yale Journal on Regulation, Vol. 6, No. 1, Winter, 1989 [hereafter cited as Viscusi 1989]. (The choice between willingness to pay and willingness to be compensated is explained in a separate section.)

21 See infra, Chapter III K., Health Risk Valuation.

22 Although economic valuations of environmental risks are emphasized in this report, we need improved understanding of the changes in physical and biological relationships that result from environmental impacts of energy resources to understand the risks.

23 Rescher, supra note 16 at p. 50.

24 Id. p. 53.

average measure of willingness to pay or willingness to be compensated for each member of the affected societal group, multiplied by the number of people in the group, yields the expected value of the social cost of the environmental risk.[25]

To summarize, economic value of environmental risks is the amount that society would be willing to pay to avoid the environmental risk or the amount society would require as compensation to incur the environmental risk voluntarily. The economic value of environmental risks can be based on a number of different measures.

2. Mitigation Costs, Control Costs, and Damage Costs

One common measure of environmental cost is the cost of coping with or mitigating the environmental effects. For example, one way to measure the environmental cost of air pollution to a farmer whose yields are reduced by a power plant's emissions is to estimate the cost of the fertilizer necessary to offset yield reductions.

A second basis for estimating costs is the cost of preventing the effects from occurring.[26] This requires estimating the costs of reducing emissions to zero, or to some benign level at which the effects would not occur. This cost might be based on the cost of a series of scrubbers or other measures installed to remove pollutants from the emissions stream, or by the cost of using non-polluting resources. In general, society is willing to pay for the lowest cost of these measures. The typical challenge of environmental cost analysis, however, is to determine the value of the residual environmental risks after controls have been implemented by the utility.

Because utilities do not account for the environmental costs of their resources (that is, after all, what makes them externalities), they do not select control measures based on the potential environmental benefits of those controls. Utilities generally have no incentive to pay for controls beyond those required by regulatory authorities. Consequently, because the amount and type of controls to be put in place is already determined, the cost of additional controls is largely irrelevant. Moreover, the potential benefits of using controls are the damages avoided. One cannot determine the benefits of controls by defining them to be equal to their cost. One of the valuable purposes of estimating environmental cost is to help determine the economically efficient level of controls, which requires determining the amount of damage avoided as a result of the controls. It is that damage that we seek to value through environmental costing procedures.

A third measure is the net economic damage created by the environmental effects of an energy resource. Continuing the example of crop losses, the economic damage

---

25 Often several groups must be identified so that within each group all persons share approximately the same risk. But different groups may share different risks. For example, population groups living in concentric rings around a power plant may be identified. Those living closest to the plant would bear greater health risks than those living further away. Similarly, population groups may be aggregated by age factors. Children and the elderly may face greater risks than middle age people exposed to the same level of pollutants. Thus, the society at large whose values are being counted may require grouping, but the same concepts apply: The average value of the risk borne by members of the group is multiplied by the number in the group to yield the group's willingness to pay or willingness to be compensated.

26 Chernick, P. and E. Caverhill, The Valuation of Externalities from Energy Production, Delivery, and Use, for Boston Gas Co., Boston, Mass., December 22, 1989, p. 38.

would be valued by the product of lost yield and crop prices, which is the lost economic value of the farmer's product. Because there is no reason to believe that control costs and the amount of economic damage associated with most environmental risks will be related, damage costs are more likely to represent the real cost of environmental risks faced by society. In the absence of damage cost estimates, however, control costs may be the best available measures of environmental costs. It is not possible to estimate damage costs of global warming, for example, as its potential costs are unknown and highly speculative.[27] What is known is that the costs could be catastrophic. If society chooses to avoid the greenhouse risk, then the relevant measure of its costs would be the cost of prevention. The goal would be to prevent or, if prevention is impossible, to slow the onset of climatic change at the least cost. This is the methodology used for global warming in this report. For other environmental costs we use damage costs as the basis for valuation.

E. WHAT ENVIRONMENTAL RISKS ARE TO BE VALUED?

Because each potential energy resource and each potential site has unique characteristics,[28] and each affected societal group has unique interests and concerns, it is not possible to list all environmental effects that may have economic value. What may have a significant economic value at site A may have little value at site B. Nevertheless, it is useful to explore some of the general characteristics of effects likely to be caused by energy resources.

1. Costs that Precede Plant Construction and Operation

Environmental costs are created during such activities as fuel extraction and in the manufacture of materials used to build power plants and to install conservation measures. These kinds of costs are problematic for environmental cost analyses because it is uncertain whether those costs should be included in the resource's environmental costs.

In principle, all costs associated with the energy resource under consideration should be accounted for.[29] This also is true for the fuel and materials required to build and operate the plant. But there are difficulties accounting for such costs as coal mining effects, pipeline leakages, coal train accidents, and so forth.

First, there is a never ending chain of effects when looking "upstream"[30] at the fuel cycle. Consider coal mining, which certainly creates some environmental costs. But the mining operation depends on manufactured materials and equipment. That

---

27 Chapter V.A. treats in full the valuation of the effects of global warming.

28 See Buchanan, supra note 1.

29 BPA, 1986a, supra note 4.

30 "Upstream effects" (also, front-end costs) occur prior to operating an energy resource. "Downstream effects" occur after constructing and operating an energy resource.

manufacturing process also creates environmental costs, and it uses tools and equipment that are manufactured somewhere else. And that process uses equipment that was manufactured somewhere else, and so on.[31]

How are the environmental costs accounted for at every stage in that process? One solution is to use an input-output model which, through the use of multipliers, can sort out this infinite chain, and yield estimates of all physical goods and processes used during the life-cycle of the energy resource. This resolves the physical entanglement of processes, providing such a model is available, but it leads to another problem.

Some of those costs are internalized in the costs of inputs. Insurance and safety expenditures incurred by the coal mining firm internalize at least some of the environmental costs associated with coal mining. These costs are passed on to the coal plant operator, and ultimately to the electric power consumers in the price of the coal. With all upstream effects, it is difficult to ensure that some costs are not counted twice, resulting in an overestimate of environmental costs.[32]

Because of these concerns, the contract under which this study was conducted, and its scope only studies of the "downstream" costs of energy resources are evaluated in this report. Upstream environmental costs not included in the values reported in this study are found by costing studies reviewed to be significant.

2. Fixed and Variable Costs

Over its life, a resource is in one of three stages: construction, operation, and decommissioning.[33] Environmental costs created by plant construction, or installation of a conservation measure, are usually one-time events. Although these costs are fixed and invariant with respect to whether and how often a plant operates, they may, however, persist over time, even beyond the life of the resource.

Construction, decommissioning, or the very existence of a power plant at a site can have a number of environmental effects including a reservoir that floods agricultural land removing it from production for at least as long as the reservoir exists; land contaminated by radiation may be permanently lost; the quality of life in a community may be reduced if there is an influx of a large, temporary construction work force, an effect known as the boomtown effect; fish and wildlife habitat may be destroyed; or, aesthetic values may be damaged, such as when a unique vista is marred, a waterfall is flooded, or when scenic sites are altered. The frequency, severity, and therefore, the costs of these effects do not depend on the amount of

---

31 Bonneville Power Administration, BPA Evaluation of Generic Environmental Costs and Benefits Studies, Portland, OR, 1986b, [hereafter cited as BPA, 1986b].

32 ECO Northwest, Economic Analysis of the Environmental Effects of the Coal-Fired Electric Generator at Boardman, Oregon, for Bonneville Power Administration, DE-AC79-83BP11551, Portland, OR, 1983, p. IV-3, [hereafter cited as ECO Northwest 1983].

33 BPA, 1986a, supra note 4 at p. 16.

energy produced by the plant, although they may be correlated with plant capacity, if the effects depend on plant size.[34]

With few exceptions, environmental effects associated with plant operation vary directly with plant output because air and watersheds are affected directly by plant operation. Most of the effluents and their ensuing effects can be traced from their emission from the plant to their final physical effects. The correlation of plant output and environmental costs can usually be expressed on a per kilowatt-hour basis, which is useful when determining the levelized costs of a resource's environmental costs.[35] Costs in this report have been converted to costs per kilowatt-hour, expressed in 1989 dollars.

3. Direct Costs, Indirect Costs, and Transfer Costs

The net change in the economic value of environmental risks from construction, operation, or decommissioning of an electric power resource includes only the costs and benefits directly attributable to the resource. Direct costs are the net change in economic value resulting from the production, consumption, or exchange of an economic good or service.[36] Indirect costs are the changes associated with ensuing rounds of production, consumption, or exchange of other goods and services. In a perfect economic analysis, all effects would be traced out and the net change in value across the entire economy would be measured. In the real world, however, indirect costs and benefits tend to cancel each other out.

For example, a reservoir created as part of a hydroelectric project may generate direct benefits in the form of increased recreation values afforded vacationing boaters and prospective boaters.[37] Indirect effects include the increased retail opportunities to serve the influx of boaters. Whether to count those indirect effects as benefits depends on the analytic perspective.

From a national perspective, the increase in recreation value experienced by boaters at the reservoir would be included as direct benefits, and the increased income of area residents who sell goods and services to the new boaters would be indirect benefits. Although these represent real gains to the community, they are costs to the boaters. Indeed, the increased incomes for local residents are exactly offset by the costs incurred by the boaters.[38] If, however, the state where the reservoir is located

---

[34] BPA, 1985, supra note 6.

[35] "Levelized costs" are costs expressed on a per kilowatt-hour basis. Cost levelization converts uneven streams of costs into streams of equal payments for each unit of energy produced, enabling comparison of resources having different capital and operating costs. For example, the costs of a hydroelectric facility are almost entirely capital costs, while a combustion turbine is dominated by operating costs. Their costs can be compared by levelizing their capital and operating costs over the energy produced by each plant.

[36] Campen, J., Benefit, Cost, and Beyond, Ballinger Publishing Co., Cambridge, Mass., 1986, p. 33.

[37] Knetsch, J., Economics of Outdoor Recreation, Johns Hopkins University Press for Resources for the Future, Baltimore, MD, 1966.

[38] BPA, 1986b, supra note 31.

decided that only benefits and costs to its residents are to be counted, the direct benefits to all state residents would be counted, while the direct benefits to out-of-state boaters would not be counted. Boating services payments by state residents would not be counted because the local income gain would be exactly offset by the costs incurred by other residents. Conversely, the local income gains created by the spending of another state's residents would be counted because expenditures by non-residents would be ignored, and so would not offset the local income gains.

If the reservoir were in another state, the situation would differ in only one respect. Direct benefits would be counted as before: the benefits to state residents who use the site would be counted. Neither direct nor indirect benefits to out of staters would be counted because they would accrue entirely to residents of another state, who, by definition, have not been included in the perspective.

Because the impulse to treat expenditures as benefits is prevalent,[39] exploring the example a little further may bring some clarity to the issue. Transfer costs and benefits merely take money out of one pocket and put it into another, with no net change in economic benefits or costs.[40] Had the reservoir not been created, the boaters would not have been attracted to this location and would have spent their money somewhere else. The money might have been spent at an existing reservoir for similar goods and services such as food, fuel, or equipment. Alternatively, the money might have been spent in an altogether different way, such as building a backyard swimming pool, but someone else would have received the revenues and the resulting benefit, so the retailers' increased incomes at the new reservoir represent forgone incomes to other retailers. One set of businesses has gained at the expense of another set. This is known as an income transfer.[41] Incomes that would have been created elsewhere or spent on other goods and services would have been transferred to the new locality. From a global perspective, however, no net change in income will have occurred.

There are sound theoretical and pragmatic reasons for counting only direct effects and excluding indirect effects and transfer costs from the evaluation of environmental costs and benefits in general.[42] First, there is no evidence that alternative expenditure patterns would create a significantly different economic equilibrium with or without the good or service under consideration (in our example, the reservoir).[43] On the average, people will spend the same amount of money elsewhere; on the average, people will spend their money similarly (on boating in this example); and, on the average, the indirect and transfer costs will all cancel each other out.[44]

Moreover, the complexity of tracing out all effects and measuring the resulting change in value is enormous. In principle, an input-output model of the economy

---

[39] Id.

[40] Id.

[41] Campen, supra note 36 at p. 33.

[42] Id.

[43] BPA, 1986b, supra note 31 at p. 6.

[44] Id.

could be developed to estimate all the interactions among all the economic agents and economic variables involved, which would enable an analyst not only to estimate the increases in local proprietary income but to estimate how it will be spent and how recipients of the income spent by the proprietor spent their income, how those recipients spent their income, etc. After several rounds of spending, the effects would become negligible.

Describing these effects is a useful and often necessary task, especially when the goal is regional or industrial development.[45] It is, however, exceedingly difficult, costly, and time-consuming. And, while necessary to perform a complete and perfect economic analysis, it is not sufficient. More difficult, still, would be identifying each and every alternative expenditure pattern: if recreators did not have the new reservoir available, where and how would they spend their money?

Measuring only direct effects avoids these difficulties with little loss of accuracy.[46] Excluding indirect and transfer costs means that the net economic value of an effect, whether it be recreation, health, ecosystem damage, or any other effect, is captured by an estimate of the direct costs and benefits alone. It is not only unnecessary to capture indirect effects, it is incorrect to do so because, unless the nearly impossible conditions for a full analysis can be met, valuing indirect effects as part of the environmental costs and benefits of a project results in double counting of benefits or costs.

F. PERSPECTIVE

1. Environmental Costs Imply a Social Cost Perspective

The issue of whose benefits and costs to count when estimating environmental benefits and costs is called the perspective issue. One may define the perspective for analysis in a variety of ways but the most common definition would be by political units.[47] Costs borne by economic agents residing within those units are counted; costs borne by economic agents beyond those boundaries are ignored.

One definition of the relevant political boundary is the service territory of the utility, but with that perspective, the incentive for utilities simply to develop resources elsewhere is obvious. Moreover, it is a ratepayer perspective. There would be no accounting for the environmental costs of resources developed beyond the utility's service territory except when such resources create risks for people within the service territory --i.e., ratepayers--and this is the situation that accounting for environmental costs is intended to correct.

---

45 Id. It would also be necessary to perform this task for every single effect of every single resource.

46 Id.

47 Buchanan, supra note 1 at p. 4.

Another perspective is that of the state. Under this perspective, costs borne by out-of-state residents would be ignored. Only those costs incurred by residents or other businesses in the state would be counted.[48]

State regulatory commissions have required utilities to consider all costs from utility operations, not confined to any political boundaries. [49] Why would a state select a national or international perspective for evaluating environmental costs and benefits? To address that question it is useful to examine how environmental costs may be borne by out-of-state residents.

The energy resource, or some components of it, may be produced or located out-of-state. A coal mine in Pennsylvania may supply a coal plant in New York. A coal plant in Wyoming may supply electric power to consumers in Oregon. Environmental costs associated with energy resources or fuels located in other states are knowingly and willingly incurred by residents of those states and that the profits on the plant or fuels, as well as the mitigation measures undertaken by the host state to compensate for those costs, are internalized in the price of fuel or electricity, so it would be double-counting to treat them as environmental externality costs.[50]

To the extent that such costs truly are internalized, they should not be counted as environmental costs. The conditions under which such costs are internalized are restrictive, however. First, the people affected must be aware of the risks associated with environmental effects. Risks imposed on an unsuspecting public can not be considered to be internalized.[51] Second, for costs to be internalized, those who bear risks must bear the costs. The compensation value of those costs must be included in the price of the services rendered by the entity creating the costs in the first place. This may sometimes be accomplished by insurance. But insurance premiums are based on the amount of claims paid. Even though real public costs may be incurred when a natural asset such as a waterway is damaged, seldom is the public fully compensated by insurance claims. Thus, insurance costs are unlikely to cover the full amount of potential damages associated with environmental effects, and therefore, do not fully account for the costs of the risk thereby created.

Third, many environmental effects may be created elsewhere and are not confined to local boundaries. This leads to the second way in which out-of-state residents may incur environmental costs. Energy resources may cause acid rain or deplete anadromous fish stocks, creating costs to people far from where the pollutant is emitted. Emissions of greenhouse gases and ozone depleting substances affect everyone.

States might choose to account for costs imposed on out-of-state residents, because externalities are considered in the acquisition of energy resources, and because energy is a regulated, public good, directly affecting the public's interests. The nature of

---

48 Id.

49 See Chapter X.

50 ECO Northwest, 1983, supra note 32 at p. IV-3.

51 Measures of WTP and WTC require conditions under which transactions would occur voluntarily. Samuelson, supra note 13.

interstate commerce implies that costs incurred by one state should be evaluated as they would be if they were borne by another state.

Another pragmatic reason to account for all environmental costs, even those borne by out-of-state residents, is to anticipate future environmental laws and regulations. Environmental regulations enacted during the past two decades were implemented to reduce real environmental costs. When real economic damage occurs the political and social processes respond and statutes and regulations are enacted to reduce the severity of damage costs. As more is learned about environmental risks, there is every reason to believe this trend will continue.

Moreover, to the extent that decision processes ignore social costs, social costs will not be minimized. Utility resource decisions send clear and strong price signals to the market. A selection process which ignores external costs sends misleading price signals to the market.[52]

From a national perspective, costs borne by all United States citizens are counted and counted equally. Costs to Pennsylvania citizens count as much as those to New York citizens; costs to Wyoming citizens count as much as those to Oregon citizens. Moreover, the most efficient national market results when prices reflect the true costs of production, consumption, and exchange.[53] Therefore, a national or international perspective is consistent with least social cost planning.

A global perspective may be preferred to a national perspective and, in fact, has been adopted by the state regulatory commission, as previously mentioned.[54] Many environmental risks do not respect national boundaries. Hydroelectric facilities may harm anadromous fish and affect both foreign and domestic fishing enterprises. Emissions from coal plants in the United States may cause acid rain in Canada. Carbon dioxide emissions contribute to global climate change. To the extent that these costs, and others like them, are known, it makes sense economically to include them as resource costs.

None of these arguments implies using a single national or world price. Costs that differ among regions because of different physical impacts or regional variations in the value of those impacts are appropriately reflected in the valuation of environmental effects. The point is that failure to include all costs, regardless of who bears those costs, distorts price signals and impedes economic efficiency improvements that could result from selection of least social cost resources.[55]

---

[52] While the focus of this report is on economic efficiency, equity and fairness are also important considerations when making economic decisions. Whether to count the costs of environmental risks borne by citizens of other states certainly qualifies as an equity issue.

[53] Samuelson, supra note 13.

[54] Buchanan, supra note 1 at p. 4.

[55] The foregoing discussion concerns the perspective for evaluating environmental costs and benefits in the context of utility resource planning. This is distinct from regulating such environmental costs. Although increasingly wide regulatory perspectives require higher levels of government involvement, no such dependence on higher levels of government exists for utility planning purposes. The selection of a political boundary is a choice to be made by the utility or by its regulatory body.

2. Temporal Perspective

Another perspective issue is how to evaluate costs to future generations. Future generations will bear some of the costs imposed by energy resources planned today. Such costs are taken into account when internal costs of energy resources are evaluated--the costs to future ratepayers are explicitly taken into account. Similar procedures should be applied to environmental costs that will be borne by future citizens, and they also must be included as part of the social cost of a prospective energy resource.

3. Willingness to Pay and Willingness to be Compensated

Another significant issue related to choice of an analytical perspective is whether to value environmental risks with measures based on willingness to pay (WTP) or willingness to be compensated (WTC). Benefits (or costs) are usually expressed as a maximum WTP or a minimum WTC. The choice involves determining property rights which, for many collectively held goods and services, are not always clearly defined.

Historically, economists have assumed WTP and WTC measures to be nearly identical. Theoretical support for that view was provided by Willig,[56] whose analysis appeared to show that as long as consumers' changes in income have no effect on their demand for a good and as long as any price change has a small effect on the income available to spend on other goods and services the two measures would not differ significantly. Even when those conditions were only approximated, the difference between WTP and WTC would be small. These findings were consistent with what economists had long observed with respect to market goods and services. Consequently, the two measures were assumed to be substitutes.

That changed with the advent of contingent valuation, the only technique capable of measuring both WTC and WTP. One of the first studies to estimate both measures found WTC values to be about four times greater than WTP values.[57] Researchers discovered that, contrary to expectations, WTC values were consistently higher than WTP measures. At first, these findings were dismissed as anomalous because Willig's 1976 work convinced many that such an outcome had to be either a fluke or the result of poor methodology. Subsequent contingent valuation studies, however, consistently showed high WTC values relative to WTP values. Accordingly, researchers began to seek explanations for the phenomenon.[58]

---

[56] Willig, R., "Consumers' Surplus Without Apology", American Economic Review, Vol. 66, No. 4, September, 1976, p. 589.

[57] Hammack, J. and G. Brown, Waterfowl and Wetlands: Toward Bioeconomic Analysis, Johns Hopkins, Baltimore, Md., 1974.

[58] Mitchell, R. and R. Carson, Using Surveys to Value Public Goods: The Contingent Valuation Method, Resources for the Future, Washington, D.C., 1989 [hereafter cited to as Mitchell].

a. Why WTP May Not Equal WTC

Several reasons for the discrepancy between the two measures have been identified. Extremely high--sometimes infinitely high--WTC values may indicate a rejection of the proposal. These bids (answers to survey questions about willingness to be compensated) are often referred to as protest bids, in which the respondent apparently views the proposed action as implausible or illegitimate.[59] Such bids are significant for energy resource planning as they may indicate public rejection of an environmental risk.

In some cases high, but not extraordinarily high, WTC values have been found.[60] A "cautious consumer" hypothesis may explain these further discrepancies. It argues that respondents often do not have sufficient familiarity with contingent value questions, may be uncertain, do not have time to optimize the decision about the good in question, or may be risk averse.[61] Each of these characteristics may result in higher WTC values with respect to WTP values than would occur if risk neutrality, certainty, and sufficient time were available.

Prospect theory, also used to explain the discrepancy between WTP and WTC,[62] proposes that the welfare reduction of an absolute amount of loss is greater than the welfare improvement of an equivalent absolute amount of gain. In other words, a dollar lost hurts more than a dollar gained helps. As a result, if the contingent valuation format implies that the individual must give up a good he now holds or to which he is entitled, a higher amount of compensation will be required than would be paid to obtain the good. This outcome is even more likely with respect to natural resource public goods because the issue often involves an all-or-nothing outcome, exacerbating the perceived degree of loss that must be compensated.

Another explanation is the price flexibility of income, which consists of a measure of income elasticity and the elasticity of substitution between the public good and all other goods in the economy.[63] If there are frequent opportunities to benefit from the good in question or others like it, the elasticity of substitution is likely to be high. If there is nothing particularly unique about the good a number of other goods can, with some degree of imperfection, substitute for the good. A high elasticity of substitution results in small differences between WTC and WTP. If, however, the proposed action involves large, irreversible changes, and if the good has few substitutes, then the elasticity of substitution is likely to be small. These circumstances predictably result in large differences between WTP and WTC. If substitution possibilities diminish or

---

59 Id.

60 Bishop, R. and T. Heberlein, "Measuring Values of Extramarket Goods: Are Indirect Measures Biased?", American Journal of Agricultural Economics, Vol. 61, 1979, p. 926.

61 Hoehn, J. and A. Randall, Incentives and Performance in Contingent Valuation, mimeo, University of Kentucky, February 1983.

62 Kahneman, D. and A. Tversky, "Prospect Theory: An Analysis of Decision Under Risk", Econometrica, Vol. 47, No. 2, March 1979, [hereafter cited as Kahneman].

63 Hanemann, W., Willingness to Pay and Willingness to Accept: How Much Can They Differ?, University of California, Working Paper No. 328, Berkeley, Cal., March 1986.

if natural resources become increasingly scarce, the disparity will increase between the two measures.

Another factor that increases the difference between WTP and WTC is when large or irreversible actions will destroy the good in question or alter it significantly. Confiscation of property is more costly than a voluntary sale because the inequity must be compensated for, even if it is only a perceived inequity.

b. Choosing Between WTP and WTC

The choice between WTP and WTC depends on legal, philosophical, and availability criteria. Certain federal agencies, for example, are barred by the Interior Department Inter Agency Task Force from using WTC values.[64] Similarly, a state regulatory body may mandate the use of one measure or the other or define the circumstances under which either measure can be used.

A desire for consistency may guide regulators in establishing the criteria previously described. In citing an example of site restoration, Fisher argues that WTC measures should be more widely applied.[65] Cost estimates to restore a site implicitly use WTC measures. These are the payments required to compensate for wages, payments for materials, and so forth. The owners of those goods and services will not expend them voluntarily unless sufficient compensation is forthcoming. Consistency requires that when non-market goods and services are valued in such a context, WTC measures be used.

The recognition of existing or perceived property rights may also dictate the measure to be used. Holders of the property rights to a resource may be entitled to the existing form, quality, and quantity of the resource in question. If an action would destroy the resource, asking how much one would pay to avoid the action could be considered economic racketeering, like, "How much will you pay me not to burn your house down?"

However, often the property rights to the good in question are unclear. Common property resources have no well defined property right holders.[66] In such cases, it may be necessary to compute both WTP and WTC measures. WTP measures would be construed as minimum values, while WTC measures would be construed as maximum values. Neither measure may be entirely correct; neither may be completely incorrect.

While value-neutral economic analysis has no theoretical basis by which to select the measure to be used when property rights are not well-defined, explicit decisions regarding the designation of property rights holders are within the purview of decision makers, at least with respect to deciding which value to use. Indeed, explicit decisions

---

[64] Carson, R. and P. Navarro, "Natural Resources Damage Assessment", Natural Resources Journal, Fall 1988, p. 815 [hereafter cited as Carson].

[65] Fisher, A., "Energy and Environment in the Long Term", Energy Policy, Vol. 17, No. 2, April 1989, p. 84.

[66] Coase, R., "The Problem of Social Cost," The Journal of Law and Economics. Vol. III, 1960 and Randall, A., "Market Solutions to Externality Problems: Theory and Practice," American Journal of Agricultural Economics, Vol. 54, 1972, p. 175.

may be necessary, to decide which measure to use. This means that the utility or its regulatory body must define either the polluter or the public as the property right owner. If a polluter has the property right to pollute, the cost of the pollution borne by others, who by assumption do not hold a property right to a clean environment, must be valued by their willingness to pay to avoid the pollution. Conversely, if the affected public holds the property right instead of the polluter, then the cost of pollution is measured by society's willingness to be compensated for the pollution.[67]

In sum, WTP values are most appropriate when those bearing the costs of environmental risks do not hold property rights to the degraded natural asset. WTC values are the most appropriate when those bearing the costs of environmental risks hold property rights.[68]

However, WTP values are likely to be the only values available to the analyst. The preponderance of studies derive WTP values whereas only a limited number have estimated WTC values. Without a contingent valuation study[69], there may be no way to estimate WTC values. In such cases the analyst has little choice but to use WTP values. In such cases, WTP usually underestimates damages, perhaps significantly. If the cost effectiveness of a potential energy resource is sensitive to a value based on WTP, further work to derive a WTC value may be necessary.

G. CHARACTERIZING ENERGY RESOURCES

1. Generic vs. Site-Specific Analyses

In planning for new energy resources, utilities determine the cost effectiveness of a range of possible resources, which is likely to include both actual, site-specific resources, and generic resources.[70] Generic resources represent typical, but hypothetical facilities. They are useful for developing supply functions because they focus on significant characteristics such as capital, operating, and fuel costs; plant capacity; energy output; construction lead-time; expected facility life; and environmental costs and benefits. By reducing information needs to a few salient characteristics, analysts can evaluate efficiently a range of available resource choices.

However, the ease of forecasting for a generic resource is counterbalanced by the greater accuracy and reliability of forecasts made for site-specific resources. This is especially true for environmental costs and benefits. Many environmental costs and benefits depend on both the resource type and its site.[71] The same generic facility

---

67 The social and economic difficulties that arise with common property resources are described elegantly in Hardin, G., "Tragedy of the Commons", Science, Vol. 162, 1968.

68 Carson, supra note 64.

69 See Section I.4.c.below.

70 See, for example, Bonneville Power Administration, "WNP-1 and -3 Study", 1987 Resource Strategy, Portland, OR, May, 1987.

71 BPA, 1985, supra note 6.

could produce vastly different environmental effects, depending upon climate, geography, soil types, ecosystem types, wind patterns, size and proximity of the exposed human population, affected fish and wildlife populations, local economics, and demographic characteristics. If site characteristics, not generic characteristics, determine the type and magnitude of environmental costs, estimates based only on generic resource characteristics will be less reliable.

Generic analyses may be more likely to underestimate environmental costs. Almost by definition, a generic site, which is selected largely because of the lack of significant impediments to siting the facility at that location, has no locally significant effects, while many environmental costs are a function of site. Consequently, when estimating the environmental effects associated with the resource, only effects that are generally expected to occur, and which do not depend on site characteristics, will be accounted for. Specific and locally significant effects will be accounted for only when site-specific plants are analyzed, so to the extent that site characteristics determine the type and magnitude of environmental costs, estimates based only on prototype resource characteristics will be unreliable.[72]

Developing estimates of environmental costs is a dynamic process. First-cut estimates can be developed generically. Resources whose generic environmental costs are high enough to make them cost-ineffective often can be eliminated because subsequent site-specific costs will likely be even higher. Generic analyses are also useful for guiding site-specific analyses; sensitivity analyses of potentially significant variables at the generic analysis stage can point to factors which may be significant at the site-specific level. For example, a particular pollutant from a power plant may travel only short distances after emission. A generic analysis can determine threshold levels of local population beyond which the pollutant's costs become significant.[73] Similarly, generic analyses can guide siting decisions. Significant cost factors identified in generic analyses can be considered in siting actual resources. For example, the size of local populations may be a significant determinant of environmental costs. Or, aesthetic factors may be identified as a potentially significant cost. Considering such factors during site selection offers the possibility of reducing costs by avoiding certain locations.

By defination, generic analyses identify average costs, whereas site-specific analyses identify the costs associated with marginal impacts. At a policy level, however, the average effects are paramount because policies address average, not marginal effects. Therefore, generic analyses are useful at the policy level even if significant site-specific effects are overlooked. On the other hand, for environmental costing purposes marginal costs are sought where possible, because it is the environmental cost of a new proposed resource that must be selected and costed.

Finally, generic estimates of environmental costs are often the only estimates available. In the absence of site-specific estimates of environmental risks, generic estimates must be used.

---

[72] BPA, 1986b, supra note 31 at p. 1.

[73] ECO Northwest 1987, supra note 19 at p. 32.

2. Costs of Joint Products

When two or more products are created by the same process, it may not be clear how to allocate costs to each product.[74] The problem of allocating joint production costs nearly always arises with cogeneration which, by its very definition means that more than one product is being produced, and may sometimes be an issue with conservation measures. Usually, the joint products are electricity and thermal power.[75]

All cost allocation methods first separate the costs that are related to one product. The separable costs of each product are those incurred in producing that product and that product only. A turbine-generator is a separable cost because it would not be incurred if only thermal power were being produced. Similarly, when the cogeneration plant produces just one product, environmental costs are allocated fully to that product. If, for example, the plant were operating to produce electric power but no thermal power, the costs of atmospheric emissions would be charged fully to the electric power.[76]

Sometimes the environmental cost of electric power production determining how often the plant produces a single product can be calculated. When that product is electricity, all environmental costs of plant operation are charged to electrical production. During those periods when no electricity is produced, none of the environmental costs of plant operation are charged to electrical production.[77]

Most of the time, however, a cogenerator operates in a joint production mode. One method of allocating joint costs is according to the economic **value of the product**. If, for example, 60 percent of the total value is from electricity sales, then 60 percent of the costs are allocated to electricity. It is a relatively straightforward task to determine the total value of each product, its proportion of the total value of the productive process, and to allocate that proportion of environmental costs to that product. However, this method may generate inconsistent values for environmental costs when comparing those costs to environmental costs produced by other energy resources, because the price received for electricity sales by the cogenerator may not reflect the social value of the power, or tax incentives may distort the respective values of electric and thermal power, leading to over- or under-estimates of the environmental cost of electricity.

---

[74] BPA, 1986b, supra note 31 at p. 26.

[75] This section on joint products assumes such a process. Other forms of cogeneration do exist, however. Geothermal processes can produce steam for both electric power and direct space and water heating. Solar arrays could do much the same thing. Most hydroelectric projects are really cogenerators, providing power, irrigation, flood control or other benefits. As diverse as these and other cogeneration configurations can be, however, the environmental costs and benefits of each can be assessed using the principles and methods put forth in this section.

[76] BPA, 1986b, supra note 31.

[77] Id.

Another method allocates costs according to the primary **purpose** of the plant.[78] The environmental costs assigned to producing electric power would be the incremental costs incurred because of the decision to produce electricity. If the purpose of a plant is to use process heat and it would be used for that purpose regardless of production of electricity, then one could impute to electricity no environmental costs for electrical production. A possible objection to this method is that it may require inferring how the plant would have been configured and operated in the absence of an electrical generation process. It might be impossible to know what the amount and timing of emissions would be in the absence of electric power production.

If two important assumptions are met, the plant's **heat rate** can be used to allocate environmental costs.[79] First, one must assume that thermal power would be produced whether or not electric power is produced. Second, one must assume that the effluents emitted by the production of thermal power are emitted during cogeneration. The heat rate for the thermal process alone is subtracted from the total plant heat rate, or total amount of heat, measured in btu's, used to generate each kilowatt-hour. Assume, for example, that in the cogeneration mode the plant uses 12,000 btu for each kWh produced and the thermal process uses 7,000 btu to obtain the amount of thermal power produced when one kWh of electric power is produced. Subtracting 7,000 btu from 12,000btu leaves 5,000btu applicable to electricity production. This heat rate can then be used in the modeling of the environmental costs created by emissions from the plant. The resulting estimate of those costs will automatically be the cost of electricity production, net of the thermal production.

A specific formula for calculating the net emissions from a cogenerator as a function of plant and boiler heat rate is provided by the Energy Systems Research Group in a study prepared for the State of Vermont:[80]

$$En = Eg - Eb \times (Sc / Sb)$$

Where En = Net emissions from a cogenerator
Eg = Gross emissions from a cogenerator
Eb = Gross emissions from the average avoided boiler
Sc = Overall steam efficiency of cogenerator
Sb = Overall steam efficiency of boiler

This method relies on the heat rates of both the avoided boiler and the actual cogeneration unit.

---

78 Buchanan, supra note 1 at p. 12.

79 TechPlan Associates, Assessment of Commercial and Industrial Cogeneration Potential in the Pacific Northwest, for U.S. Dept. of Energy, DE-AC79-88BP40040, March, 1989, p. II-19.

80 Energy Systems Research Group, The Role of Hydro-Quebec Power in a Least-Cost Energy Resource Plan for Vermont, prepared for Dept. of Public Service, State of Vermont, January 19, 1990, p. 9-29.

3. Conclusion

The over-arching principle in estimating environmental costs of cogenerated electricity is to count only those costs that are incurred as a result of electricity production. Nearly all environmental costs are associated with fuel combustion. When the cogenerated product is thermal power, the thermal needs of the plant are readily identifiable. If the assumptions about the thermal joint product are met, the heat rate applicable to the electrical portion of the cogenerating process can be used. The heat rate method is generally accurate and suitable for modeling with atmospheric dispersion models.

H. SELECTING VALUATION METHODS

1. Introduction

The environmental risks associated with an energy resource have been identified, analysts must select methods to estimate the economic value of those risks. This section is intended to guide selection of those methods.[81] It is important to note at the outset that choosing appropriate and workable methods requires some artfulness in balancing ease of estimation, accuracy, and theoretical appropriateness. There is no established formula for selecting methods, although some general guidelines can be provided.

2. Use of Market Prices

The environmental effects of energy resources are:

1) Those for which market prices exist;
2) Those for which prices can be derived; and,
3) Those for which credible prices cannot be derived.

Only the first two categories will be discussed here. The third will be discussed in Section K, Non-priced effects.

Market prices for environmental effects often can be used directly. If, for example, one effect is reduced yields of a commercial crop, one can multiply the observed market prices of the crop by the yield reduction to estimate the cost. Direct application of market prices is not appropriate in all cases, however. If the reduction in yields is large, applying market prices will overstate the true cost,[82] because, first,

---

[81] This section addresses economic valuation methods, alone, because that is the purpose of this report. Other approaches to incorporating externalities exist. As explained in Section K on Non-Price Effects, externalities are fundamentally an economic issue because when utilities make resource selection decisions, economic impact result.

[82] Freeman, A., The Benefits of Environmental Improvement, Johns Hopkins Press, Baltimore, MD 1979 [hereafter cited as Freeman].

lower yields also may reduce the grower's variable production costs--a lower yield costs less to harvest. Second, large reductions in yields may induce the grower to change production methods or to switch crops. Third, if the yield reductions are widespread, market prices may change. In a large market, such as the corn or wheat market, changes affecting only a few growers would not affect market prices because yield reductions would not be large enough to affect significantly the total market supply. But, if the yield reduction is significant, market prices will overstate the economic loss associated with the yield reduction.

In most cases, yield reductions will be small[83] and amenable to application of market prices, because for a small reduction the change in variable costs will be trivial, and if the reduction is small enough to be unnoticeable, the grower will not change either production methods or crops. Finally, if overall supply does not change significantly, market prices will remain constant.

The change in total crop value with and without the yield reductions represents the environmental costs associated with the crop reduction. Large changes may require estimating supply and demand functions for the new equilibrium price and cost levels.

3. Use of Published Values

The second category of effects are of those for which no observable market prices are available, but for which prices can be derived using non-market valuation techniques to estimate environmental costs. Environmental economists have estimated the economic value of various environmental goods and services.[84] As a result of those studies, a large number of published estimates of value exist. Whether to use published values or to develop values specific to the case at hand is of considerable importance, considering both the number of effects that may require valuation and the expense that may be involved in producing original estimates of value.[85]

Except for global impacts such as ozone depletion and global warming which do not depend on the actions of the local population, it is unlikely that a published value will be available for the specific environmental risk under consideration, simply because impacts are so site-specific. Previous work, however, may have established a cost per individual of some effect, which can be applied to the population size for the case at hand but care must be taken to assure that the conditions and populations are comparable. Or, because many utilities build new power plants adjacent to other plants, published values may be available for a similar plant in a similar location.

Published values also exist for a variety of environmental goods and services and most likely exist for crops and timber, materials damage from air pollution, commercial and sport fish and wildlife, and health risks. But before using them, it is critical to determine whether the published values are relevant to the environmental goods at

83 ECO Northwest, 1987, supra note 19 at pp. 2-27.

84 See, for example, Krutilla, J. and A. Fisher, The Economics of Natural Environments, Resources for the Future, Johns Hopkins University Press, Baltimore, MD 1979.

85 Studies such as this one hopefully will lead to the creation of data bases which will accomplish the objective of having enough published data to perform most routine environmental cost analyses.

hand, and, if possible, the analyst should review the original study to evaluate its methodology, assumptions, and data. If published values can be found, and if they meet the criteria suggested later in this section, they should be used to avoid costly and time-consuming duplication of effort.

It also is likely that published values exist for one or more of the steps between emission of a pollutant and the resulting environmental cost. Analysts familiar with local resources and research can determine the availability of published response data. Published estimates and the characteristics of the energy resource, its site, and the potentially exposed populations may be combined to derive the cost of the environmental risk.

Emissions data are likely to exist because many analyses of the composition of all fuels have been conducted.[86] Any generating utility will have such information readily available. Furthermore, the environmental documentation required for plant licensing and siting will provide all or most of the necessary emissions data, since licensing requirements include documentation on air quality effects associated with large plants. Similar data are usually available for non-atmospheric emissions, including emissions to waterways as well as radioactive emissions.

Meteorological data required to estimate the dispersal of pollutants throughout an airshed are available for some locations. These data include the direction and magnitude of local wind regimes as well as topographical data on terrain conditions. In the absence of published data, and in the absence of an original study to obtain such data, most pollution dispersal models use random wind and terrain conditions to estimate the dispersal and resulting concentrations of atmospheric pollutants.

Human population data are published for almost any political unit. Estimates of wildlife population densities also are available.

Dose-response coefficients exist for many pollutants. Analysts use published coefficients because of the high cost of original research to estimate them. Dose-response coefficients are available for both crops and humans. Other response estimates also may be available, such as for the effects of changes in water temperature on different species of fish. The amount of lost wildlife is calculated by estimating the loss of habitat caused by an energy resource.

Some environmental effects cannot be valued by reference to published values. Risks such as impacts on unique natural resources or resources with high aesthetic or cultural values, will usually require using a method such as revealed preference or contingent valuation techniques, which will be discussed below. Whatever method is selected must be theoretically correct, credible, and legal. It is desirable for the method also to be ethically acceptable, capable of measuring the value of interest, easily understood, and economical to implement.

---

[86] Meridian Corporation, Energy System Emissions and Material Requirements, for U.S. Dept. of Energy, Washington, D.C., February 1989.

4. Methods

The methods available for calculating the economic value of non-market goods and services are: 1) accounting methods; 2) revealed preference methods, including hedonic pricing methods; 3) contingent valuation methods; and, 4) award methods.

A brief overview is presented to provide analysts and other interested parties with a working knowledge of basic valuation methods.[87]

a. Accounting Methods

Accounting methods are based on calculating expenditures required to cope with or mitigate damage caused by an environmental effect. This method is straightforward and easy to understand and implement. Costs such as medical expenditures, maintenance costs, replacement costs, crop and timber losses, and lost economic production, are estimated by calculating what those costs (or benefits) would be with and without the environmental effects. Accounting methods are not generally useful for estimating society's WTP or WTC for environmental risks because they are limited to cases where estimates of market prices and costs are available, and they do not account for diminished quality or other intangible costs.

b. Revealed Preference Methods

The revealed preference method, developed to calculate the value of non-market goods and services, was first used to estimate the value of recreation sites by the travel costs incurred by visitors.[88] Revealed preference techniques are based on observed behavior--for example, the observed frequency and distance that people travel to enjoy a recreation site. A demand function that can be used to value the site can be derived by relating the rate of use for visitors to their cost of traveling to the site.

Hedonic pricing methods are a subset of revealed preference methods. They use market-based prices to impute prices to non-market goods and services by comparing the market price of a good which embodies the non-market service to the price of the same good which does not embody the non-market service.[89] The difference between the two prices represents the value of the non-market service. For example, wages of workers exposed to an occupational risk can be compared to wages of workers who are not exposed to the risk. The difference is an estimate of the value of the risk to workers in that occupation, assuming all other factors are equal. Changes in property

---

[87] For a discussion of valuation methods, see Freeman, supra note 82; Mitchell, R. and R. Carson, Using Surveys to Value Public Goods: The Contingent Valuation Method, Resources for the Future, Washington, D.C. 1989; and Prest, A. and R. Turvey, "Cost-Benefit Analysis: A Survey", Surveys of Economic Theory, Vol. I, St. Martin's Press, N.Y. 1967.

[88] Clawson, M. and J. Knetsch, Economics of Outdoor Recreation, Resources for the Future, Johns Hopkins University Press, Baltimore, 1966.

[89] Carson, supra note 64.

values may also be explained by the presence or absence of a non-market good or service. For example, the selling prices of homes commanding a scenic view can be compared to the selling prices of homes with otherwise equal amenities to determine the value of the scenic view.

The principal difficulty in applying hedonic methods is ensuring that, except for the attribute being valued, all other effects are similar. Compared properties must be of similar size, have similar neighborhoods, similar travel distances, similar shopping opportunities, and so forth. Econometric methods can be used to control for these differences, if the equations are properly specified to ensure that no significant variables that may affect prices are overlooked. If proper specification can be achieved, hedonic methods are widely accepted because they are based on observable rather than inferred or hypothesized market prices.

c. Contingent Valuation Methods

Contingent valuation methods use survey techniques to elicit values from a sample population.[90] Respondents are asked directly to value a non-market good or service, by answering a question such as, "how much would you pay to receive [some benefit]?" The resulting values do not depend on actual behavior or prices revealed in a market.

Contingent valuation methods are subject to a variety of biases, although considerable progress has been made in controlling them.[91] The principal disadvantages of contingent valuation are first, that the biases may not be controlled, and second, that the respondents may have little motivation to reveal their true preferences. These are related criticisms. One concern is that respondents may state values for strategic purposes. If, for example, respondents believe their response may prevent an undesirable action, they may state an excessively high cost. Or, they may believe they will have to pay an amount based on the estimated value and might understate the value. The question format may also result in responses that do not indicate the respondent's true value. Careful study design and application of appropriate statistical and survey techniques can reduce biases significantly.[92]

The principal advantages of contingent valuation methods are that estimates can be obtained for environmental goods and services that have no market counterpart, and estimates of existence and compensation values can be derived. Of great importance is the fact that contingent valuation is the sole method capable of producing both WTP and WTC estimates.[93]

Another advantage of contingent valuation methods is that they can be used to estimate a single value for a fairly complex bundle of attributes or amenities associated with an environmental effect. For example, citizens have expressed concern for an

---

90 Mitchell, supra note 58.

91 Id.

92 Id.

93 Id.

array of issues related to nuclear power, including routine emissions of radioactive substances, catastrophic accidents, hazardous waste disposal, nuclear weapons fuel proliferation, and decommissioning reactors. Evaluation of each component of concern is difficult, especially when relying on observed behavior and prices. Contingent valuation can be used to estimate WTP or WTC values for the whole bundle of attributes, without the need to separate them. Similarly, contingent value estimates of health risks do not require separating components such as health care expenditures, lost productivity, reduced quality of life, and so forth. One estimate of value covers all dimensions of the cost. Thus, despite its drawbacks, contingent valuation is increasingly useful for estimating the value of non-market goods and services.

d. Awards Methods

Awards methods reflect jury awards to set damage costs, principally those related to health and safety concerns.[94] Such estimates may be interesting and somewhat useful in establishing compensation levels for injuries caused by negligence, but there are problems using them to determine the value of environmental health risks, or any other risks. An environmental cost analysis is prospective and the specific individuals who might eventually be affected are unknown. Jury awards, however, represent compensation to a known individual affected by a known event and are fundamentally different from prospectively valuing a risk that is simultaneously faced by large numbers of people of whom none, all, or some may actually suffer adverse consequences. Jury awards can be as unreliable as using the amounts people are willing to spend on mine safety, and the amounts they are willing to spend to rescue a trapped miner.

I. ADJUSTING ENVIRONMENTAL COST ESTIMATES

1. Introduction

Adjustments of environmental cost estimates sometimes may be necessary. Some experts maintain that the treatment of future environmental costs, for example, requires selection of a discount rate. Also, because prices change over time, adjustments for real price changes must be made. In addition, there are aspects of risk that must be considered, including risk aversion, catastrophic events, and apparent zero and infinite costs. Finally, there is an issue regarding the aggregation of environmental costs across members of society. These issues are explored in this section.

---

[94] Viscusi, 1989, supra note 20.

2. Risk Characteristics

a. Uncertainty of Physical Relationships

Risk is the set of all possible responses, and their associated probabilities, to an environmental intrusion. Deriving a risk function that describes physical responses to physical stimuli is an imposing task for physical scientists, and the difficulty of predicting the ecosystem's response to environmental intrusions may be the greatest barrier to estimating the environmental costs of energy resources.[95] Science's ability to measure and predict outcomes for exposures to everything from acid rain to zirconium is severely tested by the task. Consequently, it is not surprising that, as research continues, new estimates--new probability functions--emerge. However, the difficulty and inherent uncertainty of understanding and predicting the environmental risks of energy resources is no more daunting than coping with uncertainty in load growth and fuel prices. The more sophisticated current resource planning models explicitly address uncertainty in such variables; there is no reason that the same can not be done with environmental costs.

b. Perceived vs. Actuarial Risks

Most estimates used in environmental cost analyses are expected values based on expert findings.[96] Some are well understood, predictable outcomes described by physical laws. Others are statistically based, with varying degrees of accuracy. Still others are really nothing more than educated guesses. Insurance companies determine premiums, in part, by the expected value of a loss which is, in turn, based on both the probabilities and costs of various outcomes. This value might be termed an actuarial value.

The members of the public who bear the risks may see them quite differently, however.[97] Outcomes not considered by the experts may concern the public. Similarly, the probability associated with various outcomes may be perceived to be significantly higher than the actuarial risk. This disparity between perceived and actual risk may induce a willingness to pay to avoid the risk that exceeds the actuarial value of the risk. Consequently, economic behavior can be affected directly by risk perceptions. It might appear that if all decisions were made by experts, the risks perceived by the public would not matter, because the experts would be using the "correct" probabilities. But if people are willing to pay to avoid risks, and they perceive those risks to be greater than the expert or actuarial risk, then using the actuarial risk underestimates the risk's economic value. Conversely, if they perceive risks to be lower than they are, then the risk's economic value is overestimated.

---

[95] Buchanan, supra note 1 at p. 8.

[96] Gregory, R., R. Mendelsohn, and P. Slovic, Review of Uncertainty and Risk in BPA-Sponsored Analyses of Energy Resources, for Bonneville Power Administration, Portland, OR, November 18, 1987, [hereafter cited as Gregory].

[97] Id.

Consequently, while actuarial values are objective measures and appropriate in most instances, decision makers must be aware of and account for circumstances in which people's perceived risks diverge significantly from actuarial risks.

c. Infinite Costs

The expected value of an estimate is typically used in economic analyses because it is an unbiased estimate of the variable.[98] Expected values may be the single most useful estimator, but they do not represent the variability of possible outcomes. For example, the proportion of a fish run that actually may be lost because of a new hydroelectric facility may differ from the predicted amount.

In the extreme, the use of expected values may mask low probability, high cost outcomes.[99] The potential for catastrophic outcomes is well recognized.[100] Most environmental documents address "worst case" outcomes, which, if severe enough, may be avoided by resorting to alternatives.

An environmental cost may be considered infinite when either the cost of the environmental risk is so great that no amount of income would be sufficient compensation, or when the environmental risk is prohibited by moral or legal considerations. For instance, under the Endangered Species Act,[101] no energy resource owner may harm a threatened or endangered species; even if the owner were willing to suffer legal sanctions, no licenses or permits would be issued by the relevant government agencies that would make it impossible to build or operate the plant.

Moral considerations, in addition to legal prohibitions, may also imply infinite costs, which are problematic for contingent valuation estimates of WTC values. Typically, such studies attempt to derive average compensatory values for a population sample, which are then applied to the population to estimate the total compensation required for the population to be willing to suffer the environmental risk. The CVM question is usually framed as: "How much money would it take to compensate you for suffering (some environmental risk)?" Respondents sometimes reply that no amount would be sufficient--the cost is infinite. Applying even a single infinite value means that the social value is infinite. Traditionally, analysts have simply thrown out such responses, viewing them as protest bids, not legitimate attempts to express an economic value.[102] If a significant number of responses are infinite, the problem that elicited the infinite responses may be inappropriate for economic analysis and more properly addressed as a political question.

---

[98] Rescher, supra note 16 at p. 50.

[99] Id. at p. 11.

[100] Id. at p. 64.

[101] 16 U.S.C. §§ 1531 - 1544.

[102] Mitchell, supra note 58.

The uniqueness of the resource in question seems to be correlated with extremely high values that are effectively infinite.[103] Surveys have provided strong empirical evidence that as the existence of the last remnants of a resource is threatened, people place very large values on it.--indeed, value may increase exponentially.[104] Uniqueness and the perception of strongly held property rights may indicate the need for extreme care in valuing the resource. Regardless of how they are treated, values which effectively are infinite can and do result from standard non-market valuation techniques under circumstances that are not far-fetched or even unusual.

d. Zero Costs

If either the probability of an outcome or its cost is close to zero, the value of the risk also will be zero.[105] A meteor hitting a power plant may have a positive probability yet be small enough to ignore. People living upwind and far from a power plant have exposure probabilities close to zero. It may be reasonable to establish threshold probabilities for routine risks, below which risks are deemed to be zero. A dilemma results when the actuarial probability is effectively zero, but the consequences are judged to be catastrophic. Probabilities close to zero may translate into zero value of risk. But unacceptable outcomes translate into infinitely high values. In such cases, the analyst has little choice but to report the range of possible outcomes and describe the nature of the associated probabilities and costs. Such risks are addressed most effectively outside the economic valuation process.

It is important to distinguish between environmental costs that may be significant to those who bear them and environmental costs that are significant in the economic context of the energy resource.[106] Some costs may be extremely high for those who must bear them, yet be trivial in the context of the other costs of the energy resource. Localized effects that disturb only a few individuals are not likely to be economically significant risks. Although the environmental effects may be extremely costly to a few affected individuals, the social cost may be insignificant when levelized over the output associated with the resources.[107]

Conversely, aggregation and rounding errors may lead to false estimates of zero cost in a situation where a small amount of damage is experienced by each of a large

---

[103] Haneman, U., Willingness to Pay and Willingness to Accept: How Much Can They Differ?, University of California, Working Paper No. 328, Berkeley, CA, March 1986.

[104] Meyer, P. and E. Cheslak, et. al., Calculation of Environmental Costs and Benefits Associated with Hydropower Development in the Pacific Northwest, for Bonneville Power Administration, DE-AC79-83BP11546, Portland, OR, 1986, p. 84, [hereafter cited as Meyer].

[105] Rescher, supra note 16 at p. 114.

[106] ECO Northwest, 1986, supra note 7 at p. 1-4.

[107] This does not have anything to do with the potential criminal or civil liability for taking an individual life or the value society places on every human being. It has only to do with valuation of the risk to life for purposes of influencing utility resource selections. The value of the risk of loss to a very few individuals simply isn't large enough to affect the economics of choosing one kind of utility resource over another. Mitigation measures may be entirely appropriate and economically efficient in such circumstances because they likely would add little to the overall costs of the project.

number of people. Rounding individuals' costs to zero, instead of aggregating the small costs across everyone in the affected population, could lead to a false estimate of zero.

Erroneous interpretations of regulatory standards also may lead to false estimates of zero costs, a situation most frequently encountered with respect to emissions limits. Emission standards set in a political process denote an acceptable emissions level; rarely are these standards set at levels expected to result in no effects. Yet environmental costs reflect the value of the risks borne by society as a result of the emissions, irrespective of the permissible level of emissions. Any positive quantity of emissions may create risk, no matter how small. Emissions standards reduce the magnitude of the risks that might otherwise have occurred, but they seldom reduce risks to zero.

Zero cost values may be mandated by statute or regulation. A regulatory agency may deem that costs borne by residents of another jurisdiction not be counted. For example, regulatory bodies need not compel utilities to consider the effect of their emissions on Canada. Similarly, environmental costs imposed on illegal activities may be deemed zero, or a regulatory agency may decide that exposure to an arbitrarily small amount of some substance poses zero risk.

Finally, zero costs may result from an inability to derive economic value for some environmental risks. Lack of theoretical guidance, data, or methods may make any positive estimate of cost indefensible. Treatment of such non-priceable effects is discussed in Section III.K.

e. Risk Aversion

Even within less extreme ranges of probabilities, risks exhibit certain attributes that affect how people respond to and value them. Most notably, people are risk averse.[108] This does not mean simply that people do not like bad outcomes. Rather, bad outcomes are "worse" than equivalent good outcomes are "better". The potential loss of a dollar may be thought to reduce well-being more than the potential equal gain of a dollar may be perceived to improve well-being. Risk aversion is one explanation for the sometimes significant difference between compensatory values and willingness to pay values.[109]

As the size of the risk grows, the cost of the risk to the individual also grows. In other words, as risks grow, successive increases will have greater value. The marginal cost of the risk is increasing.[110] Increasing marginal costs are referred to as the cumulative effects problem. For example, the effect of a dam on the ecosystem depends not only on itself but on other dams in the system, including planned ones.[111]

---

108 Kahneman, <u>supra</u> note 62.

109 Carson, <u>supra</u> note 64.

110 Kahneman, <u>supra</u> note 62.

111 Meyer, <u>supra</u> note 104 at p. 97.

Similarly, the incremental value of a health risk may increase as the background level of health risks increases.

Some aspects of risk may cause people to respond differently even to risks of equal probability and cost. Among those factors are dread, controllability, newness of the risk, understanding, and irreversibility.[112] People respond to these risk dimensions in predictable ways. For example, dreaded risk is positively correlated with perceived risk. Because higher perceived risks evoke a strong desire to reduce risks, people are willing to accept regulations designed to do so.[113] Such factors probably affect people's willingness to pay to avoid risks, or their willingness to be compensated to incur them.[114] Although no studies have been found which attempt to quantify how these dimensions of risk affect economic values, such research might be fruitful. Until that research becomes available, there is reason to adjust risk values for these considerations. Nevertheless, analysts should attempt to ensure that risk values for "normal" or "undreaded" risks are not applied to dread risks, and vice versa.

3. Aggregating Individual Environmental Cost Values

Another issue is how to aggregate measures of individually held values of social risk. The aggregate social value of a public good is given by the sum of all individual values for a given quantity of the good.[115] In current economic practice there are two schools of thought. One holds that social value is the sum of all individual values.[116] This is equivalent to estimating a mean individual value and multiplying it by the relevant population. Thus, its basis is the sample or population mean.

The median voter theory, a competing view,[117] rests on the proposition that issues can be presented and evaluated as an economic referendum. The median voter tips the balance, determining the outcome of the vote. Similarly, if the expressed economic values of all individuals were arrayed, the median value would constitute the critical social value. A payment or compensation just above or below this value would be sufficient to affect the outcome of a decision. This procedure has merit because it conforms with the political system and therefore, has an instinctive appeal. Moreover, it avoids the problems created by infinite and zero values. The analyst is not required to determine the motives of respondents who give what may appear to be absurdly or irrationally high or low values.

---

[112] Slovik, P., B. Fischoff, and S. Lichtenstein, "Characterizing Perceived Risk", in Perilous Progress, R.W. Kates, et. al. eds., Westview, Boulder, Colorado 1985.

[113] Id.

[114] Gregory, supra note 96.

[115] Samuelson, P., "A Diagrammatic Exposition of a Theory of Public Expenditure," The Review of Economics and Statistics, Vol. XXXVII, No. 4, November, 1955.

[116] Carson, supra note 64.

[117] Id.

Median voter theory, however, does not conform precisely with current economic theory. Most economists would argue that the social value of environmental risk is the total payment or compensation applicable to the relevant population. This is simply the aggregate of the individual values which, in turn, are based on a well established theory of individual choice and preference. It is a richer and more widely accepted body of theory than the median voter theory. However, median voter theory is accepted by many public sector economists, who argue that this is the correct way to to evaluate social needs and programs.[118]

Regardless, median values offer the analyst a choice of measurements and measurement techniques. There is nothing inherently erroneous or in violation of theory with using median values. Although not as widely accepted among economists, median voter-based values are legitimate.

4. Discount Rates

a. The Social Rate of Time Preference

Discount rates are used to compare future economic benefits and costs with today's benefits and costs. Low discount rates weigh the future more heavily than high discount rates. A discount rate can be measured by: 1) the social rate of time preference; 2) the consumption rate of interest; 3) the marginal private rate of return on investment; or, 4) the opportunity cost of public investment.[119]

The social rate of time preference is the rate at which society is willing to exchange present consumption for future consumption. The consumption rate of interest is the corresponding rate of time preference for individuals. The marginal private rate of return on investment is the effective rate of interest earned on business investments by individuals and corporations. The opportunity cost of public investment is the return on private investment forgone by the investment in a public project.

Discounting environmental costs and benefits introduces considerations different from traditional regulatory concerns. Specifically, the value of future environmental costs and benefits of an energy resource is independent of and distinct from the financial interests of the utility. The value of environmental costs and benefits to the public are evaluated (and discounted) not the investments of the utility. It is the public, or a portion of the public, that bears the costs of environmental risks. The tradeoff between present and future suffering bears no relation to the utility's opportunity costs. Therefore, the utility'smarginal private rate of return on investment is irrelevant.

The financial outlays and returns of the utility still would be discounted at the opportunity cost of capital. The introduction of an additional class of costs--externality

---

118 Id.

119 Lind, R., Discounting for Time and Risk in Energy Policy, Resources for the Future, Washington, D.C., 1982, p. 21, [hereafter cited as Lind].

costs--need not affect the choice of a financial discount rate.[120] Some economists maintain that it is appropriate to discount different classes of economic costs at different rates.[121] Traditional financial concerns of a utility may still be assessed using traditional financial criteria. Adding a new class of costs and benefits does not eliminate the desirability of earning a profitable rate of return for the utility. For example, a utility may reduce environmental damage through abatement, mitigation, or compensation, and those costs will be included in the rate base and treated as traditional financial costs, discounted at the opportunity cost of capital. Not incidentally, such costs may then earn a rate of return for the utility.

The same logic means that the opportunity cost of public investment is considered by some economists to be inappropriate for discounting environmental externality costs. To consider this a legitimate element of an environmental cost discount rate, one would have to demonstrate that bearing environmental risks somehow displaces private investment with public investment.

The consumption rate of interest is also considered inappropriate for discounting environmental costs and benefits by some economists because it is based on narrow and private self-interests rather than collective interests. Environmental damage risks will be faced by the collective membership of the affected society. It will surely be possible to identify specific gainers or losers.

There are at least two reasons why many economists maintain that a social rate of time preference should be applied to environmental externalities. First, individuals make investments that yield returns from which they do not benefit directly. For example, people pay taxes to support schools, even though some taxpayers may not attend the schools, may have no children in school, and may never receive the benefits of the educated society for which they are paying. That people support public investments implies that they are willing to sacrifice private consumption for future benefits. Individuals will sometimes support expenditures for which they will derive no benefits. The willingness to forgo current consumption for a payoff that may take years to be realized, and may never be realized in some cases, is evidence that the social rate of time preference is lower than the consumption rate of interest.

Second, the interests of future generations are not accounted for in the market, since future generations are not market participants. A social rate of time preference is consistent with society's concerns with the interests of future generations, because use of a social discount rate means that a lower discount rate will be used to evaluate

---

[120] Some economists would disagree with this position, saying that using different discount rates for different cost elements may distort the relative weight of each cost element. As a practical matter discount rates do not affect the estimates of the levelized cost of environmental externalities presented in this report. Nearly all of the environmental costs reviewed are annual costs, directly related to plant output. Consequently, discounting has no effect on the levelized costs reported. Discounting does affect present values of resource costs, and the application of different discount rates to different cost elements can change resource cost-effectiveness rankings.

[121] Id.

environmental costs.[122] Using higher market rates of interest ignores a significant portion of future values: the values held by tomorrow's citizenry.[123]

b. Risk Free Discount Rates

Discount rates typically are adjusted to account for risk. Theoretically risk should not be used to adjust the discount rate for environmental costs. It is important to distinguish between project risk and environmental risk. Project risk implies variability of the investor's portfolio,[124] which concerns the utility but not those who bear the environmental risks. If it is desirable, cash flow analysis can account for a project's financial risk. Risk to the utility, however, is not to be confused with the environmental risks borne by the public.

The public's environmental risks have economic value that may be based on the public's perceived certainty of the risks. In other words, the magnitude of the economic value collectively assigned to the environmental risk may reflect a host of considerations, including its effect on the variability of the public's incomes or wealth; i.e., on the variability of the public's "portfolio." But in such cases the risk is already reflected in the value of the environmental risk; to account for that risk again when discounting risks over time, would be redundant.

Moreover, risk neutrality--i.e., not adjusting the discount rate for risk--may be justified when the value to each individual in the exposed population of the risk of a perspective harm is so small it does not cause risk aversion. This argument is called risk spreading.[125]

Another argument against risk adjustment is called risk pooling.[126] The typical situation will involve risks faced by a large number of citizens. Using unbiased estimates of cost per individual means that individual uncertainty no longer matters. As the number of individuals increases, the average cost will tend towards the expected or mean estimated value, an inevitable consequence of the law of large numbers. Some individuals will suffer greater than expected damage; others will suffer less or even no damage. In the aggregate, the group's valuation of the risk will tend toward the average damage value.

---

122 Shuman, M., and R. Cavanagh, A Model Conservation and Electric Power Plan for the Pacific Northwest, Northwest Conservation Act Coalition, Seattle, Washington, November 1982, at p. 1, [hereafter cited as Shuman].

123 A discussion of using zero discount rates vs. the social rates of time preference or market rates is contained in the Executive Summary, Chapter II. In brief, advocates of a zero discount rate maintain that sound environmental stewardship requires valuing future environmental damages as high as present damages. Id.

124 Lind, supra note 119.

125 Arrow, K. and R. Lind, "Uncertainty in Public Investment", The American Economic Review, Vol. 60, 1970, p. 364.

126 Samuelson, P. and W. Vickrey, "Discussion", The American Economic Review, Vol. 54, 1964, p. 88.

The foregoing does not mean that the estimated costs will be correct, but means simply that if unbiased estimates are used, there is no need to adjust them because of uncertainty. The uncertainty inherent in such estimates is addressed separately.

c. Quantifying the Social Rate of Time Preference

To determine a reasonable estimate of the social rate of time preference, one must use a long-term, risk-neutral rate that reflects the public's time preferences used.[127] Using observed market interest rates as proxies for the social rate of time preference has inherent difficulties. One is defining the time period over which the review should take place. Interest rates are not constant from year to year, so a case can be made for almost any interest rate if the time period is selected carefully. Second, the observed interest rates are nominal interest rates. That is, the observed rates include expected inflation.

The real rate of interest is the nominal rate minus inflation. For example, if the nominal rate is 8 %, and inflation is constant at 5 %, then the real rate is 2.9 % (1.08/1.05 = 1.029). The difficulty is that the actual inflation rate may differ from the investors expectations since they demand a rate of return over and above the inflation rate. It is impossible to determine from nominal interest rates what investors believe is the inflationary component.

A third difficulty is that tax laws at the federal and state level change over time. This means that required rates of return vary over time according to, among other things, the marginal tax rate. Thus, the effect of tax rates cannot truly be assessed with regard to measures of the social rate of time preference.

Finally, there are several indices of long-term, low-risk interest rates. There is no compelling reason to believe that any is <u>the</u> measure of the social rate of time preference. A review of several such indices must be made. One such review[128] showed that the historical average annual real rate of interest on 20-year government bonds is 2.2%; on AAA bonds it is 2.9%; and, on 12-month Treasury bills it is 1.8%. Reviews of other rates showed similar results. For example 2-year municipal bonds sold in 1979 at a real interest rate of <u>minus</u> 2%. Real interest on those bonds increased to just over 6% in 1984, and has since declined to approximately 3%. Forecasts of the real rate for the next decade are also in the 3% range.[129]

The historical record presents a compelling case for real discount rates of close to 3%. Real rates of return on long-term, low-risk investments have approximated that level for most of this century. Although year-to-year variation in those rates occurs, those variations are probably because of different inflationary expectations from year to year, inflationary expectations that differ from the actual inflation rate, and the availability of different investment opportunities over time. There is no strong

---

127 This measure can be determined administratively if desired.

128 Bonneville Power Administration, <u>Internal Review of Discount Rate Practices</u>, Portland, Ore., 1986c [hereafter cited as BPA 1986c].

129 Data Resources, Inc., "Implicit Price Deflator for GNP", in <u>Long-Term Forecast of U.S. Economy</u>, Lexington, Mass., 1990.

evidence, however, that the social rate of time preference also varies over time. Consequently, the evidence suggests a real discount rate for environmental cost analyses on the order of 3%.

d. Practices of Other Entities

A survey of utilities and agencies that employ discounting procedures is summarized in Table 1.[130] The range of discount rates shown is from 0% to 10%. At the low end, The Natural Resources Defense Council contends that the discount rate for health risks should be zero because a positive rate unjustly transfers life-threatening hazards from current generations to future generations. Because human lives can not be banked at interest to provide returns at a later date, NRDC maintains that it is immoral to discount those lives. This is discussed further in Chapter III.K.5.

TABLE 1

REAL DISCOUNT RATES BY SOURCE

ORGANIZATION	REAL DISCOUNT RATE
Northwest Power Planning Council	3%
Bonneville Power Administration	3%
Seattle City Light Co.	3%
Eugene Water and Electric Board	3%
Clark County (WA) Public Utility District	6%
Portland (OR) General Electric	6%
Office of Management and Budget	10%
U.S Forest Service	4% to 8%
Natural Resource Defense Council	1%
Natural Resource Defense Council (Health Risks)	0%
Robert C. Lind, et. al. in Discounting for Time and Risk in Energy Policy	1% to 4.6%

Source: Bonneville Power Administration, Internal Review of Discount Rate Practices, 1986c.

---

130 BPA, 1986c *supra* note 128.

Several public agencies and utilities use a 3% real rate of interest to discount future costs and benefits. Of those, only BPA estimates environmental costs; the other entities apply discount rates only to utility financial costs. Other utilities were found to use a 6% real rate of interest for discounting, but not to estimate environmental costs. The Forest Service attempts to measure environmental costs and benefits. It uses two discount rates; one is 4%, the other is just under 8%. The Office of Management and Budget (OMB) uses a real rate of 10%, well above those used by any other entity surveyed, but again not to value environmental damages. It is not clear why OMB's rate is so high, although its primary interest in short-term budgetary considerations would be consistent with a high discount rate. Finally, Lind maintains that most energy projects should use discount rates of between 1% and 4.6%.[131] His arguments apply generally to actual cash flows of the project sponsor, not necessarily to the public's cost of environmental externalities.

The discount rates used by most entities are not, strictly speaking, relevant to environmental cost evaluations because most entities apply these rates only to financial outlays and returns. The review shows that a real rate of about 3% is consistent with actual practices. Thus, there is ample evidence that a real rate of about 3% is supported by historical rates of return on long-term, low-risk investments as well as by common utility and agency practice.[132]

5. Real Value Escalation

Prices and costs of economic goods and services change over time. Most energy resource planning is conducted in the context of real prices and costs,[133] calculated by selecting a base year and converting all prices and costs to that year's dollars, thereby removing the effect of inflation. Real cost escalation is then applied to each cost component according to forecasts of how that component's costs are expected to change over time, relative to all other goods and services in the economy. If an escalation rate of 2%, for example, is applied to fuel prices, that means that fuel prices are expected to increase by 2% per year above the inflation rate. Forecasts for escalation rates are available for most significant cost components. Major econometric forecasting groups regularly provide clients with price forecasts.[134] If escalation rates are applied to various cost components, it would be appropriate to apply escalation rates to environmental costs and benefits if such rates can be determined credibly.

The real economic value of goods and services may be affected by changes in demand, changes in supply, or both. Increasing scarcity is typical of many environmental goods and services. Many natural assets can shrink, but as a practical matter, they cannot grow. Examples include old growth forests, free flowing rivers, pristine recreational areas, wetlands, and unique resources such as the Grand Canyon.

---

131 Lind, supra note 119.

132 As noted, the choice of discount rate does not affect the levelized environmental cost associated with annual energy output. Such costs constitute the vast majority of environmental costs in this report.

133 BPA, 1986a supra note 7 at p. 4.

134 See, for example, Data Resources, Inc., supra note 129.

Wilderness had little value 100 years ago. Today, wilderness is scarce and so its marginal value is higher.

Individual shifts in demand can lead to real value changes. The aggregate, or social, demand may change as the number of people who demand the good or service change. An individual's demand for an environmental good or service depends on personal tastes, income, and prices of other goods and services. Over the past generation, Americans have exhibited a growing predilection toward recreational and outdoor activities.[135] This may indicate changes in taste if, for example, lifestyles become increasingly oriented toward enjoyment of natural resources.

The social value is the sum of the values held by all individuals in society. If population grows, aggregate demand also grows, potentially leading to higher values for environmental costs and benefits.

Increasing natural resource scarcity, increasing individual demand, and increasing population size may push the real value of most natural resources upward. Still, it is uncertain whether trends will continue, or whether values of different uses will merely shift with no change in net real value. Population continues to increase but future changes in taste are impossible to predict. Changes in taste could either accelerate or negate the changes in value that would otherwise follow upward trends in income and population.

Indexing real dollar values to the rate of growth in population is the method preferred by many economists. This is done by multiplying the net benefit for an average individual by the size of the population forecast for each future year. If, for example, today's population is 2 million people and the average individual net benefit is $0.50, the current value is $1 million. The population in five years might be 2.2 million. Multiplying that figure by $0.50 gives a $1.1 million value for the resource in that year.

As information about individual shifts in demand is available, both that shift and population growth rates can be used. The growth in individual demand can be applied to individual benefit estimates which can then be multiplied by the relevant population figures.

No indices were found for forecasting individual demand or supply functions. Consequently, it is not now possible to forecast changes in real value over time for individuals. In the absence of such indices, analysts can reflect only changes in aggregate value related to incre[illegible] in population.

The preceding discussion ap[illegible] real, or constant dollar, values. Real values use some year as the base value, [illegible] values converted to equivalent values in that year's dollars. Adjustments to [illegible]at value must be made whenever the base year changes. If, for example, value[illegible] [illegible]ressed in 1980 dollars but the resource cost effectiveness analysis uses 198[illegible] [illegible] the values must be adjusted for inflation between 1980 and 1989. The G[illegible] [illegible]tor for the entire economy is often used, which is equivalent to assuming that e[illegible] [illegible]tal costs and benefits retain a constant value relative to all goods and service[illegible] economy.

---

[135] Meyer, supra note 104 at p. 8[illegible]

J. NON-PRICED EFFECTS

Some environmental risks seem to defy economic valuation, either because the risk itself defies measurement or because the risk has no economic counterpart. Or, an economic assessment may be deemed inappropriate for reasons including ethical considerations, political sensitivity, or lack of adequate time and resources to conduct a study. Effects unlikely to be priceable include nuclear proliferation, losses of cultural and archaeological resources, global climate change, risks of radioactive waste disposal, and risks involving physical interactions that are poorly understood and impossible to predict.

1. Consideration of Non-Priced Effects in Resource Planning

In most utility least cost planning analyses undertaken to date environmental effects have not been priced.[136] Environmental risks may be considered when ranking and selecting resources, but few attempts have been made to include them in an economic calculus of social costs. If effects that are priceable were included, the number of non-priced effects would have been reduced, facilitating analyses of the tradeoffs involved in selecting one resource over another. However, some identified risks that are not priceable, for any of the reasons mentioned above, may remain and need to be contended with.

In some cases, the inability to price environmental risks does not matter. If when all environmental costs of a given resource have been priced, and that resource is still the lowest cost resource under consideration, it does not matter whether the environmental risks of more costly resources have been priced. Any positive environmental cost associated with those resources would simply increase the cost advantage of the first resource. Of course, this can not be known unless the environmental damages are valued.

Sensitivity analysis can be used for empirical effect. The unquantified effects can be approximated by a reasonable range of values to see if cost effectiveness rankings change. As an analytical learning device, proxy costs can be useful and can help direct further research to where it would be most useful. The analysis will lose credibility, however, if proxy costs are treated as actual values, because with no real basis for them, no consensus can be reached on either the values themselves or the study's conclusions. Proxy costs are most useful in a "What if?" scenario to guide rational and informed decision making.

When several effects are non-priced, or when several resources with non-priced effects are being considered, other methods of comparative assessment can be used. The utility or regulatory body may use existing methods to evaluate the relative significance and importance of the environmental effects. Methodologies developed for federal or state environmental impact statements could be used, with an

---

136 See Chapter X.

accompanying Record of Decision to explain the procedures used, to evaluate the effects and look at tradeoffs.

The problem with these other methods is that they are subjective. There is no objective standard, such as dollars, by which criteria can be judged. It is exceedingly difficult to elicit weights from decision makers, especially if they are influenced by political or other non-economic goals. Decisions based on weights viewed as arbitrary or capricious will have little support among the public, potentially embroiling a resource selection process in unnecessary and undesirable conflict.[137] In addition, decision makers tend to view explicit statements of weights as potentially limiting their ability to make future decisions. They worry that they will be forced to continue using weights that may no longer be appropriate, or be criticized as inconsistent if they change the weights. An objective analysis avoids these concerns.[138]

Finally, as discussed in Section III.J., risk considerations have several dimensions which may be especially relevant to non-priceable effects. Is the risk a potentially catastrophic risk? Is the risk likely to be persistent or irreversible? Is the risk too small to be considered? Are the risks dreaded, unknown, controllable, or familiar? To the extent that risks can be characterized in this fashion, the decision maker can determine the subjective acceptability and significance of the risk. Decision makers must consider the ethics of imposing certain risks on society. Is the risk likely to be disproportionately shared by certain members of society? Does the risk discriminate against certain members of society? Does the risk entail benefits for a few at a cost to many? Does the risk burden future generations to a socially unacceptable extent? These considerations require an explicit subjective judgment on the part of the decision maker.

2. Conclusion

Consideration of non-priced environmental risks requires subjective judgment, but that judgment is no more severe or difficult than that required without economic valuation of externalities. The problem is reduced to the extent that externalities not valued under current practices are valued in a social cost framework.

Regardless of the decision making framework, non-priceable effects are not non-cost effects. The environmental risks imposed by energy resources result in costs for someone, regardless of whether analysts are willing or able to estimate the costs. Whenever a resource with non-priced environmental risks is selected, an implicit decision is made that those non-priced effects are less costly than the difference in cost between that resource and the next cheapest resource. Whether the decision to count those effects as having lower costs than the competing resource is made explicitly or implicitly, there is no denying that a tradeoff has been made.

---

137 Buchanan, supra note 1 at p. 10.

138 Id.

Consider Figure 2. Resource B has the lower social cost when the non-priced effects are ignored. Resource A has no non-priced effects. Selection of Resource B is equivalent to saying that the cost of the non-priced effects is less than the difference in the social cost of Resource A and Resource B. Selection of Resource A is equivalent to determining that the additional cost of Resource A is worth incurring to avoid the non-priced effects of Resource B. So, in the first case, the cost advantage is sufficient to compensate for the additional non-priced effects. In the second case, the cost penalty is acceptable to enable avoiding the non-priced effects of Resource B. An economic cost or benefit is implied even for non-priced effects.

The most precise method of treating environmental externalities in utility least-cost planning is to assign costs to all environmental risks wherever possible. Decision makers must then determine whether the remaining non-priced environmental risks are worth paying to avoid, or are adequately compensated by lower measurable environmental costs.

K. HEALTH RISK VALUATION

1. Introduction: Risk as the Basis for Valuation

One of the most significant and controversial components of many environmental cost analyses is the valuation of human health risks. They are significant because of their magnitude in comparison to other risks in many instances. Studies of environmental costs associated with coal plants in the Pacific Northwest, for example, indicate that as much as 95% of the quantifiable environmental costs associated with such plants are attributable to human health risks.[139] The values are controversial because they are often confused with values of human life, not risks to human life. Most people are skeptical of attempts to value how much a person is worth.

The value of human health risks must be estimated, not by the value of a life, but by the value of the risks to life. Specifically, the economic value of health risks consists of either society's willingness to pay to avoid the risk, or willingness to be compensated to suffer the risk.[140] The economic value of a health risk is not the value of a certain death, it is the value of a risk shared by members of an exposed population. The value is based on everyone sharing the risk, without knowing the specific individuals who will suffer death or injury.

As with other environmental risks, the value an individual places on a health risk depends on the likelihood and magnitude of its expected damages. These damages include real economic costs such as increased medical expenditures, loss of income and other economic products, as well as decreases in the quality or quantity of life.[141] Early

---

139 ECO Northwest, 1987, supra note 19 at p. iii.

140 Viscusi, 1989, supra note 20.

141 Cannon, James S., The Health Costs of Air Pollution, American Lung Association, New York, January, 1990.

attempts to derive health risk values were based largely on an accounting of these costs. Individuals take such considerations into account to determine their willingness to pay to avoid or willingness to be compensated for health risks.

Health risk values are often expressed as values per human life. This is convenient but inaccurate terminology. Aggregating values to a single life facilitates comparision, but it creates the impression that human life itself is being valued. Risk values are typically calculated for very small risks. An analyst may determine, for example, that each increment of risk of 1/100,000 probability of fatality has a value of $40. If that risk were imposed on a population of 100,000, it would be expected that one person would die. Since that amounts to 100,000 people each with a $40 value, the total risk value would be $4,000,000. Thus, the value for the statistical life would be $4,000,000.

FIGURE 1

HYPOTHETICAL RESOURCE COST COMPARISONS

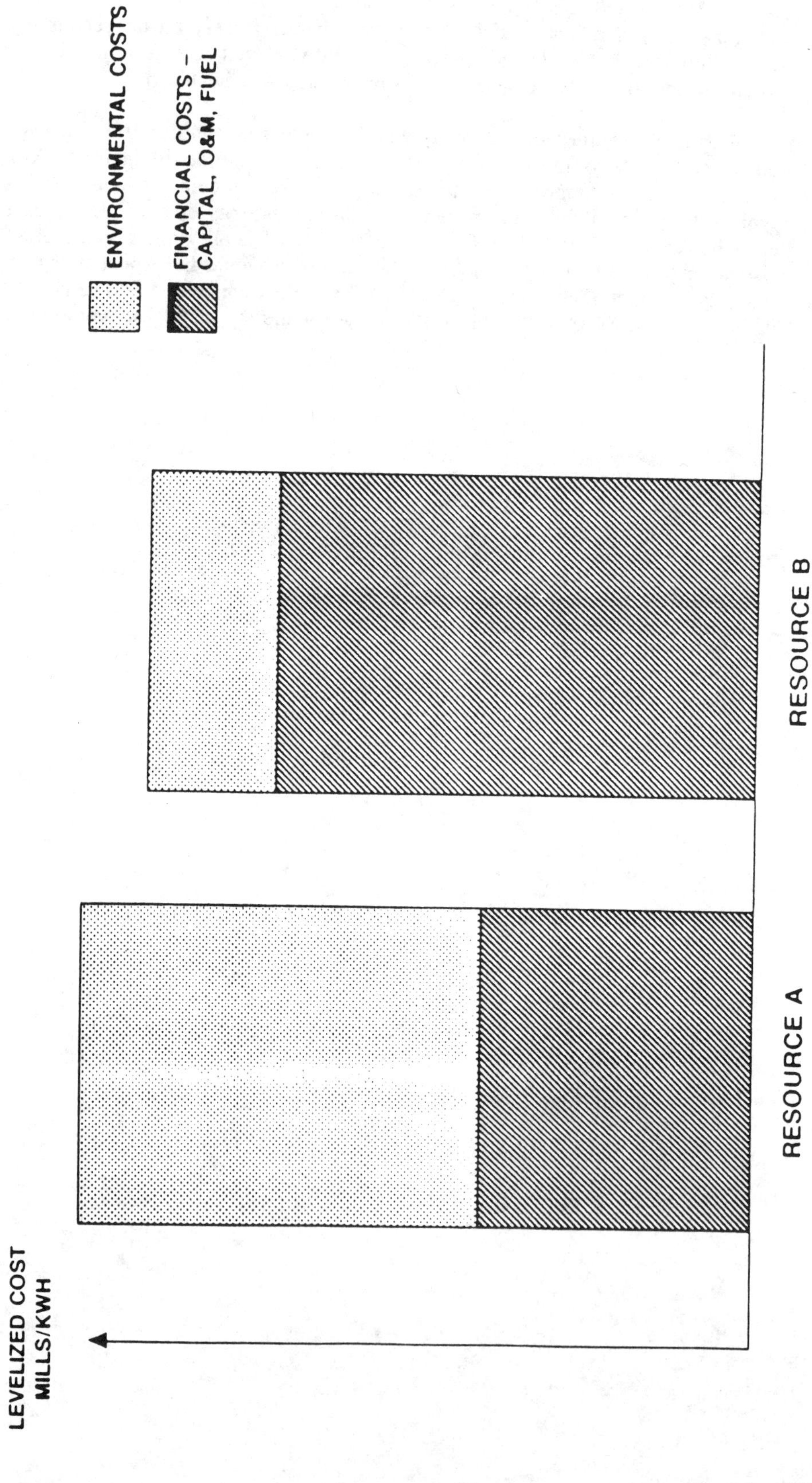

FIGURE 2

HYPOTHETICAL RESOURCE COST COMPARISONS

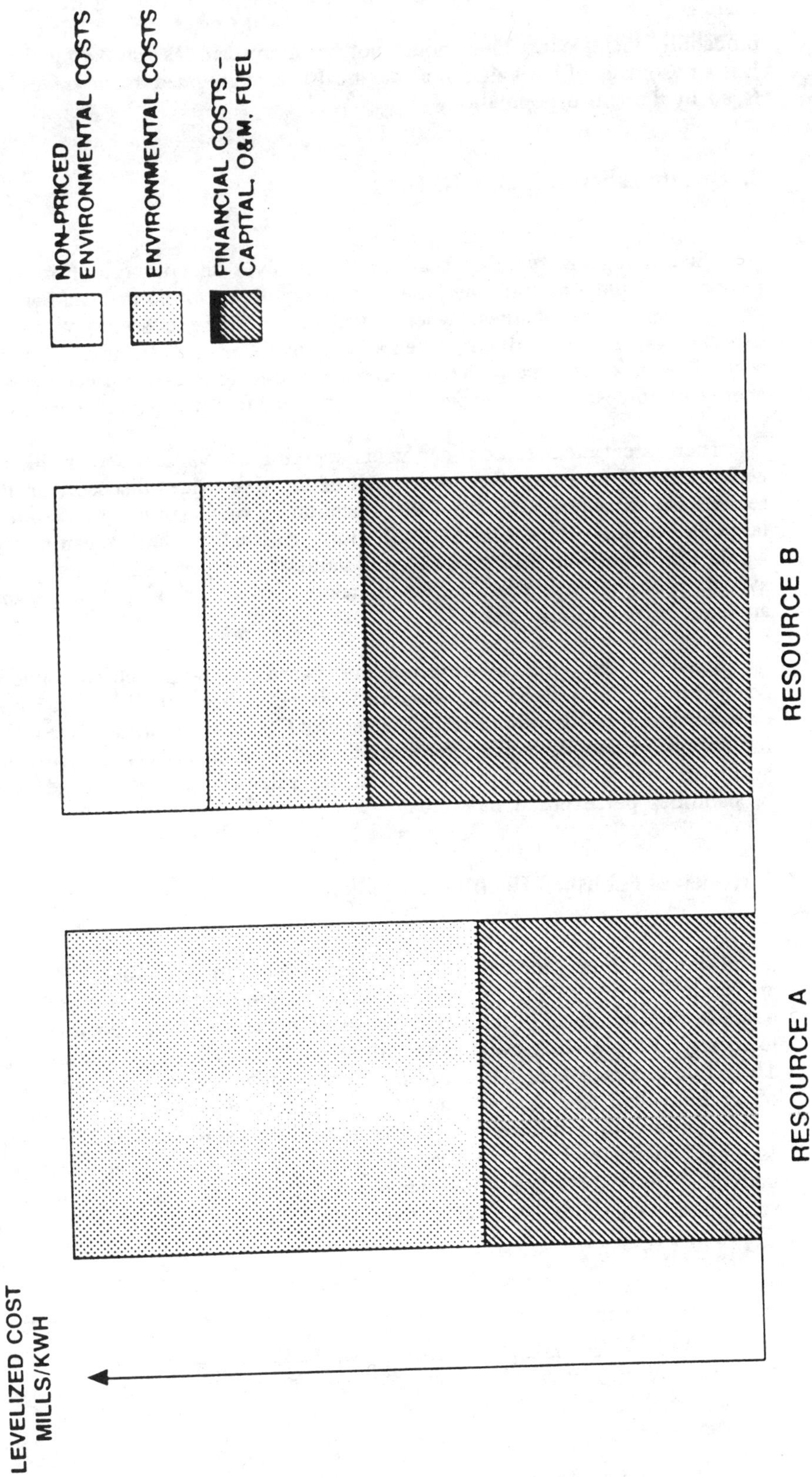

In this report, values for statistical lives are used to compare estimates and to avoid having to specify both a probability of fatality and the associated value for that probability increment. This should not be interpreted as estimating the value of life. It is an estimate of the value of a statistical life, aggregated from values for small risks faced by the entire population.

2. Quantification of Health Risks

Quantifying and valuing health risks involves uncertainty. For example, dose-response calculations must be based on extrapolation of animal studies to humans or on epidemiological studies, where available. If the dose-response functions are expected values, they will not systematically over- or under-estimate physical risk. As such, they are consistent with other measures used in the cost effectiveness analyses of energy resources, such as expected load growth, fuel prices, and construction costs.

There are factors to consider when applying the values used in this report to the health risks of an energy resource. All of the risk values discussed in the next sub-section are values built up from the valuation of small risks. If risks are likely to be large, the values derived here may not apply. At least two factors can be identified that would lead to higher than proportional values for larger risks. First, people are risk averse. As fatal risk probabilities increase, people would pay increasing marginal amounts to avoid those risks.[142]

Some of the studies reviewed are based on wage compensation for risky occupations. The idea is that workers must be compensated to incur greater health or safety risks, and the amount of the required compensation implies a value for that incremental risk. Both risk adverseness and income effects combine to make the health risk values derived from such studies relevant only within the range of small probabilities per exposed individual.

3. Review of Published Health Risk Values

There are three general methods of deriving health risk values. The human capital approach was one of the original bases for valuing a statistical life. This approach assumes that the value of individuals is given by their expected economic contribution to society. People are viewed as factors of production, hence the term human capital. The value of a statistical life is given, approximately, by the expected lifetime income of an individual (the human capital approach ignores the cost of maintaining the human factor of production over a lifetime). Because it is based on expected lifetime earnings, this method assumes that minorities are worth less than others, handicapped individuals are worth less, older people--especially retired people--have little or no value, and even young housewives have little value.

---

[142] Viscusi, W., The Valuation of Risks to Life and Health: Guidelines for Policy Analysis, Paper prepared for National Science Foundation, 1984.

Second, one could attempt to estimate the costs associated with various health effects. These costs include medical expenditures, loss of income, and other increased costs of living. Such methods do not account for suffering either in anticipation of the effect or following manifestation of the effect. The method also ignores other diminutions in the quality of life as well as costs of which the analyst may be unaware or can not measure. While medical costs, etc., may influence the amount that an individual would pay to avoid a risk, they do not measure the value of the risk, the primary measure of economic value.

A third method is based on tort awards. However, as discussed in Section I.3.d., above, tort awards do not value risks, they value the cost of damage to a known individual, which is not relevant to risk valuation.

The methods for valuing human health risks used in this report identify the amount people will pay to avoid a risk or accept as compensation for the risk. Many such studies are based on wage differentials for risky occupations. Several such studies are presented in Table 2.

All of the studies, except for the last two, are based on wage/risk compensation. The last two studies derive values from other published studies, principally wage compensation studies.

The range of values estimated from the different studies is wide. The lowest values indicated are $440,000 and $700,000 and go as high as $12,800,000.

The Thaler and Rosen result is significant because it was one of the first values derived by a wage compensation methodology.[143] It examined only high-risk occupations, rather than a broad base of occupations. Workers who are risk-seekers--that is, workers who enjoy risks--may tend to select high risk occupations. Consequently, smaller wage increments are necessary to induce such workers to enter those occupations, which results in values that are skewed downward.

The highest values, on the other hand, are at the extreme upper end of values typically derived in such studies. Although they cannot be rejected simply because they are high, they must be viewed with some skepticism.

---

143 Thaler, R. and S. Rosen, "The Value of Saving a Life: Evidence from the Labor Market", in Household Production and Consumption, N. Terlecky, ed., Columbia University Press, New York, 1976, p. 265 [hereafter cited as Thaler & Rosen].

TABLE 2

SUMMARY OF PUBLISHED HEALTH RISK VALUES
(Expressed as Value Per Statistical Life)

Study	Value Per Life (Millions of 1989$)
Brown (1980)	1.3 to 1.9
Olson (1981)	9.1
Smith (1976)	9.4
Thaler and Rosen (1976)	0.7
Viscusi (1979)	3.6 to 4.9
Viscusi (1983)	8.5 to 12.8
Moore and Viscusi (1988a)	4.6 [1/]
Moore and Viscusi (1988b)	5.3 to 6.4
Shuman and Cavanagh	.44 to 4.4
ECO Northwest (1987)	3.3

Value of $200,000per life year in original study. Value of $4.6 million per life derived by discounting the $200,000 annual payment over our assumed remaining life of 40 years, at a three percent real discount rate.

SOURCE: Thaler and Rosen, supra note 143.

4. Derived Health Risk Value

This report uses a statistical life value of $4,000,000 in 1989 dollars, a value consistent with values reported in the literature. It exceeds the values derived by Thaler and Rosen,[144] Brown,[145] and ECO Northwest,[146] although it exceeds the ECO value by only a small amount. It is less than the values found by Olson,[147] Smith,[148] Viscusi (1983),[149] and two Moore and Viscusi studies.[150] Those studies, however, report ranges whose low end is slightly greater than used here. Finally, the value used in this report is within the range computed by Viscusi in 1979.[151]

Because primary research into the value of health risks was beyond the scope of this report, judgment as to a reasonable value was required.[152] This judgment was based on review of the literature. It's a middle ground, selecting a wide range of value for sensitivity analyses, and a specific mid-range value around which most empirical estimates are apparently clustered.[153]

---

144 Id.

145 Brown, Charles, "Equalizing Differences in the Labor Market", Quarterly Journal of Economics, Vol. 94, February 1980, p. 113.

146 ECO Northwest, 1987 supra note 19 at p. 3-5.

147 Olson, C., "An Analysis of Wage Differentials Received by Workers on Dangerous Jobs", The Journal of Human Resources, Vol. 16, No. 2, 1981.

148 Smith, R., The Occupational Safety and Health Act: Its Goals and Achievements, cited by Viscusi, 1989, supra note 20.

149 Viscusi, W., Risk by Choice: Regulating Health and Safety in the Workplace, cited by Viscusi, 1989, supra note 20.

150 Moore and W. Viscusi, "The Quantity Adjusted Value of a Life", Economic Enquiry, Vol. 26, No. 369, 1988a. and Moore and W. Viscusi, "Doubling the Estimated Value of Life: The Implications of New Occupational Fatality Data", Journal of Policy Analysis and Management, Vol. 7, 1988b.

151 Viscusi, W., Employment Hazards: An Investigation of Market Performance, cited by Viscusi, 1989; supra note 20.

152 In a review of the draft of this report, the New York Power Pool criticized the value selected, arguing that it is too high because it exceeds the discounted value of lost earnings. As discussed in this section, there are serious problems with use and lost earnings as a basis for health risk values because lost earnings are only one of the many costs associated with health risks and they seriously under value non-earners and low-earners. The adopted value is not precise and certain, but it appears to be conservative based on analyses of the studies reviewed.

153 See, Morrall, J., "A Review of the Record," Regulation, November/December 1986, p.25. According to Morrall, Table 4, at p. 30, the cost of various federal health and safety regulations per life saved ranges from $100,000for steering column protection to $132,000,000for DES in cattle feed (1984$). Proposed regulations would entail a cost per life saved of as high as $72,000,000,000(1984$) for formaldehyde. If federal regulations represent a kind of revealed preference study of risk values, these figures suggest that a value of $4,000,000(1989$) per life is not unreasonable.

Although there is considerable evidence that the true value is greater, there is some evidence that it could be smaller. Because the credibility of the value and its application in environmental cost studies is crucial, a conservative estimate was adopted. Although underestimating the cost of health risks may result in somewhat inefficient resource allocations, lack of analytical credibility is viewed as a fatal flaw for any analysis.

As with any uncertain estimates, sensitivity analysis may be performed if health risk values are a significant component of environmental costs. A reasonable range for sensitivity analyses from the studies reviewed is from $1,000,000 to $10,000,000. This range spans an order of magnitude reported on the studies. Few studies derive values for statistical lives outside this recommended range.

For morbidity, or non-fatal health risks, a value of $400,000per statistical injury is adopted. This is one-tenth the value of a fatal health risk. Shuman and Cavanagh[154] recommend a morbidity value equivalent to one-tenth the value of a fatal health risk. The estimate for morbidity risks is imperfect. Little research has been done in this area to support any empirical value. It is also clear that there is a vast difference between the risk of irritated eyes and permanent paralysis. No single value can possibly cover the full range of risks. While some injury risks might have little cost, others could have costs greater than fatal health risks. Indeed, it is not uncommon to hear people express a preference for death over certain debilitating conditions. Until such time as better values are derived, a value of $400,000per statistical injury appears from the studies to be reasonable.

5. Discounting Health Risk Values

In Chapter III, J.4.d., a social time preference rate for discounting future environmental costs and benefits was discussed. This is the rate used to compare future environmental costs with today's environmental costs. Environmental costing practitioners disagree as to whether health risk values or any environmental risks should be discounted at all.

Advocates of discounting at a positive rate believe that if health risks are treated as economic values, then they should be consistent with other economic values. They maintain that, from an economic efficiency viewpoint, health risks created during, say, the fortieth and final year of a plant operation should be discounted because the present value of the cost could be invested for 40 years and used to compensate future risk bearers. Therefore, from a pure equity point of view, future health risk costs should be discounted because the opportunity cost of the present investment would exceed the health risk cost in the future. They further argue that failure to discount would be tantamount to valuing future health risks more than current health risks.

Proponents of a positive discount rate point out that risk of a human fatality ten thousand years from now is not likely to cause any but the most philosophical among us to grieve. They assert that few people would be willing to pay any compensation

---

[154] Shuman, supra note 122.

for the risk of a loss of life that far into the future. The distance in time is too abstract, civilization may have ended before that, and technological advances could neutralize the risk. If a fatal risk that far in the future has little value to people then the question becomes, at what point would it not be discounted?

Others maintain that a zero discount rate should be used, particularly as applied to human life and health risks, as a matter of morality, because a life in the future is as valuable as a present life.[155] They maintain that sound environmental stewardship mandates that the value of future lives and other environmental assets be weighted as heavily as the value of present lives. Furthermore, they maintain that discounting (at rates higher than zero), double-discounts future risks since, in the risk calculation, risk is already reduced by the likelihood that the risk may not be realized. The calculation of the value of risk to a statistical life is, by the means it is calculated, already reduced to present value. Finally, they assert that it is inappropriate to discount long-lasting risks, such as those from high level nuclear wastes or risk of nuclear proliferation that pose risks for millennia.[156]

A third treatment of discounting is suggested by the kinds of risks at issue in the debate. Most pollutants cause health risks on a one-time basis; for example, each sulfate molecule formed from coal plant emissions that is breathed once by one person causes no further damage to anyone else. Nor do the sulfates linger in the environment for long periods of time. Such risks are not persistent. Risks may be long lasting in the sense that cancers may take years to form following exposure to a substance, but they do not persist in the sense that the same substances continue to pose risks to the public. Future generations can avoid non-persistent risks simply by ceasing to produce them. Some risks however, <u>are</u> persistent, radioactive waste being the most striking example of such risk. Once created, hazardous wastes may impose risks on future generations that they can not avoid.

Using this view one would begin discounting from the time when the risks are created[157] whether a risk is to an individual exposed to a substance that has a delayed effect or a risk that is persistent and faced by numbers of people over time. Once the risk is created, it would be discounted from that moment and no later. This means that if the risk is borne immediately--such as when sulfates are inhaled--regardless of how long it takes effects to manifest themselves--its value would be discounted from

---

155 <u>See</u>, Shuman, <u>supra</u> note 122. Weiss, E., <u>In Fairness to Future Generations: International Law, Common Patrimony, and Intergenerational Equity</u>, Dobbs Ferry, NY, 1989, pp. 152-153.

156 That risk to life must be given a dollar value in order to include loss of life in the calculation of the cost of environmental impacts, does not mean that loss of life is a strictly economic commodity, any more than jury awards for pain and suffering mean that one's suffering is a purely economic commodity. The inadequacy of current micro and macroeconomic theory to encompass environmental degradation and the need for a new pre-analytic vision of environmental economics was presented by Herman Daly at a conference of The International Society for Ecological Economics (ISEE), "The Ecological Economics of Sustainability," The World Bank, Washington, D.C., May 21-23, 1990; an argument that environmental costs should be discounted in a "fiduciary trust framework" and not in a "utilitarian market framework" is advanced in an unpublished paper presented at the same conference, <u>Fiduciary Responsibilities and the Greenhouse Effect</u> by Peter G. Brown, Director of Environmental Programs, School of Environmental Affairs, University of Maryland, College Park.

157 <u>Id</u>.

the time of exposure, not from the later period when the health effects occur. It is not the health effects that are valued, but the health risks.[158]

A simple example demonstrates the practical effect of this procedure. Assume that the health risk is valued at $100. If it is created today, its cost is the present value or $100. If the health risk is created 40 years from today, its present value is $31, using 3%. If the effect, rather than the risk, were valued, and the effect takes 20 years to manifest itself, but has the same $100 cost, what would its present value be? If the risk is created today but the health effect occurs 20 years from today, its present value would be $55. In the case of a risk created 40 years hence, the effect would not manifest until the 60th year. Its present value would be $17. Clearly, it makes a difference whether it is the risk or the effect that is valued.

This procedure may overcome some of the concerns expressed by Shuman and others without sacrificing economic efficiency or equity. First, the approach is consistent with procedures that value risks to health, not the loss of life itself. Second, risk valuation studies estimate the value of the risks that are immediately incurred, not the latent health effects. Finally, the most conservative approach is to value health risks when they occur.

Advocates of this view assert that by discounting from the time when risks are first created, most objections to discounting are removed: future generations will always have the option of avoiding those risks; They can do so by no longer operating plants that create those risks. Also, because it is health risks that are valued, not the health effects, health risks associated with effects that take years to manifest themselves, such as cancer, are not discounted more than health risks associated with more immediate effects such as construction fatalities. Health risks associated with persistent effects, such as those associated with nuclear waste, would be discounted from the time when the waste is generated, not from the time years hence when their health effects may result.

L. CONCLUSION

Health risks are legitimate economic costs. To assure a full account of environmental externality damages, the studies reviewed find that health risks should be measured in the same way that other environmental risks are measured: by society's willingness to pay to avoid them, or willingness to accept compensation to incur them voluntarily. Health risk values in the literature range from about $1 million to $12 million for a statistical life. For costing purposes in this report, a mid-range figure of $4 million is used for mortality risks and $400,000 for mortality damages.

---

158 Id.

M. REFERENCES

Alchian, A. and W. Allen, Exchange and Production: Theory in Use, Wadsworth, Belmont, California, 1969.

Arrow, K. and R. Lind, "Uncertainty in Public Investment," The American Economic Review, Vol. 60, pp. 364-378, 1970.

Bator, M., "The Anatomy of Market Failure," Quarterly Journal of Economics, Vol. 72, pp. 351-379, 1958.

Bishop R. and T. Heberlein, "Measuring Values of Extramarket Goods: Are Indirect Measures Biased?," American Journal of Agricultural Economics, Vol. 61, pp. 926-930, 1979.

Bonneville Power Administration (BPA), Issue Backgrounder: Counting the Costs--How BPA Performs Environmental Cost Analysis, DOE/BP-405, June, 1985.

Bonneville Power Administration (BPA), Cost Effectiveness Methodology, DOE/BP-751, December, 1986a.

Bonneville Power Administration (BPA), BPA Evaluation of Generic Environmental Costs and Benefits Studies, Portland, Oregon, 1986b.

Bonneville Power Administration (BPA), Internal review of discount rate practices, 1986c.

Bonneville Power Administration (BPA), "WNP-1 and -3 Study," 1987 Resource Strategy, USDOE/BPA, May, 1987.

Bower, B. and A. Kneese, Managing Water Quality, Johns Hopkins Press, Baltimore, 1968.

Brown, C., "Equalizing Differences in the Labor Market," Quarterly Journal of Economics, Vol. 94, pp. 113-134, Feb., 1980.

Buchanan, S., "Accounting for External Costs of Energy Resources in Utility Least-Cost Planning." for Executive Office of Energy Resources, Commonwealth of Massachusetts, March, 1988.

Campen, J., Benefit, Cost, and Beyond, Ballinger Publishing Co., Cambridge, Ma., 1986.

Cannon, J., The Health Costs of Air Pollution, American Lung Association, New York, January, 1990.

Carson, R. and P. Navarro, "Natural Resources Damage Assessment," Natural Resources Journal, pp. 815-836, Fall, 1988.

Chernick, P., and E. Caverhill, The Valuation of Externalities from Energy Production, Delivery, and Use, for Boston Gas Co., Boston, Mass., December 22, 1989.

Clawson, M. and J. Knetsch, Economics of Outdoor Recreation, Johns Hopkins University Press for Resources for the Future, Baltimore, 1966.

Coase, R., "The Problem of Social Cost," The Journal of Law and Economics, Vol. III, 1960.

Data Resources, Ind., "Implicit Price Deflator for GNP", in Long-Term Forecast of U.S. Economy, Lexington, Mass., 1990.

ECO Northwest, Economic Analysis of the Environmental Effects of the Coal-Fired Electric Generator at Boardman, Oregon, for Bonneville Power Administration, December, 1983.

ECO Northwest, Estimating Environmental Costs and Benefits for Five Generating Resources, for Bonneville Power Administration, DOE/BP-11551-1, Portland, Oregon, April, 1986.

ECO Northwest, Generic Coal Study, for Bonneville Power Administration, DE-AM79-86BP62884, Portland, Oregon, 1987.

Energy Systems Research Group, The Role of Hydro-Quebec Power in a Least-Cost Energy Resource Plan for Vermont", prepared for Dept. of Public Service, State of Vermont, January 19, 1990.

Fisher, A., "Energy and Environment in the Long Term," Energy Policy, Vol. 17, No. 2, pp. 84-87, April, 1989.

Freeman, A., The Benefits of Environmental Improvement, Johns Hopkins Press, Baltimore, 1979.

Georgescu-Roegen, N., The Entropy Law and the Economic Process, Harvard University Press, Cambridge, 1971.

Gregory, R., R. Mendelsohn, and P. Slovic, Review of Uncertainty and Risk in BPA-Sponsored Analyses of Energy Resources," for Bonneville Power Administration, November, 18, 1987.

Hammack, J., and G. Brown, Waterfowl and Wetlands: Toward Bioeconomic Analysis, Johns Hopkins, Baltimore, Md. 1974.

Hanemann, W., Willingness to Pay and Willingness to Accept: How Much Can They Differ?," University of California, Working Paper No. 328, Berkeley, March, 1986.

Hardin, G., "Tragedy of the Commons", Science, Vol. 162, 1968.

Hoehn, J. and A. Randall, Incentives and Performance in Contingent Valuation, mimeo, University of Kentucky, February, 1983.

Kahneman, D. and A. Tversky, "Prospect Theory: An Analysis of Decision Under Risk," Econometrica, Vol. 47, No. 2, March, 1979.

Knetsch, J., Economics of Outdoor Recreation, Johns Hopkins University Press for Resources for the Future, Baltimore, Md., 1966.

Krutilla, J. and A. Fisher, The Economics of Natural Environments, Resources for the Future, Johns Hopkins University Press, Baltimore, Md., 1975.

Lind, R., Discounting for Time and Risk in Energy Policy, Resources for the Future, Washington, D.C., 1982.

Meridian Corporation, "Energy System Emissions and Material Requirements", for U.S. Dept. of Energy, Washington, D.C., February, 1989.

Meyer, P. and E. Cheslak, et. al., Calculation of Environmental Costs and Benefits Associated with Hydropower Development in the Pacific Northwest", for Bonneville Power Administration, DE-AC79-83BP11546, Portland, Ore., 1986.

Mishan, E.J., "The Postwar Literature on Externalities: An Interpretive Essay," Journal of Economic Literature, Vol. 9, pp. 1-28, 1971.

Mitchell, R. and R. Carson, Using Surveys to Value Public Goods: The Contingent Valuation Method, Resources for the Future, Washington, D.C., 1989.

Moore and W. Viscusi, "The Quantity Adjusted Value of Life," Economic Enquiry, Vol. 26, No. 369, 1988a.

Moore and W. Viscusi, "Doubling the Estimated Value of Life: The Implications of New Occupational Fatality Data," Journal of Policy Analysis and Management, Vol. 7, 1988b.

Olson, C., "An Analysis of Wage Differentials Received by Workers on Dangerous Jobs." The Journal of Human Resources, Vol. 16, No.2 1981.

Prest, A.R. and R. Turvey, "Cost-Benefit Analysis: A Survey." Surveys of Economic Theory, Vol. I. St. Martin's Press, New York, 1967.

Randall, A., "Market Solutions to Externality Problems: Theory and Practice," American Journal of Agricultural Economics, Vol. 54, pp. 175-183, 1972.

Rescher, N., Risk: A Philosophical Introduction to the Theory of Risk Evaluation and Management, University Press of America, Lanham, Md., 1983.

Samuelson, P., "A Diagrammatic Exposition of a Theory of Public Expenditure," The Review of Economics and Statistics, Vol. XXXVII, No. 4, November, 1955.

Samuelson, P., and W. Vickrey, "Discussion," The American Economic Review, Vol. 54, pp. 88-96, 1964.

Samuelson, P., Economics, McGraw-Hill, New York, 1973.

Seneca, J. and M. Taussig, Environmental Economics, Prentice-Hall, Englewood Cliffs, N.J., 1974.

Shuman, M., and R. Cavanagh, A Model Conservation and Electric Power Plan for the Pacific Northwest, for Natural Resources Defense Council (NRDC), 1981.

Slovic, P., B. Fischoff, and S. Lichtenstein, "Characterizing Perceived Risk," in Perilous Progress, (R.W. Kates, et. al. eds.), Westview, Boulder, Colorado, 1985.

Smith, R., The Occupational Safety and Health Act: Its Goals and Achievements, 1976.

Techplan Associates, Assessment of Commercial and Industrial Cogeneration Potential in the Pacific Northwest, for U.S. Dept. of Energy, DE-AC79-88BP40040, March, 1989.

Thaler, R. and S. Rosen, "The Value of Saving a Life: Evidence from the Labor Market." in Household Production and Consumption, (N. Terleckyj, ed.) Columbia University Press, New York, 1976, pp. 265-298.

Turvey, R., "On Divergences Between Social Cost and Private Cost," Economica, Vol. 30, pp. 309-313, August, 1963.

Varner, G., "Do Species Have Standing?," Environmental Ethics, Vol. 9. No. 1, Spring, 1987.

Viscusi, W., Employment Hazards: An Investigation of Market Performance, 1979.

Viscusi, W., Risk by Choice: Regulating Health and Safety in the Workplace, 1983.

Viscusi, W., "The Valuation of Risks to Life and Health: Guidelines for Policy Analysis," Paper prepared for National Science Foundation, 1984.

Viscusi, W., "Toward a Diminished Role for Tort Liability: Social Insurance, Government Regulation, and Contemporary Risks to Health and Safety," Yale Journal on Regulation, Vol. 6. No.1. Winter, 1989.

von Mises, L., Human Action, Yale University Press, New Haven, 1949.

Willig, R., "Consumers' Surplus Without Apology," American Economic Review, Vol. 66, No. 4, September, 1976, pp. 589-597.

IV. FOSSIL FUEL EMISSIONS

IV. FOSSIL FUEL EMISSIONS

A. DISCUSSION

An objective of environmental costing is to arrive at a social cost figure expressed in cents per kilowatt hour for each type of electric generation option. This figure can then be applied to incorporate environmental costs in utility planning and resource acquisition procedures to permit selection of the options that are of least cost to society.

To arrive at externality costs expressed in cents per kilowatt hour, the analyst must first ascertain the pounds of each pollutant of concern emitted per kilowatt hour for each technology. This chapter addresses air pollutant emissions for fossil fuel-fired power plants.[1] Chapter V. A.-E. treats the costs to society of each major fossil fuel plant air pollutant in dollars per pound. Then, Chapter VI. A.- C. combines the air emissions figures of this chapter with the cost figures from Chapter V to arrive at the cents per kilowatt hour figures that can be used by utilities and regulators. All the above emissions and valuation figures are derived from identified studies reviewed.

Table 1 describes five types of air pollutant emissions, and three types of solid waste generated by coal-fired steam plants. The heat rate and sulfur content assumptions used in calculating these figures are also given. The table relies on figures established in two separate documents. One (PLC) was written by Paul Chernick and Emily Caverhill of PLC, Inc. These individuals also authored several portions of this report as consultants to the Center for Environmental Legal Studies, Pace University School of Law. The second (DOE/PEIA) was prepared by Oak Ridge National Laboratories for the U.S. Department of Energy. Complete citations to these documents, and to studies relied upon in subsequent tables are listed in the References at the end of this chapter.

Table 2 provides essentially the same information for two types of "clean coal" combustion technologies. These are newly demonstrated or experimental types of coal-fired power plants, which utilize combustion techniques which greatly reduce sulfur dioxide emissions. Atmospheric Fluidized Bed Combustion (AFBC) is a system in which particles of pulverized coal are suspended along with similarly sized bed material of sorbent (crushed limestone or dolomite) in a continuously moving mass of air. The sorbent captures a portion of the sulfur dioxide generated during combustion. The system has lower combustion temperatures which serve to minimize nitrogen oxide formation.[2]

Integrated Gasification Combined Cycle (IGCC) plants mix ground coal in a water slurry and feed it into a gasifier, where it is partially burned with oxygen into a mixture of carbon monoxide and hydrogen. Sulfur in the fuel is converted to hydrogen sulfide

---

[1] Data on water pollution effluents and land use per kilowatt generated from fossil-fuel power plants as well as estimates of their costs/kWh where available are provided in Chapter V.G.

[2] U.S. DOE, Energy Technology Characterization Handbook: Environmental Pollution and Control Factors, DOE/EP-0093, March, 1983, p. 83.

hydrogen sulfide, which is later converted to elemental sulfur (a marketable product). The remaining hydrogen is burned in a gas turbine.[3]

Table 3 sets forth the air emissions for Gas-Fired Generation. The figures are developed by PLC, Inc. and the U.S. Department of Energy. Gas-fired plants do not generate solid or liquid combustion wastes.

Table 4 sets forth the emissions from Oil-Fired Generators. Three separate figures are provided by PLC, Inc., based on different sulfur-in-fuel assumptions.

Table 5 breaks out into a single table the carbon dioxide emissions for eight different power generation options. The source from which each figure is derived is indicated on the table. Differences in amount of carbon/kWh are due primarily to different estimates for the heat rate, or efficiency, of a particular technology.

Tables 6 and 7 describe air toxic emissions for coal- and oil-fired plants in pounds per 10^{12} BTU. The data were obtained form the April, 1989 EPA report, "Estimating Air Toxic Emissions from Coal and Oil Combustion Sources." Air toxics include metals as well as polycyclic organic matter (POM) and formaldehyde. POM is a very broad category of organic structures that are formed from two or more compounds, but those most common in fuel combustion emissions are poly-aromatic hydrocarbons (PAH), composed of only carbon and hydrogen, and their PAH-nitrogen analogs. POM can be emitted in either a gaseous or a particulate phase.

The EPA report points out that the trace element content of coal varies significantly among coal mines as well as within a single coal seam. There is less variation in emissions among heating oils of different origins.

Uncontrolled metals emissions, or emissions from plants equipped only with an ESP, are generally much higher than emissions from scrubber-equipped plants. The variation can be as high as one to two orders of magnitude. Though an externality value for air toxics has not been assessed, emissions of metals, POM and formaldehyde have significant health impacts. Their valuation merits future research.

---

[3] Siegart, R., Cool Water Achievements: Impressive Past for a Promising Future, presentation to Alternative Energy 1989 Conference, Tuscon, AZ, April 1989, p. 7.

TABLE 1

EMISSIONS FOR COAL-FIRED STEAM PLANTS

		Uncontrolled		With FGD\ESP		NSPS
	UNITS	DOE/PEIA	AP-42	DOE/PEIA	AP-42	PLC
Heat Rate	BTU/kWh	9,400	10,000	9,400	10,000	10,000
Coal Sulfur Content		2.5%	1.2%	2.5%	1.2	any
SO_2 (1)	lb SO_2/kWh	4.65×10^{-2}	1.8×10^{-2}	4.65×10^{-3}	1.8×10^{-3}	1.2×10^{-2}
NO_x	lb NO_x/kWh	9.40×10^{-3}	6.07×10^{-3}	9.40×10^{-3}	6.07×10^{-3}	6.00×10^{-3}
CO_2 (2)	lb C/kWh	0.53	0.57	0.53	0.57	0.57
(3)	lb CO_2/kWh	1.96	2.09	1.96	2.09	2.09
Methane	lb CH_4/kWh	n.a.	1.6×10^{-3}	n.a.	1.60×10^{-3}	1.60×10^{-3}
Particulates (4)	lb TSP/kWh	9.40×10^{-4}	5.0×10^{-4} - 4.0×10^{-2}	7.52×10^{-5}	3.0×10^{-4}	3.0×10^{-2}
Solid Waste						
Bottom Ash	lb/kWh	2.26×10^{-2}	n.a.	2.26×10^{-2}	n.a.	n.a.
Fly Ash	lb/kWh	8.84×10^{-2}	n.a.	8.84×10^{-2}		
Sulfur Byproducts (5)	lb/kWh	--	n.a.	9.4×10^{-2}		

n.a. = Not available from source.

-- = Not relevant to type of generation.

TABLE 1 - NOTES

(1) PLC lists SO_2 in units of lbs sulfur/10^6 BTU. Pounds of sulfur were converted to lbs SO_2 by multiplying by a factor of 2 based on 64g SO_2/32 g S. DOE\PEIA assumes a 90% SO_2 removal resulting from Flu Gas Desulfurization (FGD). Figures in the NSPS column reflect the maximum allowable emission rates. Actual emissions will vary depending on coal sulfur content.

(2) PLC assumes a typical value of 57 lb C/10^6 BTU for coal. Values listed under DOE/PEIA were derived by applying 57 lb C/10^6 BTU to the DOE/PEIA heat rate.

(3) Pounds of carbon were converted to lbs CO_2 by multiplying by a factor of 3.67 based on 44 g CO_2/12 g C. This ratio assumes that all carbon is converted to CO_2.

(4) FGD emissions assumes fabric filter particulate control, see DOE/PEIA at pp. 2-30, 2-32. Uncontrolled emissions in the AP-42 column represent a range dependent upon the sulfur and ash content.

(5) Dry FGD waste.

Derived from PLC at Table 9.1 ("Coal plant from NESCAUM 1986, lowest coal emissions without least emissions dispatch") and at Table 9.4(NSPS); DOE/PEIA at p. 2-9 (Uncontrolled pulverized coal fired plant) and at p. 2-6 (with wet lime/limestone FGD). Values for FGD-equipped plant in DOE/PEIA are given as a percent reduction and were applied to the baseline values for the uncontrolled plant.

TABLE 2

NEW COAL PLANT EMISSIONS

		AFBC		IGCC	
	Units	PLC	DOE/PEIA	PLC	DOE/PEIA
Heat Rate	BTU/kWh	10,000	9,400	10,000	9,010
Coal Sulfur Content		1.1%	2.5%	.45%	any
SO_2 (1)	lb S/kWh	$2.75x10^{-3}$		$1.85x10^{-3}$	
	lb SO_2/kWh	$5.50x10^{-3}$	$4.65x10^{-3}$	$3.7x10^{-3}$	$1.34x10^{-3}$
NO_x	lb NO_x/kWh	$3.00x10^{-3}$	$3.76x10^{-3}$	$6.00x10^{-4}$	$4.51x10^{-4}$
CO_2 (2)	lb C/kWh	0.57	0.53	0.57	0.51
(3)	lb CO_2/kWh	2.09	1.96	2.09	1.88
Methane	lb CH_4/kWh	$1.6x10^{-3}$	n.a.	$1.6x10^{-3}$	n.a.
Particulate	lb TSP/kWh	$1.5x10^{-3}$	$2.82x10^{-4}$	$1.5x10^{-3}$	$9.01x10^{-5}$
Solid Waste	lb/kWh	n.a.	0.24	n.a.	0.11
Sulfur Byproducts	lb/kWh	--	--	n.a.	$1.98x10^{-2}$

n.a. = Not available from source.

-- = Not relevant to type of generation.

TABLE 2 - NOTES

(1) PLC lists SO_2 in units of lbs carbon/10^6 BTU. Pounds of sulfur were converted to lbs SO_2 by multiplying by a factor of 2 based on 64g SO_2/32 g S.

(2) PLC assumes a typical value of 57 lb C/ 10^6 BTU for coal. Values listed under DOE/PEIA were derived by applying 57 lb C/10^6 BTU to the DOE/PEIA heat rate.

(3) Pounds of carbon were converted to lbs CO_2 by multiplying by a factor of 3.67 based on 44 g CO_2/12 g C.

Derived from PLC at Table 9.4 and DOE/PEIA at p. 2-12 (AFBC) and p. 2-20 (IGCC). The DOE/PEIA figures are expressed in terms of percent reduction. Values were derived by applying the reductions to the baseline uncontrolled pulverized coal-fired plant at p. 2-9 in DOE/PEIA. Basic data for this baseline plant are presented in Table 1 under the column title "Uncontrolled".

TABLE 3

EMISSIONS FOR NATURAL GAS-FIRED GENERATION

	UNITS	Steam Plant		Combined Cycle(PLC)		
		PLC	DOE/Char*	Existing	NSPS	BACT**
Heat Rate	BTU/kW	10,400	9,224	9,000	9,000	9000
SO_2	lb sulfur/kWh lb SO_2/kWh	---	$5.40x10^{-6}$	---	---	---
NO_x	lb NO_x/kWh	$2.6x10^{-3}$	$6.2x10^{-3}$	$3.8x10^{-3}$	$1.8x10^{-3}$	$2.5x10^{-4}$
CO_2 (1) (2)	lb C/kWh lb CO_2/kWh	0.312 1.14	0.27 0.99	0.27 0.99	0.27 0.99	0.27 0.99
Methane	lb CH_4/kWh	---	$8.98x10^{-6}$	---	---	---
Carbon Monoxide	lb CO/kWh	n.a.	$1.53x10^{-4}$	n.a.	n.a.	n.a.
Particulate	lb TSP/kWh	0	$2.93x10^{-4}$	0	0	0

n.a.= Not available from source.

-- = Not relevant to type of generation.

TABLE 3 - NOTES

(1) PLC derives emissions of CO_2 in lbs C/10^6 BTU. For natural gas, PLC calculates 0.03 lb C/cf or 30 lb C/10^6 BTU, assuming 1000 BTU/cf. PLC at 5. Using the PLC figure for lb C/cf, values listed under DOE/Char were calculated from annual natural gas usage, annual kWh production, and heat content of 1020 BTU/cf provided in DOE/Char.

(2) Pounds of carbon were converted to lbs CO_2 by multiplying by a factor of 3.67 based on 44 g CO_2/12 g C.

*DOE/Char gives emissions by technology in tons/year and also gives annual production of kWh. Heat rate was derived for comparative purposes by dividing 3413 kWh/BTU by 37% (the facility efficiency).

**Best Available Control Technology (BACT) is defined in PLC for gas-fired Combined Cycle as selective catalytic injection (SCR) and steam water injection (SWI).

Derived from PLC at Table 9.1 (Steam Plant) and Table 9.4 (Combined Cycle); DOE/Char at pp. 134-135 (Steam Plant).

TABLE 4

EMISSIONS FOR OIL-FIRED GENERATION

			Steam Plant - # 6 Oil			Combustion Turbine #2 Diesel
	UNITS	DOE/Char*	PLC	PLC	PLC	PLC
Heat Rate	BTU/kWh	9,840	10,400	10,400	10,400	13,600
Oil-Sulfur Content	%S	2%	2.2%	1.0%	0.5%	0.3%
SO_2 (1)	lb S/kWh		1.24×10^{-2}	5.19×10^{-3}	1.77×10^{-3}	2.18×10^{-3}
	lb SO_2/kWh	2.54×10^{-2}	2.48×10^{-2}	3.54×10^{-3}	1.04×10^{-2}	4.36×10^{-3}
NO_x	lb NO_x/kWh	2.95×10^{-3}	3.71×10^{-3}	2.98×10^{-3}	3.71×10^{-3}	6.77×10^{-3}
CO_2 (2)	lb C/kWh	0.45	0.48	0.48	0.48	0.60
(3)	lb CO_2/kWh	1.65	1.75	1.75	1.75	2.19
Hydrocarbon	lb CH_4/kWh	n.a.	3.54×10^{-3}	3.02×10^{-3}	3.02×10^{-3}	3.94×10^{-3}
	lb hydro-carbon/kWh	6.75×10^{-5}	n.a.	n.a.	n.a.	n.a.
Carbon Monoxide	lb CO/kWh	3.37×10^{-4}	n.a.	n.a.	n.a.	n.a.
Parti- (4) culates	lb TSP/kWh	2.8×10^{-3}	1.8×10^{-3}	9.4×10^{-4}	5.72×10^{-4}	3.7×10^{-4}
Solid (5) Waste	lb/kWh	0.11	n.a.	n.a.	n.a.	n.a.

n.a. = Not available from source.

TABLE 4 - NOTES

(1) PLC lists SO_2 in units of lbs sulfur/10^6 BTU fuel input. Pounds sulfur were converted to lbs SO_2 by multiplying by a factor of 2 based on 64 g SO_2/32 g S.

(2) PLC lists CO_2 in units of lbs carbon/10^6 BTU fuel input. PLC calculates 46 lb C/10^6 BTU fuel input for residual oil #6 and 44 lb C/10^6 BTU for diesel or #2 fuel oil. PLC at p. 5 and Table 9.1. Value under DOE/Char was calculated by applying the DOE/Char heat rate to the PLC carbon calculation. DOE/Char does not calculate carbon dioxide emissions.

(3) Pounds of carbon were converted to lbs CO_2 by multiplying by a factor of 3.67 based on 48 g CO_2/12 g C.

(4) DOE/Char provides values for total suspended particulates and also gives annual levels in tons for some particulates by composition. In lbs/yr, the DOE/Char oil-fired generator produces the following particulate air pollutants: 254 lbs arsenic; 202 lbs beryllium; 7,580 lbs cadmium; 40.4 lbs lead; 254 lbs mercury; 75,800 lbs nickel; 254 lbs maganese; 594 lbs chromium; 594 lbs copper; and 1,196 lbs vanadium.

(5) DOE/Char gives solid waste in terms of scrubber sludge and particulate control waste combined. The plant has a sulfur dioxide scrubber and an electrostatic precipitator.

DOE/Char provides emissions values in tons/year and gives annual energy production in kWh. Heat rate was derived for comparative purposes by dividing 3413 kWh/BTU by 34.7%, the plant efficiency provided in DOE/Char.

Derived from PLC Table 9.1 (Existing Steam Plants and Oil-fired Combustion Turbine) and DOE/Char pp.at 114-115 (Oil-fired Steam Electric Plant).

TABLE 5

CARBON EMISSIONS FROM OPERATION OF ELECTRIC GENERATORS

Type of Generation			lb C/kWh
COAL:			
	Uncontrolled Coal/Steam		
		DOE/PEIA	0.53
	Coal/Steam with FGD		
		DOE/PEIA	0.53
		PLC	0.57
		San Martin	0.58
	AFBC		
		DOE/PEA	0.53
		PLC	0.57
		San Martin	0.58
	IGCC		
		DOE/PEIA	0.51
		PLC	0.57
		San Martin	0.58
OIL:	No. 6 Residual/Steam		
		DOE/PEIA	0.45
		PLC	0.44
		San Martin	0.43
	No. 2 Residual (diesel)/ Combustion Turbine		
		PLC	0.60
NATURAL GAS:	Steam		
		DOE/Char	0.27
		PLC	0.31
		San Martin	0.29
	Combined Cycle		
		PLC	0.27

Derived from emissions charts titled "Emissions for Coal-Fired Steam Plants"; "Clean Coal Emissions"; "Emissions for Oil-Fired Generation"; and "Natural Gas-Fired Generation" and San Martin, Table 1. San Martin gives emissions in metric tons of CO_2/Gwh. These values were converted to lbs C/kWh using the following factors: 2200 lbs/metric ton; 10^6 kWh/Gwh; and 0.272 based 12 g C/44 g CO_2.

TABLE 6

METALS AND TOXIC EMISSIONS FROM COAL-FIRED PLANTS
(Bituminous Coal)

	Emissions (1) ($lb/10^{12}$ BTU)			Emissions (5) (lbs/Kwh)
	Uncontrolled	ESP	Scrubbers	Scrubbers
Arsenic	684	40.1	17.2	1.72×10^{-7}
Beryllium	81	3.0	.11	1.1×10^{-9}
Cadmium	44.4	9.2	.35-1.6	3.5×10^{-9} - 1.6×10^{-8}
Chromium (2)	1250-1570	356-447	102-129	1.02×10^{-8} - 1.29×10^{-6}
Copper	848	194	24	2.4×10^{-7}
Mercury	16	8-16	.96-7.4	9.6×10^{-9} - 7.4×10^{-8}
Manganese	2980	642	36	3.6×10^{-7}
Nickel	1030-1290	280-352	37-46	3.7×10^{-7} - 4.6×10^{-7}
Lead	316	49	16.8	1.68×10^{-7}
POM (3)	n.a.	.03	18.6	1.86×10^{-7}
Formaldehyde	130	n.a.	n.a.	n.a.
Radionuclides (4)				
Uranium-238	n.a.	295.3	73.7	7.37×10^{-7}
Thoruium-232	n.a.	170.0	36.5	3.65×10^{-7}

n.a.= not available from source.

TABLE 6 - NOTES

(1) Factors represent emissions for pulverized dry bottom coal-fired boilers which predominate in the utility sector.

(2) Factors for chromium, mercury, nickel and POM are ranges for boilers tested, all other factors are averages.

(3) POM stands for Polycyclic Organic Matter.

(4) Radionuclide factors are in pCi/10^6 BTU.

(5) Assuming a heat rate of 10,000 BTU/kWh.

DOE/Char provides values for total suspended particulates and also gives annual levels in tons for some particulates by composition. In lbs/yr, the DOE/Char oil-fired generator produces the following particulate air pollutants: 254 lbs arsenic; 202 lbs beryllium; 7,580 lbs cadmium; 40.4 lbs lead; 254 lbs mercury; 75,800lbs nickel; 254 lbs maganese; 594 lbs chromium; 594 lbs copper; and 1,196 lbs vanadium.

Source: U.S. EPA, Estimating Air Toxics from Coal and Oil Combustion Sources, Office of Air Quality Planning and Standards, Research Triangle Park, NC, EPA-450/2-89-001. April 1989, Table 4-38, 4-47, 4-56, 4-65, 4-76, 4-93, 4-85, 4-102, 4-116, 4-120, 4-121, 4-122 and 4-123.

TABLE 7

METALS AND TOXIC EMISSIONS
Oil-Fired Plants
(Residual Oil)

	Emission Factor $lb \backslash 10^{12}$ BTU
Arsenic	19
Beryllium	4.2
Cadmium	15.7
Chromium	21
Copper	280
Mercury	3.2
Manganese	26
Nickel	1260
Lead (1)	9.3-47
POM	8.4
Formaldehyde (2)	405
Radionuclides	n.a.

n.a. = not available from source

Source: U.S. EPA, Estimating Air Toxic from Coal and Oil Combustion Sources, Office of Air Quality Planning and Standards, EPA-450/2-89-001, April 1989, Table 4-1, p. 4-2; Table 117, p. 4-175.

TABLE 7 - NOTES

(1) The range for lead represents ESP controlled, and uncontrolled plants. All other emission factors are averages for uncontrolled emissions.

(2) Formaldehyde factors are averages based on very limited and relatively old data.

B. REFERENCES

Chernick, P., and E. Caverhill, The Valuation of Externalities from Energy Production, Delivery, and Use: Fall, 1989 Update. Report to the Boston Gas Company. Boston: PLC, Inc., December 22, 1989 [cited as PLC].

San Martin, R., Environmental Emissions from Energy Technology Systems: The Total Fuel Cycle. Washington, DC: U.S. Department of Energy, April, 1989 [cited as San Martin].

U.S. Department of Energy (DOE), draft, Energy System Emissions and Materiel Requirements, prepared Meridian Corporation. Alexandria, VA: February, 1989 [cited as DOE/Materiel].

U.S. Department of Energy (DOE), Fossil Energy, Innovative Clean Coal Technology: Programmatic Environmental Impact Analysis (PEIA), prepared by Oak Ridge National Laboratory. September, 1988 [cited as DOE/PEIA].

U.S. Department of Energy (DOE), Office of Environmental Protection, Safety, and Emergency Preparedness, Office of Environmental Analysis, Energy Technology Characterizations Handbook: Environmental Pollution and Control Factors, 3d ed., prepared with assistance from Aerospace Corporation and Mueller Associates, Inc. DOE/EP-009. Washington, DC: DOE, March, 1983 [cited as DOE/Char].

U.S. EPA, Estimating Air Toxics from Coal and Oil Combustion Sources, Office of Air Quality Planning and Standards, Research Triangle Park, North Carolina, EPA-450/2-89-001, April, 1989, Table 4-1, p. 4-2; Table 117, p. 4-175.

V. EXTERNALITY COSTS BY POLLUTANT

A. GLOBAL WARMING

V. EXTERNALITY COSTS BY POLLUTANT

A. GLOBAL WARMING

1. Introduction: The Prospect of Global Warming

The earth's atmosphere is a global commons into which the world's population emits the gaseous by-products of its activities on the erroneous assumption that the atmosphere has limitless capacity to absorb invisible gaseous wastes without changing its characteristics, and that air pollution is cost-free waste disposal. However, all of these emissions effect changes in the world's ecosystems, and some of the emissions, in particular emissions from electric power production, may radically alter the world's climate. If one could determine the cost of the global climatic environmental impacts resulting from electricity production using fossil fuel, then the institutional structures of the electric power industry could be modified to incorporate that cost into the price of electricity and into decisions concerning how to provide electric power services. It is that cost that this chapter will attempt to determine.[1]

Many of the gases we emit, particularly carbon dioxide (CO_2), methane (CH_4), nitrous oxide (N_2O), tropospheric ozone (0_3), and chlorofluorocarbons (CFCs), absorb infrared radiation (heat) created when visible light of the sun strikes the earth. This absorption and reradiation prevents some of that heat energy from radiating back into space and causes the temperature of the earth's surface to rise. Without this "greenhouse" effect, the earth would be some 30°C cooler than it is.[2] Although there is uncertainty about many of its details, the greenhouse effect is one of the "most well-established theories in atmospheric science." There is scientific consensus that increases in greenhouse gas emissions will result in climate change,[3] although the

---

[1] The specific legal and policy questions arising out of the restructuring of the electric power industry to correct its failure to internalize the global warming effects of its activities are too broad to be answered here. The wide range of questions, such as whether the Clean Air Act, 42 U.S.C. § 7401 et seq., is an appropriate vehicle to control CO_2 emissions and how one modifies power plant dispatch orders in interstate power pools and in intrastate, intra-utility structures needs to be addressed in a comprehensive, integrated fashion so that market and policy signals are consistent at each level of decisionmaking.

[2] United States Environmental Protection Agency, Office of Policy, Planning and Evaluation, Policy Options for Stabilizing Global Change, Draft Report to Congress (February, 1989) at I-2 (hereafter cited as EPA Report.) Although the Draft Report is marked "DRAFT-DO NOT QUOTE OR CITE," it has been presented to Congress (see Policy Options For Stabilizing Coastal Climate, Hearing before the Subcommittee on Public Works, United States Senate, 101st Congress, 1st Session, March 17, 1989, testimony of William K. Reilly, EPA Administrator, and is widely used as the most comprehensive work covering the state of knowledge on climate change. It is believed that the final report will be issued in several months; when issued, the only changes will be modifications of certain model projections showing a somewhat greater climate change impact than was previously predicted. Conversation with Daniel Lashof, "Responding to Climate Change," conference, University of Maryland School of Law, Baltimore, MD, (November 17, 1989).

[3] Schneider, "The Greenhouse Effect: Science and Policy," 243 Science 771 (February 10, 1984); Intergovernmental Panel on Climate Change, Working Group 1, Scientific Assessment of Climate Change (June 1990).

nature and extent of the change, as well as its ramifications for human well-being are uncertain.[4]

As a result of industrial activity over the last century, the atmospheric concentration of each of these greenhouse gases has increased. For instance, as shown in Figure 1, it is well documented that the concentration of CO_2 in the atmosphere has increased by 25% since the industrial revolution, and is increasing at the rate of 0.4% per year.[5] Similarly, methane, which has a per mole global warming potential 3.7 times that of CO_2,[6] has more than doubled over the last three hundred years and is expected to increase by 1% per year due to emissions from rice paddies, cows and other livestock, landfills, coal mine seams, melting areas of permafrost, natural gas wells and pipeline leaks, and forest clearing.[7] N_2O, which has a global warming potential per mole 180 times that of CO_2,[8] has increased to 5 to 10% since the industrial revolution and is increasing at the rate of 0.25% per year, due to use of nitrogen-based fertilizer, land clearing, biomass burning and fossil fuel combustion.[9] Additionally, there are now a variety of CFCs emitted into the atmosphere, none of which existed until the middle of the twentieth century. Although their concentrations are tiny, they are about 25,000 times more potent greenhouse gases than CO_2, are increasing at the rate of 5% per year, and have the potential to deplete stratospheric ozone.[10] Tropospheric ozone has greenhouse gas capability but its contribution to global warming is uncertain.[11]

---

[4] EPA Report, supra note 2 at pp. II-2, II-22-28; Intergovernmental Panel on Climate Change, Working Group 2, Potential Impacts of Climate Change, (June 1990).

[5] Id. at pp. II-2, II-7-8.

[6] Lashof and Ahuja, "Relative Contributions of Greenhouse Gas Emissions to Global Warming," 344 Nature 529 (April 5, 1990). The relative global warming potential of CO_2 will be reduced to the extent future warming is discounted and current radiative forcing is considered more important than radiative forcing in the future. The article notes that "intergenerational equity issues and the likelihood that the value placed on limiting climate change will grow with economic output, however, argues against discounting future forcing."

[7] EPA Report, supra note 2 at pp. II-2, II-22-28.

[8] Lashof and Ahuja, supra note 6. Fertilizers and deposition of oxides of nitrogen may contribute to increased warming.

[9] EPA Report, supra note 2 at pp. II-3, II-30-36.

[10] EPA Report, supra note 2 at pp. II-3, II-21, II-36-40. Lashof and Ahuja, supra note 6, calculate CFC-12 as having 10,000 times the global warming potential, per mole, of CO_2.

[11] Id. at pp. II-40-45; Hansen et al., Evidence for Future Warming: How Large and When, in Shands & Hoffman (ed.), The Greenhouse Effect, Climate Change and United States Forests, 1987, 66-67 [hereafter cited as Greenhouse].

FIGURE 1

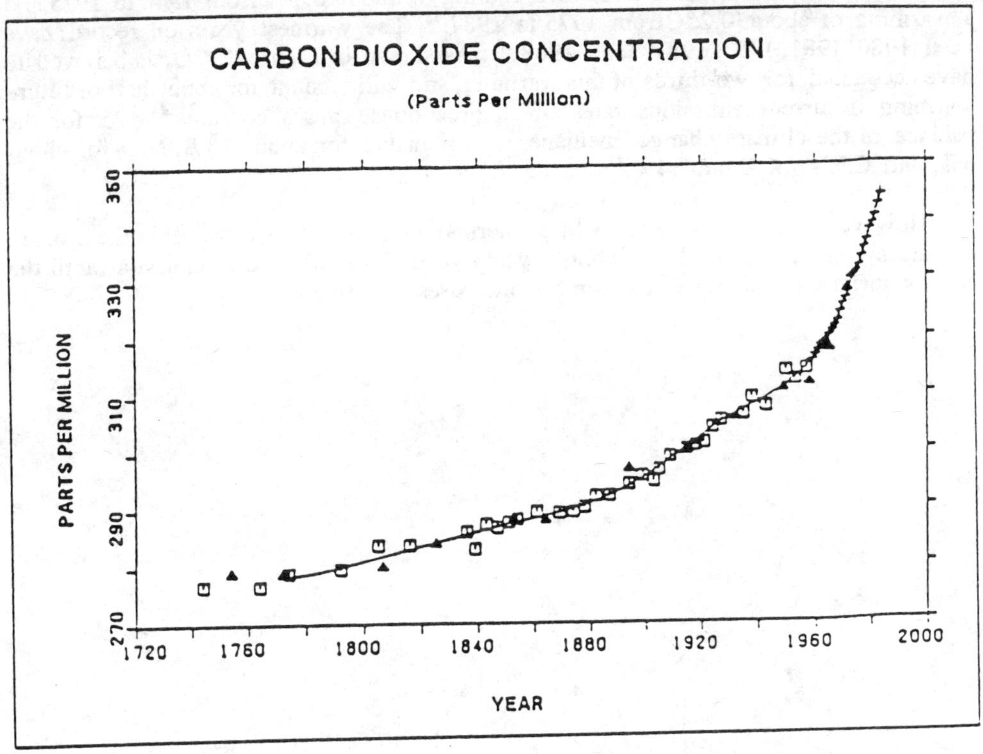

The history of atmospheric CO_2 presented here is based on ice core measurements (open spaces, closed triangles) and atmospheric measurements (crosses). The data show that CO_2 began to increase in the 1800s with the conversion of forests to agricultural land. The rapid rise since the 1950s, due primarily to fossil fuel combustion, is at a rate unprecedented in the ice core record, (Sources: Neftel et al., 1985; Friedli et al., 1986; Keeling, pers. communication; as cited in: Siegenthaler and Oeschger, 1987).

Source: EPA Report at II-11 (EPA Figure 2-2)

As a consequence of this increase in atmospheric concentration of greenhouse gases, the average temperature of the world has increased between 0.3° and 0.7°C since the industrial revolution;[12] Figure 2 portrays the relationship between CO_2 and temperature. The most complete global surface air temperature records show a global warming of 0.3°C from 1900 to 1940, a cooling of about 0.1°C from 1940 to 1975 and a warming of about 0.2°C from 1975 to 1987.[13] The warmest years on record have been 1980, 1981, 1983, 1987,[14] and 1988.[15] As shown in Figure 3, CO_2 is believed to have accounted for two-thirds of this warming, and will account for about half of future warming if current emissions rates of all greenhouse gases continue.[16] As for the balance of the climate change, methane is responsible for about 18%, N_2O for about 6%, and CFCs for about 14%.[17]

However, because the ocean's huge thermal mass acts as a flywheel in the world's climate system, there is a lag of about twenty years from the date of emission until the earth's surface temperature measurably increases due to that

---

12 EPA Report, supra note 2 at p. III-6. The range is due to uncertainty in the data arising from lack of temperature stations in some areas, changes in location and quantity of stations, growth of urban heat islands, and changes in measurement techniques over time. See also Schneider, supra note 3.

13 Jones, et al., "Evidence for Global Warming in the Past Decade", 332 Nature 790 (1988).

14 EPA Report, supra note 2 at p. III-6.

15 Schneider, supra note 3 at p. 772.

16 EPA Report, supra note 2 at p. II-6. If relative greenhouse forcing potential of CO_2 is used, CO_2 could account for 80% of future warming. See, supra, note 6

17 Id. The parties to the 1987 Montreal Protocol on Substances that Deplete the Ozone Layer have agreed to phase out CFCs by 2006 (developing countries will have an additional 10 years as a grace period), which requires a 50% reduction in use of certain CFCs, is amended as proposed, production of the most potent CFCs will be eliminated over time, thereby eventually diminishing the contribution of CFCs to global warming. International Environmental Reporter [Current Report] Bureau of National Affairs, Vol. 13. No. 7, p. 275 (July 11, 1990). However, because CFCs can survive in the atmosphere for 50 to 100 years (EPA Report, Id. at p. II-38), even if production were halted today, CFCs already in the atmosphere, and those released over time from air conditioners and refrigerators (it takes one to three years for the CFCs to migrate from the earth's surface to the stratosphere, Id., II-39), will continue to warm the globe through the next century. Moreover, the class of CFC replacements known as HCFCs are also potent greenhouse gases, so a shift to HCFCs will only marginally reduce the radiative forcing from CFCs. Id. at 276; New York Times, April 5, 1990 at p. D6.

FIGURE 2

CARBON DIOXIDE LEVELS COMPARED WITH TEMPERATURE

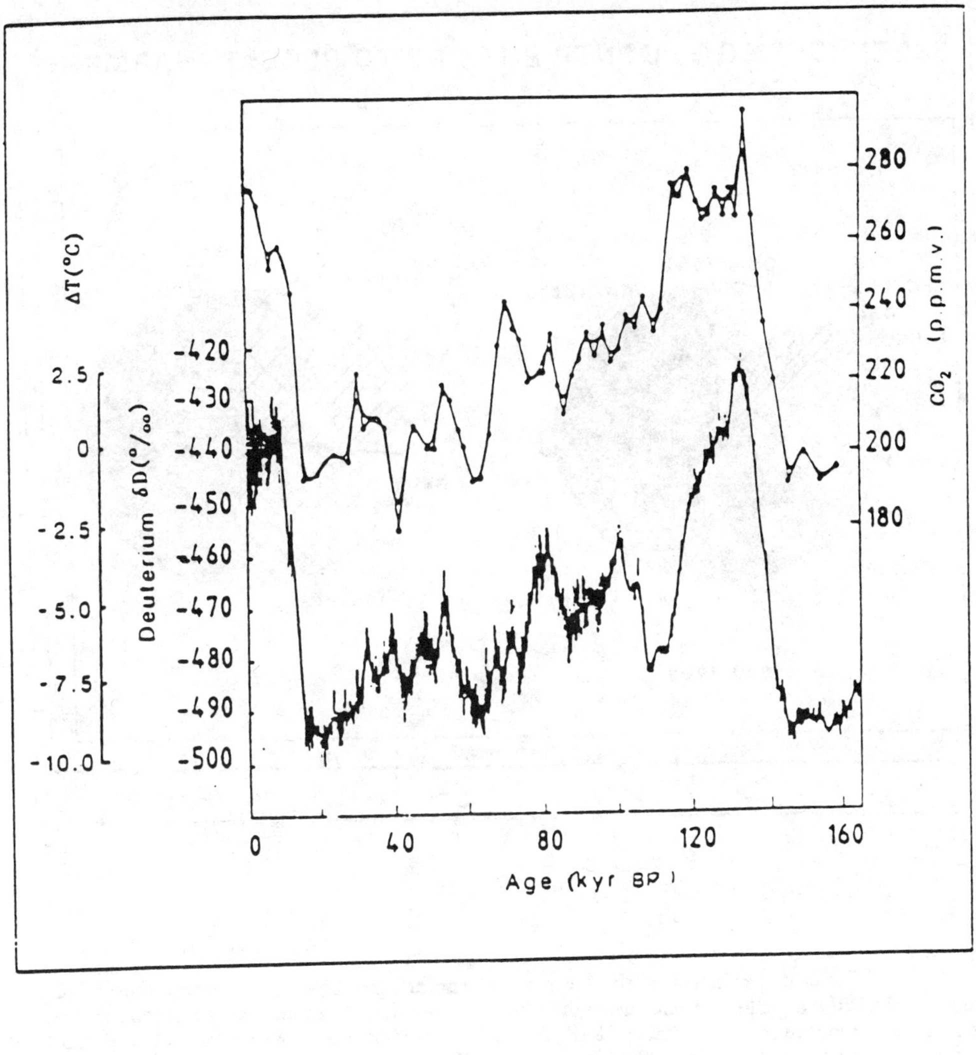

Carbon dioxide levels and temperatures over the last 160,000 years from Vostok 5 Ice Core in Antarctica. The temperature scale is for Antarctica; the corresponding amplitude of global temperatures swings is thought to be about 5°C. (Source: Barnola et al., 1987.)

Source: EPA Report at III-10 (EPA Figure 3-3)

FIGURE 3

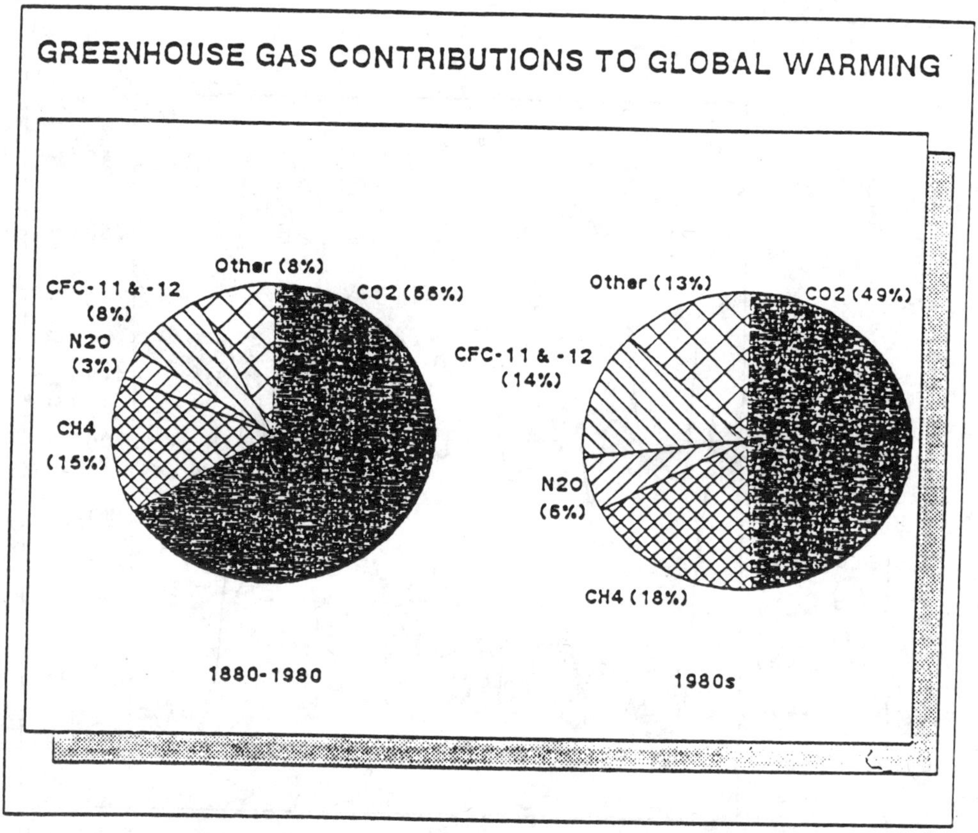

Based on estimates of the increase in concentration of each gas during the specified period. The "Other" category includes other halons, tropospheric ozone, and stratospheric water vapor. The contribution to warming of the "Other" category is highly uncertain. (Sources: 1880-1980: Ramanathan et al., 1985; 1980s: Hansen et al., 1988.)

Source: EPA Report at II-6, Figure 2-1

emission.[18] Data based on core samples deep sea sediments and from Greenland glaciers indicate that over the last 700,000years the maximum global temperature has varied by about 5°C, with the coldest times being at the peaks of ice ages and the warmest times being the present and the warm peaks between ice ages.[19] (See Figure 4). Because of the emission of greenhouse gases since the industrial revolution began, and if current trends in greenhouse gas emissions continue, the average equilibrium global temperature (i.e., the full warming impact from a change in greenhouse gas concentrations) will rise above this level of historic variability by 1.5°to 5°C by 2030,[20] which is a 3° to 9°F rise above the pre-industrial level. Over the next century, if CO_2 doubles in the atmosphere, global temperatures could rise an average of 5.5°C(9°F).[21] All computer models evaluating the rate and size of global climate warming indicate that "by early in the next century the Earth could be warmer than at any time during the last million years or more, and that the rate of change could be unprecedented in Earth history."[22]

If this warming were to occur over the next 10,000-20,000years, as it has over the last 18,000 years, ecosystems and economics would have time to adapt with

---

[18] Mintzer, I., Weathering the Storms in a Warming World, 46:6 Public Power at 16 (Nov. - Dec., 1988); EPA Report, supra note 2 at III-32; Krause, et al., Energy Policy in the Greenhouse, El Cerrito, CA, International Project for Sustainable Energy Paths (IPSEP), September, 1989, Vol. 1 at p. I.2-6-9 [hereafter cited as Energy Policy].

[19] Hansen, et al., supra note 11 at 62.

[20] Mintzer, supra note 18 at p. 1; Hansen, supra note 11, at 67. This is the equilibrium-warming the earth will be committed to; when this warming will be fully realized depends on the thermal lag caused by the oceans. There is considerable uncertainty and scientific controversy over how much lag will result from the thermal mass of the oceans. Depending upon assumptions, the lag could range from twenty to 75 years.

[21] Hansen, supra note 11 at p. 67; EPA Report, supra note 2 at p. III-2, III-31. Although global circulation models have revealed a climate equilibrium sensitivity from a doubling of atmospheric CO_2 of 1.8°to 5.2°C,reviews of these results in National Academy of Sciences, Carbon Dioxide and Climate: A Scientific Assessment (1979), NAS, Changing Climate (1983) and in NAS, Current issues in Atmospheric Change (1987) concluded that a more likely range is 1.5°to 4.5°C. A similar conclusion was reached in MacCracken and Luther, Projecting the Climate Effects of Increasing Carbon Dioxide (1985). However, another analyses suggests that a range of 1.5°to 5.5°C is more likely. Dickinson, "The Climate System and Modelling of Future Climate" in Bolin et al., The Greenhouse Effect, Climate Change, and Ecosystems (1986). In its draft report to Congress EPA adopted a 2°to 4°C temperature rise as most likely on the statistical basis that this range covered one standard deviation. However, EPA acknowledges that possible biochemical feedbacks could drive up the temperature as much as 8°to 10°C. EPA Report, supra note 2 at p. III-31. Others believe that 1.5°C warming is more realistic because the models that predict 1.5°C warming for a doubling of CO_2 also predict a 0.5°C warming from preindustrial levels by 1980, which is approximately what has been measured. Krause, et al., Energy Policy in the Greenhouse, supra note 18 at p. I.2-2. See also, IPPC Working Group I Report, supra. note 3.

[22] EPA Report, supra note 2, at III-36.

FIGURE 4

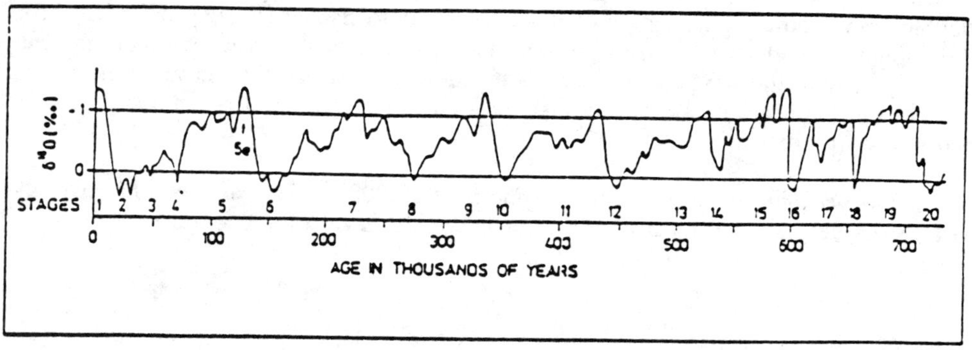

Composite $\delta^{18}O$ record of Emiliani (1978) as given by Berger (1982). This comes from deep sea sediment cores and is an index of global temperature, with the temperature range from stage 1 (present) to stage 2 (18,000 years ago) equal to about 5°C.

Source: EPA Report at III-11

little difficulty.[23] However, the temperature change equivalent of going from a full ice age to maximum global warmth will now occur during the span of a human life. Ten to twenty millennia of climate changes in temperature, precipitation patterns, wind patterns,[24] storm severity and ecological responses will occur over decades, or a century at most, a rate 1,000 to 2,000 more rapid than human beings, flora, fauna and regional ecosystems previously have experienced.[25] This relatively lightning-like pace of climate change has the potential to alter all aspects of human and natural existence.[26]

2. Electricity's Contribution to Global Warming

To avoid this massive, rapid climate change it is necessary to reduce promptly greenhouse gas emissions into the atmosphere.[27] Not only will achieving these reductions require separate emission reduction strategies for each of the diverse sources of greenhouse gases, but for each gas no single strategy will be sufficient to achieve even a 20% reduction in radiative forcing.[28] Obviously, the first strategies developed should be aimed at the most significant sources of greenhouse gases. In terms of overall impact on global warming, CO_2 is the most significant greenhouse gas,

---

23 The historic rates of change are based upon analysis of ice cores and deep sea sediments. (EPA Report, supra note 2 at p. III-8, Figure 3-4 at p. III-11, Figure 3-2 at p. III-9) Analysis of a 2083 meter deep ice core in Antarctica indicates that CO_2 levels over the last 160,000 years ranged from as low as about 180 parts per million (ppm) to as high as 285 ppm. The changes from about 195 to 285 ppm about 140,000 years ago occurred rapidly, in about 10,000 years. More recently, CO_2 levels changed from about 195 to about 280 ppm, where it remained stable until the start of the industrial revolution at the end of the eighteenth century, over about 20,000 years. Over the last 160,000 years, temperature changes have paralleled, although slightly lagged, CO_2 concentration changes. Current levels of CO_2 are higher than they have been in the last 160,000 years. (EPA Report, supra note 2 at p. II-10).

24 Mintzer, supra note 18, suggests that warming at high latitudes will be two to three times the global average, while the tropics will only warm by 50 to 75% of the average. This will shift the traditional regional patterns of wind, rain and ocean currents. Although global rainfall may increase slightly, mid-continent, mid-latitude areas like the U.S. Midwest, the Soviet grainbelt and prime Chinese agricultural areas may become hotter and drier in the summer.

25 Krause et al., note that a 1° to 1.5°C warming would represent a climate not experienced since the beginning of agricultural civilization some 6000 years ago; a 2° to 2.5°C warming would represent a climate not experienced since humans lived in hunter-gatherer societies 125,000 years ago, when the West Antarctic ice sheet may have partially disintegrated and sea-levels were elevated by five to seven meters; a 3° to 4°C warming would represent a climate not experienced since 3 to 5 million years ago (human beings appeared on the earth about 2 million years ago); and a global warming of 5°C or more would represent a climate not experienced for tens of millions of years, when there were no glaciers on the polar land masses or major mountain ranges. Energy Policy, supra note 18 at p. II-15.

26 Sen. Wirth (D-Colo) and Sen. Heinz (R-Pa), Project 88: Harnessing Market Forces to Protect Our Environment, December, 1988, at p. 10 [hereafter cited as Project 88]: "Short of nuclear war, it is difficult to imagine a more sweeping transformation of the earth as we know it than that forecast to result from global warming."

27 If emissions were reduced today sufficiently to stabilize the climate, the warming already built into the system nevertheless would be about 1.5°C. If the stabilization occurred in thirty years, world temperatures are predicted to increase 2.5°C. Stabilization will require a 50-80% reduction in CO_2 emissions, a 10 to 20% reduction in methane, a 80 to 85% reduction in nitrous oxide, a 75 to 100% reduction in CFCs and a freeze of CO and NO_x. John Hoffman, U.S. EPA, Responding to Global Change, University of Maryland School of Law, Baltimore, MD (November 17, 1989).

28 EPA Report, supra note 2 at pp. VII-6 - 7.

having accounted for two-thirds of the warming to date, and predicted to account for about 80% of future warming if current greenhouse gas emission rates continue.[29] The major human source of CO_2 emissions into the atmosphere is the burning of fossil fuels (e.g. coal, oil, natural gas),[30] which accounts for 5 of the 6 to 8 billion tons of carbon emitted annually as a result of human activity,[31] and which is growing annually at the rate of about 3.6% per year.[32] In the United States, electric utilities account for one-third of all the carbon emitted from fossil fuels, and, in 1986, for about 1.275 billion tons of carbon.[33] United States fossil fuel burning accounts for about one-third of all fossil fuel emissions in the world, with CO_2 accounting for 80% of future warming. Thus, the generation of electricity by United States electric utilities accounts for about 8.9% of future global warming, and if carbon emission from the entire fuel cycle were included, electricity's contribution would be much larger.[34] Coal-fired plants contribute about 84% of all electric utility carbon emissions.[35] Because the electric power industry is such a significant contributor to climate change, it is important that the external environmental costs of the activities be internalized into its decision making structure.[36]

Currently, there are no restrictions on the use of fossil fuels or on emission of CO_2 from fossil fuel combustion, nor are the costs of the effects of global warming included in the cost of electricity derived from fossil fuel combustion. If the full cost of global warming were included in the cost of fossil fuel combustion, decisions related to the generation and use of electricity would change.[37] For instance, although 84% of the current CO_2 emissions created by electric generation come from coal-fired power plants,[38] the same amount of electric power could be produced by burning oil or natural gas, reducing emissions by about 20% and 40% respectively.[39] Moreover,

---

29 Lashof and Ahuja, supra note 6. Because of CO_2's extraordinarily long life in the atmosphere, CO_2 accounts for 80% of the warming potential resulting from 1985 emissions of greenhouse gases.

30 EPA Report, supra note 2 at p. IV-14.

31 Id. at p. IV-2. Carbon releases from deforestation are highly uncertain, as is the rate of carbon uptake by the oceans and terrestrial ecosystems.

32 Id. at p. IV-15.

33 Machado and Piltz, Reducing the Rate of Global Warming: The States' Role, RenewAmerica, Washington, DC (November, 1988).

34 California Energy Commission, 1988 Inventory of California Greenhouse Gas Emissions, draft report (May, 1990). Carbon emissions attributable to an electricity generating resource can change dramatically if the resource is evaluated from the perspective of the complete fuel cycle (an analysis beyond the scope of this study). See, Critical Mass Energy Bulletin, March, 1990 at p. 5.

35 Id. at p. 10.

36 Although this report focuses on the global warming costs to be internalized by the electric power industry, the external costing analysis is equally applicable to other fossil fuel based activities, such as motor vehicle transportation.

37 EPA Report, supra note 2 at p. VIII-8-9.

38 Id. The reductions would be greater if the oil/gas technology were combined-cycle or other efficient technology.

39 Id. at p. VIII-22.

emissions and costs could be further reduced if the energy services currently powered by this electricity, such as light and heat, were provided by new efficient technology.[40] However, the benefits of both reduced CO_2 emissions and lower cost from fuel switching and efficiency improvements are not being realized, in part because of false economic signals given by present market prices for energy and energy use that do not reflect the true social costs, including environmental costs associated with global warming of fossil fuel-fired electricity.[41]

If fuel costs included the full cost of the environmental consequences of the combustion of the fuel, there would be no marginal benefit to increased use of currently low cost fuels such as coal that emit large amounts of CO_2 into the global atmospheric commons. Unfortunately, the tragedy the world faces now is that the economic benefits that each electricity generator derives from emitting more CO_2 are greater than the harm to it resulting from the increased emissions.[42] As a result, the economic costs of reduced carbon emissions are not offset by an economic benefit to the emitter from improved environmental quality.[43] If the environmental cost of the use of fossil fuel were included in its price, then the market would encourage energy use decisions that would increase the efficiency of use of energy services and reduce the environmental cost, resulting in lower total costs of energy services to society.[44] This section seeks to measure the environmental costs of global warming that should be included in the evaluations of the costs of electricity production and fossil fuel, so that energy production and use decisions will reflect their effect from global warming.

---

40 Rosenfeld & Mowris, "Energy Efficiency: The Best Way to Save Money and Slow Global Warming," 18-3 Physics and Society (July, 1989) (in press). According to Rosenfeld and Mowris, energy efficiency improvements since the 1973 Arab oil embargo and oil price increases have reduced our electricity bills 50% from 1973 projections, a $100 billion savings equivalent to the annual output of 250 base load power plants.

41 Project 88, supra note 26 at p. 12. Even with proper pricing, market imperfections will produce inadequate investment in end-use efficiency. Plunkett and Chernick, "The Role of Revenue Losses in Evaluating Demand-Side Resources: An Economic Reappraisal", Proceedings of the 1988 Summer Study on Energy Efficiency in Buildings, Vol. 8, 1988, p. 197.

42 See Hardin, "The Tragedy of the Commons," 162 Science 1243-1248 (1968).

43 EPA Report, supra note 2 at p. VIII-7; the "Tragedy of the Commons" exists on the international scale, as well, because no single country enjoys enough benefits from reduced CO_2 emissions to justify unilateral action, even though the global benefits could be substantial.

44 Utility and government intervention also will be required to achieve cost-effective and end-use efficiency decisions. Plunkett and Chernick, supra note 41.

3. Methods of Measuring The Cost of Global Warming

a. Damage Costs

There are at least three general approaches to measuring the societal cost of CO_2 emissions. The mitigation approach is to predict the environmental impacts of global warming and to calculate the cost of enduring or repairing the harm. The control cost approach is to calculate the cost of reducing greenhouse gas emissions, such as by using pollution control technology to remove CO_2 from fossil fuel exhaust gas or by using efficiency improvements that reduce emissions resulting from the generation and use of energy. The approach we adopt here is to calculate the cost of sequestering the CO_2 emitted into the atmosphere by planting trees or other vegetation that will remove CO_2 from the atmosphere during photosynthesis and store it in plant material.

The problem with the first approach, calculating the cost of the effects of global warming, is that the effects are both speculative and enormous. If the total economic cost of global warming could be calculated, then a power plant's proportional role in global warming could be determined and the environmental costs charged against that power plant as the product of the total environmental costs times that plant's proportional contribution.[45] However, all predicted effects of global warming are based on computer-based analysis known as general circulation models, which are able to predict only relatively large scale weather phenomena such as seasonal temperature changes and broad rainfall patterns.[46] The models crudely describe ocean/air interaction, evolution and migration of vegetation, cloud and ice formation and melting. They are not sufficiently refined to determine the effects of cloud cover, permit regional climate forecasts or to identify specific global warming impacts.[47] Because the process of climate change varies regionally, is not necessarily linear - an area may become wetter before it becomes drier or colder before warmer - and because the data are not detailed enough to describe regional results, the models are unreliable for regional analysis of the impacts of climate change.[48] Periods of climate transition may produce unstable weather patterns, with alternating droughts and floods, heat waves and late frosts.

Moreover, even if regional climate change could be predicted accurately, the impacts of those changes are speculative and unmeasurable in dollars. For instance, forest growth patterns may shift unpredictably and dramatically,[49] potentially dooming

---

[45] Buchanan, S. Costs of Mitigating Greenhouse Effect for Generic Coal, Oil, and Gas-Fired Plants at p. 1 (draft of January 24, 1989). (Unpublished report.)

[46] Gibbs and Hoffman, An Approach for Generating Climate Change Hypothetical Given Limitations in Current Climate Models in Shands and Hoffman (ed.), supra note 11 at p. 95 (1987).

[47] Id. at p. 97. Moreover, the models provide little insight into possible nonlinear, chaotic bio-geo-chemical planetary feedback systems that may affect the climate; scientists can only speculate as to the surprises nature has in store for the world. R. Coppock (National Academy of Sciences), in letter to Richard L. Ottinger, April 6, 1990.

[48] Id. at p. 101.

[49] Id. at pp. 113-153.

many forests in many regions.[50] A modest sea level rise could mean the loss of up to 15,400 square miles in the United States alone, including 76% of our remaining wetlands.[51] Adverse climate conditions caused by global warming may reduce crop yields and alter the demand for and supply of water for irrigation, causing billions of dollars of agricultural losses, in addition to degradation of the environmental and natural resources in many regions.[52] If major portions of the Antarctic ice shelf melted, the seas could rise five to eight meters, with catastrophic effects.[53] Even a sea level rise of one meter, (which the world will experience due to thermal expansion of water even if the effect of greenhouse gas emissions were stabilized today), could have such catastrophic effects as inundating the coastal areas of Egypt (which contain about 13% of its population and 15% of its economic wealth[54]) or intensifying storm flooding in Bangladesh, with the potential of creating ten to thirty million environmental refugees.[55] Scientists expect that the frequency and severity of storms will increase so that 50-year floods will become twenty-year floods, 100-year storms will become 50-year storms, and long stretches of extreme weather will become more frequent.[56] In developed countries, hotter summers will cause higher peak demand for electricity for air conditioning, and, if traditional utility planning prevails and the electricity is generated from coal, more CO_2 emissions will occur, causing a dangerous positive feedback loop that will only accelerate global warming.[57] By 2055, the national increase in annual fuel costs attributed to global warming might be $33 to 73 billion, and a total of $175 to 325 billion would be required for additional power plants.[58] Other factors that would need to be valued are the loss of biodiversity from rapid ecosystem change; the impact of warming on fresh-water and salt-water fisheries, migratory birds, coastal wetlands,

---

50 "How Fast Can Trees Migrate?", 243 Science, pp. 735-737 (Feb. 10, 1989).

51 Smith and Tirpak (eds.), U.S.E.P.A., The Potential Effects of Global Climate Change on the United States, (Executive Summary) at p. 16 (October, 1989). There is great uncertainty about the impact of global warming on regional agriculture, although it is certain that the effects will vary by crop, region and ecosystems.

52 Adams, et al., "Implications of Global Climate Change for Western Agriculture", 13(2) Western J. of Agric. Econ. 348-386 (1988). There is great uncertainty about the impact of global warming on regional agriculture, although it is certain that the effects will vary by crop, region and ecosystem. Smit, B., Ludlow, L. & M. Brklacich, "Implications of a Global Climatic Warming for Agriculture: A Review and Appraisal," 17 J. Environ. Qual. 519 (1988).

53 Schneider and Chen, "Carbon Dioxide Warming and Coastline Flooding: Physical Factors and Climatic Impact," 5 Ann. Rev. Energy 107, 135 (1980). This outcome is now considered unlikely for some centuries.

54 Mintzer, I., Responding to Global Change, University of Maryland School of Law, Baltimore, MD, November 17, 1989.

55 Id. The influx of environmental refugees into already stressed developing countries could cause political changes in the affected countries, destabilize regions or, potentially, trigger armed conflict.

56 Mintzer, supra note 18 at pp. 15, 16 (Nov.- Dec., 1988)

57 See, e.g., Electric Power Research Institute, Potential Impacts of Climate Change on Electric Utilities, pp. 4-19 (January, 1989). See footnote 283, infra.

58 Smith and Tirpak, supra note 51 at pp. 26-28 (1988)

coastal estuaries, and fresh water resources; increased weather-affected illness;[59] and the effects of altered rainfall patterns.[60] It is not currently possible to predict accurately the costs associated with these effects in the United States, let alone the world.[61]

b. Control Costs

The alternative of scrubbing exhaust gas to remove CO_2 has been almost universally dismissed as too costly, at $240 per ton of carbon, and too technically difficult to be practical.[62] One currently conceived technique for disposing of significant amounts of CO_2 is to pump it in liquid form under high pressure in a pipe 100 miles out to sea, where it would be discharged at least 500 feet below sea level, to dissolve in sea water.[63] Although neither the technical feasibility nor the reliability of the cost estimates for an undertaking of this size have been demonstrated,[64] the estimated capital costs of such a project are between $890 and $1520/KW for the CO_2 scrubbing and pipeline disposal, in addition to a 25% energy penalty, a 22% capacity penalty and operational and maintenance costs of at least $10 per kW year.[65] For comparison purposes, CO_2 scrubbing is 3.5 to 4.5 times more expensive than SO_2 scrubbing, as illustrated in Table 1. Other suggestions include dumping a high density solution of seawater and CO_2 into the ocean floor, dumping solidified blocks of CO_2-hydrate that would sink to the ocean floor or dumping blocks of solidified CO_2 (dry ice) into the

---

[59] Id. The health effects of global warming, potentially great but speculative, may include increases in mortality from heat stress, morbidity and mortality from lung diseases, malnutrition and hunger from diminished food production, and increases in water borne disease as water supplies deteriorate due to sea level rise, floods and larger spring melt runoff. Leaf, A., "Potential Health Effects of Global Climatic and Environmental Changes," Vol. 321 (23), The New England Journal of Medicine 1577 (Dec. 7, 1989).

[60] Although the world on average may become somewhat wetter, North America may become 30 to 60% dryer, and tropical regions may become somewhat wetter. (Mintzer, supra note 54) Moreover, it may rain at different times and places than at present, and spring snow melt patterns may change. For instance, rainfall may become more concentrated, as occurred recently in Sudan, where the country's entire annual rainfall fell in one three-day period, causing flash floods and erosion of already thin top soil. (Id.) Alternatively, the monsoons in India may occur out of sequence with established growing patterns. (Id.)

[61] For instance, a 4°C warming may push regional temperatures in Southeast Asia and India above the maximum temperature at which rice flowers, potentially causing up to a 90% loss of certain rice crops. (Mintzer, supra note 54.) It is difficult to imagine the human and economic disaster that could result from such a loss of a regional rice crop.

[62] See, e.g., New York State Energy Office, Staff Report, Draft New York State Energy Plan, Vol. VI, p. 39 (1989). Control of other greenhouse gases may be feasible, but the costs have not generally been determined.

[63] Steinberg, M. and H. Cheng, A Systems Study for the Removal, Recovery, and Disposal of Carbon Dioxide from Fossil Fuel Power Plants in the U.S., Brookhaven National Laboratory, Department of Applied Science, Process Sciences Division, BNL 35666 (February, 1985).

[64] Id. Moreover, there is no discussion of the long-term effect on or capacity of the oceans' ability to act as a CO_2 sink.

[65] EPA Report, supra note 2 at p. VII-135, Table 7-9. Chernick, P. and E. Caverhill, The Valuation of Externalities From Energy Production, Delivery, and Use, Boston, MA: PLC, Inc., December, 1989. The cost of scrubbing is estimated to be $200-500 per ton of carbon.

TABLE 1

CO_2 SCRUBBER COSTS COMPARED TO SO_2 SCRUBBER COSTS[a]

	CO_2 Scrubber[b]	SO_2 Scrubber[c]
Capital Cost ($/KW)[d]		
Scrubber	810	220
Pipeline/Disposal	80-710	N/A
Variable Operation & Maintenance Costs (mills/kWh)	N/A	3.5
Energy Penalty (%)	25	4.5
Capacity Penalty (%)	22	2.5
Fixed Operation & Maintenance Costs ($/kWh)	N/A	10
Total Cost (mills/kWh)[e]	36-47	20.7

a 90 percent removal of both CO_2 and SO_2.

b Steinberg, Cherg, Horn, 1984.

c 1987 EPA Interim Acid Rain Base Case Estimates.

d Greenfield Site.

e 65 percent capacity factor, 9 percent capital charge rate; incremental power costs 65 mills per kilowatt-hour; new plant costs of $1,200/KW; fixed O&M for CO_2 scrubber is assumed to be ten dollars per kilowatt-year for comparison purposes only, actual costs could well be higher, 1988 dollars assumed to be worth 42 percent less than 1980 dollars.

Source: EPA Report at p. VII-135 (EPA Figure 7-9).

ocean, where they would sink to the ocean floor.[66] None of these suggestions is considered feasible because of the lack of knowledge of the ocean processes, the immense energy required to run such an operation (30 to 45% of the total electric energy produced would be required to operate this disposal system), and because of the unknown ecological effects (such as shifts in plankton populations) of rapidly increasing the CO_2 content of the oceans.[67]

The cost of supply side[68] and demand side efficiency improvements,[69] and emission offsets in other economic sectors could be used as a measure of CO_2 control costs; however, this approach presents several analytical problems. The data is sparse and the analytical models used are fraught with both uncertainty and questionable analytical assumptions.[70] More importantly, even if all the available supply and demand-side improvements were implemented, which assumes that major institutional obstacles to conservation are removed,[71] further measures would still be necessary to achieve even a 20% reduction in CO_2 emissions from the level of 1990.[72] As for offsets, opportunities in other economic sectors or in other regions of the world are vast (from more efficient cars to improved electric generation facilities in Eastern Europe to introducing more efficient cooking stoves in developing countries). On the other hand, the cost of planting trees to sequester carbon is a measure that is independent of fuel, power production and use, so it provides a yard stick against which to measure the seemingly infinite variety of efficiency and offset options available in the market.

Although a detailed analysis of these options from a carbon perspective is beyond the scope of this report, several efforts have been made to estimate these costs.[73]

---

[66] de Baar, H. and M. Stoll, "Storage of Carbon Dioxide in the Oceans" in Okken, P.A., R.J. Swart and S. Zwerver (eds.), Climate and Energy (1989).

[67] Id.

[68] Supply-side improvements include renewable energy sources (such as hydropower and pumped storage, biomass/biofuels, geothermal, ocean energy, solar thermal electric, wind energy, photovoltaics, solar heat, and associated technologies such as energy storage, hydrogen, fuel cells, and transmission and distribution improvements), advanced coal and gas-fired electricity generation technologies and fuel switching. See EPA Report, supra note 2 and U.S. Dept. of Energy, The Potential of Renewable Energy: An Interlaboratory White Paper, DE90000322, SERI/TP-260-3674, March, 1990.

[69] See Chapter VI.G. for a review of the externalities associated with some demand-side management options.

[70] Zimmerman, M., Assessing the Costs of Climate Policies: The Uses and Limits of Models, The Alliance to Save Energy, (April 10, 1990).

[71] See Chapter X.C. infra.

[72] EPA Report, supra note 2. For an analysis from a Netherlands perspective of the difficult task of achieving CO_2 emission reductions, and a preliminary carbon reduction cost supply curve, see, Swart, R., R. Maas, & H. de Vries, "From Global to National Climate Policy," paper presented at International Society of Ecological Economics Conference on The Ecological Economics of Sustainability: Making Local and Short-term Goals Consistent with Global and Long-term Goals, World Bank, Washington, DC, May 21-23, 1990.

[73] For a more detailed discussion of energy efficiency supply curves see, Ledbetter, M. and M. Ross, "Supply Curves of Conserved Energy from Automobiles," paper prepared for Lawrence Berkeley Laboratory Applied Science Division, Berkeley, CA (March, 1990); Rosenfeld, A. and R. Mowris, "Energy Efficiency: The Best Way to Save Money and Slow Global Warming," Testimony for Hearing on an

Dudek, LeBlanc and Miller concluded after reviewing data from conservation programs in the Mid-West, Pacific Northwest and New York State that the average cost of reducing carbon emissions is \$23.17 per ton.[74] They calculate the cost of fuel switching to be \$18.11 per ton of carbon reduced.[75] In terms of offsets, Ledbetter and Ross calculated that it would cost \$0.53 per gallon to improve automobile efficiency to 44 miles per gallon, saving twenty-two pounds of CO_2 per gallon, for a cost of \$176 per ton of carbon saved.[76]

The approach for valuing the effects of global warming, which we adopt, is to price the cost of reducing climate change by sequestering carbon in trees. If the cost of burning fuel includes the full cost of capturing released CO_2, then choices of energy services will reflect the total costs, including the costs imposed by CO_2 emissions. This approach will reduce the extent of climate change, even if no trees are actually planted, because the reordering of energy decisions will reduce emissions. To the extent that power producers do, in fact, plant trees, their power plant emissions will be offset by sequestration, thereby further mitigating the climate change that would otherwise occur.

Although forestry is not the sole or complete solution to the problem of global warming, it can significantly delay the effects of global warming.[77] By providing a measure of the external costs of fossil fuel combustion, forestry can reduce CO_2 emissions by providing a means to internalize those effects into the market for energy services. Tree cultivation, a long-known art that does not require the use of unproven new technology,[78] is an approach far more susceptible to concrete cost analysis than either CO_2 scrubbing or measuring environmental harm from global warming.

Integrated National Energy Efficiency Strategy before Subcommittee on Energy and Power, Committee on Energy and Commerce, United States House of Representatives (June 23, 1989); Vine, E. and J. Harris, "Evaluating Energy and Non-energy Impacts of Energy Conservation Programs: A Supply Curve Framework of Analysis," paper presented at 1989 Energy Conservation Program Evaluation Conference, Chicago, Il (August 23-25, 1989); Geller, H. & S. Nadel, "Energy Conservation: Potential vs. Achievement," ACEEE, paper prepared for NARUC Least Cost Utility Planning Conference, Charleston, SC, Sept. 11-13, 1989; Krause, F. and J. Koomey, "Unit Costs of Carbon Savings From Urban Trees, Rural Trees, and Electricity Conservation: A Utility Perspective" Energy Analysis Program, Lawrence Berkeley Laboratory, Berkeley, CA, Feb 24, 1989; and Nixon, E. & C. Neme, An Efficient Approach to Reducing Acid Rain: The Environmental Benefits of Energy Conservation, Center for Clean Air Policy, May, 1989.

[74] Dudek, D., A. LeBlanc, P. Miller, CO_2 and SO_2: Consistent Policy Making in a Greenhouse, Environmental Defense Fund (January, 1990) at p. 9.

[75] Id. at p. 10.

[76] Telephone conversation with Marc Ledbetter, ACEEE, June 7, 1990; Ledbetter and Ross, supra note 73.

[77] Marland, The Prospect of Solving the CO_2 Problem Through Global Reforestation, U.S. Dept. of Energy, DDE/NBB-0082, 1988.

[78] However, there are many technical problems with selection of the right tree species for particular locations and with maintenance of the tree populations. There is also danger that if tree planting is concentrated in monoculture plantations supported by pesticides, herbicides and fertilizers, species diversity may be diminished and ecosystem stability jeopardized. We must act carefully to avoid creating new environmental problems from the technological fixes to current environmental problems, i.e., the environmental equivalent of iatrogenic disease--disease caused by medical treatment.

4. General Forestation Issues

At first glance, the idea of using the cost of planting trees as a measure of the societal environmental cost of releasing CO_2 into the atmosphere seems simple and elegant. By adding the cost of trees onto the cost of generating electricity, society creates a seemingly objective, easily calculable dollar amount that can be internalized readily into the economics of electricity generation. The tree-planting standard provides double environmental benefits: mitigating the effects of CO_2 emissions and driving market decisions that will enhance energy supply and efficiency investments and reduce energy consumption.[79] An increased carbon sink in forests (and forest products) instead of in the air will postpone climate warming[80] and offer the world additional time to switch its energy source to non-fossil fuels.[81]

However, there is no worldwide tree planting market that establishes a market clearing price for the cost of capturing a ton of carbon in trees. The cost of cultivating trees is as diverse as the worldwide variety of ecosystems, tree species, soil conditions, harvesting patterns, maintenance practices and tree end-uses. This portion of the report will examine factors and policies that can vary the cost of carbon fixation and sequestration.[82]

Forests affect atmospheric carbon levels in two ways: carbon released by deforestation and wood combustion increases carbon levels, while carbon captured by growing trees, and by the related ecosystems, reduces atmospheric carbon. Yet worldwide deforestation has been and continues to be enormous. Over centuries, worldwide and United States forest land has decreased rapidly as population has increased and people have converted forest land to agricultural and commercial use.[83] The historic clearing of temperate forests in Europe, Asia and North America, which has caused a release of perhaps 120 x 10^9 tons of carbon,[84] has now ended, and

---

79 Shands, Forests--The Momentum for a Greenhouse Effect: Physical, Economic and Political Limits to Curtailing the Magnitude of Global Warming, in Shands and Hoffman (ed.); Greenhouse, supra note 11 at p. 44.

80 However, if warming is more rapid than existing forests can handle not only will it be difficult to increase the extent of forest cover, but more likely, existing forest will be lost. Deumling, D. letter to Richard L. Ottinger, May 2, 1990, and Deumling, D., "Risks For Future Forestry," July, 1989 (unpublished paper).

81 Sedjo and Solomon, Climate & Forests in Rosenberg et al (ed.); Greenhouse Warming: Abatement and Adaptation, Resources for the Future, (Washington, D.C. 1989).

82 "Fixation" refers to the ability of a tree to absorb carbon, whereas "sequestration" refers to the ability of an ecosystem to retain the carbon over time. For instance, a rapidly growing tree may fix carbon at a high rate, but release it quickly when it is burned for firewood, perhaps resulting in no sequestration, but still displacing fossil fuel and reducing atmospheric carbon levels. In comparison, a slow growing hardwood may fix carbon at a low rate each year, but hold it for 100 years in a forest, and for decades more in the form of furniture and construction lumber, resulting in a high, long term sequestration rate.

83 Sedjo and Solomon, supra note 81 at p. 3. Estimates of global decline vary from 15% (700 million hectares)(one hectare equals 2.47 acres; there are 259 hectares in a square mile) to 50%, citing, respectively, Matthews, "Global Vegetation and Land Use: New High Resolution Data Base for Climate Studies," J. Climate and Applied Meteorology 474-487 (1983) and Olson, et al., Carbon in Live Vegetation of Major World Ecosystems, Report ORNL-5862, Oak Ridge National Laboratory, Oak Ridge, TN, 1983.

84 Marland, supra note 77 at p. 55.

temperate forests are increasing modestly in North America, Western Europe and Siberia.[85] But in the tropics, land use patterns favoring the clearing of forest for agricultural use are causing an estimated loss of 0.6 to 2.0 x 10^9 tons of carbon per year.[86] The tropical release of carbon from deforestation may account for 10 to 20% of the annual release of carbon to the atmosphere.[87] One could reduce carbon emission by halting the deforestation of a tropical rain forest, that would be far more effective than planting on cleared land since it only takes minutes to sell a tree, but it may take decades to grow one, and deforesting is far more certain than afforestation. Over a small margin, the price of halting deforestation would represent the cost of offsetting carbon emission reduction.

Merely offsetting current deforestation, however, will reduce, but not halt, global warming. Eliminating deforestation cannot offset current or prior carbon emissions from fossil fuel combustion, or historic destruction of forests. If a utility is required only to plant trees or halt deforestation in an amount equal to its present emissions, then there will be no net reduction of atmospheric carbon.[88] But if the cost reflects an additional amount to offset prior emissions or deforestation, then total atmospheric carbon will be reduced, thereby assuring progress towards combating climate change.[89] The cost will depend on how much carbon a utility is required to offset.

Pricing the cost of carbon sequestration is complex. Forests can consist of fast or slow growing trees; "even a pristine landscape consists not simply of undisturbed old-growth forests, but of a variety of forests at different stages of development and growth, thus . . . sequestering very different amounts of carbon."[90] A slow-growing species may absorb less carbon each year than a faster-growing species, but will do so longer before reaching maturity. Trees can be harvested for industrial purposes, such as poles, fences, paper and construction timber, which permanently sequester some of the carbon in a non-forest location.[91] Trees can also be harvested for energy,

---

85 Sedjo & Solomon, <u>supra</u> note 81 at p. 3.

86 Marland, <u>supra</u> note 77 at p. 11.

87 <u>EPA Report,</u> <u>supra</u> note 2 at p. VII-195. The loss comes from fire, decay and soil disturbance. These estimates have recently been challenged by new data on tropical forest carbon content. Brown, S. et al., "Biomass Estimation Methods for Tropical Forests with Applications to Forest Inventory Data", <u>Forest Science</u> 35:4 (December, 1989) pp. 881-901

88 If carbon remains constant at 1989 emissions levels, the world will experience an overall temperature rise of 4°F. Rosenfeld, A., Lawrence Berkeley Laboratory, University of California at Berkeley, lecture at Electric Utility Reform Seminar, Pace University School of Law, White Plains, N.Y. (September 24, 1989).

89 This is analogous to the offset concept in the nonattainment program in Part D of the Clean Air Act, 42 U.S.C. § 7503, which requires for areas that have not attained national ambient air quality standards that total emissions after a new major source of pollution is added be less than before so as to represent "reasonable further progress" towards attainment of the air quality standard.

90 Sedjo and Solomon, <u>supra</u> note 81 at p. 4.

91 <u>Id</u>. Since about one fourth of industrial hardwood used in construction, furniture and other durable uses lasts thirty-five years after it is harvested, an amount of wood roughly one half the growing stock in all U.S. commercial forests or about 0.17 billion tons of carbon per year, is currently harvested and stored in carbon. Undecayed wood and paper products in landfills probably sequester additional carbon, but no estimate has been made of this potential sequestration.

displacing fossil fuels. However, the harvesting of mature forests results in a net release of carbon that is not recaptured by subsequent planting unless the replanted tree is allowed to grow into an old-growth tree, e.g.,after more than 250 years.[92] Thus, one of the most effective means of reducing carbon emissions might be to stop harvesting old growth timber in the Pacific Northwest.[93] Moreover, open spaces after clearcut harvesting offer new seedlings far worse conditions for growth than forest interiors, and this will be especially so in the event of global warming.[94]

The question of what happens after all available land is used to plant all possible trees must also be addressed when pricing the cost per ton of carbon sequestered. Even with slow growing hardwoods, that mature in thirty to forty years, eventually all available forestland will be used for trees. Trees could be left standing in mature forests or harvested for lumber and paper, or could be burned for fuel, releasing sequestered carbon that will not be removed from the atmosphere unless replacement trees are planted. A tree planting/burning/planting cycle would not reduce emissions, but would result in a steady state of emissions sustained by a renewable fuel. However, in areas already short of fuel sources, as is the case in most of the third world, the availability of wood fuel may not displace existing fossil fuel use, but supplement it. In that case, unless fast-rotation energy forests protect existing natural forests and/or improve living standards by displacing fossil fuel use, the fast rotation forests will not reduce CO_2 emissions but will merely delay their build-up in the atmosphere for the few years the trees are growing.[95]

An increase of forest biomass requires an increase of the forested land area, an increase of the biomass per unit of land, or both. Trees can be planted in understocked portions of existing forests, in highly managed plantations, in commercial forests, on marginal land (e.g., over-farmed, semi-arid), in the tropics or temperate zones, in agroforestry settings (e.g., in hedge-rows, and windbreaks), in urban heat islands, or even along highways. No one approach is optimal. Eventually, commercial forestry and plantations reach maturity and settle into a carbon equilibrium, when increasing carbon sequestration per acre becomes increasingly difficult.[96] Without

---

92 Oregon Energy Office, "SB 576 Working Group: Biomass Subcommittee Draft Report" (Revised April, 27, 1990) at p. 3. The net loss is caused by the large release of soil carbon and by the inevitable harvesting of the replacement trees at an earlier age than the original tree, so that the replacement trees are smaller (and therefore contain less carbon) than the original trees.

93 Id. at p. 9.

94 Deumling, D. letter, supra note 80. Deumling concludes that to protect and increase forests, forestry practices should emphasize thinning management and should severely restrict clearcutting, thereby protecting forest canopies that offer new trees a natural climate buffer.

95 Trexler et al., Forestry As A Response to Global Warming: An Analysis of the Guatemala Agroforestry and Carbon Sequestration Project, World Resources Institute, June, 1989, at 63, note 35. See Chernick and Caverhill, The Valuation of Externalities from Energy Production, Delivery and Use, PLC, Inc., Boston, MA, December, 1989 at pp. 65-66 for a discussion of the fossil fuel vs. wood fuel problem.

96 Sedjo and Solomon, supra note 81 at p. 5.

harvesting, forests will reach a maturity equilibrium, between 50 and 500 years,[97] unless the impact of climate change alters growth rates.[98]

EPA strategies for increasing carbon-sequestering trees fall into two categories of forestry options for controlling climate changes: a) to reduce demand for forest land and destructive products (especially in the tropics) and b) to increase supply of forestry land and responsibly harvested forest products.[99] Although these strategies can be pursued simultaneously, some are better suited to undeveloped countries and some are more appropriate for developing countries.[100] For instance, high volume branch trees such as Douglas fir in the Pacific Northwest grow slowly (80 to 100 years to fully mature) and provide wood most useful in industrial countries whose relatively stable political, social and economic institutions favor long-term forest protection and management.[101] However, in tropical, developing countries that need to maximize growth rates, restore deforested land and produce firewood and timber in the near term, and which have limited ability to achieve long term forest protection, short rotation forest crops are both flexible and appropriate.[102] EPA has identified several approaches to reducing demand for forest land and forest products, as shown in Table 2.[103]

The scale of forestation necessary just to offset current, let alone past, CO_2 emissions is so vast that the opportunities associated with each option will be insufficient to satisfy all the forestry offset requirements of electric utilities.[104] However, across the spectrum of technical options, there may be sufficient forestry opportunities to satisfy all electric utilities' offset needs. These carbon sequestration forestry options comprise a potential world-wide market for carbon sequestration, with marginal costs increasing as forestry options are exercised.

Each strategy for reducing demand or increasing supply can be pursued by a number of technical options, which can be region-specific.[105] We will briefly review the options and then consider specific cost estimates that have been calculated for these options.

---

97 Id. at p. 4.

98 For instance, increased concentrations of CO_2 may "fertilize trees" by enhancing photosynthesis rate, thereby causing trees to grow faster, although lower precipitation, weather extremes, hotter temperatures, and lack of sufficiently cold winter weather may impair forest growth, and, of course, lightening or man may undo a forest altogether. Sandenburgh et al., "Rising CO_2, Climate Change and Forest Management: An Overview," in The Greenhouse Effect, supra note 11 at pp. 113-127.

99 EPA Report, supra note 2 at p. VII-203.

100 Id. at p. VII-204.

101 Id.

102 Id. at pp. VII- 204-205.

103 Id. at p. VII-203.

104 In 1986, electric utilities emitted a total of 1.275×10^9 tons of carbon. Machado and Piltz, supra note 33 at p. 19.

105 EPA Report, supra note 2 at pp. VII-207-208. See Table 2 (EPA Table 7-14), supra note 2.

TABLE 2
Potential Forestry Strategies and Technical Options to Slow Climate Change

Strategy	Technical Options	Regions Most Effective In
Reduce Demand for Forest Land and Forest Products		
Substitute sustainable, integrated forest and natural resource management	• Natural forest management systems • Extractive reserves • Biosphere reserves	• Tropical moist and dry forests • Temperate forests (public or private)
Substitute sustainable agriculture	• Small-scale agroforestry • Financial incentives for swidden colonists to shift to sustainable practices • Technical aid in soil and crop selection • Plan into development projects by banks, state agencies	• Tropical moist & dry forests with strong central governments (Brazil, Colombia, Malaysia, Indonesia)
Decrease forest consumption for development	• Assistance from multilateral banks and state agencies contingent on planning. Loans contingent on minimal forest loss • Mitigation of loss by 2:1 protection of forest	• Strong central governments and banks with ability to plan and manage (Brazil, Costa Rica, India, China, Mexico)
Improve efficiency of biomass combustion	• Widely distribute efficient cookstoves • Incentives for industrial cogeneration	• Areas with inefficient current stoves, good extension, and difficult-access or expensive fuelwood (Nepal, India, Sahel, Haiti)
Decrease production of disposable forest products	• Substitute durable wood products for disposables • Establish recycling programs for wood	• Areas with cheap substitutes for wood & developed markets (industrialized areas of developing countries, Japan, U.S.)

Source: EPA Report at VII-207

TABLE 2 (Continued)
Potential Forestry Strategies and Technical Options to Slow Climate Change

Strategy	Technical Options	Regions Most Effective In
Increase Supply of Forested Land and Forest Products		
Increase forest productivity • Manage temperate forests • Apply natural forest management in tropics • Increase plantation productivity	• Intensify timber stand improvement all forests • Apply fertilizers & biotechnology to plantations • Extend natural forest management practices	• Developed countries and industrialized developing countries, with extension capability
Increase forest harvest efficiency	• Increase number of species harvested • Decrease damage to standing trees • Use harvest slash & mill scraps	• Any area, if marketed, and countries with large or multinational logging concessions (Brazil, Malaysia)
Plant trees on crop & urban lands in temperate zone • Expand tree planting programs • Reforest croplands • Reforest urban areas • Reforest highway corridors	• Reforest surplus cropland • Plant fast-growth plantations • Plant trees near buildings, highways, rivers	• Developed countries • US: Southeast, North Central states, West Coast
Reforest degraded forest lands and plant plantations in tropics	• Incentives for agroforestry • Establish extension farms & workers for agroforestry • Require commercial & village loggers to replant • Organize village tree planting • Mobilize youth and religious groups to plant trees	• Tropics, where rainfall and soils are adequate

a. Option 1 -- Slow Deforestation by Sustainable Forest Use Systems[106]

One method of reducing forest demand in developing and industrialized countries is to replace clear-cutting with sustainable natural forest management (NFM) silviculture techniques that provide a stream of forest benefits while minimizing destruction of national forests.[107] One example of NFM is the use of "extraction reverses," such as was done in Brazil, where forest reserves were established out of which nuts and rubber were permitted to be extracted. The trees remain standing while providing jobs to rubber trappers and nut collectors otherwise dependent upon logging for income.[108] Other NFM approaches use tree harvesting techniques on a twenty to forty year rotation on small swaths or parcels so that the post-harvest forest gaps are small enough to be reseeded naturally. These harvesting techniques preserve the biological diversity of the forest, minimize erosion, and present the potential for net profits of up to $3,500per hectare after the harvested wood is processed.[109] According to EPA, NFM is a promising vehicle for maintaining high-biomass standing forests, slowing deforestation and allowing the 54 million hectares of forests already logged to regenerate.[110]

b. Option 2 -- Substitute Sustainable Agriculture for Swidden Farming[111]

In tropical countries, some 41 million hectares of forest are burned annually as a result of swidden (shifting) agriculture methods in which farmers burn forest to create farm land, farm it until it is no longer productive, and then abandon it in favor of a new patch of cleared forest.[112] Swidden agriculture persists in poor countries because the burning releases nutrients stored in woody plants into the soil, thereby eliminating the need for expensive fertilizers.[113] By introducing sustainable agriculture that uses low-cost biological recycling of chemical nutrients and energy, and only naturally occurring mechanisms for protecting crops from pests, to produce sustainable annual harvests, farmers will be able to abandon their burn-and-abandon agriculture. For

---

106 Id. at p. VII-209.

107 Id. See also McNeely, J. Economic and Biological Diversity: Developing and Using Economic Incentives to Conserve Biological Resources, Inter-Union for Conservation of Nature and National Resources, Gland, Switzerland (1988).

108 EPA Report, supra note 2 at p. VII-209.

109 Id. at pp. VII-209-210.

110 Id.

111 Id. at p. VII-211.

112 Id.

113 Id. Tropical forests store up to 90% of their nutrients in woody plants, whereas in temperate forests, 97% of the nutrients are stored in the soil.

every hectare of sustainable agriculture, five to ten hectares of tropical forest might be saved.[114]

By employing agroforestry,[115] which combines agriculture and forestry techniques to produce woody plants, food or commodity crops or livestock on the same farm parcel, farmers can meet both fuel wood and food needs, while reducing environmental problems associated with monoculture row cropping. Sustainable agroforestry reduces atmospheric carbon in several ways by: (1) reducing forest burning, (2) increasing the amount of carbon stored in tropical soils, and (3) adding woody biomass.

c. Option 3 -- Decrease Forest Consumption for Development

Large development projects in the tropics can consume huge tracts of forest for roads, hydroelectric projects, reservoirs and new communities,[116] and these projects stimulate further development and more forest destruction.[117] For instance, the Mahavel project in Sri Lanka will destroy 260,000 hectares of forest (1,000 square miles) so that it can generate 466 MW of electricity and provide flood control and irrigation.[118] Changing the lending policies of multinational banks that fund these projects to require environmental impact analysis, minimal destruction of forests, and offset reforestation of other areas can reduce the incentives to destroy more forests.

d. Option 4 -- Increase Efficiency of Burning Wood as a Fuel

In many poor countries, the major source of fuel is wood, but the demand for wood exceeds the sustainable yield of the forests in those countries, causing

---

114 Id.

115 EPA defines, in EPA Report, supra note 2 at p. VII-213, three major classes of agroforestry:

a. agro-silviculture, which combines agriculture with fuel wood trees, hedgerow or "alley" intercropping, shelter belts and windbreakers;

b. silvo-pastoral, which combines livestock, fodder production, living fences and trees in pastures and;

c. agro-silvo-pastoral which involves woody hedges for grazing and mulch, and home gardens with woody plants.

116 Id. at p. VII-217.

117 Id. at p. VII-201.

118 Id. at p. VII-217. At 256 tons carbon per hectare, this project would release 66 million tons of carbon, or as much as a 591 MW coal plant operating at full capacity for forty-three years. On a present-value basis, and reflecting the fact that the hydroelectric facility will operate at less than 100% capacity, the dam will produce about five to fifteen times the CO_2 effects as the worst-case fossil plant. In addition, some of the carbon would be released as methane, which is 3.7 times as potent a greenhouse gas as is CO_2. See supra note 6.

deforestation. The use of more efficient industrial technologies and cooking stoves (presently available and economical) could reduce demand for wood by 25 to 70%.[119]

e. Option 5 -- Reduce Use of Disposable Wood Products

One of the major global warming forestry questions is what will happen to all the mature trees that are planted to sequester carbon. Disposable wood products (e.g. newsprint, paper goods, packaging, disposable chop sticks), when burned or landfilled, create greenhouse gases.[120] If the trees were dumped onto the industrial wood market as it exists today, the oversupply could have disastrous economic effects.[121]

One solution to this dilemma is to substitute durable wood products for disposable wood products, thereby reducing long-term demand for wood, while storing harvested wood in a permanent form. Another solution might be to use wood instead of plastic, metal or other products, substituting, for example, wood panelling for drywall. These practices would increase the total carbon sink as well as increase demand for harvested wood. At the same time, recycling paper would decrease deforestation pressure and increase the standing carbon sink, as well as reduce methane emissions from landfills and CO_2 emissions from landfills and incineration, and increase the amount of stored carbon, so long as the forests that would have been used to make paper remain standing or are converted to other durable products.[122]

f. Option 6 -- Manage Temperate Forests for Higher Yields

The United States, with a population of 237 million people,[123] emits 1,135 x 10^6 tons of carbon per year with a total closed forest of 195 x 10^6 hectares (0.8 hectares per person).[124] Thus, the United States emits 5.8 tons of carbon per hectare of forest at a per capita rate of almost five tons of carbon per year.[125] However, United States forests sequester carbon at the average rate of only .82 tons of carbon per hectare per year.[126] The United States would have to increase its forests some 7.5 times, to about six hectares of forest per person, to absorb current annual carbon emissions. For a population of 240 million, at six hectares per person, the U.S. would need 1,440 x 10^6

---

119 L. Brown et al., <u>State of the World 1988</u>, Worldwatch Institute (published by Norton) (1988) at p. 90.

120 CO_2 results from burning; methane results from bacterial activity in landfills.

121 Sedjo and Solomon, <u>supra</u> note 81 at p. 24.

122 <u>EPA Report,</u> <u>supra</u> note 2 at p. VII-220.

123 1985 estimate, Marland, <u>supra</u> note 77 at p. 6.

124 <u>Id</u>., 1982 figures.

125 <u>Id</u>.

126 <u>EPA Report,</u> <u>supra</u> note 2 at p. VII-221.

hectares of average forest to absorb the carbon it emits annually. Unfortunately, the total land area of the U.S. is only 913 x 10^6 hectares, and not all of this will support forests.[127]

Clearly, more intensive forestry, not just more extensive forestry will be needed.[128] Increased CO_2 concentrations may stimulate tree growth rates and lower trees' water requirements, but temperature changes and other factors may cause forest migration and loss, and temperature extremes associated with climate change may cause trees to lose vigor and become more susceptible to insects and disease.[129] Additional growth stimulation would have to come from intensive management practices such as species selection, fertilization, spacing control, genetically improved trees, and full stocking of forests.[130]

The impact of intensive management could be significant. Marland suggests that fully stocked United States forests would collect 1.35 tons of carbon per hectare per year.[131] Furthermore, according to Marland, net annual growth could be significantly higher than at present if fast-growing species were grown on optimum sites with advanced silviculture techniques such as species selection, genetic screening, spacing, thinning, pruning, weed control, fire and pest control, fertilization, irrigation, harvest cycle time control, and site preparation.[132]

---

127 Marland, supra note 77 at p. 6.

128 Id. at 31; see also Clawson, "Forests in the Long Sweep of American History," 20 Science 1168-1174 (1979), who draws four conclusions:

> 1. The total area of land in forests in the United States is now largely stabilized. Shifts to and from forest land use will be relatively modest in the future.
>
> 2. The volume of standing timber will continue to increase modestly over the next few decades or longer.
>
> 3. The trend toward increasing annual timber growth will continue, perhaps accelerate, as a consequence of improved stand management.
>
> 4. The frontier in forestry lies at the intensive, not at the extensive margin of forest practice. Productivity increases will be largely due to intensive management of the most productive sites.

129 Sandenburg et al., supra note 98 at p. 114.

130 Marland, supra note 77 at p. 27.

131 Id. at p. 32. Forests with mature trees have stored a great deal of carbon but have very low annual growth rates (mature forests can continue to accumulate carbon for long periods of time--300 to 1,000 years--but at very slow rates). On the other hand, young, vigorous forests absorb carbon much faster. This implies that to maximize the rate at which carbon is removed, mature trees should be harvested and stored in construction materials, with young trees replacing them; however, carbon lost from the soil is not made up for by the increased fixation rates from young trees. See, supra note 92. If a forest is managed to maximize a sustained yield of wood rather than to maximize carbon storage, the carbon content at maturity of the former will be about one-third the content of the latter at maturity. Forests rotated using optimal financial return on investment criteria will result in even less carbon being stored in the mature forest, since forests will be harvested to maximize their commercial value rather than their carbon sequestration rates.

132 Id. at p. 38.

However, many of these ideas may be expensive and ecologically dangerous. The cost of fertilization may equal or exceed the value of tree growth that fertilizer provides.[133] Nitrogen fertilizers release the potent greenhouse gases methane and nitrous oxide from forest soil. Labor-intensive activities will be expensive. Money spent on genetic research may improve tree growth rate, wood quality, disease and pest resistance, drought tolerance, and use of nutrients.[134] However, tropical deforestation may reduce genetic diversity among trees, thereby limiting options for genetic improvement.[135] As climate changes, genetically "improved" trees will also be vulnerable to disease, pests, toxins, or environmental conditions for which the trees are not specifically adapted.

Intensive tree plantations with improved growth rates might be sufficient to meet national, if not global carbon reduction needs. Assuming growth rates achieved by the best managed, fastest growing tropical plantations, 500 x 10^6 hectares of plantations would be needed to sequester CO_2 at the rate it is emitted by fossil fuel emissions.[136] At the growth rate equivalent to the best American plantations (Georgia Sycamore), 700 x 10^6 hectares would be required.[137] Instead of plantations on unforested land, if all the forests of the world (3000 x 10^6 hectares) were stimulated to absorb an extra 1.7 tons of carbon per hectare per year, the annual growth would fix all annual fossil fuel carbon emissions. However, once these fast plantations matured, the problem of how to store the carbon and continue fixation would remain.

Marland's calculation shows that it may be physically possible to remove 5 x 10^9 tons of carbon per year by improved intensive forest practices. But technical feasibility may be irrelevant if there are substantial political, social, economic, ecological and practical constraints to storing large quantities of harvested wood in useful, long-term projects.[138] Nevertheless, the Marland proposal is important as a relatively short-term response to the danger of severe ecological impact of long-term climate change.[139]

In the tropics, where 83% of the forests are natural, forest management, which can produce products and services that support local populations which would otherwise be destroying trees for those products and services, presents the most viable long-run option for forestry.[140] Although yields on tropical plantations can be very high,[141] most

---

133 Id. at p. 43.

134 Id. at p. 47.

135 Id. Marland notes that while there are thousands of tropical tree species, 87% of tropical forestry depends on three tree types (pine, eucalyptus and teak). In temperate forests such as in the USSR, with the worlds largest forest, there are 570 species, only thirty of which have major economic significance.

136 Id. at p. 53.

137 Id. This rate cannot be achieved in more northern climes.

138 Id. at pp. 54-58.

139 Id.

140 EPA Report, supra note 2 at p. VII-224.

forestry will have to be in villages of developing countries, where a mix of short, medium and long-rotation species will most likely provide the sustained stream of forest products and income necessary for local needs.[142]

g. Option 7 -- Improve Forest Harvest Efficiency

Tropical forestry harvesting techniques are extremely wasteful: about 85% of all wood cut goes unused as slash or waste at the mill.[143] In Malaysian and Indonesian logged forests, 45 to 75% of the standing trees are injured, and in the Amazon, for every hectare that is clear-cut, three hectares of forest are seriously damaged by logging and by colonization by peasant farmers.[144] Figure 5 illustrates this destructive cycle.

EPA believes that improved harvest efficiency could reduce tree loss and improve yields more than silvicultural innovations.[145]

h. Option 8 -- Expand Tree Planting Programs in Temperate Zones

It is believed that temperate forests in North America could be expanded because of temperate forests' large historic size.[146]

EPA's study suggests that governmental, financial, and institutional incentives could result in reforestation of up to about 1.5 million hectares over a five year period.[147] Large-scale reforestation programs, such as reforesting surplus agricultural lands, urban areas, and highway corridors, must overcome political and institutional inertia and the problems of the high costs of site preparation, planting, forest management, and site acquisition (either directly or through financial incentives to landowners).[148] Yet

---

141 Id. at p. VII-227. Although genetics has improved growth rates for temperate and tropical tree species, these rates are still not even close to Marland's target growth rates for carbon removal.

142 Id. at pp. VII-224-225; see Table 3 for a summary of forest acreage requirements to offset various CO_2 emissions goals.

143 Goldemberg, et al., Energy for a Sustainable World, 1987, at p. 382.

144 EPA Report, supra note 2 at p. VII-228; See Figure 5.

145 Id.

146 Id. at p. VII-229. For instance, France, once 80% forested, has expanded its forest cover, which was depleted to 14% in 1789, to about 25% today. See Brown, et al., supra note 119 at pp. 84, 87. Similarly, forests in the continental United States covered about 385 million hectares in 1630, but only 249 million hectares in 1920. Id. at p. 84; by 1982, United States forest area had declined to an historic low of 233 million hectares as grain exports encouraged conversion of forests to cropland and urban development encroached on forests. Id. at p. 87.

147 EPA Report, supra note 2 at pp. VII-229-30.

148 Id. at pp. VII-231-241.

TABLE 3
Estimates of Forest Acreage Required to Offset Vartious CO_2 Emissions Goals

Estimate	Location	Carbon Sequester Rate Assumed (t C/ha/yr)	Offset Goal	Hectares ($\times 10^6$)	Total Planting Cost ($ $\times 10^9$)	Average Cost/ha ($)
Dyson and Marland (1976)	Temperate Zone	7.5	5 Pg C (total annual fossil fuel use)	700		
Marland (1988)	Tropics	9.6	5 Pg C (total annual fossil fuel use)	500		
Myers (1988)[1]	Tropics	10.0	2.9 Pg (net annual increase C)	300	120	398
Sedjo and Solomon (in press)	Tropics or Temperate	6.2	2.9 Pg (net annual increase C)	465	186 tropics 372 temperate	395 800-1400[2]
Woodwell (1987)	Tropics	5.0	1-2 Pg (net annual increase C from tropics)	200-400		
Postel and Heise (Brown et al., 1988a)	Tropics	6.8	0.7 Pg (C benefits from new fuelwood plantations and restored forests)	110		
Dudek (1988a,b)	U.S.	10-12	0.05 Pg (1987-96 new electric plant C)	3.4-4.5	1.6-1.9[3]	432[3]
EPA (this study)	U.S.	3.5-10	0.05 Pg (1987-96 new electric plant C)	4.5-13	1.9-5.6[3]	432[3]

Notes:

1. See also Booth, 1988.
2. Includes $400/ha land purchase cost.
3. Assumes no cost-sharing of establishment costs, and no annual rental payments (see text).

Source: EPA Report at VII-239

FIGURE 5

POPULATION GROWTH, ROAD BUILDING, AND DEFORESTATION IN AMAZONIA

A. Growth of population and deforested area in the state of Rondônia.

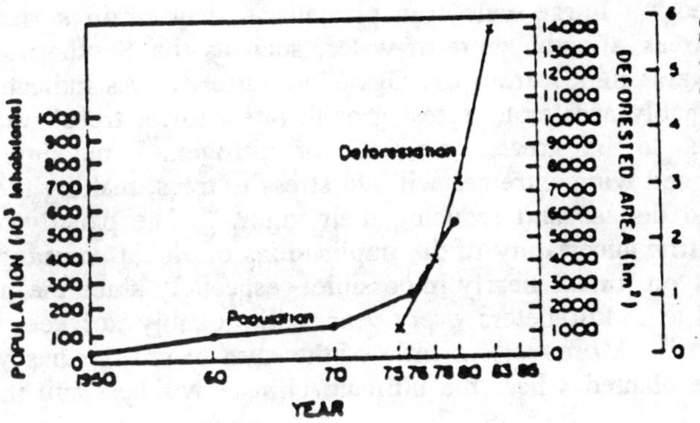

B. Causal loop diagram of the relationship between road building and deforestation.

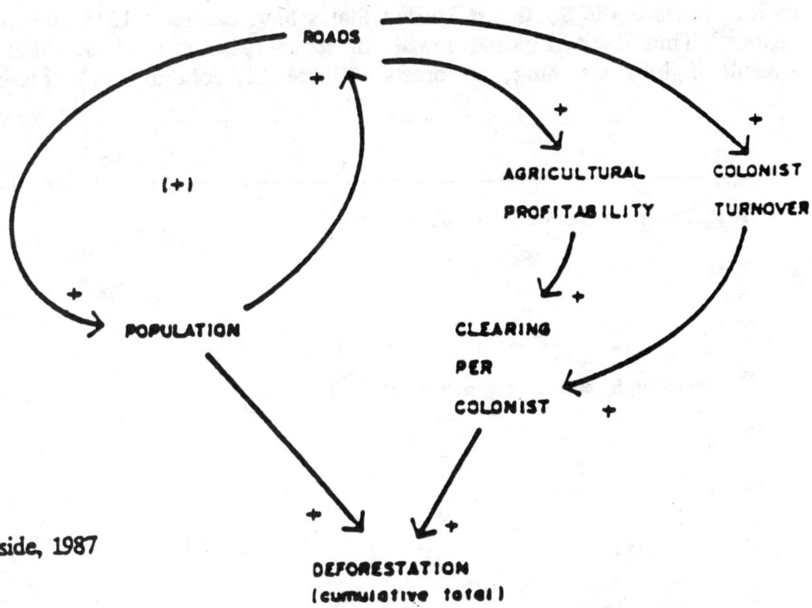

Source: Fearnside, 1987

Source: EPA Report at VII-201

despite these obstacles and even without strong financial incentives, 1.2 million hectares of trees were planted in the U.S. in 1987.[149] State foresters believe that financial incentives of $125 to $250 per hectare ($50 to $100 per acre) would significantly increase reforestation and that, with a three year lead time, existing tree nurseries could produce enough seedlings to increase tree planting by three to ten times the current yearly acreage.[150] However, there are serious ecological concerns about massive reforestation. Monoculture forests would have little genetic diversity, reducing their resistance to infestation by pests that can cause forest decline.[151] Moreover, as the climate becomes warmer, fungi and insects will increase;[152] and in those areas where climate change results in reduced precipitation, fungi, bacteria and weeds will be advantaged.[153] Large-scale tree plantations may strain surface and groundwater supplies in areas already short of water, such as the Southern Great Plains, which depend on water mined from the Ogallala aquifer.[154] As indicated before, increased CO_2 will probably accelerate forest growth rates, lower trees' water needs, and allow soil microbes to fix greater amounts of nitrogen,[155] but increased temperature, precipitation and wind extremes will add stress to trees, making them more susceptible to insects and disease and reducing their vigor.[156] The paucity of data and the high level of scientific uncertainty of the implications of global warming make prediction of the net result on forests nearly impossible - especially since the natural rate of forest migration, .1 to .4 kilometers every year, will probably not keep up with the rate of forest decline.[157] Moreover, as little of the climate change has yet occurred, forests cannot yet be planted where the ultimate climate will best suit the trees.

Air pollution, such as acid precipitation and ozone, may impede plantation and forest growth, as is evidenced by the decline in eleven important European forest tree species and eight North American species since 1979. 52% of West Germany's forests and 36% of Swiss forests were in decline by 1986, and growth rates of yellow and loblolly pines in the Southeast United States have declined 30 to 50% in the past thirty years.[158] Thus, even if global boreal forests increase in total area and tree density as a result of global warming, the forests will probably contain less biomass and fix carbon

---

149 Id. This figure seems to include replanting.

150 Id.

151 Id.

152 Sandenburgh, et al., supra note 98 at p. 115.

153 Id.

154 Id.

155 Id. at p. 114.

156 Id. at pp. 116-117.

157 EPA Report, supra note 2 at pp. VII-242-243. It has been estimated that if atmospheric CO_2 doubles, the decline in boreal forest biomass will produce a global net loss of 24 billion tons of carbon globally.

158 Id.

at lower rates than current boreal forests unless the problems of acid precipitation and ozone are reduced.[159]

Thus, reforestation may become less viable as a mitigation means, or at least become more expensive, as climatic changes occur and the rate of change accelerates.

i. Option 9 -- Reforestation in Developing Countries

The needs of developing countries for fuel wood and for restored degraded lands is already enormous, even without considering the carbon benefits from afforestation.[160] For instance, by the year 2000, the demand for fuel wood in developing countries could exceed supply by one billion cubic meters.[161] The continued destruction of the world's tropical forests is also driven by the increasing demand for agricultural land to supply the needs of rapidly growing populations.[162] By the year 2000 an estimated 2.7 billion people will be living in regions of either acute fuel wood scarcity or fuel wood deficit. Fuel wood scarcity means that fuel wood resources have been depleted to the point where fuel wood sufficient for minimum needs cannot be obtained even through overcutting. Fuel wood deficit means that minimum fuel wood needs can be met, but only by overcutting existing resources. Because the resources are insufficient to meet needs on a sustainable basis they are being depleted.[163] Although global funding for forestry by multilateral development banks and bilateral agencies was about $1 billion in 1988,[164] the rate of development of tree plantations is "barely one-tenth the rate of forest clearing."[165]

Interestingly, a recent estimate of the total area of global forest clearing to date is "virtually identical" to an independent estimate of reforestation necessary to fix enough CO_2 to equal current fuel releases;[166] thus, there is some hope of remediation. However, deforestation now occurs at ten times the rate of tropical reforestation.[167]

---

[159] Id. at p. VII-243.

[160] Id. at p. VII-236.

[161] Marland, supra note 77 at p. 12.

[162] Id.

[163] Id. at p. 15.

[164] EPA Report, supra note 2 at p. VII-236.

[165] Marland, supra note 77 at p. 19.

[166] Id. at p. 25. This and similar estimates are called into question by new data indicating that less carbon is stored than previously believed. Brown, S., "Biomass Estimation," supra. note 87; Botkin, D. and L. Simpson, The Distribution of Biomass in the North American Boreal Forest, University of California at Santa Barbara, Environmental Studies Program.

[167] Trexler, et al., supra note 95 at p. 33.

For instance, an estimated 500 million tons of carbon were released by Brazil in 1987 just from forest fires in the Amazon.[168] Thus, even if forestation were merely able to bring the world's forests into carbon balance, annual worldwide carbon emissions would be reduced significantly.

Several estimates have been made of the amount of land needed to offset the amount of carbon emitted each year by fossil fuel combustion.[169] Sedjo and Solomon, who assume that the oceans and existing forests absorb about half the carbon emitted,[170] believe the net carbon emitted (2.9 billion tons) could be sequestered for thirty years in 465 million hectares of plantations. EPA reports that Myers has suggested that "300 x 10^6 hectares of plantation eucalyptus and pine--a land mass the size of Zaire--absorbing about ten tons of carbon per hectare per year could offset 2.9 billion tons of carbon accumulated in the atmosphere annually."[171] Marland suggests that 700 x 10^6 hectares of short rotation American Sycamore, fixing 7.5 tons of carbon per hectare per year, would be needed to offset all global emissions of 5 billion tons of carbon per year.[172] At typical forest growth rates, the required land areas would be much greater.

Unfortunately, all these estimates are based on a single variable such as projected tree growth rate and do not reflect the complexity of actual forestation projects.[173] For instance, it is not clear that there is sufficient idle land available with soil and climate conditions suitable for massive tree planting. EPA suggests that in South and Southeastern Asia there are about 100 x 10^6 hectares of former forest land which are either degraded or in pasture use and not in use for crops or development.[174] In Asia, EPA estimates that if fires to create and maintain savannahs are suppressed, which is a difficult to do, then 210 to 340 x 10^6 hectares theoretically would be available.[175] Reforestable land exists in South America, where there are large deforested areas cleared by now-abandoned slash and burn logging practices.[176] It has been estimated that 758 x 10^6 hectares of degraded tropical land (including 203 x 10^6 hectares of

---

[168] Id.

[169] This assumes, of course, no reduction in fossil fuel burning in industrial countries through conservation, efficiency improvements, and the use of alternative fuels--an important additional option for mitigating carbon-based global warming that would reduce the amount of land needed for afforestation. As indicated earlier, the inclusion of the price of afforestation in utility rates and decision making would accelerate these reductions. See, discussion at 55, et seq. A detailed review of these possibilities is found in Flavin and Piltz, Sustainable Energy, RenewAmerica, Washington, DC, 1989.

[170] The "airborne fraction" of carbon remaining in the atmosphere is between 50-55% of all carbon emitted. Id. at p. 38.

[171] EPA Report, supra note 2 at p. VII-237.

[172] Marland, supra note 77 at p. 53. This is an amount equal to the total global forest cleared since agriculture began; EPA Report at p. VII-237.

[173] Trexler et al., supra note 95 at p. 33; EPA Report, supra note 2 at p. VII-237.

[174] Id. at p. VII-238.

[175] Id.

[176] Id.

previously forested land) could be reforested, although with low productivity.[177] By replacing swidden cultivation with low input agriculture, 365 x 10^6 hectares of fallow land could be reforested.[178]

In the Western Hemisphere only 2% of subtropical dry forest remains, leaving large areas available for restoration efforts. In Costa Rica, it is hoped that a plan for establishing an educational research program, reducing human-set forest fires, reducing cattle ranching and agricultural clearing, purchasing remaining dry forest habitat next to moist forest tracts or protected areas of seed sources, and stressing species diversity enable a closed canopy dry forest to evolve in ten to fifty years.[179] Hillside forest restoration projects have been successful in Africa to prevent erosion, create crop terraces and produce forest and firewood.[180]

Even if the degraded land is available for forestry, successful tropical reforestation projects must overcome many obstacles. Tropical monoculture tree plantations are susceptible to pest infestations including rats, fungus and nematodes, that have made large scale tree plantations difficult to successfully operate.[181] Other plantation problems include rapid depletion of soil nutrients by fast-growing species; reduced growth rates on hillsides at elevations above 450 meters; frost sensitivity; erosion; lack of large, contiguous land areas; poor transportation; poaching; lack of capital for establishment; and lack of educated, skilled persons to operate the plantations.[182] To reforest pastures resulting from deforestation, the resilient monoculture grasses filling the pasture must be suppressed to allow the trees to survive. Few tree seeds are naturally dispersed into large, highly degraded Amazon pastures because 85% of the seeds are dispersed by animals that do not live in pastures most seeds that do reach the pastures are eaten and water and light conditions at the soil level are different in pastures than in forests.[183] Severe economic, population and social pressures in developing countries inhibit the success of forestry projects.[184] Thus, in the tropics, the practical difficulties of increasing forested land area may equal or exceed the theoretical potential.

The realistic potential of tropical forestry to mitigate global warming can best be measured by answering the following questions raised by World Resources Institute's analysis of a forestry project in Guatemala designed to offset the CO_2 emissions of a new coal-fired power plant:[185]

---

177 Id. at p. VII-240.

178 Id.

179 Id.

180 Id. at p. VII-241.

181 Id. at p. VII-243.

182 Id.

183 Id.

184 Brown, et al., supra note 119 at p. 98.

185 Trexler et al., supra note 95 at pp. 40-42.

Land Availability and Suitability

How much land is realistically available for afforestation or reforestation? How is this land distributed by climate, soil type, human population density, and price? Will global warming, to which we are already significantly committed, reduce the productivity of existing forests or render potentially forestable areas unsuitable?

Physical and Social Feedbacks of Forestry Strategies

How would large scale reforestation and afforestation affect the planet's albedo and consequent heat balance? What would be the impacts of large-scale carbon sequestration forestry on timber, pulp, and fuel markets? What latent demand for non-carbon-sequestering wood products, e.g. firewood and charcoal, would appear in response to falling prices? How much new forest is required just to supply the existing fuel wood deficit? What would the impacts of large-scale carbon sequestration forestry be on the intensity of management of existing commercial forests, and ultimately their own carbon sequestration productivity?

Biotic Potential for Carbon Sequestration

What silvicultural growth rates can be achieved considering the range of climatic and soil conditions where land might be available? Which species, growth rates, and harvest patterns should form the basis for carbon sequestration estimates? How much and how fast can soil carbon levels be increased through forestry projects? Should low input forestry be assumed, or should extrapolations rely on the application of biotechnology and intensive plantation management to maximize carbon yields? What levels of inputs such as fertilizers will be required for alternative forestry approaches?

Accomplishing Long-term Carbon Sequestration

To what extent can the achieved carbon fixation be in the form of long-lived tree species? How much additional plantation forestry is consistent with the needs and perspectives of local peoples? What is the potential for planting fuel wood trees or pursuing agroforestry to save the large quantity of carbon currently sequestered in standing natural forest? Can such forestry be implemented on a long-term sustainable basis? What is the potential for biomass derived biofuels or electricity generation to displace the consumption of carbon-emitting fossil fuels?

<u>Basic Prognosis for Reforestation Projects</u>

What explains the failure of many past reforestation and afforestation projects? Can these problems be overcome in pursuing carbon sequestration forestry? How plausible is large-scale carbon sequestration in countries with high population growth rates, chronic fuel wood deficits, and widespread rural poverty? How much money intended for reforestation efforts can be realistically absorbed by national administrative and implementing infrastructures around the world?[186]

Despite the uncertain answers to these questions, reforestation has significant potential to mitigate CO_2 emissions. Although, as summarized on Table 3 supra and in the following Table 4, the broad-brush estimates of Marland and others confirm the abstract potential of forestry to offset carbon emissions from fossil fuel combustion, it must be remembered that reforestation or afforestation will only occur on a project by project basis, each with its own approaches to achieving carbon sequestration. Various projects might involve large-scale industrial plants to produce paper, timber, electricity, or biofuels; the regeneration or physical protection of existing natural forest; the development of woodlots and agroforestry; or urban forestry. Each project will be proposed, evaluated, and implemented individually, and despite many uncertainties.[187]

Once the CO_2 emission offset requirements are set,[188] then the marginal cost of CO_2 sequestration becomes a least-cost option against which other alternatives[189] can be measured.[190] The next section will review cost calculations of various projects in an attempt to set a numeric range, to the extent current data can support it, for the cost of sequestering carbon.

---

186 Id.

187 Id.

188 Because this is an environmental externality, the offset requirement must be imposed as a legal requirement if the remedial costs are to be internalized; the offset level will be based on value judgments that depend on whether emitters should offset past and future emissions or only a portion of them. The larger the offset ratio, the greater the cost of mitigation; as the internalized costs increase, alternative mitigation measures become marginally more beneficial, thus increasing CO_2 reductions in the atmosphere.

189 For instance, it might be less expensive per ton of carbon for a utility to retire old, inefficient cars and replace them with cars with state-of-the-art fuel efficiency than to establish and manage new forests. See text accompanying footnote 76 supra.

190 Forestry projects in developing countries may also provide important social, environmental and economic benefits that may justify the projects irrespective of carbon sequestration. However, those benefits should not be subtracted from the project costs, since they are unrelated to carbon sequestration (i.e., the prevention of global warming). Because forestry is being used as a surrogate for the external costs of global warming, only carbon sequestration-related costs and benefits should be considered in calculating the costs to be internalized by the electric power industry. This is consistent with the practice that benefits of control technology are not counted when estimating the cost of the control. Just as benefits such as enhanced employment from SO_2 scrubber construction are not subtracted from the cost of the scrubber, so the environmental benefits of using forests as carbon scrubbers should not be subtracted from the cost of sequestering carbon in trees.

TABLE 4

Approaches to Offsetting
Per Capita U.S. Carbon Emissions*

MITIGATION STRATEGY	MITIGATION REQUIREMENT
Planting temperate sycamore plantation:	1.5 acres
Planting tropical eucalyptus plantation:	0.7 acres
Foregoing driving your car (at 25 mpg):	50,000 fewer miles
Recycling rather than venting automobile air conditioning charges:	3 charge recyclings**
Replacing 75 W incandescent bulbs with 18 W fluorescent bulbs:	circa 120 bulbs

* Based on the emission of 5.0 M tons of carbon (as CO_2) per capita, or its warming equivalent in other greenhouse gases. Areas of planted trees would mitigate annual emissions as long as growth rates are maintained. Energy efficient bulbs would mitigate annual emissions over their lifetimes. The other alternatives require the mitigating measure to occur every year.

** Assumes a 2 lb CFC charge, and a molecule for molecule CFC:CO_2 warming effectiveness ratio of 20,000:1.

Source: Trexler, et,al (1989) at 41

5. Cost of Forestry Based Carbon Sequestration

a. Introduction

This section will review various attempts to calculate the cost of offsetting carbon emissions in diverse environments, ranging from the cost of establishing a Douglas Fir forest in the Pacific Northwest to establishing social forestry projects in Central America. The costs vary, depending on the assumptions made and on the nature and location of the project. This section will describe each proposal, including the proposal's assumption and calculation methods, and will convert the results, to the extent possible, into common units relevant to internalizing the costs into the electric generation decision making process.

b. Applied Energy System's Guatemala Agroforestry and Carbon Sequestration Project

The first, and currently only, forestry project designed to offset carbon emissions from an electric generation power plan was the result of Applied Energy Service's ("AES") desire to mitigate the carbon emissions of a new coal fuel power plant it was building in Connecticut. AES, an independent power producer (IPP), was the successful bidder to supply electric power at a fixed price to Connecticut Light & Power and, therefore, could not pass on to the utility the cost of the mitigation. Nevertheless, AES offered to make a $2 million grant to a project that would sequester 387,000 metric tons of carbon per year for forty years, a total of 15.5×10^6 tons.[191] Ultimately, AES, with World Resources Institute ("WRI") as project coordinator, issued a request for proposals and out of the responses selected a CARE forestry project in Guatemala that emphasized tree planting in woodlots and agroforestry, increasing sustainable biomass yields and productivity through soil conservation, protecting existing forest by forest fire brigades, developing educational and management activities, and involving women in all project activity.[192] The project, with an estimated cost of $14 million (shared between AES, CARE, Guatemala, USAID, and Peace Corps)[193], will involve 40,000 farm families planting 52×10^6 trees in wood lots for poles and timber, in agroforestry for fuel wood, fodder, and soil nitrogen fixation, in fruit and nut production, in alley cropping, and in live barriers for soil conservation and line fencing.[194] Hundreds of local forestry committees will be founded and supported by educational and technical training to meet local needs, develop and implement plans, share benefits and coordinate management of community woodlots, nurseries and fire brigades.[195]

---

191 Trexler et al., supra note 95 at p. 15.

192 Id. at p. 17.

193 The Peace Corps and CARE contributions appear to be priced below market costs.

194 Trexler et al., supra note 95 at pp. 18, 58-59.

195 Id. at p. 19.

The project envisions 24.4×10^6 trees in woodlots, 26.5×10^6 trees in agroforestry, 2,400 hectares of forest saved by fire protection and carbon added to the soils as a result of these activities.[196]

For carbon costing purposes, the major question about this project is how much carbon will be sequestered--a question more easily asked than answered. CARE said the project would sequester 33.7×10^6 tons, but WRI calculated the same project to sequester about half that amount, only 16.3×10^6 tons.[197] WRI calculated the amount of biomass in a tree by multiplying the stemwood by two, but CARE used a factor of 2.5. WRI believed the wood had an average density of 0.5 metric tons per cubic meter but CARE used 0.6. More importantly, CARE assumed that all of the planted trees would sequester carbon, whereas WRI believed that the woodlots and agroforestry were primarily aimed at reducing deforestation pressures, thereby saving wild forest from exploitation. The final difference in assumptions turned on whether CARE was double-counting trees saved by fire protection and trees either planted or saved from exploitation, thus inflating the fire protection benefits.[198]

Unlike CARE, WRI explored the fate of the carbon in the woodlot trees. It assumed that 85% of the trees would be consumed as fuel over forty years, leaving only 15% of the planted trees as a net addition to the earth's biomass, or 0.6×10^6 tons of carbon.[199] However, over the forty years, the woodlots' carbon would displace forest exploitation. WRI assumed that of the 85% of the woodlot harvested for fuel, only two-thirds of that amount contained usable wood, leaving 2.4×10^6 tons of carbon that would displace forest exploitation. WRI then assumed that if the farmers had collected wood from the forest, additional carbon would be released from the soil, roots, leaves, and destruction of other trees so that every "usable" ton of woodlot carbon would save 1.5 tons of natural forest carbon. Thus, on the assumption that the woodlots will save 3.6×10^6 tons of carbon in the forests, WRI credited the woodlots with a total of 4.2×10^6 tons of carbon sequestered compared to CARE's calculated credit of 6.4×10^6 tons.[200]

A similar analysis was performed on the agroforestry component, resulting in a credit allowed by WRI of 11.2×10^6 tons versus CARE's figure of 17×10^6.[201] Since WRI assumed that natural forest was already credited with being protected by the woodlot and agroforestry programs, it reduced CARE's credit for fire fighting to 2,400 hectares saved (0.6×10^6 tons), so that CARE would not be doubly credited for saving

---

[196] Id. at pp. 49-51. The original CARE proposal envisioned saving 19,000hectares of forest via fire protection. Id. at p. 47.

[197] Id. at pp. 23-33.

[198] Id.

[199] Id. at p. 49.

[200] Id. at pp. 47-51.

[201] Id.

the same trees.[202] Finally, WRI and CARE agreed that the forestry would increase the carbon content of affected soils by 0.3×10^6 tons.[203]

Thus, WRI's final estimate of the total long-term carbon sequestration from the project is 16.3×10^6 tons, obtained at a total cost, in cash or kind, of $14.3 million to offset the forty year CO_2 emissions of a 183 megawatt ("MW") coal-fired plant.[204] If the project is successful, the installed cost of the sequestration will be $0.78/MW or $78 per kilowatt (KW) which is 5.1% of the total project cost of $275 million, or is $4.21 per ton of carbon sequestered.[205] On a kilowatt hour basis, assuming the power plant operates at a 90% capacity factor, the cost is .12 cents/kWh over forty years. The program will cover about 385 square miles (250,000 acres or, 101,175 hectares), of which 50 miles will be woodlots, 260 agroforestry and 75 forest protection.

These cost estimates must be used cautiously because they are based on speculative assumptions made in the absence of hard data.[206] For instance, the amount of hectares and carbon to be saved by forest protection was, ultimately, a guess not supported by any meaningful data from past projects. Similarly, the woodlot and agroforestry numbers are only best-guess estimates, since there are no data on the carbon sequestration results of comparable projects.

The costs of the project are understated. For instance, there are no direct labor costs included in the project; rather, WRI assumed that the farmers' labor could be compensated with food aid. Research is under way to evaluate this and other forestry projects from the point of view of carbon sequestration, but the results will not be available for several years.[207]

However, the costs of the AES project are so low, and so under-inclusive, that few people believe that they are representative of the true costs of carbon sequestration.[208] For instance, the carbon sequestration calculations for this project do not provide for losses from pests, natural disasters, social or political unrest, or institutional barriers not adequately accounted for. Since forestry projects in tropical countries are inherently risky, only one-half to one-third of the proposal's estimate of carbon sequestration should be used in computing unit costs.[209]

---

202 This double credit issue was the subject of great debate.

203 Id.

204 Id. at p. 19.

205 $14.3 million multiplied by a typical utility's real carrying charge of 12% equals $1.72 million annually. Dividing the annualized cost by the annual carbon savings (0.41 million tons) gives $4.21/ton.

206 Conversation between Trexler and David R. Hodas, October 24, 1989.

207 Id.

208 Id. and conversation with Christopher Flavin, Worldwatch Institute, October 24, 1989.

209 Trexler conversation supra, note 206.

The WRI analysis assumes that "social forestry"--forestry pursued to meet social needs such as carbon reduction--will save natural forest from destruction by reducing pressure to clear forests for building materials, firewood, and agriculture, but does not propose how the success of a project should be measured or evaluated. Determining how much extra carbon is saved in standing forests as a result of woodlots and agroforestry will be crucial to project evaluation, because the AES project relies primarily on demand reduction to protect forest. If the woodlots and agroforestry do not offset demand, then the carbon sequestration projected in the WRI analysis will not be realized.

Expenses to help minimize the risk of failure were not included in the project. For instance, there are no provisions for forest rangers, forest fire fighters, or for any significant measures to protect the forests from destruction, measures which would add significantly to the project expenses.[210] The land on which the trees will be planted may be too depleted to support the growth rates and carbon fixation rates assumed in the calculations. The WRI calculations neither consider possible detrimental effects on carbon fixation rates of increased temperature such as changed precipitation patterns, or increased severity of storms that might occur as a result of global warming,[211] nor evaluate the risks of failure of the forestry program due to desperate political or social conditions caused by rapid population growth. If all of these factors were added into the analysis of a carbon offset forestry project, the costs could increase substantially.[212] It is reasonable to expect that the costs of the first few projects--which will tap the least expensive forestry opportunities, although at the most expensive point on the learning curve-- will be less than the cost of later projects designed to offset additional carbon releases.

Additionally, the cost of project development, proposed evaluation, and project follow-up evaluation were not included in the above figures. WRI estimates that for a 150 to 200 MW plant, the cost of project development would be about $50,000,and follow-up and tracking another $75 to $100,000.[213] These costs do not include costs for detailed verification, quality control oversight, modification or replacement of projects that break down, or implementation of other enforcement mechanisms.[214] Since the AES project is voluntary, there is no requirement for independent verification or enforcement of the carbon sequestration results,[215] a requirement that would be crucial

---

[210] Trexler conversation, id. See also discussion of World Wildlife Fund Project, and Costa Rica projects, infra.

[211] Temperature changes in the tropics are likely to be smaller than world averages, but anticipated increased precipitation and stronger hurricanes may be destructive to Central American forests. See note 20, supra.

[212] Trexler conversation, supra note 206.

[213] Id.

[214] Id.

[215] However, CARE is to provide AES with information about the pre-project status of selected evaluation sites, quarterly monitoring reports on seedling outplanting rates, soil conservation treatment and fire brigade activities, annual reports on seedling survival rates, tree growth measurements on selected plots, soil carbon changes on selected soil conservation plots and estimated carbon savings through fire protection activities, and provide three external evaluations that estimate the carbon sequestration of the project. Applied Energy Services, "Monitoring and Evaluation Plan For Carbon Flux CARE-Guatemala

if a project were to be given a carbon credit by a government agency as part of an emissions-trading or offset program.

Taken together, uncertainties about WRI's carbon-offset calculations limit the value of any results derived from them. It is clear that, generally, the cost of marginal carbon sequestration will be considerably higher than in the AES project. The complete results of the AES project evaluation will not be available for decades, at which point decades of additional CO_2 emissions will have occurred and many decisions made in the interim will be expensive or impossible to correct. To the extent that a project like this is used to establish a surrogate measure for global warming costs, the cost evaluation should allow considerable latitude for increased cost, decreased effectiveness, social, political and scientific uncertainties and for the effect of historic emissions. Although the AES project has shortcomings, AES nevertheless deserves much credit for attempting, on a voluntary and experimental basis, the first forestry carbon sequestration project to offset power plant carbon emissions.

c. Conservation Foundation/World Wildlife Fund Project

In response to the AES/WRI request for proposals, the Conservation Foundation/World Wildlife Fund (CF/WWF) submitted a carbon-sequestration proposal designed to sequester carbon by halting rampant deforestation in Costa Rica through forest management and reforestation. As with the CARE proposal, CF/WWF intended to leverage AES's $2 million grant; WWF planned to create a debt-swap endowment that would provide loans and technical assistance to small landowners. WWF hoped to sequester 10.9×10^6 tons of carbon in ten years and 21.8×10^6 tons in forty years.

At Costa Rica's current rate of deforestation of about 60,000 hectares per year, there will be no forests left by the year 2000 outside the natural parks, which are increasingly subject to deforestation by squatters and loggers.[216] At this rate of deforestation, by 1995, Costa Rica will spend more to import forest products than to import oil.[217]

Deforestation is particularly effective in releasing carbon. For example, for every tree utilized as timber by Costa Rican commercial loggers, three are destroyed and left to decay.[218] Deforestation in Costa Rica releases about 7.4×10^6 tons of carbon annually; a 5% reduction in the rate of deforestation alone would virtually offset the carbon emission of AES's proposed plant.[219]

Agroforestry and Resource Conservation Project" (undated).

216 Conservation Foundation/World Wildlife Fund, Proposal: The Forestry Fund: Endowment for Forest Protection, Management, and Reforestation in Costa Rica 1, May, 1988, [hereinafter cited as CF/WWF].

217 Id.

218 Id.

219 Id. at p. 2.

Although some reforestation takes place currently, it is insufficient to offset the rate of deforestation, which increases as population growth and wood scarcity increase pressures on forests.[220] This forest loss results in loss of diversity of flora and fauna, release of carbon to the atmosphere, foreign currency expenditures on forest products, soil erosion, siltation of hydroelectric projects and increases in flooding.[221]

The CF/WWF proposed project hopes to slow deforestation by actively protecting and managing forests, by reducing logging and clear cutting on private land and by stabilizing and reforesting land converted to pasture by clear cutting. To do this, CF/WWF proposed to leverage the AES $2 million grant to create a much larger available resource. A $500,000 (U.S.) Endowment Fund was created for technical assistance. The remaining $1.5 million was to be converted into Costa Rican Colones and supplemented through a debt swap that would create the purchasing power equivalent of $5 million to $7 million.[222] These funds (both the Colones and the dollar Endowment Fund) were to be used during the first ten years to protect 72,000hectares of forest from deforestation, to manage another 38,000 hectares and reforest 12,000 hectares; the mix of efforts in later years would be similar.[223]

The forestry project uses a two-pronged approach. The first deals with the concern that loggers pay little or nothing for the right to harvest trees, which are then sold to the mills. The mills neither own nor manage the forests, nor do the loggers, who do not live in the area and have no interest in a sustained yield from a forest; thus a "tragedy of the commons" is occurring in the form of unbridled destruction of a common resource.[224] Moreover, the logging occurs in previously inaccessible areas, that have been made accessible by the logging roads which do not prevent agricultural squatters from using slash-and-burn techniques, furthering the increase of deforestation.[225]

CF/WWF proposes to stop destruction in a national park and a forest reserve by strengthening forest protection institutions and coordinating state and national Costa Rican forest protection services. At the same time, CF/WWF proposes to stop destruction of privately held forests by providing local organizations, cooperatives and businesses with technical assistance in selective timber extraction, forest regeneration, waste reduction, and improvement of extraction efficiency.[226]

On the reforestation side, CF/WWF proposes a forestry program for small farmers. Reforestation reduces income from food crops during the seven to twenty years until the trees can be harvested. The CF/WWF endowment fund would lend

---

[220] Id. at p. 3.

[221] Id.

[222] Id. at pp. 1, 5, 11.

[223] Id. p. 4.

[224] Id. at p. 7-8.

[225] Id. at p. 8. See Figure 5, supra, which illustrates the relationship between rainforest road building and the acceleration of deforestation.

[226] Id. at p. 6.

money to farms to cover lost opportunity costs incurred from taking agriculture or pasture land out of use, taking the future value of the planted trees as collateral.[227] The plots would have a mixture of fast and slow growing trees, so that wood and crop harvests would continue from year seven to fifty, and into perpetuity as trees were replanted, with payments on the loans beginning after year ten, and then at a low interest rate.[228] CF/WWF believes that, if this approach is successful, peasant farmers will no longer need to clear-cut forests to create farms every five to ten years.[229]

In calculating the carbon-sequestration effect of this plan, CF/WWF compared the ecosystem carbon content of various land uses before and after the project. CF/WWF's basic carbon assumptions, extrapolated from a review of literature, are summarized in Tables 5 to 10.[230]

CF/WWF calculated the carbon that would be sequestered by reforesting 1,200 hectares per year for ten years as the difference in carbon content between a thirty to forty year old mature plantation (256 tons of carbon per hectare) and the existing pasture (75 tons of carbon per hectare), for a net carbon gain of 181 tons per hectare. For 12,000 hectares this is 2.2 x 10^6 tons. CF/WWF did not address what would happen to the carbon in the wood after the plantation reached maturity, i.e.,whether it would be burned as biomass fuel, thereby releasing carbon, or used as durable construction materials, thereby increasing long-term sequestration. The forest management and protection aspects of the project were analyzed by comparing the carbon content of the forest reserve and park with and without the project; the difference projected as a result of the program would be a savings of 6.2 x 10^6 tons of carbon from release by deforestation.

In the national park area, which was 100% natural forest, CF/WWF estimated that, without protection, the area would become 30% natural forest, 50% logged forest and 20% pasture. The carbon difference between 100% forest and the hypothetically lower future deforestation because of the protection of the program compared to the projected deforestation without the program's protection, produced projected carbon savings of 2.5 x 10^6 tons.

The cost of these savings, including estimated debt-swap leverage, would be about $6 million; on an annual basis the cost would be about $720,000 for 273,000 tons, or $2.64 per ton. CF/WWF expects to be able to repeat the entire process during years ten to forty in a different area of the country, to double the eventual carbon savings. Thus, the total projected carbon savings would be 21.8 x 10^6 tons for an initial investment of $6 million. Assuming the second round of reforestation starts twenty years after the first, and a 6% discount rate, the effective cost of carbon sequestration

---

227 Id. at p. 9. In comparison, in the CARE/WRI project, CARE only intends to provide food assistance to farmers for five years. (Trexler, et al., supra note 95 at p. 19). If CARE provides food for ten years, the costs would increase from $14 million to $16.3 million, a 16.4% increase. If one multiplies that amount by the previously discussed uncertainty factors, the final costs of the CARE/WRI project could be an additional 50-100%.

228 Id.

229 Id.

230 New data indicate that tropical forests contain less carbon than previously believed. Brown et al., supra note 166.

Table .6 Ecosystem carbon content under various land uses (metric tons C per hectare).

	Undisturbed Forest	Logged or Managed Forest	30-40 year old Forest Plantation	Deforested for Pasture or Agriculture
Vegetation	175	129	175	10
Soil	81	81	81	65
Total	256	210	256	75

Table 6 Land distribution on the Osa Peninsula, Costa Rica.

Golfo Dulce Forest Reserve	76,803 ha
Privately Owned	60,608 ha
Corcovado National Park	41,788 ha
Agrarian Reform Agency (IDA)[1]	1,904 ha
Guaymi Indigenous Reserve	1,100 ha
	182,203 ha

[1] IDA also controls 39,496 ha within Golfo Dulce Forest Reserve.

Source: CF/WWF Proposal

Table 7 Carbon uptake due to reforestation projected for years 1-10.

Reforestation in the Osa Peninsula	1,000 ha per year
Reforestation in Puriscal	200 ha per year
Total reforestation after ten years	12,000 ha
Carbon content of plantations after 30-40 years	256 tons per ha
Carbon content of pastures before reforestation	75 tons per ha
Net carbon sink per unit area	181 tons per ha
Net Carbon Sink for Total Reforested Area	2.2 Million Tons

Table 8 Present land cover in the 77,000 hectare Golfo Dulce Forest Reserve, and 40 year projections with and without the proposed project (% of land area).

	Present[1]	Projected with the project	Projected without the project
Mature Forest	70%	40%	10%
Logged Forest	20%	50%	30%
Pasture	10%	10%	60%

[1] Source: Tschinkel (1987) and personal observation.

Table 9 Present carbon content of the 77,000 hectare Golfo Dulce Forest Reserve, and 40 year projections with and without project (metric tons C).

	Present	Projected with the project	Projected without the project
Mature Forest	13,763,000	7,865,000	1,966,000
Logged Forest	3,226,000	8,064,000	4,839,000
Pasture	576,000	576,000	3,456,000
Total	17,562,000	16,505,000	10,261,000

C saved: 6.2×10^6 tons

Table 10 Corcovado National Park as a potential carbon source.

	Present values		Likely future values if unprotected	
	% of Area	Tons C	% of Area	Tons C
Mature Forest	100%	10,698,000	30%	3,209,000
Logged Forest	0%	0	50%	4,388,000
Pasture	0%	0	20%	627,000
Total		10,698,000		8,224,000

C saved: 2.5 x 10^6 tons

would be reduced to about $2 per ton. As with the CARE project, the costs of sequestering carbon are astoundingly low.

CF/WWF assumes that plantations and forests have a carbon content of 256 tons per hectare. By comparison, WRI assumes wood lots to have 350 tons per hectare and agro-forestry 171 tons per hectare, which average to 260, approximately the same as CF/WWF's 256 tons per hectare. While WRI and CF/WWF appear to be using similar carbon fixation rates, CF/WWF does not account for what happens to the trees that will be ready for harvest after seven to ten years, but assumes they will be harvested to provide farm income. Once harvested, if used for biomass fuels, all the carbon will be released, and no long-term sequestration will result.[231] Carbon will be sequestered in the wood used for construction materials, but even so, some carbon in the leaves, bark, and branches will be released.[232] CF/WWF provides no analysis of the steady-state level of carbon on the reforested pasture, other than to indicate that these trees will be used to reduce pressure on forests.[233] Using WRI's analysis of the disposition of woodlot carbon, CF/WWF's claimed credit of 2.2×10^6 tons would be reduced by 85% to 330,000 tons sequestered. CF/WWF separately accounts for the carbon saved through protection of existing forests.[234]

CF/WWF's analysis assumes that its project will be completely successful, even though existing forests will be rapidly and almost completely deforested without the program. CF/WWF does not include any money for fire protection, nor does it demonstrate that forestry protection and management efforts will be completely successful. As with WRI/CARE, CF/WWF does not provide a margin for risk of failure. Nevertheless, even if burdened with add-ons to account for risk and historic emissions, the CF/WWF project, if it works, appears to be a low-cost approach to mitigating the global warming problem.

As a fall-back from its social reforestation, CF/WWF assumes a cost of $700 per hectare to reforest the land areas included in its proposal. At a 3% real discount rate (4.2% carrying charge) $700 per hectare is the equivalent of $29 per hectare-year; at a 12% real carrying charge the cost would be $84 per hectare per year. If all the carbon is sequestered (181 net tons per hectare or about 4.5 tons per year over forty years), the cost would range between $6.50 and $18.70 per ton of carbon, depending on the carrying charge.

Although it is impossible to quantify the risk of failure associated with such forestry projects, there is an intuitively inverse relationship between cost and risk.[235] When the projected carbon sequestration is based exclusively on halting deforestation in the future, the uncertainty is doubled. There are both the risks that the replanting

---

231 If the biomass displaces fossil fuel, carbon will remain in the ground.

232 The roots may rot, or sprout new shoots, depending on the species.

233 CF/WWF, supra note 216 at p. 12.

234 Using WRI's analysis of natural forest saved by reforestation (Trexler, supra note 77 at p. 49), CF/WWF's 2.2×10^6 tons of carbon is multiplied by 0.66 (usable branch wood multiplier) and by 0.85 (proportion of woodlot harvested) to make 1.12×10^6 tons of woodlot carbon, or 1.68×10^6 tons of forest carbon. This is less than the savings CF/WWF projects in the park alone.

235 Trexler, supra note 77 at p. 43.

will not be as successful as envisioned, and the risks that the replanted and "protected" areas will be deforested anyway.

d. Costa Rican Government Project

Costa Rica has its own reforestation program, which in 1989 will reforest 1375 hectares divided among 435 farms.[236] This new, although modest, program is funded by the Foundation for Forest Development (FFD), created by the governments of Costa Rica and the Netherlands to reforest 3,500 hectares per year for four years.[237] The fund will give local farm-based forestry groups technical assistance, capital, and administrative help to encourage planting trees for windbreaks, firewood and agricultural forestry, which is the incorporation of trees among the other crops on a farm. The revolving fund will require that the beneficiaries contribute to the planting effort. According to FFD figures, the cost of establishing and maintaining a plantation will be 86,000 Colones per hectare,[238] broken down as follows:

Supplies (plants, medical, etc.)	21,000
Manual labor	53,000
Administration	12,000
	86,000 or $1,079 (U.S.)

The fund pays for everything except 30% of the labor costs, which the beneficiary must either pay or provide. The beneficiary's 30% of labor is 16,000 Colones or twenty-two days wages (including a 49% surcharge for social security). Ten percent of the proceeds from the final wood harvest must be paid to the local forestry group for further forestation. The project description does not discuss carbon sequestration. However, FFD assumes that each hectare planted for firewood will displace demand to deforest standing forest, thereby reducing carbon release. Each hectare for windbreaks and agroforestry will sequester carbon directly, since these uses envision long-lived trees. Since each local group or force will decide what forestry is most appropriate for its needs, there is no way of predicting the mix of uses.

Once the woodlots reach steady state, each hectare will contain about 90 tons of extra carbon. Assuming that the average tree is half-grown, the woodlots would directly add 2.25 tons per hectare per years to standing carbon inventory over a 40-year project term. Woodlots that displace forest exploitation will produce 181 x 0.66 x 0.85/20 = 5.1 tons of carbon per hectare annually.[239] This displacement of forest exploitation would start when the woodlots are reasonably mature, perhaps about year fifteen, resulting in 5.1 x 1.5 = 7.7 tons of carbon saved per hectare per year.[240] The cost of

---

236 4 Boletin Forestal 1, Costa Rica National Forestry Service (March, 1989).

237 Id. at p. 2.

238 About 80 Costa Rican Colones are equivalent to one United States dollar. (Bank of America Foreign Currency Indication Rates, November 1989.) The period of maintenance appears to be four years.

239 See WRI analysis, supra. This estimate assumes the average tree matures in twenty years.

240 The 1.5 multiplier is also from WRI.

the net carbon sequestered would be \$6.30per ton at a 4.2% carrying charge or \$23.60 at a 12% carrying charge.

e. Macro Cost Estimates

Several estimates have been made of the cost of using forest plantations to offset all carbon emissions. Marland suggests that with genetic improvements in trees and efficient forestry practices, 500 x 10^6 hectares of intensively managed, rapidly growing plantations could sequester all 5 x 10^9 tons of carbon released annually by fossil fuels.[241] Woodwell suggests that 200-400 x 10^6 hectares of rapidly developing forests could withdraw 1 to 2 x 10^9 tons of carbon from the atmosphere.[242]

Atmospheric CO_2 is rising at about 3 billion tons of carbon per year.[243] At maximal growth rates for commercial forests in the Pacific Northwest, 465 x 10^6 hectares would be needed to stabilize this growth. Depending upon location, the current cost of establishing plantations might be \$230-\$1,000per hectare with an average of \$400 per hectare,[244] plus the cost of land, \$400-\$1,000per hectare,[245] for a start-up cost in the U.S. of \$630 to \$2,000per hectare. The total cost would be at least \$372 billion for 465 x 10^6 hectare.[246]

However, as the most economical sites are used, the cost of land and planting would rise, and the productivity would tend to fall. Using degraded tropical lands for these plantations might reduce the establishment cost to as little as \$186 billion, depending on the productivity of the available land. Moreover, filling the world with the fast-growing monoculture tree plantations assumed by Marland and Sedjo is neither desirable nor feasible. Each forestry project will have to be location-specific, and in developing countries will have to be tailored to the social and economic needs of the local populations. Thus these broad, generic estimates of cost do little more than establish the scale of the problem.

---

241 Marland, supra note 77 at p. 53. Carbon releases are now probably closer to 6 million tons per year. At this 10 tons per acre sequestration rate, the forests would mature in ten years; further sequestration would depend on harvesting.

242 EPA Report, supra note 2 at p. VII-239.

243 Sedjo & Solomon, supra note 81 at p. 20. The oceans are currently absorbing 2 to 3 x 10^9 tons of carbon.

244 Id. at p. 23; Marland, supra note 77 at p. 55 notes that the cost of establishing and tending large scale plantations in the Sahel was over \$1,000per hectare for a yield of four to seven cubic meters of biomass (or 1 to 1.8 tons of carbon) per hectare per year, or \$67 to \$120 per ton of carbon.

245 Id.

246 Id., and Sedjo, "Forests: A Tool to Moderate Global Warming?," Environment, Vol. 31, No. 1, p. 14 (Jan./Feb., 1989).

EPA and the New York Energy Plan both summarize these generic estimates.[247] Chernick and Caverhill also review these macro-sequestration estimates, calculate the cost to be between $40 and $200 per ton of carbon, suggest the middle range of $120 per ton is reasonable, but adopt the more optimistic figure of $80 per ton of carbon.[248] The Tellus Institute reviewed Chernick and Caverhill and adopted $80 per ton.[249] Koomey[250] compares several generic estimates and reports Chernick and Caverhill at $84 per ton, (1989 $) Schilberg et al.,[251] at $54 per ton, and the California Energy Commission at $26 per ton.[252] The Schilberg estimate was advocated by Natural Resources Defense Council/Sierra Club before the California Energy Commission because it was based upon the estimated average cost of establishing and maintaining large stands of trees in California and the Pacific Northwest.[253] More recently, in evaluating the air quality benefits of proposed new units, the California Energy Commission adopted $54 per ton of carbon as the appropriate marginal cost.[254]

f. Pacific Northwest Forestry

The cost of sequestering carbon in the United States has been estimated for the Pacific Northwest, for existing agricultural lands, and for urban areas. Two sources have estimated the cost of planting forests in the Pacific Northwest to offset carbon emissions. One was performed by Shepard Buchanan of the Bonneville Power

---

247 Table 3 (EPA Table 7-21), supra note 142; Draft New York State Energy Plan, supra. note 62, Vol. VI, Tables 11 and A5 at App. 40 (For New York, see Table 11, infra).

248 Chernick and Caverhill, supra note 95 at p. 73.

249 Bernow, S., & D. Marron, Valuation of Environmental Externalities For Energy Planning and Operations: May 1990 Update, May 18, 1990 at p. 26.

250 Koomey, Comparative Analysis of Monetary Estimates of External Environmental Costs Associated with Combustion of Fossil Fuels, Energy Analysis Program, Applied Sciences Division, Lawrence Berkeley Laboratory, Berkeley, CA, April, 1990, at p. 27.

251 Schilberg, G., J. Nahigan & W. Marcus, Valuing Reductions in Air Emissions and Incorporation into Electric Resource Planning: Theoretical and Quantitative Aspects (re: CEC Docket 88-ER-8), JBS Energy, Inc. for the Independent Power Producers, August 25, 1989, at p. 9.

252 California Energy Commission Staff, Energy Siting and Environmental Protection Division, Valuing Emission Reductions for Electricity Report 90, Staff Issue Paper #3R, Docket #88-ER-8, November 21, 1989.

253 C. Calwell, "Valuing Reductions in Carbon Dioxide Emissions," NRDC/Sierra Club Written Testimony for the California Energy Commission Electricity Report 90 (January 11, 1990).

254 Tooker, C. & R. Buell, "LUZ SEGS Units IX and X Air Quality Benefits As Determined Under ER-7," California Energy Commission, written testimony (May 30, 1990).

TABLE 11

Reforestation Estimates for CO_2 Uptake

Source:	Fuel Type	Facility Size	Facility CO_2 Emission Rate	Tree Species	Tree CO_2 Uptake Rate	Tree Planting Costs	Unit Cost	Levelized Rate
		(MW)	(tons/mwh)		(tons/acre)	($/acre)	($/kW)	(¢/kWh)
(a) BPA	Coal	560	1.05	Douglas Fir	4.2	450	697	0.49 1/
(b) Pacific Power	Coal	300	1.50	N/A	7.5	250	375-750	0.37 2/
(c) EDF	N/A	N/A	1.28	Silver Maple	16.5 3/	275	121	N/A
(d) EPA	N/A	N/A	N/A	Silver Maple	8.2	175	N/A	N/A
Average	Coal	200	1.29	"Average"	6.6 4/	288 4/	377	0.79 5/
Average	Oil	200	0.89	"Average"	6.6 4/	288 4/	262	0.55 5/

1/ Levelized over 40 years at 3% discount rate.
2/ Levelized over 25 years at 5.5% discount rate.
3/ Not used in the calculation of average uptake rate; the author later revised the estimate to agree the EPA estimate and is quoted here only for comparison purposes.
4/ The average uptake rate and dollar per acre was applied to each generic 200 MW facility.
5/ Levelized over 40 years applying the financial planning assumptions.

N/A -- Not Available.

Sources: (a) S. Buchanan, Bonneville Power Authority (BPA), personal conversation.
(b) H.S. Reichmuth, Pacific Power, personal conversation.
(c) D.J. Dudek, Offsetting New CO_2 Emissions. Environmental Defense Fund, 1987.
(d) Environmental Protection Agency (EPA). Policy Options for Stabilizing Global Climate: Draft Report to Congress, 1989.

Source: Draft New York State Energy Plan, Vol. VI., Air Emissions From Electricity Generation, May 1989

Administration[255], and the other by Howard Reichmuth of Pacific Power and Light (PPL), and David Robison of Lambert Engineering for a west coast utility.[256]

Buchanan estimated the cost of growing trees to store carbon without harvesting.[257] Buchanan believes that planting enough trees to sequester all the carbon released world-wide by human activity would not be feasible. He uses the cost of tree planting as a "reasonable first approximation" of the environmental costs associated with the CO_2 emissions from fossil-fueled power plants.[258]

Buchanan estimated that an average mixed-age stand of Douglas Fir sequesters 2.85 tons of carbon per hectare per year or 1.14 tons of carbon per acre per year. The cost of planting commercial stands of Douglas Fir is estimated by the Forest Service at $450 per acre.[259] Buchanan annualized $450 per acre using a capital recovery factor of .043 to arrive at a cost of $19.50 per year for planting the trees, assuming a 3% real discount rate over forty years and no taxes.[260] Dividing the amortized cost of tree planting by the sequestration rate of 1.14 tons of carbon per acre per year results in a sequestration cost of $17.08 per ton. In comparison to Buchanan's 3% real discount rate, using a 6% real discount rate the cost would be $29.91 per acre per year and $26.23 per ton of carbon; at a 12% real discount rate, the cost would be $54 per acre per year and $47.40 per ton of carbon.

Buchanan estimates that a 560 MW coal plant operating at a 70% capacity factor would produce 985,535 tons of carbon per year, requiring 864,122 acres (350,000 hectares or 1350 square miles) of forest. After forty years, the sustained yield of the forest could fuel a biomass-fuel power plant of about half the size of the coal plant.[261]

These costs are based on land which is currently replanted with trees as it is clear-cut. The actual costs for marginal sites would be higher, since only higher-priced, less accessible, or less productive land would be available for planting. Another location for forestry projects is along the major highway corridors of the United States, where an estimated million hectares of trees could be planted.[262]

The Reichmuth/Robison analysis arrives at lower costs for carbon offset, because it uses different assumptions than Buchanan used. Reichmuth and Robison assume that a temperate forest can fix carbon at the average rate of 1.7 tons of carbon per acre per year. They also assume that $250 per acre ($618 per hectare) will purchase a

---

[255] Buchanan, supra. note 45.

[256] Reichmuth and Robison, Carbon Dioxide Offsets (March 2, 1989). (unpublished report; available from Reichmuth at Pacific Power and Light).

[257] Buchanan, supra note 45 at p. 1.

[258] Id.

[259] Id.

[260] Id. at p. 4.

[261] Id. at pp. 7-8. Buchanan does not evaluate the cost or feasibility of collecting wood for the plant.

[262] EPA Report, supra note 2 at p. VII-235.

"stewardship" forestation contract.[263] Amortizing the $250 per acre forestry cost over forty years at 3%, the cost per ton of carbon sequestered would be about $6.30per ton. At a 12% carrying charge, sequestration would cost $17.67 per ton. Adding in land costs at $100 per acre would increase the total cost to $8.85 per ton at a 3% real discount rate, $13.60at a 6% real discount rate, or $24.70at a 12% real discount rate.

g. Conservation Reserve Program

Another approach to offsetting carbon emissions is the proposal of Dudek and LeBlanc, of the Environmental Defense Fund,[264] to use the Conservation Reserve Program (CRP), created by the Food Security Act of 1985,[265] to subsidize the planting of trees which will reduce erosion and surplus agricultural production and sequester carbon to mitigate global warming. CRP contracts with owners of erodible cropland to retire some land for ten years, which is then to be planted with trees or other vegetation cover; the CRP pays half the planting costs and an annual rental fee to the landowners.[266] CRP aimed to have 40 to 45 million acres of cropland under contract by 1990, with 12.5% of the area devoted to trees.[267] As of May, 1989, less than one-third of the tree-planting goal had been reached.[268] Of about 5.6 million acres (2.3 million hectares) designated as eligible to be forested within the program, only 1.6 million acres (0.6 million hectares) have been enrolled.[269]

Dudek and LeBlanc proposed that the CRP be used to offset the added CO_2 emissions from oil- and coal-fired power plants planned to go on-line between 1987 and 1996. They assumed that the plants would operate at 65% capacity and would be 33% efficient.[270] Since different tree species would be planted in different regions of the country, and because of scientific uncertainty as to carbon fixation and sequestration rates, Dudek estimated the necessary acreage by using fixation rates ranging between five and fifteen tons of CO_2 per acre year, based on silver maples, the

---

[263] A "stewardship" contract includes follow-up work to ensure the survival of the planting, with the payment based on the survival rate. Reichmuth and Robison, supra note 256 at p. 3. Reichmuth and Robison provide no cite for this cost, which is inconsistent with the Forest Service data cited by Buchanan.

[264] Dudek, D. & A. LeBlanc, Offsetting New CO_2 Emissions: A Rational First Greenhouse Policy Step, Environmental Defense Fund, April, 2 1990, at p. 4.

[265] 16 U.S.C. §§ 3831 - 3836; Department of Agriculture regulations governing the Conservation Reserve Program are located at 7 CFR 704.1 et seq.

[266] Id. at pp. 6, 9.

[267] Id.

[268] Id.

[269] Id. at p. 9. The low planting rates may be due to low bid prices, farmers' reluctance to lose base acreage in U.S. crop support programs, and inadequate support from extension offices. EPA Report at p. VII-231.

[270] Id. at pp. 6-7.

least efficient tree reviewed.[271] This assumption led to the conclusion that 8.5 to 25.4 million acres (3.4 to 10.3 million hectares) could sequester the 126.8 million of annual CO_2 emissions (or 34.6 million tons of carbon) from the new coal- and oil-power plants planned to go on line through 1996.[272]

The cost of this tree planting was calculated using data from the CRP, which currently pays up to half the planting costs and $50 per acre rent, although Dudek and LeBlanc believe the rental fee must be increased to induce farmers to sign up for the program.[273] They assume planting costs of $150 per acre, annual rental costs of $100 per acre and fertilization costs of $25 per acre, all in 1985 dollars;[274] for 16.95 million acres (6.9 million hectares) the total costs are $3.5 billion to establish the trees plus $2 billion per year for rental in 1989 dollars.[275] The total cost of carbon fixation would be about $53 per ton of carbon for a 3% real discount rate (a 4.2% carrying charge over forty years), and $58 per ton for a 12% carrying charge.

h. Foresting Urban Areas

Developed urban areas create "heat islands" which in warm, mid- and low-latitude cities can increase temperature an average of 3 to 5 C, thereby adding to discomfort and increasing air conditioning loads.[276] Research indicates that by planting one shade tree on the west side of a house and two on the south side, the house's cooling energy needs can be reduced by 47% and peak load cooling reduced by 34.2%.[277] Thus, because it both absorbs carbon and reduces the need for electricity, a well placed urban tree is potentially fifteen times more valuable than a forest tree in mitigating global warming.[278] If the United States could be properly shaded, a savings of about

---

271 Id. at p. 6. These carbon-fixation rates (up to ten tons of carbon per hectare-year) require intensive plantation management (EPA Report, supra note 2 at p. VII-227) and would also result in only a few years of growth before harvesting. If the wood is burned, there would be little long-term sequestration.

272 Id.

273 Id. at p. 9.

274 Id. at p. 7. The costs do not include the cost of additional trees to offset the effect of nitrogen fertilizers, which cause forest soils to release methane, an important greenhouse gas.

275 Id. This calculation assumes 4% inflation from 1985 to 1989.

276 Akbari et al., The Impact of Summer Heat Islands on Residential Cooling Energy Consumption, presented at the 8th Miami International Conference on Alternate Energy Sources (December 14-16, 1987) [hereinafter cited as Impact]; and Taha, et al., "Residential Cooling Loads and the Urban Heat Island - - the Effects of Albedo," 23 Building and Environment 271-283 (1988).

277 Akbari et al., Strategies for Reducing Urban Islands: Savings, Conflicts and City's Role, presented at 1st National Conference on Energy Efficient Cooling, San Jose, CA, Oct. 21-22, 1987, [hereafter cited as "Strategies"].

278 Akbari et al., The Impact of Summer Heat Islands on Cooling Energy Consumption and CO_2 Emissions" presented at ACEEE Summer Study on Energy Efficient Buildings, Asilomar, CA, July 12, 1988, [hereafter cited as "ACEEE"]; EPA Report, supra note 2 at p. VII-235.

50 billion kWh might be realized.[279] Akbari, et al., estimate that planting and protecting these trees will cost up to 1.3 cents per pound of carbon conserved.[280]

Since heat-island tree planting is estimated to cost from 0.3 to 1 cent/kWh, compared to 7.5 to 10 cents/kWh for the electricity otherwise needed, the net cost of carbon emissions reduction is negative.[281] Thus, this sequestration is obtained at a net savings to society. Moreover, as atmospheric warming progresses, the savings from shade trees will increase in the ever-warmer summers: in warmer climates, the trees will have larger effects on emissions and on expenditures for fuel and capacity.[282] The Akbari proposal, if it works, should be pursued regardless of carbon-fixing requirements.

6. Conclusion

The external environmental cost of global warming should represent the cost of the marginal measures necessary to slow climate change to an acceptable rate. Neither the total requirement for reducing carbon buildup, nor the supply curve for mitigation measures, is well-understood. The most reliable estimates of sequestration costs are from temperate industrial countries, because they are more politically and socially stable then developing countries and have an established commercial forestry industry. More importantly, in the temperate zones the rate of sequestration is verifiable by direct observation of tree growth rates in new forests.

In contrast, in projects proposed for tropical countries, the sequestration rate would not be verifiable by direct measurement, since the rate is based upon estimated reductions in off-site deforestation. It may be that as more and better data are assembled on tropical social forestry, the impact of the programs will be more verifiable. However, until our verification ability improves and demonstrates that tropical social forestry sequesters carbon at identifiable rates, the cost of social forestry,

---

279 Akbari, et al., Recent Development in Heat Island Studies: Technical and Policy presented at Heat Island workshop, Berkeley, CA, (Feb. 23-24, 1989) at p. 5. Heat island effects can also be reduced by planting trees to shade streets with dark surfaces. The American Forestry Association estimates that there is room to plant one million trees along urban streets, although it might cost up to $200 to plant each urban street tree. N. Sampson, American Forestry Association, speaking at Global Warming Dialogue, Center for Clean Air Policy, Washington, DC, (December 8, 1989).

280 Impact, supra note 276.

281 Akbari and Rosenfeld, Conservation Supply Curves for Reducing CO_2 Emissions (Cost of CO_2 Emissions Reductions), Cal. En. Comm. Hearing (ER-90) (January 25, 1990).

282 Electric Power Research Institute, supra note 57. For instance, increased saturation and use of air conditioning equipment in New York State resulting from climate change could increase peak load requirements by 45%. Id. at p. 5-23. In Florida, the projected capacity does not increase caused by global warming will be 5% to 21% (Id. at pp. 4-16). The study indicates that the current cost advantages of coal will lead utility planners to meet this climate driven demand increase by building more coal-fired power plants (Id. at pp. 4-5, 4-20-22, 5-26) at a cost of $1500 per KW. (Id. at p. 4-3). However, the study fails to consider that increased coal burning will create a powerful feedback, accelerating climate change. This utility planning study is also flawed because it does not internalize any costs of CO_2 emissions, consider the possibility of using energy more efficiently, nor analyze the impact of expanding coal burning on the problem of global warming.

which is currently estimated to be relatively low (at least for small increments), should not be used as an estimate for marginal global-warming mitigation costs.

Given the potentially catastrophic consequences of global warming, any estimate of marginal control must be adopted conservatively; that is, any error should be in favor of higher costs to reflect the risk of currently unforeseen catastrophe. The higher the internalized cost, the stronger will be the signal directing decisions away from further global warming. Although the AES project is commendable, its unrepresentatively low costs, unverifiable sequestration rate, and failure to include risk of failure, all constrain its use as a sequestration model to establish a global warming externality value. The surrogate price should not include high intensity plantations, exotic genetic fencing, fertilization or other approaches discussed by Marland, since these measures raise the specter of creating new environmental problems and often high costs. Finally, the estimate should assume that all tree-planting with major advantages (e.g., lumber products) has been or will be pursued, and that marginal plantings will not yield other net benefits.

Of the American, region-specific estimates reviewed, the best appears to be the analysis of Buchanan, \$17.08 per ton of carbon for 3% financing or \$47.45 per ton for a 12% real discount rate, which is similar to Schilberg at \$54 per ton. Reichmuth and Robison's assumptions are speculative and undocumented, and their \$19-25 per ton results are unreviewable. Dudek's estimated sequestration rates are optimistically high, and the \$53-58 per ton values resulting from those estimates are correspondingly low, although the result is similar to those obtained by Buchanan (at a 12% real discount rate) and Schilberg. The Akbari figures for the cost of energy conservation through urban heat island forestry represent an attractive, low cost, conservation option, not a marginal carbon-sequestration cost.

Moreover, the Buchanan, Schilberg, and Dudek estimates are optimistic, since they use the cost of planting trees already being planted, not the cost of more expensive or less productive planting that might reasonably represent the marginal greenhouse-mitigation option. Chernick and Caverhill (1989) review a range of planting costs and productivities, and conclude that \$80-\$120 per ton is likely to represent the marginal cost of sequestration, although their calculation includes utility financing, at a rate 60 to 140% more than the lower discount rate assumptions used by Buchanan.

If conservation, tree-planting, fuel-switching (from coal to oil and gas, and from electricity to direct end uses) and low-cost renewables prove insufficient to balance the world carbon budget, the world will have to choose between higher-cost measures and the consequences of rapid warming.

7. Bibliography

Adams, et al., "Implications of Global Climate Change for Western Agriculture," 13(2) Western Journal of Agricultural Economics (1988), pp. 348-386.

Akbari, H. and A. Rosenfeld, Conservation Supply Curves for Reducing CO_2 Emission (Cost of CO_2 Emissions Reduction), Comments for a California Energy Commission Electricity Report Hearing (ER-90) Valuing Emission Reduction for Electricity Report, Sacramento, CA (January 25, 1990).

Akbari, et al., Strategies for Reducing Urban Islands: Savings, Conflicts and City's Rite, presented at 1st National Conference on Energy Efficient Cooling, San Jose, CA (Oct. 21-22, 1987).

Applied Energy Services, "Monitoring and Evaluation Plan For Carbon Flux CARE-Guatemala Agroforestry and Resource Conservation Project", undated.

_______, The Impact of Summer Heat Islands on Cooling Energy Consumption and CO_2 Emissions, presented at ACEEE Summer Study on Energy Efficiency in Buildings, Asilomar, CA (July 12, 1988).

_______, The Impact of Summer Heat Island on Residential Cooling Energy Consumption, presented at the 8th Miami International Conference on Alternate Energy Sources (December 14-16, 1987).

_______, Recent Development in Heat Island Studies: Technical and Policy presented at Heat Island Workshop, Berkeley, CA (Feb. 23-24, 1989).

Bernow, S. & D. Marron, Valuation of Environmental Externalities For Energy Planning and Operations: May 1990 Update, (May 18, 1990).

Botkin, D. and L. Simpson, The Distribution of Biomass in the North American Boreal Forest, in University of California at Santa Barbara, Environmental Studies Program.

______, Biomass of the North American Boreal Forest: A Step Toward Accurate Global Measures, University of California at Santa Barbara, Biological Sciences and Environmental Studies Program.

Brown, S., et al., "Biomass Estimation Methods for Tropical Forests with Applications to Forest Inventory Data," Forest Science 35:4, (December, 1989) pp. 881-902.

Brown, L., et al., State of the World 1988, Worldwatch Institute (published by W. W. Norton), 1988.

Buchanan, S., Cost of Mitigating Greenhouse Effect for Generic Coal, Oil-, and Gas-Fired Plants, draft January 24, 1989, unpublished, Bonneville Power Administration.

California Energy Commission, Energy Siting and Environmental Protection Division, "Valuing Emission Reductions for Electricity Report 90," Staff Issue Paper #3R, Docket #88-ER-8, (November 21, 1989).

California Energy Commission, 1988 Inventory of California Greenhouse Gas Emissions, draft report, May, 1990.

Calwell, C., "Valuing Reductions in Carbon Dioxide Emissions," NRDC/Sierra Club Written Testimony for the California Energy Commission Electricity Report 90, January 11, 1990.

Chernick, P. and E. Caverhill, The Valuation of Externalities from Energy Production, Delivery, and Use, Boston, MA: PLC, Incorporated, December, 1989.

Clawson, "Forests in the Long Sweep of American History," Science 20:1168-1174,1979.

Costa Rica National Forestry Service, 4 Boletin Forestal 1, March 1989.

Conservation Foundation/World Wildlife Fund, Proposal: The Forestry Fund: Endowment for Forest Protection, Management, and Reforestation in Costa Rica May, 1988.

Critical Mass Energy Bullentin, March, 1990.

de Baar, H. and M. Stoll, "Storage of Carbon Dioxide in the Oceans" in Okken, P., Swart, R. and S. Zwerver,(eds.), Climate and Energy, 1989.

Deumling, D., letter to Richard L. Ottinger, May 2, 1990.

Deumling, D., "Risks For Future Forestry," (unpublished paper) July, 1989 .

Dickinson, "The Climate System and Modelling of Future Climate" in Bolin et al, The Greenhouse Effect, Climate Change, and Ecosystems, 1986.

Dudek, D., A. LeBlanc, P. Miller, "CO_2 and SO_2: Consistent Policy Making in a Greenhouse," Environmental Defense Fund, January, 1990.

Electric Power Research Institute, Potential Impacts of Climate Change on Electric Utilities, January 1989.

Flavin and Piltz, Substanable Energy, RenewAmerica, Washington, DC, 1989.

Geller, H. & S. Nadel, "Energy Conservation: Potential vs. Achievement", ACEEE, paper prepared for NARUC Least Cost Utility Planning Conference, Charleston, SC, Sept. 11-13, 1989.

Gibbs and Hoffman, An Approach for Generating Climate Change Hypothetical Given Limitations in Current Climate Models in Shands and Hoffman (ed.), The Greenhouse Effect, Climate Change and United States Forests, 1987.

Goldemberg, et al., Energy for a Sustainable World, 1987.

Hansen, et al., Evidence for Future Warming: How Large and When, in Shands & Hoffman (ed.), The Greenhouse Effect, Climate Change and United States Forests, 1987.

Hardin, "The Tragedy of the Commons," 162 Science 1243-1248, 1968.

Hill, R., "The Impact of Energy on Environmental Development," paper presented at IVth Nobel Prizewinners Meeting: Man--Envionrment and Development--Towards A Global Approach, December 10-14, 1989.

Hoffman, J. and U.S. EPA, Responding to Global Change, University of Maryland School of Law, Baltimore, MD, November 17, 1989.

"How Fast Can Trees Migrate?," 243 Science 735-737, Feb. 10, 1989.

Jones, et al., "Evidence for Global Warming in the Past Decade," 332 Nature 790, 1988.

Koomey, J., Comparative Analysis of Monetary Estimates of External Costs Associated with Combustion of Fossil Fuel, Energy Analysis Program, Berkeley, CA, January 16, 1990.

_______, Comparative Analysis of Monetary Estimates of External Environmental Costs Associated with Combustion of Fossil Fuels, Energy Analysis Program, Applied Sciences Division, Lawrence Berkeley Laboratory, Berkeley, CA, April, 1990.

Krause, F., et al., Energy Policy in the Greenhouse: Volume One, International Project for Sustainable Energy Paths (IPSEP), El Cerreto, CA, September, 1989.

Krause, F. and J. Koomey, "Unit Costs of Carbon Savings From Urban Trees, Rural Trees, and Electricity Conservation: A Utility Perspective" Energy Analysis Program, Lawrence Berkeley Laboratory, Berkeley, CA, Feb 24, 1989

Lashof and Ahuja, "Relative Contributions of Greenhouse Gas Emissions to Global Warming," 344 Nature 529, April 5, 1990.

Leaf, A., "Potential Health Effects of Global Climatic and Environmental Changes," Vol. 321 No. 23 The New England Journal of Medicine 1577, Dec. 7, 1989.

Ledbetter, M. and M. Ross, "Supply Curves of Conserved Energy from Automobiles," paper prepared for Lawrence Berkeley Laboratory Applied Science Division, Berkeley, CA, March, 1990.

MacCracken and Luther, Projecting the Climate Effects of Increasing Carbon Dioxide, 1985.

Machado and Piltz, Reducing the Rate of Global Warming: The States' Role, RenewAmerica, Washington, DC, November, 1988.

Marland, The Prospect of Solving the CO_2 Problem Through Global Reforestation, U.S. DOE, DDE/NBB-0082 (1988).

Matthews, "Global Vegetation and Land Use: New High Resolution Data Base for Climate Studies," Journal of Climate and Applied Meteorology, pp. 474-487,1983.

McNeely, J. Economic and Biological Diversity: Developing and Using Economic Incentives to Conserve Biological Resources, Inter-Union for Conservation of Nature and National Resources, Gland, Switzerland, 1988.

Mintzer, I., "Weathering the Storms in a Warming World,",Public Power 46:6, Nov.-Dec. 1988.

National Academy of Sciences, Carbon Dioxide and Climate: A Scientific Assessment, 1979.

_____, Changing Climate, 1983.

_____, Current Issues in Atmospheric Change, 1987.

_____, Projecting the Climate Effects of Increasing Carbon Dioxide, 1985.

New York State Energy Office, Staff Report, Draft New York State Energy Plan, Vol. VI (May 1989).

Nixon, E. and C. Neme, An Efficient Approach to Reducing Acid Rain: The Environmental Benefits of Energy Conservation, Center for Clean Air Policy, May, 1989.

Olson, et al., Carbon in Live Vegetation of Major World Ecosystems, Report ORNL-5862, Oak Ridge National Laboratory, Oak Ridge, TN, 1983.

Oregon Energy Office, "SB576 Working Group: Biomass Subcommittee Draft Report", revised April, 27, 1990.

Plunkett, J. and P. Chernick, The Role of Revenue Losses in Evaluating Demand-Side Resources: An Economic Re-Appraisal, proceedings of the 1988 Summer Study on Energy Efficiency in Buildings, American Council for an Energy Efficient Economy, 1988.

Policy Options For Stabilizing Coastal Climate, Hearing before the Subcommittee on Public Works, United States Senate, 101st Congress, 1st Session, March 17, 1989. Reichmuth and Robison, Carbon Dioxide Offsets, unpublished report for Pacific Power and Light, March 2, 1989.

Rosenfeld, A., and R. Mowris, "Energy Efficiency: The Best Way to Save Money and Slow Global Warming," 18-3 Physics and Society, July, 1989 (in press).

_______, "Energy Efficiency: The Best Way to Save Money and Slow Global Warming," Testimony for Hearing on an Integrated National Energy Efficiency Strategy before Subcommittee on Energy and Power, Committee on Energy and Commerce, United States House of Representatives, June 23, 1989.

Rosenfeld, A., Lawrence Berkeley Laboratory, University of California at Berkeley, lecture at Electric Utility Reform Seminar, Pace University School of Law, White Plains, NY, September 24, 1989.

Sandenburg, et al., Rising CO_2, Climate Change and Forest Management: An Overview, in Shands & Hoffman, ed., The Greenhouse Effect, Climate Change and U.S. Forests, The Conservation Foundation, Washington, DC, 1987.

Schilberg, G., J. Nahigan, and W. Marcus, Valuing Reductions in Air Emissions and Incorporation into Electric Resource Planning: Theoretical and Quantitative Aspects (re: CEC Docket 88-ER-8), JBS Energy, Inc. for the Independent Power Producers, August 25, 1989

Schneider, "The Greenhouse Effect: Science and Policy," 243 Science 771, 10 February 1984.

Schneider and Chen, "Carbon Dioxide Warming and Coastline Flooding: Physical Factors and Climatic Impact," 5 Ann. Rev. Energy 107, 1980.

Sedjo, "Forests: A Tool to Moderate Global Warming?," Environment, Vol. 31, No. 1 p. 14, Jan./Feb. 1989.

Sedjo and Solomon, Climate & Forests in Rosenberg et al., (ed.) Greenhouse Warming: Abatement and Adaptation, Resources for the Future, Washington, DC, 1989.

Sen. Wirth (D-Colo) and Sen. Heinz (R-Pa), Project 88: Harnessing Market Forces to Protect Our Environment, December, 1988.

Shands, Forests -- The Momentum for a Greenhouse Effect: Physical, Economic and Political Limits to Curtailing the Magnitude of Global Warming, in Shands and Hoffman (ed.), Greenhouse Effect, Climate Change and U.S. Forests, Conservation Foundation, 1987.

Smit, B., L. Ludlow, and M. Brklacich, "Implications of a Global Climatic Warming for Agriculture: A Review and Appraisal," 17 J. Environ. Qual. 519, 1988.

Smith and Tirpak (eds.), The Potential Effects of Global Climate Change on the United States, Executive Summary, U.S. EPA, October, 1989.

Steinberg, M. and Cheng, H.C. A Systems Study for the Removal, Recovery, and Disposal of Carbon Dioxide from Fossil Fuel Power Plants in the U.S., BNL 35666, Brookhaven National Laboratory, Department of Applied Science, Process Sciences Division, NY, February, 1985.

Swart, R., R. Maas, and H. de Vries, "From Global to National Climate Policy," paper presented at the International Society of Ecological Economics Conference on the Ecological Economics of Sustainability: Making Local and Short-Term Goals Consistent with Global and Lon-Term goals, World Bank, Washington, DC, May 21-23, 1990.

Taha, et al., "Residential Cooling Loads and the Urban Heat Island -- the Effects of Albedo," 23 Building and Environment 271-283, 1988.

Tooker, C. & R. Buell, "LUZ SEGS Units IX and X Air Quality Benefits As Determined Under ER-7," California Energy Commission (written testimony), May 30, 1990.

Trexler, et al., Forestry As A Response to Global Warming: An Analysis of the Guatemala Agroforestry and Carbon Sequestration Project, World Resources Institute, June, 1989.

U.S. Dept. of Energy, The Potential of Renewable Energy: An Interlaboratory White Paper, DE90000322, SERI/TP-260-3674, March, 1990.

U. S. Environmental Protection Agency, Office of Policy, Planning and Evaluation, Policy Options for Stabilizing Global Change, Draft Report to Congress, February 1989).

Vine, E. and J. Harris, Evaluating Energy and Non-energy Impacts of Energy Conservation Programs: A Supply Curve Framework of Analysis, paper presented at 1989 Energy Conservation Program Evaluation Conference, Chicago, IL, August 23-25, 1989.

Zimmerman, M., Assessing the Costs of Climate Policies: The Uses and Limites of Models, The Alliance to Save Energy, April 10, 1990.

V. EXTERNALITY COSTS BY EMISSION

B. SULFUR DIOXIDE (EXCLUDING ACID RAIN EFFECTS)

V. EXTERNALITY COSTS BY EMISSION

B. SULFUR DIOXIDE (EXCLUDING ACID RAIN EFFECTS)

1. Introduction

Sulfur dioxide (SO_2) has many deleterious impacts on humans and their environment. It is the major cause of acid rain (discussed in Chapter V.D.), SO_2 and sulfates (SO_4), which are particulates produced by reactions of SO_2 in the atmosphere. They also cause human respiratory health problems, degrade visibility and cause vegetation and materials damage through deposition on plant and material surfaces. The deposition of SO_2 and sulfates change plant and animal habitats, which affects ecosystems and wildlife.[1]

The primary sources of SO_2 emissions are the combustion of sulfur-containing coal and oil. Other major sources of SO_2 emissions are copper, lead and zinc smelting, and emissions from the extraction, processing and transportation of coal, oil and natural gas. Electricity generation facilities are the largest source of SO_2 emissions.[2]

This chapter reviews various direct costing studies of the damage caused by SO_2 and sulfate deposition to human health, materials, crops and visibility. Since so much has been written about SO_2's contributions to acid rain, the costs of acid rain are discussed in Chapter V.D. of this report. Acid rain effects have been excluded from the estimates presented here, whenever possible.[3] The methodology, scope and results of each study are set forth, and where possible a cost per lb of SO_2 is extracted from the data. All dollar figures are stated in the year in which they were reported in the respective study, unless otherwise noted.[4]

2. Survey of Individual Studies

a. Human Health

Many air pollutants affect human health; generally, they affect respiratory function, causing symptoms such as impaired breathing, coughing, chest tightness, and reduced

---

[1] Northwest Power Planning Council, New Resources: Supply Curves and Environmental Effects, Staff Issue Paper, Portland, OR, February 1990.

[2] Wellburn, A., Air Pollution and Acid Rain, 1988.

[3] In some cases the damages associated with particulates emissions, also discussed in this report, include damages due to sulfates. This overlap must be considered when estimating a "total" externalities value for a particular supply option, as in Chapter VI.

[4] Costs are inflated to 1989$ using the Consumer Price Index, unless otherwise noted.

productivity and activity. Since many air pollutants can potentially affect respiratory functions, it is difficult to attribute specific effects to specific pollutants.

SO_2, itself, is not generally believed to be one of the major causes of air pollution-related health effects. Rather, ozone and particulates under 10 microns in diameter (PM10) are most often recognized as the major causes of air pollution-related health effects. Emissions of SO_2 contribute to ambient levels of PM10 by reacting in the atmosphere to form sulfates, which are believed to be a significant portion of PM10, in terms of both volume and toxicity to humans.[5]

Graham et. al., in a report for the National Acid Precipitation Assessment Program (NAPAP), discusses the health effects of ambient levels of SO_2. He reports that the National Ambient Air Quality Standards (NAAQS) for SO_2 provides "an adequate margin of safety against effects observed in . . . epidemiological studies" and that "qualitative information suggests that health risks would be small at concentrations at or below the current SO_2 standard."[6] Because this study reports a small health effect of SO_2 when emissions are within limits set to meet the NAAQS, New York Power Pool argues that the health effects of SO_2 should not be included in any calculations of the environmental externalities of SO_2 emissions.[7] However, the analytical framework of this report requires reporting all emissions effects even if they are within regulatory limits.

Graham also reports that SO_2, and especially acid aerosols and sulfates (both of which are partly derived from SO_2 emissions) are particularly suspect for negative health effects. The EPA is considering adopting a 1-hr SO_2 standard to protect susceptible individuals from acute SO_2 exposure. The health effects of sulfur-derived acid aerosols may lead the EPA to modify existing or issue new NAAQSs to protect sensitive populations (particularly asthmatic children) from the effects of acid aerosols.[8]

Hodas (1989)[9] provides a thorough discussion of the health effects of acid aerosols, but does not attempt to estimate the magnitude or costs to society of acid-aerosol-related health effects. He provides a detailed discussion of the formation and residence of acid aerosols in the atmosphere under different humidity conditions and the effects on the human respiratory tract and on human health. He concludes that

---

[5] The health effects of PM10 are discussed in Section V.E.

[6] Graham, J., L. Grant, J. Folinsbee, D. Gardner, R. Schlesinger, J. Overton, S. Lounsburry, T. McCurdy, V. Hasselblad, D. McKee, H. Richmond, B. Polkowsky, A. Marcus, Direct Health Effects of Air Pollutants Associated with Acidic Precursor Emissions, National Acid Precipitation Assessment Program (NAPAP), State-of-Science Technology Report 22, Vol. II, Secs. 4,5,6,and Appendix A, U.S.E.P.A.,NC, December, 1989.

[7] A. Telitsky, Chairperson, New York Power Pool Task Force on Environmental Externalities, in letter to David R. Wolcott, May 15, 1990.

[8] The "best scientific judgment" of the United States Environmental Protection Agency's Clean Air Scientific Advisory Committee and its Acid Aerosols Subcommittee is that the sulfur-derived acid particle/droplet portion of acid aerosols have the potential to cause health effects of public concern and that EPA should start the process of developing new or modifying existing NAAQSs that address these detrimental effects. United States Environmental Protection Agency, Clean Air Scientific Advisory Committee (U.S. E.P.A. CASAC), Acid Aerosol Subcommittee, minutes of public meeting, Washington, DC, June 14-15, 1988, and U.S. E.P.A. CASAC, transcript of public meeting, October 6, 1988.

[9] Hodas, D. The Health Effects of Acid Aerosols, unpublished paper prepared for LL.M. in Environmental Law, Pace University School of Law, 1989.

the effects on the human respiratory tract and on human health. He concludes that while the "scientificdata base" does not contain any one study that definitely establishes that acid aerosols endanger public health, important circumstantial and qualitative evidence representing the weight of the science evolving from animal toxicology, human clinical studies, and epidemiology points to potential health effects from acid aerosols at or near ambient levels.

Any attempt to value the health effects of SO_2 emissions must address the synergistic effects of SO_2 and acid aerosols, since it is nearly impossible to segregate precisely the health effects of SO_2 from the effects of sulfur-derived acid aerosols. With this uncertainty, the results of studies that report the health effects of SO_2 emissions from power plants are not zero are discussed.

The Bonneville Power Administration (BPA) commissioned ECO Northwest to study the direct effects of power plant studies on human health, materials, visibility, wildlife and ecosystems. Three of their were reviewed: a study of an existing coal-fired facility in Oregon (the Boardman plant), ECO (1983) [10]; a study of an existing gas and oil-fired facility in Washington state (the Frederickson plant in Pierce County, Washington), ECO (1984)[11]; and a study of a generic coal plant located in several hypothetical locations around Washington state, ECO (1987).[12] In each study, health effects were estimated by modeling the dispersion and reactions of pollutant emissions (including SO_2 and sulfates) in the atmosphere and relating the resulting ground-level concentration of pollutants to impacts on humans and their environment, including effects on human health.

The models used in the ECO studies for transmission of the pollutants through the atmosphere were not reviewed. The dose-response relationships used in ECO (1987) for SO_2 effects are linear. This may be an acceptable assumption over the range of ambient air qualities considered in this study, but would not hold in areas with different ambient air pollutant concentrations. ECO cites but does not review mortality estimates done by Lave and Seskin (1978), Lipfert (1984), and Mendelsohn and Orcutt (1979). ECO (1987) relies on the SO_2 and sulfate results from Mendelsohn and Orcutt, who give a risk of mortality for sulfates of 100×10^{-6} per microgram/m^3 of SO_4 per year and estimate the risk from SO_2 to be an order of magnitude lower. Variations in these assumptions could have a significant impact on the total mortality effects.

ECO uses different values for mortality and morbidity effects in its different studies. These values range from $1 million per life lost plus $75 per lost activity day in its 1984 study of the Frederickson plant, to $3 million per life lost and no additional

---

[10] ECO Northwest et al., Final Report: Economic Analysis of the Environmental Effects of the Coal-Fired Electric Generator at Boardman, Oregon, Report commissioned by Bonneville Power Administration, December 29, 1983 [hereafter cited as ECO (1983)].

[11] ECO Northwest et al., Economic Analysis of the Environmental Effects of a Combustion-Turbine Generating Station at Frederickson Industrial Park, Pierce County, Washington: Final Report, Report commissioned by Bonneville Power Administration, March 26, 1984 [hereafter cited to as ECO (1984)].

[12] ECO Northwest et al, Generic Coal Study: Quantification and Valuation of Environmental Impacts, Report commissioned by Bonneville Power Administration, January 31, 1987 [hereafter cited as ECO (1987)]. This report concentrates mostly on data from ECO (1987), since it is the most recent ECO study available.

morbidity in its 1987 Generic Coal Plant study. ECO (1987) cites several hedonic wage studies as the basis for its estimates of the value of health and reducing the risk of death (value of a life). ECO relies on a study by Violette and Chestnut (1983) that reviews other valuation studies to determine that its chosen value, \$30 for reduced risk of 1/100,000, or \$3,000,000per life, is reasonable. If we adjust these values of \$4 million (1989\$) per life, and \$400,000 (1989\$) for morbidity, as selected in Section III.F. of this report, the Generic Coal study implies an annual mortality cost of about \$82.8 million due to SO_2 emissions for a generic plant located near a highly populated area in Washington State.[13] Based on ECO (1987)'s estimated annual emissions of 24,040 tons/year, the mortality damage due to SO_2 is on the order of \$1.72/lb SO_2 (1989\$), including damages due to both SO_2 and sulfates.[14] See Table 1.

---

[13] The population within 187 km of the plant was assumed to be 3.7 million people.

[14] This is appropriate given that both pollutants are emitted from the stack as SO_2, some of which is then converted to sulfate. On the other hand, the sulfate costs may overlap with estimates discussed for particulates in Chapter V.E.

TABLE 1: DIRECT COSTS OF SO2 EMISSIONS
ECO NORTHWEST: GENERIC COAL STUDY, 1987
(All figures restated in 1989$)

	WEST SIDE, LARGE CITY				OUTSIDE TERRITORY, SMALL CITY			
RESPONSE	INCIDENTS (NUMBER)	UNIT VALUE (1989$)	DAMAGES DUE TO SO2 ($)	$/lb SO2	INCIDENTS (NUMBER)	UNIT VALUE (1989$)	DAMAGES DUE TO SO2 ($)	$/lb SO2
	[1]	[2]	[3]	[4]	[5]	[6]	[7]	[8]
MORTALITY	20.7	4,000,000	$82,800,000	$1.72	1.4	4,000,000	$5,720,000	$0.12
MORBIDITY	5.9	400,000	$2,360,000	$0.05	0.5	400,000	$181,640	$0.00
CROP LOSSES	0.0		0		0.0		0	
LIVESTOCK	5.6		$389	$0.00	5.3		$1,728	$0.00
TIMBER	0.0		0		0.0		0	
MATERIALS			$803,385	$0.017			$58,320	$0.001
ECOSYSTEMS	0.0		0		0.0		0	
VISIBILITY			NA				NA	
TOTAL			$85,963,774	$1.79			$5,961,688	$0.12

[1]: ECO Table 3-3A; Morbidity units are "200 short duration (average 3-day) illnesses."
[2], [6]: Unit Values. Blanks indicate ECO unit values were used, and inflated to 1989$.
[3]: [1]*[2]; Except for Material Damage (see ECO Table 3.1).
[4], [8]: ($ Damages due to SO2)/(48,080,000 lbs SO2/yr emissions).
[5]: ECO Table 3-3F.
[7]: [5]*[6]; Except for Material Damage (see ECO Table 3.1).

ECO (1983) and the other cases in ECO (1987) report lower costs than the high population density case of the generic study, primarily due to significantly lower population densities surrounding the facilities. Since the Northeast region of the U.S. has a population two to ten times larger than even the most populated region analyzed in ECO (1987), equivalent emissions would affect two to ten times more people for roughly two to ten times the direct cost,[15] assuming a linear relationship between the number of health impacts and population density. In fact, the health impacts may increase faster than the population density due to corresponding increases in ambient levels of pollution from automobiles and other sources. Based on the ECO (1987) study, the direct health effects of SO_2 pollution, including the effects of sulfates, are likely to be in the range of $1.72/lb SO_2 (reflecting the ECO (1987) results) to $17.20/ lb SO_2 (ten times the ECO (1987) estimate) for typical to high density areas.[16]

Krawiec (1980)[17] presents work done by Waddell (1974)[18], who estimates health effects of SO_2 from studies done by Lave and Seskin (1977)[19] on mortality and the EPA "CHESS" program on morbidity. Waddell estimates national human morbidity costs due to SO_2, particulates and sulfates to be $0.9 to $3.2 billion (1970$). Krawiec does not attempt to disaggregate the estimate into costs from each pollutant.

Krawiec uses health cost estimates that are based on epidemiologic studies that use regression analyses that correct for variables such as personal attributes, socioeconomic factors, demographics and climate. As reviewed in Krawiec, Lave and Seskin conducted a study of the health impacts of air pollution in several cities, including Chicago, Denver, Philadelphia, St. Louis, and Washington, D.C. The study's results, corrected for weather and day of the week, concluded that a decrease of 0.092 parts per million in mean concentration of sulfur dioxide is associated with 6.3 fewer deaths per day in Chicago.[20] This estimate relates 10.8% of the total mortality in Chicago to SO_2. An alternative estimate is provided by Lipfert (1990)[21] for a mean concentration of SO_2 in Chicago of 0.167 ppm. In Lipfert's study, 3.5% of the total mortality in Chicago is related to SO_2 alone, or roughly 1/3 of that reported by Lave and Seskin. As in many of the studies reviewed, no emissions figures were given, so we cannot estimate a cost per lb SO_2 emitted.

---

15 Assuming the same dose-response relationships.

16 This analysis, and all subsequent analyses of the ECO studies, is based largely on work begun in Chernick and Caverhill, The Valuation of Externalities From Energy Production, Delivery, and Use, PLC, Inc., Boston, Massachusetts, December 22, 1989.

17 Krawiec, F., Economic Measurement of Environmental Damages, Golden, Colorado, Solar Energy Research Institute, May 1980 [hereafter cited as Krawiec].

18 Waddell, T., The Economic Damages of Air Pollution, EPA.

19 Lave, L., and E. Seskin, Air Pollution and Human Health, Johns Hopkins Press, Baltimore, 1978.

20 Krawiec (1980) appears to have made a mistake reporting Lave and Seskin's figure as 63 deaths per day, rather than 6.3.

21 Lipfert, F., Correspondence to Richard L. Ottinger, Pace University School of Law, March 1990.

Mendelsohn (1979)[22] provides estimates of the damages caused by the uncontrolled emissions from a coal-fired utility plant near New Haven, Connecticut. New Haven is an area of high population density, but a large fraction of emissions from this site blow to sea on the prevailing wind. Mendelsohn reports incidence figures for mortality and three-month, and acute illnesses. For these effects we have used our standard values of $4 million per death and $400,000per longer-term illness to estimate the mortality costs. Adjusting Mendelsohn's dollar values (apparently 1979$) to 1989$, we find the mortality due to SO_2 and sulfates has a cost of $192.8million, while morbidity damages are valued at $456.5 million. In relation to Mendelsohn's reported annual emissions of 72,140 tons of SO_2, the health damage due to SO_2 is $1.34/lb for mortality and $3.16/lb for morbidity.[23] Power plants located farther west will have higher mortality and morbidity costs.

The studies reviewed that do supply estimates of damages from SO_2 emissions imply health effects ranging from $1.34/lb SO_2 to $17.20/lb SO_2.

b. Agriculture

Crop damage from SO_2 emissions includes acidification of soils, damage due to direct deposition on plant foliage, and materials soiling. These effects, apparently caused for the most part by acid rain deposition, generally result in negligibly reduced yields of particular crops. Several studies of SO_2 impacts are reviewed, most of which do not differentiate between acid rain effects and direct SO_2 and sulfate effects.

Page et al. (1980)[24] estimated the economic losses to the agricultural sector from airborne residuals in the Ohio River Basin Region (ORB). The ORB (referred to as the ORBES region in the study) includes Kentucky, and portions of Illinois, Indiana, Ohio, Pennsylvania and West Virginia. The study assumes a fixed growth rate of electrical capacity as well as compliance with state emission criteria. It projects monetary losses to agricultural producers from 1976 to 2000.

Their study is based on four assumptions: 1) that regional agricultural producers are price takers and that variations in individual farmer's production will not affect the price of produce; 2) that the price of crops rises with the rate of inflation; 3) that the present discounted value of cumulative producer surplus losses can be measured by the sum of the discounted losses from 1976-2000; and, 4) that the size of the regional agricultural sector will stay the same.

---

22 Mendelsohn, R., "An Economic Analysis of Air Pollution from Coal-Fired Power Plant," Journal of Environmental Economics and Management, 7:30-43, 1980 [hereafter cited as Mendelsohn].

23 Mendelsohn's estimates seem reasonable compared with estimates based on the data from ECO. However, Mendelsohn reports net negative health impacts (or benefits) from NO_x emissions, and no health impacts from particulates. The effects of NO_x and particulates seem implausible and, by association, cast doubt on Mendelsohn's SO_2 estimates.

24 Page, Arbogast, Fabian and Cieka, "Estimation of Economic Losses to the Agricultural Sector from Airborne Residuals in the Ohio River Basin Region," Journal of the Air Pollution Control Association, 32: No.2, February, 1982, p. 151.

With these assumptions the crop loss from sulfur dioxide in the ORBES region is calculated to be $20.9 million net present value for the period 1976-2000, assuming a discount rate of 10%. This represents 26% of total crop losses in the region or 64% of total crop losses associated with electric utility plants.

The estimates in the study for total crop damage may be slightly understated in that they reflect SO_2 effects on only corn, soybeans and wheat. The damage functions cannot be applied to other crops in the region since other crops have differing susceptibilities to sulfur deposition.

Page et al. appear to have assumed emissions levels for the two cases presented, but do not provide SO_2 emissions figures for the region. Without these figures the emissions and the implied value of crop damage/lb SO_2 cannot be approximated.

Krawiec (1980)[25] provides an extensive survey of air pollution costing studies that gives us some information about damage due to SO_2. The results are being reported here without prior examination of all the underlying documents. In those studies reviewed, crops are generally valued at their market price. This may understate their value, since crops may provide benefits such as soil retention and aesthetic value.

Krawiec cites a Stanford Research Institute (SRI) study by Waddell (1974) that estimates the total national economic loss to agricultural crops at $85.5 million (1964$) and to ornamental plants at $46 million. Damages due to SO_2 were estimated to be $3.3 million and $3.0 million (1964$) of the totals, respectively. Krawiec asserts that these figures understate the total damage to crops and ornamental plants because they do not consider costs associated with grower relocation, crop substitution, reduction in productivity and erosion.

As explained by Krawiec, the assumptions and methodology used in Waddell were based on a prior study at SRI conducted by Benedict, Miller and Smith (1973). In order to ensure national coverage in the survey by county, they selected counties in which the major air pollutants (oxidants, sulfur dioxide and fluorides) were likely to reach plant-damaging concentrations because of fuel consumption and large single-source emitters.

According to Krawiec, the national SRI figures are consistent with individual crop damage estimates for California (Middleton and Paulus 1956; Millican, 1971), Pennsylvania (Lacasse and Weidensoul 1970), New Jersey (Feliciano 1972; Dell 1973) and New England (Naegele, Feder and Brandt 1972). However, Krawiec points out that the state-specific estimates of losses of ornamentals generated by the SRI model are higher than those developed by the studies for the individual states.

Krawiec does not give national pollution emissions figures related to the SRI (or any other) study. A very rough estimate of the average cost of SO_2 damages can be found by comparing the cost estimates to national emissions figures.

In 1964, national SO_2 emissions were approximately 25 million tons. Based on the annual damage costs of $3.3 million calculated in the SRI study, the average damage costs to agricultural crops would be $0.13/ton SO_2 (1964$) or a very small cost/lb. For ornamental plants, the cost/lb is on the same order of magnitude. This is a very rough

[25] Krawiec, supra note 17.

calculation to illustrate the order of magnitude of national damages. Marginal damages in areas with higher SO_2 emissions and more valuable crops such as vegetables and fruits would be significantly greater.

Krawiec also presents work by Heintz, Hershaft and Horak (1976) on national air pollution damages to vegetation in 1973. The total damages due to all air pollutants estimated by Heintz et al. are $2.9 billion, with SO_2 (including that in acid rain) responsible for $10 million in damage to forests. The damages due to SO_2 and acid rain were not separated. According to Krawiec, new data on rural oxidant levels and the results of yield loss experiments are responsible for the differences between Heintz et al. and Waddell.

These figures capture only the physical effect of air pollution on the magnitude of outputs (e.g., agricultural production) and inputs (e.g., replacement plantings). Determination of price effects requires outside econometric models. Heintz et al. did not include the cost of developing resistant plant varieties because of the difficulty of assigning a dollar value to such an activity.

ECO (in its three aforementioned reports for BPA)[26] and the Charles River Association (CRA) (1984)[27] all assume that SO_2 causes no damage to crops or forests. This may be a reasonable assumption for areas where a certain plant-damaging threshold of ambient pollution has not been reached, such as in Washington state especially if acid rain effects are excluded.

Mendelsohn[28] also provides an estimate for vegetation damage due to SO_2 and sulfates. Damage to crops and ornamental plants in the New Haven, Connecticut region is $449,000(1979$), ($700,000,1989$), without accounting for changes in crop types or amounts. Thus, the vegetation damage due to SO_2 in the New Haven area, based on Mendelsohn's estimate of 72,140 tons/year SO_2 emissions, is $9.70/ton (1989$) or 0.5 cents/lb. Mendelsohn also does not separate the damages due to acid rain from other SO_2 damages.

In summary, the effect of SO_2 on crops appears to be significantly less than the effects on health. There are no current estimates of the marginal cost of SO_2 crop damage, except zero. The cost per pound of SO_2 emitted may be negligible if acid rain effects are excluded.

c. Materials

Sulfur oxides combine with oxidants and moisture to form sulfuric acid, which causes corrosion to metals, damage to electrical contacts, deterioration of paper, textiles, leather, finishes and coatings, and erosion of building stone strength. It

---

[26] ECO (1983), ECO (1984), ECO (1987), <u>supra</u> notes 10-12.

[27] Charles River Associates (CRA), <u>Benefits and costs of Externalities and Intangibles Associated with Southern California Edison's 1985 and 1986 Conservation and Load Management Programs,</u> CRA Report #792, May 15, 1984.

[28] Mendelsohn, <u>supra</u> note 22.

appears that this effect can occur on a micro level (on a surface such as a car or building) or generally as an acid fog or acid rain. We have not attempted to separate these effects in this chapter, if indeed they could be separated. Among the four major criteria pollutants--SO_2, NO_x, ozone and carbon monoxide--SO_2 causes by far the most material damage because of its effect on exposed metals.

Krawiec[29] reviews several studies on the effects of ambient SO_2 concentration on metal corrosion, including a study by Fink, Buttner and Boyd (1971) on the damage costs to galvanized steel. These authors used national shipment value data to compute average pollution costs and assumed that 80% of materials are located in polluted areas. They estimated the increased protection and maintenance costs incurred and the decrease in structure life due to acid rain corrosion. The total national corrosion cost from all air pollutants was on the order of $1.45 billion (1971$) or $7.10 per person per year. This estimate relates to damage to outdoor metalwork, chain link fencing, pole line hardware, galvanized wire and rope, steel storage tanks, bridges, streetlight fixtures, power transformers, and transmission towers.

According to Krawiec, Fink, Buttner and Boyd assert that 90% of the national economic burden imposed by air pollution corrosion is due to accelerated corrosion of zinc by SO_2. They projected the annual damage costs to metals from SO_2 for a variety of SO_2 concentration levels. Total damages from all air pollution were estimated to increase from the 1971 level of $1.45billion to $2.1 billion by 1980, if the pollution level increased by 55%. A 10% increase in the SO_2 level alone would result in an increase in annual loss of $0.3-1.73billion by 1980. Fink, Buttner and Boyd do not provide corresponding SO_2 emissions estimates.

As summarized by Krawiec, Waddell believes that the Fink, Buttner and Boyd study makes a systematic and reasonable estimate of the costs of corrosion to materials and the costs of related losses. However, Waddell identified two important weaknesses: 1) no attempt is made to relate material damage to the severity or type of air pollution and 2) the role of relative humidity in the corrosion and deterioration of materials is not considered. For these reasons, Waddell believes that the Fink, Buttner and Boyd estimates are probably understated for areas with high humidity and/or high ambient levels of pollution.

Keeping in mind these caveats, we can again derive an average materials damage cost for SO_2 per lb of emissions by comparing the Fink, et al. estimate of total costs due to SO_2 to an estimate of the national emissions of SO_2 in 1971, which were approximately 30 million tons. If the damage due to SO_2 is approximately 90% of the total cost of $1.45 billion (1971$), ($4.10 billion, 1989$), then this yields a national average estimate of $135/ton SO_2 (1971$) ($0.34/lb SO_2 1989$)) for corrosion damage. This is only a very rough estimate of average national damages, and does not represent the marginal cost in areas with high SO_2 emissions and high population and materials density.

---

29 Krawiec, supra note 17.

Krawiec also reviews Gillette and Upham (1973)[30], who used the same general approach but used a much more comprehensive assessment of the economic damages from SO_2 and relative humidity for 150 Standard Metropolitan Statistical Areas (SMSAs). Gillette and Upham assumed that materials are allocated according to human population distribution. The amount of metalwork at risk in the SMSAs was estimated from local data on population distribution, ambient sulfur dioxide levels, and average annual relative humidity.

Using damage functions for corrosion and paint deterioration, Gillette and Upham estimated for 1970 that SO_2 damage to metals and paints was approximately \$0.4 billion. They concluded that SO_2 effects on textiles, building materials, leather, paper and dyes are economically negligible because these materials are largely exposed only to indoor air and the service life of many of these materials is short.[31]

Gillette (1975) defined the ordinary use life of different materials as prescribed by the IRS, estimated the total stock of materials in use using the annual US Census of Manufacturing, allocated total materials geographically according to population density, and determined probable pollutant levels measured by the air monitoring work of the Environmental Protection Agency. Gillette argued that even though local estimates of damages based on single site data are likely to be questionable, aggregation of these estimates at the regional or national level would tend to average out the estimates made at the local or SMSA level. However, it is the latter estimates which are generally relevant for environmental costing.

Gillette assumed that most of the actual damage to materials from sulfur compounds results from the formation of sulfur acids, and, therefore, used the presence of SO_2 as the best proxy for the presence of the related sulfur compounds and derivatives.

The costs examined by Gillette were the increased expenditures for materials maintenance and from replacement and substitution resulting from sulfur damage. The damage function used by Gillette, Haynie and others for zinc or galvanized coatings exposed to ambient SO_2 incorporates coefficients for corrosion rate and for annual average relative humidity, and explained over 90% of the observed variation in the corrosion rate for zinc. Based on this model, the annual replacement costs incurred due to sulfur dioxide for galvanized products was estimated at \$6.85 per capita in 1972 dollars. Based on the 1972 national population of approximately 210 million, the total cost of SO_2 damage to galvanized products was \$1.44 billion. Relating that to total emissions of SO_2 in 1972 of approximately 30.3 million tons, Gillette estimates that the national average materials damage done by SO_2 is \$47/ton or \$0.024/lb SO_2 (1972\$). Inflating this figure to 1989\$ based on the national average growth in material wealth,[32] this cost would be \$0.12/lb SO_2.

According to Krawiec, Salmon's (1970) was the most comprehensive study of pollution damage to materials up to the time of Krawiec's 1980 review. Salmon

---

30 Gillette, "Sulfur Dioxide and Material Damage," Air Pollution Control Association Journal, December 1975, p. 1239.

31 The cultural and historical damage due to destruction of printed material is thus excluded.

32 From Statistical Abstract of the United States, 1989, Table 744.

analyzed all interactions of 53 economically important materials with pollutants and environmental parameters. The rate of economic loss ($/yr) was calculated as the product of the economic value of material exposed to air pollution ($/unit of material) and an interaction value (units lost/yr). The interaction value was calculated by estimating the difference between the rate of materials deterioration in a polluted environment and in a clean environment. Salmon estimated that $100 billion in added cleaning costs would be necessary to keep the materials in polluted areas as clean as they would be in an unpolluted environment. Salmon also estimated that deterioration of materials causes yearly damage losses of approximately $4 billion, ($19 billion, 1989$). Paint and zinc were most affected by soiling and deterioration, accounting for greater than half of the total losses in each category. Combining the damage estimate of $4 billion (1970$) to national SO_2 emissions in 1970 of 31 million tons, Salmon's figures indicate that the average national SO_2 damage to materials is $0.064/lb SO_2 ($0.22/lb, 1989$).

In its Generic Coal study, ECO (1987)[33] estimates emissions-related material damage by assuming that materials exposure is proportional to the exposure of the population as a whole, and by estimating an average, national, per capita material damage effect per unit of pollutant. ECO estimated that SO_2 accounts for 80% of the total materials damage due to air pollution. For the generic plant located in a populous area, the damage due to SO_2 was $744,000(1987$) for emissions of 24,040 tons SO_2 per year. ECO's figures imply that the average materials damage due to SO_2 was $0.016/lb SO_2 in this case ($0.017/lb, 1989$). As for some of the figures above, all of the underlying studies have not been reviewed to assess the validity of the assumptions or the transferability of the results to other areas. These studies give only a rough idea of the order of magnitude of the <u>average</u> materials damage, and do not help form an estimate of the marginal value of reducing SO_2 emissions.

CRA (1984)[34] discusses the wide range of air pollution damages to materials, but analyzes only three major categories: soiling, ozone damage to tires, and acid deposition. Of the three, SO_2 contributes only to acid deposition; CRA used a value of zero for material damages from SO_2 since the relationship between acid precipitation and damages to materials is not known with enough certainty to include acid rain effects in the study. This is a simplification, and not a studied estimate of the damage due to SO_2, since most other sources discussed above indicate that SO_2 causes significant damage to materials.

In summary, it is difficult, and perhaps inappropriate, to distinguish between the materials damage due to acid rain (caused by emissions of SO_2), and ambient SO_2 materials damage. Some estimates have been developed for the damage caused by SO_2 emissions in general, but they are difficult to apply to specific cases or plants because: 1) many are national averages that will understate the damage in highly populated regions, while overstating the damage in other regions; and, 2) some of the estimates were made ten to twenty years ago. In order to compare these figures with other estimates for damage due to SO_2, the basis of these estimates requires significantly more research into their differences and assumptions, and application to current ambient levels of pollution. The studies reviewed that have quantified materials-related damages from SO_2 emissions estimate costs of $1.017-$0.34/lb SO_2.

---

[33] ECO (1987), <u>Supra</u> note 12.

[34] <u>Id.</u>

d. Visibility

The Generic Coal study, ECO (1987), reviewed both hedonic property value studies and preference polling studies in estimating a value for visibility. ECO (1987) summarized a number of values from various studies that employed either the contingent valuation (CV), or the hedonic pricing (HP) valuation method or both. ECO chose an average value of $10 per lost km-year per person (1987$) for the study region, from a range of $1-$79 per lost km-year per person reported in the studies reviewed, and assumed a linear relationship across all visibility ranges.[35] The visibility effect (in lost km of visibility) for the generic plant in this particular study was simply stated as 0.1 km loss for the first 50 km from the plant and 0.01 km loss thereafter (out to 187 km). ECO (1987) estimates total visibility losses of $1.38 million. It does not attribute the visibility losses to particular pollutants, so an accurate estimate of the damage due to SO_2 is not possible.

Further, the estimation of total visibilityloss in ECO (1987) appears low compared to the results in ECO (1984).[36] Both studies assume roughly the same reduction in local visibilityeven though the SO_2 emissions from the generic plant in ECO (1987) are 38 times the emissions from the Frederickson plant in ECO (1984). Higher emissions should have a higher impact on local visibility.

ECO (1984) briefly outlines a more rigorous modeling effort for lost visibility for the Frederickson generation facility. This analysis modeled the visibility loss due to each pollutant emitted from the plant, and estimated visibility effects for various distances from the plant slightly lower but on the same order of magnitude as reported in ECO (1987). At $10 per lost km-year per person for visibility, ECO (1984) estimated annual losses due to SO_2 to be $142,350 for emissions of 630 tons, or $0.11/lb SO_2 (1982$). In 1989$, this estimate would be closer to $0.14/lb SO_2, excluding regional population growth.

CRA used a hedonic property value model to estimate the combined cost of degraded visibility and soiling. However, they attribute none of the visibility effects to SO_2. Figures from Mendelsohn provide a value for lost visibility of $0.02/lb SO_2, but Mendelsohn gives no basis for his visibility impact estimate.

---

[35] The major differences in the values reported by the reviewed studies reflect different visibility ranges in different regions of the country and in some cases different survey techniques.

[36] ECO (1984), <u>supra</u> note 11.

3. General Studies

Koomey (1990)[37] summarizes ten different estimates of environmental damages associated with fossil-fuel combustion, one of which is based on the direct costing studies of Shuman and Cavanagh (1982), EPRI (1987) and Hohmeyer (1988)[38], which will be briefly discussed here.

Hohmeyer (1988) estimates total health and environmental damages from fossil-fuel and nuclear electricity generation in West Germany. Hohmeyer provides emissions figures and relative damage weights for SO_2, NO_x, particulates and VOCs. The relative weights are apparently based on the relative acute toxicity of the pollutants to humans, and are not meant as definitive estimates of the relative importance of the total health and environmental effects of the air pollutants. The implied costs for each pollutant can be estimated from the information provided in Hohmeyer's study. Koomey reports Hohmeyer's marginal damage costs, based on the information in Hohmeyer's report, as \$0.23-\$1.24/lb SO_2 (1989\$), including damages due to sulfates.

Hohmeyer's damage cost estimates are low for several reasons. Several effects, including effects on wildlife, are omitted. In addition, Hohmeyer's estimates are based on values of human life and health of about \$500,000 and \$250,000, respectively, where an illness prevents ten years of employment. Adjusting Hohmeyer's implied damage costs to reflect values of human life and health of \$4,000,000 and \$400,000 would result in a value at least double, and possibly much higher for damages caused by SO_2.[39]

Three recent studies reviewed the ECO Northwest studies: 1) PLCI (December 1989),[40] 2) PGE (Draft, April, 1990)[41] report on Least Cost Planning Treatment of Externalities, and 3) Tellus Institute (1989)[42].

PGE provides a simple summary of the ECO results (in \$/lb SO_2, NO_x and particulates) without analysis of the underlying assumptions, noting that acid rain effects are excluded from the ECO results, and that the estimates drawn from ECO are understated estimates of the direct costs of emissions from coal-fired power plants.

---

[37] Koomey, J., Comparative Analysis of Monetary Estimates of External Environmental Costs Associated with Combustion of Fossil Fuels, Berkeley, CA., April 1990.

[38] Hohmeyer, O., Social Costs of Energy Consumption, Springer-Verlag, New York, 1988.

[39] Hohmeyer does not provide enough detail for us to ascertain his assumptions regarding the types of health effects and the risk of premature deaths caused by SO_2.

[40] Chernick, P. and E. Caverhill, The Valuation of Externalities from Energy Production, PLC, Inc., Boston, MA, December, 1989.

[41] Pacific Gas & Electric, Least Cost Planning Treatment of Externalities, Preliminary Draft, April 1990.

[42] Tellus Institute (formerly Energy Systems Research Group), The Role of Hydro-Quebec Power in a Least-Cost Energy Resource Plan for Vermont, E.S.R.G. #89-078, an analysis on behalf of the Vermont Department of Public Service for Docket #5330 before the Vermont Public Service Board, December 19, 1989.

From the Generic Coal study (ECO, 1987), PGE reports a cost range of \$193-\$2,790/ton SO_2 (excluding acid rain effects).

PLCI provides an analysis and discussion of the ECO Northwest Reports and estimates the direct damage costs implied in the data supplied in the reports. PLCI adjusts the results of the ECO reports to reflect consistent valuation assumptions about the values of life and health, and combines the results from the 1987 and 1984 studies to attempt to capture better the visibility externality of the generic coal plant. The PLCI methodology has been largely followed in this report.

Tellus Institute also provides a brief review of the direct costs implied in the ECO Northwest reports. It does not provide a derivation of its estimates. The damage costs estimated from ECO (1987) are 1,000 times higher than comparable estimates from PGE and PLCI, apparently due to a mistake in the interpretation of the emissions from the generic coal plant. Otherwise, the estimates presented by Tellus generally agree with PGE and PLCI before adjustments for the values of human life and health are made. Neither Tellus nor PGE notes that ECO uses different assumptions in its various studies.

Since the results of the ECO studies are discussed directly, the results of these studies for the individual pollutants will not be reviewed.

Cannon (1990)[43] provides an excellent survey of recent studies on the health costs of air pollution. Studies reviewed include: Hall (1989), Rowe et al. (1986) and Chestnut et al. (1987) for costs in California; Deluchi (1987) for national health costs; U.S. EPA and Krupnick et al. (1988) for the northeastern United States; Bonneville Power Authority (ECO, 1987) estimates of damage caused by a power plant; and Chestnut and Rowe (1987) for the Denver area. Cannon provides a brief but informative discussion of the studies' assumptions and results. In Chapter V.C. Hall (1989)[44] and a section of Krupnick and Kopp (1988)[45] are reviewed in more detail because these studies can be related to specific pollutant emissions.

4. Results

There is considerable uncertainty in estimating and valuing the damages due to SO_2. The studies reviewed generally look at only a part of the issue. A comprehensive amalgamation of these estimates is difficult. National average damage estimates, especially those from older reports, are certainly understated for many regions due to differences in affected population densities and ambient air concentrations of SO_2 and

---

[43] Cannon, J., The Health Costs of Air Pollution: A Survey of Studies Published 1984-1989, American Lung Association, 1990.

[44] Hall, J., Economic Assessment of the Health Benefits from Improvements in Air Quality in the South Coast Air Basin, Report to the South Coast Air Quality Management District, Contract No. 5685, California State University Fullerton Foundation, Fullerton, Calif., June 1989.

[45] Krupnick, A., and R. Kopp, The Health and Agricultural Benefits of Reductions in Ambient Ozone in the United States, Prepared for OTA Contract No. H3-6820.0, June 1988.

other pollutants with similar effects. The population density and ambient air pollution concentrations are critical for the following reasons: 1) the size of the affected population affects the total number of incidences of premature death and morbidity, which critically affects the cost per lb SO_2; 2) the amount of material exposed is often assumed to be proportional to the size of the exposed population; and, 3) visibilitycosts are calculated on a per capita basis, and then multiplied by the total population. Further, the population density is sometimes inversely proportional to other effects of SO_2 emissions. Land devoted to crops and wildlife (e.g. farming in the Midwest in rural areas, or the national parks) generally have low associated population densities. In these latter areas, although the health effects will be considerably lower than in heavily populated areas, there may be significant effects on wildlife and ecosystems. The damage figures reviewed do not include any value for effects on wildlife or ecosystems (beyond a qualitative description of the potential effects), or for effects on stone monuments or other culturally significant landmarks. Even when the dose-response relationships are well understood, these effects will be difficult to aggregate and value. In any case, these effects must still be estimated and included in the damages of SO_2 emissions.

Table 2 summarizes the reviewed estimates of SO_2 damages for each effect. Aggregation of these estimates provides a rough starting point of \$2.03/lb SO_2 to use in a direct cost analysis of the environmental impacts of SO_2-emitting sources. However, the costs resulting from SO_2 emissions on humans and their environment may be found to be significantly higher once all effects are properly taken into account.

TABLE 2: SUMMARY OF DAMAGES DUE TO SO2

EFFECT	ECO (1987) [1]	ECO (1984) [2]	MENDELSOHN (1979) [3]	KRAWIEC (1980) [4]	HOHMEYER (1988) [5]	STARTING POINT [6]
	<<<< COSTS PER LB SO2 >>>>					
HEALTH						
Mortality	1.72		1.34		NA	1.72
Morbidity	0.05		3.16		NA	0.05
Total						
MATERIALS						
Corrosion	0.017		0.01	0.12 0.22 0.34	NA	0.12
VEGETATION						
Crops	0	0	0.005	0.00	NA	0
VISIBILITY		0.14	0.02		NA	0.14
OTHER						
Ecosystems	NA	NA	NA	NA	NA	NA
Historical Monuments	NA	NA	NA	NA	NA	NA
TOTAL	$1.79	$0.14	$4.54	$0.34	$0.23-1.24	$2.03

Notes: See text for description and limitations of these estimates.

[1][2][3][4][5]: Figures have been restated in 1989 dollars.

[4]: The estimates listed for corrosion are from estimates of damage provided by Gillete and Upham (1973), Salmon (1970), and Fink et. al. (1971), and reviewed in Krawiec. The Total figure represents Fink, et al.'s corrosion estimate.

[6]: The starting point figures are for a "typical" location, which we define as similar to the western Washington site in the Generic Coal Study (ECO, 1987). Population densities and other parameters will vary with location. The uncertainties associated with these estimates in the original studies are large; the studies did not have estimates for some potentially important effects; and the existence and magnitude of some of the reported effects are still in considerable dispute. These estimates should be used with great caution, as they indicate only the magnitude of the damages.

5. Bibliography for Chapters V. B, C, and E

See XV. Appendix B, page 761.

V. EXTERNALITY COSTS BY EMISSION

C. NITROGEN OXIDES AND OZONE (EXCLUDING ACID RAIN EFFECTS)

V. EXTERNALITY COSTS BY EMISSION

C. NITROGEN OXIDES AND OZONE (EXCLUDING ACID RAIN EFFECTS)

1. Introduction

Oxides of nitrogen (NO_x) are particularly troublesome pollutants since they react in the atmosphere to form tropospheric ozone and smog, and precipitate out to form acid rain. They also contribute to the greenhouse effect by their conversion to nitrous oxide (N_2O),[1] by production of ozone, and by reducing the uptake of methane, a potent greenhouse gas, in aerobic temperate forest soils.[2] Recent work suggests that NO_x also promote the growth of cancer.[3]

This chapter assesses some of the environmental impacts attributed to NO_x and tropospheric ozone. NO_x emitted from electrical generation facilities forms ozone (O_3) in the atmosphere when it reacts with volatile organic compounds (VOCs) in the presence of sunlight. The effects of NO_x and ozone are separated, where possible, in evaluating the studies reviewed.

This chapter reviews the non-acid rain, non-global warming effects of NO_x emissions and ozone formation on six areas: human health, flora (specifically agriculture, commercial timber and ornamental plants), materials and property, fauna, visibilityand ecosystems. For each effect, a brief description of the pollutants' physical damages is provided, along with a brief review and analysis of the damages assessed in other costing studies. The discussion attempts to highlight how the damage impacts of NO_x and ozone pollution differ in urban and rural locales.

2. Background

a. NO_x

Nitrogen oxides consist of chemical compounds such as nitric oxide (NO) and nitrogen dioxide (NO_2). NO is the dominant NO_x species emitted by power plants, but due to the reactivity of NO, the dominant compound in the atmosphere is NO_2. Emissions of NO_x by weight are generally stated as NO_2 equivalent. NO_x is formed during hydrocarbon fuel combustion when nitrogen in the air combines with oxygen.

---

1 N_2O is an important greenhouse gas, even though it is present in minute amounts in the atmosphere, because it absorbs approximately 180 times as much infrared radiation as does CO_2, on a volumetric basis (Lashof and Ahuja, 1990). On the other hand, NO_x tends to destroy the greenhouse gases chlorofluorocarbons (CFCs) and methane, leading to the production of ozone.

2 Steudler, P., R. Bowden, J. Melillo, and J. Aber, "Influence of Nitrogen Fertilization on Methane Uptake in Temperate Forest Soils," Nature, Vol. 341, September 28, 1989.

3 Fackelmann, K., "Air Pollution Boosts Cancer Spread," Science News, Vol. 137, April 7, 1990.

NO_x, an oxidant or bleach, is a yellowish brown gas that contributes to the summer haze and smog over most urban areas.

NO_x is produced naturally by lightning and by the interaction of sunlight with biological reactions in the soil.[4] Natural NO_x sources account for about 10% of global NO_x emissions. Anthropogenic sources of NO_x include fossil fuel combustion by highway vehicles and other transportation, power plants, appliances, heating systems and industrial processes. Electric power plant emissions account for about 33% of all anthropogenic NO_x pollution. In urban centers, anthropogenic sources dominate NO_x formation. In rural settings, natural NO_x sources play a larger role in ambient NO_x concentrations.

NO_x is a primary precursor to the formation of tropospheric ozone, nitrate particulate matter, toxic nitrogen compounds such as peroxyacetyl nitrate (PAN), peroxprionyl nitrate (PPN), and nitric acid, which is a component of acid rain. This chapter excludes, where possible, the acid rain effects of NO_x emissions, and concentrates on the direct effects of NO_x and ozone.[5]

b. Tropospheric Ozone

Ozone is present in both the stratosphere and the troposphere.[6] Stratospheric ozone is necessary for life on earth, because it shields the sun's harmful ultraviolet radiation. In this section, we are concerned with tropospheric ozone, which is generally recognized as the primary element of urban smog and regional haze. Ozone is created by the reaction of NO_2 with atmospheric oxygen in the presence of sunlight; the presence of VOCs, aldehydes or carbon monoxide (CO) aids this process significantly by providing the free radicals necessary for conversion of NO, which is produced in the combustion process, to NO_2.[7]

Tropospheric or ambient ozone can cause severe damage to human health, vegetation, rubber and other materials. Very little is known about the effects of ozone on wildlife and ecosystems.

This chapter links ozone-related damages directly to NO_x emissions. Although the relationship between NO_x emissions and ozone formation is complicated by ambient VOC and NO_x levels, climate, and area topography, NO_x clearly plays a significant role, and as a first approximation we assume that ozone-related damages can be linked directly to regional NO_x emissions. In some cases, such as estimating the

---

[4] Mackenzie, J. and M. El-Ashry, Ill Winds: Airborne Pollution's Toll on Trees and Crops, World Resources Institute, September 1988, p. 35.

[5] The environmental damage costs caused by acid rain and particulates (including the contributions of NO_x to these effects) are discussed in Chapters V.D. and V.E. of this report.

[6] The troposphere and stratosphere are two layers of the atmosphere. Troposphere describes the atmosphere for the first 10 km in altitude; stratosphere refers to the portion that is 20-50 km in altitude. The tropopause is the layer in between the two.

[7] Wellburn, A., Air Pollution and Acid Rain, 1988. The peroxyl radical (HO_2) aids the conversion of NO to NO_2.

ozone-related health effects reported for the South Coast Air Basin by Hall[8], it is assumed here that NO_x and VOC emissions reductions are equally important for ozone reduction.

3. Environmental Damages Caused by NO_x and Ozone Pollution

NO_x and ozone affect humans and their environment in several ways. NO_x emissions from fossil-fueled mobile and stationary combustion engines react in the atmosphere to form ozone and acid aerosols which harm human health. Ozone is a significant contributor to ornamental plant and forests damage, and may be the largest contributor to pollution-related crop damage nationally. NO_x emissions cause regional haze and loss of visibility, which affect recreation. NO_x may cause other less well understood effects, such as ozone damage to wild flora and fauna and to livestock. This chapter's assessment of the damage caused by NO_x and ozone pollution begins with a brief description of human health effects.

a. Human Health Effects

i. Physical Effects of Ozone and NO_x on Human Health

Ozone is an extremely reactive gas that can have substantial short-term and long-term effects on human health. There is strong evidence to suggest that exposure to high ambient ozone concentrations over a short period of time can cause temporary ailments such as lung irritation, hyperactivity, minor eye irritation, inflammation of respiratory cells, coughing, reduction of lung function, and pain upon inhalation.[9]

Moderate exposure to ozone can lead to: 1) a reduction or loss of worker productivity; 2) an increase in health care costs; and, 3) discomfort, pain and suffering.

More seriously, when ambient or tropospheric ozone is inhaled over a continuous period of time, it attaches to lung tissue through chemical reactions and causes serious damage. 90% of inhaled ozone is never exhaled.[10] Some studies on the laboratory animals' lungs (which are generally good models for human lungs)[11] indicate that long-

---

[8] Hall, J., Economic Assessment of the Health Benefits from Improvements in Air Quality in the South Coast Air Basin, Report to the South Coast Air Quality Management District, Contract No. 5685, California State University Fullerton Foundation, Fullerton, Calif., June 1989, [hereafter cited as Hall].

[9] Office of Technology Assessment, Catching Our Breath: Next Steps for Reducing Urban Ozone, Congress of the United States, August 1989.

[10] Bromberg, P., Testimony before the House Subcommittee on Environmental Protection, Energy and Commerce Committee hearing on Health Effects of Air Pollution, Washington D.C., 1989.

[11] Phalen, R., Testimony before the Subcommittee on Environmental Protection, hearing on Health Effects of Air Pollution, Washington D.C., 1989.

term exposure to ambient ozone can cause structural lung damage which may lead to chronic lung disease, lung cancer, and increased susceptibility to respiratory infections such as bronchitis and pneumonia.[12] Worldwatch reports that in cities like Athens, Bombay and Beijing, days with severe air pollution have markedly higher death rates.[13]

People who are exposed to high ambient ozone levels common in many urban centers are the most vulnerable to these effects. Frequent strenuous activity outdoors increases the ozone dose of an individual. Children are especially susceptible since human lungs are not fully developed until adulthood, and children tend to play strenuously outdoors. Together, these factors may lead to more serious long-term health effects in individuals exposed to ozone as children.

b. Studies Assessing Human Health Damages

Long-term effects cannot be studied under controlled experimental conditions, but must be inferred from animal studies and epidemiology, and from anecdotal evidence from polluted regions of the country.

There are many studies which discuss the health effects of air pollution in general, such as those reviewed in the American Lung Association's report on the health costs of air pollution[14] (Cannon, 1990). It is often difficult to identify the cause of observed health effects such as coughing, eye irritation or aggravated bronchial distress. Even more difficult is attributing effects to specific air pollutants. However, ozone and NO_x clearly have effects on human health, and ozone has been the primary air pollutant of interest in many studies. Here we review studies which provide an idea of the costs of ozone damage to human health.

i. Mortality Costs of NO_x and Ozone Pollution

Given that exposure to ambient ozone poses severe threats to the respiratory system, such as susceptibility to lung cancer, structural tissue damage, and bacterial and viral infections, medical and circumstantial evidence indicates that human exposure to NO_x and ozone pollution may lead to premature death.[15] While the extreme ozone conditions that occur in cities give evidence that ozone can cause premature death in susceptible individuals, the effects of ozone in less extreme conditions is more difficult

---

[12] Godar, T., Testimony on behalf of the American Lung Association before the House Subcommittee on Environmental Protection, Energy and Commerce Committee hearing on Health Effects of Air Pollution, Washington D.C., 1989.

[13] French, H., "You Are What You Breathe," Worldwatch, May-June 1990.

[14] Cannon, J., The Health Costs of Air Pollution: A Survey of Studies Published 1984-1989, American Lung Association, 1990.

[15] Jacobson, B., "The Role of Air Pollution and Other Factors in Local Variations in General Mortality and Cancer Mortality," Archives of Environmental Health, Vol. 39, No. 4, August 1984, pp. 306-313.

to determine. NO_x and ozone exposure does not cause sudden death in healthy individuals. Rather, it contributes to the initiation of chronic respiratory problems, aggravates respiratory conditions in individuals with existing respiratory problems, and increases the susceptibility of the ill and elderly to life-threatening pneumonia and other respiratory infections.

ECO Northwest (ECO) prepared several reports for the Bonneville Power Administration (BPA) on the direct costs of air pollution emissions from power plants in the Northwest,[16] as discussed in Chapter V.B.2. These studies provide estimates of NO_x and ozone damages for several effects, and the level of NO_x emissions responsible for the ambient levels of NO_x and ozone causing the predicted effects. Since the plant's VOC emissions would be negligible (and are not even computed by ECO), all ozone effects are NO_x-related.

ECO estimates no mortality effects in locations with low population densities, such as in the 1983 report and in several cases in the 1987 report. This estimate may be appropriate for the areas reviewed if: 1) in the absence of significant ambient VOC concentration, negligible ozone will form from the plant's emissions or, 2) humans have a health effects tolerance below a threshold level of ozone. Even if these assumptions are valid for the study regions of the Northwest, they are not valid for areas with heavier population densities and much higher ambient pollution levels that occur more often.

The ECO (1987) report estimates the ozone-related mortality from a generic coal plant in a variety of locations around Washington state. In its highest population density case it estimates that the ozone caused by the NO_x emissions from the generic plant would cause 1.88 deaths per year over the life of the plant.[17] ECO found no evidence to suggest that NO_x has direct effects on mortality. At $4 million per life lost, the cost of ozone-related death would be $7.5 million (1989$) per year. ECO estimates that these effects are caused by NO_x emissions of 11,024tons/year. The mortality cost alone of the NO_x emissions from the Generic Coal Plant in the high population density location is thus $0.34/lb (1989$). This calculation is shown in Table 1, along with the results for the other effects of NO_x reported in this study. This estimate depends heavily on population density. For instance, in the Northeast, where the population densities affected by new power plants is between two and ten times higher than that

---

[16] ECO Northwest et al., Final Report: Economic Analysis of the Environmental Effects of the Coal-Fired Electric Generator at Boardman, Oregon, report commissioned by Bonneville Power Administration], December 29, 1983, [hereafter cited as ECO (1983)]; ECO Northwest et al., Economic Analysis of the Environmental Effects of a Combustion-Turbine Generating Station at Frederickson Industrial Park, Pierce County, Washington: Final Report, report commissioned by Bonneville Power Administration, March 26, 1984, [hereafter cited as ECO (1984)]; ECO Northwest, et al., Final Report: Description of Generic Generation Resources, Their Likely Significant Environmental Effects, and the Economic Value of Their Effects, Report commissioned by Bonneville Power Administration, March, 1986, [hereafter cited as ECO (1986)]; ECO Northwest et al., Generic Coal Study: Quantification and Valuation of Environmental Impacts, report commissioned by Bonneville Power Administration, January 31, 1987, [hereafter cited as ECO (1987)].

[17] Id., Table 2-5A. ECO provides a very sketchy basis for its dose-response functions for ozone mortality, but appears to have averaged the findings of Lipfert (1984) and Lave and Seskin (1978) and Mendelsohn and Orcutt (1979). ECO did not include mortality effects for persons under the age of eighteen.

on the west side of Washington state, the fatalities would be correspondingly greater.[18]

The ECO (1984) report provides a similar analysis for a plant located in Pierce County in Washington state, an area with the same population density as the high population density case in the 1987 report. However, in this report ECO attributes no mortality effects to either NO_x or ozone. It is assumed here that the mortality estimated in the latter study ECO (1987) is valid.

ii. Morbidity Costs of No_x and Ozone Pollution

While the mortality effects of NO_x and ozone are difficult to separate from other respiratory-related causes of death, there have been several estimates of morbidity damages; primarily ozone-related.

Recent studies of the South Coast Air Basin (SoCAB) region in California estimate that the health benefits of achieving the ambient federal and state ambient levels for ozone and PM10 (particulate matter under 10 microns in size) would be significant. Hall focused on ozone and PM10 as the primary pollutants causing health impacts in the SoCAB region, and estimated that the annual health benefits of achieving the federal ambient standards for ozone alone would be in the range of $1.1 to $5.4 billion, with a "best" estimate of $2.4 billion[19]. This estimate includes short-term health effects, but does not include any benefits related to the mitigation of the long-term chronic health effects or the reduced lung functioning potentially caused by ozone. Hall reports that attaining the California state standard for ozone would have slightly higher expected benefits at $2.6 billion.

South Coast Air Quality Management District (SCAQMD) finalized its strategy for attaining federal and state air pollution targets[20]. SCAQMD reports that emissions reductions required for SoCAB to meet the federal ozone standard by 2010 from a 1985 baseline are 836 T/day NO_x and 1,064 T/day of VOC, or about 693,500T/yr of ozone precursors.[21] If reductions of NO_x and VOC are equally important (on a weight basis) for ozone reduction, then the estimated average benefit of attaining the federal ozone standard in SoCAB is $2.4 billion per year divided by 693,500T/yr, or $3,460/T ($1.73/lb) of ozone precursor. The benefit of reducing ambient ozone levels immediately will be higher than the average benefit of reaching the standard. The emissions reductions required to meet the California state ozone standard are higher than those attainable with Tier III control measures, and are not provided in the SCAQMD report.

---

[18] Assuming the same dose-response relationship.

[19] Hall, supra note 8, Table 7.2-23.

[20] South Coast Air Quality Management District, Air Quality Management Plan: South Coast Air Basin, Southern California Association of Governments, March 1989.

[21] Emissions reductions reflect adoption of Tier III measures OF SCAQMD which will bring California into compliance with the federal ozone standard (SCAB, 1989, Tables 3.2 and 4.14). The term reactive organic gases (ROGs) is commonly used in California and is equivalent to volatile organic compounds (VOCs).

TABLE 1: DIRECT COSTS OF NOx EMISSIONS
ECO NORTHWEST: GENERIC COAL STUDY, 1987
(All figures restated in 1989$)

RESPONSE	WEST SIDE, LARGE CITY				OUTSIDE TERRITORY, SMALL CITY			
	INCIDENTS (NUMBER)	UNIT VALUE (1989$)	DAMAGES DUE TO NOx ($)	$/lb NOx	INCIDENTS (NUMBER)	UNIT VALUE (1989$)	DAMAGES DUE TO NOx ($)	$/lb NOx
	[1]	[2]	[3]	[4]	[5]	[6]	[7]	[8]
MORTALITY	1.9	4,000,000	$7,520,000	$0.34	0.09	4,000,000	$360,000	$0.016
MORBIDITY	0.0	400,000	$0		0.00	400,000	$0	$0
CROP LOSSES	NA		$141,331	$0.01	NA		$43,906	$0.002
LIVESTOCK	3.3		$229	$0.00	1.60		$517	$0.000
TIMBER	NA		$5,625	$0.00	NA		$129	$0.000
MATERIALS	NA		$199,229	$0.01	NA		$12,960	$0.001
ECOSYSTEMS	0.0		$0		0.00		$0	$0
VISIBILITY	NA		$1,488,116	$0.07	NA		$73,821	$0.003
TOTAL			$9,354,529	$0.42			$491,334	$0.022

[1]: ECO Table 3-3A; Morbidity units are "200 short duration (average 3-day) illnesses."
[2], [6]: Unit Values. Blanks indicate ECO unit values were used, and inflated to 1989$.
[3]: [1]*[2] for Mortality and Morbidity; Others are taken from ECO Tables 3-1, 3-3A, and 3-3f.
[4], [8]: ($ Damages due to NOx)/(22,048,000 lbs NOx/yr emissions).
[5]: ECO Table 3-3F.
[7]: [5]*[6]; Except for Material Damage (see ECO Table 3.1).

Harrison and Nichols of National Economic Research Associates[22] provide a summary and critique of the Hall study. Harrison and Nichols conclude that Hall's estimates are significantly overstated and that the uncertainty associated with the figures presented by Hall is understated. Harrison and Nichols argue that the work on which the Hall study is based "has been given little weight by the U.S. EPA and its advisors."[23] Based on a study done by Krupnick and Kopp,[24] Harrison and Nichols estimate that the annual health benefits to SoCAB of achieving the federal ambient ozone standard would be in the range from $0.045 to $1.7 billion, with a "mid-range" estimate of $0.37 billion. Using SCAQMD's required emissions reductions of ozone precursors, Harrison and Nichols' benefit estimate suggests a benefit of $602/ton, or $0.30/lb of ozone precursor.

Hall and Krupnick and Kopp review essentially the same willingness-to-pay (WTP) studies to determine values for lost or restricted activity days. The values chosen by Hall and by Krupnick and Kopp are based on these studies and are slightly different. The values used by Hall were slightly higher. Hall, Harrison and Nichols, and Krupnick and Kopp provide discussions of the studies on which they base their estimates and provide a rationale for their conclusions.

The ECO (1987) report does not estimate morbidity damages due to NO_x directly, and it estimates that ozone has no morbidity effects.[25] Although more densely populated areas have adverse health effects associated with ambient ozone levels, it does not provide useable information for estimating morbidity effects. It only provides a qualitative discussion of the influence of ambient levels of a pollutant such as ozone on the marginal direct effects and costs of that pollutant. It seems implausible that ECO reports ozone-related deaths without ozone-related illness, especially since ozone does not cause sudden death but rather aggravates other conditions.

The ECO (1983) and (1984) and other ECO studies also assume no health damages due to NO_x and ozone.[26] Berrett and Weddell[27] assume no health damages due to NO_x emissions. However, the state of knowledge on the health effects of ozone has grown considerably in the last twenty years, so that older studies must be used very carefully, if at all.

---

[22] Harrison, D., and A. Nichols, <u>Benefits of the 1989 Air Quality Management Plan for the South Coast Air Basin: A Reassessment,</u> Prepared for California Council for Environmental and Economic Balance, National Economic Research Associates, Inc., Cambridge, Mass., February 1990.

[23] <u>Id</u>., p. E-3

[24] Krupnick, A., and R. Kopp, <u>The Health and Agricultural Benefits of Reductions in Ambient Ozone in the United States,</u> Prepared for OTA Contract No. H3-6820.0, June 1988.

[25] ECO (1987), <u>supra</u> note 16, Table 2-5.

[26] ECO (1983) and ECO (1984), <u>supra</u> note 16.

[27] Berrett, L. and T. Weddell, <u>Costs of Air Pollution Damage: A Status Report,</u> U.S.E.P.A., National Environmental Research Center, Research Triangle Park, North Carolina, February 1973, p. 59.

4. Flora Damage

NO_x and ozone cause damage to agricultural crops, commercial timber and natural forests, ornamental plants, and other natural flora. The studies reviewed here primarily focus on economic damages to crops, commercial timber and ornamental plants. A brief description of the other potentially significant damages, such as aesthetic damage and loss of habitat will be provided in this section. Unless otherwise noted, the cost figures presented in this section represent the economic cost of the reduced crop yields only. The figures do not account for other market reactions such as price impacts, crop substitution, use of growth stimulants, or farmer relocation.

a. Physical Effects of NO_x and Ozone Pollution on Flora

Damage to vegetation from ozone pollution may include leaf necrosis or injury, reductions in plant growth and vigor, reduction in plant yield, and increased susceptibility to biotic and abiotic stresses.[28] Factors such as light, plant variety, other stresses (e.g., acid rain), pollutant concentration, and amount of rain or irrigation may increase the level of the pollutant absorbed by a plant and therefore effect the amount of damage. These factors must be considered when assessing the level of damage or crop loss.

b. Studies Assessing Flora Damage Due to NO_x and Ozone

The ECO (1987)[29] report attributes all observed crop damage to ozone. It looks at approximately thirty crop varieties, including grain, fruit, vegetable and seed crops and estimates that the annual crop losses due to ozone are highest in its highest population density case because of the value of vegetables, fruits and grasses that are grown in this area. Based on ECO (1987)'s estimated damages of $141,000 (1987$), NO_x emissions of 11,024 tons/year, the crop damages due to ozone are approximately are approximately $12.80/ton (1987$) or $14/ton (1989$) in the high density case. The other cases reviewed in that report have lower crop losses, based on lower ambient pollution and different resident crops, which are largely wheat and barley (Table 1).

In the ECO (1983) report,[30] the annual ozone-related damages to several crops surrounding the Boardman power plant were estimated to be $7,130/yr (1982$), based on emissions of 6,000 tons of NO_x per year. These damages are ozone-related and not direct NO_x effects. However, if we relate these damages to NO_x emissions, these costs translate into a cost of $1.19/ton NO_x (1982$) or $1.51/ton NO_x (1989$). In ECO

---

[28] Energy and Resource Consultants, Inc., The Benefits of Air Pollution Control in California, Prepared for the California Air Resources Board, December, 1986, pp. 2-28., [hereafter cited as Benefits].

[29] ECO (1987), supra note 16.

[30] ECO (1983), supra note 16.

(1984)[31] the ozone-related damages to crops surrounding that plant for both cases (natural gas and oil-fired) were on the order of $30/yr (1982$), which translates into about $0.10/ton NO_x (1989$). There is considerable disparity in ECO's various estimates of NO_x and ozone-related damages, which related to the value of affected crops.

5. Material and Property Damage

a. Physical Effects of NO_x and Ozone Pollution on Materials

Materials damaged by NO_x and ozone include rubber products, dyes and paints,[32] textile fabrics, plastics and electrical components. NO_x damages outdoor art works, monuments, and historic structures by inducing corrosion, fading, soiling, and spalling (small fragmentary surface and corner cracks).

Ozone weakens, soils and fades textiles.[33] Exposure to ambient ozone concentrations causes the dye molecules in textiles to be converted through oxidation to a less deeply colored molecule. Dyes in cotton, rayon and nylon fibers are particularly susceptible to ozone damage, while dyes in fibers such as modacrylic, polyester, nylon 66 and acrylic are not.

Ozone is also the leading hazard to elastomers,[34] which include natural or synthetic rubber substances such as natural rubber and neoprene. Natural rubber has a low resistance to ozone which causes it to crack during ozone exposure. Highly unsaturated elastomers such as neoprene, polybutadiene, nitrile and polyisoprene are more subject to ozone damage than are saturated elastomers. Materials such as metal or steel, cement, glass, graphite, stone and brick appear to be resistant to damage from exposure to ozone.

b. Damage Costs

i. Cost Estimation

Damage costs to materials and property can be estimated using a combination of several different measures: 1) material replacement costs; 2) the cost of periodic repainting or cleaning; 3) the loss of consumer perceived value of the material; or 4) the cost of developing ozone and NO_x resistant materials, such as fade-resistent dyes.

---

[31] ECO (1984), supra note 16.

[32] NO_x is the primary cause of damages to exterior paints and dyes. National Academy of Sciences, "Effects of Photochemical Oxidants on Materials," Ozone and Other Photochemical Oxidants, Washington, D.C., Chapter 13, p. 653, [hereafter cited as Oxidants].

[33] Benefits, supra note 28, pp. 2-34.

[34] Oxidants, supra note 32 at p. 665.

Calculation of losses to materials caused by NO_x and ozone pollution must exclude effects that would otherwise have occurred, such as natural weathering of materials from environmental factors such as temperature, sunlight, humidity, salt, mildew, and wear. On the other hand, the acceleration of natural degradation of materials by the presence of NO_x and ozone must be accounted for in an assessment of direct costs of damage due to NO_x and ozone.

ii. Studies Assessing Material Damage

Table 3-1 of the ECO (1987) report[35] assesses the annual materials damage due to "Nitrogen Compounds" as $184,471(1987$) for the highest population density case. ECO admits that its materials damages estimates are rough because they are based on the national average per capita material damage estimated using figures by Waddell[36] and assume that material damage due to NO_x is approximately 20% of the total damage (with SO_2 and particulate damage making up the remainder). Based on this estimate, NO_x-related damages are on the order of $19/ton NO_x in 1989$. (See Table 1).

The ECO (1983) report[37] estimates an almost negligible materials loss (Table 2). This low estimate is based on the low population density surrounding the Boardman power plant and the direct relationship ECO assumes between materials damage and population density. The ECO (1984)[38] study estimates material damage by a method similar to those used in the ECO 1987 report, but reports significantly lower damages (compare Tables 1 and 2). The reason for the difference in these estimates is not obvious. For the purposes of this report, since the population densities of the two plants are roughly comparable, the later study, ECO (1987) is used, providing the best estimate for material damages at $19/ton NO_x.

Another study which assessed the material damage caused by NO_x and ozone is a 1970 report issued by the Midwest Research Institute (MRI), which is reviewed in a National Academy of Sciences publication.[39] MRI assessed economic effects of oxidant pollution on materials such as paint, elastomers, textile fibers, dyes and other materials. The study concluded that the value of the exposed materials was the product of four multipliers: The annual production of the material, the average economic life of the material, the fraction of the material exposed to oxidant pollution and the labor cost of installing the material. After defining the value of the materials exposed to air pollution, the MRI study assessed the damage costs as a product of the material value and the percentage reduction in the economic life per year of exposure.

---

[35] ECO (1987), supra note 16.

[36] Waddell, T., The Economic Damages of Air Pollution, EPA, 1974.

[37] ECO (1983), supra note 16.

[38] ECO (1984), supra note 16.

[39] Oxidants, supra note 34, p. 665.

The MRI study used research prepared by Spence and Haynie[40] to conclude that the damage costs to exterior paints such as automotive refinishing, household paints, coil coating and industrial maintenance paints, caused by all air pollution, totalled $225 million (1970$) in 1968. The material value does not account for the value of exposed paint in rural areas and therefore understated the total damage to paint caused by oxidant pollution.

The 1968 national NO_x and VOC emissions were approximately nineteen million tons and thirty million tons, respectively, or forty-nine million tons of ozone precursors. Assuming that NO_x and VOCs contribute equally to ozone formation, and that ozone is the predominant pollutant responsible for damages to paints, then the average cost of ozone-related damage to paints is on the order of $4.60/ton ozone precursor (1970$) or roughly $23/ton ozone precursor (1989$). The marginal damages to paint materials in areas with high ambient ozone levels and high population and materials density could be significantly higher.

The total damage cost figure represents the 1968 manufacturer's cost, which may understate the actual damage costs inflicted on exterior paint because it does not include the damages suffered by consumers. Spence and Haynie estimated that the loss at the consumer level, i.e.,the cost of the paint applied to surfaces, including labor, was three times the manufacturers' cost. Thus, the damage cost to exterior paint for manufacturers and consumers would be closer to $70/ton ozone precursor (1989$).

The National Academy of Sciences' report also assessed the economic damage to elastomers caused by ozone, based on a study conducted by Mueller and Stickney in 1970,[41] which concluded that the total retail cost of ozone damage to elastomers in 1969 was $596 million. This figure included retail costs of $257 million for special formulations and $339 million for early replacements.[42] Special formulation costs represented the cost to the manufacturer of avoiding ozone damage to rubber products by introducing ozone resistant chemicals such as polymers and antiozonants and changes in rubber production techniques such as paper wrapping, protective finishes, compound development, and waxing. Mueller and Stickney assessed the special formulation costs as $34.1 million for antiozonants, $5 million for waxing, $20.6 million for special polymers, and $26 million for the combination of protective finishes, paper wrapping, and compound development. Early replacement costs included labor costs for replacement and replacement costs for entire assemblies and failed parts.

Mueller and Stickney predicted future ozone damage to rubber products by approximating the percentage increase in rubber production over a fixed period of time and then multiplying that number by $596 million or the total retail damage cost

---

[40] Spence, J. and F. Haynie, Paint Technology and Air Pollution: Survey and Economic Assessment, EPA-AP-103, Research Triangle Park, N.C., U.S.E.P.A., 1972.

[41] Mueller, W., and P. Stickney, Final Report on a Survey and Economic Assessment of the Effects of Air Pollution on Elastomers, National Air Pollution Control Association, Contract CPA-22-69-146, Battelle Memorial Institute, Columbus, Ohio, 1970.

[42] The cost to the manufacturer for special formulations was $85.7 million in 1969. The retail costs were derived by multiplying the manufacturer's costs by a labor factor of 3.0. The manufacturer's cost for early replacements was $225.7 million in 1969. The retail costs were calculated by multiplying the manufacturer's costs by a labor factor of 1.5. This means that the cost to the manufacturer for ozone damage to elastomers does not include the cost of labor. For example, the manufacturer's cost for early replacement does not include the labor cost for actual replacement.

in 1969. For example, based on then expected growth of rubber production of 25% over 1968 levels, the study concluded that in 1975 the cost of ozone damage to elastomers would be $750 million (1969$). Using 1968 national NO_x and VOC combined emissions of forty-nine million tons of ozone precursors, the ozone damage to rubber products was on the order of $15.30/ton of ozone precursor (1969$) or roughly $77/ton (1989$). The marginal ozone-related damage to rubber in areas with high ambient ozone levels and high population and materials density could be significantly higher.

Ozone does not generally cause damage to historical monuments. However, NO_x emissions contribute to such damage through the formation of acid rain and nitrates. The damage caused by nitrate particulates is discussed in Chapter V.D. and the damage caused by acid rain is discussed in Chapter V.B.

6. Visibility Damage

The ECO 1987[43] report uses an admittedly simplistic method for estimating the visibility lost due to the pollutants from its generic coal plant, as discussed in the visibility section for SO_2 damages, Chapter V.B. A more rigorous method is employed by ECO in its 1984 study. ECO 1984 estimates that the value of annual visibility losses due to NO_x emissions from the Frederickson plant under the oil-fired scenario is about $115,000(1982$). Based on NO_x emissions of 440 tons/year, the cost of the visibility loss due to the Frederickson plant is $0.13/lb NO_x (1982$), or about $0.17/lb in 1989$ (Table 2). These estimates are based on a value for visibility of $10/person km year (1982$) estimated by ECO after a survey of willingness-to-pay (WPT) and contingent valuation (CV) studies. The natural gas-fired case has slightly fewer (on the order of 15% fewer) visibility effects than does the oil-fired case.

7. Ecosystems

ECO (1987) provides a discussion of the difficulties involved in the valuation of ecosystems and wildlife and places a value only on the availability of game animals for human recreation. Ecosystem and wildlife valuations are potentially very important to the analysis of the effects of NO_x and ozone on ecosystems and wildlife, and must be estimated in future valuation efforts for the results to be meaningful. No studies attempted to relate air pollution damages to wildlife to ambient ozone or NO_x levels.

8. Results

Chapter V.B., pertaining to SO_2 damages, provides a discussion of the uncertainties inherent in all of the estimates presented in this report regarding dose-response relationships, population density and effects not valued. These considerable uncertainties apply to the estimates presented in this section.

---

43 ECO (1987), supra note 16.

TABLE 2: DIRECT COSTS OF NOx EMISSIONS

ECO NORTHWEST: BOARDMAN PLANT (1983), AND FREDERICKSON PLANT (1984)

(All figures restated in 1989$)

RESPONSE	BOARDMAN COAL PLANT, 1983				FREDERICKSON PLANT, 1984 OIL-FIRED CASE			
	INCIDENTS (NUMBER)	UNIT VALUE (1989$)	DAMAGES DUE TO NOx ($)	$/lb NOx	INCIDENTS (NUMBER)	UNIT VALUE (1989$)	DAMAGES DUE TO NOx ($)	$/lb NOx
	[1]	[2]	[3]	[4]	[5]	[6]	[7]	[8]
MORTALITY	0.0	4,000,000	$0	$0	0	4,000,000	$0	$0.000
MORBIDITY	0.0	400,000	$0	$0	0.01	400,000	$4,000	$0.005
CROP LOSSES			$9,055	$0.0008			$39	$0.000
LIVESTOCK			NA				NA	
TIMBER			NA				NA	
MATERIALS			$89	$0.0000			$91	$0.000
ECOSYSTEMS			$445	$0.0000			$140	$0.000
VISIBILITY			$2,604	$0.0002			$145,631	$0.165
TOTAL			$12,192	$0.0010			$149,901	$0.170

[1]: ECO (1983) Table III-6; Morbidity units are "200 short duration (average 3-day) illnesses."

[2], [6]: Unit Values. Blanks indicate ECO unit values were used, and inflated to 1989$.

[3]: [1]*[2] for Mortality and Morbidity; Others are taken from ECO (1983) Table III-8 (AND INFLATED TO 1989$).

[4]: [3]/(12,000,000 lbs NOx/yr emissions).

[5]: ECO (1984) OIL-FIRED CASE; Table III-5. GAS-FIRED CASE has similar (lower by about 15%) results.

[7]: [5]*[6] for Mortality and Morbidity; Others are taken from ECO (1984) Table III-7 (and inflated to 1989$).

[8]: [7]/(880,000 lbs NOx/yr emissions).

Table 3 summarizes the reviewed estimates of NO_x damages for each effect. Aggregation of these estimates provides a very rough starting point of $0.82/lb NOx for use in a direct cost analysis of the environmental impacts of NO_x-emitting sources. However, the costs resulting from NO_x emissions on humans and their environment may be found to be significantly higher once all effects are properly taken into account.

TABLE 3; SUMMARY OF DAMAGES DUE TO NOx AND OZONE

EFFECT	ECO(1987) BIG CITY	ECO(1987) SMALL CITY	ECO (1983)	ECO(1984) OIL CASE	HALL (1989)	HARRISON & NICHOLS (1990)	NAS	STARTING POINT
	<<<<< COSTS PER LB NOx >>>>>							
	[1]	[2]	[3]	[4]	[5]	[6]	[7]	[8]
HEALTH								
Mortality	0.34	0.016	0	0	0	0		0.34
Morbidity	0	0	0	0.005	1.73	0.29		0.29
Total								
MATERIALS								
Paint							0.035	
Rubber							0.04	
Total	0.01	0.001	0	0			0.075	0.01
VEGETATION								
Crops	0.01	0.002	0.0008	0				0.01
Ornamental								
Forests	0	0	0	0				NA
Total								
VISIBILITY	0.07	0.003	0.0002	0.17				0.17
OTHER								
Ecosystems	0	0	0	0				NA
Livestock	0	0	0	0				NA
TOTAL	**0.43**	**0.022**	**0,001**	**0,175**	**1,73**	**0.29**	**0.075**	**0.82**

Notes: See text for description and limitations of these estimates.
All figures have been restated in 1989$

[1] [2] [3] [4]: Taken from Tables 1 and 2.

[5] [6] [7]: Derived in the text.

[8]: The starting point figures are for a "typical" location, which we define as similar to the western Washington site in the Generic Coal Study (ECO, 1987). Population densities and other parameters will vary with location. The uncertainties associated with these estimates in the original studies are large; the studies did not have estimates for some potentially important effects; and the existence and magnitude of some of the reported effects are still in considerable dispute. These estimates should be used with great caution, as they indicate only the magnitude of damages.

V. EXTERNALITY COSTS BY EMISSION

D. ACID DEPOSITION

V. EXTERNALITY COSTS BY EMISSION

D. ACID DEPOSITION

1. Introduction

The purpose of this section is to review and evaluate the literature that has estimated an important component of the external costs of various energy production technologies, namely the effects of acid deposition. Acid deposition is commonly referred to as acid rain. The terms are used interchangeably here. Included in the section are discussions of studies that value effects on aquatic ecosystems (by necessity our focus is primarily on recreational fishing effects), forests, crops and materials. Other sections of this report examine effects on human health and visibility.

Such costs must be in terms of the dollars per unit of emissions -- emissions, that is, of the precursors of acid deposition, sulfur dioxide and nitrogen oxides -- to be useful for comparing alternatives. Valuation requires an understanding of the sequence of events by which emissions of these precursor compounds are converted to acidic compounds and the pathways by which such compounds can cause damages which people are willing to pay money to avoid.

Three functional relationships must be established in order to quantify the relationship between emissions and valuation. These are the relationships:

- between emissions and acid burden;
- between acid burden and physical or biological effects; and,
- between physical effects and monetary valuation.

If any of these linkages is missing, then the calculation of the external costs of acid deposition cannot be completed. Not all linkages must be made in the same study, but there must be a set of studies that can be combined in a consistent way in order to calculate acid deposition's external costs. Overall, we find no studies or sets of studies that permit us to make these linkages in a consistent manner.

2. The Science of Acid Deposition

The following discussion of the science of acid deposition and effects is not intended to be comprehensive, but rather is included to enable the reader to understand the complexities associated with estimating the economic benefits of curbing acid deposition. Detail on the scientific aspects associated with acid deposition is presented in the National Acid Precipitation Assessment Program's (NAPAP) State of Science (SOS) reports[1] which are the most recent and complete compendium of scientific knowledge on the subject. Note, however, that the reports are neither fully comprehensive nor uncontroversial.

a. From Emissions to Acid Deposition

Acid rain, or acid deposition, results from emissions of sulfur dioxide (SO_2) and nitrogen oxides (NO_x), primarily from power plants, vehicles, and industry. In 1985, 68% of U.S. SO_2 emissions were from electric utility plants, and 32% from vehicles and industry. In 1985, 33% of U.S. NO_x emissions were from electric utility plants, 36% from vehicles and 31% from industry. Total national SO_2 emissions in 1985 were 23,699,000tons, of which 16,204,000tons were from electric utilities. Total national NO_x emissions were 21,054,000 tons, of which 6,989,000 tons were from electric utilities.[2] The contribution of emissions from different sectors varies across the country.

SO_2 and NO_2 combine with moisture in the atmosphere and are then deposited as acids in the precipitation. In eastern North America, about two-thirds of precipitation acidity is associated with sulfate, and one-third with nitrate.[3]

These acid precursors are carried in the atmosphere for one to ten days before being deposited.[4] These residence times indicate that the sulfur precursors of acid rain (the acidity of acid rain in the United States is primarily due to sulfuric acid) can be deposited 1000 km or more from the source. Thus, out-of-state damages caused by acid deposition will be a large part of total damages. About one sixth of sulfur emissions in the eastern United States are deposited in Canada, and a third make it to the Atlantic Ocean.[5]

Because of prevailing winds, the northeastern United States and Canada receive significant quantities of acid precursors from the band of heavily industrialized and coal-using states stretching from Missouri to Pennsylvania. Nonetheless, the relative contribution of regional versus local sources must be determined before damages can be assigned to emissions from a particular source. For instance, Feely and Bogen

---

[1] U.S. EPA et al., National Acid Precipitation Assessment Program, State of Science/Technology, Washington, DC, 1989 [hereafter cited as U.S.E.P.A. 1989].

[2] U.S. EPA et al., National Acid Precipitation Assessment Program (NAPAP), Interim Assessment, Washington, D.C., 1987.

[3] Lipfert, F., "Effects of Acidic Deposition on the Atmospheric Deterioration of Materials", Materials Performance, July, 1987, pp. 12-19 [hereafter cited as Lipfert].

[4] Berner, E. and R. Berner, The Global Water Cycle: Geochemistry and Environment, Prentice-Hall, Inc., 1987, pp. 89, 113 [hereafter cited as Berner].

[5] National Research Council, Acid Deposition Atmospheric Processes in Eastern North America, National Academy Press, Washington, DC, 1983, p. 57 [hereafter cited as Acid Deposition].

(1989) have estimated that the fraction of the sulfate and hydrogen ion from local, urban sources in the New York City area is between 30% and 45%.[6]

In 1980, the average pH of annual precipitation over the eastern U.S. was as low as 4.1 in some locations.[7] Although pure water is neutral, with a pH of 7,[8] normal rainwater is slightly acidic, with a pH of 5.6, as a result of being in equilibrium with atmospheric CO_2.[9] Local natural effects make it either somewhat more acidic, or slightly more basic. Consequently, "acid rain" resulting from anthropogenic emissions of sulfur and nitrogen oxides has a pH less than 5.6.

Attempts to link utility emissions and acid deposition have been controversial. Proposals to reduce acid rain have relied on the "linearity hypothesis," which asserts that reducing acid precursors would have a proportionate effect on reducing acid rain in sensitive areas. There are numerous examples of theoretical considerations and empirical evidence for and against this hypothesis.

The National Academy of Science study (NAS, 1983)[10] concluded that if all sources of acid precursors reduced their emissions by the same fraction, then acid deposition would fall correspondingly. The linearity hypothesis has been given further support by NAPAP research, which predicts that a 50% decline in precursor emissions would result in a total reduction in acid burden of about 40%.

However, the linearity hypothesis is applicable to total emissions, not emissions from particular sources, and it is the latter that is often required for environmental costing. As the 1983 NAS study put it, the application of "linearity" is limited to "circumstances in which the spatial distribution of emissions is not changed." In the case of site-specific environmental costing, the spatial distribution of emissions would be changed with decisions on the location and type of new generation. However, if the costing analysis is being performed to judge the effect of existing sources, or if it is based on a generic plant approach, then this may be less of a problem.[11]

If the linearity hypothesis is inappropriate for environmental costing, then a set of "transfer coefficients" is needed to link emissions at a source to acid deposition at

---

[6] Feely, H., and D. Bogen, Contributions of Local Sources to the Acidity of Rain in an Urban Area, paper abstract presented at the NADP Technical Committee Meeting, Provincetown, MA, October 23-26, 1989.

[7] Berner, supra note 4 at p. 126-7.

[8] The pH scale is a logarithmic measure of the concentration of hydrogen ions: $pH=-\log[H^+]$. pH of 6 is ten times more acidic than pH of 7, etc.

[9] See, Berner, supra note 4 at p. 121 for the calculation.

[10] Acid Deposition, supra note 5.

[11] See Analytical Framework, Chapter. III and Sulpher Dioxide, Chapter V.B.

receptors. On this matter, extensive research and development activities regarding the regional acid deposition models are being conducted by NAPAP.[12]

Previous modeling efforts appear to predict seasonal and annual totals of sulfur wet deposition fairly well (explaining 60% of the variance in deposition during the warm seasons, but about half of this percentage during the cold seasons). However, they do a relatively poor job of predicting dry deposition and, in general, are too rudimentary to provide reliable transfer coefficients. NAPAP is now developing a sophisticated new model, the Regional Acid Deposition Model (RADM), that holds promise in calculating acid precipitation events but requires additional models to translate these events into changes in seasonal and annual total deposition over the eastern U.S. and southeastern Canada associated with changes in regional emissions.

The first phase of evaluation of this model should be completed in the Spring of 1990, but preliminary findings indicate that while the model has no major flaws and produces reasonable predictions of pH, the extensive testing to date has been insufficient to determine the model's accuracy.[13]

b. From Deposition to Damage

The second link comprises the effects of the cumulative acid burden in wet and dry deposition on aquatic and forest environments, crops, and materials (visibility and possible health effects are discussed elsewhere in this report). For example, acid lakes have difficulty supporting fish; increased acid inputs may slow tree growth and damage soils; acid rain may reduce crop yields, and possibly damage plants; and acid attacks exposed building materials, especially limestone and gypsum.

Although the types of effects and the underlying mechanisms are fairly well understood, the ability of scientists to quantify the physical damages from acid rain is far from perfect. Indeed, as one report pointed out five years ago: "the speculative and uncertain nature of these possible [pollutant/plant] relationships cannot be over-emphasized".[14] While considerable progress has been made since then, especially

---

[12] Brown, G. et al., National Acid Precipitation Assessment Program State-of-Science/Technology Report 27 Part B: Methods For Valuing Acidic Deposition and Air Pollution Effects, 1989, [hereafter cited as Methods].

[13] U.S.E.P.A. 1989, supra, note 1, vol. 5. Also see Methods, supra note 12, for summary of the models. RADM is a three-dimensional non-linear dynamic model. It also includes ozone formation equations and accounts for the effects of cloud processes. Its limitations include a large grid size (80x80 km) that cannot resolve urban plumes, limited representation of aerosol products, and simplified representations of cloud effects. As in any model of this class, a massive and detailed speciated emissions inventory is required to run the model. When, as is often the case, this information is unavailable, assumptions and "literature values" must be relied upon. Another consequence of the use of this type of model is that only short acid episodes can be modeled, with fairly arbitrary links needed to bridge the gap between episodic effects and seasonal or annual effects.

The RADM model concept has been criticized. See comments of Donald Peterson, RCG/Hagler, Bailly, on the draft of this report, in a letter to Ottinger of May 15, 1990.

[14] Chapman, D. and R. Kohut, Ozone and Acid Deposition: An Economic Perspective on Agricultural and Forestry Impacts, Cornell Agricultural Economic Staff Paper, No. 84-28, 1984; at p. 15 [hereafter cited as Chapman].

as a result of the National Acid Precipitation Assessment Program, that generalization is still true.

Further, uncertainties are not limited to those associated with physical damages to individual plants, lakes or materials. Reliable inventories of how much of which types of materials are exposed have been difficult to obtain. Like the damage relationships, progress has been made during the last decade, much of which has been integrated in NAPAP's State of Science (SOS) reports.[15]

The complexity of acid deposition phenomena has several implications for valuation. The first has to do with the relationship between the source area -- where emissions are generated, and the receptor area -- where the chemically transformed emissions do economic damage. If external costs of emissions from a designated source area are to have any meaning, then the cost estimate of a unit of emissions must reflect marginal damage in each receptor area, weighted by the relative contribution of that source area to each receptor area. For example, it may not be sufficient to determine only the acid rain damages in the Adirondacks, as long as the precursor emissions also adversely affect the southern Appalachians.

An additional implication is to beware of sunk costs. In the Adirondacks, for example, it has been noted that numerous lakes no longer support fish life. Attempts to estimate damages by computing the lost fishing opportunity at these sites are not consistent with the frequently made allegations of irreversible damage to the same lakes. If the damage is truly irreversible, then the monetized damage to such lakes is probably irrelevant. What is relevant is the damage that still can be prevented to lakes that have not yet been degraded biologically.

The complex, highly nonlinear environmental system that both creates and is affected by acid rain implies that the marginal approach to valuation is essential. That is, the damages from each incremental unit of pollution, rather than the total or average damages per receptor unit, need to be quantified, since the damages per receptor unit are generally not constant as the pollution increases.

Even when the physical damages per receptor unit are constant with increasing exposure to acidity, the valuation of those physical damages may not be. As examples of problems of nonlinear physical damages, lakes have thresholds at which point the input of acid surpasses the buffering capacity. Depending on the type of materials, the damage functions as a result of contact with acidity are not necessarily linear.

The complexity of the science also means that there have been few studies valuing acid rain damages starting with the emissions themselves. Only one study was found incorporating all the linkages between emissions and valuation, and this study applies to Norway rather than the U.S.[16] Further, existing U.S. studies on the individual links are not of sufficient quality and detail that they can be linked to produce damage estimates. However, it is clear that a better job could be done linking studies of each

---

[15] U.S.E.P.A. 1989, supra note 1.

[16] Navrud, S., Estimating Social Benefits of Environmental Improvements from Reduced Acid Deposition: A Contingent Valuation Survey, contained in Folmer, H., and E. Ierland, Valuation Methods and Policy Making in Environmental Economics, Elsevier, Amsterdam, Holland, 1989 [hereafter cited as Narrud].

of the necessary parts. Work to be completed in Fall, 1990 under the auspices of the NAPAP program should greatly improve the situation.[17]

c. From Damage to Value

Our focus on the complexities associated with the science is not intended to suggest that with greater scientific certainty the valuation step would be easy. The studies that will be discussed attempt to put an economic value on the various categories of damages caused by acid deposition. Unfortunately, they do not link these estimates to the quantity of pollutants released upwind, or examine how the damages vary by quantity of emissions.

While acid deposition includes both wet and dry deposition, most of the economic studies on acid rain do not specify that they include dry deposition, or what they consider the acid burden to be. These studies do not permit a calculation of marginal damages. Instead, most researchers in this field compare damages from a particular level of pH to a base case of no acid rain, or calculate the costs of restoration to a pre-acid rain state. These approaches are problematical for application to environmental costing because of their failure to link emissions to damages.

These studies have another common problem: their results cannot be generalized with any confidence. The size of the areas for which damages from acid rain were calculated in the specific studies varies from one Metropolitan Statistical Area (e.g. New Haven-West Haven, Connecticut) up to the Adirondacks.[18] In order to compare one study to another, or combine estimates for different categories of damages, the results need to be generalized to different sized areas and other locations. Depending on the type of damage, different scaling factors could be used for this purpose. For instance, the valuation of aquatic damages could be scaled by the surface area of lakes in the appropriate area, damages to forests or crops by acres of forest or farmland undercultivation, and damages to materials by the size of the population living in an affected city.

All of these methods for scaling have their problems, however. Lakes have different capacities for buffering and, consequently, the same input of acid rain could cause very different damages in different lakes. Materials are used in different proportions in different cities, so population is not necessarily a good proxy for the amount of a particular building material to be found. Soil type, quantity of rainfall, and types of crops grown vary across regions. The problems of generalization will be discussed in greater detail in the sections devoted to each category of damage.

---

[17] Mary Jo Kealy, NAPAP, personal communication.

[18] Lipfert, supra note 3; Menz, F. and J. Mullen, Acidification Impact on Fisheries, in Economic Perspectives on Acid Deposition Control, Crocker, T., ed., Butterworth Publishers; Boston, Mass., 1985, pp 135-56 [hereafter cited as Menz]; Violette, D., A Model Estimating the Economic Impacts of Current Levels of Acidification on Recreational Fishing in the Adirondack Mountains, U.S. EPA, Washington, D.C., 1985 [hereafter cited as Violette].

3. Overview of the Studies

This section examines the small literature that focuses on economic damages from acid rain. Heavy reliance was placed on the National Acid Precipitation Assessment Program State of Science/Technology report on economics[19] and the papers described within that report. Finally, the Agricola index, compiled by the National Agriculture Library, was searched for journal articles and papers.

Table 1 summarizes the studies of greatest interest in each damage category, and Table 2 categorizes the studies by damage category. Forster (1984a)[20] presents some crude calculations for aquatics and crops in eastern Canada. Crocker and Regens (1985)[21] generalize estimates of all acid-induced damages to the Eastern third of the United States. Lipfert (1987)[22] focuses solely on materials damage in New Haven, Connecticut. Menz and Mullen (1984),[23] Violette (1985),[24] and Morey and Shaw [25](forthcoming) present damage estimates for the Adirondack fishery.

In addition, Navrud's examination of acid precipitation damages to freshwater fishing in Norway is briefly discussed.[26] Adams, Callaway and McCarl (1986),[27] and Chapman and Kohut (1984)[28] focus on crop damages, and Callaway, Darwin and Nesse (1986)[29] examine forest damage. The NAPAP report itself does not present dollar

---

[19] Methods, supra note 12.

[20] Forster, B., Economic Impact of Acid Precipitation: A Canadian Perspective, in Economic Perspectives on Acid Deposition Control, 1984a, pp. 97-121, [hereafter cited as Forster].

[21] Crocker, T., and Regens, J., "Benefit Cost Analyses of Acid Deposition Control: A Benefit-Cost Analysis: Its Prospects and Limits," Environmental Science and Technology , February 19, 1985, pp. 112-16 [hereafter cited as Crocker].

[22] Lipfert, supra, note 3.

[23] Menz, supra note 18.

[24] Violette, supra note 18.

[25] Morey, E. and W. Shaw, An Economic Model to Assess the Impact of Acid Rain: A Characteristics Approach to Estimating the Demand for and Benefits from Recreational Fishing, in Smith, V. and Witte, A., eds., Advances in Applied Microeconomic Theory, Vol. 8, JAI Press Inc., Greenwich, CT, (forthcoming)[hereafter cited as Morey].

[26] Navrud, supra note 16.

[27] Adams, R., J. Callaway, and B. McCarl, "Pollution, Agriculture and Social Welfare: The Case of Acid Deposition", Canadian Journal of Agricultural Economics, Vol. 34, March, 1986, pp. 3-19 [hereafter cited as Adams et al.].

[28] Chapman, supra, note 14.

[29] Callaway, J., R. Darwin, and R. Nesse, Economic Effects of Hypothetical Reductions in Tree Growth in the Northeastern and Southeastern United States, Pacific Northwest Laboratory, Richland, Washington, PNL-5939, 1986 [hereafter cited as Callaway et al.].

TABLE 1

SUMMARY OF ACID RAIN VALUATION STUDIES

Study	Scenario	Cost/Benefit Estimates/yr.	Area	$year	Method	Assumptions
Aquatics						
Crocker & Regens 1985	100% reduction in acid deposition	$250 million	Eastern US	1978	Menz & Mullen (1984) scaled up	see Menz & Mullen scaling assumptions
Forster 1984	varies	$28-100 million (Canadian$?)	Ontario & Quebec	varies	cost of liming tourist revenues	liming is effective
Menz & Mullen 1984	recreation sites with pH<5; 5% change in lake area	$1.7-3.2 million	Adirondacks	1982	travel cost	substitution only within fishery only recreation only licensed fishermen
Morey & Shaw	25% change in catch	$8.70/person per season	a few lakes in Adirondacks		share model	
Navrud 1989	30-50% reductions in S emissions in Europe	$16-48/fish per household	Norway	CV		
Violette 1985	100% reduction	$.8-11.6 million	Adirondacks	1984	travel cost participation model	
Welle 1985	moderate to severe changes	$30-36/non-user $91-120/user	Minnesota	CV		
Forests						
Callaway, Darwin, and Neese 1986	unknown hypothetical growth reductions	$3.4-5 billion present value 2030 to	Eastern US	forest sector model	10% discount rate	
Crocker & Regens 1985	100% reduction in acid deposition	$1.75 billion	Eastern US	1978	market value of timber; method of valuing other uses unspecified	

Crops

Adams, Callaway, & McCarl 1986	0-40% decrease from 1980 emissions	$48 million best $19-142 million range from yield reductions, $24 million cost of liming, fertilization benefit > $200 million	United States	1980	sector model	mix of seven soybean types
Chapman & Kohut 1984	4% increase in lime	$1-2 million	New York		cost of liming	sulfur sufficient soil
Crocker & Regens 1985	100% reduction in acid deposition	$1 billion	Eastern US	1978	unspecified	acid damage = ozone damages
Forster 1984	10% of Ontario fields need lime	$8.6 million (Canadian$?)	Ontario, Nova Scotia Quebec	1980	cost of liming	labor costs excluded

Materials

Crocker & Regens 1985	100% reduction in acid deposition	$2 billion	Eastern US	1978		
Lipfert 1987	100% reduction in SO_2 & H^+	$6.1 million $8.50/person for H^+ $6.50/person for SO_2	New Haven	1980?	damage functions only buildings and fences ground truth samples no Cu or Al	

TABLE 2

CATEGORIES VALUED BY STUDIES

Study	Aquatics	Forests	Crops	Materials
Adams, Callaway and McCarl (1986)			X	
Callaway, Darwin, and Nesse (1986)		X		
Chapman and Kohut (1984)			X	
Crocker & Regens (1985)	X	X	X	X
Forster (1984)	X		X	
Lipfert (1987)				X
Menz & Mullen (1984)	X			
Morey & Shaw (forthcoming)	X			
Navrud (1989)	X			
Violette (1985)	X			
Welle (1985)	X			

estimates for any of the categories, but focuses instead on describing and criticizing studies and methodologies.

It is no accident that most economic studies have been done on aquatic damages, for which the effects of increased acidity are most established, and the fewest have been done on crops and forests, where the results of scientific studies have been more contradictory, and on materials, where the link from physical effects to changes in behavior in response to materials damage is uncertain and thus difficult to value.

4. Damage Categories

a. Aquatics

i. Science

Lakes receive acid inputs both directly from deposition from the atmosphere, and from runoff from the surrounding watershed. The Adirondacks, New England and eastern Canada are areas where lakes are particularly susceptible to acidification because of the geology and the soil. Soils are better at neutralizing acid precipitation than lake water. The more the water in a lake comes from runoff, rather than direct deposition, the less acid the lake will be. According to NAPAP, acid lakes were concentrated not only in the Northeast, but also in Appalachia, on the mid-Atlantic coastal plain, in northern Florida, and parts of northern Wisconsin and the Upper Peninsula of Michigan. In areas receiving acid rain, 2.7% of the streams were also acidified.[30]

The change in pH in a lake as a result of a particular quantity of acid input depends on how well the lake is buffered. Bicarbonate buffering is most effective in the range of pH 6 to 8.5.[31] Oligotrophic lakes (lakes which have a low concentration of nutrient elements, such as nitrogen and phosphorous) and streams in areas underlain by noncalcareous granite rocks are very poorly buffered, so acid rain can have a profound effect.[32]

Lakes of this type which have been exposed to acid rain have, on average, experienced a drop in pH of two units. That is, the level of acidity is now about 100-fold above the estimated acidity in pristine conditions. There is no buffering capacity in these lakes below pH 5.15. Lakes that are less susceptible to acidification because they are underlain by calcareous rock continue to have buffering down to pH

---

[30] Methods, supra note 12.

[31] Berner, supra note 4 at p. 276.

[32] Kimmins, J., Forest Ecology, Macmillan Publishing Company, New York, 1987 at p. 118 [hereafter cited as Kimmins].

4.65. When calcareous rocks are present, the buffering capacity of the lake effectively is infinite since the rocks can replenish the bicarbonate lost to buffering.[33]

Because of the buffering capacity of lakes, there is a threshold effect for the damages. As a result, in order to know the physical damages to a lake from an extra quantity of pollution, one needs to know the pH and buffering capacity before the acid precursors are added. To know the damages, it is necessary to know how close a lake is to exhausting its buffering capacity. Extrapolating the problem to more than one lake, to come up with the physical damages for a region, the initial state of each lake must be known.

Tolerance of fish to low pH varies by species, with reproductive failure of the most sensitive occurring at pH 6. Fish species increasingly experience reproductive failure as acidity increases. At the most acid-tolerant end of the scale, lake herring, yellow perch, and lake chub do not start to have difficulty reproducing until the pH drops to 4.7-4.5.[34] One would expect that effects on other inhabitants of lakes would also vary with pH. For instance, when the pH drops below about 4, the increased mortality of frogs' eggs causes problems with their reproduction. In addition, at lower pH's, heavy metal ions such as aluminum become available to fish and other aquatic organisms in harmful concentrations.[35]

A problem with generalizing to areas not directly studied stems from the types of fish in the lakes. The composition of species inhabiting the lakes will affect both the physical damages and the economic damages from acidification. On the physical side, some species are more tolerant of acidity than others, so the species composition of a certain lake will determine how sensitive it is to an incremental change in pH. As some species start to die out in a lake, while other species continue to live, the character of the lake is likely to change. In order to calculate the effects on recreational fishing during this intermediate period when there are still fish, one needs to link biological abundance to catch rates.

On the valuation side, both use and non-use values are likely to be affected by the change in character of water bodies. For instance, fishermen have different preferences for types of fish. To value losses, the effects on species composition are needed. In addition, a study of a lake with one composition of species may not be subject to generalization to give economic damages to lakes with a different mix of species. Furthermore, recreational fishing is not confined to lakes. Extrapolating from an economic study of lake fishing to stream fishing raises further problems.

ii. Valuation Studies

Most of the studies of aquatic damages have concentrated solely on the value of lakes for recreational fishing. The value of other water recreational activities (such as swimming or boating) that may decline in quality as a result of acid rain is largely

---

[33] Berner, supra note 4 at p. 276.

[34] Forster, supra note 20 at p. 111.

[35] Id.

ignored in the economic literature as are the non-use values. The former omission stems primarily from lack of knowledge about the linkages between acid deposition, physical effects, and economic impacts. As NAPAP points out, fish populations have been studied most heavily because they are high in the food chain, and serve as integrators of ecosystem function.

No non-use values have been quantified for particular areas, although several studies use the contingent valuation method to calculate per person existence values for changes in the ecological quality of lakes. NAPAP notes that excluding existence values in an assessment of acid deposition damages could lead to potentially large underestimates of damages.[36] The economic value of streams is also ignored because of the uncertainty of the effects from acid deposition.

It is difficult to compare the dollar figures given for damages in the studies since they are not all valuing the same things. Menz and Mullen and Violette[37] both use the travel cost method to value recreational fishing in the Adirondacks, and present similar annual dollar damage estimates of under $15 million. The estimates from Welle's[38] contingent valuation studies of willingness to pay for environmental quality range from a low of $30 per person to a high of $36. Navrud[39] presents median use value estimates of $16 to $48 per fish per household, and median non-use values of $12 to $36. Forster's estimates of damages in the Adirondacks ranges from $28 to $100 million per year.

However, in order to be able to generalize and to link the estimates of damages back to emissions, the dollar values per person should be summed over the people appropriately included for each area, and that figure allocated by the sources of the pollutant load. Not enough information is given in all of the reports to calculate a dollar value per person.

Mullen and Menz (MM) (1985)[40] use data from a 1976 New York State Anglers' Survey[41] to estimate a relationship between an individual's fishing days and site availability, which is measured as the sum of acres of fishable water (for four different kinds of fishing), weighted by the travel cost from each site (or collection of sites) to the individual's residence. This is converted to a demand function by adding a price term to the weights and using the estimated relationship to determine changes in visitation as a function of the price. In the next step they remove from the available fishable waters all sites where pH has fallen below 5 in measurements made since 1976,

---

[36] Methods, supra note 12 at p. 6-34.

[37] Menz and Violette, supra note 18.

[38] Welle, P., Potential Economic Impacts of Acid Rain in Minnesota: The Minnesota Acid Rain Survey, unpublished manuscript, Department of Economics, Bemidji State University, Bemidji, MN, 1985 [hereafter cited as Welle].

[39] Navrud, supra, note 16.

[40] Mullen, J. and Menz, F., "The Effect of Acidification Damages on the Economic Value of the Adirondack Fishery to New York Anglers," American Journal of Agricultural Economics, February, 1985.

[41] 1976-77 New York Angler Survey Final Report, N.Y. State Bureau of Fisheries, Albany, NY, 1981.

according to surveys of Adirondack lakes made since 1976. A new demand curve is calculated and the economic losses due to acidification are estimated by the area between the two curves.

This analysis is not very useful for making estimates of external costs, although in fairness to the authors it should be noted that this was not their purpose. The analysis of Menz and Mullen (MM) has been vigorously criticized by Shaw (1989)[42], who argues that their demand curve is not consistently derived from economic theory and is not really a demand curve at all. However, this argument is of secondary importance in evaluating the use of MM for purposes of making external cost estimates. Far more important are the authors' failure to make a linkage back to emissions and their inattention to the sunk cost problem, i.e.:

(1) There is no observed connection between physical damages and recreation behavior. MM assume a decline in recreation visits is associated with acidification; they do not observe it. Of the lakes removed from the supply of fishable water, it does not appear from their article that they can assert that these lakes are not being fished today or that they were being fished prior to 1976.

(2) MM value the damages that they believe have already occurred to Adirondack lakes. As explained above, a far more useful concept is the valuation of lakes that would not become acidic if emissions were reduced because the damages to be valued are the future damages from electric power production.

Violette (1985)[43] applies two models, a travel cost model with site characteristics and a simpler participation model, to fishing sites in the Adirondack Mountains of New York. This method only considers use values, although Violette notes that the non-use values may exceed the use values. Acid rain was assumed to affect both the number of sites available for fishing and the characteristics of the sites. Only lakes are included in the analysis. Sites were characterized by the number of lakes they contained with certain characteristics, for instance acres of cold water, and two story or warm water lakes. Site characteristics were obtained from the Adirondack Lake and Pond Survey. The economic damages were calculated by changing the characteristics of the sites, for instance by changing the fishable acres of cold water lakes. The characteristics did not include catch rates.

For the fishermen, Violette uses the same data set as MM, the 1976-77 New York Angler's Survey. The survey was mailed to a 3% sample of fishermen licensed in New York State, and asked questions on fishing activities, expenditures, preferences, attitudes and opinions, and participant background. Violette designed the model to yield an upper bound estimate for damages. For instance, he did not take substitutability of fishing sites into account. The estimates of damages from the travel cost model ($.8 to $11.6 million) and the participation model ($1.7 to $10.5 million) are about the same.

[42] Shaw, W., "Valuing the Effect of Acidification Damages on the Adirondack Fishery: Comment," American Journal of Agricultural Economics, February 1989.

[43] Violette, supra note 18.

Like MM, Violette's work appears to be interesting and competently done. However it is no more useful for estimation of external cost because it, too, does not link his estimates of economic damages either to acid deposition in the region or to emissions. In addition, the Lake and Pond Survey is not a very comprehensive or up-to-date data set. Not all lakes and ponds are surveyed each year or necessarily within the last twenty years. Data on pH existed for only 35% of measured surface area and information on alkalinity was available for only 52%. This lack of information is a problem since what the Lake and Pond Survey records as the state of the lake may have no relationship to its actual state at the time anglers were making a recreation decision.

Morey and Shaw,[44] using the 1976-77 New York Anglers Survey -- the same data as Violette and Mullen and Menz -- estimate a share model for seven lakes or sets of lakes in the Adirondacks and for eight varieties of sport fish. Each fisherman allocates a fixed recreational budget to alternate sites, and the model estimates the effect of site characteristics on shares. The site characteristics Morey and Shaw consider are fishable acreage and average catch rate for the individual's first and second most preferred species at the site. Morey and Shaw estimate the willingness to pay for a 25% increase in catch rate per season at $8.68 per fisherman; for a 50% increase, $15.61.

Morey and Shaw did not link acidity to fish populations or fish populations to catch rates, so the study is only useful as a demonstration of the sensitivity of benefit estimates to catch rates. Because there is no link between physical and economic damages, the study does not in and of itself produce useable results for environmental costing. Once such links are available, however, this study may become quite valuable despite its limitations. One such limitation is the assumption of a fixed recreation budget. This is bound to underestimate benefits of improvements, owing to substitution between fishing and other activities. However, the effect is not likely to be large. The approach also assumes an exogenous total number of recreation trips.

Forster (1984a)[45] produces an estimate of damages to aquatics using a less systematic method than all of the studies discussed to this point. In fact, he does not present a single dollar value for the damages, choosing to list economic disadvantages of acidification, and then providing estimates of the costs of liming to repair the damage. He includes in his list commercial fishing, sport-fishing expenditures by travelers, annual fishing licenses, and fishing lodge industry revenues and the direct and indirect effects of its loss. The low end of his estimates is from the fishing lodge industry revenues, and the high end is from the cost of liming.

The sport-fishing expenditures by travelers do not include the costs of travelling to the location, so even combined with the cost of annual fishing licenses, and fishing lodge industry revenues, these expenditures do not represent the price that any angler pays to go fishing. These lost revenues are simply the local economic impact on a region that relies on tourism for business, and do not represent the value of the fishing site.

---

[44] Morey, supra note 25.

[45] Forster, supra note 20.

There are several problems with using the cost of liming as a measure of benefits. It is difficult to ermine if people are liming in response to increased acid deposition. If people are liming in response to the acid input, and no physical damages are observed, then the economic damages are equal to the cost of liming. If people are not liming, it may be because the resource damage is less than the cost of liming. Even if liming takes place, it is not clear that the resource value of the lakes will be fully restored.[46]

Welle (1985),[47] calculates existence values for the environmental quality of lakes in Minnesota, which may be affected by acid rain.[48] About 1000 Minnesota residents were asked how much they would be willing to pay to prevent declines in the environmental quality of Minnesota lakes from acid rain. The changes in environmental quality were listed on an "environmental quality ladder." In addition, they were asked to characterize themselves as users or non-users, and the bids of non-users were characterized as existence values by Welle. The mean bids for non-users ranged from $30 to $36 depending on the degree of damage, and for users the bids were $91 to $120. The range of damages was unspecified in NAPAP's summary of the report. NAPAP described the study as limited in terms of the population and the scope of the effects of acid deposition to which they can be applied.[49] In addition, the questions asked in this study were only loosely tied to theory, so the existence values calculated may not be near the true existence values.

Navrud's study of willingness to pay (WTP) of households in Norway for incremental improvements in freshwater fish populations[50] calculated median non-use values of $12 to $36 per fish per household, per year. The author asked respondents to indicate the maximum amount of money they would pay for improvements from liming, and to divide their total bid into use, option, and existence and bequest values. The improvements were equal to the expected effects of 30%, 50%, and 70% reductions in sulphur emissions in Europe, although the empirical basis for this linkage is not discussed, nor are any literature citations provided. Median WTP for the 30%-equivalent reduction was 100 to 300 Kroner, depending on the starting option given. This translates into a range of $16 to $48 at the exchange rate in effect in April 1988 when the survey was conducted.[51] Respondents reported 12% of WTP to be recreational value, 12% option value and 76% existence value.

Assuming Americans have the same preferences as Norwegians, it would seem that these results can be used in environmental costing applications in the U.S. However, two vital pieces of information are still needed. First, we need to know how many people should be included in the population giving value to the resource. Second, we still need the "transfer coefficient" relating changes in emissions to changes

---

[46] Id.

[47] Welle, supra note 38.

[48] Methods, supra note 12 at p. 6-34.

[49] Id. at p. 6-34.

[50] Navrud, supra note 16.

[51] Purchasing power parity would provide a more meaningful comparison but is not as readily available.

in water quality. The link between water quality improvements and the 30, 50 and 70% emission reductions assumed by Navrud are not justified in the paper, and even if they can be they relate only to European, not American, experience.

Crocker and Regens (1985)[52] produced an estimate of damages for aquatics based on Menz and Mullen's estimate. As we have already explained, the MM study cannot be used for environmental cost purposes, and therefore Crocker and Regens is similarly flawed. Nevertheless, the Crocker and Regens study can serve as a useful example of the difficulties with attempting to generalize. Since Menz and Mullen's figures were for the Adirondacks, and Crocker and Regens were studying damages in the eastern third of the United States, they had to scale their numbers up. Crocker and Regens did not explain their procedure for scaling. Their damage estimate for the eastern third of the United States was about 116 times the maximum damages that Menz and Mullen presented for the Adirondacks.

The scaling factor that Crocker and Regens used seems high for several reasons. The land area of the eastern United States is about 95 times the land area of the Adirondacks, a bit lower than the ratio of 116 to 1 for the damage estimate. If Crocker and Regens used the water area instead, their scaled up damage estimate should be lower still since proportionate to land area there are fewer lakes in the South, for example, than there are in the Adirondacks. They should also have taken into account the exposure of the region to acid deposition, and the susceptibility of the lakes to acidification.

Considering that the Adirondacks were receiving acid rain longer than much of the eastern United States, and as of 1980, were at the low end of the scale for the average pH of rainfall in the east, the exposure of the Adirondacks is more extreme than the area which Crocker and Regens studied. In addition, the lakes in the Adirondacks are more susceptible to acidification than lakes in the Southeast.

The Adirondacks should be viewed as a worst case, and any extrapolation to the rest of the country should account for the differences. The studies discussed above consider the effects of acid rain on recreational fishing. There are basically two models of these effects. Increases in acid rain may reduce the supply of fishable lakes, holding catch rates constant at the lakes remaining, or increases in acid rain may reduce catch rates, keeping the supply of lakes constant. (Obviously, both types of models could be needed to describe the actual situation). Menz and Mullen is an example of the former approach. To apply the latter approach, one needs estimates of the willingness to pay (WTP) for increases in catch rate (or to avoid reductions in catch rate) and a function relating acid rain to catch rate. A large number of studies have estimated the WTP for a change in catch rate.

Table 3, taken from the NAPAP report,[53] lists six of the most recent and best studies estimating WTP for changes in catch rate. All but Huppert (1988)[54] address

---

[52] Crocker, supra note 21.

[53] Methods, supra note 12.

[54] Huppert, D., Two Empirical Issues in Recreational Fisheries Economics: Mail Survey Self-Selection Bias And Divergence Between WTP and WTA, EPA 230-08-88-034, U.S. EPA, Washington, DC, Fourth Annual Area Workshop: Marine Sport Fisheries, Economic Evaluation and Management, Seattle, WA June 23-24, 1988.

TABLE 3 - Comparison of Benefit Estimates of Changes in Catch Rates

Study	Date	Location	Species Type	Model(a)	Scenario	Value
Bockstael, McConnell & Strand (1988a)	1980	Chesapeake Bay	Striped Bass	CTC	+(20%)	(per trip) $ 2.00 to $ 6.30
Bockstael, McConnell & Strand (1988b)	Nov./Dec. 1987	Florida (Atlantic coast)	Big Game	RUM	+(20%)	(per trip)
			Small Game	Nested Logit	catch rate	$ 1.56 $ 0.33
			Nontargeted Small Game			$ 0.32
			Bottom fish (from boat)			$ 1.27
Smith & Palmquist (1988)	Summer 1981 & 1982	Albemarle/Pamlico Estuary	All Species	RUM	+(25%)	(per trip)
		All Sites Closest 4 Sites		Nested Logit	catch rate	$ 2.43 $ 0.60
		Outer Banks Range Across Most Sites	All Species	CTC		$ 1.74 to $ 38.07
		Pamlico Range Across Most Sites	All Species	CTC		$ 1.99 to $ 14.24
Huppert (1988)	July 1985-June 1986	San Francisco Bay and Ocean Area	Anadromous Fish Runs (Salmon & Striped Bass)	CVM		(per year)
				EV CV	-(50%)	$ 37.12 $ 83.71
				CV	+(100%)	$ 43.05
				CTC		
				EV CV	-(50%)	$126.76 $127.34
				CV	+(100%)	$ 69.58
Morey & Shaw (forthcoming)	1976/77	Adirondacks (Saranac, Raquette, Lake Placid & Piseco)	Brook & Lake Trout (Average)	SHR		(per season)
					+(25%)	$ 8.68
					+(50%)	$ 15.51
Milon (1988)	1981 & 1986	Gulf of Mexico	King Mackeral	RUM		(per trip)
			Average for 4 Sites		+(25%) +(50%)	$ 5.40 $ 16.70

(a) The guide to symbols is RUM for Random Utility Model; CTC for Conventional Travel Cost (includes Simple Travel Cost and Varying Parameter/Regional Travel Cost Models); CVM for Contingent Valuation Method (EV for Equivalent Variation and CV for Compensating Variation); SHR for Share Model.

increases in catch rate. To interpret the information on this table, consider Bockstael, McConnell, and Strand (1988a).[55] They found, using the conventional travel cost model, that a recreational fisherman fishing for striped bass in the Chesapeake Bay would be willing to pay from $2.00 to $6.30 per trip for an increase in catch rate of 25%.

b. Forests

i. Science

The net effect of acid rain on forest ecosystems is not well established in the United States. The NAPAP assessment concluded that, with the exception of red spruce at high elevations, there is no evidence that acid rain has caused a general decline in American forests.[56] The report has been criticized for not discussing possible effects that will not be visible in the short run, and for inadequately dealing with the effect of acid deposition on the nutrients in the soil.

Europeans have seen a greater decline in their forests than generally has been observed in the United States. New types of forest damage were observed in West Germany starting in the mid-1970s. By 1986, 54% of the forest area contained trees with at least slight foliage loss. Within central Europe, the German and the Dutch experiences have been most severe. While acid rain has been implicated in the damages, scientists generally agree that no single cause can be blamed. Damages are site specific, and are tied to the stress factors present.[57]

The acidity has a direct effect on plants as well as an indirect one as a result of influence on soil. In a typical forest, the average raindrop comes in contact with three tiers of leaves before it hits the ground.[58] It therefore has a triple-effect on the leaves.

Acidic precipitation has a direct adverse effect on vegetation, by damaging leaf surfaces, interfering with the normal operation of guard cells, poisoning plant cells, disturbing the normal metabolic or growth processes, interfering with reproduction, and interacting with other environmental stresses.

Acid rain may accelerate leaching of calcium and other cations out of soil, and also may make aluminum available to plants. The aluminum is toxic to fine roots, and when these roots die, the trees become more susceptible to drought and have a

---

[55] Bockstael, N., K. McConnell, and I. Strand, Benefits from Improvements in Chesapeake Bay Water Quality, Report for EPA under Cooperative Agreement CR-811043-01-0 with the University of Maryland, College Park, MD, 1988.

[56] Methods, supra note 12. See also, Stevens, W., "Worst Fears on Acid Rain Unrealized", New York Times, February 20, 1990 at pp. C1, C11.

[57] MacKenzie, J. and M. El-Ashry, eds., Air Pollution's Toll on Forests and Crops, Yale University Press, New Haven, CT, 1989, at p. 64.

[58] Chapman, supra note 14 at p. 2.

reduced ability to absorb nutrients.[59] On the other hand, acid deposition is in part associated with nitrogen. Nitrogen, which contributes about 1/3 of overall rainfall acidity, can be the limiting factor in forest growth, and the input of this nutrient may have a beneficial initial effect, although it may be injurious in the long run.

ii. Valuation Studies

In part, because the U.S. damage studies are so equivocal, there are no credible economic estimates that value acid deposition damages to forests. Crocker and Regens[60] use estimates by Crocker and Forster[61] assuming a 5% growth reduction. Crocker & Regens include losses in timber production, recreation, water storage, habitats, and other forest services in their estimate of damages from acid rain. Of these categories, the only one explained in the 1985 article is timber. They use the National Academy of Sciences estimate of a 5% reduction in tree growth rates, and assess its market value.[62]

The NAPAP state of science/technology assessment[63] discusses a study by Callaway, Darwin, and Nesse[64] that uses the Timber Assessment Market Model (TAMM) to estimate the economic effects of hypothetical reductions in tree growth in the northeastern and southeastern United States. The TAMM is a forest sector model. Using a timber inventory projection system, the effect of lower growth from acid rain effects on the inventory of timber is modelled. This stock of timber is fed into the economic model of the timber market. The present value of damages (assuming a 10% discount rate) between 1985 and 2030 ranged from $3.4 billion to a little more than $5.0 billion depending on the severity of the hypothetical growth reduction. The NAPAP report does not specify the assumed growth reductions.

NAPAP could not find a single study that quantified the change in appearance of a recreational site caused by acid rain. Because of this void in the literature, they surveyed studies that placed a value on forest recreation. They felt there were four difficulties in generalizing the effects of acid rain which are important to keep in mind while trying to apply these other studies to acid rain damages.[65]

First of all, most of the studies estimate the net benefits which would be lost if an entire recreational site were eliminated. As acid rain would only change the characteristics of a site, this is an inappropriate perspective. The second point is that most studies on recreation estimate the value of a recreational site at the margin,

---

[59] Kimmins, <u>supra</u> note 32 at p. 118.

[60] Crocker, <u>supra</u> note 21.

[61] No cite given.

[62] Crocker, <u>supra</u> note 21 at p. 114.

[63] <u>Methods</u>, <u>supra</u> note 12.

[64] Callaway et al., <u>supra</u> note 29 at p. 178.

[65] <u>Methods</u>, <u>supra</u> note 12 at p. 2-19.

rather than looking at a system wide change, where all substitutes have experienced the same change.

Acid rain would affect an entire region rather than just one site. The third point is that when valuing the changes from acid rain, changing use levels and congestion should also be taken into account. Finally, there is significant overlap between forest recreation and activities such as fishing, and calculating the values of each separately and adding them together will not yield the correct total value.

NAPAP grouped studies that assessed the effect of changes in the appearance of a recreational site into four categories: fire studies, psychologically based studies that rate the scenic beauty of different forest stands, ozone damage studies, and insect damage studies.[66] After discussing the insect damage studies, NAPAP concluded that the types of damage from insects and from acid deposition were too different to transfer values from insect studies for use in acid rain studies.

The fire studies document that there is an effect on recreational value of changes in appearance, but the quantitative results cannot be transferred to acid rain caused damage because the change in physical appearance is so different resulting from the two disturbances. Fire first devastates the forest, and then allows it to regrow. Damage from acid deposition remains as long as the input of acids continues. There is no progress to a healthier or more beautiful forest as long as the deposition continues.

The scenic beauty research likewise cannot give quantitative economic damages to acid rain-induced damage. NAPAP has only found one study that links measures of scenic beauty to economic value.[67] An early study that did not make that link noted that the first signs of damage caused the greatest decline in the rating of scenic quality. Increased damage also caused a decline in the ratings, but at a slower rate. NAPAP concluded from this that the marginal damages caused by acidic damage may be greatest when the effects first become visible.

Brown, Richards, and Daniel[68] interviewed 1464 recreationists in Arizona, asking them to rate scenic beauty and to give willingness to pay for access to those sites. They concluded that scenic beauty accounts for 33% of the variance in willingness to pay. The problem with relating these scenic beauty studies to acid rain is that the connection between physical damage from acid deposition (as opposed to other causes) and changes in scenic beauty is not definitively established.

The two ozone damage studies discussed by NAPAP both have problems that limit their usefulness. Crocker[69] asked recreationists how much more they would be willing to pay above existing costs if the area looked like each of three photographs of

---

[66] Methods, supra note 12 at p. 2-20.

[67] Id. at p. 2-21.

[68] Brown, T., M. Richards, and T. Daniel, Scenic Beauty and Recreation Value: Assessing the Relationship, unpublished manuscript, USDA Forest Service, Rocky Mountain Forest and Range Experiment Station, Fort Collins, CO, 1989.

[69] Crocker, T.D., "On the Value of the Condition of a Forest Stock", Land Economics, 61(3), 1985 at pp. 244-254.

high, medium, and low levels of ozone damage. They were not permitted to give negative answers, so the mean willingness to pay figures were probably affected. The other study on ozone damage, Peterson et al.,[70] did not separate recreational effects from ecological and health effects.

c. Crops

i. Science

Acid deposition can, in theory, cause both direct and indirect effects on agriculture. Considerable research has been directed at direct damage to crops from acidity. Indirect effects include a fertilizer effect from greater inputs of the nitrogen nutrients, and acidification of soil, requiring additional lime to be applied. The treatment of inputs to the production of crops needs to be carefully thought out.

The science underlying direct damage to crops has progressed over the last decade, rendering economic studies based on early scientific results incorrect. Prior to 1983, agricultural damage was demonstrated at pH levels between 2 and 3.[71] The early studies also demonstrated that depending on the types of ions being deposited, and their ratio, beneficial effects of increased acidity are possible. Experiments done on radishes found increases in yield when the acid solution contained sulfuric acid and nitric acid in a 2:1 ratio, and decreases in yield only when sulfuric acid alone was used.[72]

More recent experiments under conditions resembling commercial production indicate that soybean is the only crop to show a response to changes in ambient pH.[73] The current NAPAP assessment concludes that there is no evidence that acid rain in the United States is harming crops.

Irving (1983)[74], in a summary of crop responses based on research prior to 1983, notes that the response of plants to acid rain may depend on soil types, climatic conditions and ozone concentrations. The link between ozone and crops is quite well established, so a complete assessment should take ozone into account as well. In fact, most economic studies of the damages from acid rain on crops at least pay lip service to ozone, and NAPAP devotes a significant section to discussing ozone studies.

---

[70] Peterson, D. et al., Improving Accuracy and Reducing Costs of Environmental Benefit Assessments, Office of Policy, Planning and Evaluation, U.S. Environmental Protection Agency, Washington, DC, 1987.

[71] Crocker, supra note 21 at p. 114.

[72] Forster, supra note 20 at p. 106.

[73] Adams et al., supra note 27 at p. 7.

[74] Irving, P., "Acidic Precipitation Effects on Crops: A Review and Analysis of Research," Journal of Environmental Quality, Vol. 12, no. 4, 1983 [hereafter cited as Irving].

In terms of the indirect effects, NAPAP cites McFee[75] who asserts that a change in liming as a result of a change in acid deposition is a small proportion of total liming required to counteract soil acidification. Fertilizer applied to crops increases the acidity of the soil, and lime is commonly applied to fields to prevent acidification. If lime is not used, in the long term, acidic precipitation may leach soil nutrients or mobilize toxic metals.[76]

ii. Valuation Studies

Studies that were done before the NAPAP research on the direct physical effects on crops was completed, relied on data that have since been refuted because the crops were grown under conditions that did not resemble commercial agriculture.[77] Forster (1984a),[78] Chapman and Kohut (1984),[79] and Crocker and Regens (1985)[80] fall into this category. Adams, Callaway and McCarl (1986)[81] use the newer scientific information.

Forster discusses his 1984 research in both a journal article[82] and in a chapter in a book.[83] In the book, Forster explains in great detail how he calculates his estimates. While he starts by discussing the underlying science, he abandons that approach because the net effects of acid rain on crops are so unclear. Forster also mentions the possibility of comparing costs across farms, and attributes part of the differences to increased acidity. Again, he finds problems with this approach because it seemed likely to him that there would not be sufficient variation across farms since pH is likely to have only small variations over large geographic areas. Finally, Forster resorts to estimates of the additional quantity of lime required per eastern province. His dollar figures include the costs of this lime, but not the labor needed to apply it.

A Cornell Agricultural Economics staff paper by Chapman and Kohut (1984)[84] also discusses liming. They "speculate" that acid deposition on normally

---

[75] McFee, W., Acid Precipitation in Relation to Agriculture, Forestry and Aquatic Biology, Report No. 100, Council for Agricultural Science and Technology, Ames, Iowa, 1984.

[76] Irving, supra note 74 at pp. 447, 452.

[77] Adams et al., supra note 27.

[78] Forster, supra note 20.

[79] Chapman, supra note 14.

[80] Crocker, supra note 21.

[81] Adams et al., supra note 27.

[82] Forster, supra note 20.

[83] Forster, B., "An Economic Assessment of the Significance of Long-Range Transported Air Pollutants for Agriculture in Eastern Canada," Canadian Journal of Agricultural Economics, Vol. 32, November, 1984.

[84] Chapman, supra note 14.

sulfur-sufficient soil requires a 4% increase in liming. From that figure, and assumptions on the cost of lime and the size of the typical 90-cow dairy farm, they calculate that this increase in liming would add about $150 per year to the costs of the farm. For New York, they estimate that acid deposition is probably adding between one and two million dollars annually to the costs of liming.

Crocker & Regens (1985)[85] asserted that no scientific studies had demonstrated a consistent sensitivity of crops to acid deposition. Nevertheless, they presented a damage figure. What this number is based on is not explained in their article. According to Adams, Callaway and McCarl[86], however, Crocker and Regens used ozone pollutant damages as a surrogate for damages from acid deposition.[87]

To date, it appears as though ozone is far worse for plants than acid rain. Separate from their presentation of the damage estimate, Crocker and Regens discuss substitutions among crops, and price effects if yields are affected. This sidelight does not appear to have any connection to the actual dollar estimate.

Adams, Callaway, and McCarl think there may be a net economic benefit to annual crops from acid deposition. Work is currently being done for the 1990 NAPAP report to update this study.

Adams, Callaway, and McCarl use a mathematical programming sector model of the United States agricultural economy to make their calculations of damages to crops. The model was originally used by Adams, Hamilton, and McCarl (1984, 1986)[88] to simulate the least cost allocation of agricultural resources for the base case and cases with alternative ozone concentrations.

The agricultural economy is modeled as a set of primary crop markets which supply commodities to livestock markets and other secondary markets as well as to consumers. Exports of commodities are specifically taken into account. Primary crop producers in each region are aggregated into regional farms. As is typical of activity analysis representations of production, constant returns to scale, divisibility of production processes, and additivity of two or more processes are assumed. A finite set of possible crop mix alternatives available to each regional farm is also assumed.

With its own price elasticities of domestic and export demand, zero cross-price elasticities, and supply elasticities for labor, land, and other inputs given, a competitive equilibrium results which simultaneously maximizes the sum of consumers' and producers' surplus over all modeled agricultural activities over all regions. In all, welfare changes are estimated for ten primary commodities and sixteen secondary commodities.

---

[85] Crocker, supra note 21.

[86] Adams et al., supra note 27.

[87] Id. at p. 16.

[88] Adams, R., S. Hamilton, and B. McCarl, The Economic Effects of Ozone on Agriculture, U.S.E.P.A., EPA-600/3-84-090, Corvallis Environmental Research Laboratory, 1984. Adams, R., S. Hamilton and B. McCarl, "The Benefits of Ozone Control: The Case of U.S. Agriculture", American Journal of Agricultural Economics, 1986.

Demand for commodities is assumed to have either constant or perfect elasticity or, as a third alternative, to be a step function. Constant elasticity curves are truncated arbitrarily (at about three times the 1980 price) to permit calculation of consumer's surplus. The producer's surplus (quasi-rents) is measured as production cost minus the sum of the crop's factor supply curve. These supply curves are assumed to have constant elasticity with the curves truncated at about one-third the 1980 price.

A mathematical programming model is used to determine, for the base case, the optimal allocation of resources to activities, as well as prices, outputs, input quantities, and the welfare measure. To model the optimal allocation of resources to activities when ozone levels change, the baseline yield/acre coefficients are modified according to the dictates of the NCLAN[89] dose-response functions and the programming model is solved again for new prices, outputs, inputs, and the welfare measure. The effect of the ozone change policy on social welfare is then calculated by subtracting the base case welfare measure from the new welfare measure. This approach appears to be reasonable.

For acid rain, this same model is applied using the effects on crops from acid deposition. Only soybean yields are assumed to change with increased acidity. Adams, Calloway and McCarl use, as their base case of acid deposition, a 50% reduction from 1980 conditions. Soybean yields were reduced from the base case to reflect increases in acid deposition of 10, 30, and 50% from the base case. Economic damages from yield reductions, assuming a mix of types of soybeans, ranged from $19 million to $142 million depending on the amount of acidity.

Besides this direct effect, Adams, Callaway, and McCarl calculated indirect effects of fertilizer cost reductions (benefits) from increased deposition of nitrogen and sulfur and increased liming costs. They estimate that the benefits of the free fertilizer exceed $200 million, although that figure is biased upward because the deposition is year round instead of just during the growing season, and some crops do not need fertilization. The extra liming involved is calculated to reduce producers' surplus by $15 million and consumers' surplus by $9 million. Thus, on net, increasing acid rain decreases agricultural costs.

d. Materials

Acid rain affects many types of materials. This section deals only with materials used in buildings or other man-made structures. There are two categories of materials of concern: damage to historical, artistic, or irreplaceable objects, and damage to other more ordinary items. No studies were located that value damages to the first category of objects, although certainly damage does occur.

---

[89] See Heck, "Assessing Impacts of Ozone Control on Agricultural Crops: II. Crop Yield Functions and Alternative Exposure Statistics," Journal of the Air Pollution Control Association, Vol. 34, 1984, at pp. 810-817.

i. Science

For stone, acid rain deposits ions which then react with the minerals present. The rate of corrosion is affected by the relative reactivity of the material to acid, delivery of moisture, gases, and particles to the surface, the physical force of delivery, and the intensity, duration and amount of rain. Calcium carbonate, as in limestone, and calcium sulfate, as in gypsum, are particularly susceptible to acid rain. Although limestone and gypsum are most susceptible, other materials are also damaged by the acidity.

One complication that can arise when valuing damages to materials from acid rain is that corrosion can occur at pH levels higher than those caused by the increased acidity. For instance, concrete is corroded at pH levels less than 6, but since ordinary rainwater has a pH of 5.6, "acid" rain is not the only kind of precipitation that will corrode concrete. On the other hand, some materials do not show any effects until the pH drops below the level that could be considered natural. At pH levels less than 5, zinc, commonly used as a protective coating for steel, will also begin to dissolve.[90]

ii. Valuation Studies

The most thorough study of materials damage is Lipfert (1987)[91], which values SO_2 and acid rain damages to materials (paint, galvanized steel, mortar, and stone) in the New Haven, CT region. Lipfert uses damage functions estimated by combining data from eight test programs comprising 72 different test sites in many countries. Most of the programs used data based on the deterioration of test samples exposed on racks, mounted at 30 to 45 degrees to the horizontal, facing south.

The materials distribution to calculate the dollar value of damages to materials in the New Haven-West Haven, CT metropolitan statistical area (MSA) was broken down into five-by-five kilometer grid squares on the basis of census tract centroid locations.[92] The damages are calculated relative to a zero pollution environment, based on 1980 pollution levels, although the damage functions are approximately linear, so intermediate levels of pollution can be calculated.

The unit cost factors, which are based on the costs of repainting or replacing, are as follows: $\$1/ft^2$ for repainting 15% of the total area, $\$3/ft^2$ for repainting mortar, $\$4/ft^2$ for replacing galvanized steel, and $\$22/ft^2$ for replacing stone facing. Lipfert did not cite unit cost factors for concrete and structural steel, although he briefly discussed the physical damages to structural steel.

As Lipfert noted, carbon steel is not normally used in an unprotected state, so information on its corrosion is useful primarily as a reference for the deterioration

---

[90] McCormick, J., Acid Earth: The Global Threat of Acid Pollution, Earthscan, London, U.K., 1985 at pp. 37-39.

[91] Lipfert, supra note 3.

[92] Lipfert cites Merry, C. and P. Lapotin, A Description of the New Haven, CT Building Material Data Base, Draft Report, US Army Cold Regions Research and Engineering Laboratory, Hanover, NH, 1985.

rates of steel with different degrees of protection. Because neither copper nor aluminum were found in large quantities in the area, the replacement or repair costs to these materials were not valued.

Lipfert finds that the costs from H^+ (hydrogen ions) alone are $3.42 million annually, about $8.50 per capita, with total costs from SO_2 and H^+ about $6 million, or $15 per capita. Repainting is responsible for the lion's share of the costs. With the linear damage function assumption, the benefits of a 50% reduction in acid rain would be about $4.25 per capita.

This study is a reasonable example of an "engineering" approach to damage valuation, in that damage functions are linked to unit values for repainting and replacement, but these values have no behavioral content. These unit values do not reflect the frequency and type of responses made by building owners to signs of materials damage or to the prospect that acid rain may damage materials in the future. Therefore, the above estimate of materials repainting and replacement costs may be a poor estimate of the actual benefits of a reduction in acid rain, even in New Haven. There are examples of materials damage estimates that do rely on behavioral models, but these apply to soiling damages from particulates, not acid rain.

The results of the Lipfert study can be generalized to other areas, using population as a scaling factor, particularly to cities of about the same average age and size as New Haven. It should be recognized, however, that these estimates will reflect the mix of materials and the ratio of population to affected materials found in New Haven. Further, as Lipfert does not link acid rain reductions back to SO_2 emissions, the results of this study need to be linked with an SO_2/acid deposition model to be applied to other areas.

While Crocker & Regens (1985)[93] discuss various aspects of valuing damages to materials, they do not describe their approach. They discuss the ability to substitute less vulnerable materials in new construction versus mitigation for existing buildings, and mention the problem of valuing objects that are linked to "cultural heritage". These are the kind of impacts that it is important to measure in future research.

The quantity of materials that may be damaged in New York and New England is enormous. For cultural resources, 20% of historic stone buildings are located in Massachusetts, and 19% are located in New York.[94]

5. Future Prospects for Better Estimates

Although some of the studies reviewed estimate the externality costs of acid deposition, an attempt to derive values from existing data runs two risks. On the one hand, both the scientific and economic data are inadequate. On the other hand, an estimate that consists only of damage components and values that can be rigorously defended will necessarily be an underestimate of social costs and may thereby trivialize

---

[93] Crocker, supra note 21.

[94] Methods, supra note 12 at pp. 4-3.

the problem of acid deposition by making the costs seem smaller than they really are. Nonetheless, where there is scientific and economic data available, making a start in the right direction will stimulate a demand for better data and methods.

For aquatic and materials damages, especially the former, studies now in progress offer the prospect of substantially improving the information base for benefit estimation. This work, conducted jointly by the EPA and Batelle Institute for NAPAP, is expected to be completed by September 1, 1990, when a report is due to be submitted to Congress.

The EPA/Batelle study will examine freshwater fishing benefits in four states: New York, Maine, Vermont and New Hampshire. A telephone survey of 7000 people selected randomly from the general population has been conducted, and about 1000 anglers were identified. A detailed questionnaire concerning fishing participation was then distributed to the angler subset.[95] The data will be used to generate demand functions for freshwater fishing by employing for comparative purposes, three different estimation methods: the random utility model, the share model, and the hedonic travel cost model.

In this study, the acid rain damages to recreational fishing are assumed to work through fishing success. If the catch rate declines at a recreational site, presumably the site becomes less attractive and less visited.

To connect catch rate with the physical effects of acid deposition the EPA-Batelle study willutilize work recently completed by NAPAP estimating a biological abundance index for a subset of lakes in the study area. Based on lake characteristics, such an index can be calculated for each lake in the study area. The angler survey will then be used to associate estimated biological abundance to the catch rate.

NAPAP studies now complete or soon to be completed will also permit links between the biological abundance index and water chemistry, water chemistry and acid burden, and acid burden and emissions. When these studies are combined with the economic study, there may finally be established a link between emissions and valuation, at least for aquatic damages in the Northeast.

Matters should soon be improving for materials damage as well. Materials inventories are steadily improving, and dose-response functions are improving also. These functions now can rely not only on laboratory experiments but extensive field data on a variety of materials at sites around the country. What is missing are the behavioral components: the study of individual actions as indicators of how people value damage to materials, including how they attempt to protect themselves against such damage.

Empirical methods developed for particulate soiling studies could usefully be applied here. We believe, in fact, that work of this sort is currently the most urgent research need for development of benefit estimates.

---

[95] The initial survey is said to contain some questions that would permit a contingent valuation of benefits among nonusers, but analysis of this data set will not be attempted this summer.

6. Conclusion

The studies reviewed do not provide a comprehensive and credible estimate of external costs; adequate data is not yet available. The paucity of studies even attempting economic evaluation of acid deposition effects is surprising. The main obstacle to such estimates is the difficulty of linking emissions to effects that can be valued. Construction of a chain of cause and effect is exceedingly complex, requiring linkage between emissions and acid formation, between acid formation and acid deposition, between acid deposition and physical/biological effects, and between physical effects and willingness to pay. Construction of such estimates may be possible in the near future, at least for freshwater fishing and materials damage. Studies to be completed by NAPAP by the end of the summer should make it possible to estimate economic damages in these important categories of effects.

7. References

Adams, R., J. Callaway and B. McCarl,"Pollution, Agriculture and Social Welfare: The Case of Acid Deposition," Canadian Journal of Agricultural Economics Vol. 34 March, 1986, pp. 3-19.

Adams, R., S. Hamilton and B. McCarl, The Economic Effects of Ozone on Agriculture, U.S.E.P.A., EPA-600/3-84-090, Corvallis Environmental Research Laboratory, 1984.

Adams, R., S. Hamilton and B. McCarl, "The Benefits of Ozone Control: The Case of U.S. Agriculture," American Journal of Agricultural Economics, 1986.

Berner, E. and R. Berner, The Global Water Cycle: Geochemistry and Environment, Prentice-Hall, Inc., 1987.

Bockstael, N., K. McConnell and I. Strand, Benefits from Improvements in Chesapeake Bay Water Quality, Report for EPA under Cooperative Agreement CR-811043-01-0 with the University of Maryland, College Park, MD, 1988.

Brown, G., et al., National Acid Precipitation Assessment Program State-of-Science/Technology Report 27 Part B: Methods For Valuing Acidic Deposition and Air Pollution Effects, 1989.

Brown, T., M. Richards and T. Daniel, Scenic Beauty and Recreation Value: Assessing the Relationship, unpublished manuscript, USDA Forest Service, Rocky Mountain Forest and Range Experiment Station, Fort Collins, CO, 1989.

Callaway, J., R. Darwin and R. Nesse, Economic Effects of Hypothetical Reductions in Tree Growth in the Northeastern and Southeastern United States, PNL-5939, Pacific Northwest Laboratory, Richland, WA, 1986.

Chapman, D. and R. Kohut, Ozone and Acid Deposition: An Economic Perspective on Agricultural and Forestry Impact, Cornell Agricultural Economics Staff Paper, No. 84-28, 1984.

Crocker, T., "On the Value of the Condition of a Forest Stock," Land Economics 61(3), 1985.

Crocker, T., and J. Regens, "Benefit-Cost Analyses of Acid Deposition Control: A Benefit-Cost Analysis: Its Prospects and Limits," Environmental Science and Technology, Vol. 19, February 1985.

Feely, H., and D. Bogen, Contributions of Local Sources to the Acidity of Rain in an Urban Area, paper abstract presented at the NADP Technical Committee Meeting, Provincetown, MA, October 23-26, 1989.

Forster, B., "An Economic Assessment of the Significance of Long-Range Transported Air Pollutants for Agriculture in Eastern Canada," Canadian Journal of Agricultural Economics Vol. 32, November, 1984.

Forster, B., Economic Impact of Acid Precipitation: A Canadian Perspective in Economic Perspectives on Acid Deposition Control, 1984.

Harrington, W., Acid Rain: Science and Policy A Primer, Resources For the Future, Washington, DC, 1989.

Heck, "Assessing Impacts of Ozone Control on Agricultural Crops: II. Crop Yield Functions and Alternative Exposure Statistics," Journal of the Air Pollution Control Association Vol. 34, 1984.

Huppert, D., Two Empirical Issues in Recreational Fisheries Economics: Mail Survey Self-Selection Bias And Divergence Between WTP and WTA, EPA 230-08-88-034, U.S. EPA, Washington, DC, Fourth Annual Area Workshop: Marine Sport Fisheries, Economic Evaluation and Management, Seattle, WA, June 23-24, 1988.

Irving, P., "Acidic Precipitation Effects on Crops: A Review and Analysis of Research," Journal of Environmental Quality, Vol. 12, no. 4, 1983.

Kealy, M., J. Dovidio and M. Rockel, "Willingness to Pay to Prevent Additional Damages to the Adirondacks From Acid Rain," Reg. Sci. Rev., 1987.

Kimmins, J., Forest Ecology, Macmillan Publishing Company, New York, 1987.

Lipfert, F., Effects of Acidic Deposition on the Atmospheric Deterioration of Materials, Materials Performance, July 1987.

MacKenzie, J. and M. El-Ashry, eds., Air Pollution's Toll on Forests and Crops, Yale University Press, New Haven, CT, 1989.

McCormick, J., Acid Earth: The Global Threat of Acid Pollution, Earthscan, London, U.K., 1985.

McFee, W., Acid Precipitation in Relation to Agriculture, Forestry and Aquatic Biology, Report No. 100, Council for Agricultural Science and Technology, Ames, Iowa, 1984.

Menz, F. and J. Mullen, Acidification Impact on Fisheries, in Economic Perspectives on Acid Deposition Control, Crocker, T., ed., Butterworth Publishers, Boston, MA, 1984.

Menz, F. and J. Mullen, "Valuing the Effect of Acidification Damages in the Adirondack Fishery: Reply," American Journal of Agricultural Economics, February, 1989.

Merry, C. and P. Lapotin, A Descrition of the New Haven, CT Building and Material Data Base, Draft Report, U.S. Army Cold Regions Research and Engineering Laboratory, Hanover, NH, 1985.

Morey, E., and W. Shaw, "An Economic Model to Assess the Impact of Acid Rain: A Characteristics Approach to Estimating the Demand for and Benefits from Recreational Fishing," In: V. Smith and A. Witte, eds., Advances in Applied Microeconomic Theory, Vol. 8, JAI Press Inc., Greenwich, Connecticut (forthcoming).

Mullen, J. and F. Menz, "The Effect of Acidification Damages on the Economic Value of the Adirondack Fishery to New York Anglers," American Journal of Agricultural Economics, February, 1985.

National Research Council, Acid Deposition Atmospheric Processes in Eastern North America, National Academy Press, Washington, DC, 1983.

Navrud, S., "Estimating Social Benefits of Environmental Improvements from Reduced Acid Depositions: A Contingent Valuation Survey," in Folmer, H. and E. van Ierland, Valuation Methods and Policy Making in Environmental Economics, Elsevier, Amsterdam, Holland, 1989.

Office of Technology Assessment, Acid Rain and Transported Air Pollutants: Implications for Public Policy, Washington, DC, 1984.

Peterson, D., et al., Improving Accuracy and Reducing Costs of Environmental Benefit Assessments, Office of Policy, Planning and Evaluation, U.S.E.P.A., Washington, DC, 1987.

Phillips, T. and B. Forster, "Economic Impacts of Acid Rain on Forest, Aquatic, and Agricultural Ecosystems in Canada," American Journal of Agricultural Economics, December, 1987.

Shaw, W., "Valuing the Effect of Acidification Damages on the Adirondack Fishery: Comment," American Journal of Agricultural Economics, February 1989.

State of the Environment: A View toward the Nineties, The Conservation Foundation, Washington, DC, 1987.

Stevens, W., "Worst Fears on Acid Rain Unrealized," New York Times, February 20, 1990.

U.S.E.P.A. et al., National Acid Precipitation Assessment Program (NAPAP), Interim Assessment, Washington, D.C., 1987.

U.S.E.P.A. et al., National Acid Precipitation Assessment Program (NAPAP), State of Science/Technology, Washington, DC, 1989.

Violette, D., A Model Estimating the Economic Impacts of Current Levels of Acidification on Recreational Fishing in the Adirondack Mountains, U.S.E.P.A., Washington, DC, 1985.

Welle, P., Potential Economic Impacts of Acid Rain in Minnesota: The Minnesota Acid Rain Survey, unpublished manuscript, Department of Economics, Bemidji State University, Bemidji, Minnesota, 1985.

1976-77 New York Angler Survey Final Report, New York State Bureau of Fisheries, Albany, New York, 1981.

V. EXTERNALITY COSTS BY EMISSION

E. PARTICULATES

V. EXTERNALITY COSTS BY EMISSION

E. PARTICULATES

1. Introduction

Fossil-fuel-fired electricity generating systems, particularly coal and oil-fired facilities, are significant emitters of particulate matter. The major components of particulate emissions from a power plant include ash, which is made up of heavy metals, radioactive isotopes and hydrocarbons, and sulfates (SO_4) and nitrates (NO_3), which are formed by the reaction of sulfur dioxide (SO_2) and nitrogen oxides (NO_x) in the atmosphere. The smallest ash particulates (including sulfates and nitrates) cause human respiratory effects and impaired visibility. Other effects may include materials damage due to soiling and possibly corrosion, damage to domestic and wild flora through deposition of particulates on foliage, and possible health effects on domestic animals and wild fauna.

Several studies focus on the direct effects of high ambient levels of small particulates. This chapter reviews the available literature on the effects of particulate emissions on humans and their environment, and attempts to assign a cost figure to the environmental effects and human health impairments associated with particulate matter emissions. Specifically, this report focuses on the effects of particulates related to human health, visibility, flora, fauna and materials.

2. Composition of Particulates

This report focuses on the man-made emissions of particulate matter from fossil-fuel fired electricity generating systems, since the literature suggests that these are some of the largest producers and emitters of particulate matter. Particulate matter emitted into the atmosphere by these systems can be dispersed and deposited at various distances up to hundreds of miles away. Other sources, including industrial boilers, solid waste combustion and the production of biomass fuel are also significant sources of particulate emissions.

Particulates are very fine solid particles ranging in size from 1 to 100 microns with extremely varied chemical properties. They are categorized as either primary of secondary, depending on their physical and chemical properties and their size.

Primary particulates are injected directly into the atmosphere by chemical or physical processes and are generally greater than 2.0 microns in diameter. Data on the chemical composition of primary particulates is sparse even though their environmental effects are widely known.

Secondary particulates are mainly formed by the combination of sunlight with chemicals such as sulphur dioxide (SO_2), ammonia (NO_4), nitric oxides (NO_x), water and hydrocarbons, and are predominantly 0.005-2.0 microns in diameter.[1] They have life spans of approximately one week to forty days before they are deposited by rain or combine to form large particles and eventually settle out of the atmosphere as dry deposition.

In general, smaller particles are more hazardous to human health and visibility because they enter the human respiratory system more easily than larger particles, which can be filtered out. However, larger particles are more important in soiling. All particulates contribute to visibility impairment.

3. Particulate Emissions

Particulates are generally referred to in the literature as total suspended particulates (TSP) or particulate matter (PM). These terms refer to both primary and secondary particulates, and particulate matter smaller than 10 microns, or PM10. PM10 constitutes virtually all of particulate emissions from gas and oil-fired combustion processes, and ranges from approximately 45% to 65% of particulate emissions from coal-fired sources.

The amount of particulates emissions must be known in order to estimate the effects caused by the particulates emissions. While damages attributed to particulates generally include damages caused by sulfates and nitrates, emissions figures generally do not include all of the SO_4 and NO_3 produced from a plant. Some of the sulfates and nitrates are formed in the atmosphere from emissions of SO_2 and NO_x. Estimates of the effects of the major energy-related secondary particulates, sulfates and nitrates may overlap with the damages reported in Sections V.B and V.C. on damages caused by SO_2 and NO_x, respectively. An effort has been made to eliminate any duplication in the figures.

4. Particulate Effects

a. Human Health Effects

Particulates, like other airborne pollutants, enter the lungs and cause reduced respiratory function in healthy humans, and aggravate respiratory conditions in those with existing respiratory ailments. The smaller particles, PM10, are believed to account for the majority of particulate-related health problems, for two reasons: the smaller particles remain suspended in the air longer, so their chances of being inhaled and absorbed are increased as they are filtered out; and the acidic secondary particulates are very damaging to lung tissue.

---

[1] Cadle, R., "Particulate Matter in the Lower Stratosphere," Chemistry of the Lower Stratosphere, ed. S.I. Rassol. N.Y., Plenum Press, 1973.

As discussed in previous sections, there are many studies that review the health effects of existing pollution levels, for instance Cannon (1990)[2]; or the benefits of pollution reduction, such as Hall (1989)[3], Krupnick and Kopp (1988)[4] and Rowe et al. (1986).[5] It is useful to discuss the results of these studies to understand the issues surrounding the direct cost estimates. However, as pointed out in the SO_2 and NO_x sections, we are able to take advantage of the results of only some of these reports to estimate the direct cost of pollutant emissions. Many of the studies do not divide the damages among contributing pollutants and/or do not provide related emissions figures of the specific pollutants.[6] Here we review the studies that do estimate damages caused by particulates.

Hall (1989) estimates that 1,062 premature deaths caused by PM10 would be avoided each year in the South Coast Air Basin (SoCAB) if the federal standard for PM10 were achieved in that area. If the California standard were met, Hall estimates that 1,802 PM10-related deaths would be avoided annually. Hall bases her dose-response relationships on work done by Evans et al. (1984)[7], which reports high uncertainties in the dose-response relationships presented. Hall uses Evans "best" estimate of PM10 mortality to estimate mortality benefits of reducing ambient particulate levels, although according to Evan's results, mortality could plausibly be zero. Hall gives a range of mortality benefits of meeting the federal standard for PM10 of $967 million to $13.9 billion, which correspond to values of avoiding premature death of about $900,000to $13 million. At a value of $4 million per avoided death, as developed in Section III, Hall's avoided mortality estimate implies $4.25 billion (1989) in mortality benefits.

In Section V.C.,we dealt with Hall's estimate of the benefits of reducing ambient ozone by estimating a benefit per pound of ozone precursor, including NO_x and VOCs. For PM10, we can estimate the mortality benefit in a similar manner. SCAQMD

---

[2] Cannon, J., The Health Costs of Air Pollution: A Survey of Studies Published 1978-1983, American Lung Association, August 1985, pp. 12-14.

[3] Hall, J., Economic Assessment of the Health Benefits from Improvements in Air Quality in the South Coast Air Basin, Report to the South Coast Air Quality Management District, Contract No. 5685, California State University Fullerton Foundation, Fullerton, CA, June 1989.

[4] Krupnick, A., and R. Kopp, The Health and Agricultural Benefits of Reductions in Ambient Ozone in the United States, Prepared for OTA COntract No. H3-6820.0,June 1988.

[5] Rowe, R., and L. Chestnut, The Value of Visibility: Economic Theory for Air Pollution Control, Cambridge, MA, Abt. Books, 1982.

[6] Although much of this information is not available for this report, obtaining comparable emissions estimates is technically possible.

[7] Evans, J., T. Tosteson, and P. Kinney, "Cross Sectional Mortality Studies and Air Pollution Risk Assessment", Environmental International, Vol. 10, pp. 55-83.

(1989)[8] reports that the emissions reductions required for SoCAB to meet the federal PM10 standard by 2010 from a 1985 baseline are 230 T/day for PM, 74 T/day for SO_x, and 715 T/day for NO_x. We can estimate a plausible range of PM10 emissions reductions from these emissions: 1) If all of the SO_x and NO_x were converted to SO_4 and NO_3, respectively, and all of the PM reported in SCAQMD were smaller than 10 microns (or PM10), then SCAQMD (1989) implies PM10 emissions reductions of 1305 T/day PM10 (230 T/day PM + 111 T/day SO_4 + 964 T/day NO_3);[9] 2) If 45% of the PM emissions reductions are PM10, which is implied in SCAQMD (1989, Table 3.1), and SO_4 and NO_3 emissions are included in this figure, then PM10 emissions reductions are 45% of 230 T/day, or 103 T/day.

The former PM10 emissions estimate of 1305 T/day almost certainly overstates actual PM10 emissions, but provides a maximum value. The latter estimate of 103 T/day ignores the contribution to ambient PM10 made by the formation of SO_4 and NO_3 in the atmosphere, and is a very low estimate of the PM10 emissions responsible for the health effects in the SoCAB region.[10] However, the PM10 emissions reductions in SoCAB required to meet the federal PM10 standard by 2010 should fall in the range 103-1305 T/day, or 37,595-476,325 T/year PM10.

Relating the emissions figures to Hall's estimated mortality benefits of $4.25billion (adjusted to reflect a value per life of $4 million) Hall's results imply that the average benefit of attaining the federal PM10 standard is in the range $4.50-$57/lb PM10 (1989$) for mortality alone. The marginal benefit of reducing ambient PM10 levels today is likely to be higher than the average benefit of achieving the federal PM10 standards in SoCAB.

The emissions reductions required to meet the California PM10 standard are higher than those attainable with either the Tier II or Tier III of SCAQMD control measures, and are not provided in SCAQMD (1989). Therefore, we are unable to estimate a per-pound benefit of achieving the California standards.

Harrison and Nichols[11] (1990) of NERA review Hall's study, and report that Hall's estimates of mortality due to PM10 are not well supported based on the uncertainties in the results of Evans, et. al. (1984). Harrison and Nichols choose to assume that until a more definitive analysis is performed, the "best" estimate is that there are no particulate-related mortalities.

For other health benefits of meeting PM10 regulations, Hall estimates that the annual reduction in restricted activity days (RADs) would be 14.6 million days for

---

[8] South Coast Air Quality Management District, Air Quality Management Plan: South Coast Air Basin, Southern California Association of Governments, March 1985 [hereafter cited as SCAQMD, 1989].

[9] One ton of SO_x converts to 1.5 tons of SO_4; one ton of NO_x converts to 1.35 tons of NO_3.

[10] Hall assumes that particulate health effects are due to PM10.

[11] Harrison, D., and A. Nichols, Benefits of the 1989 Air Quality Management Plan for the South Coast Air Basin: A Reassessment, Prepared for the California Counsel for Environmental and Economic Balance, National Economic Research Association Inc., Cambridge, MA, February 1990.

attainment of the federal PM10 standard, and 24.7 million RADs for attainment of the California PM10 standard. Valuing RADs at $66 per day, Hall estimates that morbidity benefits of attaining the federal standard are $967 million, and $1.63 billion for the California standards. Dividing the morbidity benefits of achieving the federal PM10 standards by the PM10 emissions reductions estimated above, the unit benefits are $1.01-12.90/lb PM10. We cannot estimate the unit benefits of achieving the California standard, as noted above.

As discussed in Chapters V.B. and V.C., ECO Northwest performed several studies on the environmental costs of emissions from power plants (ECO, 1983, 1984, 1987). ECO (1987)[12] estimates the damages caused by particulates emissions from a generic coal-fired plant in or near Washington state for seven cases. For the plant located in the most highly populated location, annual particulate-related deaths were estimated to be 0.2, or 1 death every five years over the operating life of the plant. Valued at $4 million per premature death, the annual mortality costs associated with this plant are $776,000 (1989$). Based on particulate emissions of 1,193 T/yr, the cost of particulate-related mortality is $0.33/lb (1989$). The same study estimates that the particulate emissions for the same case will cause 31 cases of bronchitis which, when valued at $400,000 per 200 acute illnesses, are worth $62,000, or about $0.03/lb particulates.[13] The lowest population density case results presented in this study are on the order of about one-tenth the high-density case (Table 1).

ECO (1984)[14] estimates the pollution-related damages from the Frederickson plant located in Pierce County, Washington, an area similar to the ECO (1987) high-density case. ECO (1983)[15] estimates pollution-related damages for the Boardman coal-fired plant in Oregon. Both of these reports estimate that no human mortalities occur, or no risk of mortality is assumed by residents, as a result of the operation of these power plants. The Boardman study also estimates no morbidity, while the Frederickson study estimates the morbidity to be the same as ECO (1987) high-density case, $0.03/lb particulates.

b. Visibility

Estimates of damages related to visibility focus on the occurrence of regional haze, or the loss of visibility over distance. The aesthetic impact of the plume from a power plant stack may also be important. However, the effects of a plume are very site-specific and are not necessarily negative because in some regions the plume of a

---

[12] ECO Northwest et al., Generic Coal Study: Quantification and Valuation of ENvironmental Impacts, report commissioned by Bonneville Power Administration, January 31, 1987 [hereafter cited as ECO (1987)].

[13] $400,000 per 200 acute illnesses is equivalent to $2,000 per acute illness.

[14] ECO Northwest et al., Economic Analysis of the Environmental Effects of a Combustion Turbine Generating Station at Frederickson Industrial Park, Pierce County, Washington: Final Report, report commissioned by Bonneville Power Administration, March 26, 1984 [hereafter cited as ECO (1984)].

[15] ECO Northwest et al., Final Report Economic Analysis of the Environmental Effects of the Coal Fired Electric Generator at Boardman, Oregon, report commissioned by Bonneville Power Administration, December 1983 [hereafter cited as ECO (1983)].

TABLE 1: DIRECT COSTS OF PARTICULATE EMISSIONS
ECO NORTHWEST: GENERIC COAL STUDY, 1987
(All figures stated in 1989$)

RESPONSE	WEST SIDE, LARGE CITY				OUTSIDE TERRITORY, SMALL CITY			
	INCIDENTS (NUMBER)	UNIT VALUE (1989$)	DAMAGES ($)	$/lb PARTICULATES	INCIDENTS (NUMBER)	UNIT VALUE (1989$)	DAMAGES ($)	$/lb PARTICULATES
	[1]	[2]	[3]	[4]	[5]	[6]	[7]	[8]
MORTALITY	0.194	4,000,000	$776,000	$0.33	0.013	4,000,000	$52,000	$0.02
MORBIDITY	0.155	400,000	$62,000	$0.03	0.011	400,000	$4,500	$0.00
CROP LOSSES	0		0	0	0		0	0
LIVESTOCK			$17	$0.00			$83	$0.00
TIMBER	0		0	0	0		0	0
MATERIALS			$3,740	$0.00			$274	$0.00
ECOSYSTEMS	0		0	$0.00	0		0	0
VISIBILITY	NA		NA	NA	NA		NA	NA
TOTAL			$841,757	$0.35			$56,857	$0.02

[1]: ECO Table 3-3A; Morbidity units are "200 short duration (average 3-day) illnesses."
[2], [6]: Unit Values. Blanks indicate ECO unit values were used, and inflated to 1989$.
[3]: [1]*[2] For Mortality and Morbidity; for Material Damage see ECO Table 3.1.
[4], [8]: ($ Damages)/2,386,000 lbs particulates/yr.
[5]: ECO Table 3-3F.
[7]: [5]*[6] For Mortality and Morbidity; for Material Damage see ECO Table 3.1.

power plant (or another plant) is considered by some people to be a positive sign of economic health.

The two primary approaches used to value changes in visibility in a residential or recreational setting, as discussed previously, are hedonic property value (HPV) studies and contingent valuation (CV) studies.[16] In HPV studies, the premise is that residents' preferences toward air quality will be reflected in the market prices for homes and property. In CV studies, residents of, and visitors to an area are asked how much they would be willing to pay to improve visibility from one level to another (say from 1km to 5km, or 10km to 20km). A value "per person-km-year" is then estimated, and can be used to generalize between results from different studies.

The ECO studies reviewed here are concerned only with the effect of general visibility loss. ECO (1987) uses a crude guess, for which it provides no basis, to estimate reductions in visibility to be 0.1 km for the first 50 km from the plant and 0.01 km thereafter. Multiplying the populations at various distances from the plant by these distances gives the number of person-kms by which visibility will be reduced. Since the estimate of the visibility effect in ECO (1987) is not well supported, we will rely on the apparently more rigorous air quality modeling analysis performed by ECO in its 1984 study.

ECO (1984) estimates separate impairment factors for each pollutant contributing to visibility reduction, including particulates. It estimates that 10,000 person-kms will be lost annually due to particulate emissions. Valued at $10/person-km (1987$) or $10.80/person-km (1989$) this translates into a cost of $0.83/lb particulates (1989$).

c. Flora

ECO, in the studies we have reviewed (1983, 1984, 1987), estimates particulate emissions damages to crops, commercial forests and ecosystems to be zero. We have found no other useful estimates for the crop damage due to particulates.

d. Materials

ECO (1983, 1984, 1987) assume material damages are proportional to the population surrounding the plant sites, and applies a national average material damage per capita estimated by Waddell (1974) to the population in order to estimate the materials damage.[17] To at least two decimal places, ECO estimates that the materials damage due to particulates is zero in each of the studies.

---

[16] See, Chapter III for further discussion.

[17] Waddell, T., The Economic Damages of Air Pollution, U.S.E.P.A., 1974.

e. Wildlife, Endangered Species, and Ecosystems

ECO (1987) discusses dose-response relationships and assumes that wild animals have the same sensitivity to air pollutants (including particulates) as do humans, and that wild plants have the same sensitivity as do cultivated crops. ECO (1987) outlines the potential effects of a power plant on an ecosystem: potential loss of individuals of a species which is not endangered but is generally acknowledged to have considerable value; upset of the role different ecosystems play in production of various environmental services such as water, soil fertility and waste recycling; and the reduction of the perceived "naturalness" of a valued area. ECO estimates in this report, and in the 1983 and 1984 reports, that particulate-related damages to ecosystems are zero.

5. Summary

Damages due to particulates are presented in Table 2. They are strongly dominated by health effects and visibility losses since many of the other damages are poorly understood (and have not been valued) or are very small (so they are shown as a zero value).

Our use of the damage estimates from the reports reviewed to estimate the damages/lb particulates is strongly limited by the uncertainties associated with the underlying assumptions and the estimates themselves. Many of the uncertainties inherent in the use of damage estimates from the studies are discussed in Chapter V.B.4 for SO_2 emissions. Specifically important for particulate emissions, the visibility valuation is very regional, and even site-specific, as it is based on the general level of visibility, and the preferences of residents and visitors. The health effects are also very site-specific, in the sense that the physical features of the site determine the transport of the pollutant through the air, its direction, distance, concentration (and potentially even composition) when it contacts humans. Also, other effects such as damages to wildlife and ecosystems are not well understood, and are potentially highly undervalued. Finally, the assignment of damages between primary and secondary particulates, and between emissions of particulates and SO_x or NO_x, is tentative and may result in either double counting or complete omission of some effects.

In summary, we have reported estimates for particulate damages on humans and their environment. Aggregation of these estimates provides a very rough starting point of $1.18/lb of emissions for use in a direct cost analysis of the environmental impacts of particulate emitting sources (Table 3). The damages could be much higher: 1) for a plant located in a more highly populated area; 2) in a region where visibility is highly valued; and, 3) once other potential effects of particulates are understood.

TABLE 2: DIRECT COSTS OF PARTICULATE EMISSIONS
ECO NORTHWEST: FREDERICKSON, OIL-FIRED CASE, 1983
(All figures stated in 1989$)

RESPONSE	FREDERICKSON, OIL-FIRED CASE, ECO (1984)				BOARDMAN COAL-FIRED PLANT, ECO (1983)			
	INCIDENTS (NUMBER)	UNIT VALUE (1989$)	DAMAGES ($)	$/lb PARTICULATES	INCIDENTS (NUMBER)	UNIT VALUE (1989$)	DAMAGES ($)	$/lb PARTICULATES
	[1]	[2]	[3]	[4]	[5]	[6]	[7]	[8]
MORTALITY	0	4,000,000	$0	$0.00	0	4,000,000	0	0
MORBIDITY	0.010	400,000	$4,000	$0.03	0	400,000	0	0
CROP LOSSES	0		0	0	0		0	0
LIVESTOCK	NA		NA	NA	NA		NA	NA
TIMBER	NA		NA	NA	NA		NA	NA
MATERIALS			$1	$0.00			$10	$0.00
ECOSYSTEMS	0		0	0	0		0	0
VISIBILITY	10,000	10.80	$108,000	$0.83	4.0	10.80	$43	$0.00
TOTAL			$112,001	$0.86			$53	$0.00

[1]: ECO (1983) Table III-6; Morbidity units are "200 short duration (average 3-day) illnesses."

[2], [6]: Unit Values. Blanks indicate ECO unit values were used, and inflated to 1989$.

[3]: [1]*[2] for Mortality and Morbidity; Others are taken from ECO (1983) Table III-8 (AND INFLATED TO 1989$).

[4]: [3]/130,000 lbs particulates/yr.

[5]: ECO (1984) OIL-FIRED CASE; Table III-5. GAS-FIRED CASE has similar (lower by about 15%) results.

[7]: [5]*[6] for Mortality and Morbidity; Others are taken from ECO (1984) Table III-7 (and inflated to 1989$).

[8]: [7]/246,000 lbs particulates/yr.

NA: Indicates no estimate attempted by ECO.

TABLE 3: SUMMARY OF DAMAGES DUE TO PARTICULATES

<<<< COSTS PER LB PARTICULATES >>>>

EFFECT	ECO(1987) LARGE CITY [1]	ECO(1987) SMALL CITY [2]	ECO(1983) [3]	ECO(1984) OIL CASE [4]	HALL (1989) [5]	STARTING POINT [6]
HEALTH						
Mortality	0.33	0.02	0	0	4.50	0.33
Morbidity	0.03	0	0	0.03	1.01	0.03
Total						
MATERIALS	0	0	0	0		0.00
VEGETATION						
Crops	0	0	0	0		0.00
Ornamentals						
Forests	0	0	NA	NA		0.00
Total						
VISIBILITY	NA	NA	0	0.83		0.83
OTHER						
Ecosystems	0	0	0	0		0
Livestock	0	0	0	NA		0
TOTAL	$0.36	$0.02	$0.00	$0.86	$5.51	$1.19

Notes: See text for description and limitations of these estimates.

[1][2][3][4]: Figures have been restated in 1989 dollars.

[5]: Hall's figures imply mortality damages of $4.50-$57/lb PM10,and morbidity benefits of $1.01-$12.90/lb PM10. Harrison and Nichols estimate no effects.

[6]: The starting point figures are for a "typical" location, which we define as similar to the western Washington site in the Generic Coal Study (ECO, 1987). Population densities and other parameters will vary with location. The uncertainties associated with these estimates in the original studies are large; the studies did not have estimates for some potentially important effects; and the existence and magnitude of some of the reported effects are still in considerable dispute. The estimates should be used with great caution, as they indicate only a possible magnitude of the damages.

V. EXTERNALITY COSTS BY EMISSION

F. LAND USE AND WATER POLLUTION IMPACTS

V. EXTERNALITY COSTS BY EMISSION

F. LAND USE AND WATER POLLUTION IMPACTS

1. Introduction

This section discusses the environmental impacts associated with solid and liquid combustion wastes and cooling system discharges from nuclear, coal, oil, and gas fired power plants. This chapter also presents data for land use requirements for these types of power plants. Solar, wind, hydro and biomass power supply technologies also have some land use and water impacts, but the impacts vary greatly in kind and degree from conventional power technologies. For this reason the water and land externalities of these technologies are discussed in subchapter VI.E.

Coal, oil and nuclear power plants also generate a variety of solid wastes from power generation and maintenance operations. These solid wastes must be disposed of in landfills, which may have a variety of adverse effects on surface water, groundwater, and land use. Power plants also require significant amounts of land for plant sites, fuel storage, transmission lines, and waste disposal.

These effects are highly site specific. For example, the potential for groundwater contamination by combustion wastes may depend on local hydrogeologic conditions. The impacts of thermal discharges vary with the size of the receiving water body, cooling water volume and plant operation schedules. Land use impacts will depend on the nature of surrounding geography, demographics, and wildlife needs. The impacts will also vary greatly depending upon the stringency of mitigation measures required by state and local government.

Large fossil fuel and nuclear plants require large quantities of water for cooling and maintenance. The removal from and return of cooling water to rivers, streams and lakes may have adverse effects on fish populations and other aspects of aquatic ecosystems. Other water impacts include pollution of surface water from coal storage pile and plant site run-off, and wastewater discharges of acids, organics, suspended solids and metals derived from boiler or cooling system maintenance procedures.

For these reasons it is very difficult to determine a generally applicable externality cost figure for land and water impacts of electric power plants. The New York Public Service Commission (NYPSC) appears to have made the only effort to do so. Its estimate was based on control and mitigation costs, rather than on estimates of damages. The NYPSC conclusion is summarized in the next part of this subchapter. Our review of the literature does not reveal damage based externality costs for any land or water effects. In the area of cooling water intake effects (fish impaction and entrainment) the literature provides for a range of control or mitigation based externality costs. A discussion of that literature is contained in part 3. The remainder of this subchapter consists of a general discussion of thermal, waste disposal, land consumption and wastewater effects of fossil and nuclear plants.

2. Land and Water Externality Values Adopted by the New York Public Service Commission

The NYPSC has adopted figures for land use and water pollution externalities of fossil fuel plants for use in new capacity bidding programs. It assigned a .1 cent per kilowatt hour externality to water-related impacts and a .4 cent per kilowatt hour for land use-related impacts.[1] These figures were derived from studies by the Bonneville Power Authority (BPA),[2] based on the cost of controlling or mitigating residual water discharges and land use impacts. The land use externality figure was extrapolated from a BPA case study of land use related social costs of a nuclear power plant, which BPA estimated to range from 0.1 to 0.44 cents per kilowatt hour.[3] In adopting these estimates for water and land impacts, the NYPSC acknowledged the difficulties in assigning these values. In early spring of 1989 it ordered the utilities to fund and participate with state agency staff in a state-wide "pooled effort to develop estimates of external environmental costs for all electric supply and demand options."[4]

3. Impacts of Water Intake

Thermal electric generating facilities use heat to convert water into steam to drive electric generating turbines. This steam must be condensed back into water in order to be cycled through the turbines again. Condensing is accomplished through a heat exchange process that relies on another, separate, body of water to absorb the heat of the steam. This body of water can either be a closed system of cooling water, or water drawn continuously from a nearby water source in a once-through cooling process.

Once-through cooling, by far the most common cooling systems in power plants, can have three major types of environmental impacts: water use/consumption; impingement/entrainment; and thermal pollution. The costs of these damages are largely external to the cost of electricity.

When water is drawn from lakes, rivers, estuaries, or the ocean, it must be screened in order to prevent debris from entering the relatively delicate condenser/heat exchange system. In screening the cooling water, aquatic organisms can be pinned against the screening devices and can be injured or die. This effect is known as "impingement". Organisms, primarily eggs and small larval fish too small to be excluded by the screens, can also be drawn through the heat exchange system to suffer

---

[1] Putta, S. Competition In Electric Generation--Environmental Externalities, New York State Public Service Commission staff paper, October 1988, pp. 9-10.

[2] Quantification and Economic Valuation of Selected Environmental Impacts/Effects, Bonneville Power Administration Contract No. DE-AC79-83BPIN552.

[3] New York State Public Service Commission, Consideration of Environmental Externalities in Competitive Bidding Program of Orange and Rockland Utilities, (undated) pp. 4-5.

[4] Case 28223, Electric Utility Conservation Programs, Opinion No. 89-15 (issued May 23, 1989), p. 40. See also, Putta, S., supra note 1 at p. 10.

thermal, mechanical and pressure shocks--a process often fatal to the organism involved. This effect is termed "entrainment".

Finally, the heated water discharged from the system can upset the normal balance of aquatic life in the receiving waters by destroying vegetation, causing nitrogen embolisms, oxygen depletion, and leaving fish subject to cold shocks when facility operation is interrupted. Figure 1 represents environmental impacts associated with various components of a once-through cooling system. Thermal discharge impacts are discussed in part 4 of this section.

Closed-cycle cooling systems, using mechanical draft or hyperbolic cooling towers, greatly reduce the amount of water drawn through the cooling system--on the order of 2 to 4% of the water required for once-through cooling.[5] Basically, only that water necessary to offset evaporative losses is required. Yet, closed-cycle cooling systems impose other environmental costs not associated with once-through systems. Coastal facilities are believed to cause salt drift, where salt bearing steam drifts across neighboring lands, damaging agricultural capacity. Cooling towers are capable of causing increased local fogs and road icing under certain climatic conditions. Finally, closed-cycle cooling often involves cooling towers, large structures which may carry a negative aesthetic component. Closed-cycle cooling systems are seldom installed at generating facilities because of their high construction costs. See Table 11 infra. The authors are unaware of any attempts to quantify the negative environmental impacts associated with these structures. Their construction and operation costs, however, can be considered a measure of the mitigation cost of the water consumption, impingement/entrainment and thermal pollution impacts of once-through systems.

In next section, we review studies which attempt to quantify some of the environmental costs associated with the once-through cooling process at thermal electric generating facilities. Damage cost estimations are not available for the impacts of this process.

[5] Sharma, et al., Survey of Fish Impingement at Power Plants in the United States, Argonne National Laboratory, ANL/ES-56 (3 volumes), 1977.

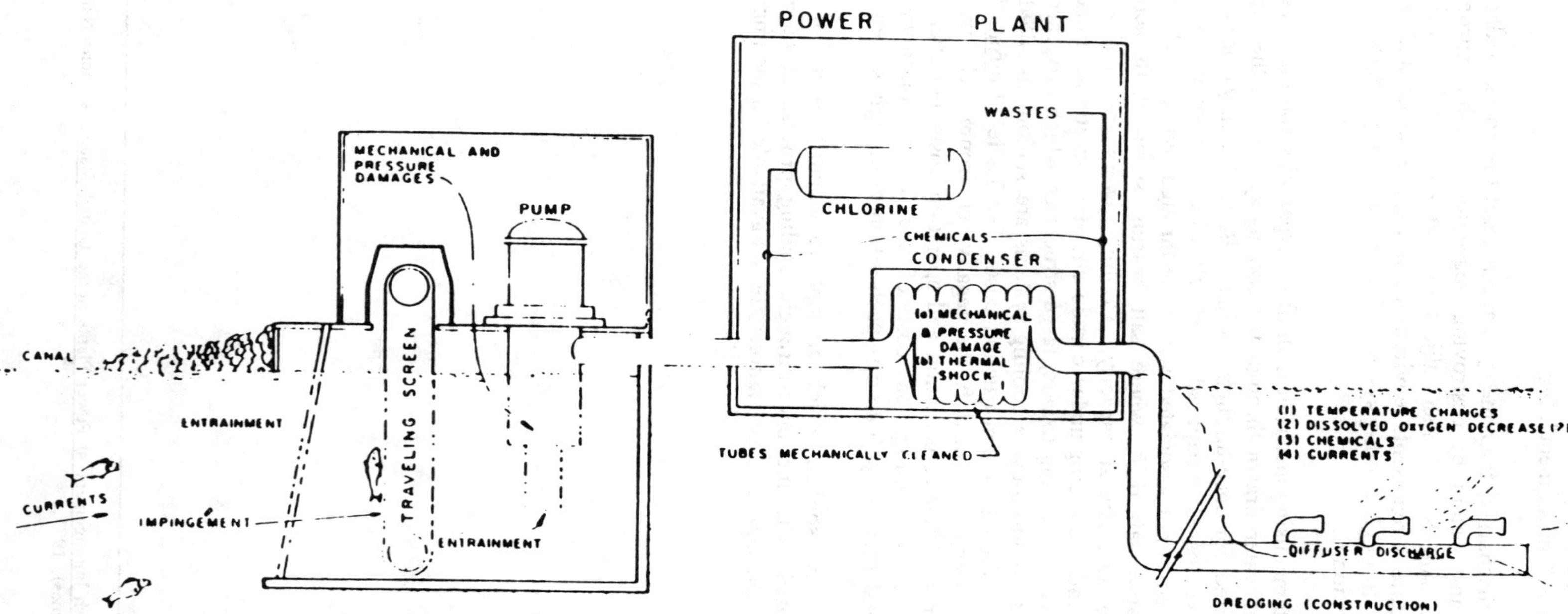

Figure 1.

Schematic Representation of a Typical Once Through Cooling System and Sources of Potential Biological Damage.

Source: Clark, J. & W. Brownell. 1973. Electric Power Plants in the Coastal Zone: Environmental Issues. American Littoral Society Special Publication No. 7. Fig. III-9.

a. Water Consumption and Use

i. Water Consumption

Data has been collected estimating the amount of water consumption for various combustion-based and nuclear generation methods. Water consumption primarily occurs through evaporative losses from the cooling system. Department of Energy studies estimate fossil combustion water consumption to range from $.779 \times 10^{-6}$ acre feet/kWh to 3.097×10^{-6} acre feet/kWh. For nuclear generation, the range is from 2.63 $\times 10^{-6}$ acre feet/kWh to 4.078×10^{-6} acre feet/kWh.[6] When converted to gallons per kilowatt hour, these figures appear small indeed, ranging from .254 gal/kWh to 1.009 gal/kWh for fossil plants and .854 gal/kWh to 1.329 gal/kWh for nuclear plants.[7] In order to develop a cost for water consumption, an average cost per gallon of untreated water from the local source could be applied to these gallon per kilowatt figures. In some areas where water is in short supply the water consumption may be a significant externality. We did not discover any study which attempts to apply such prices to develop an externality cost for water consumption. A graphic description of water consumption for various generating technologies is provided in Table 1.

ii. Water Use

Although total water consumption is relatively small, the amount of water which passes through the once-through-cooling systems is quite large. In the Hudson estuary, for example, during summer peaking periods, the water diversions of the several

---

[6] The following Department of Energy studies formed the basis for Tables 1, 15, 16, 17, 18, 19 and 20:

San Martin, R., Environmental Emissions from Energy Technology Systems: The Total Fuel Cycle. Washington, DC: U.S. Department of Energy, April 1989 [hereafter cited as San Martin].

U.S. Department of Energy (DOE), draft, Energy System Emissions and Material Requirements, prepared Meridian Corporation, Alexandria, VA: February, 1989 [hereafter cited as DOE/Material].

U.S. Department of Energy (DOE), Fossil Energy, Innovative Clean Coal Technology: Programmatic Environmental Impact Analysis (PEIA), prepared by Oak Ridge National Laboratory, September 1988 [hereafter cited as DOE/PEIA].

U.S. Department of Energy (DOE), Office of Environmental Protection, Safety, and Emergency Preparedness, Office of Environmental Analysis, Energy Technology Characterizations Handbook: Environmental Pollution and Control Factors, 3d ed., prepared with assistance from Aerospace Corporation and Mueller Associates, Inc., DOE/EP-009, Washington, DC: DOE, March 1983 [hereafter cited as DOE/Char].

[7] An example is the WPPSS-2 nuclear plant, Its environmental impact statement reported that the unit would evaporate 160 million gallons of water annually. Sharma, K.J., Environmental Costs and Benefits Case Study: Nuclear Power Plants--Quantification and Economic Valuation of Selected Environmental Impacts/Effects, Nero and Associates, Inc., Portland, OR, 1984, p. 4, Appendix B.

Hudson River power plants reportedly often exceed fresh water input to the river.[8] Data from a study by Argonne National Laboratories shows that nuclear plants use approximately 76.45 gallons of water per kilowatt hour of energy produced. Fossil fuel plants use about 57.46 gallons per kilowatt hour.[9] Data collected by the Hudson Riverkeeper Fund's Atlantic Coast Power Plant project shows an average water use of 78.73 gallons and 57.65 gallons per kilowatt hour for nuclear and fossil plants respectively.[10] Data on water use by waste-to-energy plants is not readily available.

Although these water uses are large, they do not directly constitute a cost associated with electricity generation. The water is returned to the water body from which it was withdrawn and thus is available for its original uses. The true costs associated with water use for once-through cooling systems are best reflected in the costs associated with impingement and entrainment effects, thermal effluent effects and chemical discharge effects.

---

[8] Hutchinson, J., "Technical Descriptions of Hudson River Electricity Generating Stations", American Fisheries Society Monograph 4:113, at App. 1; and Cooper, J., et al., "Overview of the Hudson Estuary", American Fisheries Society Monograph 4:11, 1988, at Table 2.

[9] Sharma, et al., supra note 5. These are average figures. usage for individual plants can be much lower. This is especially true in northern states, where, during colder months, plants may use considerably less cooling water. Personal communication with Edward Raidle, Supervising Aquatic Biologist, New York State Department of Environmental Conservation, June 21, 1990.

[10] Data collected as part of the Hudson Riverkeeper Fund's Atlantic Coast Power Plant Project by Karl Rabago and Diana Leicht. This data consists of available reports and statistics drawn from the Utility Data Institute, a utility information database, and through records searches at State regulatory agency offices. Copies of reports and other data may be obtained from the Hudson Riverkeeper Fund, P.O. Box 130, Garrison, New York 10524,
(914) 424-4149.

TABLE 1

WATER USE FOR COMBUSTION-BASED GENERATION

		Water Consumption (acre-ft/Kwh)
COAL-BASED GENERATION		
Steam with FGD		
DOE/Materiel	(1)	3.097×10^{-6}
DOE/Char (Eastern Coal)	(2)	2.36×10^{-6}
DOE/Char (Western Coal)	(3)	1.52×10^{-6}
AFBC		
DOE/Materiel (Ill. Coal)	(4)	3.097×10^{-6}
DOE/Char (Ill. No. 6)	(5)	1.63×10^{-6}
DOE/Char (Subbituminous Western)	(6)	1.99×10^{-6}
IGCC		
DOE/Materiel	(7)	1.856×10^{-6}
OIL-BASED GENERATION		
Steam with FGD		
DOE/Char	(8)	0.857×10^{-6}
NATURAL GAS BASED GENERATION		
Steam		
DOE/Char	(9)	0.779×10^{-6}
NUCLEAR (For comparison)		
Boiling Water Reactor		
DOE/Materiel	(10)	4.078×10^{-6}
DOE/Char	(11)	2.76×10^{-6}
Pressurized Water Reactor		
DOE/Char	(12)	2.62×10^{-6}

(1) Figure is "water demand" for a conventional 500 MW facility producing 3.5×10^9 Kwh of electricity annually "built to meet or exceed existing environmental standards and to maximize performance" and using a wet lime/limestone scrubber. DOE/Materiel at 12 and 23, Figure 9.

(2) Power plant make-up consumption for a 500 MWe conventional steam electric facility with onsite water treatment and recirculation facility to minimize liquid discharges. Plant is located at mine-mouth and fired with typical eastern bituminous coal. Source notes an additional 58-138 acre-ft/year of water would be consumed in coal preparation. Annual electricity production is 3.52×10^9 Kwh. DOE/Char at 91-92 (Coal-fired Power Plant-Eastern Coal).

(Continued on next page)

(3) Conventional steam electric 500 MWe facility using western low sulfur (0.63% S) coal with wet lime/limestone scrubbers and onsite water treatment and recirculation. Data is for cooling tower makeup consumption and includes 445 acre-ft/yr for dust control and SO2 control makeup. Annual electricity production is 3.52 x 10^9 Kwh. DOE/Char at 93-94 (Coal-fired Power Plant - Western Coal).

(4) "Water demand" for 500 MW AFBC plant with annual energy production of 3.5 x 10^9 Kwh. DOE/Materiel at 13 and 23, Figure 9.

(5) Consumptive water uses for 814 MWe steam electric facility with AFBC and conventional water treatment as necessary, producing 4.63 x 10^9 Kwh/yr. DOE/Char at 83-84 (Atmospheric Fluidized Bed Combustion - Bituminous Coal).

(6) Consumptive water uses for 536 MWe steam electric facility with AFBC and conventional water treatment as necessary producing 4.45 x 10^9 Kwh/yr. DOE/Char at 85-86 (Atmospheric Fluidized Bed Combustion - Western Subbituminous Coal).

(7) "Water demand" for 945 MW IGCC plant producing approximately 6.7 x 10^9 Kwh/yr. DOE/Material at 13 and 23, Figure 9.

(8) Cooling tower make-up for mechanical draft cooling towers for 800 MWe oil-fired steam electric plant operating with an annual capacity factor of 55 percent. DOE/Char at 114 (Oil-Fired Steam Electric Plant).

(9) Once through (consumptive water use only) for 800 MWe gas-fired steam electric plant operating with an annual capacity factor of 55 percent. Source notes that "cooling towers can also be used as cooling system." DOE/Char at 134 (Gas-Fired Steam Electric Plant).

(10) "Water demand" for 1000 MW BWR producing 6.13 x 10^9 Kwh/yr. DOE/Materiel at 13 and 23, Figure 9.

(11) Make-up water for cooling tower and miscellaneous plant services for 1000 MW BWR (GE Mark III design) operating at 70 percent capacity. Plant has natural draft wet cooling towers and onsite treatment of river supply water. DOE/Char at 19-21 (Boiling Water Nuclear Power Plant).

(12) Make up water for cooling and miscellaneous plant services for 1000 MW PWR operating at 70 percent capacity. Plant has natural draft wet cooling towers and onsite treatment of river supply water. DOE/Char at 17-18.(Pressurized Water Reactor Nuclear Power Plant).

b. Impingement and Entrainment Impacts

Impingement and entrainment losses caused by cooling water intake structures can have significant effects on populations of fish in the source water body. For example, water demand at the Salem nuclear plant accounts for an estimated 11% direct reduction in the Delaware estuary year-classes of weakfish (Cynoscion regalis) and a 31% direct reduction of the bay anchovy (Anchoa mitchilli)[11].

In the Hudson estuary, impingement cropping alone is reported to reduce the annual year-class abundances of Hudson River white perch (Morone americana) by 20% or more.[12] At the Indian Point 2 and 3 reactor on the Hudson River fish impingement for 1987 totaled 1,539,162 fish, at a rate of 848 fish per 1,000,000 cubic meters of water. These losses occurred in spite of the installation of a screening device designed to avoid some impingement.[13] The year-class losses of striped bass (Morone saxatilis) to both impingement and entrainment range from 10 to 15% in the Hudson River.[14] At the 90 thermal electric generating facilities using once-through-cooling on the Great Lakes, reports indicate that in excess of 40 million fish per year were lost to impingement. Estimates suggest this figure could range as high as 100 million fish, accounting for an equivalent loss of 7,500 metric tons of fish per year. By comparison, the annual harvest for all fish species in the Great Lakes is estimated at 50,000 metric tons.[15]

Estimates at the Brunswick nuclear generating facility in North Carolina suggest that the plant's once-through-cooling system would result in a loss of 46% to 99% of the larvae in the Cape Fear River estuary. For spot, croaker, trout and shrimp, entrainment was estimated to cause a 3.07 million pound reduction. Impingement estimates at that plant suggested a reduction from 8.1 million to 3.1 million for the number of juvenile fish, or some 66% of the estuary population.[16]

---

11 Versar, Inc., Technical Review of Thermal Effects Studies and Cooling Water Intake Structure Demonstration of Impact for the Salem Nuclear Generating Station, Versar, Inc., Columbia, Md, 1986.

12 Van Winkle, W. et al., Evaluation of Impingement Losses of White Perch at the Indian Point Nuclear Station and Other Hudson River Power Plants, Environmental Sciences Division, Oak Ridge National Laboratory, ORNL/NUREG/TM-361, Oak Ridge, Tennessee, 1980.

13 Fletcher, R., On the Reconfiguration and Empirical Evaluation of Prototype Screening Device at Indian Point Nuclear Unit 2, Final Report to the Hudson River Fisherman's Assn., 1986.

14 Barnthouse, L. and W. Van Winkle, "Analysis of Impingement Impacts on Hudson River Fish Populations", American Fisheries Society Monograph 4:274-279,1988. Boreman, J. and C. Goodyear," Estimates of Entrainment Mortality for Striped Bass and Other Fish Species Inhabiting the Hudson River Estuary", American Fisheries Society Monograph 4:162-160,1988.

15 Gates, D., Energy and Ecology, Sinauer Associates, Inc., 1985.

16 Decision of the EPA Regional Administrator (Region IV), In the Matter of: Carolina Power and Light Company, Brunswick Steam Electric Plant, Units 1 & 2, 1977, [hereafter cited as EPA/Carolina].

Studies in the early 1970's at the Brayton Point plant facility on Mount Hope Bay, Massachusetts, established a record high of 164.5 million fish impinged on a single day. On several other days, kills ranged from 7 to 28 million per day.[17]

Most of the information on impingement and entrainment losses is anecdotal. A serious effort to account for nation-wide losses, initiated at Argonne National Laboratories in the late 1970's,[18] ended before sophisticated analysis of the collected data was completed. This was coincidental with the remand of the Federal regulations governing cooling water intakes, discussed below. As a result, the data collected for that analysis is outdated. Most of the other studies occurred in the mid to late 1970's. With improvements in water quality occurring since that time, it is likely that the data on impingement losses reported from those studies are extremely conservative for present day conditions.

Cooling water intake structures are governed by section 316(b) of the Clean Water Act.[19] Section 316(b) requires that cooling water intakes reflect the best technology available for minimizing adverse environmental impact. The EPA promulgated regulations under this provision in 1976. But the regulations were remanded to the EPA under a 1977 court order[20] and were withdrawn by the EPA in 1979. No federal regulations have been promulgated in their place.

Most states have authority delegated from the EPA to administer NPDES (National Pollution Discharge Elimination System) programs. A survey of the water protection laws on the east coast revealed only two states with specific provisions relating to cooling water intakes. New York has a regulatory provision that mimics the language of section 316(b) in the Clean Water Act (CWA). Maryland has adopted regulations requiring utility investment in impingement mitigation technology, depending upon the number of fish impinged at the plants. Additionally, Delaware has recently undertaken a review of their CWA section 316 program.[21]

Most regulation of cooling water intakes, therefore, occurs under the "case by case" provisions of section 402 of the Clean Water Act.[22] That section, and the regulations implementing it, allow state and federal agencies to set "best professional judgment" standards where no federal regulations exist. Current regulatory practice in this area is in the nature of a variance proceeding. Essentially, utilities applying for NPDES permits undertake studies to determine the impacts of impingement and

---

[17] Clark, J. and W. Brownell, Electric Power Plants in the Coastal Zone: Environmental Issues, American Littoral Society Special Publication No. 7, 1973, [hereafter cited as Clark & Brownell].

[18] Sharma, et al., supra note 5.

[19] 33 U.S.C. 1326(b).

[20] Appalachian Power Co. v. Train, 566 F.2d 451 (4th Cir. 1977).

[21] Survey conducted by Versar, Inc., ESM Operations, Columbia, Maryland, April 1990.

[22] 33 U.S.C. 1342.

entrainment on water sources. These "Section 316(b) Demonstrations" generally attempt to show that the intake structure satisfies the requirements of § 316(b) thereby avoiding a closed-cycle cooling requirement as might otherwise be imposed under the "best professional judgement" standard. Agencies review the Demonstration reports and make determinations on a case-by-case basis. It is fairly clear that closed-cycle cooling is the most effective means currently available for minimizing impingement/entrainment and thermal pollution impacts. The section 316(b) standard, however, has been interpreted in EPA administrative decisions to be limited by what is "economically achievable." Therefore, the utility demonstrations focus on attempting to show that any minimization of environmental impacts avoided by closed-cycle cooling is disproportionate to the costs of such systems.

The resulting regulatory structure varies from state to state, infrequently considers cumulative effects of multiple plants, and is seldom invoked absent some public agitation. There has been no general trend toward the installation of closed-cycle cooling systems in new or existing large power plants, nor has significant effort been devoted to the reduction of impingement and entrainment effects caused by once-through systems, except in limited areas such as the Hudson River.[23] By and large, once a plant has had its cooling water intake structure approved by the appropriate regulatory agency, the issue of impingement and entrainment is never revisited on permit renewal.[24]

c. Estimates of Costs

We have attempted to collect and consolidate the available data on impingement and entrainment effects. Major sources include the Argonne Labs study (Table 2.), discussed above, various professional writings and reports on the subject, and data collected by the Hudson Riverkeeper Fund's Atlantic Coast Power Plant Project (Table 3).[25] Perhaps the only comprehensive estuary-wide research available is that stemming from studies mandated by the Hudson River Settlement Agreement, which temporarily ended the dispute over the installation of cooling towers at the various Hudson River plants.

For impingement, the data consists of current information on file in regulatory agencies on the east coast, and information contained in miscellaneous reports and other documents. Power capacity and water intake figures were taken directly or indirectly from utility data plate information. Annual kWh production estimates were derived by multiplying MW capacity by 5,343,600 (24x365x1000x.61), under a

---

[23] Biological monitoring, surveys and studies are a required component of the Hudson River Settlement Agreement. This effort has resulted in the development of an extensive body of information on the Hudson River estuary ecosystem.

[24] New York appears to be an exception. Powerplants there undergo a 316(a) and (b) review (for mitigations of aquatic effects every time the state water discharge permit is renewed. Personal communication with Edward Raidle, Supervising Aquatic Biologist, New York Department of Environmental Conservation, June 21, 1990.

[25] See, Sharma, supra note 5.

continuous operation and average 61% load factor assumption. Average impingement per kWh figures for costing analysis were derived only from those facilities from which both entrainment and impingement data were available, under an assumption that this data might have been more accurately obtained.

All reported cost estimations are for impingement effects, and are therefore quite conservative as to total aquatic impacts. The end result of our estimation process is an impingement per kWh figure for a hypothetical 500 megawatt plant (Table 4). Table 5 shows anecdotal information concerning screen mortalities collected by Clark & Brownell, and demonstrates the degree of variation from the estimated impingement rates that is possible at specific sites.[26]

For entrainment, we discovered no cost estimation methodologies. Table 6 reflects a collection of anecdotal information on inner plant kills collected by Clark & Brownell. Ecologically, entrainment effects can be quite significant in two ways. First, in estuarine systems, although fecundity can be quite high, with each female of some species producing thousands or millions of eggs, natural mortalities of eggs, larvae, and early juveniles are also quite high--greater than 95% in some species. Therefore, success of some fish species depends on an extremely small margin of natural survival. When once-through cooling systems located in major spawning grounds entrain eggs, yolk-sac, post yolk-sac larvae, and early juveniles, they impose significant added mortalities. Models have been developed which can predict the added conditional mortality imposed on fish populations by entrainment.[27] The conditional mortality is the fraction of an initial population that would be killed by entrainment during the year if no other sources of mortality operated.

Further research into the valuation of individual species stocks could be applied to these conditional mortality rates to estimate the cost per kWh of electricity. It must be stressed that due to ecosystem, spatial and temporal variances among generating

---

[26] See, EPA/Carolina, supra note 16.

[27] See generally, Boreman and Goodyear, "Estimates of Entrainment Mortality for Striped Bass and Other Fish Species Inhabiting the Hudson River Estuary", American Fisheries Society Monograph 1988, 4:152; Vaughn, "Introduction to Section 3: Entrainment and Impingement Impacts", American Fisheries Society Monograph 1988,4:121; Muessig, et al., "Advances in Field and Analytical Methods for Estimating Entrainment Mortality", American Fisheries Society Monograph 4:125, 1988; Christensen and Englert, "Historical Development of Entrainment Models for Hudson River Striped Bass", American Fisheries Society Monograph 1988, 4:133-142. See also Englert and Boreman, "Historical Review of Entrainment Impact Estimates and the Factors Influencing Them", American Fisheries Society Monograph 1988, 4:143-151; Barnthouse, "An Analysis of Factors that Influence Impingement Estimates at Hudson River Power Plants", in The Impact of Entrainment and Impingement on Fish Populations in the Hudson River Estuary ch. I (Oak Ridge Nat'l Lab., NUREG/CR-2220, TM-385/V2, 1982) [hereafter cited as Oak Ridge Report, 1982]; Van Winkle and Barnthouse, "Evaluation of Impingement Losses of White Perch at Hudson River Power Plants," ch. II, Oak Ridge Report, 1982; Barnthouse and Van Winkle, "Impingement Impact Estimates for Seven Hudson River Fish Species," ch. III, Oak Ridge Report, 1982; Cada and Lee, "Alternative Screening Devices at Indian Point Units 2 and 3, Bowline Point, and Roseton Generating Stations," ch. IV, Oak Ridge Report, 1982; Barnthouse, "Density-Dependent Growth: A Critique of the Utilities' Empirical Evidence," ch. V, Oak Ridge Report, 1982; Golumbek and Christensen, "A Critical Review of the Utilities' Age Composition Analysis of the Hudson River Striped Bass Population," ch. VI, Oak Ridge Report, 1982; Golumbek, et al., "A Critical Evaluation of the Lawler, Matusky and Skelly Two-Dimensional, Real-Time, Life-Cycle Model of the Hudson River Striped Bass Population," ch. VII, Oak Ridge Report, 1982.

facilities, the most useful information is that developed for a specific site [28] and applied to an entire fishery.[29]

Second, entrainment losses have the potential for adversely affecting adult populations by destroying the underlying food sources for adults. This impact is particularly difficult to estimate in estuarine and coastal ecosystems due to the abundance of life forms in these regions, and the fact that the effects are delayed and indirect in nature. A pictorial diagram of these effects appears in Figure 2.

[28] Goodyear, "Implications of Power Plant Mortality for Management of the Hudson River Striped Bass Fishery", American Fisheries Society Monograph, 1988, 4:245-254.

[29] Van Winkle, et al., "Relative Contributions of Hudson River and Chesapeake Bay Striped Bass Stocks to the Atlantic Coastal Population", American Fisheries Society Monograph, 1988, 4:255-266.

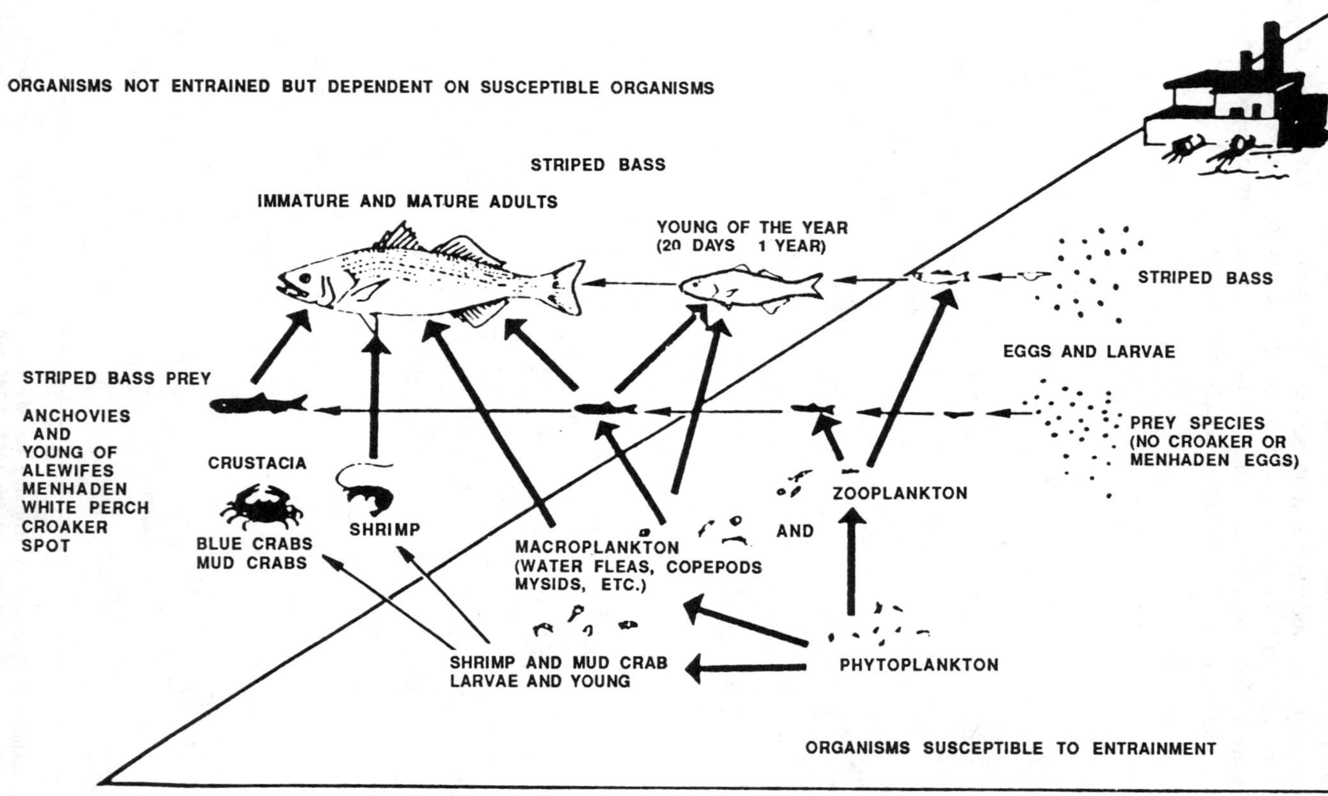

Figure 2.

Diagram Showing Areas of Potential Power Plant Impact on Striped Bass and Associated Food Items.

Source: Clark, J. & W. Brownell. 1973. Electric Power Plants in the Coastal Zone: Environmental Issues. American Littoral Society Special Publication No. 7. Fig. V-9.

TABLE 2a

Plant and Impingement Data from Argonne Labs

No.	Fuel	MW	Kwh/Year	Gal/Year	Gal/Kwh	Fish Impinged	Fish Impinged/ Kwh
27	Nuclear	29444.0	157,336,958,400	12,028,586,212,800	76.45	70,631,620	0.0004
45	Fossil	46692.6	249,506,577,360	14,337,793,519,200	57.46	173,585,760	0.0007
72	N & F	76136.6	406,843,535,760	26,366,379,732,000	64.81	244,217,380	0.0006

TABLE 2b

Estimates for a 500 MW Plant Based on Data From Argonne Labs

Fuel	MW	Kwh/Year	Gal/Hour	Gal/Kwh	Fish Impinged	Fish Impinged/ Kwh
Nuclear	500.0	2,671,800,000	204,262,094,362	76.45	1,199,423	0.0004
Fossil	500.0	2,671,800,000	153,533,895,298	57.46	1,858,814	0.0007
N & F	500.0	2,671,800,000	173,151,806,963	64.81	1,603,811	0.0006

Source: Sharma, et al. 1977. Survey of Fish Impingement at Power Plants in the United States, Argonne National Laboratory ANL/ES-56 (3 volumes).

TABLE 3

Impingement and Entrainment Effects Based On Hudson Riverkeeper Fund Data

Data Available	Fuel	MW	Kwh/Year	Impingement	Impingement/ Kwh	Entrainment	Entrainment/ Kwh
Impingement & Entrainment	N	6890.4	36,819,541,440	22,364,700	0.00061	35,484,620,000	0.96374
Impingement	N	13815.4	73,823,971,440	47,424,790	0.00064		

TABLE 4

Estimates for a 500 MW Plant Based on Hudson Riverkeeper Fund Data

Type	MW	Kwh/Year	Impingement	Impingement/ Kwh	Entrainment	Entrainment Kwh
Nuclear	500.0	2,671,800,000	1,622,888	0.00061	2,574,931,789	0.96374

Type	MW	Kwh/Year	Impingement	Entrainment	Gallons/Year	Gallons/Kwh	Impinge./ Gal	Entrain./ Gal.
Nuclear	500.0	2,671,800,000	1,622,888	2,574,931,789	210,336,399,818	78.725	0.000008	0.012242

Table 5

Reports and Predictions of Screen Kills of Estuarine Species

Power Plant	Impingement Event	Period	Comments
Millstone, Niantic Bay, CT	Massive kill of small menhaden (more than 2.0 million), screens clogged	1971	Occurring late summer, early fall; plant shut down on 8/21/71; cause unknown persistent low kill of 10 other species.
P.H. Robinson, Galveston Bay, TX	7,191,785 fish impinged in one year	1969-70	Projected from sampling of operating plant; principal species were menhaden anchovy, croaker; highest in March.
Indian Point, No. 1 Hudson River, NY	Yearly kill of 1.0 to 1.5 million fish	Jan. 71	Primarily white perch with 4-10% striped bass.
	Kill of 1.3 million in 9.5 weeks		10% striped bass; plant closed Feb. 8.
Indian Point, No. 2	Massive kills; maximum per day 120,000	Jan. 71	Testing cooling system of new plant (no heat); white perch & other species.
	175,000 fish killed in 5 days	Feb. 72	Testing again (no heat) Con. Ed. fined $1.6 million by NY for kills.
Indian Point, Nos. 1 & 2	Predicted total kill 6.5 million fish/yr		With both plants in full operation; no settlement agreement.
Port Jefferson, Long Island, NY	2 truckloads (at least) of fish killed on screens in 3 days	Jan 26-28, 1966	Mostly small menhaden; also white perch.
Crystal River, (near) Cedar Key, FL	Predicted annual kill of 400,000 fish and 100,000 shellfish	1969	Based upon operation of 3 units (2 units destroy 1/2 amount (1973)).
Brayton Point, Mt. Hope Bay, MA	350,000 fish impinged in one year; mostly menhaden	1971-72	Heaviest from Nov-Mar; flounder, silverside, & others also impinged.
Oyster Creek, Barnegat Bay, NJ	10,000 fish, 5,000 crabs, destroyed per month in spring and summer	1971	Estimated from 19 days of sampling; screen kill in cold season unknown.
Surry Power Station, James River, VA	6 million river herring destroyed in 2-3 months	Oct-Dec, 1972	Estimated by AEC from screen samplings during partial power runs.

Source: Clark, J. & W. Brownell, Electric Power Plants in the Coastal Zone: Environmental Issues, American Littoral Society Special Publication No. 7, Table V-B, 1973.

Table 6

Reports and Predictions of Inner Plant Kills of Estuarine Species

Power Plant	Event	Date	Comments
Brayton Point, Mt. Hope Bay, MA	7.0 to 165.5 million menhaden (some river herring) killed per day	Summer, 1971	Est. from EPA's sampling techniques 164.5 million kill on July 2; fish mangled.
	50 million fish killed in 11 days	Aug 10-21, 1971	Estimated from net tons at discharge; menhaden and blueback herring; tests showed all fish died.
Millstone, Niantic Bay, CT	36 million fish killed in 16 days (probably menhaden and blueback herring)	Nov 2-18, 1971	Estimated by sampling of vertebrae of dead fish in discharge canal.
	2.5 million flounder entrained	Apr-Jun, 1972	Death rate not estimated.
Connecticut Yankee, Conn. River, CT	179 million fish larvae killed per year	1969 & 1970	Estimated by B. Marcy.
Indian Point, Hudson River, NY	Predicted 7.3 million striped bass killed per year (larvae & juveniles)	Future (no settlement agmt)	For Units 1 & 2; estimated from estuary sampling in 1966 & 1967
Seabrook, Hampton-Seabrook Estuary, NH	Predicted kill of 74 million clam larvae per day	Future	Estimated from proposed plant; 74 million is initial kill at plant startup, lower rate after equilibrium reached

Source: Clark, J. & W. Brownell, Electric Power Plants in the Coastal Zone: Environmental Issues, American Littoral Society Special Publication No. 7, Table V-C, 1973.

i. Control Cost Estimation

This study generally does not focus on nor subscribe to the use of mitigation costs to establish externality values. Nevertheless, in the absence of other valuation estimates, the following mitigation costs are noted and provided in Table 12.

Maryland Regulatory Approach

The State of Maryland has recently adopted new regulations pertaining to impingement effects at cooling water intake structures.[30] Maryland chose to require operators of cooling water intake structures to derive a level of mitigation expenditure, required for a five year period, from a formula which uses impingement counts multiplied by a set of factors depending on the nature of the fish (Table 7). This approach derives a simple annual requirement for impingement mitigation expenditures that ranges from $ .75 to $1.00 per fish impinged. The Maryland regulatory multipliers assign greater value to commercial and recreational fish, and less to forage species. This may be an ecologically unsound approach, since forage species are often part of the food chain supporting the larger recreational and commercial species. The figures are then applied to the data derived for a hypothetical 500 MW plant described in Table 8.

---

[30] Code of Maryland Regulations (COMAR), Title 26, Subtitle 08, section .05, 1990.

TABLE 7

Maryland Regulatory Cost Factor for Impingment Effects

Species Function	Factor (Multiplier)
Recreational Only	1.00
Commercial and Recreational	1.00
Commercial Only	1.00
Commercial, Recreational, and Forage	0.80
Commercial and Forage	0.75
Recreational and Forage	0.75
Forage	0.75

Source: Code of Maryland Regulations (COMAR), Title 26, Subtitle 08, section .05 (1990).

TABLE 8

Maryland Regulatory Cost Factor Applied to Hudson Riverkeeper Fund Data for 500 MW Plant

Type	MW	Kwh/Year	Impingement	Impingement/ Kwh	Adjustment Factor	Multiplier	Annual Cost Requirement	Cost/ Kwh
Nuclear	500.0	2,671,800,000	1,622,888	0.00061	High	1.000	$1,622,888.00	$0.00061
Nuclear	500.0	2,671,800,000	1,622,888	0.00061	Low	0.750	$1,217,166.00	$0.00046
Nuclear	500.0	2,671,800,000	1,622,888	0.00061	Average	0.875	$1,420,027.00	$0.00053

Hatchery Replacement Cost Analysis

As part of the Hudson River Power Plant Case Settlement Agreement, utilities with plants in the vicinity of Indian Point, New York began a striped bass hatchery program in an attempt to compensate for impingement losses.[31] Expenses and stocking quantities [32] were analyzed in order to determine an average cost per fish stocked, as described in Table 9.[33] This cost was then applied to estimates for fish impinged per kWh (Table 10). While this method is limited in that it cannot accurately account for the cost to stock all the various species of fish impinged at power plants, it does offer an opportunity for further study, and provides an example of compensatory costing for damage inflicted by once-through cooling. Costs for raising other species of fish in hatcheries may be less or greater than those for striped bass. Finally, there is some question about the effect of large influxes of hatchery reared fish as an adequate substitute for indigenous populations destroyed by intake structures.

Modifications to Once-Through Cooling Systems

The financial requirements of the Hudson River Settlement Agreement provide an insightful estimation of the costs of various mitigative technologies. This estimate can serve as the lowest end of the range of impingement costs associated with electric power production. Included in the Settlement Agreement were provisions for planned outages during spawning season, the cost of establishing a hatchery, and other modifications to plant operations and intake structures.[34] We analyzed that data using the methodology described above regarding Table 4 to obtain the cost per kWh figure shown in Table 11.

Closed-Cycle Cooling

The costs associated with the construction and operation of closed-cycle cooling represent what industry generally considers to be the upper extreme of control costs for impingement and entrainment impacts. Data concerning the estimates of costs for closed-cycle cooling at the Hudson River Plants were analyzed to derive a cost per kWh for this mitigative technology (Table 11).[35] These mitigation cost figures are summarized in Table 12.

---

[31] Barnthouse, J., et al., "Hudson River Settlement Agreement: Technical Rationale and Cost Considerations", American Fisheries Society Monograph 4:267,1988.

[32] EA Engineering, Science, and Technology, Final Hudson River Striped Bass Hatchery 1989 Overview, EA Report No. 60013.03,1990.

[33] Barnthouse, supra note 31 at Table 86.

[34] Table 11 summarizes cost data reported by Barnthouse, et al.

[35] Id.

TABLE 9

Hudson River Hatchery Results
Cost per Fish Stocked Data

Year	No. of Fish Stocked	Annual Cost	Cost/Fish
1983	61,357	$700,000.00	$11.41
1984	147,153	$600,000.00	$4.08
1985	284,578	$600,000.00	$2.11
1986	529,563	$600,000.00	$1.13
1987	324,800	$600,000.00	$1.85
1988	48,611	$600,000.00	$12.34
1989	202,068	$600,000.00	$2.97
AVG	228,304	$614,285.71	$2.69

TABLE 10

Cost Factor Based on Hatchery Costs per Fish Stocked (Applied to Hudson Riverkeeper Fund Data for 500 MW Plant)

Type	MW	Kwh/Year	Impingement	Impingement/ Kwh	Cost per Stocked Fish	Annual Replacement Cost	Cost/ Kwh
Nuclear	500.0	2,671,800,000	1,622,888	0.00061	$2.69	$4,365,568.72	$0.00164

TABLE 11

Closed Cycle Cooling Costs for Hudson River Plants Based on Utility Estimates

Unit Type	Unit MW	Kwh	Capital Construction	Capital Const./ Kwh	Total Revenue Requirement	Total Rev. Req./ Kwh	Annual Levelized Cost	Ann. Lev. Cost/ Kwh
Nuclear	2026.0	216,522,672,000	$320,100,000	$0.00148	$1,296,800,000	$0.00599	$126,034,839	$0.00058

Estimated Costs for Settlement Agreement at Hudson River Plants

Type	Unit MW	Kwh	Baseyear & Capital Construction	Base & Cap. Const./ Kwh	Total Revenue Requirement	Total Rev. Req./ Kwh	Annual Levelized Cost	Ann. Lev. Cost/ Kwh
Nuclear	2026.0	216,522,672,000	$39,424,040	$0.00018	$132,859,376	$0.00061	$12,906,756	$0.000060
All Plants	4426.0	473,015,472,000	$56,800,000	$0.00012	$182,200,000	$0.00039	$17,700,000	$0.000037

ii. Damage Cost Methodologies for Fish Population Losses

This section discusses alternative costing methodologies for recreational and commercial fisheries. The costing data generated from these damage based methodologies is separated from the control costs discussed above because these damage based methodologies do not yield the kind of data which is readily reducible to cents per kilowatt hour. An attempt is made, however, to discuss the type of information that is missing from selected alternative methodologies which, if provided by future research efforts, would produce a cents per kilowatt hour figure.

Fee

A basic methodology available to value a day of fishing is to equate the value of the recreation resource with the fee charged for a day's use. Some economists believe that this methodology is insufficient because it tends not to consider the richness and variety of the fishing area and, therefore, drastically undervalues the resource. The fee charged to engage in a day of fishing must, therefore, only reflect the minimum value of the resource.[36]

Travel Cost

If the fishing area charges no fee for its use, economists look to the cost of travel from one's home to a fishing site. Increased travel costs result from reductions in fish populations caused by impingement and entrainment effects, which require recreational and commercial fishermen to travel further to catch fish. The costs of travel include the amount of money spent on gasoline for travel to an alternate recreation site, or the amount of time consumed in the travel. More sophisticated travel cost methodologies attempt to extend their analyses to include the effects on costing of visitation to multiple sites with differing characteristics.[37] Gibbons maintains that the travel cost methodology is superior when costs differ significantly across users, when non-use values are minor (i.e. it is assumed that if persons take the time to drive to a recreation area, they will use it), and when single-site trips are the norm. Gibbons supports the consumer survey approach when consumer travel behavior is homogeneous and consumers visit multiple sites in a particular trip.[38]

---

[36] Gibbons, D., The Economic Value of Water, Resources for the Future, Inc., Washington, D.C., 1986, p. 67.

[37] Vaughn, W. and C. Russel, Freshwater Recreational Fishing: The National Benefits of Water Pollution Control, Resources for the Future, Inc., Washington, D.C., 1982, p. 131.

[38] Gibbons, supra note 36 at p. 67.

TABLE 12

Summary of Cost Estimation Results

Methodology	Cost per Kilowatt Hour Nuclear	Fossil
Maryland Regulatory Cost Factor - High	$0.000610	$0.000220
Maryland Regulatory Cost Factor - Low	$0.000460	$0.000170
Maryland Regulatory Cost Factor - Average	$0.000530	$0.000190
Hatchery Costs per Fish Stocked	$0.001640	$0.000590
Hudson River Settlement Agreement Costs	$0.000060	$0.000019
Hudson River Closed Cycle Cooling Costs	$0.000580	$0.000190

Contingent Evaluation

The contingent evaluation method uses surveys to value a day of fishing by hypothetical willingness to pay. The results of this method most closely approximate the true value of a recreational fishing site. In the National Wildlife Service's 1975 "National Survey of Hunting, Fishing and Wildlife-Associated Recreation", a typical question was: "Having thought about how much this activity cost you in 1975, how much more money would you be willing to spend annually on your very favorite activity before deciding to stop doing it because it is too expensive?"[39] The responses are expected to increase in value as power plant mortalities require increased effort and expense to engage in a continuous level of fishing success.

Potential Uses of Methods of Valuing Impingement and Entrainment

Although critics may argue about the relative accuracy of the fee, travel cost, and consumer survey methods in particular sets of circumstances, each has the potential to provide some value for a given fishing location. Presumably, if one multiplies the results of either the payment of one fee, the calculation of a day's travel for one person, or value attributed to one person's fishing experience for the day by the number of persons engaged in fishing at a particular location, this will provide an estimation of the value of that particular fishing resource.

If data is available on the catch-rate of the particular fishing site, and some correlation exists between the catch-rate and the value of the fishing site, then one could arrive at a cost for impingement and entrainment by determining a percentage reduction of the population resulting from impingement and entrainment.

Valuation of Hudson River Fishery Resources

One way to determine the number of persons engaged in recreational fisheries is to conduct aerial overflights on a regular basis and literally count the number of anglers in the water at any given time. This procedure was performed on the Middle Hudson recreational fishery from 1972 to 1974. During the period from April to September (except for April, 1972), researchers counted boat and shore anglers along the Hudson between the Troy Dam and the Tappan Zee Bridge.[40]

According to the aerial count, the Middle Hudson recreational fishery averaged about 4603 angler days for 1972 and 1973. The author of the study cautioned that the overflight counting results should be considered minimal because each count reflects an instantaneous survey of the number of anglers. He maintained the adjusted annual range should amount to 20,000 to 40,000 angler-days for an adjusted average of

---

[39] Vaughn and Russel, <u>supra</u> note 37 at p. 129.

[40] Sheppard, J., <u>Valuation of the Hudson River Fishery Resources: Past, Present and Future,</u> Bureau of Fisheries, New York Department of Environmental Conservation, Albany, New York, April 1976, p. 30.

30,000 angler-days, per-year,[41] assumed a $10.00 value per angler-day, for a total value of about $300,000 for the Middle Hudson recreational fishery (1976 $s).[42]

The author also used an alternative method to value the Middle Hudson. He stated that the number of angler days can be derived from the following formula:

$$\text{Number of Angler Days} = \frac{\text{Est. annual fish production x percent rec. fish}}{\text{Average weight of fish/angler day}}$$

When considering average values for each of the components, Sheppard developed the formula in this way: the annual fish production is about 200 lbs/acre; about 20% of the annual fish production is recreation fish; the average daily weight requirement is 1.0 - 1.5 lbs./angler; and the average value of an angler-day is $12.50 (1976 $s). With these figures, the Middle Hudson fishery possesses a recreational capability of 880,000 - 1,320,000 angler-days, with an economic value of $11.0 - 16.5 million (1976 $s).[43]

Percentage Reduction Analysis of the Cost of Impingement and Entrainment

The percent reduction of an entire recreational fishery, as a result of impingement and entrainment, can be subtracted from the total value of the fishery to arrive at a total cost for impingement and entrainment. Calculations of these impacts are made more complex if efforts are made to value forage species upon which recreational species depend.

A site specific study on the J.R. Whiting power plant in Monroe County, Michigan attempted to quantify the loss to the yellow perch population as a result of impingement and entrainment in the waters of Lake Erie for a period of one year.[44] Using the logistic surplus production model (LSPM) [45] the yellow perch population was estimated to be 1.074×10^{10} fish. To determine the loss to the yellow perch population caused by impingement and entrainment, the study averaged the percent reduction in the population per year for twenty-five years. The authors then subtracted impingement and entrainment numbers during a specified year from the population

---

[41] Id.

[42] Id.

[43] Id. at p. 32.

[44] Stanford, R., "The Bioeconomic Impact of Impingement and Entrainment on Yellow Perch in Lake Erie", North American Journal of Fisheries Management, Vol, 2, 1982, pp. 285-293.

[45] For a detailed discussion of the LSPM, see id. at pp. 285-6.

during year zero. The result is an annual 1.7% loss in the adult yellow perch numbers.[46]

The Whiting plant study makes the assumption that a 1.7% loss in population will cause a 1.7% reduction in the sport catch-rate of yellow perch. The authors state that they are not aware of studies that relate population size to reduction in catch rate, but they consider it both logical and conservative to assume a direct relationship between the two.[47] The 1.7% reduction in the yellow perch catch-rate results in a monetary loss of $25,000-$96,000 per year.[48]

The J.R. Whiting study example illustrates the potential for future costing methodologies. Future research should be expanded to include all important species and derive individual effects for each. These impacts must then be divided into plant power production to arrive at a cents per kilowatt hour figure. Finally, an additional cost should be attached to the figures for losses occasioned by impingement and entrainment of forage species upon which commercial species depend.

d. Conclusion

Table 12 reflects a summary of the estimated costs per kWh for each of the mitigation cost methodologies. The reader should bear in mind that none of these estimates represents a complete value of the water impacts of fossil and the nuclear plant cooling systems. There is no generally applicable value for entrainment impacts and other water pollution effects discussed in this report. Further research into ecological and economic impacts of impingement and entrainment effects, as well as thermal effluent effects (discussed below) is warranted. Due to the site specific nature of these impacts, individual study and analysis by utilities is required. Additionally, analysis of cumulative impacts of multiple plants located near each other is also required. Unfortunately, the state of Federal and State regulation is such that these assessments are infrequently conducted or updated. The authors therefore conclude that the best cost factor to apply, absent proof of accurate assessment of impacts, is that associated with the cost of the most effective mitigation technique--closed-cycle cooling systems.

4. Thermal Impacts of Cooling Water Discharge

Data on the quantity of cooling water discharges from electric power plants is presented in part 3, a, ii, of this section. When released, cooling water is substantially warmer than when it was collected from the source. The warm water (typically about 40 degrees celsius) can have both positive and negative effects on fish populations. It

---

[46] Stanford at p. 286.

[47] Id. at p. 289.

[48] Id. at p. 286.

may create more favorable feeding and breeding conditions for some species. The benefit, however, may turn to disaster when the plant ceases discharges due to maintenance, refueling or unplanned outages. A radical drop in water temperature can cause fish kills.[49]

The text below describes other adverse effects which may result from thermal discharges from once-through cooling systems. These effects are largely site specific. The magnitude of the effect is highly dependent on the characteristics of the water body into which the effluent is being discharged (e.g. the size of the water body, water flow rates, water temperature, and makeup of the plant and animal communities). Effects are also dependent on the volume and temperature of the discharged effluent, and plant operation schedules.[50] Due to the site specific nature of these factors, it is difficult to make generalizations about the effects of thermal discharges, and the literature on the subject does not attempt to place a monetary value on power plant thermal discharges.[51]

The most complete discussion of thermal wastewater effects is contained in the "Comprehensive Cooling Water Study", conducted in 1987 by the Savannah River Laboratory. That study examined the various effects which could result from thermal discharges from nuclear production reactors and powerhouse operations on the Savannah River in Georgia.[52] The following section is largely a summary of the effects discussed in this study.

Water temperature is an important controlling factor in regulating ecosystem structure and function. In the water bodies affected by the Savannah River plant, the discharge of thermal effluents was found to have an adverse impact on aquatic foodchains. The streams affected by thermal discharges were found to have lower organic content than the unaffected streams. The particulate matter which was present in the thermally impacted streams was largely comprised of silt and sand.[53] Thermal discharges have adverse effects on the lower food chain organisms, which in turn have a significant effect on the structure and function of aquatic ecosystems.

---

[49] Ramsay, W., Unpaid Costs of Electrical Energy: Health and Environmental Impacts from Coal and Nuclear Power, Resources for the Future, Washington, DC, 1979, pp. 92, 93.

[50] On the Hudson River plant shut downs are planned to minimize the cold shock effect on fish populations drawn to and acclimatized to thermal discharges.

[51] Clark and Brownell, supra note 17 at Chapter VI, p. 2-3.

[52] U.S.D.O.E., Comprehensive Cooling Water Study, Savannah River Laboratory, Aiken SC, 1987, [hereafter cited as Comprehensive Cooling Water Study]. This report comprises eight volumes. The first is a summary of environmental effects. The other volumes address the effect of cooling water on water quality, radionuclide and heavy metal transport, wetlands, aquatic ecology, federally endangered species, ecology of Par Pond, and waterfowl. Thermal discharges from conventional fossil fuel and nuclear power plants would not necessarily have all of the effects observed by the Savannah River Laboratory Report.

[53] Id. at Vol. 1, p. xii.

a. Effects on Wetlands

The Savannah River Study supports the conclusion that thermal discharges may have particularly pronounced adverse effects when the discharge contacts wetland areas.[54] Temperature alteration is particularly critical in wetland areas because of the high concentration of life in protected and shallow waters, and because many important species resort to estuaries for certain key life functions.[55] In the Comprehensive Cooling Water Study, major differences were noted in species composition and diversity between areas which received thermal effluents and those areas which did not.

One of the most pronounced wetland effects of thermal discharges was the impact on the wetland plant communities. The most obvious effect was canopy loss from wetland tree species.[56] Approximately 1,020ha of wetland tree canopy exhibited some degree of canopy loss. Canopy loss is continuing at a rate of approximately 10 to 11 ha/yr.[57] Closed canopy forest has been replaced by algal mat, thermally tolerant herbaceous plants, and scrub-shrub communities. Little regeneration of the original climax community of cypress-tupelo forest occurred once discharge of thermal effluent had ceased.[58] Changes in the plant community structure were reflected in the utilization by various animals, such as aquatic insects and birds.

Death of riparian zone trees removed an important allochthonous energy source from the system, in the form of dead leaves.[59] Processing of leaves and other organic matter into food was also affected. At very high temperatures microbial and macroinvertebrate processing of organic matter is slowed.[60] The diversity of the foodchain was reduced and dominance was switched to a food web which was dependent on allochthonous material, instead of a food chain dependent on autotrophs. This was also due to the dominance of blue-green algae, which is generally a poor food source.

---

[54] Id. at Chapter 1, p. xix.

[55] Clark and Brownell, supra note 17 at Chapter VI, p. 1.

[56] Comprehensive Cooling Water Study, supra note 52 at Chapter I, p. xi.

[57] Id. at Vol. IV, p. 147.

[58] Id. at Vol. 4, p. 1.

[59] Id. at Vol. 5, p. 237.

[60] Id. at Vol V, p. 230.

The discharge of thermal effluents was also found to have an impact on the periphyton communities and benthic plantlife.[61] The non-thermal streams were characterized by green algae and diatoms. In the cooler thermal streams the periphyton biomass was found to be high and dominated by blue green algae. The periphyton biomass was found to be low in the hottest streams.

Macroinvertebrate communities were also adversely impacted by the thermal discharges. Extremely high temperatures may eliminate all or most species. At extreme temperatures normal stream organisms were excluded from the channels and a very simplified food chain existed in the restricted habitat available.[62] The macroinvertegrates were found to have greatly reduced species richness, low biomass, and low densities of organisms, with the exception of a few heat tolerant taxa such as oligochaetes, nematodes, and some chironomids.[63]

b. Effects on Fish

The effect on fish communities can be divided into two parts: effects on adult fish and effects on ichthyoplankton, which includes fish eggs and larvae. The effects on ichthyoplankton are mostly the result of entrainment into the cooling system, but extreme temperatures may directly kill the organisms.

Streams near the Savannah River Plant were mostly devoid of fish during reactor operation, except for mosquito fish which occupied the limited cooler backwater areas. In cooler seasons, fish were attracted to the warmer effluent waters and subjected to thermal shock if there was a reactor shutdown. The warmer waters can also alter spawning activities, which are largely temperature controlled. The warmer thermal waters can lead to spawning earlier than would normally take place, which may stress the fish fry when they hatch due to lack of food sources that would normally be available with later spawning.[64]

Adult fish can also be impacted by nitrogen embolism. This impact was not addressed in the Comprehensive Cooling Water Study. This is an indirect effect of the higher temperatures of the effluent. The heated water holds less oxygen, and may become supersaturated with nitrogen. The excess nitrogen is taken into the blood stream of the fish and "boils out" into the tissues and organs.[65] This causes disequilibrium and death. In colder seasons, the fish occupying the discharge plume

[61] Id. at Vol. V, p. 85.

[62] Id. at Vol. V, p. 237.

[63] Id. at Vol. V, p. 158.

[64] Clark and Brownell, supra note 17 at Chapter VI, p. 4.

[65] Id. at Chapter VI, p. 18.

become acclimated to it and cannot make a sudden transition to the colder waters outside the plume. Thus, they may not leave the plume to escape the nitrogen excess without suffering thermal shock. The potential for nitrogen embolism is increased by high turbulence in the cooling system, which enhances the formation of gas bubbles under super-saturation.[66] Anecdotal information concerning discharge related mortalities appears in Table 13.

Small to moderate increases in temperature, as a result of thermal pollution, can also result in adverse biological intensification. Increased temperature increases the reaction rates of all types of biological reactions, and can intensify decay processes and bacterial action, affect gas balance, and increase the impact of pathogens and toxins.[67]

The impacts of thermal pollution can be greatly increased through synergistic interaction of these impacts with one another. Thermal impacts can also synergistically interact with physical factors associated with cooling water intake, such as erosion, flooding, and sedimentation.[68]

c. Regulatory Setting

We have examined the regulatory structure governing power plant thermal discharges, in order to determine whether these effects are internalized into electric power cost through regulation. The following summarizes the results of this inquiry.

In establishing limitations for particular sources, regulators develop best professional judgment ("BPJ") standards under section 402 of the Clean Water Act.[69] Today virtually all dischargers with a heat effluent apply for variances under section 316(a) of the Clean Water Act,[70] fearing that any BPJ limitation would be more stringent than a limit derived under section 316(a). Closed-cycle-cooling is probably the best technology for "ensuring the protection and propagation of a balanced, indigenous population of shellfish, fish, and wildlife in and on"[71] the receiving water body. In the vast majority of cases, however, variances are granted and once-through-cooling is employed. Discharge permits usually contain delta-T provisions setting out the maximum allowable increase in ambient water temperature in the thermal effluent

---

66 Id. at Chapter VI, p. 20.

67 Id. at Chapter VI, p. 9.

68 Comprehensive Cooling Water Study, supra note 52 at Vol. I, p. xi.

69 33 U.S.C. 1342.

70 33 U.S.C. 1326(a).

71 This is the language of the section 316(a) standard for a variance. 33 U.S.C. 1326(a).

Table 13

Discharge Related Mortality Events at Power Plants Located on Estuarine Waters

Power Plant	Event	Date	Comments
Oyster Creek, Barnegat Bay, NJ	100,000-200,000 menhaden killed	Jan. 28-30, 1972	Cold shock following winter plant shutdown. Fish were resident in plume. Approx. 25°F drop in temp. Continuing winter 1973.
Northport, Long Island Sound, NY	10,000 bluefish killed	Jan. 17, 1972	Cold shock caused by sudden shifting of plume (delta T 25°F) due to winds and tide Fish resident in plume exposed to cold. Bodies on bottom; count made by diver.
Millstone Point, Long Island Sound, NY	tens of thousands of adult menhaden killed	Spring, 1972	No reason given (nitrogen gas embolism suspected).
Turkey Point, Biscayne Bay, FL	thousands of dead fish	June 26, 1969	High temperature shock, apparently Plant discharge temperature 95-100°F
Lovett, Hudson River, NY	1,000 fish killed	June 7, 1971	Species not given. Power plant caused. Lovett assumed responsible; closed plant to Thompkins Cove, where reported.
P.H. Robinson, Galveston Bay, TX	significant kill of menhaden	August 21, 1968	Unknown quantity. Cause given as high temperature shock.
Pilgrim, Cape Cod Bay, MA	from "thousands" to 75,000 or more adult menhaden		Smithsonian report, 1,000's; press, "...fight for life...school in excess of 75,000." Apparent cause nitrogen embolism.
Cape Cod Canal, Cape Cod Canal, MA	kill of several hundred to several thousand menhaden per treatment	Aug/Sept 1968	Chlorine treatment (residual Cl=0.8-1.5 ppm) twice daily; kills occurred at high water slack.
	repeated mortality of large schools of silversides and menhaden	late summer, 1968	Near discharge; lethal temperatures 90-94°F; predation by gulls.
Chalk Point, Patuxent River, MD	40,000 blue crabs killed, minimum		Cause not determined; probably chlorine.

Source: Clark, J. & W. Brownell, Electric Power Plants in the Coastal Zone: Environmental Issues, American Littoral Society Special Publication No. 7, Table VI-A, 1973.

and most states have promulgated temperature standards for water quality, and have imposed these limits on thermal dischargers. However, since thermal discharges are reduced by increasing intake volume, which increases impingement and entrainment impacts, thermal effluent regulation without intake structure regulation affords no real net protection to the aquatic environment.

The costs associated with thermal effluents are difficult to assess. Most environmental damages reported are isolated incidents, such as those resulting from cold shocks during rapid plant shutdown or improper chlorination kills. (See Table 13.) The literature, however, does not give a clear picture of the magnitude of effects or how to value them. It may be that thermal impacts are so site specific and variable that it will be impossible to establish a generally applicable externality value, and the authors have found no studies attempting to do so.[72] As with entrainment and impingement impacts, the cost of closed-cycle-cooling may provide the best surrogate value available, since this technology would eliminate negative impacts of once-through-cooling systems, including thermal effects.

5. Waste Water Contaminant Discharges

Fossil fuel and nuclear plants produce a variety of water pollutants. No studies were discovered which attempted to value the environmental effects of these pollutants. The following describes in general terms the types and quantities of liquid waste discharges.

a. Coal-Fired Plant Effluents

Coal-fired plants generate wastewater discharges in the form of boiler blowdown, coal pile run-off, cooling tower blowdown, demineralized regenerants and rinses, metal and boiler cleaning wastes, pyrite transport water and sump effluents. In common industry terminology, these wastes are referred to as low volume wastes even though some wastes, such as cooling tower blowdown, are generated in substantial quantities.[73] For low volume wastes, quantity, and type of waste varies widely depending on plant size, boiler type, age of equipment, maintenance schedule, operating conditions, and other factors.[74]

Boiler blowdown is a fairly alkaline liquid with a low level of total suspended solids, containing certain chemical additives that control scale and corrosion. Trace elements in boiler blowdown include copper, iron, and nickel. This waste stream

---

[72] See, Clark & Brownell, supra note 17 at pp. VI-14 to VI-26.

[73] EPA, Report to Congress, Wastes from the Combustion of Coal by Electric Utility Power Plants (Final Report), Feb. 1988, [hereafter cited as EPA, Coal Combustion Wastes] at p. 3 - 2.

[74] Id. at pp. 3-41 - 3-42.

results from periodic purging of impurities that become concentrated in boiler systems that recirculate water for steam production.[75]

Coal pile runoff is formed when water comes into contact with coal storage piles maintained on the power plant site. Depending on the plant, coal piles are usually 25 to 40 feet high and can cover up to 75 acres of land. Inactive piles, used to store a 60 to 90 day coal supply, are generally sealed to protect the coal against weather; active piles, used to supply the plant's immediate needs, are usually open to the elements. One estimate concludes that 73% of the rainfall on active coal piles becomes coal pile runoff. Characteristics of the runoff depend on coal composition and pile drainage patterns as well as on the amount of water to which the pile is exposed. Runoff from bituminous coals is usually acidic, while runoff from sub-bituminous coals may be neutral or alkaline. High concentrations of copper, zinc, magnesium, aluminum, chloride, iron, sodium, and sulfate may also be found in coal pile runoff.[76]

Cooling tower blowdown refers to the wastewaters produced by all recirculating cooling systems, whether the system involves a cooling pond or a cooling tower. Only about one-third of utility power plants use a recirculating system, but this percentage may increase due to concern over water availability and thermal discharges. Composition and quantity of cooling tower blowdown reflects the composition of makeup water (fresh, saline, or brackish), chemicals added to prevent biological growth in the towers and to prevent corrosion in condensers, the condition of the cooling system, and the amount of water evaporated. Chemical additives include chlorine, chromate, zinc, phosphate, and silicate.

Demineralized regenerants and rinses are chemicals employed to purify waters used as makeup water for the cooling system. Wastes may be acidic or alkaline. Use of sulfuric acid as the regenerant results in precipitation of calcium into the waste stream.

Metal and boiler cleaning wastes are among the coal combustion waste products which the EPA has concluded may exhibit RCRA Subsection C characteristics of corrosivity or EP toxicity. Gas-side wastes are produced during maintenance of the gas-side of the boiler, which includes the air preheater, economizer, superheater and stack. Residues such as soot and fly ash must periodically be removed, usually with plain water containing no chemical additives. Gas-side cleaning is done approximately twice a year. Volume of waste varies with number of rinses. The composition of the waste directly reflects the composition of the soot and fly ash residues, which depend in turn on the coal burned. Water-side wastes derive from cleaning scale and corrosion products from the water-side of the boiler, which includes the boiler tubes, the super heater, and the condenser. Cleaning solutions contain chemical additives that vary with the type of scale to be removed. An alkaline solution containing ammonium salts, an oxidizing agent, and nitrates or nitrites is used for scale containing high levels of metallic copper. Scale caused by hard water, iron oxides, and copper oxides is removed with an acid cleaning solution, usually hydrochloric acid. Hydrofluoric acid or fluoride salts are used to remove silica deposits. In addition, alkaline cleaning rinses and

---

[75] Id. at p. 3-45.

[76] Id. at p. 3-47.

passivating rinses may be used to remove iron and copper compounds and silica and to neutralize residual acidity from acid cleanings.

Pryite transport water, a result of coal cleaning processes, contains suspended solids, sulfate, and a variety of heavy metals (including cadmium) and other contaminants.

Sump effluents are wastes collected by floor and yard drains and reflect rainfall, groundwater seepage, process spills and leaks, and small equipment cleaning operations. Frequency, quantity, and composition are very plant specific. These waste streams may contain coal dust, fly ash, oil, and detergents.

These types of water pollution discharges are subject to state water pollution controls which vary from state to state and from site to site. Presumably some fraction of power plant wastewater contaminants escape into surface waters or municipal waste treatment systems (though some are configured as zero discharge systems).[77] Treatment technologies include filtration, iron exchange, reverse osmosis, electrodialysis, biological processes, coagulation/sedimentation, and neutralization. These technologies have removal efficiencies which typically range from 75 - 95%.[78] New source performance standards are applicable to wastewater emissions from electric utility plants. These standards allow for limited discharges of suspended solids, oil and grease, copper, iron, chlorine, zinc, chromium, and water with elevated pH. The standards do not apply to overflow of coal pile runoff caused by a heavy storm, such as a "ten year, 24 hour rainfall event."[79]

EPA estimates the following average annual low-volume waste generation for a 500 MW power plant operating at 70 % capacity. See Table 14.

---

[77] DOE/Char, supra note 6 at p. 251.

[78] Id. at p. 253.

[79] 40 C.F.R. § 423.15 (1989). See also, 47 Fed. Reg. 52304 (November 19, 1982).

TABLE 14

LOW VOLUME LIQUID WASTE GENERATION

Discharge Types	Average Annual Production	Production per mWh
Boiler Blowdown	11 million gals.	25.6 gals.
Coal Pile Runoff	20 in.	4.66×10^{-6} in.
Cooling Tower Blowdown	2.6 billion gals.	6.06×10^{3} gals.
Demineralized Regenerant	5 million gals.	11.7 gals.
Gas-side Boiler Cleaning	700,000 gals.	1.63 gals.
Water-side Boiler Cleaning	180,000 gals.	.42 gals.

Source: Based on EPA Coal Combustion Waste, supra note 51, at 3 - 44. Production per mWh was calculated based on 429,240 mWh/yr. This document also provides tables describing the chemical characteristics of each type of wastewater listed in the text above. These figures would be useful in assigning an externality figure, once a cost per level of contamination were established. Since we have not discovered such a figure, the extensive tables have not been reproduced here. (The figure for coal pile runoff does not appear to be complete).

b. Oil-Fired Effluents

For oil-fired units, effluent rates were not available in the same units as for coal-fired plants. DOE estimated in 1983 that an 800 megawatt oil-fired plant would discharge water pollutants having the following annual effluent characteristics:[80]

TABLE 15

OIL-FIRED PLANT EFFLUENT CHARACTERISTICS

Characteristic	Annual Discharge
Biochemical Oxygen Demand	67.8 tons
Chemical Oxygen Demand	509 tons
Total Suspended Solids	910 tons
Total Dissolved Solids	5.06 x 10^3 tons
Ammonia	977 tons

[80] These figures are based on an 800 MW oil-fired steam electric plant with closed-cycle cooling system, operating at 55% capacity, with a wastewater treatment system and a sludge dewatering system. DOE/CHAR, supra note 6 at pp. 114-115. The report also calculates these effluents as tons per 10^{12} BTU produced.

c. Gas-Fired Effluents

The annual effluent characteristics for gas-fired steam plants are much lower for biochemical oxygen demand, total dissolved solids, and ammonia.[81]

TABLE 16

GAS-FIRED EFFLUENT CHARACTERISTICS

Characteristics	Annual Discharge
Biochemical Oxygen Demand	5.21 tons
Chemical Oxygen Demand	439 tons
Total Suspended Solids	909 tons
Total Dissolved Solids	849 tons
Ammonia	0.973 tons

The authors have discovered no studies which attempt to value the environmental cost of these residual discharges from fossil fuel plant wastewaters. A description of the environmental impacts of coal combustion wastes is contained in Subsection 7 infra, but the literature does not distinguish between impacts due to liquid and solid wastes.

d. Nuclear Plant Effluents

In 1983 DOE estimated that a 1000 MW pressurized water nuclear power plant would discharge water pollutants having the following annual effluent characteristics:

TABLE 17

PRESSURIZED WATER REACTOR EFFLUENTS

Characteristics	Annual Discharge
Total Dissolved Solids	2860 mg/l.
Iron	180 mg/l.
Chloride	360 mg/l.

---

[81] These figures were based on an 800 MW gas-fired steam electric plant operating at 55% capacity, using an open-cycle cooling system. DOE/CHAR, supra note 6 at p. 135. The report also calculates these effluents as tons per 10^{12} BTU produced.

TABLE 17 (continued)

PRESSURIZED WATER REACTOR EFFLUENTS

Characteristics	Annual Discharge
Chromium	.30 mg/l.
Copper	.73 mg/l.
Zinc	.84 mg/l.

The amount discharged per 10^{12} BTUs of energy was not calculated. The report states that the figure depends on flow, which varies widely from plant to plant.[82] For Boiling Water Reactors, however, DOE does provide an annual effluent per 10^{12} BTUs of energy output.[83]

TABLE 18

BOILING WATER REACTION EFFLUENTS

Effluent	Annual Level (Tons)	Tons Per 10^{12} BTU
Sulfates	23	1.1
Chlorine	.9	.04
Sodium	11	.53
Other	5.8	.28

Nuclear plants also release small quantities of radiation carried in routine plant wastewater discharges. The following data in Table 19 is from the DOE/Char Report, supra note 6 at pages 18 -19. A different set of data is provided in the DOE/Material Report, supra note 6 at page 27. That report describes radioactive water emissions for a boiling water reactor at .002 tons tritium per gigawatt.

[82] DOE/Char, supra note 6 at p. 18. The report assumes a 70% annual capacity factor. Allowable increases in river concentrations are governed by 40 CFR part 423.

[83] DOE/Char, supra note 6 at p. 20.

TABLE 19

RADIOACTIVE WATER POLLUTANT RELEASES

Pollutant	Boiling Water Reactors		Pressurized Water Reactors	
	ANNUAL	PER 10^{12} BTU	ANNUAL	PER 10^{12} BTU
Activated Corrosion & Fission Products	.1 ci	5×10^3 ci	.12 ci	.0006 ci
Tritium	35 ci	1.7 ci	302 ci	14.4 ci

Tables 20 and 21 illustrate more recent liquid radioactive effluent data from both boiling water reactors and pressurized water reactors.[84] The NRC study provides site specific data for all operating nuclear power plants in the United States.

The NRC study cautions that one should not attempt to undertake a generic analysis of radioactive emissions based on plant size and yearly energy production. Various site-specific factors influence routine annual radiation emissions, including the fuel condition, primary system integrity, treatment systems for effluent and radioactive waste, and the extent to which facilities put these systems to use.[85] The study gives annual emissions data for the period 1970-1987. We selected the most recent year (1987) merely to illustrate the magnitude of the discharge. The annual releases will vary widely from year to year for any given plant. Variations between plants may occur because of differences in analytical methods, operating histories, and effluent and emission control methods.[86].

[84] See, Tichler, J. et al., Radioactive Materials Released from Nuclear Power Plants: Annual Report 1987. Prepared by the Brookhaven National Laboratory for the U.S. Nuclear Regulatory Commission, NUREG/CR-2907 BNL-NUREG-51581 Vol. 8.

[85] Id. at p. 2.

[86] Id. at p. 3.

TABLE 20

LIQUID TRITIUM EFFLUENTS FROM BOILING WATERREACTORS

1987 data (in curies)

Facility	Tritium	Power(MWT)	MWh Produced
Big Rock Pt 1	0.6	240	375,000
Browns Ferry 1,2,3	2.03	9879	0
Brunswick 1,2	19.3	4872	9,740,000
Clinton 1	1.87	2894	684,000
Cooper	5.02	2381	5,520,000
Dresden 1	N/D	700	0
Dresden 2,3	22.3	5054	7,740,000
Duane Arnold	N/D	1658	2,540,000
Edwin I Hatch 1	20.1	2436	5,080,000
Edwin I Hatch 2	8.1	2436	5,760,000
Fermi 2	1.05	3292	1,390,000
Grand Gulf 1	18.3	3833	7,730,000
Hope Creek 1	9.53	3293	7,280,000
Humboldt Bay 3	0.0007	220	0
Fitzpatrick	2.48	N/D	4,200,000
Lacrosse	46.6	165	N/D
Lasalle 1,2	1.1	6646	8,620,000
Limerick 1	6.02	3293	5,320,000
Millstone	17.8	2011	4,380,000
Monticello	N/D	1670	3,530,000
9 Mile Pt 1	N/D	1850	4,620,000
9 Mile Pt 2	0.05	3323	261,000
Oyster Creek 1	1.96	1930	3,110,000
Peach Bottom 2,3	46.4	6586	3,010,000
Perry 1	2.93	3579	828,000
Pilgrim 1	3.21	1998	0
Quad-Cities 1,2	6.92	5022	9,410,000
River Bend 1	6.92	2894	4,960,000
Shoreham 1	0.006	121	N/D
Susquehanna 1,2	18.7	6586	14,730,000
Vermont Yankee 1	N/D	1593	3,400,000
WNP-2	1.21	3323	5,400,000
Fort St. Vrain*	56.1	N/D	181,000

N/D = Not Detectable
* = High Temperature Gas-Cooled Reactor

TABLE 21

LIQUID TRITIUM EFFLUENTS FROM PRESSURIZED WATER REACTORS

1987 data (in curies)

Facility	Tritium	Licensed Power(MWT)	MWh Produced
Arkansas One 1	150	2568	4,760,000
Arkansas One 2	352	2815	6,610,000
Beaver Valley 1,2	572	5320	6,358,000
Braidwood 1	41.2	3411	1,460,000
Byron 1,2	410	6822	7,300,000
Callaway 1	448	3565	6,320,000
Calvert Cliffs 1,2	738	5400	10,100,000
Catawba 1	364	3411	6,380,000
Catawba 2	364	3411	7,170,000
Crystal River 3	356	2452	3,620,000
Davis-Besse 1	246	2772	5,060,000
Diablo Canyon 1,2	691	6749	14,000,000
Donald Cook 1,2	1970	6641	10,060,000
Fort Calhoun 1	228	1500	3,060,000
H.B. Robinson 2	274	2300	4,230,000
Haddam Neck	3170	1825	2,530,000
Harris 1	248	2775	3,380,000
Indian Point 1,2	563	3373	5,150,000
Indian Point 3	340	2760	4,850,000
Joseph Farley 1	637	2652	6,440,000
Joseph Farley 2	505	2652	4,900,000
Kewaunee	351	1650	4,010,000
Maine Yankee	118	2630	4,040,000
McGuire 1	492	3411	7,350,000
McGuire 2	492	3411	7,570,000
Millstone 2	286	2700	6,890,000
Millstone 3	590	3411	6,740,000
North Anna 1,2	836	5786	9,220,000
Oconee 1,2,3	949	7704	16,340,000
Palisades	119	2530	2,630,000
Palo Verde 1	N/D	3800	5,270,000
Palo Verde 2	N/D	3800	8,190,000
Palo Verde 3	N/D	3800	320,000
Point Beach 1,2	709	3161	7,180,000
Prairie Island 1,2	446	3300	8,020,000
R.E. Ginna	564	1520	3,800,000
Rancho Seco 1	18.3	2772	0
Salem 1	379	3338	6,210,000
Salem 2	661	3338	6,170,000
San Onofre 1	2270	1347	2,710,000
San Onofre 2,3	820	6800	13,750,000
Sequoyah 1,2	119	5630	0
St. Lucie 1	338	2560	5,720,000
St. Lucie 2	338	2700	5,950,000
Summer 1	736	2775	5,150,000
Surry 1,2	815	4882	9,420,000
TMI 1	197	2535	5,030,000
TMI 2	0.001	2772	0
TMI 2/Epicor	**	**	**
Trojan	175	3411	4,350,000
Turkey Point 3,4	N/D	N/D	N/D

TABLE 21 (continued)

LIQUID TRITIUM EFFLUENTS FROM PRESSURIZED WATER REACTORS

1987 data (in curies)

Facility	Tritium	Licensed Power(MWT)	MWh Produced
Turkey Point 3	269	2200	856,000
Turkey Point 4	269	2200	2,640,000
Vogtle 1	321	3411	3,920,000
Waterford 3	525	3390	7,430,000
Wolf Creek 1	317	3411	6,500,000
Yankee Rowe 1	219	600	1,140,000
Zion 1,2	656	6500	11,170,000

N/D = Not Detectable
** = Included with Three Mile Island 2 Total

6. Dedication of Land for Generation, Transmission and Waste Disposal

Electric power plants require sizeable acreage for plant sites, transmission facilities, landfills for disposal of ash and slag, and evaporation ponds or other treatment facilities for waste water discharges. DOE estimates that a typical 500 megawatt coal-fired plant will occupy 849 acres for coal storage, fuel preparation, solid waste disposal, and power plant. Oil-fired plants require significantly less acreage, estimated at 96 acres for an 800 megawatt plant.[87]

A study by ESRG estimated land use implications of new steam coal-fired plants at 1.24 acres per megawatt, and 1.00 acres per megawatt for fluidized bed coal plants (not including indirect land use for waste disposal).[88] A figure of 1.00 acre per megawatt was also assigned to oil and gas fired plants. This indicates that the primary reason for increased land use requirements (for coal vs. oil and gas plants) is the land needed for waste disposal.[89] Table 22 presents the data on land use in terms of acres per kilowatt. The references for the studies relied upon occur at footnote 6 supra. A discussion of the land use implication of nuclear plants is contained in Chapter VI. D. In summary that discussion states that a typical 1000 MW nuclear plant will need 1000 acres for plant site and 1800 acres for transmission lines. At some plants cooling ponds will require up to 2500 acres. The discussion notes that some of this land use is internalized. No cost figure is assigned to land use effects.

---

[87] DOE/Char, supra note 6 at pp. 91, 114.

[88] ESRG (Tellus Institute), The Role of Hydro-Quebec Power in a Least Cost Energy Resource Plan for Vermont, prepared for Department of Public Service, State of Vermont, January 19, 1990; Tellus Institute Study No. 89-078, Boston, MA, pp. 9-5. 9-37. ESRG estimates were based in part on the previously cited DOE Energy Technology Characterizations Handbook (DOE/Char).

ESRG notes that the Center for Global Change at the University of Maryland has researched land and water impacts of fossil fuel plants on behalf of the Vermont Agency of Natural Resources. The Center recently presented testimony before the Vermont Public Service Commission, including tables on air, water and land use impacts of eighteen different types of energy supply options.

[89] Id. at p. 9-5.

TABLE 22

LAND USE FOR COMBUSTION-BASED GENERATION

Resource Type	Acres/kWh
COAL	
Steam with FGD	
Including coal preparation	(1) 8.0×10^{-9}
Only power plant and associated solid waste disposal	(2) 3.49×10^{-9}
AFBC	
DOE/Material	(3) 8.0×10^{-9}
DOE/Char (Ill. No. 6)	(4) 3.38×10^{-9}
DOE/Char (Western Subbituminous)	(5) 4.97×10^{-9}
IGCC	
DOE/Material	(6) 8.0×10^{-9}
OIL	
Steam with FGD	(7) 0.71×10^{-9}
NATURAL GAS	
Steam	(8) 0.66×10^{-9}
NUCLEAR	
BWR	(9) 12.0×10^{-9}

(1) Total land requirement for a generic conventional 500 MW coal plant using on-site coal preparation which generates substantial waste and on-site disposal of ash and scrubber sludge. DOE/Material at pp. 12, 22, Figure 7. This value is apparently derived from the same values as DOE/Char gives for a mine-mouth conventional coal plant using typical eastern bituminous coal. See DOE/Char at pp. 91-92; DOE/Material at p. 12 n. 27.

(2) Based on total lifetime land requirement of 369 acres for plant and associated scrubber sludge and fly ash disposal for a 500 MW steam electric plant producing 3.52 x 10^9 kWh/yr and with a 30 year lifetime. DOE/Char at pp. 91-92.

(3) For 500 MW AFBC plant producing 3.5 x 10^9 kWh/yr and with a 30 year life. Source assumes acreage for waste disposal are similar to that of conventional plant. DOE/Material at pp. 12, 22, Figure 7; see also, note 1 supra.

(4) Based on total land requirement of 246 acres for 814 MW steam electric facility with AFBC producing 4.63 x 10^9 kWh/yr and with a 20 year life. DOE/Char at pp. 83-84 (Atmospheric Fluidized Bed Combustion-Bituminous Coal).

TABLE 22 (continuation of notes)

(5) Based on total land requirement of 442 acres for 536 MW steam electric facility with AFBC producing 4.45 x 10^9 kWh/yr and a 20 year life. DOE/Char at pp. 85-86 (Atmospheric Fluidized Bed Combustion-Western Subbituminous Coal).

(6) For 945 MW IGCC plant producing 6.7 x 10^9 kWh/yr and with a 30 year life. Source states that space requirements for the IGCC plant are comparable to land requirements of a conventional plant with scrubber. DOE/Material at pp. 12-13, 22, Figure 7; see also, note 1 supra.

(7) Land area based on mechanical draft cooling tower for 800 MW oil-fired steam electric plant producing 3.85 x 10^9 kWh/yr over 35 year life. Although plant has a sludge dewatering system and solid waste disposal system, total land usage of 96 acres does not appear to include land requirements for the 216,000 tons/yr of solid waste produced by the scrubber and particulate control system. DOE/Char at pp. 114-15.

(8) Fixed land area including average of land range given for cooling towers for 800 MW gas-fired steam electric plant producing 3.85 x 10^9 kWh/yr over 35 year lifetime. Total land usage given is 88.8 acres. DOE/Char at p. 134.

(9) Land area for 1000 MW BWR producing 6.13 x 10^9 kWh/yr with a 30 year lifetime. Value does not include land use for permanent waste storage and plant decommissioning. DOE/Material at pp. 13 and 22, Figure 7. Land areas in DOE/Char are similar: 1,850 acres total or 0.01 x 10^{-6} acre/kWh for a 1000 MW PWR with river supply. DOE/Char at pp. 19-20. DOE/Char also gives values for a 1000 MW BWR but value includes site land requirement for two 1,250 MW units with cooling towers and transmission route: 3,380 acres total or 0.018 x 10^{-6} acre/kWh. DOE/Char at pp. 19-21.

Although the cost of the land for these facilities is incorporated into the capital costs, a number of external land use costs remain. Plant sites, combustion waste dumps, fuel piles and power lines often have the effect of lowering surrounding land values, due to aesthetic impacts of construction, operation and maintenance. Some facilities may be located so as to consume open space or agricultural land, which may impact upon wildlife (including endangered species) and diminish present and future local food production.

Due to their need for cooling water, fossil fuel nuclear plants are often located on or near waterways,[90] yet because rivers, streams, and lakes typically provide much of the natural beauty to an area, scenic and recreational values are undoubtedly reduced by power plant construction and operation.

Combustion wastes from fossil fuel plants (particularly coal-fired units) must be landfilled. This shortens the life of landfills, consuming space that could otherwise be devoted to municipal solid waste disposal, and accelerates the need for additional future landfill siting. Current land disposal requirements for coal combustion waste are estimated to be 1595 acres per year for ash disposal and 590 acres per year for flue gas desulfurization wastes. These requirements are projected to increase to 2710 and 4340 acres per year by 2010.[91] These land use costs are not incurred by Demand Side Management supply options.

7. Solid Wastes from Coal Combustion

a. Introduction

Combustion of fuel in utility plants produces solid wastes, both directly from combustion and indirectly from other operation-related practices. The basic types of waste generated directly from coal combustion are fly ash, bottom ash, boiler slag and flue gas desulfurization (FGD) sludge. These solid wastes are often referred to as high volume wastes. Fly ash, produced in varying degrees by all coal and oil plants consists of small non-combustible particles entrained by exhaust gas system. Larger particles that settle to the bottom of the boiler become bottom ash. If the particles melt they become boiler slag.[92] FGD sludge is produced when chemicals are introduced into combustion gases to react with and capture sulfur dioxide emissions. FGD sludge may

---

[90] EPA, Coal Combustion Wastes, supra note 73 at pp. 5-71 - 5-73.

[91] Department of Energy, Fossil Energy, Innovative Coal Technology, Programmatic Environmental Impact Statement Analysis (PEIA), September 1988, pp. 3-24, 5-6 to 5-7. DOE assumes a land use rate of 18 acres per 10^6 tons of ash and 38 acres per 10^6 tons for FGD waste.

[92] EPA, Coal Combustion Wastes, supra note 73 at p. 3-7.

also contain water and flyash.[93] Some coal-fired plants also produce pyrites during on-site coal preparation.[94]

This section reviews the types and characteristics of wastes associated with coal combustion, the primary methods of disposal, and the environmental consequences associated with that disposal. At the end of this part we briefly provide data on low level radioactive solid wastes. This subject is addressed, more fully in the section of Chapter VI. D. on Nuclear Power Plants.

b. Coal Combustion Waste Characteristics

Most solid wastes associated with fossil fuel combustion arise from coal-fired generation. Approximately 1% of utility fossil fuel wastes were from oil-fired generation with the remainder attributable to coal-fired generation.[95] Coal-fired utility plants produce large volumes of ash and flue gas desulfurization wastes. In 1984 coal-fired power plants nationally generated 69 million tons of ash and 16 million tons of flue gas desulfurization wastes. By the year 2000 these are expected to increase 120 million and 50 million tons respectively.[96]

The increase in national ash and flue gas desulfurization sludge wastes from fossil fuel plants is due both to increases in coal use and increasingly stringent air pollution control requirements.[97] A typical coal-fired power plant will annually produce 308 tons of fly ash, 77 tons of bottom ash and 364 tons of flue gas desulfurization wastes for landfilling per megawatt.[98] For a 500 megawatt plant this amounts to 317,000 tons of waste per year.[99]

---

[93] Id. at p. 3-33.

[94] Pyrites are solid mineral compounds present in raw coal and are separated out before coal is burned. Some removal takes place at the power plant just before coal is pulverized. An average 500 mWh plant will have annual production of pyrites of between 30,000 and 100,000 tons per year. EPA Coal Combustion Wastes, supra note 73 at p. 3-60.

[95] EPA, Coal Combustion Wastes, supra note 73, at p. 1-10, at. 10, citing Physical - Chemical Characteristics of Utility Solid Wastes (by Tetratech, Inc. for EPRI, Sept., 1983).

[96] Id. at p. xii.

[97] EPA, Coal Combustion Wastes, supra note 73 at pp. 3-8, 3-29.

[98] Arthur D. Little, Inc. Full-Scale Field Evaluation of Waste Disposal from Coal-Fired Electric Generating Plants, EPA 600/7-85-028, June 1985. Amounts will vary depending upon coal quality, emission control technology, boiler type and other factors. This figure is used in Coal Combustion Wastes to calculate utility waste disposal costs. Id. at p. 6-7.

[99] DOE/Char, supra note 6, at p. 92.

Fossil plants also generate smaller waste streams from equipment maintenance and cleaning activities. About one-fifth of coal generation waste is reused as cement additives, road construction material, and blasting grit; the remainder is disposed of in landfills or surface impoundments, often near or at the plant site.[100]

Coal combustion waste streams may create significant environmental pollution impacts and occupy large amounts of land for disposal sites.[101] 95% of coal ash is composed of silicon, aluminum, iron, and calcium--materials generally considered nonhazardous. Other constituents of coal combustion waste include arsenic, barium, cadmium, chromium, lead, mercury and selenium. These "trace" materials have toxic effects, particularly if they leach out of the disposal site and migrate into water supplies in sufficient concentrations.[102]

Utility waste management sites generally do not provide a high level of protection against leaching. Only 25% of all coal-fired utility waste disposal facilities have liners to protect against off-site leachate migration. Only about 15% have leachate collection systems; and about 33% have groundwater monitoring systems. Liners, collection systems, and monitoring systems are more common at newer facilities.[103]

At present, special categories of large volume industrial wastes, including all coal combustion wastes, are exempt from disposal requirements applicable to other industrial hazardous wastes under the Resource Conservation and Recovery Act (RCRA).[104] A recent EPA Report to Congress describes the application of RCRA standards to coal combustion waste, and makes recommendations as to possible regulatory changes.[105] The report noted that laboratory tests have found cadmium and arsenic in ash and sludge samples at levels which would normally be considered hazardous for other types of waste under RCRA.[106]

---

[100] Id. at p. ES-2

[101] A recent Wisconsin PSC order took note of the use of prime agricultural land for ash and scrubber sludge as one factor in assigning a 15% credit to non-combustion source costs in its least cost plans. Public Service Commission of Wisconsin, Advance Plans for Construction of Facilities, Docket 05-EP-5, Slip Op. at p. 11, C-2 (Wisc. PSC April 6, 1989). The 15% level was based on the Northwest Power Planning Council (NWPPC) policy. Neither the NWPPC nor the Wisconsin PSC assign a specific figure to the land and water portion of the total externality figure.

[102] EPA, Coal Combustion Wastes, supra note 73, at p. ES-3.

[103] Id.

[104] 42 U.S.C. § 6924(x).

[105] EPA, Coal Combustion Wastes, supra note 73. 42 U.S.C. § 6982(n) of RCRA, added in 1980, instructed the EPA administrator to conduct a "detailed and comprehensive" study on adverse effects on human health and the environment from waste and byproduct materials generated from the combustion of coal or other fossil fuels.

[106] Id. at p. ES-4.

EPA indicated that disposal of the low volume cleaning wastes were of possible concern, and perhaps inappropriately excluded from RCRA hazardous waste disposal requirements. The low volume waste stream associated with coal combustion is similar to industrial boiler cleaning and process wastes. Boiler cleaning waste from coal plants contains chromium and lead, often at RCRA hazardous levels, and is highly corrosive.[107] Most of the low volume wastes occur as water discharges and are discussed above in part 5 of this section.

The EPA Report is the most recent and comprehensive document on coal combustion waste available at the time this section was drafted. Consequently, this section relies heavily on that document and the studies it summarizes.

c. Environmental Consequences of Coal Combustion Waste

EPA's Report to Congress[108] surveys the literature evaluating potential dangers to human health and the environment associated with coal combustion waste. First, the EPA report reviews laboratory studies of the characteristics of coal combustion related wastes and evaluates the results in comparison to RCRA requirements for industrial wastes. The report also analyzes the concentration of coal waste pollutants monitored in groundwater and surface water around coal combustion waste disposal sites, in relation to Safe Drinking Water Act standards.[109] EPA's Report reviews studies that compiled and evaluated the incidence of water contamination due to coal combustion waste. Finally, the report examines environmental settings and population data for 100 randomly chosen coal-fired utility power plants to determine qualitatively the exposure of humans, animals and plants to contaminants from coal combustion waste.

The EPA selected 100 coal-fired utility plants randomly from the Utility Data Institute Power Statistics Database and evaluated waste disposal sites to determine exposure potential for humans and the environment. For power plants where waste was disposed of on-site, information was collected for the plant location. If off-site disposal was used, EPA assumed, absent other information, that disposal took place at the nearest municipal landfill. Data collected included distance to surface water; flow to surface water; depth to groundwater; hydraulic conductivity (the rate at which water travels through the aquifer); net recharge (the amount of water absorbed into the ground annually); location of private and public drinking water systems; groundwater hardness (if water is hard, treatment systems already in place may also address waste-related contaminants); type of surrounding natural ecosystems; and location of human population.[110]

---

[107] Id. at p. ES-3. The EPA noted tests indicating that when boiler cleaning wastes were co-disposed with high volume wastes, the cleaning wastes did not exhibit hazardous characteristics. Id. at p. ES - 4.

[108] Id.

[109] 33 U.S.C. § 1445 et. seq.

[110] EPA, Coal Combustion Wastes, supra note 73 at pp. 5-68 - 5-70.

The 100 plant study characterizes sites but does not measure actual contaminants or exposure at those sites. Moreover, as summarized, the data does not indicate control mechanisms in place at the disposal sites.

i. Possible Exposure Related to Surface Water Contamination

Utility plants need a source of cooling water and are therefore located near water sources. Consequently, most disposal sites identified in the 100 plant study were close to surface water. Over 50% of the disposal sites were within 500 meters of surface water; over 70% were within 1,000 meters of surface water. EPA suggests that the proximity of sites to surface water could pose a threat to aquatic life and humans using surface water if dangerous quantities of contaminants are entering the surface water.[111]

Concentration of contaminants in surface water is dependent on the water body's flow, expressed in terms of cubic feet per second (cfs). The study showed 19% of the sites as having a flow of zero, indicating a lake, swamp, marsh, or possibly a seasonal stream. 41% of the surface water bodies had a flow of 1 to 1,000cfs; 21% had a flow of 1,000to 10,000cfs; and 18% had a flow of over 10,000cfs.[112] Because of the nature of the study, actual concentration of contaminants in relation to flow cannot be determined from this report.

According to EPA, if the waste site is located very near to a surface water body, the opportunity for use of contaminated groundwater as a drinking water supply is reduced.[113] EPA concluded that "it is not common" to locate drinking water wells between the disposal site and the nearest downgradient surface body.[114] However, 34% of the 100 sites had public drinking water intakes downgradient from the disposal site and within a 500 meter radius.[115] EPA notes that flow of surface water would "tend to dilute the concentrations of trace metals to levels that satisfy drinking water standards."[116]

---

[111] Id. at p. 5-70.

[112] Id. at p. 5-73.

[113] Id. at p. 5-71.

[114] Id. at p. 5-96.

[115] Id. at p. 5-89. 15% of the 100 sites were within 500 meters of systems serving over 5,000 people; 19% were within the radius for systems serving fewer than 5,000.

[116] Id. at pp. 5-96 to 5-97. Data on population, hydrogeological, surface water characteristics, and location of public water systems is presented on a plant by plant basis in tabular form. See EPA, Coal Combustion Wastes, supra note 57, at Vol. 2, App. F. Data presented, however, does not include the ecological characterization discussed infra on a plant by plant basis. The EPA presentation also does not indicate leachate control systems which may be in place at particular sites.

The largest potential impact of contaminated surface water could be to nearby ecological communities. The presentation of the EPA data from the 100 plant study makes it impossible to directly correlate surface water characteristics with ecological characteristics. However, some troublesome relations may be suggested. A high percentage of the 100 sites have rare plant and animal communities within a five kilometer radius.

Working with state Heritage Programs, EPA developed data for 85 of the 100 sample sites on rare or endangered species within a 500 meter radius of the waste sites. Sample sites were grouped into four categories based on Heritage Program data. 12% of the sites were within Category 1, sites having federally designated threatened or endangered species within a 500 meter radius. Category 2 included sites having no federally designated species within the radius, but containing species or natural communities designated by state Heritage Offices as critically endangered in the state. 29% of the sites were in Category 2. 32% of the sites were in Category 3 which consisted of sites "for which there are species or natural communities of concern in the area." Category 4 included sites for which there was "no record of the existence of species of concern" within the 500 meter area. 12% of the sites were in category 4; no information was available for 15% of the sites.[117]

73% of the sites fell into categories which reflect the potential for impact on noteworthy species or ecological communities.[118] EPA notes that the proximity of disposal sites to surface-water bodies which provide animals with drinking water suggests a "high potential for species exposure to coal combustion constituents."[119] In addition, it would be interesting to know the relationship between these sites and sites with zero or low surface flow, which could be wetlands or other ecological niches which often harbor threatened systems.

ii. Possible Exposure Related to Groundwater Contamination

Leachates from a waste site can contaminate groundwater used as a source for drinking water. Both hydrogeologic factors and the characteristics of the groundwater affect whether migrating leachate will result in exposures dangerous to humans. It is worth reiterating that the EPA 100 plant study does not quantify actual leachate or contamination levels.

Hydrogeological factors that affect the potential for groundwater contamination include depth to groundwater, hydraulic conductivity, and net recharge. The EPA 100 site study separately evaluates the possible impact of each of these characteristics on

---

[117] EPA, Coal Combustion Wastes, supra note 73 p. at 5-91. The EPA notes that completeness of data available from different states varies substantially because some state Heritage Programs are still in the preliminary stages of basic data collection. Id. at p. 5-89.

[118] Percentage is the sum of sites in Categories 1, 2, and 3.

[119] EPA, Coal Combustion Waste, supra note 73 at p. 5-93.

groundwater contamination. The study also reviews the potential impact of depth to groundwater and net recharge combined with groundwater hardness.

Depth to groundwater is the distance from ground level to the water table. A small depth to groundwater increases the risk that leachate could reach groundwater at harmful concentrations. A larger depth to groundwater increases the time needed for leachates to reach the aquifer and allows filtration by the soil and for more dispersion of the leachate before reaching the aquifer.[120] In over 80% of the 100 site sample, the depth to groundwater from the site was less than 30 feet. According to the EPA, this result indicates "a reasonably high potential" that leachate would reach groundwater.[121]

Hydraulic conductivity is an indication of the rate at which groundwater travels. A high hydraulic conductivity means contaminants may travel more quickly thus more readily reaching drinking water wells. As with surface water flow, however, high conductivity may also indicate a more rapid dilution of contamination concentration.[122] The 100 site study found a wide range of conductivity values, indicating hydrogeologic diversity among sites.[123] The movement of contaminants is complicated by interactions between contaminants and soil particles, as affected by site-specific water chemistry. These interactions could slow contaminant velocity in relation to groundwater velocity, but will not eliminate the movement of contaminants through the water table.[124]

Net recharge measures how much water is absorbed annually into the ground and affects exposure potential in terms of concentration of leachate, and flow or travel time through the ground to the aquifer. Low net recharge results in smaller volumes of more concentrated leachate which may be quickly diluted if the aquifer is deep or has a high velocity. High net recharge produces more leachate with a greater potential for dilution, and may indicate that the area has a higher groundwater flow.[125] More than 80% of the 100 sites had net recharge levels of over four inches; over 50% had recharge levels of over seven inches.[126] According to the EPA, these results imply that

---

[120] Id. note 73, at pp. 5 - 69, 5 - 75.

[121] Id. at p. 5 - 76.

[122] Id. at pp. 5 - 69, 5 - 76.

[123] Id. at p. 5 - 76. 35% of the sites had hydraulic conductivity of 700 to 1,000 gallons per day per square foot; 27% had conductivities between 1,000 to 2,000 gallons per day per square foot; 19% had conductivities of 1 to 100 gallons per day per square foot. Id. at p. 5 - 78, Exhibit 5 - 20.

[124] Id. at p. 5 - 79.

[125] Id. at pp. 5 -70, 5 - 79.

[126] Id. at p. 5-80. 37% of the sites fell in the four to seven inch range for net recharge; 23% were in the seven to ten inch range; 27% were over ten inches. Id. at p. 5-81, Exhibit 5-21.

leachate constituents will be more quickly carried to the water table, but the higher recharge rate will also result in greater dilution of leachate.[127]

Groundwater hardness, measured in parts per million (ppm) of calcium carbonate ($CaCO_3$), is also relevant to evaluating potential exposure to contaminated drinking water. Treatment of hard water tends to remove other contaminants. Public drinking water systems typically treat groundwater supplies with a hardness of over 240 ppm of $CaCO_3$. 45% of the sampled sites had groundwater hardness in the over 240 ppm range. Groundwater with hardness in the range of 180 to 240 ppm of $CaCO_3$ may be treated, but is less likely to be treated than the higher range.[128] 22% of the sites were in this range. The EPA concludes that groundwater used by a drinking water supply in the vicinity of a coal combustion waste disposal site "would often require treatment before being used" due to high levels of $CaCO_3$.[129] 33%, however, fell below 180 ppm and presumably would not need to be treated.

The 100 site study concluded that potential human exposure through contaminated drinking water appeared to be even less when proximity of drinking water systems, water hardness, and hydrogeologic characteristics were examined simultaneously.[130] Of the 100 sites examined, 18% had public drinking water systems within 500 meters of the waste site and had groundwater which might not be treated (under 240 ppm $CaCO_3$). Sites with a net recharge greater than seven inches and a depth to groundwater of fifteen or less feet were chosen as having hydrogeological factors indicating that the sites were more likely to develop groundwater contamination from leachate. Two-thirds of the sites with the drinking water systems within 500 meters and the possibility of untreated water (or 12% of the total sample) also had the high risk hydrogeologic characteristics.[131] EPA concluded that this multivariate analysis illustrated the "limited potential for human health risk through drinking water."[132]

d. Documented Cases of Damage From Coal Combustion Wastes

The EPA literature survey examines documented cases of proven damage to the environment or to human health from surface runoff or leachate from the disposal of coal combustion wastes. The EPA report does not include damage costs or sufficient information to generate generic damage cost figures. The survey does, however,

---

[127] Id. at p. 5 - 80.

[128] Id. at pp. 5 - 80, 5 - 83.

[129] Id. at p. 5 - 83.

[130] Id. at p. 5 - 97.

[131] Id. at p. 5 - 94.

[132] Id.

purport to comprehensively summarize damage cases documented prior to 1987. For this reason, the literature survey and its results are summarized briefly in this chapter. This summary may provide a qualitative indication of risks associated with coal combustion waste disposal.

EPA reviewed two "major" studies conducted for the Utility Solid Waste Activities Group (USWAG) one in 1979 by Envirosphere, Inc., and another in 1982 by Dames & Moore. EPA supplemented these studies with a 1987 literature review of "all readily-available sources," which identified two additional case studies of damages occurring in 1980 and in 1981.[133] No attempt was made to compile a "complete census" of current damage cases through field studies. The literature survey, however, found no "proven" damage cases in the seven years between 1981 and 1988. The EPA cautions that "it is not always clear whether damages would occur under current management practices or whether they are attributable to practices no longer used."[134]

The 1979 Envirosphere study reviewed EPA's damage incident files, identifying nine cases of apparent damage to the environment. The Envirosphere study also reviewed environmental monitoring studies from utility disposal sites and other available research and contacted state regulatory agencies. Envirosphere concluded it is not clear that the identified impacts can be attributed to utility disposal practices.[135]

The Dames & Moore study relied on three major data sources: computer databases used to search for publicly available sources; federal agencies such as the EPA, the U.S. Geological Survey, and the Tennessee Valley Authority, and twelve state agencies. Dames & Moore used four criteria to evaluate whether a record contained "documented" evidence proving danger to health or the environment: (1) the report existed in the public record; (2) the case involved high volume utility wastes; (3) information available permitted determination of possible health or environmental risks; and (4) the possible risks were caused by leachate migration or runoff from the utility disposal site. Dames & Moore identified seven cases that presented a potential danger to human health and the environment: six potential groundwater impacts and

---

[133] EPA, Coal Combustion Wastes, supra note 73 at p. 5 - 33. Complete citation information on four studies in the order mentioned in text is taken from p. 5 - 100, n. 27 -30. Envirosphere Company, Environmental Effects of Utility Solid Waste Disposal, prepared for USWAG and Edison Electric Institute (July 1979); Dames & Moore, Review of Existing Literature & Published Data to Determine if Proven Documented Cases of Danger to Human Health and the Environment Exist as a Result of Disposal of Fossil Fuel Combustion Wastes, in USWAG, Report and Technical Studies on Disposal and Utilization of Fossil Fuel Combustion By-Products, Appendix B (Oct. 26, 1982); D.S. Cherkauer, "The Effect of Fly Ash Disposal on a Shallow Ground-Water System", 18 Ground Water 544 - 50 (1980); G.H. Groenewold and B.W. Rehm, Applicability of Column Leaching Data in the Design of Fly Ash and FGD Waste Disposal Sites in Surface Mined Areas, in Proceedings of the Low-Rank Coal Technology Development Workshop at pp. 3-79 - 3-95 (1981) (DOE/ET/17086-1932, CONF -8106235).

[134] EPA, Coal Combustion Wastes, supra note 73, at p. 5 - 54.

[135] Id. at pp. 5 - 54 to 5 - 55. Text summarizes five examples from the Envirosphere report. Two incidents involved failure of containment mechanisms at disposal ponds, one with catastrophic consequences. Another incident involved groundwater contamination resulting from the leachate of two large unlined disposal ponds. Other examples included illegal disposal in a tidal wetland area by a private waste handler and a marshlands municipal landfill which accepted large quantities of fly ash. Id. at pp. 5 - 55 to 5 - 56.

one surface water case. Dames & Moore examined all seven sites in detail even though none of the cases met all the criteria for a "documented" case of such danger.[136]

The EPA literature survey also summarizes two independent case studies of groundwater contamination at utility disposal sites. The first study was a fly ash landfill in an abandoned sand and gravel pit in southeastern Wisconsin. Part of the pit was in direct contact with the aquifer. Most groundwater flow beneath the site surfaced in a marsh area. After eight years of disposal, iron, manganese and zinc were found in detectable levels in downgradient off-site wells. Sediments in the aquifer neutralized the acidic leachate, probably precipitating the trace metals and other constituents of the leachate. Clay in the sediments also helped to stabilize the leachate plume.[137]

The second study involved fly ash deposited in a surface mine pit between mine ash piles. An FGD waste site at the pit was also monitored. Monitoring wells at the site showed high concentrations of sulfate and trace elements, particularly from the fly ash leachate. The EPA summary notes that a high pH often characterizes leachate from fly ash of western coals and tends to cause the release of many potentially harmful constituents. In this case, arsenic, selenium, iron and manganese were identified.[138]

From the sixteen cases identified by the studies described above, EPA concluded that two cases showed documentation of significant harm to environment: the Chisman Creek and Clinch River sites in Virginia.[139] The Chisman Creek site in Virginia consisted of four separate fly ash disposal pits on both sides of the creek. The site was active as a depository for fly ash and bottom ash from both coal combustion and petroleum coke (a residual of oil distillation). In 1980, drinking water wells around the site turned green from vanadium and selenium contamination; some wells also showed elevated levels of sulfates. The site is on the CERLA National Priorities List and residents no longer use groundwater for drinking water.[140]

In 1967, 130 million gallons of caustic solution entered the Clinch River when a dike surrounding a fly ash settling lagoon collapsed. Fish kills extended over a distance of 90 miles from the site; virtually all bottom dwelling fish food organisms were eliminated for a distance of three to four miles. Natural processes diluted, dispersed

---

[136] Id. at p. 5 - 57. The seven site findings are summarized in detail at pp. 5 - 57 to 5 - 63. The sites were: Chisman Creek Disposal Site, York County, Virginia which is on the CERCLA National Priorities List;, Pierce Site, Wallingford, Connecticut; Michigan City Site, Michigan City, Indiana; Bally Site, Dune Acres, Indiana; Zullinger Quarry Fly Ash Disposal Site, Franklin County, Pennsylvania; Conesville Site, Conesville, Ohio (stabilized FGD sludge deposited next to fly ash pond); and Hunt's Brook Watershed, Monteville, Waterford, Connecticut (disposal of fly ash at three sites along different tributaries from 1960-1969).

[137] Id. at pp. 5 - 63 to 5 - 65 (Cedarsank Site, Southeastern Wisconsin).

[138] Id. at pp. 5 - 65 to 5 - 67 (Center Mine, Center, North Dakota).

[139] Id. at p. 5 - 67.

[140] Id. at pp. 5 - 57 to 5 - 58, 5 - 67.

and neutralized the waste, but the river had not fully recovered, two years after the spill.[141]

With respect to the other cases identified by the EPA's survey, the EPA concluded that "constituents from coal combustion waste disposal sites have been detected in both on-site and off-site ground and surface water."[142] Contaminants that exceeded drinking water standards seldom exceeded the standards more than ten times, but total number of exceedances was "quite small" compared to the total number of monitoring wells and samples.[143] Exceedances appeared to correlate with acidic or alkaline pH levels which can contribute to metal solubility at fly ash disposal sites.[144]

8. Nuclear Power Plant Solid Waste

Section D of Chapter VI. D. provides a general discussion of nuclear plant radioactive solid wastes. The data in Table 23 on low level wastes comes from the DOE/Material Report, supra note 6 at 57.

TABLE 23

RADIOACTIVESOLID WASTE - BOILING WATERREACTOR

Low Level Radioactive Waste	3.638 Tons per gigawatt
Radioactive Filter Waste	.003 Tons per gigawatt

Tables 24 and 25 summarize the total volumes and activity of solid wastes for each operating nuclear power plant in the U.S. in 1987. No attempt is made to derive an environmental cost from the data, but the data can assist future costing experiments.[145]

---

[141] Id. at pp. 5 - 55 to 5 - 56, 5 - 67.

[142] Id. at p. 5 - 67.

[143] Id.

[144] Id.

[145] Supra note 79.

TABLE 24

SOLID WASTE SUMMARY FOR BOILING WATER REACTORS

1987 Data

Facility	Volume Cubic Meters	Activity Curies	Licensed Power (MWT)	mWh Produced
Big Rock Pt 1	74	2,330	240	375,000
Browns Ferry 1,2,3	1,320	644	9,879	0
Brunswick 1,2	843	44,800	4,872	9,740,000
Clinton 1	51	0.01	2,894	684,000
Cooper	341	360	2,381	5,520,000
Dresden 1,2,3	1,800	826	5,754	7,740,000
Duane Arnold	494	262	1,658	2,540,000
Edwin I Hatch 1,2	778	1,820	4,872	10,840,000
Fermi 2	236	93.7	3,292	1,390,000
Grand Gulf 1	392	1,650	3,833	7,730,000
Hope Creek 1	421	363	3,293	7,280,000
Humboldt Bay 3	0	0	0	0
Fitzpatrick	513	644	N/D	4,200,000
Lacrosse	29.3	0.0003	165	N/D
Lasalle 1,2	766	2,300	6,646	8,620,000
Limerick 1	381	2,510	3,293	5,320,000
Millstone	666	505	2,011	4,380,000
Monticello	219	566	1,670	3,530,000
9 Mile Pt 1	507	230	1,850	4,620,000
9 Mile Pt 2	98.9	11.4	3,323	261,000
Oyster Creek 1	236	34,800	1,930	3,110,000
Peach Bottom 2,3	1,590	3,890	6,586	3,010,000
Perry 1	489	45.2	3,579	828,000
Pilgrim 1	527	315	1,998	0
Quad-Cities 1,2	919	29,000	5,022	9,410,000
River Bend 1	407	354	2,894	4,960,000
Shoreham 1	62.1	0.1	121	N/D
Susquehanna 1,2	718	2,110	6,586	14,730,000
Vermont Yankee 1	223	11,900	1,593	3,400,000
WNP-2	375	1,090	3,323	5,400,000
Fort St. Vrain*	30.2	103	N/D	181,000

N/D = Not Detectable
* = High Temperature Gas-Cooled Reactor

TABLE 25

SOLID WASTE SUMMARY FOR PRESSURIZED WATER REACTORS

1987 Data

Facility	Volume Cubic Meters	Activity Curies	Licensed Power (MWT)	mWh Produced
Arkansas One 1,2	523	1,630	5,378	13,370,000
Beaver Valley 1,2	76.5	32.2	5,320	6,358,000
Braidwood 1	0	0	3,411	1,460,000
Byron 1,2	306	865	6,822	7,300,000
Callaway 1	220	312	3,565	6,320,000
Calvert Clifs 1,2	244	641	5,400	10,100,000
Catawba 1,2	273	279	6,822	13,550,000
Crystal River 3	290	675	2,452	3,620,000
Davis-Besse 1	84.8	3.2	2,772	5,060,000
Diablo Canyon 1,2	165	121	6,749	14,000,000
Donald Cook 1,2	463	2,330	6,641	10,060,000
Fort Calhoun 1	126	547	1,500	3,060,000
H.B. Robinson 2	101	259	2,300	4,230,000
Haddam Neck	320	545	1,825	2,530,000
Harris 1	105	2.6	2,775	3,380,000
Indian Point 1,2	230	834	3,373	5,150,000
Indian Point 3	317	333	2,760	4,850,000
Joseph Farley 1,2	532	334	2,652	11,340,000
Kewaunee	82.5	45.8	1,650	4,010,000
Maine Yankee	75	19	2,630	4,040,000
McGuire 1,2	692	323	8,715	14,920,000
Millstone 2	138	2,130	2,700	6,890,000
Millstone 3	99.5	59.1	3,411	6,740,000
North Anna 1,2	489	1,640	5,786	9,220,000
Oconee 1,2,3	853	2,010	7,704	16,340,000
Palisades	223	106	2,530	2,630,000
Palo Verde 1,2,3	463	976	11,400	13,780,000
Point Beach 1,2	155	1,430	3,161	7,180,000
Prairie Island 1,2	142	430	3,300	8,020,000
R.E. Ginna	165	216	1,520	3,800,000
Rancho Seco 1	159	3.5	2,722	0
Salem 1,2	329	969	6,676	12,380,000
San Onofre 1	36.9	49.8	1,347	2,710,000
San Onofre 2,3	245	271	6,800	13,750,000
Sequoyah 1,2	412	976	5,630	0
Saint Lucie 1,2	353	1,050	4,260	11,670,000
Summer 1	380	676	2,775	5,150,000
Surry 1,2	515	29,400	4,882	9,420,000
TMI 1	249	238	2,535	5,030,000
TMI 2	659	318	2,772	0
Trojan	331	409	3,411	4,350,000
Turkey Point 3,4	307	932	4,400	3,496,000
Vogtle 1	0	0	3,411	3,920,000
Waterford 3	383	178	3,390	7,430,000
Wolf Creek 1	128	15.5	3,411	6,500,000
Yankee Rowe 1	186	8.8	600	1,140,000
Zion 1,2	411	713	6,500	11,170,000

9. Externalities of Power Transmission

A variety of adverse, or potentially adverse environmental effects are associated with the transmission of electric power. These adverse effects include possible health effects from exposure to electromagnetic fields (EMFs), water pollution, land use and wildlife habitat effects from powerline construction and maintenance. Certain power line construction practices also create potential for health effects from human exposure to herbicides.

The following brief discussion has been included in the Chapter on Land and Water Effects primarily because the effects are not specific to any particular generation type (as are discussed in Chapter VI) and are not in the nature of air pollution effects discussed in the other section of this chapter. Transmission effects are a subject which was not addressed in the draft report. Awareness of the need to make some comments on transmission issues arose from comments on the draft.

Several special valuation problems apply to transmission effects. In the health effects area, very little is known about the effect of human exposure to low levels of herbicide and to EMFs. The present state of knowledge regarding exposure and dose response prevent formulation of externality values.

We have not discovered studies which assign a value to adverse effects of power line construction and maintenance on wildlife. The issue is complex partly because herbicide maintenance practices appear to be shifting away from broadcast herbicide applications, and because the valuation must also consider the beneficial effect of power line "edge" and shrub communities for some species. Powerline construction and maintenance practices vary widely; careful operations are able to minimize corrosion and runoff problems, while poorly executed operations can have significant offsite impacts.

The land use effects are to some degree internalized since the purchase of the title or easement is reflected in the price of electricity. The remainder is often limited to aesthetic impairments, which are highly site specific and difficult to value.

Another difficulty is that virtually any generation source which feeds into a power grid contributes in some degree to transmission impacts. This raises difficult allocation issues. If one assigns externality values proportional to the amount of generation, then all generation types would receive the same externality value per kilowatt hour. This would be relatively useless to a regulator in deciding between competing power sources in a bidding process for new capacity. The value might, however, be useful if externalities were to be incorporated through tax or pollution mitigation funds.

Another issue is whether widely dispensed small generating sources (in close proximity to point of use) should bear the same externality as large central generating stations which would appear to require greater transmission infrastructure, at higher voltages. Many volumes have been written on environmental effects of powerline construction and maintenance. Time did not allow us to even begin to survey that literature. We include this discussion merely to raise the issue for consideration by future researchers.

Finally, in the case of electric and magnetic fields, it is not yet clear whether the largest threat is associated with large voltage lines, or smaller fields associated with distribution lines, interior wiring or even lighting and appliances. If it is the end use which is determinative, how can one allocate that externality among the variety of contributing generation sources?

On electric and magnetic fields we have located and summarized three recent studies, but did not complete a thorough review of the literature. The following subsection will briefly summarize the present state of knowledge on the effects of EMF's reflected in reports from the Office of Technology Assessment[146], the New York State Power Lines Project[147], and the Washington State Institute for Public Policy.[148] Time did not allow us to critically review the studies. Our intent was to provide an overview so that future researchers may be acquainted with the general dimensions of the issue.

a. Electric and Magnetic Field Effects

Organisms and individual cells maintain EMFs[149], and natural background levels of EMF's occur everywhere on earth. However, the levels emitted from transmission/distribution lines and some electrical appliances are greatly in excess of naturally occurring levels. Measurements reported in the New York Power Lines Project report indicate that levels of electric field strengths three feet above ground under a 765kV line may be as much as 7-8 orders of magnitude greater than the typical natural 60Hz field strengths.[150] The magnetic field strengths at three feet above the ground under a 765kV, 600A line may be as much as five to six orders of magnitude greater than the magnetic field emitted from a naturally occurring 60Hz field.[151]

Appliances are another major source of EMF exposure. Although the field strengths around appliances are greater than those around power lines, their levels fall off much more rapidly than do those of power lines. This is because power lines

---

146 U.S. Congress, Office of Technology Assessment, Biological Effects of Power Frequency Electric & Magnetic Fields--Background Paper, OTA-BP-E-53, Washington DC, U.S. Government Printing Office, 1989, p. 1, [hereafter cited as OTA].

147 New York State Power Lines Project Scientific Advisory Panel, Biological Effects of Power Line Fields, Final Report, Prepared for the NYS Power Lines Project, Albany NY, NYS Department of Health, 1987, [hereafter cited as New York].

148 Sykes, Thomas and Li, Ping, Possible health Effects of Electric and Magnetic Fields from Electric Power Lines: A Summary of Scientific Studies, Washington Institute for Public Policy, The Evergreen State College, January 1990, [hereafter cited as Sykes].

149 OTA, supra note 145 at p. 1.

150 New York, supra note 147 at p. 47.

151 Id. at p. 50.

are more extended in space than are appliances.[152] Another difference is that exposure to EMFs from appliances may be intermittent where appliances are not constantly running or in close proximity to the user.

Several effects of electrical power line EMFs are known. These effects include audible noise, television and radio interference and induced shock.[153] Also of concern are contact currents below power lines which may not only be unpleasant but may surpass the "let-go" threshold of some children, meaning that they can not "let-go" of a gripped object.[154] No information was discovered which quantified or valued these effects.

i. Cellular Level Effects

Cellular effects have been studied in numerous experiments. These experiments have found that EMFs can alter ion and protein flow over cell membranes, rates of DNA synthesis and RNA transcription, cell responses to hormones and neurotransmitter, cell immune response and rates of cancer promotion.[155] Cellular responses often do not exhibit a dose response relationship. Experiments show that results may depend on factors such as:

* a "window-effect", where exposure to a specific range of frequencies and intensities may cause effects but not exposure to higher or lower frequencies and intensities;

* the duration of exposure;

* the existence of a time threshold; and

* the existence of a field threshold.[156]

The effects found on the cellular level may not occur in whole organisms due to counteracting physiological processes.[157] Additionally, these effects may be temporary or permanent. Extrapolating cellular level results to whole animals is not possible because of these factors.

---

[152] OTA, supra note 146 at p. 8.

[153] Id. at p. 1.

[154] Id. at p. 19.

[155] Id. at pp. 25-34.

[156] Id. at pp. 20-25.

[157] Id. at p. 2.

ii. Whole Animal Effects

Several whole animal experiments have also been conducted. The studies have found that EMFs can alter hormone levels and hormonal circadian rhythms, embryonic brain and central nervous system (CNS) development, learning, alertness, reaction and heartbeat rate.[158] These experiments have been performed on various organisms and have sometimes produced conflicting results. The experiments also do not always exhibit dose-response relationships and may have permanent or temporary effects. Therefore, attempting to quantify these effects and relate them to field exposures near electrical transmission sources is not possible.

iii. Epidemiological Studies

Several epidemiological studies were discussed in the reports reviewed for this study. The results have shown an association between children living near electric power lines and rates of childhood cancer. The normal rate of cancer in children between 0 and 15 years of age is about 1 per 10,000 per person year.[159] Children studied living near electric power lines showed an increased cancer risk of about 2.0. If a causal relationship exists, electric power lines could account for 10-15% of all childhood cancer cases.[160] These studies cannot be applied to other environments because they do not consistently show a direct association between EMF levels and increased cancer rates and because no causal mechanism is known by which EMFs would cause cancer.[161]

Some appliances have raised concern as sources of continuous, proximate exposure. These include heating blankets, heating pads and waterbed heaters. Epidemiological studies involving these appliances and high appliance use have shown mixed results but do suggest an association with cancer risk.[162]

iv. Summary of Effects

Experiments on the effects of EMFs have produced conflicting, inconclusive, and complicated results. Electric and magnetic fields behave in complex manners and their

---

[158] Id. at pp. 36-51.

[159] New York, supra note 147 at p. 85.

[160] Id.

[161] OTA, supra note 146 at p. 61.

[162] Id.

effects may depend on various threshold levels and "window-effects". Induction of electric and magnetic fields by an organism, tissue or cell can vary greatly depending on its size, shape and position in relation to the field direction.[163] The effects found cannot be extrapolated to conditions of animal and human exposure near electric power lines or appliances. For these reasons, quantification and regulation of EMFs have not occurred to a substantial degree.

v. Regulation of Electromagnetic Fields

Many states are recommending and beginning to study EMF exposure effects, exposure levels, possible regulatory and engineering approaches, and economic, health and legal implications of mitigation options.[164] Several states have regulated electric field intensities from electrical transmission lines. Recently, Florida has also regulated magnetic field intensities from transmission lines.[165] At the present time, the New York Public Service Commission is proposing an interim magnetic field standard for future transmission lines.[166] However, future research on dose-effect relationships is necessary to examine whether such decreases in exposure actually decrease the harmful effects of EMFs.

10. Conclusion

Valuation of land and water impacts of fossil fuel-fired-power plants has not advanced nearly as far as other categories of externalities. This is probably because these impacts are small in comparison to the air pollution consequences of fossil fuel use. Nevertheless, these impacts deserve further attention. In particular, additional research is needed to assess the externalities of coal combustion and maintenance wastes and fish impingement.

---

[163] Id. at p. 52.

[164] Sykes, supra note 148 at pp. 33-39.

[165] Id. at p. 39.

[166] "New York PSC Proposes to Limit Magnetic Fields for Future Transmission Lines in the State; Requests Public Comments", Issues Review and Tracking: The Energy Newsbrief, NARUC No. 21-1990, Vol. 5, Issue 14, May 21, 1990, p. 6.

VI. EXTERNALITY COSTS BY RESOURCE

A. COAL PLANT OPERATIONS

VI. EXTERNALITY COSTS BY RESOURCE

A. COAL PLANT OPERATIONS

1. Table Summary

The major externalities related to air emissions from typical existing and new coal-fired facilities are summarized in Table A. The air emissions reported in this summary are sulfur dioxide (SO_2), nitrogen oxides (NO_x), particulates, and the major greenhouse gas, CO_2. The unit values for each externality are the "starting point" estimates developed in Chapter V. For CO_2 the value used in Table A ($50/ton of carbon) is near the middle of the range of costs described in the studies summarized at the end of Chapter V.A.[1] The emissions for each technology are adapted from Chapter IV and are originally from Chernick and Caverhill (1989) or other sources, as indicated. No scrubber control equipment is used on the example plants for SO_2, NO_x or CO_2 except that a scrubber is assumed for the New Source Performance Standards (NSPS) Plant.[2] However, emissions of SO_2 are dependent on coal sulfur content and, for atmospheric fluidized bed combustion (AFBC), on the amount of limestone used. For particulates, the existing boiler has installed an electrostatic precipitator (ESP) with an efficiency of 90%, and the AFBC and integrated gas combined cycle (IGCC) plants have fabric filters with an efficiency of 98%. The particulate emissions are strongly dependent on the ash and sulfur content of the coal, so the emissions quoted here may be very different under different assumptions.

Table A shows estimates of the externalities from three different coal-fired technologies. The externalities from a coal-fired boiler, with a heat rate of 10,000 BTU/kWh and burning 1.2% sulfur coal, are on the order of 5.8 cents/kWh (generated). For an AFBC plant with the same heat rate and burning 1.1% sulfur coal, the externalities are on the order of 2.8 cents/kWh (generated). For an IGCC plant with the same heat rate and sulfur content of 0.45% sulfur the externalities are on the order of 2.5 cents/kWh (generated).

2. Exclusions

These estimates do not consider overlap between the effects of SO_2 emissions and particulate emissions, particularly the health and visibility effects related to sulfate deposition. However, since the particulate cost estimate excludes the potentially significant health effects of sulfates, and so is based entirely on visibilityeffects, and the SO_2 value is dominated by health effects, we do not anticipate that these effects are double counted.

---

[1] In the table this $50/ton of carbon is converted to 2.5 cents per pound of carbon or .68 cents per carbon dioxide.

[2] The emissions figures are based on a plant that is just meeting the NSPS SO_2 limit.

In addition, these externality estimates leave out so many potential externality effects that they are likely to be conservative rather than overstated. Other externalities should be incorporated into future externalities estimates. These include: air emissions from coal combustion not estimated here, such as the greenhouse gases methane (from coal mining) and N_2O; air toxics including heavy metals; the other primary ozone precursor, VOC; other externalities related to coal combustion, such as water use, land use, and solid waste disposal; and externalities related to the other stages of the coal fuel cycle, including extraction, processing and transportation.[3]

[3] Several of these effects, including air toxics emissions, water use, land use and solid waste disposal, are discussed in this report, but costs could not be estimated from the reports reviewed.

TABLE 1

EXTERNALITYCOST FOR COAL-FIREDUNITS
(Emissions - lbs/MMBTU)

Externality	$/lb	Existing Boiler (1.2% S)	AFBC (1.1% S)	IGCC (.45% S)	NSPS (N/A)
	[A]	[B]	[C]	[D]	[E]
[1] SO_2	$ 2.03	1.80	0.55	0.48	1.2
[2] NO_x	$ 0.82	0.607	0.3	0.06	0.006
[3] Particulates	$ 1.19	0.15	0.01	0.01	0.03
[4] CO_2	$ 0.0068	209	209	209	209
Totals:					
[5] $/MMBTU Input		$ 5.76	$ 2.80	$ 2.46	$ 3.90
[6] Heat Rate (BTU/kWh)		10,000	10,000	10,000	10,000
[7] $/kWh Generated		$ 0.058	$ 0.028	$ 0.025	$ 0.039
[8] $kWh Delivered		$ 0.068	$ 0.033	$ 0.028	$ 0.045

Notes:

[A]: Unit Values derived in Chapter V.
[B][C][D][E]: Emissions are from PLC (1989); SO_2 and CO_2 emissions have been restated as lbs SO_2 and lbs CO_2. All emissions are expressed as lbs/MMBTU fuel input.
[E]: NSPS regulations require 1.2 lbs/MMBTU and 90% reduction for plants with emissions greater than 0.6 lb/MMBTU; for plants with emissions less than 0.6 lb/MMBTU; NSPS requires 70% reduction in emissions.
[1]: No SO_2 scrubbers are installed on the first three plants.
[2]: NO_x emissions are uncontrolled in each case.
[3]: Particulates emissions vary widely and are extremely dependent on the ash content and sulfur content and sulfur content of the coal. NSPS requires 0.03 lbs/MMBTU and 90% reduction.
[4]: CO_2 emissions are derived in PLC (1989).
[5]: Sum of (value x emissions for each externality) for each plant.
[6]: Assumed heat rates for each plant.
[7]: [5] x [6]/1,000,000.
[8]: Assumes 15% marginal energy losses.

VI. EXTERNALITY COSTS BY RESOURCE

B. OIL PLANT OPERATIONS

VI. EXTERNALITY COSTS BY RESOURCE

B. OIL PLANT OPERATIONS

1. Table Summary

The major externalities related to air emissions from existing and new oil-fired combustion facilities are summarized in Table B. The air emissions reported in this summary are sulfur dioxide (SO_2), nitrogen oxides (NO_x), particulates, and the major greenhouse gas, (CO_2). The unit values for each externality are the "starting point" estimates developed in Chapter V. The emissions for each technology are adapted from Chapter IV and are originally from Chernick and Caverhill (1989) or other sources, as indicated. No pollution control equipment is used on any of the example plants for SO_2, NO_x or CO_2. However, the SO_2 emissions are dependent on the sulfur content of the oil. For particulates, the emissions are dependent on the sulfur content of the fuel, and are calculated using the formula noted, which is taken from EPA AP-42.[1]

Table B shows estimates of the externalities from two different oil-fired technologies: boilers burning residual, or #6, oil and a combustion turbine burning distillate, or #2, oil. For the boilers, three different sulfur contents are assumed, but each boiler has a heat rate of 10,400 BTU/kWh. The externalities from the #6 oil-fired boiler burning 0.5% sulfur oil are on the order of 2.7 cents/kWh (generated). For the same boiler burning 1% sulfur oil the externalities are 3.8 cents/kWh (generated), and for the same boiler burning 2.2% sulfur oil the externalities are 6.7 cents/kWh (generated). The externalities of the combustion turbine burning distillate or #2 oil, with a heat rate of 13,600 BTU/kWh, are on the order of 2.5 cents/kWh (generated) assuming 1% sulfur.

2. Exclusions

As in the case of coal fired plant these cost estimates do not consider overlap between the effects of SO_2 emissions and particulate emissions, particularly the health and visibility effects related to sulfate deposition. However, since the particulate cost estimate excludes the potentially significant health effects of sulfates, and so is based entirely on visibility effects, and the SO_2 value is dominated by health effects, we do not anticipate that these effects are double counted.

In addition, these externality estimates leave out so many potential external effects that they are likely to be conservation rather than overstated. Other externalities should be incorporated into future externalities estimates. These include: air emissions from oil combustion not estimated here, such as the greenhouse gases methane (from oil drilling and production) and N_2O: air toxics including heavy metals:

---

[1] EPA AP-42, Compilation of Air Pollutant Emission Factors, Volume 1: Stationary Point and Area Sources, Fourth Edition, September 1985 (updated 10/86).

the other primary ozone precursor, VOC; other externalities related to oil combustion, such as water use, land use, and solid waste disposal; and externalities related to the other stages of the oil fuel cycle, including extraction, refining and transportation.[2]

[2] Several of these effects, including water use, land use and solid waste disposal, are discussed in this report, but costs could not be estimated from the reports reviewed.

TABLE 1

EXTERNALITYCOST FOR OIL-FIRED UNITS
(Emissions - lbs/MMBTU)

Externality	$/lb	Boiler # 6 Oil (.5% S)	Boiler # 6 Oil (1% S)	Boiler # 6 Oil (2.2% S)	Combustion Turbine # 2 Oil (1% S)
	[A]	[B]	[C]	[D]	[E]
[1] SO_2	$ 2.03	0.54	1.08	2.38	0.16
[2] NO_x	$ 0.82	0.357	0.287	0.357	0.498
[3] Particulates	$ 1.19	0.055	0.09	0.174	0.036
[4] CO_2	$ 0.0068	169	169	169	161
Totals:					
[5] $/MMBTU Input		$ 2.60	$ 3.68	$ 6.48	$ 1.87
[6] Heat Rate (BTU/kWh)		10,400	10,400	10,400	13,600
[7] $/kWh Generated		$ 0.027	$ 0.038	$ 0.067	$ 0.025
[8] $kWh Delivered		$ 0.032	$ 0.045	$ 0.079	$ 0.030

Notes:

[A]: Unit Values derived in Chapter V.
[B][C][D][E]: Emissions are from PLC (1989); SO_2 and CO_2 emissions have been restated as lbs SO_2 and lbs CO_2. All emissions are expressed as lbs/MMBTU fuel input.
[1]: SO_2 emissions are uncontrolled in each case.
[2]: NO_x emissions are uncontrolled in each case.
[3]: Particulates emissions are calculated from EPA Ap-42 using the formula: 0.02 + 0.07 x S, where S ia the sulfur content in percent.
[4]: CO_2 emissions are derived in PLC (1989).
[5]: Sum of (value x emissions for each externality) for each plant.
[6]: Assumed heat rates for each plant.
[7]: [5]*[6]/1,000,000.
[8]: Assumes 15% marginal energy losses.

VI. EXTERNALITY COSTS BY RESOURCE

C. NATURAL GAS PLANT OPERATIONS

VI. EXTERNALITY COSTS BY RESOURCE

C. NATURAL GAS PLANT OPERATIONS

1. Table Summary

The major externalities related to air emissions from existing and new natural gas combustion facilities are summarized in Table C. The air emissions reported in this summary are sulfur dioxide (SO_2), nitrogen oxides (NO_x), particulates, and the major greenhouse gas, CO_2. The unit values for each externality are the "starting point" estimates developed in Chapter V. The emissions for each technology are adapted from Chapter IV and are originally from Chernick and Caverhill (1989) or other sources, as indicated. No special NO_x-control equipment is used on the boiler or the combined cycle. However, selective catalytic reduction (SCR) and steam water injection (SWI) are applied on the BACT unit, which is a combined cycle unit fitted with best available control technology. SO_2 emissions from natural gas combustion are negligible.

Table C shows estimates of the externalities from two different natural gas-fired technologies: boilers (steam plants) and combined cycle. For the combined cycle plant, two different plants are illustrated: a plant with no add-on controls, and a plant with the best available control technology for NO_x and particulate control. The externalities from the natural gas-fired steam plant, with a heat rate of 10,400 BTU/kWh, are on the order of 1.0 cents/kWh (generated). For the combined cycle unit, with a heat rate of 9,000BTU/kWh, externalities are estimated to be on the order of 1.0 cents/kWh (generated) also. For the combined cycle unit fitted with SCR and SWI, the externalities drop to 0.7 cents/kWh (generated). The externality values estimated for natural gas units are strongly dominated by the CO_2 emissions, which vary only with the heat rates of the different plants.

2. Exclusions

These externality estimates are likely to be conservative because of the external effects that are not included. Other potentially important natural gas combustion externalities should be incorporated into future externalities estimates. These include other air emissions, such as the greenhouse gases, methane from production and pipeline losses and N_2O; the other major ozone precursor, VOC; other externalities related to gas combustion, such as water use and land use; and externalities related to the other stages of the natural gas fuel cycle including extraction and transportation.[1]

---

[1] Several of these effects, including water use and land use, are discussed in this report, but costs could not be estimated from the reports reviewed.

TABLE 1

EXTERNALITYCOST FOR NATURALGAS-FIRED UNITS
(Emissions - lbs/MMBTU)

Externality	$/lb	Existing Steam Plant	Combined Cycle	BACT (SCR, SWI)
	[A]	[B]	[C]	[D]
[1] SO_2	$ 2.03	0	0	0
[2] NO_x	$ 0.82	0.248	0.42	0.042
[3] Particulates	$ 1.19	0.003	0.003	0.0002
[4] CO_2	$ 0.0068	110	110	110
Totals:				
[5] $/MMBTU Input		$ 0.95	$ 1.10	$ 0.78
[6] Heat Rate (BTU/kWh)		10,400	9,000	9,000
[7] $/kWh Generated		$ 0.010	$ 0.010	$ 0.007
[8] $kWh Delivered		$ 0.012	$ 0.011	$ 0.008

Notes:

[A]: Unit Values derived in Chapter V.
[B][C][D]: Emissions are from PLC (1989); SO_2 and CO_2 emissions have been restated as lbs SO_2 and lbs CO_2. All emissions are expressed as lbs/MMBTU fuel input.
[1]: SO_2 emissions are zero from gas combustion.
[2]: NO_x emissions are uncontrolled in the first two cases; For the BACT case, Selective Catalytic Reduction and Steam Water injection are assumed.
[3]: Particulates emissions are estimated for CEC (1989). BACT assumes fabric filter control.
[4]: CO_2 emissions are derived in PLC (1989).
[5]: Sum of (value x emissions for each externality) for each plant.
[6]: Assumed heat rates for each plant.
[7]: [5]*[6]/1,000,000.
[8]: Assumes 15% marginal energy losses.

VI. EXTERNALITY COSTS BY RESOURCE

D. NUCLEAR PLANT OPERATIONS

VI. EXTERNALITY COSTS BY RESOURCE

D. NUCLEAR PLANT OPERATIONS

1. Introduction

This section presents a review of studies conducted within the past two decades which assign dollar values to environmental damages caused by electric utility nuclear power generation. External costs included in this report are divided into the following categories: 1) public and occupational health costs caused by routine radiation emissions; 2) public and occupational health costs caused by non-routine radiation emissions; 3) property damage caused by routine operations; 4) worldwide health impacts as a result of nuclear accidents; and 5) agricultural and other property damage caused by nuclear accidents.[1] Discussion of potential externality costs of decommissioning and waste storage and disposal are also presented, although the data available are not sufficient to assess these costs. A glossary of terms is provided at the end of the chapter.

This analysis is restricted to the direct effects of plant operation and from releases to the environment during operation. All effects of uranium mining, mill tailings, processing and enrichment, and waste disposal are omitted because they are beyond the scope of this report.[2]

The environmental impacts of the operation of nuclear power plants are much more difficult to quantify than those of fossil-fueled power plants. This difficulty stems from: 1) the difficulty of determining the frequency and magnitude of non-routine releases of radioactivity; 2) the even greater difficulty of determining the probability and consequences of major nuclear accidents; 3) uncertainty of the health effects of low radiation doses; and 4) the lack of an accepted plan for long-term high level waste storage and disposal, implementation of the low level waste disposal legislation and decommissioning plants.

In many instances the literature does not adequately provide a cents/kWh figure. Thus, it was necessary to convert the figures in the studies reviewed to a cents/kWh figure. In other cases, the studies reviewed do not give costing figures, so only impacts are discussed.

From the cents/kWh figures derived from the studies reviewed, "starting point" values are stated. "Starting point" values, as used in this report, are the values concluded best to represent the range of figures presented in the studies reviewed, considering the location for which the studies were done, their documentation, vintage and thoroughness.

---

[1] Fish losses caused by impingement in nuclear water uptake equipment are covered in Chapter V.F.

[2] The studies reviewed indicate that, for the front end of the nuclear fuel cycle, the generation of pollutants is very significant, since all stages of the extraction and preparation of nuclear fuel are highly energy intensive. For a discussion of nuclear power front end cots see text accompanying footnote 39 in Chpater II.

2. External Costs of Routine Operation

This section discusses the external costs of the routine operation of nuclear power stations. Routine operation includes the daily workings and maintenance of a nuclear power station. Subsection a. discusses routine health impacts in the occupational and public sectors. Subsection b. assesses property damage from routine operations and on-site storage of radioactive waste. Other routine operational impacts on the aqueous environment are discussed in Chapter V.G., Land and Water Pollution Impacts.

As with costing all resources damages the calculations must start with ascertainment of emissions. Tables 1 and 2 illustrate the routine emissions of airborne radioactive emissions from both boiling water reactors and pressurized water reactors.[3] The NRC study provides site-specific data for all operating nuclear power plants in the United States.

The NRC study cautions that radiation emissions will vary from year to year and are not directly related to plant size. Various site-specific factors influence routine radiation emissions, including the fuel condition, primary system integrity, treatment systems for effluent and radioactive waste, and the extent to which facilities put these systems to use.[4] Other variations occur because of differences in analytical methods among plants, different operating histories, and different effluent and emission control methods.[5]

---

[3] See Tichler, J. et al., Radioactive Materials Released from Nuclear Power Plants: Annual Report 1987, prepared by the Brookhaven National Laboratory for the U.S. Nuclear Regulatory Commission, NUREG/CR-2907 BNL-NUREG-51581 Vol. 8, 1987 [hereafter cited as NRC Study].

[4] Id. at p. 2.

[5] Id. at p. 3.

TABLE 1

AIRBORNE RADIOACTIVE EMISSIONS FROM BOILING WATER REACTORS

1987 data (in curies)

Facility	Fission and Activation Gases	I-131 and Particulates	Licenced Power(MWT)	MWh Produced
Big Rock Pt 1	8350	0.0294	240	375,000
Browns Ferry 1-3	0.3	0.002	9879	0
Brunswick 1,2	26,400	0.02	4872	9,740,000
Clinton 1	6.83	0.0003	2894	684,000
Cooper	1200	0.03	2381	5,520,000
Dresden 1	N/D	+	700	0
Dresden 2,3	277	0.15	5054	7,740,000
Duane Arnold	219	0.14	1658	2,540,000
Edwin I Hatch 1	7400	0.254	2436	5,080,000
Edwin I Hatch 2	13,700	0.12	2436	5,760,000
Fermi 2	N/D	0.009	3292	1,390,000
Grand Gulf 1	208	0.004	3833	7,730,000
Hope Creek 1	1190	N/D	3293	7,280,000
Humboldt Bay 3	N/D	0.00007	220	0
Fitzpatrick	4720	0.14	N/D	4,200,000
Lacrosse	2330	0.0023	165	N/D
Lasalle 1,2	6510	0.05	6646	8,620,000
Limerick 1	24.1	0.0012	3293	5,320,000
Millstone	5840	0.03	2011	4,380,000
Monticello	3950	0.02	1670	3,530,000
9 Mile Pt 1	197	0.02	1850	4,620,000
9 Mile Pt 2	6	5.17	3323	261,000
Oyster Creek 1	3390	0.1	1930	3,110,000
Peach Bottom 2,3	11,500	0.002	6586	3,010,000
Perry 1	10.6	0.00005	3579	828,000
Pilgrim 1	N/D	<0.0008	1998	0
Quad-Cities 1,2	373	0.009	5022	9,410,000
River Bend 1	1.39	0.0004	2894	4,960,000
Shoreham 1	N/D	N/D	121	N/D
Susquehanna 1,2	123	0.0061	6586	14,730,000
Vermont Yankee 1	N/D	0.001	1593	3,400,000
WNP-2	535	0.08	3323	5,400,000
Fort St. Vrain*	203	N/D	N/D	181,000

Source: Tichler, J. et al., Radioactive Materials Released from Nuclear Power Plants: Annual Report 1987, prepared by the Brookhaven National Laboratory for the U.S. Nuclear Regulatory Commission, NUREG/CR-2907 BNL-NUREG-51581 Vol. 8, 1987.

ND = Not Detectable
+ = Included in Dresden 2,3 total.
* = High Temperature Gas-Cooled Reactor.

TABLE 2

AIRBORNE RADIOACTIVE EMISSIONS FROM PRESSURIZED WATER REACTORS

1987 data (in curies)

Facility	Fission and Activation Gases	I-131 and Particulates	Licenced Power(MWT)	MWh Produced
Arkansas One 1	326	0.00031	2568	4,760,000
Arkansas One 2	206	0.00005	2815	6,610,000
Beaver Valley 1,2	225	0.014	5320	6,358,000
Braidwood 1	0.28	0.00001	3411	1,460,000
Byron 1,2	1300	0.009	6822	7,300,000
Callaway 1	2900	0.00045	3565	6,320,000
Calvert Cliffs 1,2	4550	0.09	5400	10,100,000
Catawba 1	2410	0.007	3411	6,380,000
Catawba 2	2410	0.007	3411	7,170,000
Crystal River 3	1100	0.0035	2452	3,620,000
Davis-Besse 1	380	0.001	2772	5,060,000
Diablo Canyon 1,2	714	0.0024	6749	14,000,000
Donald Cook 1,2	875	0.060	6641	10,060,000
Fort Calhoun 1	423	0.005	1500	3,060,000
H.B. Robinson 2	770	0.0021	2300	4,230,000
Haddam Neck	3580	0.0014	1825	2,530,000
Harris 1	1710	0.000004	2775	3,380,000
Indian Point 1,2	4680	0.02	3373	5,150,000
Indian Point 3	1820	0.0021	2760	4,850,000
Joseph Farley 1	1330	0.0004	2652	6,440,000
Joseph Farley 2	722	0.0002	2652	4,900,000
Kewaunee	<31.9	< 0.012	1650	4,010,000
Maine Yankee	780	0.003	2630	4,040,000
McGuire 1	2040	0.061	3411	7,350,000
McGuire 2	2040	0.061	3411	7,570,000
Millstone 2	397	0.007	2700	6,890,000
Millstone 3	105	0.0051	3411	6,740,000
North Anna 1,2	1050	0.02	5786	9,220,000
Oconee 1,2,3	10,500	0.2	7704	16,340,000
Palisades	1750	0.03	2530	2,630,000
Palo Verde 1	1270	0.06	3800	5,270,000
Palo Verde 2	5470	0.0134	3800	8,190,000
Palo Verde 3	0.03	N/D	3800	320,000
Point Beach 1,2	48.2	0.0031	3161	7,180,000
Prairie Island 1,2	0.9	0.002	3300	8,020,000
R.E. Ginna	177	0.01	1520	3,800,000
Rancho Seco 1	0.02	0.000002	2772	0
Salem 1	3640	0.002	3338	6,210,000
Salem 2	1060	0.002	3338	6,170,000
San Onofre 1	981	0.0004	1347	2,710,000
San Onofre 2,3	21,800	0.4	6800	13,750,000
Sequoyah 1,2	N/D	0.0005	5630	0
St. Lucie 1	6210	0.04	2560	5,720,000
St. Lucie 2	8600	0.06	2700	5,950,000
Summer 1	634	0.0007	2775	5,150,000
Surry 1,2	308	0.02	4882	9,420,000
TMI 1	789	0.00013	2535	5,030,000
TMI 2	N/D	0.000073	2772	0

TABLE 2 (continued)

AIRBORNE RADIOACTIVE EMISSIONS FROM PRESSURIZED WATER REACTORS

1987 data (in curies)

Facility	Fission and Activation Gases	I-131 and Particulates	Licenced Power(MWT)	MWh Produced
TMI 2/Epicor	**	**	**	**
Trojan	249	0.0022	3411	4,350,000
Turkey Point 3,4	N/D	N/D	N/D	N/D
Turkey Point 3	938	0.012	2200	856,000
Turkey Point 4	786	0.00014	2200	2,640,000
Vogtle 1	107	0.0002	3411	3,920,000
Waterford 3	5630	0.001	3390	7,430,000
Wolf Creek 1	173	0.0002	3411	6,500,000
Yankee Rowe 1	384	0.00004	600	1,140,000
Zion 1,2	118	0.0041	6500	11,170,000

Source: Tichler, J. et al., Radioactive Materials Released from Nuclear Power Plants: Annual Report 1987, prepared by the Brookhaven National Laboratory for the U.S. Nuclear Regulatory Commission, NUREG/CR-2907 BNL-NUREG-51581 Vol. 8, 1987.

ND = Not Detectable
** = Included in Three Mile Island 2 total.

a. Health Costs

This section discusses health costs in both the occupational and public sectors. The occupational sector discussion considers occupational mortality, both immediate and latent, and occupational morbidity. The public sector discussion describes the public health costs attributable to routine radiation emissions from nuclear power stations.[6]

An important component in determining both occupational and public health costs is a "value of human life" estimate, or VHL. This issue is dealt with in Section III, in which values of $4 million (1989$) per premature death and $400,000 per major illness are adopted for this report.

The health effects of nuclear power are dependent on the sensitivity of human beings to radiation exposure. These dose-response relationships are important determinants of latent occupational mortality, occupational morbidity, and public health effects, while immediate occupational mortalities result mainly from falls and non-radiological explosions.

Dose-response relationships for radiation are subject to considerable uncertainties. The importance of small individual exposures has been particularly controversial. Some analysts maintain that small amounts of radiation are insignificant, either because they believe that exposures far below natural background radiation are harmless, or because they believe that health effects below some level are socially "acceptable," a view propounded primarily in the late 1960s, that risks which are smaller than those assumed voluntarily (e.g., driving cars, living in brick houses) must be of little or no consequence. These positions have been essentially laid to rest by the recent BEIR report[7] which finds that all levels of radiation can have harmful health effects.

Most information on the induction of cancer in humans by radiation has been from observations in which humans were exposed to doses in excess of 100 rem, delivered in seconds or minutes. These include the nuclear weapons effects at Hiroshima and Nagasaki as well as several series of medical exposures from treatments for various ailments.[8] Studies have shown that, over the range of 100 to 300 rem, the probability of induction of cancer increases in a linear fashion with increasing doses.

---

[6] A new book by Jay Gould suggests that radioactive emissions and resulting mortality effects from routine operation of nuclear power plants are much higher than discussed above. One of Gould's statistics is that routine emissions or radiation cause over 9000 excess deaths in the U.S. each year. Because of the recent publication date of this work, it was not reviewed and the figures from it are not reflected in this report. See Gould, Jay, Deadly Deceit: Low-Level Radiation, High-Level Coverup, Four Walls Eight Windows Publishers, New York, 1990.

[7] National Research Council, Health Effects of Exposure To Low Levels of Ionizing Radiation (BEIR V), National Academy Press, Washington, D.C., 1990, at p. 20 [hereafter cited as BEIR]. For a particularly well-known and methodologically deficient example of this genre, see Starr, C. "Social Benefit Versus Technological Risk -- What Is Our Science Willing to Pay for Safety?", Science, vol. 165, September 19, 1969, pp. 1232-1238.

[8] Id.

Recent reinterpretation of data from the nuclear attacks on Hiroshima and Nagasaki indicates that the effects continue to be linear to much lower levels.[9]

i. Occupational Health Effects

aa. Occupational Mortality (Immediate)

Three studies were received which estimated the number of immediate occupational deaths at large nuclear plants per Gigawatt-year. Immediate occupational deaths are generally the result of accidents, including falls and explosions. The earliest study conducted was the WASH-1224 report, which estimated 0.1 non-radiological deaths per 0.75 Gigawatt-year, or 0.13 deaths/GW-yr.[10]

Shuman and Cavanagh estimated immediate occupational mortality per Gigawatt-year to be 0.01 to 0.15 persons, based on data developed by the British Health and Safety Executive.[11] These values exclude the front end of the nuclear fuel cycle. If front end deaths are included, the range is from 0.05 to 0.47 deaths/gw year. The original source of these data is Cohen and Pritchard.[12] Shuman and Cavanagh stated that they adjusted the figures from Cohen and Pritchard to reflect a 55% capacity factor, but do not describe the adjustment, so it is not possible to determine whether Shuman and Cavanagh used the GW-yr unit as a measure of energy (as do NSIC and Spangler), or as a measure of capacity.

Spangler's estimate that 0.01 non-radiological mortalities occur per 0.8 Gigawatt-year (or 0.012 deaths/GW-yr), for a 1000 MWe plant operating at 80% capacity factor, corresponds with the lower end of Shuman and Cavanagh's range.[13] Spangler estimates that front-end fuel cycle activities (which are not included in the 0.012 deaths/GW-yr) account for about 21 times as many occupational deaths as does power production at the plant itself. He also notes that any attempt to arrive at routine occupational mortality figures is full of uncertainty because of the lack of an

---

[9] BEIR V, supra, note 7 at pp. 20-26.

[10] U.S. Atomic Energy Commission, Office of Energy Systems Analysis, Division of Reactor Research and Development, Comparative Risk-Cost-Benefit Study of Alternative Sources of Electrical Energy: A Compilation of Normalized Cost and Impact Data for Current Types of Powerplants and their Supporting Fuel Cycles, WASH-1224, December, 1974. See NSIC staff, "Comparative Risk-Cost-Benefit Study of Alternative Sources of Electric Energy," Nuclear Safety, no. 2, March-April 1976, p. 17.

Shuman and Cavanagh estimated the immediate occupational mortality per Gigawatt-year to be 0.01 to 0.15 persons, based on a 1000 MW plant operating at 75% capacity factor. Shuman, M. and Cavanagh, R., A Model Electric Power and Conservation Plan for the Pacific Northwest: Environmental Costs, Appendix 2, Northwest Conservation Act Coalition, Seattle, WA, November, 1982 [hereafter cited as Shuman and Cavanagh], p. 26.

[11] Id.

[12] Cohen, A. and D. Pritchard, Comparative Risks of Electricity Production Systems: A Critical Survey of the Literature, Her Majesty's Stationery Office, December, 1980.

[13] Spangler, M., "A Critique of Methods in the Quantification of Risks, Costs, and Benefits in the Societal Choice of Energy Options," Annual Nuclear Energy, v. 10, no. 3,4, 1983, p. 135. (These figures were derived from USNRC, January, 1979a, Report NUREG-0512, pp. 9-17.)

adequate data base in certain areas of the fuel cycle. Spangler does not describe in any detail the methodology used in the development of his estimates, which come from an older cited study.[14] Using an 80% capacity factor appears to be unrealistically high, and could translate into a significant underestimation of this risk.

Table 3 displays the immediate occupational mortality costs derived from the studies reviewed.[15]

TABLE 3

OCCUPATION MORTALITY
(Immediate)

Study	Deaths/GW-YR	Cost(1989$)	Cents/kWh
WASH-1224	0.13	$520,000	0.0059
Spangler	0.012	$48,000	0.0005
Shuman & Cavanagh	0.01-0.15	$40,000- $600,000	0.0005- 0.0068
RANGE	0.01-0.15	$40,000- $600,000	0.0005- 0.0068

(See text for references)

[14] Hamilton, L., The Health and Environmental Effects of Electricity Generation: A Preliminary Report, Brookhaven National Laboratory, July, 1974.

[15] Each death figure from the study was multiplied by the value of human life (VHL) used in this study and then adjusted to arrive at a total cost in 1989$. The total cost is also converted into cents per kWh.

All of the underlying sources of data for these studies are somewhat dated. Shuman and Cavanagh (1982) relied on the study by Cohen and Pritchard (1980), which used still older data. Thus, none of these studies reflects the future level of occupational injuries and deaths because of the aging of nuclear power plants. In 1973, the latest year from which data would have been available for the study which Spangler chiefly cited, the oldest US commercial nuclear unit was thirteen years old, and 50% of U.S. nuclear plants were under six years old. In 1990, 19% of the licensed nuclear power plants operating within the United States are over ten years old, and 40% are over fifteen years old. Serious deterioration of equipment has become evident at many aging plants, resulting in worker injuries and deaths -- a situation that is apt to worsen as plants continue to age.[16]

The events of December 9, 1986 at the Surry nuclear power station serve as an example of the aging problem. The closure of a valve in the main steam line increased pressures in the line, rupturing a sixteen-inch diameter pipe. The rupture released 30,000 gallons of superheated water, which flashed into steam and scalded eight plant workers, four of whom later died from their injuries. Corrosion of the feedwater pipe caused the accident; the pipe, which was one-half inch thick when installed, had thinned to less than one-sixteenth of an inch at the time of the accident.[17]

Though less catastrophic, similar problems at a number of plants have arisen in the late 1980s from aging, maintenance deficiencies, and poor management. While these incidents may not readily be converted into health cost figures, they do suggest that occupational mortality and morbidity rates for nuclear plants may already be higher than in the 1970s, and may continue to increase.[18]

Another consideration in selecting any occupational mortality value for nuclear power plants is that the risk per GW-yr will vary with the capacity factor of the plant. At high capacity factors, any given number of deaths per plant-year will be spread over more kWhs. At lower capacity factors, the number of deaths may decline somewhat, but not as much as energy output declines. This relationship is far from clear, however. A low capacity factor may be associated with extensive maintenance, which exposes more workers to more dangerous operations. Low capacity factors may also result from many start-ups and shut-downs, conditions which are particularly likely to stress plant components, accelerate aging and cause accidents. The average capacity factor for large US nuclear units is about 60%, which is closer to Shuman and Cavanagh's 55% value than to the 75 to 80% values used in the other two studies.[19]

Considering the vintage and capacity-factor assumptions of the estimates, and the emergence of aging problems, the report uses Shuman and Cavanagh's high-end rate

---

[16] Riccio, J. and S. Murphy, The Aging of Nuclear Power Plants: A Citizens' Guide to Causes and Effects, Nuclear Information and Resources Service, Washington, D.C., 1987.

[17] Gordon, J. et al., 1986 Nuclear Power Safety Report, Public Citizen Critical Mass Energy Report, September, 1987.

[18] Id.

[19] Nuclear Regulatory Commission, Technology, Safety, and Costs of Decommissioning a Reference Pressurized Water Reactor Power Station, NUREG/CR-0130M and addenda, June 1978.

of 0.15 deaths/GW-Yr as a "starting point" value. Converting this figure using our $4 million value per life, this rate is equivalent to 0.0068 cents/kWh.

bb. Occupational Mortality (Latent)

A study for the Bonneville Power Authority (BPA) quantified latent occupational radiological health impacts resulting from the operation of the 1100 MW Unit 2 of the Washington Public Power Supply System (WPPSS) described by Sharma.[20] Sharma estimated 0.165 deaths per Gigawatt-year from a dose-response function of 10,000 person-rems of radiation per cancer death; this estimate was derived from the work of the International Commission of Radiological Protection (ICRP), which the author considered to be of intermediate magnitude in relation to other studies available at the time. However, new data and analyses have caused even official estimates of this ratio to fall to 1300 person-rems per cancer (or 770 cancers per million person-rem), raising the death rate to 1.45 deaths/GW-yr if all cancers are fatal.[21]

Shuman and Cavanagh estimated 0.03 to 0.39 deaths per Gigawatt-year.[22] Their figure (again from Cohen and Pritchard) reflects delayed cancer deaths. Assuming that these mortality figures are based on dose-response relationships equivalent to those used in the 1980 BEIR III report, the updated BEIR values would increase the mortality values by a factor of about 5 to 0.15 to 1.95 deaths/GW-yr.

Spangler estimated occupational mortality of about 0.061 deaths/GW-yr.[23] Assuming that these values were based on the dose response relationships in BEIR III, the updated estimate would be about 0.31 deaths/GW-yr. However, Spangler's data was from a 1979 NRC publication, so may assume even lower human sensitivity to radiation.

Table 4 displays the latent occupational mortality costs derived from the studies reviewed. As in Table 3, the number of deaths is converted to total cost and then to cents per kWh.

---

[20] Sharma, K., Environmental Costs and Benefits Case Study: Nuclear Power Plants -- Quantification and Economic Valuation of Selected Environmental Impacts/Effects, Nero & Associates, Inc., Portland, Ore., 1984, p. ES-1.

[21] National Academy of Sciences, Biological Effects of Ionizing Radiation (BEIR), vol. III, National Academy Press, 1989 [hereafter cited as BEIR III].

[22] Shuman & Cavanagh, supra note 10. This figure excludes the front end of the fuel cycle. If front end latent mortalities are included, the range is from 0.018 to 3.17.

[23] Spangler, supra note 13.

TABLE 4

OCCUPATIONAL MORTALITY
(Latent)

STUDY	DEATHS/GW-YR	COST (1989$10^6)	CENTS/KWH
Sharma	1.45	5.8	0.066
Shuman & Cavanagh	0.15-1.95	0.6-7.8	0.0068-0.089
Spangler	0.31	1.2	0.014
RANGE	0.15-1.95	0.6-7.8	0.0068-0.089

(See text for references)

cc. Occupational Morbidity

Shuman and Cavanagh estimated occupational morbidity at 0.51 to 8.10 injuries per Gigawatt-year.[24] Immediate injuries result from non-radiological accidents, while latent injuries are caused by cancer. It is not clear whether any of these occupational injuries develop into deaths that would be double-counted with latent occupational mortalities.

Multiplying Shuman and Cavanagh's morbidity range by our $400,000 morbidity valuation[25] produces a range of values from $204,000 to $3.24 million per GW-yr, or 0.0023 to 0.037 cents/kWh. Some portion of this morbidity would be increased by the BEIR III revised dose-response relationships.[26] Assuming that double-counting and increased cancer incidence roughly cancel each other out, the middle of the range of the Shuman and Cavanagh values would be 0.02 cents/kWh, which is adopted as the "starting point" value.

ii. Public Sector

Most of the literature reviewed asserts that the routine operation of a nuclear power plant has no significant negative public health impact. Excluding the front-end of the nuclear fuel cycle, Shuman and Cavanagh predicted zero mortality and zero

---

[24] Shuman & Cavanagh, supra note 10.

[25] See Section III for a discussion of the derivation of morbidity values.

[26] BEIR III, supra note 21.

morbidity from routine public exposure per Gigawatt-year.[27] However, Spangler estimated 0.016 to 0.020 public deaths from plant operation per 0.8 GW-yr, or 0.020 to 0.025 deaths per GW-yr.[28] At $4 million per life, this range of mortalities is $80,000 to $100,000 per GW-yr, or 0.0009 to 0.0011 cents/kWh. Public morbidity and birth defects should be added to this total.[29]

b. Property Damage

Most of the property damage associated with the routine operation of nuclear power plants is related to loss of land from permanent contamination. The studies reviewed indicate that the property damage caused by the routine emissions of radiation from nuclear power plants is negligible. Shuman and Cavanagh assumed that routine nuclear power plant operation causes no significant property damage.[30] The authors did not detail how they arrived at this assumption, but it is consistent with their conclusions regarding the effects on human health caused by routine operations.

According to Ramsay, utility companies must set aside at least 1000 acres for each 1000 MW light water reactor (LWR) at a site, including 130 acres for the reactor cooler alone.[31] Utilities must also allow for another 1800 acres for transmission lines to reach the neighboring power grid.[32] In addition, at some plants land is required for cooling ponds which in one case uses about 2500 acres.[33]

The NSIC staff report divided land use into two categories.[34] The first includes land which is dominated by the power plant itself and its supporting fuel cycle; the second describes land "consumed" by surface mining and land which acts as a disposal site for fuel cycle residues. For the power plant, the NSIC assigned a loss of about 1000 acres. A loss of twelve acres results from activities in the second category. Aside

---

[27] Shuman & Cavanagh, supra note 10 at p. 28. If front-end health costs are considered, Shuman and Cavanagh estimate 0.01 deaths per GW/yr, and from zero to 0.06 injuries per GW/yr.

[28] Spangler, supra note 13.

[29] Data on radiation releases in routine nuclear plant waste discharges are included in Tables 18-21, chapter V.F.5.d. Data on radioactive solid waste is included in chapter V.F.8.

[30] Shuman & Cavanagh, supra note 10 at p. 32.

[31] Ramsay, W., Unpaid Costs of Electrical Energy: Health and Environmental Impacts from /Coal and Nuclear Power, Resources for the Future, Washington, D.C., 1979. See also U.S. Atomic Energy Commission, Nuclear Power Facility Performance, pp. 4-94 - 4-96. (The requirements are apparently not normalized to generation capacity, but are averaged over all existing stations of all sizes), [hereafter cited as Ramsay].

[32] Ibid. at p. 99.

[33] U.S. Nuclear Regulatory Commission, Office of Nuclear Reactor Regulation, Final Environmental Impact Statement Related to the Operation of Wolf Creek Generating Station, NUREG 0878, Docket 50-483, June 1982, p. iii.

[34] NSIC Staff, supra note 10.

from the explanation about what these categories include, the NSIC report detailed neither how the group derived these acreage figures, nor how it assigned dollar value for the acreage lost.[35]

Evidence of property value loss resulting from perceived hazards of proximity to a nuclear waste transport route was admitted in a Texas court in 1977.[36] The plaintiff allegedly lost 38% of his property value, as compared to similar properties away from the railroad track (from $1,060 to $1,700 per acre in 1989$), due to disruptions in agricultural output caused by placing the waste transport route over his property. The second loss claimed was a 19% decline in value (from $740 to $1,060 per acre) attributed to the fear of nuclear danger from possible sabotage or from accidents during transport of waste across the land. The jury decided in favor of the property owner, but damages awarded were in the amount of only $640 (1989$) per acre.[37]

In 1976, a real estate appraiser claimed that one land owner would lose 44% of his property value (from $1560 to $2760 in 1989 dollars) due to the "prospect" of the expansion of a nearby low level waste disposal facility.[38]

Interestingly, following the evacuation of 200,000 residents living within twenty miles of the Three Mile Island nuclear power facility, empirical studies conducted by the Pennsylvania Department of Community Affairs and Pennsylvania State University found no negative impacts on local property values.[39]

Thus, while it may not be concluded that property values near nuclear facilities are negatively impacted, there is some evidence of costs, derived from litigation of external costs, from the public fear of the presence of nuclear materials; but there is insufficient data on property costs of routine nuclear plant operations for use in determining their environmental externality values.

c. Wildlife Costs

Since routine radiation emissions from nuclear power plants are considered to have no significant impact on humans, it is not surprising that few studies have been

---

[35] See U.S. Nuclear Regulatory Commission, Final Generic Environmental Statement on the Use of Recycle Plutonium in Mixed Oxide Fuel in Light Water Cooled Reactors: Health, Safety and Environment, Washington, D.C., August, 1976, pp. IV F-16, 22; and Pohl, R., "Land Use for Nuclear and Solar Energy," Environmental Conservation, Spring, 1977, pp. 7-8: 334,000acres are disturbed to produce 4.036 GW-years, and about 40 tons of uranium concentrate (U_3O_8) are produced for each acre of tailings (per 0.09 GW-yr.).

[36] Texas Electric Service Co. v. Helon, 546 S.W.2d 864 (Tex. Ct. App. 1977), reh.den., March 4, 1977.

[37] Hageman, R., "Nuclear Waste Disposal: Potential Property Value Impacts", Natural Resources Journal, v. 21, October 1981, p. 800, [hereafter cited as Hageman].

[38] Id. at p. 801.

[39] Nuclear Regulatory Commission, The Social and Economic Effects of the Accident at Three Mile Island, U.S. Government Printing Office, January, 1980. Conducted immediately following the TMI incident.

done on biotic community impacts,[40] and none quantifies damage to wildlife. Since even small doses of radioactivity may adversely affect human beings, especially their genetic material, wildlife may experience similar effects. However, the low values generally attributed to animal lives, as compared to human lives, suggest that the value of radiological effects on wildlife is likely to be low.

Water uptake at nuclear power plants clearly produces quantifiable external costs, such as net water losses, thermal pollution, chemical pollution (especially from biocides used to clean condensers), and particularly fish losses due to impingement and entrainment.[41]

3. Non-Routine Operations

Numerous events that are not part of routine operations occur at nuclear power plants and release extra radiation to the environment, but do not constitute major accidents. Examples include spills of mildly radioactive water, venting of radioactive gases, bad fuel cladding, and equipment failure. No comprehensive review of these releases was located.[42]

4. Accident Costs

This section considers four issues: 1) the probability of a major nuclear accident; 2) the health effects of a severe melt-down core accident; 3) preliminary estimates of property damage; and 4) estimates of accident-related health and property costs, in cents per kilowatt-hour.

a. Nuclear Accident Probability

Estimating the probability of future nuclear accidents which are serious enough to cause severe damage to the reactor and release a significant fraction of the reactor's inventory of radioactivity is extremely difficult and much disputed. Major reactor accidents, or even near-accidents, are rare enough to render statistical analyses suspect. Reactor design and operation change over time, and vary among countries and manufacturers.

Uncertainties in probability estimates may also result from insufficient data for component and system failure rates, human error, operator intervention, and severe external events, such as earthquakes. Finally, probabilistic risk assessments (PRAs) for nuclear units can only hope to be valid for the accident sequences modeled; since

---

[40] See Westman, W. and W. Conn, Quantifying Benefits of Controlling Air and Water Pollution from Energy Production and Use, Energy Resources Conservation and Development Commission, Sacramento, CA, 1976, pp. 35-38.

[41] These issues are covered in Section V.F., under Land and Water Pollution Impacts.

[42] Gordon, J., et. al., supra, note 17.

many important accident sequences were not imagined or modeled before they occurred, PRAs will tend to produce accident probabilities that are understated by an unknown factor.[43]

Despite these problems, various sources do offer estimates of the probabilities of severe accidents. For example, the NRC has concluded that a severe reactor core meltdown has about a 45% chance of occurring in the next twenty years at one of the 109 U.S. reactors. This estimate is based on the assumption that the chance of a severe core melt accident at any particular reactor is 1 in 3333 per year.[44]

Hohmeyer used an accident probability range, derived from several risk studies,[45] of 1 in 2000 to 20,000 unit-years for reactors in the Federal Republic of Germany.[46] Hohmeyer also estimated that the Chernobyl accident represents one major accident in 3000 reactor years, or a probability of 1/3000 per unit-year.

The Hohmeyer and NRC estimates are less than the market-based estimates of Chernick, et al., who found that insurers act as if a broader category of accidents, including the Three Mile Island accident, has a probability of about 1/1000 per unit-year.[47]

For the purposes of this section, the NRC estimate of 1 in 3333 reactor-years is used for the probability of a severe core-melt accident in the United States.

b. Health Costs

The impact on human health from a nuclear accident can be catastrophic, as seen in the Chernobyl accident, the most significant nuclear power plant accident to date. It began on April 26, 1986 at the 1000 MWe Unit 4, one of the four RBMK-1000

---

[43] Examples of unforeseen safety problems include the 1975 cable fire at TVA's Browns Ferry, Ala. Nuclear Facility, Lindeman, E., "TVA Finds Lack of Cable Separation at Sequoya, Violations of Appendix R," Inside NRC, McGraw-Hill, Inc., Vol. 12, No. 4, February 12, 1990, p. 6; the 1979 accident sequence at Three Mile Island 2, Lindeman, E. and Franklin, B., "NRC Commission Decides to Appeal Public Citizen Suit Despite Legal Advice," Inside NRC, McGraw-Hill, Inc., Vol. 12, No. 11, May 21, 1990, p. 1; and the 1986 failures of vital SCRAM mechanisms at the Salem 1 & 2 nuclear facilities, Airozo, D. and Jordan, B., "Rogers says NRC Should Focus on Management, Not New Regulations,", Inside NRC, McGraw-Hill, Inc., Vol. 9, No. 18, August 31, 1987, p. 10.

[44] Nucleonics Week, April 25, 1985. This probabilistic risk assessment (indeed, any generic risk assessment) was called into question in a letter dated June 14, 1990, from Kenneth M. Carr, Chairman of the NRC, to Dr. Albert L. Babb of the National Research Council. Chairman Carr stated that major accident risks have to be measured on a plant-specific basis, referring to a study, NUREG-1150, about to be completed for five nuclear plants as the preferred method of risk assessment. He stated that no figure should be used for an "average" severe core damage frequency, and he implied that compliance with NRC regulations is now so good that there is no figure appropriate for assessing probability of a major nuclear accident.

[45] Birkhofer, A., Was Leisten Risikostudien?, atomwirtshaft-atomechnik, v. 31, 1986, pp. 8,9,440-445.

[46] Hohmeyer, O., Social Costs of Energy Consumption, Springer-Verlag, New York, 1988.

[47] Chernick, P., W. Fairley, M. Meyer, and L. Scharff, Design, Costs and Acceptability of an Electric Utility Self-Insurance Pool for Assuring the Adequacy of Funds for Nuclear Power Plan Decommissioning Expense, NUREG/CR-2370, U.S. Nuclear Regulatory Commission, December, 1981.

units[48] at the site. On the first day, 25% of the radiation was released, while the remaining 75% was released over the next nine days. The accident released 3 to 5% of the reactor core, 40 to 50% of the volatile radionuclides -- principally radio-cesium and radio-iodine -- and all noble gases.[49]

As a result of the blast, two people died immediately from burns and trauma, while 29 others died over the next two months from severe thermal and beta-radiation burns. Two hundred more persons had to be hospitalized because of injuries sustained while fire-fighting and attempting rescues.[50]

Of the 135,000 Soviet citizens who were evacuated from a 30-km area around the plant, about 24,000 persons received average individual doses of about 45 rad. The average individual dose in the remaining population was about 4 rad.[51]

In addition to the evacuees, the forty to fifty thousand persons who participated in the cleanup of the area surrounding the reactor incurred considerable risk, compounded by the existence of "hot pockets" of radiation produced by the uneven dispersion of the radioactive materials.[52] According to the radiation detection devices installed around the plant, the radiation exposure risk ranged from 10 to 100 rems.[53]

Hohmeyer estimated worldwide exposure of 240 million person-rem as a result of Chernobyl. He estimated the incidence of cancer as 200 to 3700 per million person-rem, from a variety of sources, for a total of 50,000 to 900,000 incidents of cancer.[54] Hohmeyer assumed a mortality rate of 50% from induced cancers. At BEIR V's ratio of 770 cancers per million person-rem, 185,000 cancers and 92, 500 deaths would be expected. At our values of $4 million per death and $400,000 per non-fatal illness, 92,500 deaths and an equal number of illnesses would be worth $407 billion as the costs derived from the Hohmeyer data. These values do not include any non-cancer effects, such as retardation or genetic disorders.

---

[48] RBMK is the Russian acronym for the Soviet graphite-modified reactor design.

[49] U.S. Department of Energy, Health and Environmental Consequences of the Chernobyl Nuclear Power Plant Accident, Washington, D.C. 1987, Executive Summary, at p. vii [hereafter cited as DOE Chernobyl Report].

[50] Ibid. Recent reports indicate that over 200 people have died as a result of the accident (Hohmeyer, personal communication).

[51] Ibid. at viii.

[52] Hearing before the Committee on Labor and Human Resources, U.S. Senate, 100th Congress, 1st Session, on Reviewing the Causes and Consequences of the Chernobyl Nuclear Plant Accident, January 20, 1987, [hereafter cited as U.S. Senate Hearings] pp. 9-13. Recent Soviet information indicates that 600,000 Soviet citizens took part in the Chernobyl recovery efforts and that 300 workers died from Chernobyl effects. "USSR Marks Chernobyl Date With Closure Promise, Pleas for Help," Nucleonics Week, Vol. 31, No. 18, May 3, 1990, pp.2-4.

[53] Ferguson, J., "The Impact of Decommissioning Policy on the Cost of Nuclear Power," Public Utilities Fortnightly, September 1, 1988, p. 41.

[54] Hohmeyer, O., supra note 46.

DOE has also estimated the projected health impacts of the Chernobyl accident on people throughout the northern hemisphere.[55] Of the 3.5 billion people in the northern hemisphere, DOE expects 600 million to die of cancer from non-radiological causes. As a result of the Chernobyl accident, DOE projects an additional 28,000 fatal cancers. The revised BEIR dose-response relationships would raise this to about 140,000 additional cancers. Some 340,000 children would have suffered from severe mental retardation in the next generation, to which Chernobyl would add 700 more. Similarly, Chernobyl would add 1,900 to the 180,000,000 people DOE expects to be born with genetic disorders.[56]

Assuming that DOE's estimate of excess mortality (corrected for BEIR V), that the remainder of the 185,000 cancers predicted above will be non-fatal, and that the other effects DOE identifies are properly treated as standard morbidities, the worldwide damage from Chernobyl, from the DOE report, would include: $560 billion from cancer fatalities, $18 billion from non-fatal cancers, $280 million from severe mental retardation, and $760 million from genetic disorders, for a total of $579 billion.

Given the NRC's accident probability of 1/3333 per unit-year, these costs correspond to 2.1 cents/kWh for the Hohmeyer estimate,[57] and 3.1 cents/kWh for the data derived from DOE.

Extrapolating from the results of the Chernobyl Soviet RBMK reactor to a domestic LWR is somewhat speculative. For example, LWRs do not contain as large a mass of flammable material as do RBMKs. Domestic LWRs have better containments than RBMKs, and are also subject to more safety regulation than Chernobyl appears to have been. However, Hohmeyer claims that unpublished results of the German Risk Study B suggest that LWR accidents can release even more radiation than was released at Chernobyl.[58]

On the whole, and subject to a wide range of uncertainties, literature supports value of 2 cents/kWh as a "starting point" estimate of the expected human health externality costs from major nuclear accidents at U.S. reactors.

---

[55] DOE Chernobyl Report, Supra note 49 at pp. ix-x.

[56] Id. at p. xii; BEIR V, supra, note 7. Note that the DOE study uses the non-threshold linear dose-effect model. If the BEIR V dose-response hypothesis were used, these figures may be considerably lower. The DOE report states that "caution must be exercised in attributing too much validity to projections of health effects from radiation exposures yet to be received in distant time periods." Thus, the non-threshold linear dose-effect model most likely leads to "upper" estimates of health impacts.

[57] The Hohmeyer estimates were 0.63 - 6.3 cents/kWh based on a wider range of dose-response relationships. See Hohmeyer, supra note 46.

[58] Hohmeyer, O., personal communication.

c. Property Damage

The loss to Western Europe in contaminated food and environmental damage due to the Chernobyl accident has been reported to be $500 million, apparently in 1986/87 dollars.[59] The source of these figures does not describe their derivation.

Another estimate predicts that a major accident at a nuclear power plant in the United States such as the Salem Units 1 and 2 in southern New Jersey could result in property losses totalling $300 billion. The source does not detail the derivation of this figure, nor does it state the year which the dollar figures represent.[60]

Heising and George's study[61] assigned $3 billion per reactor-year for off-site accident costs, which includes property damage from land interdiction, decontamination, and damage to crops. The figure was derived by doubling the $1.5 billion property damage estimate in the Rasmussen study, WASH 1400.[62]

Shuman and Cavanagh calculated property damage from a reactor accident by first citing the Rasmussen report estimate that a $21.5 billion maximum credible accident could happen once every two million reactor years. They adjusted accident probability by a factor of 1000, which is suggested by several critics of WASH 1400.[63] This accident would, therefore, occur between 2×10^5 and 2×10^{11} reactor years. Even at the high end of the range, expected property damage is only $108,000 per reactor year, or under 1 mill per kWh, which Shuman and Cavanagh consider to be insignificant.[64]

One portion of the property damage loss as a result of the Chernobyl accident was damage to Soviet grain crops. According to John M. Urbanchuk, the Director of International Agriculture at Wharton Econometrics Forecasting Associates, the Soviet Union can expect a potential maximum loss of 10% of their annual grain crop as a result of the Chernobyl accident. This loss amounts to about twenty million metric tons, or 790 million bushels per year.[65]

---

[59] U.S. Senate Hearings, supra note 52 at p. 15.

[60] Hearing before the U.S. House of Representatives, Subcommittee on Oversight and Investigations, Calculation of Reactor Accident Consequences for U.S. Nuclear Power Plants (Health Effects and Costs), November 1, 1982. This hearing cites a report prepared by the Sandia Laboratory for the NRC.

[61] Heising, C. and V. George, "Nuclear Financial Risk: Economy-Wide Costs of Reactor Accidents," Energy Policy, February, 1986, p. 47.

[62] Nuclear Regulatory Commission, Reactor Safety Study: An Assessment of Accident Risks in U.S. Commercial Nuclear Power Plants, WASH-1400, NUREG 75/014 October, 1975, p. 75.

[63] See Shuman and Cavanagh, supra note 10.

[64] Id. at p. 35.

[65] Hearings before the U.S. Congress, Subcommittee on Agriculture and Transportation and Joint Economic Committee, The Chernobyl Disaster: Implications for World Food Security and the U.S. Farm Economy, May 5, 1986, at p. 14. The total U.S.S.R. land and agricultural loss from the Chernobyl accident has been reported in a recent Soviet study to amount to $96-$157 billion at the official rate of exchange.

Since the grain crop most affected by the Chernobyl accident was wheat, the price per bushel of wheat will be used to calculate the total economic loss to the grain crop reported in the Wharton report. Furthermore, because the Soviet Union must replace its lost grain crop by importing from other countries, the accident tended to increase grain prices. If the Soviet Union were to increase its wheat imports from the United States by 78 million bushels, the U.S. wheat price would rise by fourteen cents per bushel to $2.91 (1989$).[66]

If the 790 million bushels lost are worth $2.91/bushel, the annual loss derived from the Wharton report is $2.2 billion, or (at a discount rate of 3% to 6.5%), $34 billion to $73 billion in total present value. At the accident probability and capacity factors cited above, the agricultural cost of Chernobyl would be 0.18 to 0.38 cents/kWh. There are no studies that estimate the other property-related costs of the accident.

Thus, based on the reviewed studies, the "starting point" total accident damage cost estimate from a major nuclear accident is about 2.3 cents/kWh, composed of 2 cents/kWh for health damages and roughly 0.3 cents/kWh for damages to agriculture.[67]

5. Decommissioning and Waste Disposal Costs

The NRC defines decommissioning as that portion of the dismantling of nuclear plants that is necessary to remove radioactivity to the extent that the site can be released for unrestricted use.[68] The actual cost of decommissioning a large reactor is unknown because no large reactor has yet been decommissioned.[69] While it is generally accepted that decommissioning adds about one-quarter to one-third to the dismantling costs,[70] estimates of what percent decommissioning contributes to the total cost of the nuclear fuel cycle range from 5-100%: Worldwatch Institute: 5-25%, 40% for all waste disposal;[71] Williams & LaGuardia: 20%;[72] and Chapman: 100%[73]).[74]

"Cost of Chernobyl Nuclear Disaster Soars in New Study," Wall Street Journal, March 29, 1990.

66 Id.

67 A new study released by the U.S.S.R. indicates total costs from the Chernobyl accident at 170-215 billion rubles ($283-358 billion at the official rate of exchange). The report estimated lost land value and agricultural losses as 57.5-94.5 billion rubles ($96-$157 billion), contaminating 31,000 sq. km. (12,400 sq. mi.) of land, and lost electricity production at 66.8 billion rubles ($111 billion) through the year 2000. Wall Street Journal, supra note 65. These figures would indicate much higher accident costs than used in this report. The components of the U.S.S.R. costs were not stated, however, so there is no way of knowing how much of these costs can be attributed to environmental externalities. The figures, therefore, were not used in this study. This is an obvious area for future research.

68 Nixon, M., "Financing of Nuclear Decommissioning Costs," Public Utilities Fortnightly, March 20, 1986, p. 57 [hereafter cited as Nixon].

69 Id. at p. 47.

70 Id.

71 Pollock, C., Decommissioning Nuclear Power's Missing Link, Worldwatch Institute, 1986, p. 26. See also, Pollock, C., The Closing Act: Decommissioning Nuclear Power Plants, Environment, v. 28, no. 2, March 1986, p. 15 [hereafter cited as Pollock].

The NRC's final rule for decommissioning allows power reactor licensees to base funding plans on a set cost of decontamination that varies with reactor type and size. The costs were estimated by Battelle for the NRC, at 1986 price levels, at $86.6 million to $105 million for pressurized water reactors (PWRs) and $114.8 million to $135 million for boiling water reactors (BWRs).[75]

10 CFR §30 et seq. sets forth the NRC guidelines for financing the decommissioning of licensed nuclear facilities.[76] The NRC requires nuclear facilities to set aside of $100 million ($117 million in 1989 dollars) for a basic decommissioning fund. This cost would usually be covered in rates. This report will use the $117 million base figure as the internalized cost; therefore, any estimated cost which exceeds this base will be considered an externality. Individual utilities may reserve larger decommissioning funds.

A utility must provide for decommissioning at the outset of plant operation in order to allocate the estimated cost equitably to ratepayers.[77] Unfortunately, many plant owners had operated throughout the years without putting money aside for decommissioning; if allowed to continue, this pattern would have caused "aftershock" for ratepayers when decommissioning became necessary.[78] Some utility representatives now argue that decommissioning costs will exceed current estimates and that regulators should allow for unknown and unexpected expenses in setting decommissioning costs to be recovered through current rates.[79]

Nuclear plant operators have three options for decommissioning a plant. First, immediately after the plant shuts down, the owner can promptly decontaminate and dismantle the entire facility. Second, the owner can place the contents of the plant in storage ("mothballing") so that the radioactive materials can decay for several decades prior to dismantlement. Third, the owner can "entomb" (i.e., seal all the entrances with thick layers of concrete) the plant by sealing it for 30 to 100 years.[80]

---

[72] Id. See Williams and LaGuardia, Guidelines for Producing Commercial Nuclear Powerplant Decommissioning Cost Estimates, AIF, Bethesda, Md., March 1985.

[73] Id. See Chapman, Nuclear Economics, cited in Pollock, infra, note 73.

[74] Pollock, C., The Closing Act: Decommissioning Nuclear Power Plants, Environment, v. 28, no. 2, March 1986, p. 15.

[75] Ferguson, J., "The Impact of Decommissioning Policy on the Cost of Nuclear Power," Public Utilities Fortnightly, September 1, 1988, p. 41.

[76] Federal Register, v. 53, no. 123, 1988; 10 CFR Parts 30, 40, 50, 51, 70 & 72.; 26 USC 468A(e)(Supp. V. 1988) requires establishment of the decommissioning fund.

[77] Nixon, supra note 68 at p. 57.

[78] Pollock, supra note 71 at p. 42. Some nuclear units (e.g., the Yankee plants) are owned by utilities with no other assets. The cost of decommissioning these units may result in corporate bankruptcy and may have to be borne by the government. Id.

[79] Nixon, supra, note 68 at p. 57.

[80] Pollock, supra, note 71 at p. 21.

a. Decommissioning Costs for Large Reactors

This section reports comparative estimates for pressurized water reactors (PWRs) and boiling water reactors (BWRs). Because of the nature of their design, BWRs generally have higher decommissioning costs than PWRs. An attempt is to arrange the estimated costs according to decommissioning method (mothballing, etc.), as well as reactor size (1000 or 1100 MW).

Mothballing cost estimates in 1986 were $87 million to $112 million for a PWR and $114 to $144 million for a BWR (1989$).[81]

Entombment, and 100-year surveillance for a large reactor (ca. 1000 MW) were estimated by the Worldwatch Institute to cost $64 million to $66 million for a PWR and $91 million to $94 million for a BWR.[82] EPRI's estimate for entombment and 100-year surveillance of a PWR, was $72 to $75 million.[83]

Other studies which have estimated decommissioning costs specifically for PWRs and BWRs include a Battelle study, which incorporated both EPRI and NRC estimates.[84] In 1985, EPRI estimated a cost range of $92 to $170 million (1989$) for decommissioning a 1000 MW PWR. For decommissioning a 1100 MW BWR, Battelle estimated $156 million, while EPRI estimated $113 to $228 million for prompt decommissioning, and alternatively $103 to $106 million for entombment and 100 year surveillance.[85]

These 1985-1986 decommissioning cost estimates are likely to be significantly understated. Utility estimates of decommissioning costs have been escalating at 19% in real terms.[86]

Based on these studies, a "starting point" estimate for decommissioning large nuclear plants is estimated to be $.50/kWh (in excess of costs internalized by the Nuclear Decommissioning Fund).

---

[81] Ibid. Earlier estimates by the federal Energy Research and Development Administration (ERDA, now part of the Department of Energy) are much lower for mothballing: 5.9 to $6.6 million. See ERDA, Cleaning up the Remains of Nuclear Facilities -- A Multibillion Dollar Problem, Comptroller General of the U.S. Report to Congress, June 16, 1977, at p. 14.

[82] Pollock, supra note 71 at p. 21; ERDA estimated $15 to $20 million for entombment. ERDA warned, however, that the cost for each reactor will vary depending on its characteristics. See ERDA, supra note 79.

[83] EPRI Journal, Decommissioning Nuclear Power Plants, July/August, 1985.

[84] Id.

[85] Smith, R., et al., Updated Costs for Decommissioning Nuclear Power Facilities, EPRI, May, 1985.

[86] Chernick, P., and J. Wallach, Testimony on behalf of the Massachusetts Executive Office of Energy Resources, MDPU 89-100, June 30, 1989.

b. Decommissioning Costs for Actual Reactors

While no large nuclear reactor has been decommissioned, several small reactor sites have undergone decommissioning under a variety of circumstances. These costs are mentioned below. Because of the difficulty of extrapolating larger reactor costs from small reactor data these actual reactor estimates are not used in our final "starting point" external cost summary.

Figures estimated by the DOE for the 22 MW LWR Elk River plant in Minnesota, the only LWR thus far that has undergone a process of full decontamination and dismantlement, were $6.15 million. The process took three years and only included removal of the eight-foot-thick concrete containment building walls.[87]

The first power reactor in the nation, the Shippingport reactor in Shippingport, Pennsylvania, is also the largest power reactor ever decommissioned in the United States. The 72 MW light water breeder cost an estimated $98 million, or $1,400/kW, to decommission, even though the reactor pressure vessel did not need to be disassembled.[88]

Decommissioning of the 12.5 MW Japan Power Demonstration Reactor (JPDR) started in 1986 and is expected to take until 1992. This BWR only produced 140 GWH (about as much as a large reactor would produce in a typical week) over an operating life of 13 years, and was not operated for the last ten years prior to decommissioning. Despite all of these factors, disassembling the plant is expected to cost $133.33million, or $10,700/kW.[89]

Assuming an economies-of-scale factor of 0.5, the Shippingport cost would imply a decommissioning cost for a 1 GW unit of about $365 million, while that of the JPDR would imply a cost of $1.2 billion.[90] The decommissioning costs of typical commercial nuclear units would tend to be higher than for these test and demonstration reactors, since 1) they will tend to operate longer and hence become more radioactive; 2) they are more robustly constructed and contain more safety equipment, requiring more disassembly; and unlike Shippingport, they are too large to bury intact.

Long Island Lighting Company recently stated that its controversial Shoreham plant on Long Island will cost at least $400 million to decommission if dismantled now even though it operated at low power for just 30 hours.[91]

---

[87] EPRI Journal, supra note 83 at p. 17.

[88] Id. at p. 48.

[89] Usui, N., "JPDR Pressure Vessel Decommissioning Starts," Nucleonics Week, June 14, 1990.

[90] See Chernick, et al., Design, Costs, and Acceptability of an Electric Utility Self-Insurance Pool for Assuring the Adequacy of Funds for Nuclear Power Plant Decommissioning Expense, Report NUREG/CR-2370, U.S. Nuclear Regulatory Commission, December 1981.

[91] Sperber, M., "Shoreham Deal is Consummated, But Faces Opposition," Inside NRC, McGraw Hill, Inc., July 3, 1989, vol. 11, No.14, p. 1.

The costs associated with the clean-up operations at Three Mile Island are by far the most expensive.[92] The Shuman and Cavanagh study estimate the direct accident cost of Three Mile Island to be $3.2 billion, most of which is related to decontaminating the reactor.[93]

As previously stated, no "starting point" estimates can be made from these figures.

c. Waste Storage and Disposal Costs

In 1985, domestic nuclear power plants generated 1348 metric tons of high-level waste (HLW). Even with no new power plant orders, by the year 2000 there will be an estimated 41,000 metric tons of unstored waste.[94] The average nuclear power reactor produces about 30 to 40 tons of high-level waste annually.

Radioactive waste that contains plutonium and other elements with long half-lives complicates the disposal process because of the heat dissipation demands that radioactive decay places on permanent storage systems.[95] Therefore, researchers have considered many options over the years for the storage of nuclear waste. Among the options are storage in salt beds, rock formations, ice caps, the ocean floor, or outer space.[96]

The Nuclear Waste Policy Act of 1982 established a process for selecting sites for the disposal in geologic repositories of spent nuclear fuel and high level waste.[97] The general guidelines were issued in November 1984 as Title 10 of the Code of Federal Regulations, Part 960. The DOE is now proceeding with the next step in the site-selection process for the first repository. In 1988, the DOE nominated a site at Yucca Mountain in Nye County, Nevada, as its sole proposed site for characterization, but the site has run into both technical and political problems. DOE, recently announced that a site will not be ready for use until 2010.[98]

The environmental externality cost cannot yet be reasonably calculated for high level waste disposal because of the uncertainty of site selection, disposal method, and the security of the repository. However, it is likely that the internal cost of fuel

---

[92] Bureau of National Affairs, Environmental Reporter, Washington, D.C., March 3, 1989, p. 2348.

[93] Shuman and Cavanagh, supra note 10 at p. 34.

[94] Radar, N., et al., Turning Down the Heat -- Solutions to Global Warming: An Analysis of Energy Efficiency, Renewable Resources, and Other Options Versus New Nuclear Power Development, Public Citizen, Washington, D.C., 1988.

[95] Ramsay, supra note 31 at p. 60.

[96] Id. at p. 62.

[97] 42 USC 10101 et seq. A Nuclear Waste Fund has been established by a fee on nuclear power plants. This will, of course, reduce the externality costs. 42 USC 1022 (c) (1986).

[98] Chicago Tribune, "Nevada Sues Energy Chief Over Nuclear Dump Efforts," December 29, 1989, p. 14. See also IRT Publications, Nuclear Waste: Yucca Mountain, December, 1989.

disposal will be greater than current estimates, and that the disposal process will produce some residual environmental costs and risks.

d. Low Level Waste Disposal Costs

Low level waste (LLW) disposal is regulated by 10 CFR §61. There are only three LLW disposal facilities in the United States: at Barnwell, South Carolina; Beatty, Nevada; and Richland, Washington. The Low Level Radioactive Waste Policy Amendments Act of 1985 provided that states, either singly or in regional combinations, undertake responsibility for disposal of low level waste by January, 1993, or be subject to large and increasingly prohibitive fees for storage at the existing sites.[99] The states have started to implement this legislation by establishing their own (as in New York) or regional sites.[100]

It is too early to determine the environmental externality costs of low level waste disposal at this time because of the uncertainty regarding the location, security and management of the sites. Experience with leakage at the retired low-level burial site at West Valley in New York and the Hanford, Washington, federal nuclear disposal site suggests that there will be environmental externality costs.[101]

The inadequacy of utility-financed decommissioning reserves, which are intended to cover disposal of the large volume of waste from the decommissioning, will be aggravated by any environmental costs which are internalized in waste disposal fees, either for mitigation or for compensation.

6. Summary

a. Routine Operations

The "starting point" estimates, concluded from the studies reviewed, of the total external costs of routine operations include: human health costs, 0.098 cents/kWh; and wildlife damage, 0.01 cents/kWh. The total "starting point" external costs of routine nuclear power plant operations are thus approximately 0.11 cents per kWh.

The "starting point" health costs of the routine operations of a nuclear power plant break down as follows: 0.007 cents/kWh for immediate occupational mortality; 0.07 cents per kWh for latent occupational mortality; 0.02 cents per kWh for occupational morbidity; and 0.001 cents/kWh for public mortality.

---

[99] 42 U.S.C. §2021b et seq.

[100] BNA, <u>DOE Releases State, Regional Guidance on Compliance with Low Level Waste Act</u>, vol. 10, No. 24, October 8, 1987, p. 1516.

[101] <u>New York Times</u>, September 10, 1989, p. 40.

b. Accidents

Based on the health impact data compiled from the Chernobyl accident in 1986, the "starting point" value is 2 cents/kwh as an expected human health externality from major nuclear accidents at US reactors. The property damage costs derived from the Chernobyl accident damage to the Soviet wheat crop is about 0.3 cents/kWh. Thus, total "starting point" accident costs based on a Chernobyl-scale accident are 2.3 cents/kwh.[102]

c. Decommissioning and Waste Disposal

Differences in nuclear plant decommissioning cost estimates are in part the result of differences in report format, scope of the estimated work, plant characteristics, radiation protection of workers, and site features.[103]

In 1985, the NRC required utilities to establish plans for funding decommissioning at $117 million (1989 dollars). Actual costs from small reactors that have been or will soon be dismantled indicate that true decommissioning costs may be even higher, although these costs are not used here to establish "starting point" estimates. The experience at the JPDR suggests that 1000 MW BWRs will cost about $1.2 billion to decommission.

Based on these studies it appears that the decommissioning cost is likely to exceed the NRC decommissioning guideline by as much as $1.1 billion, or 0.65/kWh over a 30-year plant life. Actual costs will vary, due to site-specific factors, so the overrun at some plants may be even larger. On the other hand, at least some utilities will establish larger decommissioning reserves than currently required by the NRC. Thus, some of the cost difference is likely to be internalized for ratepayers in the near future or late in the operation of the nuclear unit. The remainder of the cost will either be internalized by ratepayers following retirement of the plant, partially absorbed by utility shareholders. The "starting point" value of 0.50 cents/kWh represents the additional costs of decommissioning which are not currently internalized, which may be thought of as economic externalities imposed on the future by current plant operation.

The "starting point" environmental externality costs of decommissioning and of high and low-level waste disposal cannot yet be determined because of the uncertainties in decommissioning technology and in the disposal programs which have not been dealt with in the studies reviewed.

---

[102] Re larger recent U.S.S.R. Chernobyl accident cost estimates, see supra note 65.

[103] Sieving, K., "Estimating the Funding Levels for Nuclear Plant Decommissioning," Public Utilities Fortnightly, August 20, 1987, p. 18.

7. Conclusions

Based upon the reviewed studies, the "starting point" environmental externality costs of nuclear power plant operations, decommissioning and waste disposal are estimated at 2.91 cents/kWh, as follows:

Routine Operations	0.11
Accidents	2.30
Decommissioning	0.50
TOTAL	2.91

8. Research Needs

Excluded from this literature review are all front-end nuclear costs such as damages from mining accidents and releases, environmental releases from disposal of mining and mill tailings, and transportation of nuclear materials to a nuclear plant. Due to the lack of studies the costs of controls and mitigation measures for environmental releases from operation of nuclear plants, nuclear plant accidents and disposal of nuclear plant wastes were not discussed or estimated. All these omitted externality costs require research if the total environmental costs of nuclear operations are to be ascertained.

Further analysis is also needed to treat other wildlife issues in at least as much detail as fish impingement, covered in Section V.G. 1, explicitly deriving a dollar value on the population effects for fish and other species. There is inadequate information to assign a dollar value to thermal pollution damages at this time and that also requires research.

No studies were found to quantify any property damage cost from routine operations. Efforts have recently been made to establish property value loss regarding areas located very close to nuclear facilities or waste transport routes, but his another area ripe for future investigation.[104]

[104] Hageman, supra, note 37 at p. 769.

9. Glossary of Terms

From: Office of Technology Assessment, Managing the Nation's Commercial High-Level Radioactive Waste, Washington DC, 1985 (Appendix H).

AEC: Atomic Energy Commission; its functions have been assumed by the Department of Energy and Nuclear Regulatory Commission.

activity (radioactivity): the rate at which radioactive material emits radiation, given in terms of the number of nuclear disintegrations occurring in a unit of time; the common unit of radioactivity is the curie (Ci).

background radiation (natural): nuclear radiation due to the natural environment and to naturally occurring radioactivity within the body.

BWR: boiling water reactor.

curie: the unit of radioactivity, abbreviated Ci. One curie equals 37,000,000,000 nuclear transformations per second. uCi (microcurie) = 1 millionth of a Ci, mCi (millicurie) = 1 thousandth of a Ci, MCi (megacurie) = 1 million Ci. The number of radionuclei corresponding to 1 Ci depends directly on the half-life. That is, the longer the half-life, the more radionuclei are necessary for a disintegration rate of 1 Ci.

decommissioning: the process of removing a facility from operation; its contents may be entombed, decontaminated and dismantled, or converted to another use.

DEIS: Draft Environmental Impact Statement.

deuterium: a natural isotope of hydrogen with one neutron and one proton in its nucleus (atomic weight = 2).

disposal: operations designed to provide final isolation by relying on a combination of manmade and natural barriers rather than on continuous human control and maintenance to ensure the isolation of the waste; the Nuclear Waste Policy Act specifies emplacement in mined geologic repositories. Disposal sites and facilities may also be used for storage prior to disposal.

DOE: U.S. Department of Energy.

dose rate: the rate of delivery of dose is referred to as dose rate and is specified in dose units per unit time.

EPA: U.S. Environmental Protection Agency.

ERDA: U.S. Energy Research and Development Administration, now DOE.

front end of the fuel cycle:
: mining, milling, enrichment, fabrication of nuclear reactor fuel and disposal of the wastes and tailings therefrom (excluded from this report).

fuel assembly:
: a grouping of fuel rods which is not taken apart during the charging and discharging of a reactor core.

fuel cycle: the uranium fuel cycle to support the operation of light water reactors involves a number of stages, including: mining, milling, conversion, enrichment, fuel fabrication, nuclear reactor operation, waste management, and transportation between stages; fuel reprocessing and re-use in breeder reactors is not presently pursued in the U.S.

GESMO: Generic Environmental Statement on the Use of Recycle Plutonium in Mixed Oxide Fuel in Light Water Cooled Reactors, NUREG-0002.

GWe: gigawatts electric, i.e., 1 billion (10E9) watts or 1,000 megawatts.

half-life: the time interval required for the number of radionuclides in a sample (and thus the rate of emitted radiation) to decrease by a factor of one-half.

high-level waste (HLW):
: highly radioactive material residues from all stages of the nuclear fuel cycle.

kWh: kilowatt-hour, a unit of one thousand watts of energy generation or consumption in a given hour.

long lived nucleides:
: radioactive isotopes with half-lives greater than 30 years.

low-level waste (LLW):
: residues of the nuclear fuel cycle (and other commercial activities using radioactive materials) with low levels of radioactivity. For the nuclear fuel cycle, this includes irradiated components and piping, shielding, resins, sludges, filters from cleansing and circulating water around the irradiated fuel and in the fuel pool.

LWR: light water reactor.

metric ton (MT):
: unit of weight; 1 MT = 1,000 kilograms.

mrem: millirem, one-thousandth of a rem.

MRS: monitored retrievable storage of high level wastes, usually above ground, where the wastes can be retrieved for reprocessing or eventual permanent storage.

MWe: megawatt electric (1MW = 1 million watts), a unit of energy production or consumption.

NEPA: National Environmental Policy Act of 1969.

OCRWM: Office of Civilian Radioactive Waste Management; part of the DOE.

Population Dose:
the sum of the radiation dose times the number of persons exposed to that dose.

PWR: pressurized water reactor: a reactor system that uses a pressurized water primary cooling system.

rad: radiation absorbed dose: a unit of absorbed dose of ionizing radiation, equivalent to the absorption of 100 ergs of radiation.

rem: roentgen equivalent man: a quantity used to express the effective dose equivalent for all forms of ionizing radiation.

roentgen: a unit for measuring gamma or X-ray radiation by calculating the effect of the radiation on air.

Sievert: 100 rems.

U.S.W.: U.S. Wattage (= 2 trillion kilowatt hours).

VI. EXTERNALITY COSTS BY RESOURCE

E. RENEWABLE GENERATION RESOURCES

VI. EXTERNALITY COST BY RESOURCE

E. RENEWABLE GENERATION RESOURCES

1. Introduction and Summary Charts

This chapter describes the environmental impacts associated with operation of renewable energy technologies. Renewable energy technologies currently supply 8% of U.S. total energy usage and that figure is certain to grow. The rate of growth will depend heavily on the availability of research and development funds, and could reach 28% of U.S. energy demands by 2030.[1] Renewable generation resources include hydroelectric development, solar energy technologies, wind conversion facilities, and biomass fueled generation.[2] A task force of personnel from five national labratories recently concluded that renewable energy technologies generally have lower environmental impacts than do fossil fuel energy systems. The task force also stated that a comprehensive and comparative analysis of environmental impacts is needed and would strengthen the National Energy Strategy.[3]

This chapter summarizes some of the available literature on costing the environmental externalities associated with hydro, solar, wind, and biomass facilities. The less prevalent renewable energy technologies, including geothermal and ocean energy technologies, were not researched. The cost ranges identified are summarized in Table 1. The Table does not include a value for hydroelectric energy. The one study which attempted to value hydroelectric externalities was highly site-specific and has been criticized for having vastly overstated the value of the externalities.[4] In reviewing the figures in the Summary Table, it is important to note that the figures may not have been developed on comparable bases and may not have included the same aspects of the fuel cycle. The discussion below describes how the data for Table 1 were derived. A qualitative discussion of the types of impacts common to these technologies has been developed and included in each renewable energy technology section in this chapter.

---

[1] U.S. Department of Energy (DOE), The Potential of Renewable Energy, An Interlaboratory White Paper, SERI/TP-260-3674, March, 1990 at p. 45 [hereafter cited as PRE Study]. Renewable energy source contributes 9.9% to total utility electric generation in the U.S. (All but 4.6% of this figure is hydro power.) U.S.D.O.E., Monthly Energy Review, National Energy Information Review, Washington DC, February, 1990.

[2] Although waste-to-energy plants are often described as a renewable technology the label is probably inappropriate. Waste-to-energy plants are discussed in a separate section of this report. See Chapter VI. G.

[3] PRE STUDY, supra note 1 generally.

[4] BPA, Methods for Valuation of Environmental Costs and Benefits of Hydroelectric Facilities: A Case Study of the Sultan River Project, Final Report, prepared by Biosystem Analysis, Inc., et al., DOE/BP-266, June, 1984 [hereafter cited as Sultan River Case Study].

TABLE 1

SUMMARY OF ENVIRONMENTAL COSTS FOR SOLAR, WIND, AND BIOMASS

Technology Type	Cents/kWh
Solar Technologies	0 to 0.4
Wind Generation	0 to 0.1
Biomass	0 to 0.7

For renewable technologies, the literature suggests that land and material requirements and their associated ecological impacts are often the most significant environmental impacts. For this reason some front-end impacts for renewables are pointed out, although discussion of front-end impacts has been generally excluded from this report.

Water use is not a major externality for renewables. To aid in comparing renewables to fossil and nuclear technologies, Table 2 describes water use for photovaltaic, solar thermal, wind, and wood-fired steam renewable energy technologies. Water used for small hydroelectric facilities is given for comparison, though this is a nonconsumptive use. Some of the sources cited provide the data in acre-feet per 10^{12} BTU of energy produced. These figures have been converted to acre feet per kilowatt hour for convenience of future research efforts.

TABLE 2

WATER USE FOR RENEWABLE GENERATION

Renewable Energy Technology	Water Consumption (acre-ft/kWh)
PV Central Station DOE/Materiel (1)	0.102×10^{-6}
Solar Thermal-Central Station DOE/Char (2)	0.069×10^{-6}
Wind Conversion DOE/Char (3)	- 0 -
Wood-Fired Steam DOE/Char (4)	8.403×10^{-6}
Small Hydroelectric (nonconsumptive) DOE/Char (5)	0.066

(1) For 100 mWe photovoltaic facility in Barstow, California with 209 gWh/yr generation, maximum water usage is for array washing and potable water needs. DOE/Materiel at pp. 13, 23, Figure 9. DOE/Char does not quantify water consumption but indicates that periodic washing of photovoltaic panels may be necessary. DOE/Char at p. 179.

(2) Process and maintenance water consumption associated with boiler make-up and heliostat washing for a 100,000kWe solar thermal central facility located in the southwestern United States operating at 50% capacity. Boiler blowdown accounts for an additional 29 acre-ft/yr or 0.066×10^{-6} acre-ft/kWh. DOE/Char at pp. 177-178.

(3) Data for 1.5×10^{3} kWe capacity wind machine using compressed air energy storage instead of batteries. Source notes that alternate storage systems such as pumped hydro could require significant water usage. DOE/Char at p. 175.

(4) For a 63 mWe wood-fired steam electric plant operating at 80% capacity. This plant would generate 4.439×10^{-6} acre-ft/kWh in aqueous waste. DOE/Char at pp. 173-74.

(5) "Feed water" which contributes the kinetic energy of flowing or falling water to power a 4 mWe small hydroelectric plant with a dam height not more than 65 feet producing 0.012×10^{9} kWh/yr is provided for comparative purposes only. DOE/Char at pp. 196-97.

Table 3 describes land use for photovaltaic stations, solar thermal, wind, wood fired steam, large hydroelectric and pumped storage. The figures are provided in acres per kilowatt hour. A figure for land use was not available for small hydroelectric. To a certain extent these land uses should be considered front-end costs. In comparing these values to those for fossil and nuclear generation of electricity, bear in mind that the front-end land costs for coal and uranium are not included in our table but are quite large due to mining impacts, permanent waste storage, and plant decommissioning. See Table 22 in Chapter V.F. At the end of this chapter there are full citations for the studies which are referred to in abbrievated form in the Tables.

TABLE 3

LAND USE FOR RENEWABLE GENERATION
(acres/kWh)

Renewable Energy Technology		Acres/kWh
PV Central Station		
DOE/Materiel	(1)	0.080×10^{-6}
DOE/Char	(2)	0.033×10^{-6}
Solar-Thermal Central Station		
DOE/Char	(3)	0.076×10^{-6}
Wind Conversion		
DOE/Char	(4)	0.006×10^{-6}
Wood-Fired Steam		
DOE/Char	(5)	0.013×10^{-6}
BPA/ECO	(6)	0.009×10^{-6}
Large Hydroelectric		
DOE/Char	(7)	0.007×10^{-6}
Pumped Storage		
DOE/Char	(8)	0.029×10^{-6}
Small Hydroelectric	(9)	n.a.

(1) For a 100 mWe photovoltaic facility in Barstow, California producing 0.209×10^9 kWh/yr and with a thirty year life. DOE/Materiel at pp. 13, 22, Figure 7.

(2) For a 109 mWe photovoltaic facility in Phoenix, Arizona producing 0.23×10^9 kWh/yr and with a thirty year life based on total land use of 230 acres. DOE/Char at pp. 179-80.

(3) For a 100 mWe solar-thermal power plant producing 0.44×10^9 kWh/yr and with a thirty year life based on total land use of 1000 acres. DOE/Char at pp. 177-78.

(4) For a 1.5 mWe wind machine producing 2.9×10^6 kWh/yr at low wind and with a thirty year life based on total land use of 0.51 acre. DOE/Char at pp. 175-76.

(5) For a 63 mWe wood-fired steam electric plant producing 401×10^6 kWh/yr and with a twenty year life based on total land use of 102 acres for storage and plant. DOE/Char at pp. 173-74.

(6) For a 12 mWe wood-fired cogeneration facility with a thirty year life producing 89.4×10^6 kWh/yr based on a 25 acre site. BPA/ECO at pp. 2-3 - 2-5.

(7) For a 200 mWe run-of-river hydroelectric consisting of dam, spillway, intakes, and powerhouse producing 0.98 x 10^9 kWh/yr and with a sixty year life based on a total lifetime use of 397 acres. DOE/Char at pp. 198-99.

(8) For a pumped storage hydroelectric plant consisting of four 250 MW pumps and drivers producing 1.14 x 10^9 kWh/yr and with a sixty year life based on a total lifetime use of 2000 acres. DOE/Char at p. 200.

(9) Land requirements for hydroelectric facilities with less than 15 MW capacity were not available in sources consulted.

Although this Chapter focuses on the adverse environmental effects of renewable energy technology, it is important to keep in mind that the literature shows that there are substantial positive externalities from renewables. Positive externalities include avoided greenhouse gas emissions, acid rain precursor emissions, trace metal emissions, cooling water impacts, nuclear accident risk, and radioactive waste disposal problems.

One study estimates that renewable energy produced in the U.S. currently reduces CO_2 emissions by 550 million tons per year. This is the equivalent of the CO_2 output of 138 typical coal-fired power plants.[5] For example, in the case of hydropower, CO_2 emissions from construction and operation are nearly 100 times lower than are CO_2 emissions from conventional coal-fired plants. The comparison is shown in Table 4.

TABLE 4

COMPARISON OF CO_2 EMISSIONS BETWEEN CONVENTIONAL COAL AND HYDRO POWER
(CO_2 in Tons/gWh of Energy)

	Resource Extraction	Facility Construction	Facility Operations	Total
Conventional Coal Plant (with scrubber)	N/A	1.048	1057.143	1058.191
Hydro	N/A	10.95	N/A	10.95

Source: U.S. DOE, The Potential of Renewable Energy An Interlaboratory White Paper, SERI/TP-260-3674 DE 90000322, March 1990 at A-12.

Renewables compare favorably on CO_2 emissions, even with nuclear plants. A recent British study identifies the nuclear fuel cycle as a major CO_2 contributor, on a

---

[5] Public Citizen, Critical Mass Energy Project, The Power of the States: A Fifty-State Survey of Renewable Energy, Washington, DC, 1990.

par with fossil fuels.[6] The CO_2 emissions from solar and wind are virtually zero, including front-end emissions. Some conventional and toxic emissions of biomass can be troublesome and biomass technology does emit CO_2. However, control technology for conventional and toxic emissions for biomass plants is similar to that available for coal and oil plants. Unlike coal and oil plants, CO_2 emitted from biomass is removed from the atmosphere in almost equal quantities if biomass is continually regenerated in new growth.[7] Also, some agricultural wastes used in biomass plants, would, if not combusted, generate methane emissions during decomposition. Methane is a more potent greenhouse gas than CO_2. In addition, some renewables, such as distributed (on site) photovoltaics, avoid large transmission line energy losses that normally occur for conventional generating technology. The Electric Power Research Institute reports line loss amounts of up to 12.9% for peak, 12% for intermediate, and 6.1% for base loads.[8] These positive externalities should be valued and applied as offsets of the negative externalities of renewables. No studies valuing these positive externalities were found. This is a task that researchers should address in the future.

2. Environmental Impacts and Costs of Hydroelectric Technologies (Hydropower)

Hydropower has been, and remains, a crucial element in U.S. energy supply. It reached a peak of 40% of electrical supply in the 1930's. As a major electricity resource, hydropower supplied about 14% of the nations electricity in 1983 (not counting substantial Canadian hydroelectric imports).[9] Currently 9.5% of total utility electric generation comes from hydropower. The principle environmental advantage is the virtual absence of air pollution impacts and greenhouse gas effects. But, hydroelectric power developments necessarily result in long-term removal, destruction, or alteration of certain environmental resources. Environmental impacts result from: 1) changes in river flow characteristics; 2) changes in the ecosystems of land flooded to form reservoirs; and, 3) erection of barriers which interfere with the natural movements of fish and wildlife.

Commentators have dramatically different interpretations of both the magnitude and costs of these effects. Some believe that hydroelectric power is a comparatively benign alternative source of electrical generation when compared to conventional generating facilities (coal and oil), particularly if hydro's impacts are lessened by

---

[6] See supra Chapter VI.

[7] Brower, M., Coal Energy, the Renewable Solution to Global Warming, Union of Concerned Scientist, Cambridge MA, 1990, p. 64.

[8] EPRI, Strategic Assessment of Storage Plants, Economic Studies, EPRI GS-6646, January, 1990.

[9] Annual Renewable Technology Review, Renewable Energy Institute, Washington DC, 1986, p. 8. (The figures are for 1984.) 1983 appears to have been a peak year, with slight reduction since then.

careful planning, site selection and remedial and mitigation efforts.[10] Other commentators, however, have concluded that new large dams may be "... arguably the worst electricity option in terms of damage to ecosystems per unit of electricity."[11]

Two factors which merit consideration in a determination of the environmental externalities of any hydro facility are: 1) how the environmental costs should be allocated in relationship to the multiple social purposes which the facility may serve, and 2) whether the environmental impacts of the facility are offset by beneficial social uses. While hydro projects are generally created and installed for the purpose of meeting a particular area's energy requirements, they often have other, social functions. Additional social benefits that may be provided by these projects are irrigation, flow regulation (flood control), and recreation.[12] Environmental impacts of a hydro facility may be the same regardless of the uses to which the facility is put.[13] Because of this multi-use capacity, environmental impact costs of hydropower projects may be allocated either strictly to the production of power or distributed among the other social uses of the facility. (See discussion of allocation of costs to joint projects, Chapter III). And, in determining the allocation of a project's environmental costs, a major consideration is the issue of whether the beneficial social effects of the project offset the project's environmental externalities.

In assessing hydropower's environmental externalities, this study assumes that electrical generation is the primary social purpose for a hydro development unless otherwise noted. This assumption is based on a New York State Department of Environmental Conservation Staff Report on Hydro Relicensing. The Staff Report concluded that the resulting "reservoir fluctuations, interruptions to downstream flows and total diversions of the flows of most major river systems in New York occurred for the sole purpose of accomodating peak demand and network balancing requirements of power generation."[14]

---

[10] Cf Rader, N., Power Surge: The Status and Near Term Potential of Renewable Energy Technologies, rev., at p. II-29, Washington, DC: Public Citizen, May, 1989 [hereafter cited as Rader, Power Surge].

[11] OECD COMPASS Project, Environmental Impacts of Renewable Energy, at pp. 74, 81, Paris: Organization for Economic Co-operation and Development, 1988 [hereafter cited as OECD COMPASS Project].

[12] For a very recent report on the existence value for sportfishing in relation to hydroelectric plant mitigation and enhancement measures see, Summary Report: Existence and Sport Values for Doubling the Size of the Columbia River Basin Salmon and Steelhead Runs, Prepared for North Pacific Division, U.S. Army Corps of Engineers, Portland, OR, January, 1990.

[13] Id.

[14] NYS Department of Environmental Conservation (DEC), Issue 2: Hydro Relicensing Staff Report at p. 4, assisted by NYS Energy Office (SEO) and NYS Department of Public Service (DPS), [hereafter cited as DEC, Hydro Relicensing], in Draft New York State Energy Plan, Volume 6, prepared jointly by New York SEO, DPS, and DEC, May, 1989.

This section on hydropower will address both changes associated with the operation of new or expanded large hydropower facilities and, separately, the impacts associated with small hydropower facilites. (For a definition of the term small-head hydro see infra, Section C of this chapter.) This section will not address environmental effects directly associated with new project construction or with project expansion (including dust emissions, road traffic, and production of component materials), or the front-end components involved in the production, acquisition, or use of fuel for construction purposes.

This section also provides a qualitative overview of the environmental impacts associated with hydroelectric development and then reviews two studies prepared for the Bonneville Power Administration (BPA) which address valuation methodologies for environmental impacts of hydroelectric facilities. Because the environmental impacts of hydroelectric facilities are extremely site-specific, this section does not relate externality valuations.[15]

a. Overview of Environmental Impacts of Hydropower

Hydropower developments most frequently involve construction of a dam on a free-flowing stream or river, which will inevitably change aquatic and terresterial ecosystems. As one commentator notes, "The real question is not whether such developments will affect the environment, but rather how much is acceptable to society as a whole, and what countermeasures should be taken to keep adverse changes to a minimum, at a reasonable economic cost, within that acceptable range."[16]

The environmental impacts of hydroelectric facilities depend largely on project specific factors related to the engineering, design and operation of the facility and the ecological characteristics of the site. Environmental impacts of hydropower facukutues are almost exclusively related to land, water, wildlife, fish and flora. A benefit of hydropower facilities is that they do not produce air or solid waste pollution apart from that created during material preparation and facility construction.

Mitigation of some adverse environmental impacts of hydroelectric facilities can occur through use of fishladders and intake screening, stocking of fish in reservoirs, and creation of land conservation trusts to preserve ecosystems that might otherwise be lost after hydro project development. To the extent that mitigation costs are included in the cost of the facility, some environmental externalities may already be internalized. With these qualifications in mind, the following paragraphs describe the general types of environmental damages associated with hydropower.

---

[15] Although attempts were made to gather data on characteristics of small hydro facilities, time limitations prevented development of any useful values. This is an area where further research is needed.

[16] OECD COMPASS Project, supra note 11 at p. 75.

i. Land

When land behind a dam is inundated, sediments that were previously carried downstream may become trapped behind the dam. Sedimentation in the reservoir contributes to possible eutrophication and stagnation of impounded waters, a problem which also occurs in natural lakes.[17] Sediment-free water flowing downstream at higher than normal velocities may cause erosion of river beds and banks as well as of distant coastal lands such as deltas, estuaries and seashores. Downstream river bed erosion can sometimes be controlled by regulating the speed of water leaving the dam site. Additionally, in certain areas, the resulting reduction of natural flooding of downstream lands may decrease agricultural productivity because flooding helps to reduce salt content of soil and provides soil nutrients from periodic sediment deposits.[18] Lack of sediments may also contribute to significant reductions of plankton and organic carbon in downstream river and marine areas, reducing aquatic populations and affecting commercial and recreational fishing.[19]

ii. Water Quality

Thermal stratification is a problem, particularly in large reservoirs. Thermal stratification occurs when a temperature gradient forms and cold dense lower water resists mixing with warm, less dense water above it. Anoxic conditions develop in the lower waters when organic matter in the stagnant bottom water decomposes and reduces the water's dissolved oxygen content. As anaerobic activities begin to dominate the reservoir, concentrations of ammonia, hydrogen, sulfide, methane, iron, and manganese increase.[20] The resulting increase in production of gases such as methane, ammonia, and hydrogen sulfide are toxic to aquatic life and affect water quality. Poor quality water released from the reservoir must travel many miles downstream before reoxgenation restores water quality to normal levels.[21] However, development and use of new technology such as aspirating turbines may help mitigate or eliminate thermal stratification and deoxygenation problems in released water.[22] Also, the local

---

[17] Medsker, L., Side Effects of Renewable Energy Sources, EPRD Report #15, rev. ed., at p. 32 National Audubon Society, December, 1982, [hereafter cited as Medsker] .

[18] OECD COMPASS Project, supra note 11 at p. 77; Medsker, supra note 17 at p. 32 (undercutting of downstream river bed could also lower the water table).

[19] OECD COMPASS Project, supra note 11 at p. 77.

[20] Id.; U.S. DOE, Energy Technology Characterizations Handbook. U.S. Department of Energy, DOE/EP-0093, March, 1983, p. 197 [hereafter cited as DOE Characterizations Handbook].

[21] OECD COMPASS Project, supra note 11 at p. 77 (noting that this problem can be observed in Tennessee Valley Authority reservoirs).

[22] PRE Study, supra note 1, at p. A-10.

environment may be severely impacted if discharged water is a different temperature than ambient river water. Often it is warmer in the winter and cooler in the summer.[23]

iii. Impacts on Wildlife, Fish, Plantlife and Their Habitats

A wide range of impacts on the biological community are a direct result of hydro facilities and not all of these impacts are well understood. Flooding of land behind a dam may result in animal casualties and habitat destruction and the reservoir may disrupt some seasonal animal migrations. Some waterfowl habitat may be created by the reservoir but it may not be of the same quality as the compromised marshlands or stream-side nesting, brooding, and feeding grounds.[24]

Fish are significantly impacted due to changes in stream flow and formation of reservoirs. Migrating fish, such as salmon that spawn in fresh water, may be severely impacted. Impacts on migrating fish can be mitigated by provision of fish ladders, screens, managed flow and other special equipment, but these measures do not completely eliminate losses during fish migration. Resident fish in a large reservoir may initially experience population increases. Eventually eutrophication and other changes in the reservoir may result in diminished populations and fewer species of fish in the reservoir. Significant fish mortalities may also result from spill death or operation of generation turbines or pumps.[25]

Because of pervasive and long-term ecological changes resulting from hydroelectric facilities, particular care must be taken to avoid eliminating endangered or threatened species or compromising their habitat. Changes in stream flow can reduce or change critical habitat with the degradation occurring over an extended period of time. For instance, the banks of the Platte River in central Nebraska provide habitat to a number of endangered or threatened species including the whooping crane, interior least tern, the bald eagle, and the piping plover. These and other species are directly or indirectly influenced by the instream flows from projects operating upstream of the habitat.[26]

Hydropower facilities may also have direct impacts on human populations with perhaps the most serious of these impacts being the risk of catastrophic dam failure

---

[23] DOE Characterizations Handbook, supra note 20 at p. 197.

[24] Meyer, P., et al., Calculation of Environmental Costs and Benefits Associated With Hydropower Development in the Pacific Northwest, prepared for Bonneville Power Administration, April, 1986, at pp. 7-8 [hereafter cited as Generic Hydro Study].

[25] See generally, OECD COMPASS Project, supra note 11 at p. 78; see also Generic Hydro Study, supra note 24 at pp. 112-127.

[26] See Platte River Whooping Crane Critical Habitat Maintenance Trust v. Federal Energy Regulatory Commission, 876 F. 2d 109 (D.C. Cir. 1989).

and disastrous flooding.[27] As one study notes: "Hydroelectric energy is the only renewable source that presents hazards on this scale."[28] However, nearly all hydroelectric dams fall under the jurisdiction of FERC (the Federal Energy Regulatory Commission) and its construction, licensing, relicensing and operating regulations and guidelines. Thus, nearly all costs of dam safety compliance for hydro facilities tends to be internalized. Proper engineering and allowance for the seismic character of a site as well as repairs, monitoring, and preventative maintenance can help to reduce or eliminate dam failure dangers.[29]

Hydropower developments may also affect recreational and commercial opportunities. Alteration of free-flowing waters could reduce or eliminate white water recreational opportunities such as kayaking, rafting and canoeing, and recreational fishing opportunities. Other recreational activities which could be negatively affected include game and water fowl hunting opportunities and recreation associated with pristine or original habitat such as wilderness hiking and camping, and scenic viewing. Commercial fishing may be similarly affected. Additionally, economic income derived from businesses associated with the above recreational activities would be reduced or eliminated.[30]

Other potential adverse effects include flooding of religious, archeological or historically significant areas. An example would be lands having cultural or religious significance to Native American tribes.

Long-term sustainable environmental mitigation can only be achieved if ecological and environmental principles are considered over the lifetime of the facility.[31] Current federal relicensing requirements may help establish and protect aquatic resource, ecological, economic, and recreational values for existing facilities, including small hydro facilities.[32]

---

[27] Construction of large hydropower facilities may also displace significant numbers of local residents with a variety of related social effects. See OECD COMPASS Project, supra note 11 at pp. 79, 80, Table 2.21 (TVA relocated approximately 60,000 people in construction of its 20 dams); citing examples of relocations in other nations ranging from 3,000 for a facility in Mexico to 480,000 for proposed construction in Thailand and Laos.

[28] Id. at 80.

[29] See id.; OECD COMPASS Project, supra note 11 at p. 81.

[30] Andrews, S. and C. Dolcine, A Practitioners Guide to River Valuation Literature, College of the Atlantic, Bar Harbor, Maine, 1990. The guide includes a bibliography of 117 studies on valuation of river ecosystems and recreational uses. It contains a table which annotated the studies into a quick-reference guide to the type of valuation included in each study. Also included is a table which summarizes the dollar figures assigned by the various authors to the river systems under study.

[31] Id.

[32] Electric Consumer Protection Act of 1986, Pub. L. No. 99-495, 100 Stat. 1243, (1986) (Codified at 16 U.S.C. §§ 791a - 825 (1989); 18 C.F.R. §§ 16.1 - 16.16 (1989); J. Boxall, "FERC Hydro Policy: A Relicensing Rule and a Forthcoming NOPR," Pub. Util. Fort., July 20, 1989, at pp. 39-41. There is legislation pending in Congress, however, that would exempt from relicensing and thus, from

b. Hydroelectric Environmental Costs in BPA Studies

The Bonneville Power Authority (BPA) has issued two reports which address methods for valuation of environmental costs and benefits associated with hydroelectric facilities.[33] The Sultan River Case Study tests valuation techniques against a particular project. The second study, sometimes referred to as the Generic Hydro Study, makes a preliminary effort to develop economic values for environmental resources in the BPA service area and describes a model which could relate those values to potential acquisition of hydroelectric resources in the Pacific Northwest.

The BPA studies do not include a generally applicable environmental externality cost associated with hydroelectric facilities. However, they do provide a useful framework for developing regional or site-specific externality costs for hydropower.

i. The Sultan River Case Study

The Sultan River Case Study develops and tests valuation methods for external environmental costs associated with hydroelectric facilities using the Sultan River Project as an example. The Project seeks to use the water resources of the Sultan River to produce electricity. The Sultan River study notes that because the features and environmental impacts of hydroelectric projects vary with the site, the valuation methods developed in the case study may not be necessary or sufficient for all hydropower evaluations. Finally, the study cautions that its results are not a definitive estimate of the environmental costs of the Sultan River Project. Researchers concentrated their efforts on "areas considered significant." Areas for which only minimal impacts were documented or for which impacts were undocumentable were not given further consideration. For example, the study notes that because full mitigation for fisheries had already been agreed upon, researchers did not pursue methodological development in that area.[34]

The study analyzes Stage II of the Sultan River Project. Stage II proposed raising an existing 200 foot high earthfill structure another 62 feet, which would flood an additional 1,054 acres.[35] The river basin is densely forested with western hemlock, western red cedar, Douglas fir, other conifers, and various hardwoods. The basin provides a variety of habitats for wildlife and spawning and rearing grounds for many

---

environmental review, pre-1935 unimproved hydro projects on non-navigable rivers. H.R. 1069, S.635, 101st Congress, 1989.

[33] See generally, Sultan River Case Study, supra note 4; Generic Hydro Study, supra note 24.

[34] Sultan River Case Study, supra note 4 at p. 1-1.

[35] Id. at p. 1-5.

species of anadromous fish. The proposed hydropower facility was estimated to have an installed capacity of 112 MW and an annual baseload production of 436,400mWh.[36]

The report identifies eight impacts associated with the dam expansion as significant for purposes of quantifying environmental costs. These impacts are:

(1) Loss of 94 acres of old-growth forest supporting at least 25 species dependent on old-growth habitat;

(2) Reduction of black-tailed deer habitat of 991 acres, resulting in loss of up to 840 annual hunter-days from the area;

(3) Loss of 10 miles of white water rapids resulting in the loss of a Class V kayaking resource;

(4) Decline of approximately 18% in habitat productivity, expected to similarly affect the quality of general recreational experiences;

(5) Potential impact on limited trapping of fur bearers;

(6) Loss of 1,129acres of commercial timber land, and clearing and replanting of an additional 70 acres;

(7) Construction and operation impacts on human health, including injuries and statistical fatalities; and,

(8) A decline in visual quality resulting primarily from construction of the power house in Sultan Gorge.[37]

The study notes the potential for double-counting certain effects. Therefore, the study quantifies the values of old-growth habitat, black-tailed deer hunting, and kayaking separately and then subtracts those values from the value for total recreational use.[38] The measure of general decline in ecological productivity is then applied to determine remaining recreational impact values.[39]

The summary economic analysis does not include visual quality declines. Researchers conclude that although construction of a powerhouse within the deep river gorge would reduce the visual classification of a short section of the river from

---

36 Id. at p. 4-1.

37 Id. at p. 4-1.

38 Recreational fishing was also quantified independently but the impact was found to be approximately zero. Id.

39 Id.

"distinctive"to "minimal,"economic analysis of the impact was beyond the informational capabilities of the study.[40]

The study concludes that health effect and productivity costs associated with injury or death during the construction or operation of the project were already included in the cost of the project in worker wage rates and contractor bids. Therefore, the study does not consider occupational health effects as external or residual costs.[41]

Table 5 summarizes the impact valuations in 1989 dollars at a 3% discount rate.[42] Values under impact headings represent the alternative valuation approaches for the same impact and are not additive. In other words, under "General Recreation" either the value for "Demand" or the value for "Compensatory" is used in achieving the total figure, not both.

---

[40] Id. at pp. 3-26 to 3-27. Figure 3-5 on page 3-27 of the study and accompanying text describe a possible method for estimating and valuing change in recreational quality and associated lost recreation days.

[41] Id. at pp. 3-28 to 3-29.

[42] Values given in 1982 dollars were converted to 1989 dollars using a factor of 1.257.

TABLE 5

SULTAN STAGE II HYDROPOWER FACILITY ENVIRONMENTAL COST ESTIMATES[43]

Impact	Levelized Cost (mils/kWh)
(1) Old-Growth Forest	0.48
(2) Black-tailed Deer	
Willingness to Pay	0.23
Hedonic	0.39
Compensatory	0.57
(3) Kayaking	
Inferential Compensatory	0.14
(4) Whitewater	
Direct Existence Value	8.46
(5) General Recreation	
Demand	1.24
Compensatory	2.29
(6) Fur bearers	
Full loss case	0.04
No loss case	0
(7) Commercial Timber	
Mixed Stands (No Thinning)	0.33
Conifer Stands (Thinning)	0.34
TOTAL	10.87 to 12.31 (.11-.12 cents/kwh)

A critique prepared for BPA concluded that the methodologies used in the Sultan River Case Study resulted in significant overstatements of the values associated with each resource in comparison to the results achieved by other studies. Furthermore, the reviewers criticize the Sultan River study for not fully documenting the uncertainty accompanying the value estimates.[44] The critique identifies five examples of overstated valuations: Thirty black-tailed deer are valued at $6,285 each; class V kayaking is valued at $1,886 per day; white water habitat is valued at $251,400 per mile per year; Recreation days lost during construction are valued at $1,257 per day; and commercial

[43] Derived from Sultan River Case Study, supra note 4 at x, Summary Table.

[44] BPA, Review of Uncertainty and Risk in BPA-Sponsored Analyses of Energy Resources: Final Report, prepared by Decision Research, at p. 13, November 18, 1987.

timberland is valued at $32,682 per acre.[45] Although the critique indicates that these values are high in comparison to other studies, reviewers do not give any examples of values from other studies which were found to be more reasonable.

The critique identifies three principal concerns with the methodology used in the Sultan River Case Study for valuing environmental costs. First, the reported results are based heavily on responses to willingness-to-be-compensated questions. The critique alleges that "[t]here is little justification for using methods which are known to be seriously biased."[46] Second, the critique says that the Sultan River contingent valuation questions "tend to be misleading" and may have biased the answers by providing information from which inappropriate inferences could be drawn.[47] Third, the valuation survey requested respondents to provide a "fair value" for loss of old-growth. The critique concludes that this question "confounds equity and efficiency considerations as well as individual and altruistic motivations" and was not clearly designed to elicit cost per household per year.[48]

ii. Study of Environmental Costs and Benefits of Pacific Northwest Hydropower Development (Generic Hydro Study)

The original purpose of the second hydropower study prepared for the BPA was to develop economic values associated with environmental resources in the BPA service region (Washington, Oregon, Idaho, and western Montana) and to relate those values to acquisition of hydropower resources in the Pacific Northwest. The study was not intended to replace the requisite site-specific analysis of particular projects. The Generic Hydro Study first presents values for five significant environmental resource-based activities and then presents a procedural framework which can predict changes in the resource base and the associated economic values should one of the general types of hydroelectric projects be acquired.[49]

The Generic Hydro Study develops a framework for valuing "significant regional environmental products" which are characterized as "a natural resource or resource-

---

[45] Id. at p. 13. Values are assumed to be in 1982 dollars as in the Sultan River Case study and were converted using a factor of 1.257.

[46] Id. at pp. 11-12. For instance, the cost of commercial timber is generally recognized as being internalized in the purchase price or value of an acre of land purchased for the site, particularily since it is likely that timber removed from the site would be marketed. However, if the land is publicly owned land then it is conceivable that there is an externality cost associated with the shift of the land from one use to another, less valuable use. If this is what the Sultan River Study authors had in mind, the study seems to reflect an overstatement by including the commercial timber costs.

[47] Id. at p. 12.

[48] Id. at pp. 12-13.

[49] Generic Hydro Study, supra note 24 at p. ii.

based activity that is of value to Pacific Northwest residents."[50] Researchers selected five significant regional environmental resource-based activities for analysis: commercial and sport fishing for salmon and steelhead; sport fishing for resident fish; hunting for deer and elk; general recreational and aesthetic outdoors enjoyment based on riparian habitat; and recreational and aesthetic enjoyment associated with free-flowing rivers.

Four factors were used to determine regional significance. First, hydroelectric generation must significantly affect the value of environmental products. Second, the products must be found throughout the BPA service area and products of local importance would need to be assessed for specific projects. Third, the products must be important to the region's residents. Fourth, the environmental products selected should be relatively distinct.[51]

The study notes that some environmental products that may have significant value are omitted because of insufficient data, contract limitations, or non-regional site-specific considerations. For instance, hydropower development can affect waterfowl habitat. The study notes that hydro facility reservoirs may provide nesting, feeding, and resting habitat for water fowl but fluctuating water levels associated with hydroelectric facilities could seriously affect nesting, brooding, and feed areas. Also, existing habitat located along marshy shores might be compromised or lost through inundation. The BPA researchers were unable to find sufficient data to extrapolate waterfowl harvest and survivorship functions. Researchers also concluded that the normal baseline population of waterfowl and the net change resulting from hydroelectric development were not clear. Thus the study concludes that no adequate data source exists that would allow quantification of these positive and negative impacts.[52]

Table 6 below summarizes some of the average unit values developed in the Generic Hydro Study for significant regional environmental products.

---

[50] Id. at p. 3.

[51] Id. at pp. ii-iii, 3.

[52] Id. at pp. 7-8. Other environmental products not included in the Generic Hydro Study are flat water recreation other than sport fishing (not likely to be significant for new hydro developments); Native American cultural values (beyond the scope of contract); and threats to endangered species (too site-specific). Id. at pp. 8-9.

TABLE 6

GENERIC HYDRO STUDY SIGNIFICANT REGIONAL ENVIRONMENTAL PRODUCTS[53]

PRODUCT	UNIT VALUED	VALUE PER UNIT (1989 $)
Commercial chinook Salmon	one ex-vessel pound	2.75
Sport-caught Salmon and Steelhead	one fisherman day	139.99
Sport-caught resident fish	one fisherman day	43.23
Hunted deer or elk	one hunter day	63.33
Riparian habitat	one acre	4,002.00
Free-flowing river	one mile	249,504.00

The study also gives total annual values of significant regional products for the Pacific Northwest and for states within the BPA service territory, and for ecological zones and physiographic subregions.[54]

The Generic Hydro Study identifies the effect of changes in resource abundance on average non-market values developed for regionally significant environmental resources.[55] For this purpose, the researchers rely on a study estimating the marginal value changes for salmon in the Fraser River in British Columbia as a proxy for resources presumed to be in relatively healthy condition.[56] To develop marginal cost equations for resources already at a much lower level of baseline abundance, the Generic Hydro Study uses the results of values developed for old growth Douglas fir forest in Western Washington.[57] Table 7 below illustrates the effect of abundance adjustments.

---

[53] Derived from Generic Hydro Study, supra note 24 at p. iv, Executive Table 1.

[54] Id. at pp. 72-79.

[55] See id. at pp. 80-86.

[56] Id. at pp. 80-81.

[57] Id. at p. 81.

TABLE 7

EFFECT OF ABUNDANCE ON SIGNIFICANT REGIONAL ENVIRONMENTAL PRODUCTS[58]

Ratio of Present Abundance	Free Flowing Rivers ($/mile)	Salmon/Steelhead	Resident Fish	Hunting	Riparian Habitat
		($ per recreation day)			($/acre)
Present level (1.00)	249,504	139.98	43.23	63.32	4,005
5% decrease (0.95)	314,640	176.56	43.45	63.63	5,051
50% decrease (0.50)	1,131,048	634.44	66.68	97.72	18,153
5% increase (1.05)	249,504	139.98	43.01	63.00	4,005
50% increase (1.50)	249,504	139.98	40.83	59.82	4,005

At levels present when the Generic Hydro Study was done, salmon and steelhead, riparian habitat, and free flowing rivers were considered as already significantly below normal baseline levels of abundance.[59] The Generic Hydro Study found no basis for making similar adjustments based on changes in levels of abundance for marketed values of Pacific Northwest Salmon, one of the significant regional environmental resources.[60]

The Generic Hydro Study proposes a conceptual impact model which could be developed to estimate the major changes in a particular region's biological products as a result of environmental effects associated with six types of hydropower projects. The report, however, does not fully quanitify regional impacts for each hydropower project type. Researchers note that "the magnitude of specific impacts can vary depending on applied circumstances and that little or no reliable data is available on which to specify the likely range of magnitude for several impacts thought to be important."[61]

---

[58] Based on id. at p. vi, Executive Table 3. Values are assumed to be in 1986 dollars (the date of the study) and were converted to 1989 dollars using a factor of 1.104.

[59] See id. at p. 82 (explaining weighting and equation application for relative levels of abundance).

[60] Id. at p. 83.

[61] Id. at p. 15.

The study also notes that several reviewers of the draft study expressed strong reservations concerning any usefulness of generic estimates.[62] Consequently, the study concludes that "there is presently an insufficient statistical basis for development of reliable impact strategies estimates across the full range of hydroelectric acquisition types identified."[63]

The study identifies adverse environmental effects associated with new construction of six types of hydro projects: run-of-river reservoir projects; diversion or run-of-river with diversion projects; storage reservoir projects; storage reservoir with diversion projects; canal or conduit projects; and off-stream or pumped storage projects. The three significant hydrologic effects associated with these power project arrangements are impoundment of water behind dams, passage of water through turbines, and diversion of water offstream.[64]

The model employed by the study first considers unmitigated impacts and then introduces mitigation through a percent reduction in expected impact magnitude. In addition, a weighting factor (from 0 to 1) is assigned representing the proportion of the nonseparable impacts and costs allocated to hydropower as opposed to other benefits associated with a multipurpose facility. For instance, turbine mortality of fish is associated exclusively with hydropower. Examples of nonseparable costs are those costs associated with passage blockage from the dam, inundation spill deaths, and downstream gravel blockage.

The Generic Hydro Study compiles a list of potential ecological effects associated with hydropower projects. The list is not comprehensive because it omits short-term construction effects such as sedimentation. Researchers support these omissions on the basis that species and sub-ecosystems are expected to recover from these short-term effects over a relatively short period of time and current construction practices usually minimize or mitigate these short term effects. The study also omits secondary impacts such as construction of power transmission and service roads and impacts stemming from increased human access to the stream.

The list of potential effects considers long-term operational effects of hydropower development which may account for 70% to 80% of all losses associated with hydropower projects. These are losses for which the Army Corps of Engineers Hydropower Data Base Analysis System could be used to estimate the magnitude of impact.[65] The twelve impacts identified in the list are passage blockage (anadromous fish), inundation, reduced flows, change in a flow regime, reduced current, turbine passage kills, spill death, gas supersaturation (which can cause bubble disease in fish),

---

[62] Id.

[63] Id.

[64] Id. at pp. 101-105.

[65] Id. at pp. 101, 108.

change in water temperature, scour and erosion, gravel loss, and pump mortality.[66] Pump mortality refers to fish kills due to pressure and mechanical stress in the pumped storage facilities.

It is beyond the scope of this section to describe the Generic Hydro model in detail. In great simplicity, the model consists of a local abundance submodel and project impact functions. The local abundance submodel uses data on regional characteristics, project description data, and regional product data to develop an estimate of pre-project abundance. Project description data and regional products data result in impact estimates or post-project abundance. From the results of these two routines, project related loss in regional products and economic valuation can be developed.[67]

The model applies to biological products only. The regional product of free-flowing waters is not considered in this model because this resource is not biological, but rather is related to the physical and aesthetic integrity of natural rivers. Authors of the Generic Hydro Study claim that use of a biologically-based model alone to predict changes in such a resource would yield misleading results.

iii. Summary of BPA Conclusions

BPA concludes that the following values are representative of the hydropower impacted resources in the Pacific Northwest:[68]

TABLE 8

BPA VALUES FOR HYDRO IMPACTED RESOURCES

Resources		$/Unit
Resident Fish (Trout)	$	14/fish
Salmon and Steelhead	$	300/fish
Riparian Habitat	$	4,000/acre
Free Flowing Streams	$	260,000/mile

BPA attaches a high degree of confidence to these values, but concludes that "more work needs to be done in the biological field to enable reasonable and credible

[66] Id. at p. 113.

[67] Id. at pp. 98-99.

[68] Issue No. 5 in letter from Shepard C. Buchanan, Economist, BPA to Michael Nicklas, Chairman, American Solar Energy Society, dated January 20, 1989, reproduced in 1989 ASES Roundtable on Societal Costs of Energy, Proceedings of conference held in Arlington, VA, March 3, 1989, compiled by Michael Nicklas. Values are assumed to be in 1989 dollars.

predictions of the effects of new hydro facilities on fish and wildlife resources."[69] Although rough estimates can be developed for hydro facilities using the representative BPA values, environmental costs for hydroelectric facilities are best developed with site specific factors or, at least, regionally developed values. These values can serve both to ensure appropriate energy supply decisions and to ensure that mitigation efforts are undertaken.

c. Overview of Environmental Impacts of Small-Scale Hydropower

Small hydro is a term used to differentiate large scale hydropower projects from smaller scale projects. The term may refer to the height of the water level behind the dam, the height of the dam itself, or to the amount of electricity the facility will produce.

Under PURPA a small hydropower project is any project with less than 80 MW capacity.[70] As with large hydro, the presumed primary purpose of a small hydropower facility is to produce "cost-effective electric power" even though other useful social functions may be served by the facility.[71]

All new hydropower facilities work basically the same way, harnessing water power of a river system for production of electricity. Small hydropower facilities provide socioeconomic benefits and environmental impacts which may differ somewhat from those provided by large hydropower projects.

The types of enviornmental impacts of new small hydropower projects may include: inudation and loss of land, wildlife, plant life and habitats, lowered water quality, visual, aesthetic, and recreation impacts, barriers to anadromous fish migration and resultant fishery depletion, and other associated problems.[72] Although small and large hydropower projects are similar in their environmental impacts, it is possible that the impacts of small hydro may be either smaller or larger than for large hydro. Large hydro usually entails greater amounts of land inudation, but new small hydro facilites may cause effects which may be more severe in cases where many small hyropower projects are stacked along a river or its tributaries. Examples of such stacking can be seen in the Snake River Basin in Idaho where an approximately 140 mile stretch of the Snake River has eight existing hydropower projects and with two more proposed

---

[69] Id.

[70] Public Utilities Regulatory Policies Act of 1978, PL 95-617, 16 U.S.C. § 2601 et. seq. at § 2701-2705 [§ 401-405 of Act].

[71] D. Olsen, Hydroelectric Power Development on the Hamma Hamma River System: Economic & Institutional Factors Affecting the Indian, Commerical and Sport Fisheries, FERC No. 3178, Washington DC, February, 1987, p. 11 [hereafter cited as Hamma Hamma River Study].

[72] See generally, Draft Environmental Impact Statement: Milner, Twin Falls, Auger Falls, and Star Falls Hydroelectric Projects, Idaho, Office of Hydropower Licensing, FERC, No. EIS-0048S, December, 1989, pp. 5-1 to 5-20.

projects in the licensing stage.[73] Another example is the Columbia River Power System which has twenty-eight dams located on the Columbia River and its tributaries for the purpose of producing power for a four state region in the Pacific Northwest.[74]

None of the small hydropower project studies cited here attempted to quantify environmental costs for any project other than those costs imposed on the Pacific Northwest salmon and steelhead fisheries.[75] The Hamma Hamma River Study made an attempt to determine a baseline value for the Hamma Hamma River fishery and then attempted to project the "precise impact to the Hamma Hamma River system fishery resulting from the construction of the proposed projects".[76] Although the study found that the precise impact could not be determined, it did define a possible range of impacts and assigned impact costs based on that range. For example, the study estimated the economic impact of the proposed projects for a single year impact based on an average annual catch with a worst-case scenario and found that the total fishery value foregone because of project operation amounted to about 4% of the value of the combined U.S. and Canada commercial catch.[77] Although this initial research provides some information on the environmental costs of low-head hydropower, much more research is required to obtain a more complete picture of the total environmental costs of small-head hydro.

3. Environmental Impacts and Costs of Direct Solar Energy Technologies

Direct solar technology includes solar photovoltaic and solar-thermal (central station or dispersed) technologies. Direct solar energy technologies are environmentally benign in their operational phase, especially when compared to fuel burning technologies. However, direct solar energy production, like all types of energy production, does have some environmental impacts. Its most significant environmental impacts are those ocurring during fabrication of materials and construction. (Construction costs are excluded from this report.) In the operation phase of central solar facilities, the most significant impact is the facilities land requirements. Once on-line, the impacts resulting from operation of a solar plant, both in absolute terms and in terms of emissions as a function of power output, are negligible. Quantified environment externalities or environmental impact costs identified in this section range

---

[73] Id. at p. 2-5.

[74] Scott, "Columbia River Salmon: Benefit-Cost Analysis and Mitigation," 3(2) Northwest Enviornmental Journal, 121, 1989.

[75] Hamma Hamma River study, supra note 72.

[76] Id. at p. 6.

[77] Id., derived from Table 13.

approximately from 0 to 0.4 cents/kWh.[78] However, the values in the literature are largely based on estimates of front-end costs (e.g. manufacturing of photovoltaic cells), and thus are not comparable to externality values for the other generating resources identified in this report.

Although direct solar technologies take several forms, the primary focus of this section is on photovoltaic (PV) and solar thermal central station power electricity generation. These technologies can be used for utility electric generation or in dispersed/non-utility electric generation applications (such as off-grid photovoltaic roof-top installations and parabolic dish solar thermal electric generation). This section also discusses two other non-electricity solar technologies, passive solar architecture and dispersed solar thermal collectors for supplying heat or hot water to buildings. These can be used to displace electric space and water heating demands.

This section first provides a brief overview of the literature available on the costs associated with the environmental impacts of direct solar technologies. Then by technology type, this section discusses land use requirements and the potential degradation of land and habitat resulting from direct solar installations. Land use requirements and their results bridge front-end costs and operational costs and are dealt with in this report.[79] This section also catalogs the impacts on air, water, and solid waste resulting from operation and decommissioning of direct solar technologies and notes the type and magnitude of these impacts when possible.[80] Occupational and public health effects associated with operation and maintenance of solar energy facilities are also indicated. Although much of the discussion is qualitative, this section should serve as a basis for comparing the environmental impacts of solar energy technologies with the impacts of the other technologies described in this report and with conventional generation technologies.

a. Overview of Direct Solar Environmental Cost Literature

Only a few studies have attempted to quantify the costs of environmental impacts associated with direct solar technologies.[81] For the most part, the literature on solar

---

[78] For an overview of the costing literature from which these figures were derived, see subsection III. A. infra.

[79] Chapter V.F. deals with land and water values for other than direct solar technologies.

[80] Because each solar facility is somewhat unique both in facility design and site, their reported values are difficult to generalize. To the extent sources quantify impacts for generic facilities, values are provided in the text.

[81] Dina Berger, a research assistant working on the report, confirmed this impression in telephone interviews with researchers in the renewable energy field. In a personal communication with Ms. Berger on August 4, 1989, Paul D. Moskowitz of the BioMedical Assessment Laboratory of the Brookhaven National Laboratory, Upton, New York, stated that "the numbers have not been compiled" to quantify the environmental impacts of solar energy. (Mr. Moskowitz has worked in the solar energy area for 15 years.) Stephen A. Rubin of the Solar Energy Research Institute (SERI), Golden, Colorado, and Edgar DeMeo of Electric Power Research Institute (EPRI), Palo Alto, California, confirmed Moskowitz's observation during personal communications with Ms. Berger on August 12, 1989.

power emissions tends to focus on environmental effects rather than on the cost of those effects.[82]

Three studies make some rough evaluations of the environmental impact costs associated with solar technologies.[83] External environmental and health costs developed in these studies range from 0 to 0.2 cents/Kwh for solar energy. Researchers who estimate a non-zero cost caution that the cost probably overestimates the ultimate environmental impacts of solar energy.[84] Because each of these studies evaluates different solar technologies using different assumptions and incorporating different portions of the fuel cycle, the results must be compared carefully.

i. Costs Developed for PV Technologies

Two studies evaluate the environmental externalities associated with photo-voltaic (PV) solar generators. The first study, prepared for Bonneville Power Administration (BPA) in 1986, found no significant environmental effects for purposes of quantifying the impacts of a generic 100 mW PV facility.[85] Hohmeyer (1988) develops an average value of approxiamtely 0.2 cents/kWh for PV electricity.

Values derived in the Hohmeyer study are based on economic values in the Federal Republic of Germany. For purposes of this average, Hohmeyer assumes that decentralized PV installations and centralized solar facilities each generate half of the total PV electricity production. Hohmeyer's costs for decentralized facilities (0.004 cents/kWh) are based on the lost production value due to accident risk for maintenace personnel at decentralized facilities. Hohmeyer's cost for centralized facilities (0.44

---

[82] The information located in the literature search tends to be very specialized. Studies investigate only certain emissions from a particular technology without relating them to costs or other emissions or other technologies. Cf. P. Moskowitz, L. Hamilton, Photovoltaic Environmental, Health and Safety Project Bibliography, Brookhaven National Laboratory, Upton, NY, June, 1989.

[83] Hohmeyer, O., Social Costs of Energy Consumption: External Effects of Electricity Generation in the Federal Republic of Germany, 1st ed., Springer-Verlag, 1988 [hereafter cited as Hohmeyer, Social Costs]; Bonneville Power Administration (BPA), Estimating Environmental Costs and Benefits for Five Generating Resources, Final Report: Description of Generic Generating Resources, Their Likely Significant Effects, and the Economic Value of Those Effects, prepared by ECO Northwest Ltd. et al., March 1986 [hereafter cited as BPA/ECO, Five Resources]; Shuman, M. and R. Cavanagh, Environmental Costs, Appendix 2 in A Model Electric Power and Conservation Plan for the Pacific Northwest, 1984 [hereafter cited as Shuman & Cavanagh].

[84] Hohmeyer, Social Costs, supra note 83 at p. 56; Shuman & Cavanagh, supra note 83 at p. 51.

[85] BPA/ECO, Five Resources, supra note 83 at p. xiv. The BPA/ECO study also looks briefly at solar-thermal central stations and concludes that visual effects might be economically significant or insignificant depending on location. Id. at pp. 2-26. The qualitative conclusions of the BPA/ECO study are included in the appropriate sections infra detailing environmental impacts.

cents/kWh) is based on the lost opportunity costs of the land occupied by the facility derived from real estate prices.[86]

ii. Costs Developed for Solar Collectors

Shuman and Cavanagh (1984) include flat plate solar collectors as an example of a renewable technology in their comparative study. They quantify material use, air emissions in the aggregate from materials acquisition and routine fuel cycle operations, and occupational effects in the aggregate for materials acquisition, construction of facilities, and routine operation and maintenance of flat plate collectors.[87] Shuman and Cavanagh conclude that the non-radiological health costs of routine nuclear power plant operations are a "reasonably good proxy" for the full cycle health costs associated with wind and solar renewable technologies: "roughly" 0 to 0.14 cents/kWh.[88]

b. Photovoltaic Solar Installations

Photovoltaic cells are thin wafers of semiconductor material that convert sunlight directly into electricity.[89] "When sunlight hits the cell, electrons are freed in the semiconductor material, and an electric current is generated. The electricity is collected and transported by metallic contacts arranged in a grid-like system on the face of the cell. Groups of cells are mounted together on a rigid plate and are electrically interconnected to form photovoltaic modules."[90] When grouped into arrays

---

[86] Hohmeyer, Social Costs, supra note 83 at pp. 55-56. The subsection on PV solar systems discusses Hohmeyer's results in more detail. See infra Section b. Hohmeyer states in 1982 DM = 0.00007 DM/kWh for occupational effects; 0.0088 DM/kWh for land effects; and 0.0044 average. Values were converted to 1982 dollars using the average annual 1982 exchange rate of 2.2631 and then to 1989 dollars using Shepard Buchanan's recommended conversion factor of 1.257.

[87] Shuman & Cavanagh, supra note 83 at pp. 46, 51.

[88] Id. at p. 51 (nuclear health costs are assumed by Shuman and Cavanagh to be comparable to renewables' costs excluding accidents, radon emissions and proliferation). Shuman and Cavanagh's value of 0 to 0.12 cents/kWh was assumed to be in 1984 dollars and converted to 1989 dollars using a factor of 1.167.

[89] For good explanations of photovoltaic technology, see Hersch, P. and K. Zweibel, Basic Photovoltaic Principles and Methods, SERI/ SP-290-1448 (National Technical Information Service (NTIS), 1981; and Flavin, C., Electricity from Sunlight: The Emergence of Photovoltaics, SERI/SP-271-2532 NTIS, 1984.

[90] OECD COMPASS Project, supra note 11 at p. 31.

oriented towards the sun, the typical module can convert about 11% of the incoming sunlight to electricity.[91]

Most commentators identify the front-end fabrication and construction of PV facilities as the most significant environmental impacts.[92] Although the focus of this study is on the environmental impacts associated with operation through decommissioning, this section briefly summarizes the solar fabrication process and its associated environmental hazards. Those impacts would be of relevance to future research in full cycle externalities analysis. This section also includes a review of the environmental impacts associated with PV central stations (with particular emphasis on land impacts), and the possible impacts of decentralized PV installations.

i. Environmental Impacts of PV Fabrication

This section provides a brief overview of the chemicals used in the synthesis and assembly of solar modules and arrays. It discusses the potential risks to workers in fabricating facilities and to the public through routine or accidental releases. Thin film solar cells are manufactured from a variety of materials and fabricated into a variety of designs in a series of discrete production processes.[93] These processes are primarily manual even though a high degree of automation is possible.[94]

Single crystal silicon is the most commonly used PV cell fabrication material.[95] Other materials can be used in PV cell fabrication, such as galluim arsenide and cadmium sulfide. However, unlike these other materials, silicon cell production does not involve the use of arsenide, a dangerous carcinogen. Nor does it create cadmuim and arsenic waste compounds. Thus, production of silicon PV cells incurs comparatively lower health and environmental impacts than does the production of other types of PV cells.[96] If the developing technology of thin film solar cells turns away from silicon based materials, toward arsenide and cadmuim compounds, the

---

[91] Some modules containing lenses that concentrate sunlight onto solar cells can convert about 14% of the incoming sunlight. As a standard, a 10% efficient PV cell about 100 sq. cms. in size can produce one (1) watt of electricity at noon on a clear day. Id.

[92] See e.g., Energy Systems Emissions and Materiel Requirements, U.S. Department of Energy (DOE), prepared by the Meridian Corporation, Alexandria, VA, 1989 [hereafter cited as DOE/Materiel], at pp. 15, 16; OECD COMPASS Project, supra note 11 at pp. 33-35, 38.

[93] Moskowitz, P., An Environmental Source Book on the Photovoltaic Industry, BNL 52052/UC-11 (Brookhaven National Laboratory, Sept., 1986 [hereafter cited as Moskowitz, Source Book].

[94] Rose, E., Environmental Health and Safety Assessment of Photovoltaics, JPL Publication 83-88, Jet Propulsion Laboratory, 1983, (automated processes are not currently cost-effective).

[95] OECD COMPASS Project, supra note 11 at p. 32.

[96] Hohmeyer, Social Costs, supra note 83 at pp. 54-55.

potential risk of occupational and public health hazards will increase because these technologies use much larger quantities of toxic, flammable, or explosive gases than the industry has used previously.[97]

The efficiency of the PV cell fabrication processes for solar cells is very low. Because of this low efficiency, significant quantities of solid wastes are created as residuals.[98]

Occupational health hazards may arise from the large variety of toxic and hazardous gases used in PV fabrication and from their related residuals. Many materials used in PV cell manufacture or produced as residuals are listed in the Toxic Substances Control Act inventory list.[99] Serious health effects from these materials may be manifested either immediately or shortly after an accidental release or acute exposure. The actual health hazards from these substances depend on the inherent toxicologic properties of the materials and the intensity, frequency, and duration of human exposures to the materials. Industry monitoring data at present are insufficient to quantify the probability of an individual worker being exposed to these hazardous agents through routine operation or an accidental event.[100]

Accidental releases of hazardous materials may result from leakage from storage, distribution and process systems or, during abnormal conditions such as a fire or power failure, from releases from process and control equipment.[101] Administrative and engineering controls are necessary to protect workers and the public from explosiveness, corrosiveness or poisoning effects which could result from these releases.[102] In general, safe management of materials is possible if basic industrial safety practices are followed.[103] We reiterate that these are front-end costs and must

---

[97] OECD COMPASS Project, supra note 11 at p. 33.

[98] Moskowitz, Source Book, supra note 93 at pp. 28-40.

[99] Id. at p. 41; 40 C.F.R. § 716.120 (1989). For discussion of hazards associated with some PV industry fabrication processes, see also OECD COMPASS Project, supra note 11 at pp. 33-32.

[100] Id. at 48. Emission control standards developed for related industries, such as the semiconductor industry, may offer guidelines for control requirements in the PV industry. Electrical and Electronic Components - Point Source Category, 40 C.F.R. § 469 (1989).

[101] OECD COMPASS Project, supra note 11 at p. 33.

[102] EPA has not yet established emissions standards for the routine or accidental discharge of atmospheric pollutants from the PV industry. Proposed and enacted National Emission Standards for arsenic and cadmium might assist regulators in establishing PV industry emissions standards. See National Emission Standards for Hazardous Air Pollutants - Proposed Standards for Inorganic Arsenic, 48 Fed. Reg. 33,112-180(1983); Assessment of Cadmium under Section 122 of the Clean Air Act, 50 Fed. Reg. 42,000-04(1985); 40 C.F.R. §§ 61.160- 61.186(1989) (National Emission Standards for inorganic arsenic emissions from glass manufacturing plants and arsenic production facilities).

[103] See OECD COMPASS Project, supra note 11 at p. 38. Ventilation, automation, process changes, material substitutions, isolation of workers in time and space, good housekeeping and maintenance, clear decontamination and emergency procedures are all standard control approaches to reduce health and safety risks. See B. Feiner, Industrial Air Contaminant Control in N. Sax, Dangerous Properties of

be compared with comparable front-end costs of other power technologies (e.g. risks of mining coal or uranium).

ii. Environmental Impacts of PV Central Stations

Apart from fabrication related impacts, land requirements and associated ecological and aesthetic effects are the most important potential environmental impacts associated with PV central stations. Water, air, and noise impacts are minimal or nonexistent during the operation stage of the fuel cycle. Decommissioning impacts depend upon the facility's constituent materials.

The amount of land required for a PV central station depends on the geographical location, the type of facility, and the size of the facility. For example, one source estimates that for a 9.5 mWe PV station, a fixed system would require 40 to 90 acres and a tracking system would require 70 to 370 acres.[104] Another source estimates land requirements of 1,000 to 1,400 acres for 100 mWe PV stations.[105] The Department of Energy (DOE) reference system estimates 230 acres for a 109 mWe facility in Phoenix, Arizona.[106] The site of a PV central station usually excludes alternative uses until the plant is decommissioned and removed.[107] Some facilities may be constructed to allow livestock grazing on the site.[108] Also, a recent DOE study published in April 1989 concluded that on a kilowatt hour basis the land needs for a PV facility are very similar to the land needs of a coal production and combustion facility.[109] Land impacts may be reduced by siting on submarginal crop- or rangeland.

Nevertheless, on a site-specific basis, PV facilities may have microecological effects on flora, fauna, and microclimate. These effects have not been quantified but are

Industrial Materials, 5th ed. (Van Nostrand Reinhold Co., 1979.

104 U. S. Congress, Office of Technology Assessment (OTA), New Electric Power Technologies: Problems and Prospects for the 1990s, OTA-E-246, at 304, July, 1985, [hereafter cited as OTA, New Electric]. For both types of systems, the OTA low estimate is based on a DOE site in Albuquerque, New Mexico, and the high estimate on a site in Boston, Massachusetts. See id. at p. 304 n. 6 & 7.

105 See, e.g., BPA/ECO, Five Resources, supra note 83 at pp. 2-23.

106 DOE, Characterizations Handbook, chart references, supra note 20 at p. 179.

107 DOE/Materiel, chart references, supra note 92 at p. 4. Some sites, such as high desert terrain, may have limited alternative uses. See BPA/ECO, Five Resources, supra note 83 at pp. 2-23.

108 Hohmeyer, Social Costs, supra note 83 at p. 54.

109 San George, R., Environmental Emissions from Energy Technology Systems: The Total Fuel Cycle, U.S. D.O.E., Washington DC, April 1989. See also, PRE Study, supra note 1 at p. G-3.

assumed to be mitigatable by choosing "relatively unimportant" ecological sites.[110] A PV plant is prominently visible in its landscape and may be aesthetically displeasing to some people. Careful siting and screening may control these effects.

Hohmeyer quantified land-related environmental externality costs for a PV central station at 0.44 cents/kWh. Underlying this calculation is the assumption that opportunity costs of land use not covered by real estate prices are approximately 10% of the real estate price. Using a very high real estate price of approximately $66,000/acre, Hohmeyer calculates the lost opportunity cost of 0.44 cents/kWh based on the land requirements and electricity production of a 3.95 acre demonstration site producing a lifetime total of 5.5 gWh.[111] Hohmeyer notes that the 10% assumption may substantially overstate the external costs of the land use but concludes that the assumption is consistent with his study's policy of "making assumptions to the disadvantage of renewable energy."[112] Hohmeyer's real estate price of $66,000/acre may be comparable to land values in suburban areas of northeastern United States, however, the value appears unrealistically high for the more isolated acreage including farmland that might be used for a solar plant. Using a real estate price of $5,000/acre as an example, application of Hohmeyer's 10% assumption to the same facility assumptions results in an external value of 0.04 cents/kWh.[113]

The water requirements for operation of a PV central station are minimal. Only small amounts of water are needed to periodically clean the arrays and for the personal needs of on-site staff.[114] The most recent PV designs reduce or eliminate array washing requirements because washing has been found to be unnecessary or uneconomical.[115] Consequently, one recent source estimates 0.102 acre-feet/gWh as

---

[110] See Hohmeyer, Social Costs, supra note 83 at p. 54; BPA/ECO, Five Resources, supra note 83 at pp. 2-26.

[111] Hohmeyer's values were converted from 1982 DM to dollars using an exchange rate of 2.2631 DM (1982)/1.0 dollar (1982) and to 1989 dollars using a factor of 1.275. Hohmeyer's calculation of 0.0088 DM (1982)/kWh was based on a PV demonstration plant covering 16,000m^2 which produced 274,000 kWh/yr over a 20 year lifetime and a 1982 real estate value of 30 DM/m^2. Hohmeyer, Social Costs, supra note 83 at p. 56. In the text above, square meters were converted to acres.

[112] Id.

[113] Values were converted from 1987 dollars to 1989 dollars using a conversion factor of 1.068. The U.S. Department of Commerce, Bureau of Census, Statistical Abstract of the United States at 612 gives average farm real estate values on a state by state basis in the United States. Values range from $130/acre (New Mexico) to $5,683/acre (New Jersey). New York farmland has an average value of $944/acre. Solar power plants have usually been located on desert land in the United States, with real estate values far lower than for farmland.

[114] OTA, New Electric, supra note 104 at pp. 304-05; DOE/Materiel, chart references supra note 92 at p. 12.

[115] DOE/Materiel, chart references supra note 92 at 12.

the high-end value for water consumption associated with PV station operation.[116] The potential for operation-related water pollution is minimal and in surface runoff it would consist of herbicides used for vegetation control and detergent, if used in array washing.[117]

Air emissions for PV facilities are exclusively associated with construction of the plant and fabrication of its constituent materials. Noise emissions are also limited to the construction phase.

iii. Environmental Impacts of Decentralized PV Installations

The most significant environmental impact associated with operation of decentralized photovoltaic installations is the hazard associated with installing, maintaining or removing rooftop photovoltaic systems. Other possible impacts include fire hazards and aesthetic considerations.

Homeowners or contractors maintaining decentralized PV systems may be subject to risk of electric shock or other task-related accidents such as falling off the roof. The risk of electric shock is significant because photovoltaic systems begin to generate electricity immediately upon exposure to sunlight. Under normal weather conditions, the voltage generated by six average size modules connected in series could be sufficient to cause ventricular fibrillation and possible death.[118] Hohmeyer quantifies the external costs due to the accident risk of maintenance personnel of decentralized photovoltaic installations based on approximately 1.5 lost person-hours/gWh and 3.0 x 10^{-5} fatalities/gWh.[119] Hohmeyer derives a lost production value of 0.004 cents/kWh.[120]

Residential rooftop photovoltaic arrays create potential fire hazards caused by short circuits or spontaneous combustion resulting from heat build-up in dead air

---

[116] Id. at pp. 12, 23, Figure 9 (O.102 x 10^{-6} acre-ft/kWh).

[117] DOE, Characterizations Handbook, chart references, supra note 20 at p. 190.

[118] OECD COMPASS Project, supra note 11 at p. 35; citing Moskowitz, P., E. Coreney, S. Rabinowitz, and J. Barancik, "Rooftop Photovoltaic Arrays: Electric Shock and Fire Health Hazards," 9 Solar Cells at pp. 327-336, 1983. [hereafter cited as Rooftop Photovoltaic Arrays.]

[119] Hohmeyer, Social Cost, supra note 83 at pp. 55-56. Hohmeyer gives the total cost in DM/PJ and DM/kWh. The ratio of kWh to PJ is 3.589 x 10^{-9} kWh/PJ. Hohmeyer's accident figures of 423.5 person-days/PJ and 0.0085 fatalities/PJ were converted using this ratio.

[120] Id. Hohmeyer's value of 0.00007 DM (1982)/kWh was converted to 1982 dollars using a 1982 exchange rate of 2.2631 DM/dollar and then to 1989 dollars using a conversion factor of 1.257.

spaces.[121] According to a recent literature review, the probability of either risk has not been calculated for photovoltaic systems.[122] The review tentatively concludes that the health risk from fire is unlikely to present undue societal risk.[123]

Decentralized photovoltaics are generally assumed to require no additional land if mounted on roofs. Small enclosed lots are another option. Rooftop installations may be aesthetically displeasing to some people particularly if the installation is a building retrofit.[124] Decentralized photovoltaics avoid not only the emisisons from conventional power plants, but also the costs and effects of transmission lines and transmission line losses.

c. Solar-Thermal Electric Powerplants

Solar-thermal electric technologies convert solar heat energy into mechanical energy in a turbine and then into electricity using a conventional generator. The United States Department of Energy (DOE) estimates that a 1,000MW solar thermal electric plant constructed in the southwestern United States will require 1,000acres of land.[125] The most important environmental effects of solar thermal electric plants derive from these large land requirements and associated ecological and aesthetic effects.[126]

In order to better describe the environmental impacts associated with this technology, this section provides an overview of the solar-thermal electric generation process. It then discusses the environmental impacts of this process.

---

[121] OECD COMPASS Project, supra note 11 at p. 35; DOE Characterizations Handbook, chart references supra note 20 at p. 151 (noting that accidental high voltage arcing may generate ozone and fumes from burned plastics).

[122] OECD COMPASS Project, supra note 11 at p. 35.

[123] Id.; citing Rooftop Photovoltaic Arrays, supra note 118. Societal risk is defined as risk per individual per number of events.

[124] See BPA/ECO, Five Resources, supra note 83 at pp. 3-46.

[125] DOE Characterizations Handbook, chart references, supra note 20 at p. 177.

[126] Solar-thermal technologies have a potential environmentally beneficial application in the breakdown of toxic wastes, including dioxin-like compounds, and chlorofluorobarbons. Press Release dated December 13, 1988, Solar Energy Industries Association.

i. Overview of Solar-Thermal Technologies

Solar-thermal power plants generally consist of a solar field, power block, and water supply system. Focusing, concentrating collectors are necessary to obtain high temperatures (above 175 degrees Centigrade) in the working fluids. The higher the temperature in the working fluid, the greater the efficiency of the system in generating electricity.[127] Two arrangements are possible for the collectors: a central receiver arrangement, generally deemed to be the most appropriate for large scale generation and a parabolic trough or a distributed collector system arrangement, generally used in facilities rated at less than 2 MW. A plant may incorporate a storage system to store thermal energy and to allow generation of steam at night or when daytime solar radiation is inadequate.

In the central receiver or power tower design, an array of sun-tracking mirrors or heliostats reflect the solar radiation onto a tower-mounted receiver. A heat transport fluid (HTF) transfers the solar energy as heat to the steam heat exchanger located in the power block at the foot of the tower. Pressurized water absorbs the heat energy and leaves the exchanger as super-heated steam which drives a conventional steam turbine electrical generator. The spent steam from the turbine is condensed and feedwater pumps return the condensate to the heat exchanger to be transformed back into steam. The heat transport fluid may be pressurized water or, in more advanced systems, liquid sodium or a molten mixture of salts.[128] Hydrocarbon oil is sometimes proposed for a storage fluid.[129]

In the distributed collector system, trough-type collectors or dish-type collectors are connected to individual absorber pipes. The heated fluid is then carried to a single location where electricity is generated.[130]

ii. Environmental Impacts Associated With Solar-Thermal Power

This section summarizes the environmental effects associated with solar-thermal installations. The environmental impacts associated with solar-thermal plants include occupational hazards from the concentrated sunlight and superheated fluids, negative impacts on water resources, and most significant of all, the aesthetic and ecological effects of the plant's land use. The impact on water resources will vary depending on the plant's size, location and operating practices. The environmental impacts due to noise and air pollution are minimal.

---

[127] PRE Study, supra note 1 at p. E-1.

[128] OECD COMPASS Project, supra note 11 at pp. 27 - 28. See also Medsker, supra note 17 at p. 45.

[129] DOE Characterizations Handbook, chart references, supra note 20 at p. 177.

[130] OECD COMPASS Project, supra note 11 at p. 27.

Ecological and aesthetic effects associated with a solar-thermal plant and its construction and maintenance activities are highly site-specific and can only be analyzed with intimate knowledge of surrounding ecosystems. For example, a proposed 4.5MW facility in San Diego County encountered substantial delays due to investigations concerning the feared disruption of the habitats of several rare plant and animal species.[131] Ecosystem impacts can include destruction or disruption of natural habitats, loss of soil or changes to soil structure, barriers to wildlife movement or flight paths, possible micro-climactic changes due to changes in the local thermal energy balance,[132] loss of scenic or aesthetic qualities, particulate emissions, hazardous waste production, drawdown of local wells, and loss of prime agricultural land.[133] Most sites currently considered for solar-thermal installations are concentrated in arid desert areas with fragile soil and plant communities.[134]

Wildlife and habitat surveys are necessary to ensure proper siting and mitigation strategies. For example, Applications for Certification to the California Energy Commission for a solar-thermal plant permit detail a site selection process used both nationally and worldwide by Luz International, a major solar-thermal manufacturer.[135] There, Luz sought land with high insolation levels, but also with limited aesthetic value and with low diversity of biological species, both in its virgin state and in its cultivated farmland state. By siting plants far from population centers but near existing transmission corridors, Luz proposed to limit adverse impacts.[136]

Some people may find solar-thermal installations to be aesthetically displeasing.[137] This effect can be limited by locating the plant away from population centers.

---

131 See, California Energy Commission, Commission Decision, Application for Certification for Luz Engineering Corporation SEGS IX & X Projects, Harper Lake, Docket No. 89-AFC-1, February, 1990, p. 118, [hereafter cited as Commission Decision].

132 See generally Medsker, supra note 17 at pp. 45 - 48; OECD COMPASS Project, supra note 11 at p. 29. Many sites most appropriate for solar thermal plants are federal lands managed by the Bureau of Land Management (BLM), whose requirements must be addressed in siting. See, The California Desert Conservation Area Plan, BLM (1980).

133 Commission Decision, supra note 131 at pp. 14 - 320.

134 OTA, New Electric, supra note 104 at p. 91.

135 See Luz International Application to the California Energy Commission for Certification of SEGS IX and X, prepared by ENSR Consulting and Engineering, February, 1989, [hereafter cited as Luz International Application].

136 Luz also engages in affirmative mitigation actions to enhance the environment affected by its facilities. A film provided to Dina Berger, a student working on this report, by Luz demonstrated its procedure for identifying and relocating flora that were disturbed by plant construction and operations. Luz is also investigating the possibility of using water from its cooling system to supplement waters flowing to nearby wetlands created as a result of agricultural runoffs. As farms disappear from this area, the wetlands are in danger of drying up. See Luz International Application, Id. at 3-17.

137 Aesthetic concerns were one issue raised in the San Diego siting, See OTA, New Electric, supra note 104 at p. 194.

Although landscaping and other screening may also help, the need for direct sunlight may prevent such mitigation efforts or reduce their effectiveness. One source estimates that visual impact of large solar thermal electric plants will be similar to the visual impact of conventional electric generation plants.[138] However, assessment techniques developed by the Bureau of Land Management and applied by Luz show that such projects are not expected to cause significant visual impacts when properly sited and developed,[139] even though they may introduce an "industrial element" into an otherwise rural setting.[140]

A unique visual hazard associated with solar-thermal facilities is the possibility that misguided or accidentally reflected light may cause eyesight injuries and even blindness. Plants must be sited to avoid shining light at nearby residences or state highways. Workers exposed to the possibility of light hazards may need to wear special glasses for protection. These visual hazards may also limit secondary uses for land within the boundaries of the plant.[141]

Another unique health hazard associated with solar-thermal plants is the potential hazard associated with exposure to the HTFs. Contact with these fluids can occur due to failure of the heat transfer or storage systems. The chemicals used in a heat transfer system are considered to be hazardous. Along with posing a health threat, a heat transfer or heat storage system failure can also threaten soil, habitat and water contamination. In an 80 MW facility proposed for development in California's Mojave Desert, it was estimated that each of the two systems to be employed could use approximately 340,000 gallons of HTF.[142] The actual hazard resulting from such an accident would depend on the type of accident and the type of heat transfer fluid used in the facility. Important factors in evaluating this occupational health risk include temperature, pressure and toxicity of the transfer fluids released.[143]

A solar-thermal installation requires water for cooling tower and boiler operations and for mirror washing and dust control.[144] Chemical or hazardous emissions in water

---

[138] OECD COMPASS Project, supra note 11 at p. 28; see also BPA, Five Resources, supra note 93 at pp. 2-26.

[139] Commission Decisions, supra note 131 at p. 224.

[140] Id. at p. 225.

[141] See OECD COMPASS Project, supra note 11 at p. 28. Animals may also be injured by direct exposure to the concentrated light beam if the facility is not designed to keep them away from the beam. Medsker, supra note 17 at p. 47.

[142] Commission Decision, supra note 131 at p. 4.

[143] OECD COMPASS Project, supra note 11 at p. 29.

[144] See DOE Characterizations Handbook, chart references, supra note 20 at p. 177 (30.3 acre-ft./yr for a 100 MW central facility); Luz International Application, supra note 135 at pp. 5-25 (water needs would be satisfied by on-site wells). One source characterizes these needs as "large." OECD COMPASS Project, supra note 11 at p. 29.

could result from runoff containing herbicides, chemical dust suppressants, and mirror washing agents. Periodic flushing of the system may also lead to the planned or accidental release of chemicals used in the cooling tower to control algae and pH or chemicals contained in the heat transfer fluid. The nature and quantity of pollutants varies by system type and management practices. Possible pollutants include hydrocarbon oil, bactericides, glycol, and corrosion inhibitors such as chromate, borate, nitrate, nitrite, sulphate, arsenate, benzoate salts, triazolate, silicate, and phosphates.[145]

Most air emissions associated with a solar-thermal plant occur during the construction phase and are significantly below all applicable air quality standards.[146] Sources of air pollution during operation are the HTF heaters, the cooling tower, the emergency diesel generators, the diesel powered water pumps and the HTF system.[147] Additionally, fugitive HTF emissions for photochemically reactive HTFs contribute to the formation of ozone and benzene.[148] Examples of other air pollutants that could be released in the case of an accident involving the working or storage fluids are nitrogen oxides, sodium monoxides, peroxides, and sodium hydroxide mists or dusts.[149]

Solar-thermal units, as with other more traditional thermal facilities, may produce waste heat. This waste heat must be discharged into local watercourses or the atmosphere.[150] The DOE estimates that a 100 MW solar thermal plant releases 2.3×10^{12} Btu of waste heat each year.[151]

Because solar-thermal projects are generally sited in the desert environment, the potential for soil erosion and loss is high. For instance in the 80 MW proposed Mojave Desert facility, estimates of soil loss rose as high as 200 tons/acre in

---

145 DOE Characterizations Handbook, chart references, supra note 20 at p. 178; OECD COMPASS Project, supra note 11 at p. 28. The solar industry maintains that proper management techniques for these chemicals are well-established and necessary remedial actions in case of a mishap are formulated during project planning. See Luz International Application, supra note 135 at pp. 175, 177.

146 See Luz International Application, supra note 135 at pp. 5-78. The only exceedance predicted by Luz was due to fugitive dust emissions resulting from the use of heavy duty construction equipment in a desert area, which is generally a nonattainment area for particulates. Continual watering during construction operations mitigates dust emissions.

147 Commission Decision, supra note 131 at p. 32.

148 Id.

149 DOE Characterizations Handbook, chart references, supra note 20 at p. 178; OECD COMPASS Project, supra note 11 at p. 28.

150 OECD COMPASS Project, supra note 11 at p. 29.

151 DOE Characterizations Handbook, chart references, supra note 20 at p. 178.

"undeveloped and unprotected" areas during each year of construction.[152] Additional soil loss will occur due to construction and operation of transmission pipelines, towers and service roads, especially in steep areas.[153]

Noise associated with operation of a solar-thermal plant shares some characteristics of other steam-generating plants. The noise generated by power block fans, turbines, and cooling towers during peak daytime hours should be below federal residential standards.[154] At night, when people are most sensitive to noise, the plant will not be operating. Noise pollution will also be reduced by the fact that solar-thermal plants are likely to be located only in a minimally populated area.

Although siting must occur in the fragile desert environment, the land being used may not be in its wild state but may be desert previously converted to agricultural use. Siting in these pre-developed areas may dislocate prime agricultural land. Loss of farms and their runoff may lead to environmental consequences for birds, animals and other forms of life attracted to the increased availability of water near the farmland.[155]

Construction and operation of solar-thermal facilities presents both long and short term land use environmental problems. The short term impacts include dust, noise and traffic. The long term effects include permanent alteration of the character of the desert site, secondary area growth, and industrialization of the land surrounding the site.[156]

d. Other Solar Technologies

Passive solar architecture and dispersed active systems (solar collectors) do not generate electricity but may use sunlight's radiant and thermal energy to reduce electric consumption for space heating, space cooling, daylighting, high temperature industrial heating, and hot water heating.[157] Consequently, these solar technologies should be viewed as demand control strategies or alternatives to electric generation. One emerging solar technology is known as Solar Hydrogen. It involves use of PV solar

---

152 Commission Decision, supra note 131 at p. 169.

153 Id. at p. 172.

154 See OECD COMPASS Project, supra note 11 at p. 29; Luz International Application, supra note 135 at pp. 5-206; Environmental Protection Agency, Noise from Construction Equipment and Operations, Building Equipment, and Home Appliances, 1971 (HUD standards). Luz associates the highest probable noise emissions with the excavation phase of construction.

155 Commission Decisions, supra note 131 at pp. 296 - 316.

156 Id.

157 PRE Study, supra note 1 at p. H-1.

cells to generate an electric current to produce hydrogen from an electrolizer. The technology is described in detail in a recent report of the World Resources Institute, but environmental hazards and risks are not discussed there or in other studies.[158] This is a subject for future research.

i. Environmental Impacts of Passive Solar Architecture

Through use of passive solar architecture buildings are designed to take full advantage of the sun's energy and use the building's structure to collect, store, and distribute energy.[159] Orientation of building and windows, choice of construction materials to reduce heat-loss, use of heat-retaining solar walls, and improved ventilation systems are passive solar options. Widespread use of solar architecture could have an aesthetic impact in areas where regional or traditional architecture is an important aspect of the local landscape. Adaptation of technologies and materials to local preferences can limit unfavorable reactions to appearance while retaining the energy efficient characteristics of these buildings.[160]

ii. Environmental Impacts of Dispersed Active Solar Collectors

Dispersed active systems absorb solar energy, usually in copper, steel or aluminum plate collectors. The heat is then transferred through use of pumps or a heat transfer fluid and used to heat water supplies or heat or cool interior spaces. The heat transfer fluids are usually water and a range of additives or air. For example, the U.S. Department of Energy (DOE) describes a reference system for a typical residence in Denver, Colorado. A 500 square foot array of flat-plate solar collectors absorbs the solar energy. The energy is transferred by a water and glycol solution to a storage tank and then pumped upon demand through a heat exchanger to provide space heating. The DOE's reference system provides 75% of the load of the house.[161]

Environmental risks associated with operation of solar collectors relate primarily to the routine or accidental discharge of the coolant fluid. The Denver reference system assumes that coolant is replaced every three years. On this basis, the DOE

---

158 Ogden, J., and R. Williams, Solar Hydrogen: Moving Beyond Fossil Fuels, World Resources Institute, Washington DC, October, 1989.

159 PRE Study, supra note 1 at p. H-1.

160 Cf. OECD COMPASS Project, supra note 11 at p. 24. Another possible risk involves reduced air change rates and accumulation of indoor air pollutants, including radon emissions from materials used as an indoor thermal mass in solar architecture. As this risk is associated with energy efficient building shell designs, it is discussed in more detail in this report's chapter on Demand Side Management.

161 DOE Characterizations Handbook, chart references, supra note 20 at p. 142. The Characterizations Handbook also describes a system which, in addition to providing heat, could satisfy 70% of the residence's cooling load by pumping the stored energy through a lithium bromide absorption chiller. Id. at p. 144.

estimates that the system would use, on a yearly basis, 14 gallons of coolant and 7 gallons of water as a replacement fluid.[162] All systems using a heat transfer fluid are likely to contain anti-freeze, rust inhibitors, or biological growth inhibitors. As a result, discharges could contain glycol, nitrates, nitrites, chromates, sulphites, and sulphates.[163] The DOE assumes ultimate disposal of all working fluids in water and estimates a resulting chemical oxygen demand of 0.15 to 0.3 lbs/year.[164] Proper disposal can control or eliminate these impacts.

Accidental release of working fluids, particularly in the case of domestic hot water systems, could result in contamination of potable water supplies. In the event of coolant loss, these systems reach high temperatures creating a risk of fire and possibly dangerous outgassing of panel components and vaporized coolant.[165]

The studies reviewed do not estimate the environmental externality costs of dispersed active solar collectors.

4. Environmental Impacts and Costs of Wind Powered Energy Generation

Wind power generators, sometimes referred to as wind energy conversion systems, capture the energy of air movements resulting from uneven solar warming of large areas of the planet's surface and convert this energy into mechanical energy which is then used to generate electricity.[166] In the United States there are presently over 16,000 wind turbines installed with a collective capacity of 1,500 MW.[167] Windfarms surrounding the Altamonte Pass, the Tehachapi Mountains, and the San Gorgonio Pass, all in California, collectively have over 15,000 turbines.[168]

Wind energy appears to be, along with so many other renewable technologies, an environmentally benign system for electrical energy production. Wind powered generating stations have little or no effect on plant and animal life, water resources, air,

---

[162] Id. at pp. 142, 144.

[163] OECD COMPASS Project, supra note 11 at p. 26. Heat transfer fluids for higher temperature applications could use aromatic alcohols, pols, fluorocarbons, or liquid sodium. Id.

[164] DOE Characterizations Handbook, chart references, supra note 20 at pp. 143, 145.

[165] OECD COMPASS Project, supra note 11 at pp. 26-27.

[166] OECD COMPASS Project, supra note 11 at p. 39.

[167] Meridian Corporation, Characterization of U.S. Energy Resources and Reserves, at p. 33, June, 1989, (Prepared for Deputy Assistant Secretary for Renewable Energy, U.S. DOE) [hereafter cited as Meridian Characterization].

[168] See San Martin, R., Progress and Impact of Renewable Energy, Speech presented at the National Press Club, Washington, DC, December 13, 1988, at p. 11.

climate, and human health and safety. Its greatest negative impact is the noise the facility would generate and the substantial land areas it would require for operation.[169]

Two factors affect the amount of electricity generated at a particular site: the size of the wind turbine rotor and the character of the moving air (wind speed and consistency).[170] A small wind turbine generates up to 200kWe; an intermediate turbine generates from 100 to 1,000kWe; and a large turbine may produce more than 1 mWe. Intermediate-sized turbines are currently the favored option for producing cheap power without imposing unacceptable risks.[171]

Availability of wind is the primary engineering constraint in the siting of wind facilities. Wind resources are particularly plentiful near coastal and mountain areas. The best sites are areas with little ground cover such as hilltops, shorelines or arable land.[172] All major obstructions such as trees must be removed and a road must usually be constructed to allow maintenance access to the turbines. The amount of land required for a wind farm depends on land topography, prevailing wind direction, the shape and orientation of the property on which the wind farm is located, and the size of the turbines used.[173] Windfarms generally require large land areas: A typical windfarm requires between fifteen and forty--five acres per megawatt of capacity depending on the site's terrain and the size of the wind machines.[174]

This section provides mainly a qualitative review of the environmental impacts associated with wind energy development because few studies have quantified the external costs associated with these impacts. The cost ranges available are from 0 to 0.14 cents/kWh and are largely front-end costs. The studies deriving these rough estimates are summarized following the qualitative review.

---

[169] PRE Study, supra note 1 at p. F-2.

[170] Meridian Characterization, supra note 167 at p. A-24; OECD COMPASS Project, supra note 11 at p. 39.

[171] OTA, New Electric, supra note 104 at p. 92.

[172] OECD COMPASS Project, supra note 11 at p. 39.

[173] OTA, New Electric, supra note 104 at p. 93.

[174] Rader, Power Surge, supra note 10 at pp. 11-53 to 11-54; see also OTA, New Electric, supra note 104 at p. 93 (consistent estimate of acreage for a reference wind consisting of 50 turbines rated at 400 kWe).

a. Qualitative Review of Environmental Impacts of Wind Powered Energy Generation

Major environmental impacts related to wind turbines are visual intrusion, ecological impact on airborne species, and conflicts with other land uses such as farming and nature conservation. Other impacts of possible significance include noise levels and hazards associated with mechanical failures such as a blade throw. Wind facilities have little or no impact on water resources and do not generate air pollution during operation. Most wind power-associated impacts, including noise and mechanical failure, can be minimized by proper design, siting and facility orientation.

Development of wind farms could change existing land use and result in loss of resource land. Wind farm sites could displace agriculture, recreation, forest, aesthetic, or other land resources.[175] Advocates of wind power believe that adequate levels of wind can be found in the United States without resorting to lands with competing economic uses such as populated areas, irrigated crop land, or national parks.[176] Some land impacts can be mitigated by encouraging compatible uses of land such as grazing and site-suited agriculture, requiring that machines be appropriately spaced, siting the facility so as to eliminate the need for additional transmission corridors and roads, and designing roads and facilities to minimize erosion.[177]

Noise and vibration from wind machine rotors may be a substantial development constraint on wind power.[178] The most commonly cited example of possible noise effects is the U.S. DOE's MOD-1 wind turbine generator at Boone, North Carolina. This machine was found to emit vibrations which allegedly made people ill and caused windows to rattle, crockery to shake, and cows to stop giving milk. Changes in design and site orientation corrected this problem at the next DOE project, the MOD-2 site.[179] Noise levels of 56 decibels (dB) have been recorded at a distance of 400 meters (about

---

[175] BPA/ECO, Five Resources, supra note 83 at p. F-34 (noting, however, that siting wind farms in a desert environment would convert marginally productive range land to highest use and best "resource" and "economic" use of land).

[176] Rader, Power Surge, supra note 10 at p. 11-52.

[177] See OECD COMPASS Project, supra note 11 at p. 39. European developers believe that wind power generation is feasible using smaller more localized developments which reduce land impacts and visibility concerns. Another siting option which has been considered in Denmark and Sweden is the use of off-shore installations. Advocates claim that these facilities would reduce on-shore visual pollution, eliminate land use issues, and could provide higher wind speeds than land installations with less adverse noise impacts then land installations. Offshore installations may have impacts on fishing and navigation, however.

[178] Id. at p. 41.

[179] York, K. and R. Settle, Potential Legal Facilitation or Impediment of Wind Energy Conversion System Siting, 58 Washington Law Review 387, 402 (1983) [hereafter cited as York & Settle].

a quarter mile) from the MOD-2 site.[180] This effect may be roughly quantifiable for particular sites and its impact on residential developments mitigated during site selection.

In certain situations, wind systems may produce safety hazards associated with disintegrating, shedding blades or ice and snow accumulations thrown from the blades.[181] Safety systems and fenced or remote siting can prevent or reduce these hazards.

Windfarm development may disrupt ecological habitats as well as present a direct hazard to birds. Wind developments must be carefully sited to avoid hazards to protected or fragile bird populations and to avoid interfering with bird migration routes.[182] Operation of wind machines affects air circulation patterns, which could affect local weather patterns and have microclimatic effects on habitat.[183] Noise may also disrupt wildlife habitat. However, some commentators note that small wildlife populations can be expected to adapt to the noise.[184] Habitats can be protected and negative effects on them mitigated through avoidance of siting in critical habitat areas and flyways.

Operation of a wind energy generation facility generally has no associated water impacts.[185] Both water consumption and the potential for water pollution during operation would depend upon the facility's storage system, if any. For instance, a pumped hydro storage system may require significant water usage.[186] If pumped air storage is used, residual contamination in the underground storage area could pollute the aquifer.[187] Another possible cause of water pollution is the release of chemicals from the on-site storage system during a fire or other accident.[188] Proper siting of the

---

[180] OECD COMPASS Project, supra note 11 at p. 41.

[181] York & Settle, supra note 179 at pp. 400-401; OECD COMPASS Project, supra note 11 at p. 42.

[182] Cf. Gorman Wind Project Voted Down, IRT Newsbrief, August 24, 1989, at p. 1. A 77 MW windpark planned for a site north of Los Angeles was voted down by the local planning commission in part because of opposition from the Sierra Club and the Audubon Society, which expressed concerns about hazards to the California Condor. The site was also opposed by a major real estate developer who planned a housing complex adjacent to the proposed site.

[183] Medsker, supra note 17 at p. 37.

[184] BPA/ECO, Five Resources, supra note 83 at p. F-33.

[185] Id. at p. F-32.

[186] DOE Characterizations Handbook, chart references, supra note 20 at p. 175.

[187] Id. at 176 (for example, residual hydrocarbons from abandoned gas wells or mines).

[188] Medsker, supra note 17 at p. 37.

wind facility away from water supplies coupled with responsible operation would mitigate or eliminate these effects.

The only air pollution effects associated with operation of a wind facility relate to the release of storage media in the event of an accident, or the release of residuals in underground storage space if pumped air storage is used.[189] Again, possible air quality degradation can be minimized by prudent operation and by choosing sites to minimize impact on residential areas.

b. Studies Evaluating the External Costs of Wind Powered Energy Generation

Three studies evaluate the environmental impacts of wind power facilities for purposes of quantification. These studies are not directly comparable because different assumptions and methodologies underlie their respective conclusions. The values quantified range from 0 to 0.14 cents/kWh.

i. Bonneville Power Study

A 1986 study done for the Bonneville Power Administration (BPA) found no significant environmental effects for purposes of impact quantification associated with a generic 35 mW wind facility. The generic facility would operate at a capacity factor of 20 percent over a 15 year plant life generating 61,320,000kWh annually.[190] The study discusses the significance and derivation of impact costs associated with four effects: visual or aesthetic impacts; effects on the local bird population; noise generation; and hazards associated with blade breakage.

According to the study, visual effects could be the largest potential environmental effect of significant economic importance resulting from the development of windfarms. Although aesthetic effects were not valued, the study found that the visual impacts could be "economically important" where significant numbers of people perceive wind facilities to be an adverse contribution to the landscape. This reaction is most likely to occur where the public desires more pristine environments such as in the Colombia Gorge or along the southern Oregon Coast or where large numbers of individuals would be adversely affected (as in the case of motorists on a heavily travelled scenic route).[191]

Also, the study found that bird kills did not have any economically important effect. Proper siting should ensure that the wind farms will not interfere with known flyways or where rare, threatened, or endangered species are present. The study

---

[189] Id. at p. 37; DOE Characterizations Handbook, chart references, supra note 20 at p. 176.

[190] BPA/ECO, Five Resources, supra note 83 at pp. 4-10. A technical appendix catalogs impacts and their environmental significance in qualitative detail for facility construction, decommissioning, and operation.

[191] Id. at pp. 2-30.

suggests that local bird populations would adapt to air circulation patterns surrounding wind machines and notes that changes in flyway paths could have a detrimental effect on particular migratory birds.[192]

The BPA study acknowledges that noise would probably be noticeable within a half mile of a wind farm but concludes that this noise effect is not economically significant because windfarms will be located in areas of limited population. The study analogizes to previous work by the same researchers which found that noise effects were economically unimportant for carefully muffled combustion turbines in urban environments and suggests that noise levels would be similar at population centers closest to the windfarm sites.[193]

In evaluating safety hazards associated with the possibility of blade breakage the study found that the possibility of a throw coupled with the possibility of a blade striking a person is insignificant. It did note, however, that a thrown blade could damage property including possibly another wind machine.[194]

ii. Shuman and Cavanagh

Shuman and Cavanagh (1984) discuss briefly the air emissions and occupational effects associated with wind electric conversion.[195] Shuman and Cavanagh conclude that the aggregate occupational risks associated with materials acquisition, construction of facilities, and routine operation and maintenance are about half the size of the occupational risks associated with coal when stated in terms of fatalities and lost work days.[196] Occupational effects for wind and coal-fired electric generation as presented by Shuman and Cavanagh are compared in Table 9.

---

[192] Id.

[193] Id. at pp. 2-30 to 2-31, citing BPA, Economic Analysis of the Environmental Effects of a Combustion-Turbine Generating Station at Fredrickston Industrial Park, Pierce County, Washington: Final Report, prepared by ECO Northwest, et al., March 26, 1984 [hereafter cited as BPA, ECO, Combustion Turbine]. The Combustion Turbine study cites evidence that the turbines were inaudible at the nearest residence, 1600 feet away, even though noise levels outside the building were noticeable. BPA/ECO, Combustion Turbine, at p. III-7.

[194] Id. Note that this study proceeds from the assumption that occupational accidents are economically unimportant as an externality because, for the most part, such costs are already absorbed into the resource's economic profile.

[195] Shuman & Cavanagh, supra note 83 at pp. 46-51. Shuman and Cavanagh also discuss the materials requirements of wind energy systems in comparison to coal and nuclear systems. They conclude that "wind generators can be comparable to coal or nuclear plants in cumulative tonnage of metals and concrete required to produce a unit of energy. Id. at p. 50.

[196] Id. at p. 51.

TABLE 9

OCCUPATIONAL EFFECTS[197]

	FATALITIES (Deaths per GW/yr)	LOST WORK DAYS (1000 Worker Days Lost per GW/yr)
Wind	0.28 - 0.44	0.82 - 1.36
Coal	0 - 1.19	1.94 - 56.00

Shuman and Cavanagh also summarize the aggregate air pollution emissions associated with materials acquisition and routine fuel cycle operations of wind electric plants. They conclude that routine non-radiological health costs of nuclear plant construction are a reasonably good proxy for the health costs of wind energy plant construction. This value is "roughly"0 to 0.14cents/kWh. Shuman and Cavanagh state that figures now available probably overstate the ultimate environmental impacts of renewable energy sources because efforts to mitigate these impacts have just begun.[198]

iii. Hohmeyer

Hohmeyer calculates an external environmental cost of 0.005 cents/kWh for electricity generated by small wind turbines.[199] Hohmeyer identifies four significant environmental effects of wind energy: the use of land for the facility installation; infringements on the landscape caused by large groups of wind energy systems as in wind energy parks; the noise produced by the wind turbines; and interference with radio or television reception. Of these four effects, Hohmeyer concludes that only the consequences of noise generation from the wind facility are quantifiable. Hohmeyer then makes some first estimates of the external effects due to noise, pointing out that these figures are only an indication of the order of magnitude of the external environmental costs since they are dependent on the number of people affected.[200]

---

[197] Derived from id. at p. 48, Table E-8. Shuman & Cavanagh's source is Holdren, J., G. Morris, and I. Mintzer, "Environmental Aspects of Renewable Energy Sources," 5 Annual Review of Energy 241, 268, Table 5, 1980.

[198] Shuman & Cavanagh, supra note 83 at p. 51. A value of 0 to 0.12 cents/kWh was assumed to be in 1984 dollars and was converted to 1989 dollars using a factor of 1.167.

[199] Hohmeyer, Social Costs, supra note 83 at p. 58. Hohmeyer's value of 0.00009 DM (1982)/kWh was converted to 1982 dollars using an exchange rate of 2.2631 and then to 1989 dollars using a factor of 1.257.

[200] Id. at pp. 57-58.

Hohmeyer derives the external costs of noise disturbance based on a reduction in rental value of "livingquarters" affected by the noise. First, Hohmeyer assumes that 140,000wind turbines producing noise levels of 30-36 decibels (dB) at 200 meters (660 feet) are located in the sparsely populated costal areas of northern Germany.[201] A maximum total of 10,000"livingquarters" are within 200 meters of the wind turbines. Hohmeyer notes:

> As the wind turbines are likely to be situated a considerable distance from any building because of wind turbulence from buildings and the resulting extreme stress on the wind turbine construction, this may be considered a very high estimate of the number of buildings affected by the noise produce.[202]

Hohmeyer assumes that noise levels of 30-35 dB reduce the average rental value of these apartments, approximately $278/month, by 3% or approximately $100 a year for each apartment.[203] Based on an annual energy production from each system of 145 mWh, Hohmeyer derives the rough externality value of 0.005 cents/kWh.

5. Environmental Impacts and Costs of Biomass Energy Generation

This section summarizes the environmental impacts associated with biomass generation and cogeneration with emphasis on the use of wood as a fuel.[204] Residues from the wood products industry, logging residues, and crop residues constitute the largest sources of potential biomass generation in the United States.[205] Sweden has concluded that a national energy scenario specifying the use of biomass generation from unutilized forest residue products and energy plantations along with energy efficiency may best accommodate that country's low-carbon energy strategy. Sweden

---

201 Id. Hohmeyer's estimates of noise levels are based on measurements conducted at the Danish national testing site. The measurements used are for a three-bladed rotor machine with a tower height of 20 meters (66 feet) and a nominal output of 55 KW.

202 Id. at p. 58.

203 Id.

204 Other sources of biomass not discussed in this report include sewage sludge and manure and crop residues. These sources are used with some form of conversion or gasification technology to generate electricity. See generally OECD COMPASS Project, supra note 2 at pp. 45-46. For an excellent discussion of gasification technology, emissions, and rate or biomass converstion in electric supply planning, see Larson, E., P. Svenningsson, I. Bjerle, "Biomass Gasification for Gas-Turbine Power Generation", in Electricity: Efficient End-Use and New Generation Technologies and Their Planning Implications, edited by Johansson, T.B., B. Bodlund, and R. Williams, at pp. 697 - 937, Sweden: Lund University Press 1989, [hereafter cited as Electricity]. The use of solid waste as fuel is discussed in a separate chapter on "Waste-to-Energy".

205 See OECD COMPASS Project, supra note 11 at p. 51, Table 2.8. Taken together, these three potential sources could generate 11 x 10^{18} joules/year if all dry weight was available for energy production. Substantially smaller quantities of waste may actually be available due to technical and economic factors. Id.

plans to meet its national energy needs without new hydropower and with a phase-out of nuclear generation.[206]

This section first briefly discusses the relative impacts resulting from wood-fired generation and cogeneration. Next, it reviews the results of a study for Bonneville Power Administration which assigns values to the environmental impacts of biomass cogeneration facilities.

a. Overview of Environmental Impacts of Biomass Energy Generation

This report does not discuss the front-end impacts of the electrical generation fuel cycle in detail. A total environmental impact cost for this source of generation would, however, reflect the negative effects that harvesting biomass could have on local ecosystems and soil conditions.[207]

For example, if the fuel cycle associated with energy production from wood is to avoid increased carbon emissions, care must be exercised to use only wood wastes as fuel. Similarly, intensive agricultural practices associated with plantation farming of trees may use significant amounts of petroleum and petrochemicals, (in the form of fertilizers and herbicides), and water,[208] perhaps compromising the renewable character of biomass energy. The growth of crops for energy purposes and plantation farming of biomass could also result in non-sustainable water resource depletion as well as possible changes in local or regional sub-climates.[209] Finally, occupational hazards associated with agricultural and forestry production have risk levels slightly higher than the national average for other types of employment; wood cutting and gathering rivals underground coal mining as a high risk job.[210]

Unlike noncombustion-based renewable energy sources, combustion or conversion of biomass produces air and water emissions and solid waste. Woodburning need not cause serious environmental problems if appropriate combustion technology and control choices are made. Biomass can be burned in everything from inefficient home stoves to highly efficient boilers and fluidized bed combustors. Control technologies,

---

[206] Bodlund, Mills, Karlsson, and Johansson, The Challenge of Choices: Technology Options for the Swedish Electricity Sector, in Electricity, supra note 204 at pp. 883-947.

[207] See OECD COMPASS Project, supra note 11 at pp. 46-50; Medsker, supra note 17 at pp. 13-15, 1982.

[208] Strauss, C. and L. Wright, Woody Biomass Production Costs in the United States, 1990. Research sponsored by the Biofuels and Municipal Waste Technology Division, U.S. DOE, Contract # DE-AC05-840R21400 with Martin Marietta Energy Systems, Inc.

[209] OECD Compass Project, supra note 11 at pp. 49-50.

[210] Id. at pp. 48, 50. Accidental injury associated with wood may be 3 to 10 times greater per unit of energy than from coal mining, but avoids some chronic health effects, such as black lung disease, associated with coal mining. Id. at p. 48.

such as scrubber and baghouse filters or electrostatic precipitators, may be used to regulate emissions from biomass combustion. Boilers and burners of wood or other biomass fuels must obtain air permits unless they are sized for residential heating.[211]

A recent source concludes that researchers generally agree about the nature of biomass emissions, but notes that "quantification is made extremely difficult by methodological differences between the various analyses."[212] Significant air emissions from wood combustion include particulates, nitrogen dioxide and carbon monoxide. Biomass burners are likely to release higher levels of carbon monoxide than coal combustion. Experts disagree as to whether nitrogen oxide emissions are more or less than emissions from coal per unit of energy.[213] Particulate emissions are an important concern for older domestic woodstoves which lack control technologies.[214] Such emissions contain inhalable toxic pollutants including carcinogens, polycyclic aromatic hydrocarbons, and other respiratory irritants.[215] Uncontrolled wood emissions may also include a variety of organic compounds including acids, aldehydes, phenols, and carcinogens, including benzo-a-pyrene.[216] Biomass combustion produces appreciable quantities of bottom ash and fly ash which is generally easier to dispose of than coal combustion wastes because it contains smaller amounts of toxic trace substances.[217] Waste solids from wood-fired combustion are generally composed of silica and alumina oxides with minor fractions of sodium, magnesium, and potassium, and "very minor quantities" of lead.[218]

---

[211] See Environmental Regulation of Biomass Facilities: A Summary of the Current System, Biologue, February/March, 1989, at pp. 10, 12 (excerpting from Biomass Energy Project Guidebook, published by Northwest Regional Biomass Energy Program).

[212] Id. at p. 51.

[213] See Id. at p. 53.

[214] For new wood stoves, the U.S. EPA has promulgated a New Source Performance Standard that is designed to reduce emissions, increase energy efficiency and reduce fires from wood stoves.

[215] See generally Id. at 55; see also, Health Effects of Wood-Smoke, Proceedings of a conference sponsored by the Northwest Center for Occupational Health and Safety, January 10, 1988 in Seattle, Washington; Preliminary Health Effect Evaluation for Pollutants Generated by Field Burning, Slash Burning, and Residential Wood Combustion, Oregon Department of Environmental Quality, prepared by OMNI Environmental Services, July 20, 1987; and Recommendations for Assessing the Impact of Public Health from Vegetative Burning (Oregon Department of Environmental Quality, no date)(peer reviews of the OMNI Report).

[216] OECD COMPASS Project, supra note 11 at pp. 55-56.

[217] Id. at p. 56.

[218] DOE Characterizations Handbook, chart references, supra note 20 at p. 174.

Water requirements from steam-generating electric plants powered by biomass are roughly comparable per unit of energy produced to the requirements of fossil-fueled plants.[219] Runoff water from the site may present water pollution concerns and aqueous wastes from combustion may contain trace amounts of metals and metal compounds.[220] Leachate from storage piles may have to be controlled.[221]

b. BPA Analysis of Biomass Cogeneration

A 1986 report prepared for the BPA concludes that external environmental effects are probably not important for biomass cogenerators.[222] The study derives health costs for a generic biomass cogeneration facility in the range of 0 to 0.7 cents/kWh. The BPA report evaluated a generic 12 MW cogeneration facility which could be located at a mill site or near lumber, wood products, or pulp and paper industries. Fuel for the generic facility consists of mill wastes, waste liquor, and forest residue (rotten or flawed logs and trees too small to harvest for milling).[223]

The plant would have a thirty year life and operate at an 85% capacity factor generating an average annual output of 89,352,000kWh.[224] The twenty-five acre site would include fuel processing areas; power block and water treatment facilities; ash handling and storage facilities; air pollution control equipment and cooling tower; and transmission access.[225] In addition to carbon dioxide emissions which the BPA study does not quantify, but which are considerably lower than from fossil fuel combustion, air emissions associated with this facility would be particulates (18.7 tons/year); nitrogen dioxide (286 tons/year); volatile organic compounds (143 tons/year); carbon monoxide (220 tons/year); and polycyclic organic matter (0.002 tons/year).[226]

Although the generic facility would generate electricity and provide process steam for on-and-off site use, the study allocates all environmental costs to electrical

---

[219] OECD COMPASS Project, supra note 11 at p. 57.

[220] Id. at p. 57; DOE Characterizations Handbook, chart references, supra note 20 at p. 174.

[221] OECD COMPASS Project, supra note 11 at p. 50.

[222] BPA/ECO, Five Resources, supra note 83 at p. xiv.

[223] Id. at pp. 2-3 to 2-5. The study notes that a facility fueled exclusively by forest residues would require residues from up to 50,000 acres of normally scheduled timber harvest.

[224] Id. at p. xiv.

[225] Id. at p. 2-5.

[226] Id. at pp. 3-4, 3-14.

generation. The authors give a caveat that this allocation may result in a significant overstatement of environmental costs attributed to electrical generation.[227]

The BPA study identifies, specifically, four "potentially environmentally important effects" associated with operation of the biomass facility:[228] (1) Facility emissions of particulates and the potential health hazard associated with particulate emissions; (2) the potential for improved visibility resulting from replacing open burning of slash with fueling cogeneration facilities with slash; (3) water consumption and the potential for surface water pollution; and (4) occupational accident potential.

Only the economic effects of the air quality effects, health hazards and improved visibility were quantified. Occupational accidents during operation are dismissed as not being an externality. The study assumes that net effects for water quality are short-term, reversible, and will not affect a sufficiently significant population of biomass or wildlife to create an economically significant environmental impact.[229]

Impact costs for operation of the generic biomass cogeneration facility are presented in Table 10. The BPA study offsets visibility effects from emissions of the biomass cogenerator which results from using wood waste to fire the cogenerator with the reduction in haze associated with slash burning. Therefore, these costs may not be directly comparable to effects in other locations.

TABLE 10

BIOMASS-FIRED COGENERATION ENVIRONMENTAL EFFECTS
Levelized Costs in Cents/kWh[230]

Impact	Low	Expected	High
Health	0.00	0.128	0.668
Visibility	- 0.012	- 0.094	- 0.126
TOTAL	- 0.012	0.031	0.542

[227] Id. at pp. 5-4 to 5-5.

[228] Id. at p. 2-9. For discussion of the environmental effects associated with the harvesting of logging residue, the front-end of the fuel cycle, see id. at pp. 2-6 to 2-9. Of the front-end costs, only land productivity changes are deemed significant for terms of economic quantification. The researchers conclude this value is likely to be zero or insignificant. See id. at pp. C3-1 to C3-20. The report also concludes that of the effects associated with transportation of fuel, plant construction and decommissioning and occupational accidents were environmentally important but not economically significant. See id. at p. 2-9 and Technical Appendices, Appendix F, Table 1.

[229] BPA/ECO, Five Resources, supra note 83 at pp. 2-9 to 2-10.

[230] Derived from BPA/ECO, Five Resources, id. at p. 4-3, Table 4-1. Costs are levelized using a 3% discount rate. Values were assumed to be in 1986 dollars and were converted to 1989 dollars using a factor of 1.106.

The low health cost scenario is based on the assumption that existing air quality standards completely protect human health. Researchers of the BPA study, however, are of the opinion that "standards do not adequately protect society from all health effects."[231] The "expected" risk scenario uses dose-response data at normal ambient exposures. If dose-response data is not available except for unusually high exposure levels, the researchers assume a linear dose response curve with no safe threshold exposure level to derive a high estimate of risk. The high estimate is then averaged with the low to derive a best estimate of expected effects. Carbon monoxide emissions account for two-thirds of the health effects these researchers associate with biomass cogeneration.[232] To calculate the value of health effects, researchers multiplied their estimates of total increased risk by the estimate that people would pay $30 to avoid a 1 in 100,000 increase in risk of death.[233]

6. Environmental Impacts and Costs of Geothermal Energy Generation

Geothermal resources are becoming increasingly popular as a renewable energy source. As new technologies make development and design of geothermal facilities more feasible from an economic and engineering standpoint, the use of this energy source as an alternative to conventional fuels is expected to increase.

No studies have attempted to place a value on geothermal energy externalities. Some authors believe that geothermal systems in New York State should have minimum environmental impact if designed properly.[234] This chapter provides a brief outline of the potential environmental impacts of geothermal systems. The adverse environmental impacts include air pollution emissions, water use, structural impacts on land, and noise pollution problems. In addition, some abatement measures are discussed which may help to ameliorate geothermal impacts, and therefore internalize externalites as part of control costs.

a. Overview of Geothermal Energy Generation

Useful geothermal energy is derived from the ascension of heat produced by the decay of radioactive elements in the Earth's interior. At the present time, only the geothermal heat within the first 15km of the Earth's crust is accessible.[235] Geothermal resources are divided into three categories: hydrothermal, geopressured, and hot dry

---

[231] Id. at p. 4-3.

[232] Id. at pp. 3-8 to 3-10.

[233] Id. at p. 3-12.

[234] Id.

[235] Organization for Economic Co-Operation and Development, Environmental Impacts of Renewable Energy, OECD, 1988, ISBN 92-64-13151-5p. 60 [hereafter cited as Impacts, OECD].

rock. At present hydrothermal resources, underground reserves of steam and/or water with a significant geothermal gradient,[236] are the most commonly exploited type.[237]

In 1984, non-electric uses of geothermal energy in sixteen countries totalled over 6,000 mW(th), while the generating capacity of electric power plants was about 3,825 mW(e).[238] Currently about half the geothermal energy in the U.S. is in the high-temperature range of 200°C.[239]

Geothermal energy potential is usually associated with the dynamic tectonic processes of the U.S. Pacific Coast, and not with the relatively quiet Atlantic Coast. But geothermal heat may be harnessed successfully and economically for use in industrial and agricultural processes, or for heating buildings, whenever saturated porous sedimentary strata overlie geothermal gradients that exceed 20°C/km. This generally occurs at a depth of about 2.0 km. Studies conducted in New York State reveal a potential for geothermal energy to be exploited economically.[240]

The New York State Energy Research and Development Authority (NYSERDA) has studied the potential for geothermal energy development in New York State in at least two studies. The first was an examination of the geological and geophysical data of the Appalachian Basin region of western New York.[241]

In the geologic region between Saratoga Springs and Schenectady, temperature gradient measurements were used to evaluate geothermal potential.[242] Here the gradients appear to be higher than in any other area described in the Northeast, due primarily to one of the largest discovered negative anomalies in the eastern United

---

[236] Id.

[237] Id.

[238] Id. These countries are the United States, Philippines, Italy, Mexico, Japan, New Zealand El Salvador, Iceland, Nicaragua, Indonesia, Kenya, Soviet Union, China, Portugal (Azores), Turkey, and France (Guadeloupe).

[239] Id. at 63.

[240] New York State Energy Research and Development Authority, Geothermal Energy Potential in the Appalachian Basin of New York State, prepared by TAL Research and Development, New York, June, 1981, ERDA Report 81-14 306/ET-AES/81 pp. 1,5.

[241] New York State Energy Research and Development Authority, Geothermal Energy Potential in the Appalachian Basin of New York State, prepared by TAL Research and Development, New York, June, 1981, ERDA Report 81-14 306/ET-AES/81. Analogous examples of the type of geothermal energy potential that exists in New York State include an operation in the French Paris Basin. Here 70°C water is pumped from a depth of around 3000m, providing 75% of the heating load of a 10,000 unit apartment complex. And in Szeged, Hungary and in the USSR, geothermally heated sedimentary formation water is being used for space heating, green houses and agricultural processing. See Tikanov, A. and I. Dvorov, Development of Research and Utilization of Geothermal Resources in the USSR, Proc. of U.N. Symposium, Development and Utilization of Geothermal Resources, Geothermics, Special Issue 2, v. 2, 1970, pp. 1072-1078.

[242] New York State Energy Research and Development Authority, Exploration for Geothermal Resources in the Capital District of New York, prepared by Dunn Geoscience Corporation, Latham, New York, ERDA Report 81-11 221/ET-RER/80, November, 1981, p. 5-1.

States, a gravity trough which runs along the east side of the exploration area along Route 22.[243]

b. Environmental Impacts of Geothermal Energy Generation

The environmental impacts of geothermal energy generally entail airborne emissions, solid wastes, brine disposal, chemical or thermal pollution of surface and ground waters, noise, induced seismicity, and subsidence.[244] Many of these environmental impacts vary with the type of geothermal resource and the nature of the site.[245]

Subsurface geothermal fluids contain complex mixtures of dissolved gases and solids.[246] As these fluids are withdrawn from a reservoir and processed to produce electricity, the various gases volatize and are released in the atmosphere. Major gases produced are usually carbon dioxide, methane, hydrogen sulphide, ammonia, nitrogen, and hydrogen.[247] Minor concentrations of benzene, mercury, radon, and boron may also occur, depending on the type of well and the length of time that fluids have been withdrawn from the well.[248]

The greatest volume percentage of the gases emitted from most geothermal systems belongs to carbon dioxide. While the levels of CO_2 released thus far by geothermal energy is far below that emitted by fossil fuel plants, this could become significant if geothermal energy use becomes widespread.[249]

Hydrogen sulfide, a toxic gas, is a commonly emitted gas in geothermal systems. It can cause eye damage at 50 parts per million volume (ppmv) concentrations, and death at concentrations above 1,000ppmv; it also possesses a foul odor, which can be detected at levels as low as 0.002ppmv.[250] Hydrogen sulfide can be found at over half of geothermal resource areas, with concentrations in the U.S. ranging from 0.18ppmv 60.7 ppmv.[251]

---

[243] Id.

[244] Impacts, OECD, supra note 235 at p. 65.

[245] Id.

[246] Id. at p. 66.

[247] Id.

[248] Id. at p. 66.

[249] Id. at p. 69.

[250] Organization for Economic Co-Operation and Development, Environmental Impacts of Renewable Energy, OECD, 1988, ISBN 92-64-13151-5p. 66.

[251] Id.

Other gases emitted from geothermal systems include benzene, with concentrations measured in California averaging 62 ppmv,[252] mercury, with concentrations ranging from 0.002 to 0.006 ppmv, radon, ammonia, and boron.[253] The three latter emissions are not considered to be a serious environmental threat at the present time.[254]

Other non-emission impacts caused by geothermal systems have been considered but not examined in great detail. At the present time, these effects do not appear to impose substantial environmental external costs, and most of the effects can be mitigated through appropriate control designs. Perhaps the greatest hindrance to geothermal development is the problem of noise pollution. This is caused primarily by steam venting.[255] Noise levels may be controlled by the use of mufflers, although this method is costly.[256] Also to be taken into account is the fact that the primary reason for keeping the vents open is to allow rock particles to discharge themselves from the upwelling fluid or steam, and the use of mufflers tends to hinder the removal of the particles.[257]

In addition, there is a concern that removal and subsequent re-injection of crustal fluids could cause land subsidence, or more significantly, increased seismicity.[258] Land subsidence, however, is expected to be sufficiently regional that damage to land or property will not occur.[259] As far as increased seismicity, it is unknown at the present time whether there is cause for alarm, however field test have shown the injection pressures used in geothermal systems are usually far below those needed to induce seismicity.[260]

The impact of water use and the problem of wastewaters is significant. At this time such issues can only be identified, and not adequately quantified or evaluated in terms of external costs.

In conclusion, geothermal processes possess numerous environmental impacts. However, due to the relatively new development of geothermal energy as an utility resource, literature addressing the environmental costs are scarce.

---

[252] Id. at p. 68, Table 2.16.

[253] Id. at pp. 68, 69.

[254] Id.

[255] Id. at p. 71.

[256] Id.

[257] Id.

[258] Id. at p. 70.

[259] Id.

[260] Id. at p. 70.

7. Conclusion

The literature reviewed in this Chapter provides insight into the types of environmental impacts that can reasonably be expected to result from the use of renewable energy technologies. In many cases, however, there is little information on the value of the externalities. For instance, though costing methodologies exist for hydropower effects, no generally applicable cost information has been developed. For other renewables, the literature contains some limited efforts at valuation of externalities.

Many of the renewable technologies, such as wind and solar, are rapidly developing. This complicates valuation efforts since the materials used and the overall scope of these technologies may undergo change. Nevertheless, the information currently available does provide a basis for comparing the relative environmental costs of renewable energy technologies with those of conventional electric power options.

8. References for the Land Use and Water Use Charts

Bonneville Power Administration (BPA), Estimating Environmental Costs and Benefits for Five Generating Resources, Final Report, Prepared by ECO Northwest Ltd. et al., Portland, OR, March, 1986 [cited as BPA/ECO Five Resources].

U.S. Department of Energy (DOE), Office of Environmental Analysis, Office of Environmental Protection, Safety and Emergency Preparedness. Energy Technology Characterizations Handbook: Environmental Pollution and Control Factors, 3d ed. DOE/EP-0093, Washington, DC, March, 1983 [cited as DOE Characterizations Handbook].

U.S. Department of Energy (DOE), Energy System Emissions and Materiel Requirements, prepared by Meridian Corporation, Alexandria, VA, 1989 [cited as DOE/Materiel].

VI. EXTERNALITY COST BY RESOURCE

F. WASTE-TO-ENERGY FACILITIES

VI. EXTERNALITY COSTS BY RESOURCE

F. WASTE-TO-ENERGY FACILITIES

1. Introduction and Summary

This section summarizes the literature reviewed on the environmental externality costs associated with "waste-to-energy" facilities. The term "waste-to-energy" refers to incinerators which burn ordinary household, commercial and municipal waste in order to process refuse and to produce electricity and/or steam.[1]

In New York State and nationally, electrical production from incinerators is growing.[2] The draft New York State Energy Plan predicts that electric generating capacity at waste-to-energy plants will grow from about 200 megawatts in 1989, to about 341 megawatts by 2008.[3] Nationally, the number of waste incineration plants, most of which will generate electricity, is expected to grow from 111 plants in 1987 to 300 plants by the year 2000.[4]

Waste-to-energy plants are financed through revenues received from municipalities or haulers for disposing of garbage ("tipping fees"), and by sale of electric power. Sale of electric energy is usually a major part of the revenues received by waste-to-energy

---

[1] Some studies place waste-to-energy incinerators in a category of renewable energy resources. See, Public Citizen, The Power of the States: A 50 State Survey of Renewable Energy, Critical Mass Energy Project, Washington DC, June, 1990. The renewable label is probably inappropriate for waste-to-energy technology. A substantial portion of the waste stream and BTU content for incinerators is derived from fossil-fuel. Plastics constitute 12-13% of the volume of municipal solid waste. Office of Technology Assessment, Facing America's Trash, What Next For Municipal Solid Waste?, OTA-O-424, (Washington, D.C.; U.S. Government Printing Office, October, 1989), Page 242, [hereafter cited as "OTA Report"]. Incinerators also use natural gas as an auxiliary fuel at start up, shut down and at times when combustion chamber temperatures fall below specific levels. Additionally, municipal solid waste is not "renewable" in the same manner as hydroelectric, solar, wind and biomass power, as there is substantial energy and materials waste in consumer packaging. For these reasons, we have chosen to discuss waste-to-energy plants as a separate category of energy resources.

[2] As of 1987, New York State had the largest number of garbage incinerators of all states, with Florida having the largest amount of incinerator capacity, as measured in tons of refuse processed per day. U.S.E.P.A., Municipal Waste Combustion Study, Report to Congress, prepared by EPA Office of Solid Waste and Emergency Response, Office of Air and Radiation, and Office of Research & Development, EPA/530-SW-87-021a, June, 1987, p. 20 [hereafter cited as "EPA Report to Congress"]; U.S. Conference of Mayors & National Resource Recovery Assn., 1989 City Currents, Washington D.C.

[3] Draft New York State Energy Plan, Volume V, Issue 4: Solid Waste/Energy, May, 1989, p. 6, [hereafter cited as "Draft NYS Energy Plan"]. Although labelled "draft", these documents "form the basis for the recommendations and are part of the plan." Overview, Final New York State Energy Plan, (September, 1989), p. 1. The Final Plan did not include the extended discussion of waste-to-energy plants. In effect, the Volume V discussion of solid waste is a final document.

[4] EPA Report to Congress, supra note 2 at pp. 20-25. For data on the number of plants that will generate electricity, see note 12 infra.

plants. Each ton of municipal refuse, when burned in a plant equipped with steam generators, can produce approximately 500 kWh of electrical energy.[5]

In most cases, therefore, the motivation and financial ability to build a waste-to-energy plant (as opposed to other solid waste management options such as landfills or recycling facilities) is based upon a mixture of solid waste disposal and electric power functions. The text below describes several methods of allocating the costs of waste-to-energy plant externalities between electric power and solid waste functions.

Waste-to-energy plants emit a wide variety of conventional and toxic pollutants. As shown in the tables below, toxic emissions include dioxins, furans, cadmium, lead, chromium, mercury, arsenic, and nickel, as well as the conventional pollutants, sulfur oxides SO_x, hydrogen chloride (HCL), nitrogen oxides (NO_x), hydrogen fluoride, particulate matter, carbon monoxide and carbon dioxide.

In fact, state-of-the-art waste-to-energy plants emit SO_x, NO_x, HCL, lead, cadmium, copper, arsenic and mercury at higher rates per kWh generated than do well controlled coal-fired plants. Waste-to-energy plants and new coal-fired plants emit similar amounts of chromium per kWh generated. Of the metal emissions, only nickel is emitted in smaller amounts per kWh in waste-to-energy plants.

Waste-to-energy plant emissions also cause material damages. Acid gas emissions, particularly HCL, are corrosive to a wide range of metal, paint, stone, and other materials used in consumer products and structures. These damage effects vary widely depending upon stringency of acid gas control and proximity to valuable structures.[6]

Incinerators have both positive and negative effects on land use and ground and surface water quality. Waste-to-energy plants produce ash which is 30% of the original volume of municipal solid waste. This volume reduction reduces land devoted to fill and possibly lowers landfill methane emissions. Incinerator ash residue, however, must be disposed of in landfills and is high in soluble toxics. Indeed, incinerator ash is higher in toxic metals than ash from coal combustion. Incinerator ash disposal practices vary widely and determine whether the overall threat of ground and surface water contamination is increased or reduced as a result of incineration of solid waste. At present, it is reasonable to conclude that there are environmental effects of incinerator ash which are not internalized in the costs of current disposal practices. We have not, however, discovered a valuation of these impacts.

Like any steam-driven electric generation plant, a garbage incinerator requires a significant amount of cooling water. Although no figures on this usage were obtained, it is likely that waste-to-energy plants would utilize roughly the same amount of water per unit of power generated as a coal-fired power plant. The impacts on aquatic environments, in terms of thermal pollution and fish impaction, would depend upon the size of the receiving water body and the cumulative stresses from other steam generating plants. For a fuller discussion of these effects, see Chapter V.F.

---

[5] Draft NYS Energy Plan, supra note 3 at p. 6.

[6] OTA Report, supra note 1 at p. 242.

Valuation of incineration externalities and the treatment of those values in bidding programs may affect whether waste-to-energy plants can compete successfully with other supply options for new capacity. The Public Utility Regulatory Policies Act (PURPA)[7] provides a limited guarantee that incinerator operators, along with other independent power producers, may sell electricity to local utilities at the utilities' avoided cost (the price utilities would bear to generate an equivalent amount of electricity themselves).[8] A recent order of the New York State Public Service Commission determined, however, that waste-to-energy plants are subject to new capacity bidding procedures.[9] Failure to prevail in bidding may greatly reduce the revenues a plant may earn from utilities under PURPA. A reduction in electric sales revenue would require a corresponding increase in garbage tipping fees, potentially affecting the economic viability of some plants.[10]

Only one study assigns a value to the externalities of waste-to-energy plants. The "expected" cost, considering health effects, visibility and materials damages, was 11.14 cents per kilowatt hour. The study assigns approximately six cents of this figure to the power production function of the plant. Another approach to valuing the externalities is suggested by the fact that air pollution emissions and toxics in ash for incinerators are equal to or greater, on a per kilowatt hour basis, for waste-to-energy plants than for coal-fired plants.

Development of a complete externality value for incinerators is a matter of some importance given the projected growth in the incinerator industry, the developing nature of state bidding processes, and the operators' need for greater certainty regarding electric sales revenue. Further research is needed in several areas including valuation of human health affects of toxic emissions, and the effect of incinerators on lowering landfill methane emissions.

---

[7] 16 U.S.C. § 824a-3, (Supp. 1988); 18 C.F.R. § 292.303(a)(1987).

[8] New York has required utilities to purchase power from independent power producers at a higher rate than that required by PURPA. N.Y. Public Service Law § 66-C. The law was recently upheld. See, In The Matter of Long Lake Energy Corporation v. Public Service Commission of the State of New York, 148 A.D. 84, 543 N.Y.S. 755 (N.Y. App. Div. June 29, 1989), motion for leave to appeal denied Dec. 14, 1989. FERC, however, has issued a ruling prohibiting states from imposing rates that exceed avoided costs in wholesale purchases in interstate commerce. Orange and Rockland Utilities, Inc. et al, 43 F.E.R.C. P61,067 docket # EL87-53-000 (April 14, 1988).

[9] N.Y. Public Service Commission (NYPSC) Case No. 88-E-246, Opinion No. 89-30, Opinion & Order Establishing Bidding Guidelines, (Sept. 13, 1989); NYPSC Case No. 29409, Opinion No. 88-15, Order Concerning Bidding, Avoided Cost Pricing and Wheeling Issues (June, 1988). See also, NYPSC Case No. 29409, Opinion and Order No. 88-15(A), November 2, 1988, pp. 23, 30-32.

[10] See, Federal Energy Regulatory Commission, Notice of Proposed Rulemaking, Docket No. RM88-5-000, March 16, 1988.

2. Allocation of Environmental Externality costs of Waste-to-Energy Plants

Waste-to-energy plants are usually constructed to serve dual purposes: to process garbage and to sell electricity or steam. For this reason, the environmental externalities of garbage incinerators may not be solely attributable to the plant's electricity production.[11] There are several ways to allocate environmental costs between a plant's solid waste function and its electric power production. One way is to estimate the cost of environmental externalities of a waste-to-energy plant, subtract from that figure the cost that would otherwise be incurred in landfilling solid waste, and assign the entire difference to the electricity production from the plant in levelized mills per kilowatt hour. This was the approach taken in 1986 in a final report prepared by the Bonneville Power Administration.[12]

A variation on this method would be to calculate the environmental externalities of land filling refuse and to use that figure as an avoided environmental cost, representing the solid waste share of total incinerator externality costs. This figure could be subtracted from total incinerator externality costs. The remainder would represent the environmental externality of electrical production from waste-to-energy plants. Such an inquiry would need to look at groundwater impacts, land use, odor, methane emissions, and other landfill effects.

An important factor to be considered is whether incinerators reduce landfill methane emissions. If so, the value of the avoided methane (a potent global warming agent) might be used as an offset to incinerator externalities. We have not found any studies which estimate the effect of incinerators on landfill methane emissions, nor a social value for methane emissions and other avoided landfill effects.

Another approach assigns none of the environmental externality costs of waste-to-energy plants to electricity production. This approach assumes that the sole purpose of the plant is to avoid placing garbage in a landfill and that the electrical production is incidental.[13] It is unusual, however, for solid waste disposal to be the only purpose

---

[11] For a fuller discussion of allocation issues, see Chapter III of this report.

[12] Bonneville Power Administration, Estimating Environmental Costs and Benefits for Five Generating Resources, Final Report: Description of Their Likely Significant Environmental Effects, and the Economic Value of Those Effects, by ECO Northwest, Ltd., Shapiro and Associates, Inc., and Seton, Johnson and Odell, Inc., March, 1986 [hereafter cited as BPA/ECO Five Resources]. The authors state that a further allocation must be made where a plant provides both waste heat for factory processes and electrical generation. ESRG has developed a formula for allocating emissions impacts between electric and steam production from cogeneration plants. Its method offsets emission effects by the amount of fossil fuel use displaced by utilization of cogenerator waste heat. ESRG, The Role of Hydro-Quebec Power in a Least-Cost Energy Resource Plan for Vermont, prepared for Department of Public Service, State of Vermont, January 19, 1990 at p. 9-28 to 9-30.

The need to allocate between steam and electric production, however, is diminishing for waste-to-energy plants. Most municipal waste incinerators being built today are constructed solely to generate electricity. In 1986 almost two-thirds of planned resource recovery facilities (63.9%) were designed to produce only electricity, while 29.2% were designed to produce both electricity and steam. Government Advisory Associates, 1986-1987Resource Recovery Yearbook, Directory and Guide, New York, NY, 1986, p. 36 [hereafter Resource Recovery Yearbook). See also, Draft NYS Energy Plan, Vol. 5, Issue 4, supra note 3 at p.8.

[13] See, supra., Chapter III of this report.

or consideration in building an incinerator. Most communities have the option of either building a landfill or constructing a waste-to-energy plant to handle municipal refuse which cannot be disposed of through recycling. Nationally, the average tipping fee at waste-to-energy plants is approximately $39 per ton, while fees to dispose of waste in a state-of-the-art landfill are approximately $35 per ton.[14]

The importance of electric sales to incinerator revenues is also demonstrated by the size of typical electric sales. In 1986 the average electric power rating of waste-to-energy facilities in the U.S. was 25.537 megawatts.[15] This is roughly the amount of power produced by a 1000 ton per day mass burn facility. Assuming that the 1000 ton per day plant operates at 76% capacity, it would sell over 138 million kWh a year[16] and achieve annual electric sales revenue of $8,322,000(at $.06 per kilowatt hour).[17] By comparison, annual revenues from tipping fees would be $10,818,600(at $39 per ton).[18] This is confirmed by the draft New York State Energy Plan which states that electric sales revenue for waste-to-energy plants are only "slightly lower" than revenues they receive from garbage tipping fees.[19] In some areas, where garbage tipping fees are artificially low, electric sales can be as high as 70% of plant revenues.[20]

Table 1 provides data for selected waste-to-energy plants showing the typical range of electric power generating capacity for different sized plants.[21]

---

[14] Draft NYS Energy Plan, supra note 3, at p. 8.

[15] Resource Recovery Yearbook, supra note 12, at 40.

[16] For comparison, Bonneville Power Authority's study determined that the expected annual electric power output of a 500 ton per day, 10 MW incineration plant would be 65,700,000kWh. BPA/ECO Five Resources, supra. note 12, at xiv, 2-13, 4-4.

[17] The 76% capacity factor was provided by Dr. Maarten de Kadt, Inform, New York, N.Y., personal communication February 7, 1990. The calculation in the text assumes a power production rate of 500 kilowatt hours per ton of refuse. The figure would be higher for refuse derived fuel (RDF) plants whose fuel (solid waste that is processed to remove some non-combustibles) will have a higher BTU value per ton.

[18] The average tipping fees charged by mass burning plants in the U.S. was $26.64per ton. Resource Recovery Yearbook, supra note 12, at p. 96. We used the more conservative figure, $39 per ton, since that is the tipping fee charged at a recently constructed landfill in New York. See, Draft NYS Energy Plan, supra note 3, Vol. V, May, 1989.

[19] Draft NYS Energy Plan, supra note 3 at p. 8.

[20] Personal communication from Dr. Allen Herskowitz, Natural Resource Defense Counsel, February 1, 1990.

[21] List provided by Dr. Maarten de Kadt, Inform, Inc., New York, NY, personal communication, February 7, 1990.

TABLE 1

ELECTRIC POWER FROM MUNICIPAL WASTE

Plant Location	Tons/Day	Rated Electric Power Capacity (MW)
Westchester, NY	2,250	60
Baltimore, MD	2,250	60
Tampa, FL	1,000	22.5
Bitterford, SC	607 (RDF)	22.5
Marion Co, OR	550	13.3
Commerce, CA	300	11.44
Oswego, NY'	200	4.0

Electric sales revenues help keep tipping fees down, so that incinerators may compete with landfills as a cost effective solid waste option. The electricity sales, therefore, often provide the additional revenues needed to make incinerators an economically viable waste disposal choice.

In some areas, however, landfills may be prohibited (either by local geologic/groundwater conditions, or by lack of land). On Long Island, for example, the $100 per ton cost of trucking waste to remote out of state landfills is probably the primary justification for constructing a waste-to-energy plant.

Variable local landfill tipping fees, and electric sales rates make it difficult to reach a general conclusion regarding energy sales as a motivating factor in incinerator construction. One solution is to allocate externality costs on the basis of the ratio of electric sales to total plant revenue. If electric sales are expected to produce half of the revenues, then one might reasonably assume that half of the motivation for building the plant is to receive electric sales revenue. In areas where landfill shortages have escalated tipping fees, a proportionately smaller percentage of the social costs could be assigned to the electricity production from the plant.

3. Incinerator Ash

Ash from waste-to-energy plants consists of fly ash trapped by air pollution control equipment, along with combustion products and non-combustible residues left behind in the combustion chamber ("bottom ash"). Both fly ash and bottom ash contain hazardous substances. Exposure to these toxics in incinerator ash may occur through contamination of groundwater, exposure of workers to ash in waste-to-energy plants or at landfills, and exposure of the public in general windblown ash dust (particularly during transportation of ash from incinerator to landfill). When ash is disposed of in municipal solid waste landfills, the mildly acidic conditions in the fill promote movement of cadmium and lead into groundwater. These metals may be leached at rates which are sufficiently high to classify the ash as hazardous waste.[22]

---

[22] Ujihara A. and M. Gough, Managing Ash From Municipal Waste Incinerators, A Report, Resources for the Future, Center for Risk Management, Washington, DC; November 1989, [hereafter cited as Managing Ash]. The report notes three studies which conclude that worker and public exposure risks are low. It also points out that EP toxicity tests for ash have poor reducibility and may not adequately mimic the actual conditions within different types of landfills (i.e. co-disposal facilities that take (continued...)

The concentration of toxic metals in incinerator ash is much greater than in unburned garbage.[23] Some toxic organic chemicals, including dioxins and furans, are formed in the combustion process and become concentrated in ash residues. Heavy metal concentrations and leachability characteristics of incinerator ash are generally much higher than for ash generated by coal-fired power plants, This is particularly true for incinerator fly ash.[24]

An unresolved question is whether groundwater is more at risk of contamination by leachate from unburned solid waste or from incinerator ash. This, of course, depends largely on the type of landfill used for each. A full accounting of the externalities of electricity generation from an individual incinerator would require an assessment of whether the incinerator is having the effect of diverting solid waste away from preexisting, poorly designed landfills and directing incinerator ash to state-of-the-art landfills (with proper liners and groundwater monitoring safeguards). In such a case the overall effects on groundwater quality may be positive. In many cases, however, incinerator ash is disposed of in the same inadequately controlled landfill space that would have held the less toxic unburned solid waste.[25]

There is a great deal of confusion regarding legal requirements for disposal of incinerator ash.[26] Clarifying legislation is being considered in proposed amendments to both the Clean Air Act and the Resource Conservation and Recovery Act (RCRA). EPA considers ash from municipal incinerators to be exempt from hazardous waste disposal requirements unless it fails a standard EP toxicity test. But it has not enforced the requirement nor issued guidelines for disposal of ash that passes the test but contains some leachable toxic metals. This controversy is well summarized in OTA's recent report.[27]

The continuing confusion over waste-to-energy ash disposal requirements and the hodgepodge of current disposal practices make it impossible to generalize about the

---

[22](...continued)
both ash and solid waste vs. monofills restricted to ash only).

[23] Managing Ash, supra note 22 at p. 8.

[24] Bridle, T., et al., "Evaluation of Heavy Metal Leachability from Solid Wastes," Wat. Sci. Tech., Vol. 19 R, 10, pp. 1029-1036, 1987. The study was conducted by members of the Environment Canada, Environmental Protection Service, Wastewater Technology Center, Burlington, Ontario.

[25] See, U.S. Environmental Protection Agency, Characterization of Municipal Waste Combustor Ashes and Leachates From Municipal Solid Waste Landfills, Monofills, and Codisposal Sites, prepared by NUS Corp, for Office of Solid Waste and Emergency Response, EPA/530-SW-87-028A, Washington, D.C., October, 1987.

[26] See generally, Managing Ash, supra note 22. ("Federal laws and regulations that mandate how ash is to be managed are unclear and tests for determining whether it is a hazardous waste produce ambiguous results. This situation has served both to preserve use of incinerators and to delay federal action to improve ash management").

[27] OTA Report, supra note 1 at pp. 37-39, 258-259.

externalities of incinerator ash. No one has attempted to value the health or environmental risks associated with incinerator ash. Moreover, no single value would apply in all circumstances, since some disposal techniques are much less risky than others. For now, therefore, no externality value can be assigned.

4. Air Pollution Emissions: Estimates of Environmental Externality Costs

Two studies were found relevant to assigning social costs to electricity produced by waste-to-energy plants. The 1986 Bonneville Power Authority[28] study estimated human health, visibility and materials damages costs of a generic waste-to-energy plant. The generic plant characteristics were a 10 megawatt generating capacity expected to burn 500 tons per day of refuse. Emissions characteristics are shown in Table 2.

---

[28] See BPA/ECO Five Resources, supra note 12.

TABLE 2

EMISSIONS CHARACTERISTICS OF SOLID WASTE GENERIC FACILITY

	Emissions (Tons/Yr)	Tons/MWh	Increase in Morta/Morb Annual Linear dose-response
Particulates	61	9.8×10^{-4}	0.04
SO_2	220	33.5×10^{-4}	1.5
NO_2	290	44.1×10^{-4}	0
VOCs	9.6	1.46×10^{-4}	?
CO	168	25.6×10^{-4}	3.8
HCI	69	10.5×10^{-4}	0.055
H^2SO_4	5.6	0.85×10^{-4}	0.23
Lead	1.6	0.24×10^{-4}	?
Mercury	0.53	0.08×10^{-4}	0.00075
Flouride	4.8	0.73×10^{-4}	0
Dioxin	5.1×10^{-6}	0.76×10^{-10}	0.062
POM	1.8×10^{-3}	0.27×10^{-7}	0.008
Beryllium	8.8×10^{-6}	1.34×10^{-10}	0
PCB	0.01	1.52×10^{-7}	3×10^{-5}

Source: BPA/ECO, Five Resources, Technical Appendices, Appendix C, Table C1-1. Tons/mWh calculated based on average annual output of 65,700,000kWh. See BPA/ECO, Five Resources, Final Report at p. 4-4. The generic plant is equipped with scrubbers and particulate controls. Increases in morbidity/mortality are from Appendix C, Table C1-5, at C1-55 of the BPA/ECO Report.

The estimated externality costs vary from a high cost assessment of 484.199 mills per kilowatt hour to a low cost assessment of 1.854. The low cost assessment was based on an assumption that existing air pollution standards completely protect human health, a conclusion which the BPA authors considered unlikely.[29] The high cost estimate is based on a linear dose response curve with no safe threshold for exposure. The "expected" cost, 111.453 mills per kilowatt hour, was based on dose response data at projected ambient concentrations. The report notes that if larger populations are

[29] BPA/ECO Five Resources, supra note 11 at p. 4-4.

exposed to incineration emissions (BPA assumed that 75,000 persons would be exposed) then air pollution health costs would be larger.[30]

Each of these figures was then reduced by the waste reduction benefit (calculated as savings from avoidance of landfill operating costs). The report does not appear to take into account any environmental effects associated with disposal of incinerator ash. The resulting damage cost figures from the BPA study are set forth in Table 3.

TABLE 3

LEVELIZED COSTS AND BENEFITS FOR SOLID WASTE GENERIC FACILITY
(mills/kWh)

TYPE OF EFFECT	LOW	EXPECTED	HIGH
Health	.000	103.482	466.664
Visibility	1.545	6.951	15.447
Materials	.309	1.020	2.008
TOTAL COST	1.854	111.453	484.119
Waste Reduction Benefit	- 33.653	- 50.976	- 67.582
STUDY TOTAL	- 31.800	60.477	416.567

Source: BPA/ECO, Five Resources - Final Report, Table 4 - 2 at p. 4 - 6.

Emissions and control assumptions for the BPA study were based on the characteristics of a plant being constructed in 1986 at Marion County, Oregon. After the BPA study was released, EPA issued new source permitting guidelines under the federal Clean Air Act.[31] The Marion County, Oregon plant was to be equipped with scrubbers and particulate control as required by the Guidelines, but may not have included the full range of "combustion controls" that are now required to further reduce emissions of dioxin, metals, carbon monoxide, and other pollutants.

Additionally, EPA has recently proposed new source performance standards for waste-to-energy plants.[32] A court order requires these regulations to be finalized by December 31, 1990, and they will apply to any incinerator on which construction is

---

[30] BPA/ECO Five Resources, supra note 11 at Appendix C1-55, C1-63.

[31] U.S. EPA, Office of Air Quality Planning and Standards. Operational Guidance to State and Local Agencies for Best Available Control Technology Determination for Permitting New and Modified Municipal Waste Combustors, June, 1987.

[32] 54 Federal Register 52251 (December 20, 1989), Standards of Performance for New Stationary Sources; Municipal Waste Combustors. EPA also proposed standards for existing incinerators, which will require retrofit of a variety of emission controls by the mid-1990s.

begun after the date of the proposed rulemaking notice.[33] These regulations may or may not achieve a further tightening of standards relative to the guidelines or control assumptions for the generic plant in the BPA study.

The impacts assessed by the BPA analysis were based on a 500 ton per day plant. This may underestimate the impacts for larger plants. Some plants currently under construction or in planning are designed to burn in excess of 2000 tons of refuse per day.[34]

The projected emissions for the proposed 3000 ton per day Brooklyn Navy Yard Plant are set forth in Table 4. To arrive at a pound per kilowatt hour emission estimate, we have divided the Brooklyn plant emission numbers by three to estimate the emissions for a generic 1000 ton per day plant, and further divided them by a typical annual kilowatt hour production of a 1000 ton per day plant (138 millon kilowatt hours, see footnote 16 supra). Table 5 sets forth the pounds per kilowatt figures for metal emissions.

A comparison of the figures in Table 5 with the data on metals emissions from coal-fired plants show that even well controlled waste-to energy plants emit led, cadmium, copper, arsenic, and mercury at levels which far exceed those of coal-fired plants, when measured in lbs/kWh. THe level of chromium emissions for waste-to-energy incinerators appeared to fall within the range given for coal-fired plants. THe level of nickel emissions for incinerators appeared to be somewhat lower then that for coal-fired plants. The level of zinc emissions for coal-fired plants are not available from the sources we reviewed. Compare Table 6 Chapter IV, column 4 with Table 5 of this chapter infra.[35]

---

[33] Id.

[34] The Hempstead, Westchester County, and Niagara Falls plants in New York State are each designed to incinerate in excess of 2200 tons per day. These were operating in 1989. The proposed Brooklyn Navy Yard plant is projected to handle 3000 tons per day by 1993. A Staten Island plant (3000 tons per day) and a Bronx plant (2000 tons per day) are being planned for construction in 1997. Draft NYS Energy Plan, Vol. V, Issue 4, supra note 3 at p. 7.

[35] Annual emissions of selected metals from a 500 megawatt coal-fired plant as reported by DOE are as follows:

Arsenic	.1125 tons
Beryllium	.0046 tons
Cadmium	.0020 tons
Lead	.0570 tons

U.S. Department of Energy (DOE), Office of Environmental Protection, Safety, and Emergency Preparedness, Office of Environmental Analysis, Energy Technology Characterizations Handbook: Environmental Pollution and Control Factors, 3d ed., prepared with assistance from Aerospace Corporation and Mueller Associates, Inc., DOE/EP-009, Washington, DC, March, 1983, p. 92.

TABLE 4

EMISSIONS OF TOXICS FROM BROOKLYN PLANT

POLLUTANT	EMISSION RATE (Tons/Year)	EMISSION RATE (gm/sec)
Lead (Pb)	14.5	4.17×10^{-1}
Cadmium (Cd)	.49	1.40×10^{-2}
Chromium (Cr)	.24	6.85×10^{-3}
Copper (Cu)	.43	1.23×10^{-2}
Nickel (Ni)	.17	4.82×10^{-3}
Zinc (Zn)	27.9	8.02×10^{-1}
Arsenic (As)	6.30×10^{-2}	1.81×10^{-3}
Selenium (Se)	6.46×10^{-2}	1.86×10^{-3}
Mercury (Hg)	5.3	0.151
Beryllium (Be)	1.9×10^{-3}	5.51×10^{-5}
Flouride (FL)	93.2	2.68
Polyaromatic Hydrocarbons (PAH)	0.275	7.89×10^{-3}
Polychlorinated Biphenyl (PCB)	.178	5.13×10^{-3}
Polychlorinated Dibenzo - p - Dioxins (PCDD)	2.56×10^{-4}	7.36×10^{-5}
Polychlorinated Dibenzo - p - Furans (PCDF)	1.10×10^{-3}	3.17×10^{-5}
Tetrachlorinated Dibenzo - p - Dioxin (TCDD)	3.72×10^{-5}	1.07×10^{-5}
2378 TCDD (Isomeric Form)	2.43×10^{-6}	7.00×10^{-5}

Source: Final Environmental Impact Statement, Proposed Resource Recovery Facility at the Brooklyn Navy Yard, Technical Appendix, Vol. III, Appendix D, Air-Quality Related Issues, June 1985. Emission rates are based on 100% of the nominal capacity, continuous operations of the fabric filter at a 0.015 gr/dscf at 12% CO_2 particulate emission.

TABLE 5

METALS EMISSIONS FROM INCINERATORS - POUNDS PER kWh FOR GENERIC 1000 TON PER DAY PLANT

Pollutant	Emission Rate	
	lbs/Yr[1]	lbs./kWh[2]
Lead	9666.66	70×10^{-6}
Cadmium	326.66	2.4×10^{-6}
Chromium	160.00	1.2×10^{-6}
Copper	286.66	2.1×10^{-6}
Nickel	113.33	0.8×10^{-6}
Zinc	18,600	134.8×10^{-6}
Arsenic	42	$.3 \times 10^{-6}$
Mercury	3,533	25.6×10^{-6}

(1) Extrapolated from projected emissions of 3000 ton/day Brooklyn Navy Yard Plant in Table 4. The figures are 1/3 of the data reported in the Final Environmental Impact Statement, Proposed Resource Recovery Facility at Brooklyn Navy Yard, Tech. App. Vol. III, Appendix D, Air Quality Related Issues, June, 1985.

(2) Assumes annual production of 138 millon kilowatt hours.

BPA's health risk assessment concluded that nearly 95% of the health effects were attributable to sulfur dioxide and carbon monoxide emissions.[36] This contradicts a recent health risk assessment performed for EPA which appears to assume that virtually all health impacts of incinerator emissions are caused by trace metals and dioxin/furan emissions.[37] Further research should address the relative importance of conventional versus toxic pollutants in valuing the externalities of incinerator emissions.

EPA's 1987 risk assessment addresses carcinogenic and non-carcinogenic health effects for direct inhalation of four metals and six types of organic emissions. By far the greatest amount of cancer incidence risk was attributed to chlorinated dioxin and dibenzofuran emissions. EPA's "controlled scenario" assumed emission controls of metals and organics at levels comparable to those expected to be achieved by the proposed EPA new source performance standards. EPA estimated that the range of national cancer incidence for metals and organics was .3 - 1.5 cases per year for populations living within 50 kilometers of all projected waste combustors in the U.S.

---

[36] EPA/ECO, Five Resources, Technical Appendices, supra note 12, at p. C1-54.

[37] Radian Corporation, Municipal Waste Combustion Study: Assessment of Health Risks Associated with Municipal Waste Combustion Emissions, prepared for U.S.E.P.A.(EPA/530-SW-87-02) Hemisphere Publishing Corporation, Washington, D.C. 1989), [hereafter cited as EPA/Radian Report.] See and compare pp. 2-6 to 2-13 with p. 3-33.

The maximum individual risk (probability that a person exposed to the highest modeled concentration of pollutants from a municipal waste combustor will develop cancer over a 70-year lifespan) was 10^{-5} to 10^{-6}.[38]

There are several severe limitations to the EPA cancer risk estimate. EPA did not look at non-inhalation exposure ("indirect exposure" from ingestion of contaminated soil or foods, and dermal contact). EPA prepared a preliminary analysis of indirect exposure but, at least as of 1987, determined that the results could not be interpreted quantitatively. EPA's preliminary analysis suggests that for some persistent organics (dioxins, PCB's and chlorobenzene) the "indirect exposures to emissions deposited over long periods may be comparable to exposures through direct inhalation." Exposure of children to deposited lead and mercury was identified as needing further analysis.[39]

Some observers contend that indirect exposure routes, particularly bioaccumulation in the food chain, are more important pathways to adverse health effects than inhalation.[40] OTA's report, "Facing America's Trash", discusses the stable, fat-soluble characteristics of dioxins and furans, which allow them to accumulate and concentrate in the food chain. It describes an assessment of dioxin and furans emissions in Minnesota which concluded that 90% of estimated incremental cancer risk from a proposed waste combustor is associated with ingestion of these substances in food.[41] The OTA report also briefly describes two other studies, one in Pennsylvania and the other in New York, addressing deposition of dioxin and furans in agricultural areas and the potential for contamination of milk from dairy cows.[42]

Another limitation is that EPA's study, like the BPA/ECO Five Resources study, did not address health effects of exposure to incinerator ash, either from landfill leachate, or from fugitive ash losses at the plant or in transport to land disposal.[43]

---

[38] Id. at p. 2-8.

[39] U.S.E.P.A., Response to Petition for Rulemaking and Advance Notice of Proposed Rulemaking, Assessment of Municipal Waste Combustor Emissions Under the Clean Air Act, 52 Fed Reg 25399,25404 (July 7, 1987).

[40] OTA Report, supra note 1, citing Ashlander, O., The Swedish Dioxin Memorandum, paper presented at ASCE Dioxin Symposium (NY, NY, February 10, 1987); Franke, B., Review of the Environmental Impacts of Solid Waste Incinerators Proposed for Long Island and New York City, prepared for Newsday (Tacoma Park, MD); Institute for Energy and Environmental Research, Nov., 1987; Webster, T., and P. Connett, Critical Factors in the Assessment of Food Chain Contamination by PCDD/PCDF from Incinerators, paper presented at Dioxin '87 (Las Vegas, NV: October 4-9, 1987); World Health Organization, "PCDD and PCDF Emissions from Incinerators for Municipal Sewage Sludge and Solid Waste - Evaluation of Human Exposure, report on World Health Organization meeting, Naples, Mar. 17-21, 1986 (Copenhagen: Regional Office for Europe, 1987).

[41] Minnesota Pollution Control Agency, Supplemental Health Risk assessment Technical Work Paper, Volume I: Polychlorinated Dioxins/Polychlorinated Furans, Wisconsin County Resource Recovery Facility, prepared by J.B. Stevens and Associates, April 1988.

[42] OTA Report, supra note 1, at p. 241.

[43] EPA/Radian Report, supra note 37 at pp. 1-3.

There are also great uncertainties in EPA's cancer potency and exposure estimates. The assessment does not include synergistic effects of exposure to a mixture of toxic pollutants from incinerators. EPA noted that:

> a significant portion (80% or more) of the organic stack gasses emitted from municipal waste combustion have not been identified and quantified. Although some portion of the mixture may be carcinogenic, the carcinogenic fraction, its composition and its potency, remain unknown. If the unspecified organics had a carcinogenic potency equivalent to the average potency of those compounds evaluated, even including CDD/CDF, the contribution to the annual incidence estimate could be appreciable.[44]

EPA notes that a variety of inconsistencies exist between the emissions and toxicity data (involving data availability specific to pollutant subclasses), and that this is an additional uncertainty in its cancer estimates. The exposure rates also do not reflect potentially higher ambient concentrations from emissions during startup, shutdown or upset conditions. The risk assessment was based on stack sampling, which may not fully reflect dioxin emission rates. According to EPA, "actual emission levels could be higher than reported emissions by an order of magnitude."[45]

EPA's assessment of noncarcinogenic effects was limited to a comparison of modeled ambient concentrations of mercury and lead to national air quality standards for these pollutants. EPA concluded that predicted emissions would not cause exceedances of these standards. EPA also compared predicted ambient HCL concentrations to occupational exposure limits. The results of this comparison, however, are not provided. There is no discussion in the EPA study as to whether either the federal standards or the occupational HCL limitation are adequate to protect human health.

Aside from the toxics, incinerators also emit large quantities of conventional air pollution. These discharges are similar in type to emissions from coal-fired electric power plants. Table 6 describes the annual emission tonnages projected from the planned 3000 ton per day Brooklyn Navy Yard Plant in New York City.

---

[44] EPA/Report to Congress, <u>supra</u> note 2 at p. 90.

[45] <u>Id</u>. at p. 85.

TABLE 6

EMISSIONS OF CONVENTIONAL POLLUTANTS FROM BROOKLYN PLANT

Pollutant	Tons/Year
Particulate Matter	161
Sulfur Dioxide	2972
Sulfuric Acid	230
Nitrogen Dioxide	2972
Hydrogen Chloride	5370
Carbon Monoxide	368
Hydrocarbons	65.7

Source: Final Environmental Impact Statement, Brooklyn Navy Yard, supra at Table 4.

Table 7 translates these numbers into pounds emitted per kilowatt hour. It estimates the annual kilowatt hour production of a 1000 ton per day plant (see footnote 16, supra, and accompanying text). The figures in table 6 from the 3000 ton/day Brooklyn Plant have been divided by three to approximate the emissions from a well controlled 1000 ton per day plant.

TABLE 7

CONVENTIONAL INCINERATOR EMISSIONS
(lb/kWh)

Pollutant	Pounds/kWh Hr.
Particulates	7.77×10^{-4}
Sulfur Dioxide	14.35×10^{-3}
Nitrogen Dioxide	14.35×10^{-3}
Hydrocarbons	$.31 \times 10^{-3}$

Different exponents have been chosen to allow a comparison with pound per kilowatt hour values for coal-fired plants in Table 1, Chapter IV. This comparison shows that incinerators have higher levels of sulfur and nitrogen compound emissions per kilowatt hour and lower levels of particulate and hydrocarbon emissions per kilowatt hour than coal-fired plants equipped with scrubbers. The data do not allow a direct comparison for hydrocarbon emissions.

Table 8 represents a calculation from the literature reviewed, to value the externalities of these emissions using the cost factors described elsewhere in this report.[46] In the table, the same "starting point" externality value developed for materials effects of utility plant sulfur dioxide emissions has been applied to incinerator

[46] See Table V.B.2 "Summary of Damages Due to SO_2".

SO_2 and HCL emissions, on the assumption that the materials effects of the two pollutants are similar.

TABLE 8

EXTERNALITY COSTS OF CONVENTIONAL EMISSIONS FROM WASTE-TO-ENERGY PLANTS

Pollutant	Cost Per Pound[1]	lbs/kWh[2]	Externality Cost in Cents/kWh[3]
SO_2	$2.03	.014	2.84
NO_x	.82	.002	.164
HCL	.12	.077	.924
Particulate	1.18	.00075	.089
Carbon Monoxide	-	.00085	-
Volatile Organic Hydrocarbons	-	.00015	-
CO_2	-	-	-
		TOTAL	4.019

(1) Derived from Table 2, Chapter V.B. "Sulfur Oxides", Table 1, Chapter V.C. "Nitrogen Oxides" and Table 3 Chapter V.E. "Particulates" of this report. These figures do not include acid rain effects.

(2) This figure is derived from the projected annual SO_2, HCL and NO_x emissions for the 3000 ton per day Brooklyn Navy Yard Plant. It is based on 60% capacity divided by three to estimate the emissions from a typical 1000 ton per day plant, and is then further divided by the typical annual kilowatt hour production for a 1000 megawatt plant (138 million kWh/yr.). See footnote 16, supra, and accompanying text. Kilowatt hour production figures for the Brooklyn plant were unavailable as that plant will produce exclusively steam. The Brooklyn plant emission rates were chosen because of similarity between proposed emission controls and proposed EPA new source performance standards.

(3) The externality cost for hydrogen chloride (HCL) is assumed to be the same as the materials damage cost for SO_2. We have not discovered an externality value for the HCL human health effects. See Table 2, Chapter V.B. "Sulfur Oxides" of this report.

The Brooklyn plant is generally regarded as an example of a plant having controls similar to those which will be required by EPA's new source performance standards. The Brooklyn plant is not designed to produce electricity and, therefore, potential electric power outputs are not available.

Complete emissions and cost figures are not yet available for all the pollutants emitted by waste-to-energy facilities. The calculation here is based solely on the acid gas emissions, and particulates. If half of the costs in Table 8 are attributable to the electric production (as opposed to the solid waste disposal function) of the plant, then this analysis would assign a social cost of 2.01 cents per kilowatt hour just for acid gas and particulate emissions. The cost does not include an estimate for health effects of HCL. By comparison, Bonneville Power Authority's "expected" externality cost for waste-to-energy plants (for all pollutant effects) is 6.0 cents per kilowatt, and its high figure is 41.6 cents per kilowatt. See, Table 3, supra.

These cost estimates are at incomplete. To them must be added the so far uncalculated cancer and non-cancer health effects of the ultra-toxic pollutants emitted from incinerators, including those caused by indirect exposures. The social cost of these effects is likely to be at least as great as the damages from the conventional pollutants.

5. Methane Emissions

Organic municipal and industrial wastes in landfills are estimated to contribute 3-10% of methane emissions world-wide.[47] Methane is a potent greenhouse gas.[48] It is possible that by reducing placement of solid waste in landfills, incinerators could reduce overall methane emissions. No studies were found which relate the effect of incinerators to landfill methane emissions. The following general discussion may help guide future research in this area.

Methane (CH_4) production in landfills results from anaerobic biological degradation of organic waste. Approximately three-fourths of municipal solid waste is organic.[49] Organic wastes begin the decay process by undergoing aerobic degradation, which produces carbon dioxide (CO_2). This quickly depletes the oxygen and creates the anaerobic conditions which lead to the production of methane.[50]

Estimates of methane production are highly variable. Factors affecting the rate of methane production include moisture, pH, age of the material, volume of material, concentrations of nutrients and bacteria, and presence or absence of sewage sludge.[51] There is a one to two year lag period between landfilling of wastes and the beginning

---

[47] Bingemer, H. and P. Crutzen, "The Production of Methane from Solid Waste," Journal of Geophysical Research 92:2189[hereafter cited as Bingemer]. Another estimate is that landfills in the U.S. Contribute 2-6% of Global Methane Emissions. OTA Report to Congress, supra note 1 at p. 286.

[48] Bingemer, H. and P. Crutzen, as cited at Draft Policy Options, part IV, p. 40.

[49] OTA Report, supra note 1 at p. 275.

[50] Id.

[51] Id. at p. 282.

of gas generation.[52] It can take from 10 to 100 years for a landfill to produce significant amounts of methane.[53]

One study estimated the rate of methane production to be from 1,000 to 7,000 cubic feet of methane/ton of solid waste (31-218 m^3/metric ton).[54] In 1988, the U.S. produced 1.48 million tons of municipal solid waste.[55] Using these figures, total U.S. methane emissions from landfills would eventually reach 2.9 - 20.7 Tg of methane per year (1 Tg = 1 teragram = $1x10^{12}$g). Using an alternative formula proposed by Bingemer and Crutzen (1987), the same amount of solid waste would generate 7 Tg of methane.[56] This rate assumes a carbon content of 22%, that 90% of municipal solid waste is landfilled, and a conservative methane production efficiency of 0.25 ton of methane per ton of carbon.[57]

Landfill methane emissions can, however, be beneficial. Methane can be collected from large- and medium-sized landfills to be burned in small electric power generators. One study estimates that if landfill methane emissions were collected completely and processed for energy production, they would supply 5% of all natural gas consumption, or 1% of U.S. energy demand.[58] Currently, only 123 of some 6584 municipal landfills collect methane to recover energy. Many more simply vent methane or burn it off with a flare.[59] Economic viability of landfill gas recovery is dependent on landfill size, local regulations, and proximity to energy users. For a discussion of recovery costs and landfill characteristics which lend themselves to methane recovery, see EMCOM Associates and Gas Recovery Inc., Landfill Gas, Analysis of Options, prepared for New York State Energy Office, 1981.

---

[52] U.S.E.P.A.,Office of Policy, Planning and Evaluation, Policy Options for Stabilizing Global Climate: Draft Report to Congress, February, 1989, at p. 189 [hereinafter cited as Draft Policy Options].

[53] Wilkey, M., R. Zimmerman, and H. Isaacson, Methane From Landfills: Preliminary Assessment Workbook, Argonne National Laboratory, Department of Energy, 1982, as cited in Draft Policy Options, supra note 51.

[54] Id.

[55] U.S. EPA., Report to Congress: Solid Waste Disposal in the United States, Vol. II, EPA/530-SW-88-011B, Washington, DC, October, 1988 [hereafter cited as EPA, Solid Waste Disposal].

[56] Bingemer H. and P. Crutzen, supra note 47 at Part VII p. 189.

[57] Id.

[58] OTA Report, supra note 1 at p. 283, citing U.S. EPA, Office of Solid Waste, Operating Criteria (Part C) Criteria for Municipal Solid Waste Landfills, 40 CFR Part 258, EPA/530-SW-88-037, Washington DC, July, 1988.

[59] U.S. EPA, Solid Waste Disposal, Report to Congress, supra note 54.

6. Conclusion

This preliminary analysis indicates that incinerator emissions are likely to have fairly large environmental externality costs. This information appears to conflict with the practice adopted by some state utility commissions of encouraging waste-to-energy plant construction through awards of increased rates of return, or other incentives for electricity produced. Indeed, it appears that the environmental costs of waste-to-energy plants are large enough to justify rate treatment or externality cost assignment similar to a coal plant. As noted above, incinerators emit far more heavy metal air pollution and produce greater amounts of metal contaminants in solid combustion wastes (e.g. fly ash) than do coal-fired plants (as measured in pounds lbs/kWh). Similarly, incinerators produce large amounts of acid gas pollutants including SO_2, NO_x and HCL. Incinerators also emit dioxins and furans that are absent from fossil fuel plant emissions.

Additional research, however, is needed before a complete social cost figure may be assigned for waste-to-energy plant emissions.

VI. EXTERNALITY COSTS BY RESOURCE

G. DEMAND SIDE MANAGEMENT RESOURCES

VI. EXTERNALITY COSTS BY RESOURCE

G. DEMAND SIDE MANAGEMENT RESOURCES

1. Introduction and Summary

Demand Side Management ("DSM") refers to a broad range of strategies to reduce electric power consumption in homes, offices, businesses and industry. DSM is becoming a major focus of utilities efforts to balance generation capacity with consumer demand. DSM includes measures to use electricity more efficiently and measures which shift the use of electricity away from peak hours of usage. Individually sponsored DSM budgets often exceed one hundred million dollars annually in New York, California, the New England States and Wisconsin. Other states also have growing DSM programs.

The major DSM initiatives currently being undertaken or contemplated by utilities include inducements to customers for:

* weatherization of homes and businesses

* improved lighting

* improved heating ventilation and air conditioning (HVAC Equipment)

* higher efficiency consumer appliances

* higher efficiency electric motors in industries

* efficient refrigeration

* load shifting, including thermal and cool storage

This chapter surveys information available regarding the potential adverse environmental impacts of these initiatives. These impacts are found to include: indoor air pollution, including the release of toxic materials used in insulation and other materials; increased chlorofluorocarbon (CFC) emissions due to increased demand for foam insulation manufactured with CFC blowing agents, or due to early retirement and disposal of appliances containing CFC's as working fluids; and increased air pollution emissions and other environmental effects caused by increased use of fossil-fuel-base load plants due to load shifting programs.

Overall, the literature surveyed disclosed no studies which attempted to quantify environmental externalities of DSM programs in a manner that could be translated into a cents/kilowatt-hour figure, or be used as an "adder" in regulatory decision making regarding alternative methods of meeting electrical demand. In September, 1989 the American Council for An Energy-Efficient Economy completed a report for NYSERDA on DSM potential in New York State it concluded that:

> As a suggestion for follow-up work . . .it would be useful to evaluate the environmental and social costs of electricity conservation measures as well as supply options. This information could be used to estimate the broad costs and benefits of electricity conservation in New York.[1]

In most cases, however, the literature supports a conclusion that, with the exception of some load shifting measures, there are no significant adverse environmental impacts from DSM and conservation programs, provided that simple and generally low cost mitigation measures are incorporated into these programs. The following summarizes the findings of the studies reviewed.

DSM strategies can affect indoor air pollution in several ways. Adding insulation and taking other steps to reduce heat loss from homes and businesses can reduce ventilation, thereby increasing or prolonging occupant exposure to cigarette smoke, radon, consumer solvents, nitrogen oxides from gas appliances or malfunctioning oil furnaces, toxic compounds from building materials and furnishings, biological contaminants (due to excess moisture, pets or mold) and other sources of indoor air pollution. These effects were found to be economically remediable by use of ventilation systems such as heat exchangers.

No studies were discovered which provide a basis for assigning an externality cost for the effect of weatherization programs on indoor air pollution health risks. Since effects of weatherization on indoor air quality are highly site-specific, it is difficult to accurately generalize how building "tightening" may increase occupant exposure.

The studies discussed below conclude that weatherization programs by themselves are not a primary cause of indoor air pollution problems. To the extent that weatherization may aggravate pre-existing indoor air pollution problems, the studies show that there are mitigation measures available. The literature on indoor air cautions that indoor air quality is a factor to be considered when "tightening" a home or commercial building to conserve energy, and suggests that indoor air quality and efficient energy use are compatible goals.

One way that was cited to ensure that weatherization programs do not aggravate this type of environmental externality was for state utility commissions to require utility-sponsored weatherization programs to include certain mitigation measures. Mitigation measures would include the training of weatherization employees or contractors to identify and correct indoor air pollution sources and apply a remedy as part of weatherization services. The remedy may be to remove the source, or use heat exchangers, or other ventilation methods.

A related concern is whether materials used for insulation and other efficiency measures may themselves contribute directly to indoor air pollution by emitting toxic compounds or fibers. Insulation may release toxic compounds, and new lighting materials may contain toxins which could be released into the indoor environment by breakage. Off-gassing of toxins from insulation was primarily a concern in the days when urea-formaldehyde insulation was being marketed. That product, however, is

---

[1] American Council For An Energy-Efficient Economy, The Potential For Electricity Conservation in New York State, Final Report, New York State Energy Authority Report # 89-12, September 1989, p. S-14.

virtually gone from the market. The remaining concern is whether current weatherization programs which seek the additional tightening of buildings containing urea-formaldehyde insulation, will increase exposure to formaldehyde. No literature specific to this concern was found. Nevertheless this is also a problem that can be mitigated by proper training and management of weatherization crews, or by the use of exhaust heat exchangers.

The literature supports a conclusion that the use of modern efficient lighting equipment significantly lowers the overall environmental loading of mercury, and possibly polychlorinated biphenyls (PCBs). This is due to the expectation that group relamping programs inspired by conservation efforts will generally utilize superior disposal procedures for old lighting equipment. Toxic materials (primarily mercury) are contained in some modern lighting equipment, but are found to present a hazard only in the case of accidents involving the simultaneous breakage of large lamp inventories in an unventilated area. Lighting efficiency programs are found to have minimal environmental costs, so long as they incorporate proper safety precautions to avoid accidents involving large amounts of fluorescent lamp breakage.

The question has arisen as to whether increased emissions of CFC's might result from conservation programs which encourage early replacement and disposal of inefficient consumer appliances which contain CFC's as working fluids. CFC's in these appliances might conceivably be recovered by future recycling programs if appliances remain in use through their normal lifetime. Currently there are viable CFC recycling programs for residential appliances but in only a few states. The literature does not quantify the effect of appliance efficiency programs on CFC release, but suggests that any adverse effect could be mitigated by requiring utility programs to include CFC recycling as a required program component.

Although CFC's have also been used in some types of foam insulation, current energy efficiency initiatives do not create increased demands for such materials in refrigeration or construction. The studies conclude that, while past energy conservation initiatives and DSM practices probably contributed to increased CFC usage, this is no longer the case. The Montreal Protocol and anticipated follow-up legislation and treaties are found to be forcing rapid CFC phase-out, such that the continuing impact of conservation policies on CFC use is negligible.

The remaining issue is whether CFC replacements have adverse environmental effects. The substitutes being considered for CFC use in refrigeration and insulation are compounds called HCFC's. HCFC's have ozone depletion effects, but on a scale much lower than CFC's. A general discussion of studies addressing these issues is included, but no studies which attempt to place a damage cost on the emissions of these compounds, or describe the effect of energy conservation measures on the use of these compounds were discovered.

Load shifting is the one DSM measure which can in some circumstances significantly increase emissions by increased use of fossil-fuel-fired baseload electric generating plants. These impacts are found to set load shifting apart from other DSM measures as less environmentally desirable.

2. Indoor Air Quality Effects of Weatherization

None of the literature on the subject of indoor air pollution, attempts to specifically value the effect of weatherization on indoor air quality. The following general discussion may be helpful in structuring weatherization programs to mitigate adverse effects and in directing future research efforts.

Air exchange losses in buildings are estimated to account for 11% of the total annual energy consumption in the U.S.[2] One third to one half of heat loss from residential buildings is due to air exchange between indoors and out.[3] Reducing the rate of air exchange through various weatherization methods is one of the most effective mens of reducing energy use in buildings.[4]

Indoor air quality began to surface as a public issue in the late 1970's and 1980's. This coincided with an increased public awareness of environmental and health issues, and with an increased use of synthetics in building materials and consumer goods. This was also a time of energy price increases and shortages, which led to changes in the way buildings were built and operated.[5] Generally these changes made buildings "tighter" by restricting ventilation to reduce heat losses. According to an EPRI study: "Many indoor air quality problems surface when air exchange rates are drastically lowered (in the interest of energy efficiency)."[6]

An EPA study concluded that proper ventilation for indoor air quality is frequently sacrificed for energy efficiency. "Indoor air quality can be impaired greatly if indoor air concerns are subjugated to concerns for energy consumption."[7] The EPA Report goes on to state that:

---

[2] EPRI, Manual on Indoor Air Quality, EPRI EM-3469, Project #2034-3 Prepared by Lawrence Berkeley Laboratories, Final Report, February 1984 p. 1-3 [hereafter cited as EPRI Manual].

[3] Id.

[4] Id.

[5] See, Godish, T., "Indoor Air Pollution in Offices and Other Non-Residential Buildings," Journal of Environmental Health, Vol. 48 (4), pp. 190-195.

[6] EPRI Manual, Supra note at p. 1-2.

[7] U.S.E.P.A., Report to Congress on Indoor Air Quality, EPA 400/1-89-001A, B, C, D, August 1989, p. 6-12 [hereafter cited as EPA Report to Congress]. (Issued under § 403(e), Title IV of the Superfund Amendments and Reauthorization Act of 1986 {SARA}). Other studies have documented cases in which building owners or operators have, in the interest of energy conservation, shut off outside air dampers (which provide minimal make-up air to replace that used by human respiration) in violation of building code provisions. Repace, J., "Indoor Air Pollution," Environment International, Vol. 8 pp. 21-26 (1982). See also Morey, P., "Microbiological Problems in Office Buildings: Recognition and Remedial Action," pp. 445-454, Proceedings of the Energy Technology Conference XV, Government Institutes, Inc., Washington, DC, 1988; Morey, P., Woods, J., "Indoor Air Quality In Health-Care Facilities," Occupational Medicine, July - September 1987, pp. 547-563.

> Sufficient evidence exists to conclude that indoor air quality represents a major portion of the public's exposure to air pollution and may pose serious acute and chronic health risks.[8]

The EPA Report to Congress discusses health effects, risk factors, dose response relationships and lost human productivity attributable to the major indoor air pollutants. EPA has conducted a number of cancer risk assessments for indoor air pollutants.[9] However, EPA has developed an estimate of annual cancer incidence from only one indoor air pollutant -- radon.[10] Unit risk estimates (risk occurring from continuous lifetime exposure to specific air concentration) are developed for 10 pollutants. EPA estimates the annual excess cancer cases due to indoor radon at about 20,000 per year.[11] Other researchers have estimated annual cancer incidence due to environmental exposure to tobacco smoke at between 12 and 11,000.[12] EPA also presents a summary of non-cancer health effects. No attempt to quantify the number of non-cancer illnesses or deaths due to indoor air pollutants is given, due to the uncertainty in scientific knowledge.[13] Indoor air pollution also has significant economic costs. EPA concludes that economic damages from indoor air pollution may amount to tens of billions of dollars per year.[14]

For the purposes of this study, however, the central question is to what extent are these damages attributable to energy conservation efforts. No studies were found which attempt to allocate health or economic damages of indoor air pollution to conservation measures. Moreover, the literature is unanimous that efforts to reduce heat loss from buildings are only one factor in the creation of indoor air pollution problems. Several studies state that the rate of emission of air toxins in the indoor

---

[8] EPA Report to Congress, supra note 7 at p. 1 of the Executive Summary.

[9] EPA Report to Congress, supra note 7 at pp. 4-1 to 4-30. For a survey of the common type of heat effects in the home and office, see, McCunney, R., "The Role of Building Construction & Ventilation in Indoor Air Pollution," New York State Journal of Medicine, April 1987, pp. 203-208.

[10] EPA Report to Congress, supra note 7 at p. 4-11.

[11] Id. at p. 4-12.

[12] Id. at pp. 4-17 - 4-23.

[13] Id. at pp. 3-1 - 3-15.

[14] Id. at pp. 5-17 - 5-19.

environment, rather than ventilation rates, is the most important factor governing concentrations in the indoor environment.[15]

For example, older homes typically are found to have fewer sources of indoor air pollution. Carpeting and wood products are usually of older types having fewer synthetic volatile compounds or have long ago released any toxins they once contained. In these homes the experience is that weatherization which lowers ventilation rates has no adverse indoor air quality effects.[16] Problems usually occur in new homes having a combination of low ventilation rates and high emission rates from materials, appliances or products within the home. Building codes at the state and local level address ventilation for commercial and large residential buildings, but ventilation standards alone are not considered adequate to control indoor air pollution problems. Such standards are not targeted to specific pollutants and hence the mitigation effect is limited.[17]

In many cases the sources of indoor air pollution can be excluded or removed from the indoor environment or modified so that the pollution emission rate is decreased. For example, smoking can be prohibited from public buildings, formaldehyde containing wood products can be coated to reduce their emissions, and radon emitting foundations can be sealed or vented to reduce a radon build up that might reach living spaces.

Although the literature is filled with general statements that lowering ventilation rates in homes tends to increase air toxic concentrations, many studies which specifically focus on weatherization programs conclude that they do not have any significant adverse effect upon indoor air quality, at least for existing homes.[18]

The EPRI Manual states that, in general, tightening measures such as caulking and weatherstripping should not lead to serious problems, particularly where none existed before. "Current research seems to indicate that conservation measures -

---

[15] Nazaroff, "The Use of Mechanical Ventilation With Heat Recovery for Controlling Radon and Radon-Daughter Concentrations in Houses," Atmospheric Environment 15: 263-270, 1981; Walsh, P., Indoor Air Quality, CRC Press, Boca Raton, FL, 1984, p. 83; Turiel, I., Indoor Air Quality and Human Health, Stanford University Press, Stanford, CA, 1985, pp. 81-89; New York State Energy Research and Development Authority, Indoor Air Quality, Infiltration and Ventilation in Residential Buildings, prepared by W. Fleming and Associates, NYSERDA report No. 85-10, March 1985, p. S-5.

[16] Hirst, E., Energy Efficiency in Buildings, Progress, and Promise, American Council for an Energy Efficient Economy, Washington, DC 1986, p. 209; Personal communication from Bill Prendle, Alliance to Save Energy, Washington, DC, January 19, 1990.

[17] EPA Report to Congress, supra note 7 at pp. 7-25 - 7-30.

[18] See generally, Byers, R., "Results of Energy Use, Indoor Air Quality, and Ventilation Monitoring for RSDP Homes in Washington State," Proceedings of the 1988 ACEEE Summer Study on Energy Efficiency in Buildings, Vol. 1, p. 1.16 to 1.28. Rizzuto, J., "An Investigation of Infiltration and Indoor Air Quality in New York State Homes," Proceedings of the 1988 ACEEE Summer Study on Energy Efficiency in Buildings, Vol. 1, pp. 1.141 - 1.156.

unless carried out to the extremes - may have only incremental effects on indoor air quality."[19]

The most comprehensive evaluation of the indoor air quality effect of weatherization programs was prepared by the Bonneville Power Authority. One BPA study assessed the health impacts of weatherization on existing homes.[20] A second BPA report addressed a new energy-efficient homes program.[21] The assessments were limited to formaldehyde and radon. These are the pollutants over which the occupant has the least influence, are most affected by builder's construction methods, and for which researchers have developed risk factors (making it possible to quantify lifetime cancer risks). Bonneville contended that there is insufficient information to quantify accurately the health effects of indoor particulate matter, combustion gases (including tobacco smoke), household chemicals and moisture.[22]

For new home weatherization programs, BPA's research gives reason for concern about effects of advanced home infiltration control and radon exposure. BPA's assessment predicted an increased cancer risk factor in new energy efficient homes having dramatically low ventilation rates. This was largely due to increased radon concentrations. Increases in air pollutants over the baseline were estimated for homes using standard and advanced infiltration reduction techniques without ventilation. Fairly large increases in cancer risk also occurred in homes with advanced infiltration control and only intermittent exhaust or mechanical ventilation. Slight increases in cancer risk occurred in homes using standard infiltration control but only intermittent (versus continuous) exhaust or mechanical ventilation. BPA concluded that real changes in cancer risk only occur from large reductions in total effective ventilation rate (e.g. nearly 43% reduction in ventilation over baseline). Energy conservation measures did not increase cancer incidence due to formaldehyde.[23]

Bonneville's analysis shows that indoor air pollution from radon is a very serious concern for new home programs if mitigation measurements are not incorporated. The number of cancer cases due to radon was conservatively estimated to be 335 per 100,000persons for baseline homes, and as high as 767 per 100,000person for homes with advanced infiltration control without exhaust or mechanical ventilation (single family homes). The BPA study also shows that radon mitigation measures

---

[19] EPRI Manual, supra note 2 at p. v.; Grumsrud, D., et al., "A Comparison of Indoor Air Quality In Pacific Northwest Existing and New Energy Efficient Homes," Lawrence Berkeley Laboratory, Berkeley, CA, 1986.

[20] Bonneville Power Authority, Pacific Northwest Home Indoor In Quality Survey and Weatherization Sensitivity Study, prepared by Lawrence Berkeley Laboratories, Berkeley, CA, February 1988, [hereafter cited as BPA Weatherization Study].

[21] Bonneville Power Authority, Final Environmental Impact Statement on New Energy-Efficient Homes Programs, Assessing Indoor An Quality Options, DOE/EIS-0127F, August 1988, [hereafter cited as BPA New Home Study].

[22] BPA Weatherization Study, supra note 20.

[23] BPA New Home Study, supra note 21.

incorporated into building design can eliminate the additional risk due to utility-sponsored new home construction efficiency measures.[24]

For existing homes, Bonneville concluded that standard weatherization measures appeared to have only a small adverse effect on indoor air quality, and that crawl-space ventilation measures added as part of the weatherization package resulted in "greatly reduced radon levels inside homes." In homes built on basements and slab-on-grade foundations, house tightening appeared to reduce radon entry rates. But radon concentrations were observed to increase in several homes after weatherization.[25]

A study prepared for NYSERDA, assessed the effect of weatherization on mobile homes and low-income houses. Five pollutants, for which there are no indoor concentration standards in residences, were monitored.[26] The results showed that radon concentrations in houses did not significantly deviate from statewide radon assessment figures. A mobile home with a well ventilated crawl-space will not likely exceed the EPA 4 pica curies per liter (PCi/L) guideline.[27] High levels of nitrogen dioxide were associated with the heavy use of gas ranges in confined spaces. No major problems were found from formaldehyde or carbon monoxide, however, the researchers did suggest that building materials with high formaldehyde emissions be avoided.[28] High levels of respirable suspended particulates were found in low-income houses with heavy smokers. The health risk associated with these particulates were found to be the highest of the five pollutants monitored.[29]

A recent article summarizes three other studies on existing homes which show that increased air changes per hour have little or no correlation to indoor levels of formaldehyde and radon. The author emphasizes that simply increasing ventilation may not be a proper response to indoor air pollution problems.[30]

Another recent study tested the effect of reducing infiltration of air into an existing home or work space on indoor air pollutant concentrations. A March 1988 study conducted for Northeast Utilities tested 100 homes to determine whether concentrations of radon, formaldehyde, and nitrogen dioxide were increased by

---

[24] BPA New Home Study, supra note 21 at p. 4.10.

[25] BPA Weatherization Study, supra note 20.

[26] New York State Energy and Development Authority, Indoor Air Quality In Weatherization Program Homes, prepared by W.S. Fleming and Associates, NYSERDA report No. 89-7, February 1989.

[27] Id. at p. 3-3.

[28] Id. at p. 3-4.

[29] Id.

[30] Hansen, S., "Indoor Air Quality: Is Increased Ventilation the Answer, "Energy Engineering, Vol. 86, No. 6, 1989.

weatherization of the homes. Radon, formaldehyde and nitrogen dioxide were chosen because they were considered to be representative of the range of pollutants causing the greatest concern for indoor air pollution.

The study concluded that there was no meaningful correlation between the concentration of radon in the basement and the homes' infiltration rate. "This study shows that homes with low infiltration rates do not, therefore, have higher radon levels."[31] The study even suggests that insulation of the home decreases radon in the living space by reducing air flow that brings radon up from the basement. In houses experiencing a significant decrease in infiltration due to weatherization, the radon values increased at a rate that was less than the day-to-day variation of radon levels. "Weatherizing these homes, in general, may have caused radon levels to increase very slightly, though not significantly."[32]From this study it appears that weatherization of existing homes to reduce infiltration rates does not create additional radon hazard.[33]

> The lack of correlation between infiltration decrease and radon increase is not surprising. In fact, there are numerous instances in the radon literature that support a decrease in radon when a house is tightened.[34]

The lack of correlation between indoor air pollution and reduced ventilation (from weatherization), may merely be the result of the fact that many homes do not have significant pre-existing indoor air pollution problems. A more meaningful comparison would be to measure the effect of weatherization on homes known to have an indoor air pollution problem. Although no studies appear to have been designed this way, some studies have found correlations between radon containment levels and ventilation rates due to weatherization.[35] And even the Northeast Utilities data showed a doubling of radon levels after weatherization in a few homes. No publications addressed the effect of weatherization on hydrocarbons or cigarette smoke.

---

[31] Northeast Utilities Service Company, A Comparison of Two Weatherization Techniques, March 1988, p. 77, (emphasis in original), [hereafter cited as Northeast Utilities].

[32] Id. at p. 79.

[33] Id. at pp. 75-77.

[34] Id. at pp. 79-80. The study quotes from Energy Design Update, Vol. 71., 1988, p. 8, which states that a common misconception of the building community is that tight construction aggravates radon problems. The Energy Design Update concludes that the opposite is actually true. "If a house is very leaky, air exfiltration from the upper parts of the house causes infiltration to lower parts of the house including infiltration into the basement." See also, Rieland, P., et al., Preliminary Radon Testing Results for the Residential Standards Demonstration Program, Bonneville Power Administration, Department of Energy August 1985 (little significant difference in average radon concentrations between model conservation homes and other recently built homes).

[35] Nazaroff, et al. "The Use of Mechanical Ventilation With Heat Recovery for Controlling Radon and Radon Daughter Concentrations in Houses," Atmosphere Envir. 15: 263-280 (1981); Flescher, R., Mogro-Compero, A. and Turner L., "Indoor Radon Levels in the Northeast U.S.: Effects on Energy Efficiency in Homes," Health Phys., 1983, pp. 45, 407.

> Some authors are unwilling to dismiss completely the existence of radon hazards due to weatherization of existing homes. If the radon input rate is constant, the radon concentration is determined largely by the ventilation rate. Other things being equal, if the rate of air exchange with the outdoor is halved the radon concentration would double. For this reason, it has been feared that weatherization of houses for energy conservation, including weatherstripping and caulking of cracks, would lead to high radon levels.
>
> Subsequent investigations have not shown large effects from weatherization, apparently because the steps taken usually do not greatly reduce the air infiltration rates, and in some cases because radon input rate may be reduced due to increases produced in basement air pressure.[36]

The author concludes, however, that the studies do not adequately predict the consequences of weatherization on radon levels, either for individual homes or for broad categories of housing stock. The only thing which appears well established is that radon concentrations among different houses are more due to rate of radon entry than from differences in ventilation.[37]

The literature is more unanimous in rejecting effects of weatherization on other indoor air pollutants, but again, the reliance on correlations is not completely satisfying. Like the BPA study, the Northwest Utilities study concludes that "[T]here was no meaningful correlation between infiltration reduction and formaldehyde increase. We may conclude that weatherizing these homes cannot be shown to cause measurable increases of formaldehyde levels."[38]

As for nitrogen dioxide measurements, the Northeast Utility study concludes that there is "low probability that a decrease in infiltration might correlate to an increase in nitrogen dioxide concentration......thispoor correlation indicates that there really is essentially no relationship between infiltration reduction and increase in nitrogen dioxide level in the home."[39]

An EPRI study on indoor air pollution concluded that: "It is important that energy efficiency efforts not be impacted negatively in looking at this problem. There is a definite relationship between the two areas, but there is room for both healthy and energy efficient indoor environments in trying to maintain economic efficiency."[40]

---

[36] Bodansky, D., Preview of the Indoor Radon Problem, contained in Indoor Radon and Its Hazards, edited by D. Bodonsky et al., University of Washington Press, Seattle, Wash. 1987 pp. 8-9.

[37] Id. at p. 9. See also, Nero, A., et al., "Radon Concentrations and Infiltration Rates Measured in Conventional and Energy Efficient Houses," Health Phys. 1983, pp. 52-281.

[38] Northeast Utilities, supra note 31 at p. 83.

[39] Id. at p. 85.

[40] EPRI, Utility Energy Strategies: The Role of Efficiency, Productivity, and Conservation; EPRI, CU-6272, Project 2982-5, Final Report, February 1989, pp. 7-7.

One could conclude that the external costs of weatherization already internalized in the home owner's decision to invest in the weatherization. This assumes that the home owner knows what the risks of weatherization will be in terms of increased exposure to indoor air pollutants, that he or she is authorized to speak for others living in the house, and that subsequent purchasers are informed. In many cases, of course, these assumptions would be wholly unwarranted. Information might be unavailable from vendors or promoters of the weatherization programs. Knowledge of risks associated with exposure to indoor air pollutants is complex, uncertain and evolving. This information is largely inaccessible to the average home owner. Moreover, in large apartment or commercial buildings the people exposed to indoor air contaminants generally do not have knowledge or a voice in deciding what weatherization programs will be undertaken by the owner.

Another approach to environmental costs of weatherization is to assume that increased risk from indoor air pollution can be economically mitigated.[41] At least one utility (Bonneville Power Authority) requires mitigation measures for indoor air quality effects of weatherization. Technologies, including air-to-air heat exchangers and new home ventilation systems are becoming available to mitigate indoor air pollution problems. Air-to-air heat exchangers increase ventilation without significantly sacrificing energy efficiency. Exchangers capture the heat from ventilated air and transfer it to incoming fresh air. Some states and localities enforce building and ventilation codes, smoking bans and other regulations to minimize indoor pollution in homes, business or public buildings.[42] Assuming that mitigation is fully effective and required in utility sponsored weatherization programs, the environmental costs, in terms of indoor air pollution, would be zero.

Typically, however, mitigation measures do not appear to accompany the home conservation kits, audits or other weatherization programs, though in New York, homeowners receive educational materials and are offered a radon test kit as part of the residential audit program.

The literature suggests that states should consider adding an indoor air mitigation as a required part of utility sponsored new and existing home weatherization programs and as a specification for bidding programs. A mitigation program would include testing of homes prior to weatherization for pre-existing radon or other indoor air hazards (such as unvented heater, or severe moisture problems).[43] Corrections of these problems, and the promotion of homeowner awareness to the homeowner could

---

[41] In regard to radon mitigation, see EPA, A Citizens Guide to Radon, What It Is and What to Do About It, OPA-86-004 (August 1986); EPA, Radon Reduction Methods: A Homeowners Guide, OPA-86-005 (August 1986); EPA, Radon Reduction Risks for Detached Houses, Technical Guidelines, EPA/625/5-86/019, June 1986.

[42] EPA Report to Congress, supra note 7 at pp. 9-12 - 9-18, 7-25 - 7-31.

[43] Weatherization programs can be structured to mitigate effects on indoor air pollution. For example, weatherization crews can be trained to apply air-to-air heat exchanger as part of a weatherization program for homes having significant indoor air pollution sources (such as unvented kerosene or propane heaters and malfunctioning furnaces). If heat exchanger cannot be used, weatherization activities can be delayed until after significant indoor air pollution sources have been eliminated. The weatherization program might include personnel trained to adjust malfunctioning furnaces. Educational materials can be distributed to alert homeowners to dangers from indoor air pollution sources.

provide a net environmental indoor air pollution benefit and ensure that weatherization programs do not aggravate pre-existing problems.[44]

For new homes, mitigation measures might follow the example set by the Bonneville Power Authority. The BPA has instituted indoor and pollution mitigation measures for new homes built under its Model Conservation Standards. The program requires either: mechanical ventilation systems to maintain ventilation rates at levels generally found in homes built before the standards were adopted (1983); or, monitoring and mitigation of formaldehyde and radon levels above 0.1 part per million or 5 pica Curies per liter, respectively.[45] Bonneville offers consumer information packets including information on radon monitoring, radon prevention construction measures for new home foundations, exhaust fans in kitchens and bathrooms, and formaldehyde product standards for particle board and plywood.

3. Indoor Air Pollution from Conservation Materials

a. Insulation

A related indoor air pollution concern, is the potential for certain types of insulation to emit toxins into the indoor environment. A well known example is the case of urea-formaldehyde foam insulation. EPA banned the manufacture of this product in 1980. The ban was subsequently overturned by a federal court, but marketing of the product, except for some limited commercial applications, essentially ended in 1980. Urea-formaldehyde, therefore, is a concern today as an externality of conservation only to the extent that weatherization programs attempt to further tighten a structure that has previously been insulated with urea-formaldehyde insulation. Here again, weatherization crews can be trained to recognize the existence of this problem and to modify weatherization accordingly.

Concerns have been raised over phenol-formaldehyde binders used in some rockwool insulation. These products are cured to drive off binder gases that might otherwise contaminate homes after insulation. This may, of course create an air pollution emission at the manufacturing site. This would be a social cost that should be considered in future research on front-end costs. The U.S.Food and Drug Administration and Consumer Product Safety Council (CPSC) have examined this issue and concluded that the binders do not pose any risk to human health as an indoor air pollutant.

---

[44] ACEEE made this recommendation in regard to low income weatherization programs. National data indicated that at least 15% of all households have elevated levels of radon and other indoor air pollutants. Weatherization organizations are in an ideal position to assess indoor air quality in low income buildings. With adequate training they could test for radon and combustion gases during weatherization visits. Measures to mitigate identified problems could be installed by weatherization crews or other contractors specializing in indoor air quality. Chandler, W., H. Geller and M. Ledbetter, Energy Efficiency: A New Agenda. American Council for an Energy Efficient Economy, Washington, DC, July 1988 (citing U.S. General Accounting Office, Indoor Radon: Limited Federal Response to Reduce Contamination in Housing, GAO/RCED-88-103, Washington, DC, April 1988).

[45] BPA New Home Study, supra note 21 at Vol. II, appendices, p. H.1.

Finally, in recent years questions have been raised as to whether fibers from fiberglass or rockwool insulation can pose health risks when inhaled. The official position of the CPSC is that there is no evidence that fiberglass poses a risk to human health. No studies have identified fiberglass as an indoor contaminant in houses that are insulated with fiberglass. CPSC asserts that there is no evidence to suggest a health hazard from this type of insulation. Research continues, however, as the result of one occupational study suggesting slightly higher rates of cancer and non-cancerous tumors in fiberglass manufacturing workers.[46]

b. Environmental Effects of Efficient Lighting Programs

i. Introduction and Acknowledgement

A comprehensive discussion of the environmental health and safety implications of energy efficient lighting systems is contained in proprietary materials prepared by Competitek. Competitek is an information service on advanced techniques for energy efficiency, operated by the Rocky Mountain Institute, a non-profit corporation. Competitek has given the authors permission to cite and to quote from their binder of information entitled, The State of the Art: Lighting, March 1988, by Amory Lovins and Robert Sardinsky. The following discussion, unless otherwise noted, is a summary of the information contained in that title.

ii. Lighting Components of Concern to Health and Safety

A wide variety of metals and gases are used in modern lighting equipment. The only materials believed to have potential for adverse health impacts are mercury, several radioisotopes and PCBs.

The last is most easily addressed. Energy conservation efforts probably decrease the hazard of PCBs in lighting equipment. PCBs once were used in "core coil ballasts" for standard fluorescent light fixtures, in the amount of about one-and-a-half ounces per ballast. Although EPA banned the manufacture of PCB-containing ballasts in 1978, there are still many in use today. PCBs can be discharged from these ballasts if they overheat or if they are crushed in disposal.

One of the most effective ways to increase energy efficiency in fluorescent lighting is to substitute high efficiency ballasts, which do not contain PCBs. Typically, energy conservation programs involve replacing older ballasts with higher efficiency ballasts in group relamping programs, rather than unit by unit as the older equipment wears out. Conservation-stimulated group relamping programs are more likely to be planned and carried out by persons who are knowledgeable of the PCB content of the older ballasts and the need for special precautions in handling and disposal (as hazardous

---

[46] Personal communication from CPSC spokesman, January 26, 1990. See also, Industrial Health Foundation, Current Status of Health Effects of Fibrous Glass and Other Manmade Vitreous Fiber, An Annotated Bibliography, Medical Services Bulletin No. 21-82, 4th revision, 1982.

waste). It is more likely that the PCB-containing ballasts will be properly disposed of in these programs, than if individual units are replaced as they wear out by less knowledgeable maintenance personnel at the end of the equipment lifetime. In addition, early retirement of PCB-laden ballasts reduces the likelihood of leakage due to overheating. Group relamping may also reduce liability for costly clean up measures associated with leaking ballasts.

Disposal costs of PCB latent ballasts vary from $0 to $8 per ballast. The expenditure can be significant. Replacement of 175,000 ballasts, at $2 per ballast, in a Milwaukee public school district resulted in a $350,000 expenditure for disposal of PCB laden ballasts.[47]

The literature suggests that state utility commissions could encourage proper disposal by requiring utility sponsored lighting efficiency programs to include worker training in order to encourage identification and proper disposal of PCB containing fluorescent ballasts.

The impact of conservation on exposure to mercury requires a more extended discussion. Mercury is not contained in incandescent bulbs. But it is a necessary component of all fluorescent lamps, including modern high efficiency compact fluorescent, and high intensity discharge (HID) lamps (mercury vapor, metal halide and high pressure sodium). Energy conservation concerns undoubtedly have led to increased reliance on fluorescent and HID lamps, and therefore to increased amounts of mercury in lighting components.

For reasons not associated with conservation, the mercury content of fluorescent lamps has dropped dramatically over the past fifteen years. In 1970 a typical fluorescent lamp contained approximately 50 mg of mercury. The mercury content today has been reduced to about 15 mg, and to about 5 mg in compact fluorescent lamps. The mercury content of HID lamps has also fallen, partly as a result of increased reliance on high pressure sodium lamps in place of the relatively obsolete mercury vapor lamps.

Worldwide, the amount of mercury placed in discharge lamps amounts to about 30 tons per year. This compares with 6000 tons global consumption for other uses, 7000 tons released by volcanoes and other natural sources, and 3000 tons released by burning fossil fuels, mainly coal, which contain trace levels of mercury.[48]

The annual usage of mercury in fluorescent lighting therefore represents .02% of all sources.[49] The actual environmental exposure is far less than the 30 ton figure, since much of the mercury in fluorescent lamps is, during use, deposited upon the lamp walls in such a way that it enters firmly into the substance of the glass. The

---

[47] Competitek, State of the Art: Lighting Second Update, Rocky Mountain Institute, January 1990, citing Energy User News, February 1989, p. 28.

[48] Id. at p. 23.

[49] Id.

release of this mercury to the environment upon disposal of the lamp is "limited and extremely slow (except in the case of leaching by acidified water)."[50]

The actual impact on a regional or global basis is diminished further by the fact that the use of more efficient fluorescent lighting significantly reduces electric power demands, and therefore, mercury emissions from coal-fired electric power plants. Competitek estimated the amount of such emissions, if all lighting were provided by mercury-free incandescent lamps instead of fluorescent lamps:

> Generating that additional electricity by burning fossil fuel would require the burning of approximately 600 million tons of coal, or its equivalent, releasing an estimated 300 tons of uncontrollable additional mercury an order of magnitude more than the [potentially more controllable] in-lamp mercury ...[51]

In addition, atmospheric deposition of acid gas emissions from increased coal use would increase the mobilization of aluminum, mercury and other toxic metals from soils into water bodies, in regions having acid-sensitive geology.[52]

The study suggests that, for these reasons global, national or regional impacts of energy efficient lighting probably represent a net environmental benefit, in terms of total loading of mercury to the environment. The remaining question is whether efficient lighting increases the risk of exposure to mercury in micro-environmental settings, such as a work place or residence.

As noted above, over the lifetime of a fluorescent bulb, much of the "free" mercury content is incorporated into the glass and phosphor of the bulb. Upon breakage, this portion would not be available to expose workers or building occupants, nor be released as landfill gas or leachate after disposal. The concern is for the "free" mercury contained in the lamps that are broken or disposed of before all of the free mercury is used up and deposited on the walls of the lamp. Group relamping, which often occurs at 60 to 80% of rated lamp life, has the largest potential for release of the "free" mercury from fluorescent lamps. Competitek estimates that if group relamping were a universal practice, the not-yet-exhausted lamps could cause an annual mercury release of eight tons per year which would occur in widely dispersed locations and be timed so that outdoor concentrations, for example at a landfill or solid waste station, would be too small to be of concern.

The primary hazard, then, is breakage of bulbs indoors, particularly if an incident occurred in poorly ventilated space and involved a large supply of lamps. Mercury is an inhalable and cumulative poison. The 21 mg of mercury in the typical four foot fluorescent lamp, if the lamp is new, is enough to contaminate about 420 cubic meters

---

[50] Competitek, State of the Art: Lighting, Rocky Mountain Institute, March 1988, at p. 230, [hereafter cited as Competitek.]

[51] Id. at p. 231.

[52] See, National Acid Precipitation Assessment Program, Interim Assessment, The Causes and Effects of Acid Deposition, Vol. IV, Effects of Acid Deposition, p. 8-1.

of air to the National Institute of Occupational Safety and Health (NIOSH) chronic exposure limit for occupational exposure; or up to 18 cubic meters to levels that are acutely toxic if breathed for a prolonged period.

No studies have been found which address the probabilities or resulting health risks of such accidents. The effect is noted here as a means of encouraging research into this potential hazard and to encourage preventative measures in storage and handling.

Other lamp materials of concern include a variety of radio-isotopes. Krypton 85 (a gas) and promethium 147 (a solid) are contained in some compact fluorescent lamp starters. Tritium is contained in self-luminous exit signs.

Competitek credits the conclusion of manufacturers that the risk from exposure to Krypton, from the breakage of the typical compact fluorescent bulb, even under prolonged exposure in unventilated areas, is infinitesimal - amounting to about one thousandth of the natural background radiation (received out of doors during an eight hour period). Some products, however, appear to contain larger quantities of Krypton and concern would be heightened if exposure occurred by reason of a catastrophic accident in which a large quantity of lamps were broken at the same time in a poorly ventilated storage site.

According to the Competitek report the risk from promethium is even lower, since it is a solid and not likely to be inhaled upon breakage of a lamp. Furthermore, promethium's decay product has a very low specific activity. Competitek concludes that there is very low risk of exposure even from unlikely types of catastrophic releases.

Tritium, radioactive hydrogen, is used in some types of energy efficient exit signs. According to Competitek, it is of concern if inhaled or ingested from breakage of an exit sign in a confined space over a prolonged exposure period. Manufacturers dismiss the risk of such exposure as insignificant compared to yearly exposure to radiation from natural sources.[53] The Competitek discussion, indicates however, that there is some basis for some limited concern over the safety of the tritium exit signs. This is an area which may benefit from additional research.

One other potential externality of efficient lighting programs is that the retrofit of older buildings with efficient lighting will, at times, involve removal of asbestos insulation. This can greatly increase installation costs, which are normally internalized.[54] Externalities, however, can occur in the form of worker illnesses, contamination of public areas and other effects if asbestos is not handled properly.

---

[53] Competitek, supra, note 50 at pp. 236-242.

[54] Savage, J., "Unplanned Asbestos Job Hikes, Cost of Relamping South Glenn Mall, Colorado, " Energy News, Vol. 12, September 21, 1987, p. 7.

4. CFC Use and Conservation Programs

a. Appliance Efficiency Standards

Chlorofluorocarbons ("CFCs") are man-made chemicals that are known to deplete the stratospheric ozone layer. This "thinning" of the ozone layer allows greater amounts of ultraviolet radiation to reach the earth's surface, where it causes a wide variety of adverse effects, including skin cancer in humans, and damage to plants, marine and terrestrial food chains. These effects could become catastrophic if severe and prolonged ozone depletion were to occur in the future. These chemicals also play a major role in global warming, due to their effect of increasing the amount of solar radiation reaching the earth's surface and because of their heat trapping characteristics. It is estimated that CFCs may remain in the atmosphere for several decades. Essentially, they are the vehicles by which bromine and chlorine reach the upper atmosphere and deplete ozone through a series of complex reactions.

There are various chemical forms of CFCs, two of which are present in electrical household appliances. CFC-11 is used in several types of materials and products for the purpose of conserving electrical energy. Certain types of insulation for refrigeration equipment and buildings are manufactured using CFC "blowing agents". Refrigeration and air conditioning equipment use CFC-12 as the "working fluid" in the cooling mechanism. In the typical residential refrigerator, about three-fourths of CFCs are contained in the insulating foam, with the remainder contained in the working fluid. The amount of CFCs in refrigeration has increased in past years as a result of efforts to conserve energy, primarily through increased use of CFC based foam insulation in the walls of refrigerators and freezers.

> Today's refrigerators and freezers are approximately 75% more energy efficient than models of the early 1970's, largely because they contain three times the quantity of CFC's by weight . . .[55]

CFCs are also currently used as working fluids in room and "through the wall" air conditioning units, but not in residential central air units (which use HCFC R22). Air conditioners (unlike refrigerators) do not contain insulation. Thus, energy efficiency standards may have marginally increased the amount of CFC working fluids, but the increase is not large.[56] Heat pumps are currently manufactured with HCFCs, but older models in use may contain CFCs.[57]

---

[55] Cogen, D., Stoves In A Glass House: CFC's and Ozone Depletion, Investor Responsibility Research Center, p. 105.

[56] Personal communication from Mike Woodford, Air Conditioning and Refrigeration Institute, January 19, 1990.

[57] HCFCs are related chemically to CFCs but have only 2 to 10% as much potential to damage the ozone layer. HCFCs are also considered to be a "greenhouse gas".

For air conditioners and refrigerators, the substitutes for CFCs may come with an energy penalty since they are not as efficient either as insulators or as working fluids compared with CFCs. CFC reduction, however, is not an energy conservation or DSM strategy. This energy penalty is assumed to be internalized into the cost of purchasing and operating an appliance containing CFC substitutes, and is not an environmental externality of energy conservation measures. For the same reason, this study does not address the potential toxicity and flammability hazard associated with some CFC substitutes.

Manufacturers of refrigeration equipment today face the dual challenge of increasing appliance efficiency to meet federal standards and of reducing, if not eliminating, CFC use to meet federal legislation and international accords. Several proposals focus on CFCs 11 and 12 and will have a great impact on refrigeration and air conditioning industries.[58] In this respect, there are complaints that, given the limited time to research and develop new alternatives, appliance efficiency standards cannot be met without continuing current levels of CFC use.[59]

Complicating the question of conservation-imposed CFC externalities is the fact that national CFC policies are changing. Recent EPA regulations designed to achieve a 50% reduction in CFC production and use will almost certainly be superceded by a mandate for a 100% phaseout, in accord with international negotiations.[60] The phaseout may address only those CFCs having the greatest ozone depletion potential. Related chemical substitutes, generally known as HCFCs, initially may not be banned. These substitutes are recognized as a temporary solution that greatly reduce, but will not eliminate, the stratospheric ozone depletion problem. Reliance on the HCFCs is expected for the period of time it will take to develop other substitutes which have no adverse stratospheric ozone effects.

Several recent studies have suggested that appliance efficiency standards would have the effect of increasing CFC use in refrigeration by one-half to one percent of total U.S. use, due to the increase of CFC-derived insulation in the walls of refrigerator units (approximately 2.0 to 4.2 million pounds of CFCs).[61]

---

[58] Creswick, Fisher, and Sand, Potential Impacts of CFC Restrictions and Space Conditioning Equipment, Vol. II, Energy Division, Oak Ridge, TN, 1988, p. 217.

[59] Id. See also, Geller, H., "Update on National and State Minimum Efficiency Standards," Proceedings of the Fourth National Conference on Utility DSM Programs, Electric Power Research Institute, Vol. 1, April 1989, pp. 4-1.

[60] Over 52 countries have ratified the Montreal Protocol, which went into effect on January 1, 1989. 55 Fed. Reg. 18256 (May 1, 1990). See also, U.S.E.P.A., How Industry is Reducing Dependence on Ozone Depleting Chemicals, A report prepared by the Stratospheric Ozone Protection Program, May 1988. There will be required recordkeeping for producers, importers and exporters of CFCs. Additionally, future trade restrictions may be imposed on countries that have not signed the Montreal Protocol. Negotiations are currently underway to extend the phasedown to a worldwide phaseout of CFCs.

[61] U.S.E.P.A., How Industry Is Reducing Dependence On Ozone Depleting Chemicals, A Status Report Prepared by the Stratospheric Ozone Protection Project, June 1988, Office of Air and Radiation; Draft N.Y. State Energy Plan, Energy Efficiency Supply Assessment, Staff Report, May 1989, p. 11.

Other more recent studies have concluded that by 1995-96 the more aggressive CFC elimination mandates will drive manufacturers to HCFC substitutes and that there will be no increase in CFC use as a result of appliance efficiency standards.[62] The loss in efficiency due to use of the less efficient HCFCs will likely be made up by modifications to compressors, adding thickness to insulation in the refrigerator walls, better insulation of doors and other adjustments.[63]

Some substitutes for CFCs are so similar to CFCs that they may be used as "drop-in" replacements. One such candidate with no ozone depleting potential is HFC-134a. Other substitutes, such as helium coolant, however, may require entirely new systems in order to achieve compatible results. A developing technology involving various types of vacuum panels eventually could replace the need for either CFCs or HCFCs and achieve insulating efficiency at 50% energy savings.[64] However, this technology is not expected to be available for commercial use until the year 2000.[65]

Appliance efficiency standards in the past have had an adverse environmental impact by encouraging wider use of CFCs in refrigeration. For the future, however, this effect is essentially negated by the rapid phase down and ultimate elimination of all CFC uses. Even the use of HCFC substitutes is likely to have a limited lifetime given the developing technologies. For these reasons the literature suggests that the present environmental externality cost of appliance efficiency standards is negligible.

b. Appliance Rebate Programs

To encourage consumers to buy more efficient electrical appliances, many utilities are implementing appliance rebate programs.[66] If these programs cause consumers to dispose of CFC-containing appliances in favor of new, more efficient models, and are not coordinated with CFC recycling, then the question arises as to whether this will

---

62 U.S. Department of Energy, Energy Conservation Standards for Consumer Appliances, Refrigerators and Furnaces, DOE/CE-0277, Nov. 1989.

63 Personal communication from Isaac Turiel, Lawrence Berkeley Laboratory, January 18, 1990.

64 Potter, P., et al., "Impacts of Advanced Refrigerator Insulation," Proceedings of the 1988 ACEEE Summer Study on Energy Efficiency in Buildings, Vol. 4, 1988, p. 4.86; Ledbetter, M., Preparing For the Energy Challenge of the 1990's, Energy Efficiency: An Overlooked Environmental Protection Strategy, Jan. 1988, American Council for An Energy Efficient Economy.

65 Personal communication, Isaac Turiel, Lawrence Berkeley Laboratory, January 18, 1990.

66 Electric Power Research Institute, A Compilation of Utility Sponsored Energy Efficiency Rebate Programs, prepared by Consumer Energy Council of America Research Foundation and the American Council for an Energy Efficiency Economy, EPRI EM-5579, Final Report, December 1987 (A survey of 157 utilities found 59 companies with appliance efficiency programs. At the time of the survey 15 utilities had pilot or full scale rebate programs for refrigerators; five had programs for freezers; 22 had programs for room air conditioners; 23 had programs for central air conditioners and 34 had programs for heat pumps.)

increase environmental loading of CFCs by placing them beyond recovery in recycling programs. It is expected that as the price of CFCs increase, recycling or other incentive programs will be established to recover, for reuse or destruction, CFCs contained in the residential sector.[67] To the extent that rebate programs cause CFC containing appliances to be retired and disposed of (presumably in a landfill) prior to the establishment of such recycling programs, the effect could be larger CFC losses to the atmosphere than if the rebate program had not been established.[68]

For some types of rebate programs this is an unlikely result. First, many appliance programs are designed to place more energy efficient models in the market, (through "trade-ally" relationships), influencing consumer choice at the store through labeling. Such programs would encourage early retirement of older, less efficient models.[69] Second, programs to recycle CFC working fluids are already emerging. Germany and Great Britain have established recycling programs using "vampires" that suck out CFCs from appliances.[70] Milwaukee and Wisconsin have "turn-in" programs which combine a rebate program, for improved energy efficiency standards, with recaptured CFCs for recycling and reuse. The Appliance Recycling Centers of America, Inc. removed and recycled CFCs from 54000 units in a nine month period in 1989.[71] This was performed under contract with Wisconsin Electric Company, and pursuant to state law forbidding landfill disposal of appliances. Such laws promote uniform handling of large home appliances, also called white goods, and reduce the risk that hazardous elements (e.g., CFCs, PCBs) may escape into the environment.[72] Legislation to ban landfill disposal of appliances and recycling of CFCs is also being considered in several other states

---

[67] Through a purification process, CFCs can be returned to their original condition. There is, however, a need to establish a standard for appliance CFC Recycling, in order to promote and facilitate CFC recycling industries. Personal communication with Katy Boone, Appliance Recycling Centers, Inc., June 19, 1990, Minneapolis, MN.

[68] This is not a concern for commercial refrigeration, since recycling programs have already begun as part of routine maintenance.

[69] See, Conservation Law Foundation, Strategic Energy Efficiency Investment for the 1990's, January 24, 1989.

[70] Commercial refrigeration and automotive air conditioning recycling programs are rapidly emerging due to the relative low cost of purification systems and rising costs of CFCs due to their limited availability.

[71] Personal communication with Katy Boone, Appliance Recycling Centers of America, on June 19, 1990, Minneapolis, Minnesota.

[72] Goldberg, D., "Recycling Used Appliances," Waste Alternaitves: Managing Problem Wastes, September 1989; Apothekar, S., "Recycling Pathways for White Goods, " Resource Recycling Magazine, October 1989.

including Vermont, Hawaii, Connecticut, New York, Oregon, Florida, Ohio, California and Maryland.[73]

Some appliance rebate programs, however, do seem designed to encourage early retirement of CFC containing devices.[74] No studies were identified estimating the CFC emissions effect of such programs, or any data which estimate the number of appliance or tonnage of CFCs involved. An important topic for future research is to quantify the amount of CFCs likely to be released, and to identify ways to implement recycling. This research would enable state utility commissions to require CFC recycling as a mitigation measure for future appliance programs, and could eventually result in early retirement of CFC containing units.

c. CFCs in Building Insulation Materials

CFCs are used to make rigid polyurethane, polystyrene and phenolic foams for use in insulating buildings. This use constitutes 19% of national CFC usage. Some DSM programs encourage homeowners and businesses to add CFC-based insulation to existing homes. DSM programs and energy efficient building codes may cause builders to increase the amounts of insulation installed in new structures, or to select CFC-containing products over other materials to capture the higher insulation value available from CFC derived insulation. A potential adverse environmental impact of such programs, therefore, is that CFC use may be increased to the detriment of the global climate.

Studies show that past energy efficiency programs have increased CFC usage in building insulation. A 1986 article suggests that the use of CFCs in the manufacture of rigid closed cell polyurethane foam insulation, could greatly increase in future years as a result of energy efficiency programs for new home construction.[75] At this point, however, the literature suggests that the phase-down or elimination of CFC use is forcing manufacturers to turn to HCFC substitutes, lessening the influence of conservation measures on CFC production.

---

[73] Clark, S. and D. Dudek, "A Proposal for State-level Refrigerant Recycling," Environmental Defense Fund (unpublished). March 13, 1989. Concurrently, some appliance manufactures have incorporated CFC recycling into authorized servicing dealerships. Training programs for correct use of CFC collecting bags are expected to help decrease CFC-12 venting to the atmosphere.

[74] In Southern California Edison's Commercial and Industrial Rebate Program, information and rebates were given during energy surveys at customer facilities. Rebate eligible products included: space conditioning, refrigeration, air conditioners, heat pumps, coolers - all potentially CFC-containing appliances. Ignelzi, P., Ridge, R., "The Evolution of Rebate Programs: From Conservation to Customer Service through Demand-Side Management," Proceedings of the Fourth National Conference on Utility DSM Programs, Electric Power Research Institute, April 1989, Vol. I, pp. 3-1 - 3-7, [hereafter cited as Proceedings]. See also, Flaim, T., Miedema, A., and Clayton, A., "Are Appliance Rebate Programs Cost Effective? Some Experimental Results," Proceedings supra this note, at p. 28-1 (Describing a Niagara Mohawk Power Corp. pilot rebate program that was offered to residential customers through direct mail. The study concluded, however, that the program did not succeed in inducing significant numbers of early purchases.)

[75] Khalil, M. and R. Rosmussen, "The Release of Trichlorofluoro methane from Rigid Polyurethane Foams," Journal of Air Pollution Control Association, 36(2), 1986, at pp. 159-163.

Dow Chemical has begun to manufacture extruded polystyrene insulation with HCFC substitutes in place of CFC-12. Dow claims that the substitution causes "no appreciable change in strength, flammability or insulation value".[76] Another manufacturer of extruded polystyrene will convert to HCFC products by the end of 1990.[77]

Replacement of CFC-11 in making polyurethane and polyisocyanurates will take longer to achieve. Competitek reports that replacement options include HCFC-123, HCFC-1416, with blends of the two, but that these substitutes are less well tested and will probably not be available until 1993 or later.[78] The substitutes appear to have higher flammability, reduced performance, to be incompatible with various plastics, and to be subject to production problems. Similar problems exist in replacing CFC-11 and CFC-113 in phenolic foams.

Oak Ridge Laboratory is currently testing insulation materials made with CFC substitutes for insulation value. The testing revolves mostly around HCFC-123 and HCFC 1416, and blends of these compounds. Initial thermal testing has not uncovered major detriments in the substitutes. However, the substitutes still need to undergo a battery of toxicity tests, along with fire and formulation optimization testing. Thus far the tests demonstrate that the substitutes do not perform as well as CFC-11, experiencing a penalty in thermal performance of about 7 to 10%.[79]

d. HCFC Use in Insulation and Refrigeration Working Fluids

HCFCs are expected to be used, at least on an interim basis, as a substitute for CFCs in foam insulation and in the working fluids of refrigerators and other cooling devices. HCFCs have a stratospheric ozone depletion potential and greenhouse gas potency of between 2 and 10% of CFCs. According to one of the Montreal Protocol documents, approximately 30% of the substitutes for foam insulation will be HCFCs. According to Steven Siedel of EPA most of these will be at the lower end of the range of ozone depletion potential described above.[80] Most experts agree that a switch from

---

[76] Competitek, State of the Art: Space Cooling, Update, January 1990 by David Houghton and Amory Lovins, p. 4.

[77] Id.

[78] Id. at p. 4.

[79] Personal communication with Jeff Christian of Oak Ridge National Laboratory, June 5, 1990.

[80] Personal communication, January 24, 1990. See also U.S.E.P.A., Flexible and Rigid Foam - Technical Progress on Protecting the Ozone Layer, June 1989.

CFCs to HCFCs will result in a loss of efficiency in cooling devices. Estimates of the efficiency loss range from 2%[81] to 15%[82].

The use of HCFCs may itself be phased out in future years either by international agreement, unilateral congressional mandate, or regional action.[83] An amendment to the Clean Air Act, approved by an 80-16 vote, would freeze HCFC production in 2015, and would halt all production after 2030.[84] In addition, Southern California's air quality board (South Coast Air Quality Management District) has voted to ban use of CFCs and Halon gas by January 1, 1997. This measure ranks as the toughest U.S. regional action to date.[85]

No studies have attempted to quantify the amount of HCFC use in future years that would be attributable to weatherization and other energy conservation activities. This may be a valuable future research topic, since the potential global effects of HCFC are significant, and the future of HCFC use patterns and the phase out timetable are uncertain.

5. Load Shifting Externalities

The literature suggests that load shifting is a form of demand side management which has greater environmental externality costs than other DSM measures. This is because, unlike other such measures, load shifting does not decrease the consumption of electricity - rather it shifts consumption away from peak demand hours.

According to New York State agency reports, DSM strategies which attempt to shift electric load from peak to off peak hours probably result in marginal increases in combustion related air pollutants.[86]

---

[81] Dunbar, M., Chlorofluorocarbons; Heating and Ventilation Manufacturers, American Society of Heating, Refrigeration, and Air Conditioning Engineers, Energy User News, Vol. 15, No. 3, March 1990, at p. 1.

[82] Calculating the cost of CFCs and New Emission Laws, excerpts from remarks made at 1989 World Energy Engineering Conference. Energy User News, Vol. 15, No. 2, February 1990, at p. 20.

[83] Doniger, D., and D. Wirth, Cooling the Chemical Summer: Some Policy Responses to Ozone - Destroying and Greenhouse Gases, remarks presented to the UNEP/EPA International Conference on Health and Environmental Effects of Ozone Modification and Climate Change, June 20, 1986, Arlington, VA.

[84] Pitched Battle predicted in House over CFC Amendment to Clean Air Bill, Chemical Regulation Reporter, Bureau of National Affairs, Inc., Vol. 13, No. 51, March 30, 1990 at p. 1650.

[85] Southern California Board Sets CFC, Halon Gas Ban, Washington Post, April 8, 1990, Section 1, p. A8.

[86] Draft State Energy Master Plan, Vol. 1, Summary Report, May 1989, p. 124. Although labeled "draft", this document formed the basis for the recommendations and were adopted into the final plan. In effect, this is a final state document. [Hereafter cited as Draft State Energy Master Plan].

There are two primary means of achieving load shifting: (1) pricing adjustments to encourage residential and industrial consumers (either voluntarily or under control of on-site load control devices) to avoid electric consumption during peak electric demand times; and (2) installation of electric thermal storage (ETS) equipment. ETS systems allow consumers to reduce or eliminate traditional electric powered space heating in favor of systems which use electric power at off-peak times to store heat (or cold) in solid or liquid masses for release into the residence or work place at a later time. This eliminates the need for power usage at the peak demand hours for space heating.

ETS can and has also been marketed in New York to replace non-electric space heating appliances (e.g. oil furnaces, wood stoves). ICF (a Washington, P.C. consulting firm) has labeled this a "valley fill" ETS program.[87] This program should not, however, be considered either a load shifting or a DSM program since it increases base load demand and does not reduce peak load. The State Energy Master Plan criticizes such programs:

> Strategies which have the effect of displacing efficient oil and natural gas appliances with competing electric fueled appliances have potential to cause relatively large emission increases at electric generating stations.[88]

Load shifting programs can have economic benefits to consumers and utilities by avoiding the need for operation of, and in some cases, construction of additional peak demand generating capacity. Typically, such peaking generating capacity will be natural gas or oil-fired turbines or other small generating facilities that are run only a few hours a day, and are generally more expensive overall than base-load generating facilities. Load shifting is a particularly advantageous strategy for utilities whose base load plants are nearing or at capacity.

Facing a decision on what DSM programs to adopt, load shifting may appear attractive to utility managers in relation to other DSM programs. This is because load shifting does not result in lower sales of power (and therefore utility profits), such as may occur with, for example, lighting retrofits (in absence of rate incentives). Perhaps for this reason, the DSM plans submitted to date to the New York State Public Service Commission (PSC), have heavily emphasized load shifting.[89]

---

[87] "Valley Fill" ETS programs eliminate environmental costs associated with air pollution emissions from wood stoves, oil furnaces, and other on-site heating systems, but replace them with environmental externalities from increased use of centralized electric power production and transmission facilities. One study has shown that air pollution emissions for sulfur dioxide, nitrogen oxide and carbon dioxide from an ETS Valley Fill program are greater overall than the emissions which would have occurred if on-site heating systems were retained. "Valley Fill" ETS systems do, however, result in significant reductions in particulate emissions, primarily by displacing wood stoves. In other words, the elimination or reduction of on-site heating systems emissions only partially offsets the increased emissions associated with additional electric power needed to power the Valley Fill ETS program. ICF, Environmental Assessment and Review of Externalities Related to NYSEG's Electric Thermal Storage Program, Vol. I, Final Report, August, 1989, pp. 4-7 - 4-9.

[88] Draft State Energy Master Plan, supra note 86 at p. 124.

[89] Energy Systems Research Group, Inc., Review of the 1990 Integrated Demand-Side Management Plans Filed in New York Public Service Commission Case No. 28223, October 1989 at pp. 6-7, filed as part of Comments of Pace University Center for Environmental Legal Studies on 1990 Annual DSM Plans of the Seven Jurisdictional Electric Utilities, October 31, 1989. See also, Memorandum from N.Y.P.S.C.

Load-shifting, however, often also means higher air pollution emissions, because a shift in demand from peak to off-peak will usually shift electricity generation from gas-fired peaking turbines, to coal or oil-fired base-load plants. Since CO_2, SO_2, particulate matter and nitrogen oxide emissions are much higher for coal and oil-fired units, load shifting programs, particularly for utilities with coal-fired base load plants, usually result in environmental externality costs which are greater than if the load shifting program were not undertaken.

Load-shifting may also shift from peak loads to base-load nuclear plants which have their own environmental externality costs.[90]

Elimination of the need for new peaking capacity will eliminate the environmental costs of those facilities, however (typically NO_x and CO_2 emissions from a gas-fired generator). Additionally, some utility's base load and peaking plants may have similar emissions profiles. For example, if load shifting results in a shift from oil-fired peaking turbines to oil-fired base-load plants, then the emissions increase may be insignificant. Similarly, for some utilities the effect of load shifting may involve less use of gas or oil turbines in favor of a nuclear baseload plant.

A complete assessment of the environmental externalities of load shifting DSM program must account for the differences in excess generation capacity, base-load and peak-load plant characteristics and other utility specific information.

a. Price Incentives Load Management

No literature was found that specifically addresses air pollutant emissions or other environmental externalities which occur as a result of price incentives to shift electric demand.[91] An example of load management price incentives is time-of-use rates (TOU).

TOU and other similar incentive programs are large in some states. Each of the New York utilities, for example, has TOU programs which are projected to shift significant amounts of power from peak to non-peak production. The following table sets forth projected winter peak reduction due to load shifting programs for New York utilities.

Office of Energy Conservation and Environment to the Commission, Review of 1990 Annual DSM Program Plans, December 5, 1989, p. 13, attached to N.Y.P.S.C. Case 29223 Order Concerning 1990 DSM Management Plans, December 29, 1989. New York recently adopted rate incentives, however. N.Y.P.S.C. Case 89-E-041, Op. No. 89-29, Opinion and Order Approving Demand-Side Management Rate Incentives and Establishing Further Proceedings, September 12, 1989.

[90] See Chapter VI. D.

[91] Bonnie Jacobsen of ICF, who performed a literature search on this topic, in conjunction with the NYSEG ETS study discussed below, expressed confidence that there have been no other studies in this area. Personal Communication with Bonnie Jacobsen, ICF Inc. January, 1990.

TABLE 1

PROJECTED WINTER PEAK REDUCTION FROM LOAD SHIFTING PROGRAMS[1]

UTILITY NAME	KW
Con Ed[2]	0
CHGE[3]	531
LILCO[4]	7185
NYSEG[5]	8603
NiMo[6]	3054
O&R[7]	66
RG&E[8]	1248
Total	20687

(1) Unless otherwise specified, data is from the Integrated 1990 Demand Side Management Plans, filed in September, 1989 by each of the seven investor owned public utilities in New York. The numbers are aggregated for all commercial and residential load shift programs.

(2) Based on the Consolidated Edison Company's Demand Side Management Plan filed in April 1988. The company's 1990 plan states that more recent peak reduction figures have not been determined.

(3) Central Hudson Gas & Electric, residential TOU rates only.

(4) Long Island Lighting Company, TOU rate only.

(5) NYS Electric & Gas residential and commercial ETS and, direct control electric water heating.

(6) Niagara Mohawk Power Corp. residential TOU rate only.

(7) Orange and Rockland residential TOU program only.

(8) Rochester Gas & Electric voluntary and mandatory TOU and ETS.

Table 2 sets forth projected summer peak reductions for load shifting programs of New York utilities.

TABLE 2

PROJECTED SUMMER PEAK REDUCTION FROM LOAD SHIFTING PROGRAMS[1]

UTILITY NAME	KW
Con Ed[2]	633
CHGE[3]	1623
LILCO[4]	8640
NYSEG[5]	3060
NiMo[6]	2600
O&R[7]	8100
RG&E[8]	596
Total	25252

(1) Unless otherwise specified, data is from the-Integrated 1990 Demand Side Management Plans, filed in September, 1989, by each of the seven investor owned public utilities in New York. The numbers are aggregated for all commercial and residential load shift programs.

(2) Based on the Consolidated Edison Company's Demand Side Management Plan filed in April 1988. The 1990 plan states that peak reduction figures have not been determined. Con Ed's only load shifting program is a thermal coal storage program.

(3) Central Hudson Gas & Electric, residential TOU rates only.

(4) Long Island Lighting Company, optional and non-optional TOU rate for residential and commercial.

(5) NYS Electric and Gas, ETS and direct control of water heating.

(6) Niagara Mohawk Power Corp., residential TOU rate only.

(7) Orange and Rockland, non-residential peak actual rate and TOU programs.

(8) Rochester Gas & Electric Company, voluntary and mandatory TOU and ETS.

The absence of information about the air pollution effect of these TOU load shifting programs represents an important future research need. Research on this subject should determine, the extent to which TOU rates have the effect of shifting load from less-polluting peaking units to more-polluting base-load plants and the extent to which additional construction of additional peaking units may be avoided.

Load shifting may also affect the dispatching of power, not only within a utility, but among other power pool members. A forecast of this effect would also be necessary before one could estimate the air pollution emission effects of a load shifting TOU rate or related incentive programs. Calculating the effect TOU rates on air pollution emissions must also include an assessment of participation in the program. In the short term, low participation rates may significantly reduce projected load shifting effects and possibly the air pollution emissions effects of TOU rates.

b. Electric Thermal Storage

The following discussion addresses the air and water pollution effects of one utility's electric thermal storage (ETS) program. The study indicates the magnitude of emission increases associated with load shifting due to price incentives, at least for to utilities having excess generating capacity. If TOU programs have emission impacts proportionally similar to NYSEG's ETS program, then it is possible that total air pollution impacts of load shifting programs are quite significant.

A recent study estimated the environmental externalities that would result from an ETS program instituted by the New York State Electric and Gas Corporation (NYSEG).[92] For the residential and commercial programs analyzed in the ICF Report, NYSEG estimated that its ETS program would defer approximately 35 megawatts of peak load.[93] NYSEG's April 1990 long range plan described winter peak savings of 5,000 kilowatts from its residential and non-residential ETS programs. It also tested a 1010 kilowatt summer peak demand reduction from its non-residential ETS program.

The following table describes overall emissions increases resulting from the load shifting portion (excluding the "valley filling" program) of the ETS program.

---

[92] ICF, Environmental Assessment and Review of Externalities Related to NYSEG's Electric Thermal Storage Program, Vol. I, Final Report, August 1989, at p. 4-11,. [Hereafter cited as ICF.]

[93] Id., at p. 1-1.

TABLE 3

INCREASES IN STATEWIDE AIR EMISSIONS LOAD SHIFTING[94]

Pollutant (lbs)	1995	2000	2004
SO_2	162,576	56,442	117,206
NO_x	85,738	(5,839)	50,898
CO_2	25,760,101	6,426,411	19,446,859
PM	8,051	115	22,127

The lower figures for the year 2000 are due to projected changes in power plant dispatching during that period, which will shift production to gas-fired units or units which have superior air pollution controls.

The study concludes that the emissions resulting from this one utility program are "verysmall in comparison to statewide air emissions projections," amounting to less than 1%, and often less than .1% of statewide emissions, even when the sizeable emissions from the "valleyfill"portion of the program are counted. Nevertheless, the emissions are not insignificant, particularly if added to the emission effects of other utility load shifting programs.

Other environmental costs of NYSEG's load shifting ETS include a full range of water and land effects associated with increase power generation. The ICF study estimates that bottom and fly ash waste to increase by .08 and .023% of the total state production by 1995 as a result of the combined NYSEG load shifting and valley fill programs. These wastes, however, are projected to decrease by 2004 due to the dispatch of generating units in that period. Scrubber sludge will initially decline, but later increases by about .031% of statewide sludge production. ICF projects similarly small increases in water consumption. Changes in water withdrawal and consumption induced by the ETS program are "all less than .1% of total state water consumption for electric generation." ICF concludes that changes in land use are too small to alter land use patterns and may actually be positive, in terms of avoiding dedication of land for small peaking units and reduced wood consumption in the valley fill portion of the ETS program.

Non-residential ETS program impacts are parallel to residential program impacts, but smaller.

---

[94] Decreases in air emissions are placed in parenthesis.

TABLE 4

NON-RESIDENTIAL ETS LOAD SHIFT CASE INCREASE IN STATEWIDE AIR EMISSIONS[95]

Pollutant (lbs)	1995	2000	2004
SO_2	118,571	(60,239)	27,803
NO_x	53,156	882	18,248
CO_2	19,448,002	1,735,124	3,207,589
PM	7,541	(2,210)	4,725

Similar programs contained in Niagara Mohawk Power Corporation's long range plan would achieve an 174 megawatt load peak reduction by 2000.[96] These authors predict reduction peak load of 100 megawatts from NYSEG ETS and 41 megawatts for Con Ed's Thermal Cool Storage by 2000.[97] Con Edison's 1990 DSM plan includes an electric cool thermal storage program which reduces peak demand by shifting air conditioning demand to off peak in the summer.

Altogether the New York utilities load shifting programs for just four utilities are projected to reduce peak demand by 315 MW by 2000, nearly ten times the size of the program evaluated by ICF. This does not count the sizeable TOU program of LILCO.

Research is needed to determine if air emissions of these programs are comparable to those of the NYSEG programs. If so, there is a need to assess the combined environmental impacts of all the New York State utilities' ETS and TOU programs. Future research projects could expand ICF's emissions estimates to the other utility programs. This could produce an estimate of statewide emission increases due to ETS programs. The analysis presumably could be modified to estimate the emissions effect from non-ETS load shifting programs. One could then apply the environmental costs factors (for conventional air pollutant emissions) described elsewhere in this report[98], and arrive at an externality cost expressed as cents per kilowatt hour of peak demand savings. At this point, the data is not available to calculate the increased emissions that occur from other utilities' load shifting programs.

---

[95] ICF, <u>supra</u> note 92 at p. 5-10. Decreases in air emissions are shown in parenthesis.

[96] Goldman, C., E. Kahn, "Comparative Assessment of the DSM Plans of Four New York Utilities," <u>Proceedings of the Fourth National Conference on Utility DSM Programs</u>, Electric Power Research Institute, Vol. 1, April 1989, p. 21-6.

[97] <u>Id</u>.

[98] <u>See</u> Chapter IV, B and C.

The literature, however, does indicate that ETS and TOU programs can have significant adverse environmental impacts. Those impacts distinguish ETS programs from other DSM strategies. The literature suggests that it may not be appropriate to treat load shifting programs the same as other DSM measures in assigning environmental externality credits in new capacity bidding programs.

6. Conclusion

The literature supports a conclusion that, with the exception of some load-shifting measures, there are no significant environmental impacts from DSM. Studies show that weatherization programs by themselves are not a primary cause of indoor air pollution problems. Where problems do exist, mitigation measures are available. The continuing impact of construction policies on CFC use is negligible, due to the rapid advancement of CFC phase-out. Load-shifting may have greater environmental externality costs than other DSM measures. This is due to the increased emissions from greater reliance on baseload electric generating plants. Additional research is needed on this topic. See Chapter IX.

VII. EVALUATION OF ENVIRONMENTAL COSTING MODELS

VII. EVALUATION OF ENVIRONMENTAL COSTING MODELS

A. INTRODUCTION

One of the tasks of this project is to evaluate environmental models capable of yielding estimates of environmental costs and benefits associated with energy resources. Despite the plethora of models that have been built to support analyses of various environmental issues, no models have been found that could accurately be described as environmental costing models.

There are some models, however, that either address significant portions of the environmental costing problem or that could be modified to produce environmental cost estimates. Several of these models are reviewed in this section. Two of the most promising models (AERAM and TEMIS) are reviewed in some detail because of their potential to serve as environmental costing models or as a bridge to a new generation of environmental costing models.

The models are not evaluated with respect to how well they conform with physical laws because this report assumes that the models accurately portray physical relationships. The underlying theoretical and empirical relationships are also assumed to be reasonable and an evaluation of those factors is beyond the scope of this project.

Models that produce estimates of environmental costs can be distinguished from models that use estimates of environmental costs. Models that produce environmental cost estimates produce those estimates for specific plants. Using information about the plant, fuel, and site, estimates of the environmental impacts are produced and used to estimate the economic value of those impacts. It is unlikely that a single model could be used to estimate the full range of environmental costs associated with an energy resource. The kinds of impacts produced by a power plant are too diverse for a single model to capture and evaluate all the effects. Any model that did so would actually be a collection of models because models that estimate the impacts to an airshed, for example, differ markedly from models used to evaluate impacts on water bodies.

All the models reviewed during the course of this project are atmospheric models. No models of land or water use were found that could be considered environmental costing models or that could be considered useful for building environmental costing models.

Most empirical studies have shown that the preponderance of environmental costs associated with most thermal plants are created by atmospheric pollution. Consequently, models that provide estimates of effects associated with atmospheric pollution would be most useful in the evaluation of environmental costs.

Models for non-thermal (or at least non-fossil fuel) energy resources such as hydro and geothermal do not exist and probably cannot be developed. Such resources are heavily dependent on the characteristics of the site at which they are located. Predicting the impacts from such resources with a generic model would be an impossible task. For example, except under unusual circumstances, two hydroelectric plants of the same size and design would have greatly different impacts on nearby fish populations. Some factors that would have to be identical in order to compare the impacts the plants would have on the fish are: the species, the size of the population, the migration period, the migration time, the amount and timing of flows, and the water quality. Several years ago, Bonneville Power Administration, an authority on hydroelectric generation, attempted to develop such a model for new hydro sites and failed. The agency concluded that modeling generic hydro impacts is impossible.

Most environmental models used by utilities are models that use, or could use, environmental cost information. These models do not estimate the environmental costs, but could use such estimates to optimize the economic dispatch of a utility system or power pool. Adding estimates of environmental costs to such models would enable a utility or power pool to internalize environmental cost considerations in their decision processes in order to minimize the social costs of energy production.

System models, or production models, have the potential to assess the macroeconomic impacts of different policies or constraints, taking into account the level and incidence of environmental costs estimated for each plant in the system. Thus, if a utility wished to reduce CO_2 emissions by some specified amount, it could test alternatives designed to do so. System models could reveal the expected system wide reduction in CO_2 emissions, the social cost of those reductions (including both utility and external costs), and the changes in plant operations that would be effected. Therefore, system models could benefit greatly from estimates of environmental costs because they could use those costs to optimize a range of objectives. One system cost model (CCMU) is evaluated in this report to illustrate such possible applications.

The review of the models follows a brief section which lays out the attributes of an ideal environmental costing model. Such a hypothetical model serves as a reference against which to compare actual environmental models.

B. AN IDEAL MODEL

An ideal model for performing calculations of environmental costs associated with energy resources, would convert user-specified information on the resource and its location into estimates of environmental costs. Changes in the characteristics of the resource or its location would be translated into changes in the environmental costs of the resource. But the model would be more than just a black box into which one puts data and from which one receives estimates of environmental costs.

The full range of effects, from primary emissions to changes in economic value associated with environmental risks, must be clearly and explicitly shown by a model. All the linkages in that chain must be accounted for. Following the stages of analysis described in the Framework section, the ideal model would consist of the following elements.

First, it would estimate the emissions from the plant based on plant type, control technologies, and fuel characteristics. This model stage would display the pollutants that exit the stack.

The second stage would use the output of the first stage to estimate and predict the transport, transformation, and dispersal of the pollutants. Some pollutants disperse according to prevailing winds and the pollutant's size and weight. Other pollutants are the result of transformations of the stack emissions. Sulfates, for example, are formed from SO_2 after the SO_2 has been emitted from the stack. During this stage, all such transformations, and the path taken by the primary and secondary pollutants would be traced out.

The third stage would estimate exposures. The model would calculate atmospheric concentrations of the pollutants at various distances from the plant. This would inform the analyst of the amount of pollutant exposure on an hourly, daily, seasonal, or annual basis.

The exposures calculated in the third stage would be used in the following stage to estimate the response of the affected population to the exposures. This would require estimates of the size of the population exposed at various distances from the plant corresponding to various levels of exposures. "Populations" could mean human populations or it could mean populations of crops, forests, buildings, or any other variable of interest to the analyst. The result of this stage would be an estimate of the physical response of the population. For example, this stage could produce an estimate of the reduced yields of timber producing forests as a result of exposures to sulfur compounds.

Finally, the last stage of the model would assign economic values to the physical impacts. Normally, this would be accomplished by multiplying a user-specified unit value by the incremental physical change or by the incremental environmental risk. For example, the user could specify that each thousand board feet of timber is worth some value. That value would then be multiplied by the amount of timber yield reduction associated with the operation of the power plant. This would give the economic value associated with the lost timber.

There are also several characteristics common to all good models. The ideal model is logical and "true." The physical and economic relationships within the model must make sense and must conform to what is actually known about the world. The physical relationships, for example, must comply with known laws of physics. Institutional constraints must be recognized. If an entity is barred by law from engaging in some activity, then the model must not assume that the entity engages in that activity.

Second, the model must produce useful results. Estimates of variables crucial to the analysis must be provided. The estimates must be credible both to analysts and to decisionmakers. This is dependent partly on the logic of the model, partly on the quality of the data available to the model, and partly on the intuitive appeal of the results.

Third, sufficient detail must be available to the model. It must include all functional relationships that may affect outcomes, it must include sufficient data, and it must give results with sufficient detail for decision making.

Fourth, the model should be easy and fast for the user to run. This desirable characteristic is often in conflict with other features. Nevertheless, the faster the model can be run, the less expensive it is likely to be and the quicker analyses can be performed. If possible, models should reside on personal computers (PCs) to make them readily available to all potential users.

Data requirements for the ideal model would be easy to meet. In general, there is a tradeoff between accuracy and logic versus ease of operation and ease of data input. At the very least, the data requirements must be well understood by any analyst using the model, and reasonably accurate data sets must be available to the analyst.

C. A PRELIMINARY REVIEW OF ENVIRONMENTAL MODELS

Existing environmental models fall generally into one of three groups. By far the most common group consists of environmental control cost models. These models are used to estimate the cost of controlling various environmental effects. These are typically engineering models used to minimize the costs to a utility of meeting air or water quality standards through the use of various control technologies, fuel sources, or other means. Control cost models provide estimates of the utility's internal costs associated with meeting environmental quality standards or mitigating some amount of environmental costs. As such, they do not really constitute environmental costing models. Some such models can, however, be adapted to serve as environmental costing models as will be shown during the review of models in the next section. In fact, such models have some advantages, the main one being that a utility or regulatory body can compare control costs to the benefits of reducing environmental damages. In general, control costs should be undertaken when the reduction in the cost of environmental damages exceeds the costs of the controls. For example, the CCMU Model described later in this section can be used to estimate the costs of controlling SO_x emissions from the New York Power Pool or from an individual plant. If the reductions in the value of economic damage associated with the SO_x reductions are greater than the cost of those reductions, overall social costs would be reduced.

A second group, also comprising a large number of models, consists of physical models of the output of a generating plant. The most common of these models are the plume models that show how atmospheric emissions from a plant disperse through an airshed. (Similar models exist for discharges to water bodies.) This group of models is typically used to conduct analyses for environmental impact statements and other non-economic analyses. They indicate the amount of various pollutants expected to be emitted by a plant over time. For example, physical models provide estimates of the number of tons of SO_2 that will be emitted over the course of a year. More sophisticated physical models provide estimates of the dispersal of the pollutants through the airshed. These models can also be adapted to serve as environmental costing models although few have been. The UNAMAP models described below and most other plume models fall into this category.

Some models have been developed within a third group known as risk or damage assessment models. Risk assessment models provide physical assessments of the risks associated with various plant configurations, fuel types, plant locations, ambient weather conditions, control technologies, and so forth. These models lack only an economic valuation component; otherwise they strongly resemble environmental costing models. The AERAM model described in this section is a risk assessment model that could be modified to yield economic cost estimates.

1. Air Emissions Risk Assessment Model (AERAM)

The Air Emissions Risk Assessment Model (AERAM) is designed to assist utilities in determining what the most effective and economical control measures are by evaluating the risks of pollutants from fossil fuel plants. Although AERAM was developed for the purpose of implementing the most cost-effective control costs, AERAM can also be used to quantify the risks associated with atmospheric emissions from fossil-fuel-fired electric generation plants. Thus, because the model is both a control cost model and a risk assessment model, it is potentially useful for estimating environmental costs and benefits.

The model is used with an IBM-compatible PC, a feature which makes the model relatively easy to use and which makes it accessible to most utilities. Based on user supplied information, the model produces estimates of the per capita risks and aggregate risks of various ailments and diseases associated with pollutants emitted by particular plants and fuel types in conjunction with the site's topography and demographic characteristics.

AERAM consists of four sub-modules: a) the Emissions Module; b) the Air Quality Module; c) the Exposure Module; and, d) the Risk Module. These are described in the next section.

a. Emissions Module

The Emissions Module uses information on firing rates, fuel types, and plant types to produce a tabulation of particle size distribution classifications for the pollutants of interest. The Emissions Module requires significant amounts of data. Some parameters are calculated internally from exogenously supplied data, but the user must supply information on several variables including which pollutants are to be modeled. These pollutants may be those contained in the fuel or they may be those that are created during the combustion process. For example, benzo-a-pyrene, BaP, and coal can both be modeled. BaP is not present in coal but is emitted from the plant and can be measured at the outlet of the pollution control equipment. Arsenic, is contained in coal and it, too, can be modeled.

The user must also specify the control devices used. Control devices could be venturi scrubbers, electrostatic precipitators, and fabric filters or baghouses.

Fuel types must also be specified. (AERAM supposedly can be used for any fossil fuel generating plant, but the Users Guide, the Case Studies, and the available software refer only to coal-fired plants.) A wide range of coal types can be modeled. Among the available coals are Ohio, Tennessee, and Illinois bituminous, and East-Central and Wyoming sub-bituminous. Data is provided for a number of fuel elements including the percentage of sulfur, ash, carbon, hydrogen, oxygen, moisture, and nitrogen. In addition, the heating value in BTU per pound is entered.

The user can also define particle size class diameters as inputs. Default values are supplied if none are provided by the user. The smallest particle size class has a very small diameter to distinguish gaseous emissions from particulate emissions.

Other input data consists of variables such as plant size, load factors, and operating hours.

The output of this module consists of three parts. First, it provides a tabular summary of input data. This feature enables the user to be sure the correct parameters have been entered and also permits others to review the inputs. Second, it provides a summary of how each variable was calculated. Some are entered by the user and some are calculated based on the data entered by the user. Third, for each pollutant of interest, the model produces a tabulation of particle size distribution classifications. This is an input into the air quality module.

b. Air Quality Module

Two sets of inputs are required for the air quality module. First, the receptor location for the purpose of exposure assessment must be provided. This is represented by population-based receptor grids.

The population-based receptor grids are then paired with annual average climatology for the location. This is used to determine the dispersal of pollutants throughout an airshed.

The climatology data sets consist of annual-average joint frequency functions from the National Weather Service site applicable to the location. These indicate the joint frequency of specific wind speed, wind duration, and atmospheric stability categories. Several categories may be specified for each of these variables.

The user may specify several control and processing options including an annual or seasonal ambient concentration; a rural or urban dispersion coefficient; the effects of atmospheric reactivity, settling, or deposition; the effects of stack-tip downwash; and, the effects of building wake effects.

The output lists the receptor locations and the numbering of receptors in each zone. Also, it provides a listing of annual fly ash and pollutant concentrations for each receptor. Finally, it provides a ranking of fly ash and pollutant concentration from highest to lowest for each receptor location. These are used as inputs to the next module.

c. Exposure Module

In the exposure module the user specifies the population for each district for which there is at least one receptor. The user also has the option of stratifying the population into one or more subpopulations.

The ambient concentration, an output of the air quality module, is translated into an inhaled concentration per individual within each district based on an exposure factor. The exposure factor varies by age because of the difference in the amount of air breathed by people of different ages.

The output of this module consists of several elements. First, as with the other modules, it provides a tabular summary of the input data. Second, it provides a histogram of the number of people exposed per concentration range and per exposure range. Third, it provides exposure levels for each subpopulation and for the total population tabulated by district. Finally, it tabulates and displays total exposures, summed over all districts, for each subpopulation and for the total population. This information is then used in the last module, the risk module.

d. Risk Module

The risk module translates the population exposures to various pollutants into estimates of the expected value of effects resulting from those exposures. It uses dose-response data to estimate the incidence of various ailments--cancer is the disease of primary interest--from the exposure values. The user must specify the incidence for various known dosage levels. Up to three dose-response models can be fit to the data. They are the one hit (linear), log-probit, and multistage models. (These models represent various ways of characterizing the response of animals or humans to the dosage of a particular pollutant.)

In addition to the summary of input data, the module provides several different estimates of risk. First it provides estimates of the per capita risk. This could be, for example, the predicted per capita lifetime excess carcinogenic risk resulting from inhalation of a pollutant based on daily exposures to the pollutant.

It also provides a mathematical description and parameter values for the different risk models; that is, linear, log-probit, and multi-stage models. Statistical goodness of fit is estimated for each of those models using the X^2 test.

Per capita and total risk are displayed by district and the aggregated total risk, summed over all districts, is predicted by each risk model.

e. Evaluation

The output of interest is an estimate of the health risks associated with each plant modeled, at the location modeled. Because the risks are provided on both a per capita basis and on an aggregate basis, it yields the information necessary to perform an economic valuation of the health risks associated with a plant. As noted, health risks are the dominant portion of environmental costs associated with fossil fuel plants.

The only significant omission from the AERAM model is an economic evaluation module. AERAM models the emissions from the stack; transport, transformation, and dispersal throughout the airshed; exposures to the pollutant stream; and, the response of the population. This provides all the required physical information for performing environmental cost calculations. Consequently, a model such as AERAM, or one similar to it, is highly recommended for consideration as an environmental costing model for use by utilities or power pools in their least cost planning processes. Utilities could use pre-specified economic values to apply to the risks estimated by the model to obtain reasonable estimates of the environmental costs associated with atmospheric emissions from a fossil fuel electric generating plant.

2. The Total Emissions Model for Integrated Systems (TEMIS)

a. Background

The Total Emissions Model for Integrated Systems (TEMIS) was developed by the OKO Institute of West Germany. The objectives of the TEMIS project were to:

1. Define standard energy systems for space heating and electricity generation, including the total fuel cycles;

2. Establish data bases on energy, efficiency, air emissions, solid waste, and land use;

3. Estimate pollution loads associated with materials in each step of the fuel cycle;

4. Compare energy systems based on units of delivered energy; and,

5. Help integrate quantitative and qualitative impacts for improved environmental decisionmaking.

TEMIS estimates the physical effects associated with a wide variety of energy systems. It produces estimates of all quantifiable impacts in physical units. As such, it is not a complete environmental costing model capable of estimating the environmental costs of energy resources. To fulfill that task, it would require augmentation with a model capable of estimating exposures and responses to the physical impacts, as well as a model for valuing those impacts. But any environmental costing model would require estimates of the physical impacts. TEMIS is one of the most complete models available for modeling those impacts throughout the entire fuel cycle and would be an excellent basis for a larger environmental costing model.

TEMIS can be run on any IBM-compatible PC. It does not depend on other software programs; it runs independently with its own software. It is menu driven, providing interactive routines for the user. These features make it very attractive as a potential tool for conducting environmental cost analyses.

TEMIS is not an optimization model--it does not provide optimal solutions with respect to maximizing or minimizing an objective function. Unlike some models, it does not provide the "best" solutions in terms of minimizing emissions, although iterations with successive runs would allow a user to converge on an optimal solution. But the lack of optimization is not a disadvantage for models used to estimate environmental costs of energy resources. Instead, an environmental costing model need only simulate the characteristics and the impacts of the actual (or hypothetical) resources being considered for acquisition by a utility. Simulating those effects allows the analyst to examine the impacts that would result <u>if the resource, as planned, were to be constructed and operated.</u> Those impacts, and their costs, can then be compared to the simulated impacts and costs of alternative resources. To the extent that TEMIS, or any other model, accurately simulates those impacts, it will be a useful tool.

TEMIS has self-contained data bases adaptable to the user's needs. Users can augment the data bases, use their own, or simply use the model's data as is. In addition, users can store data bases for later use. These are all desirable features.

Among the data bases used by the model and adaptable to the user's needs are data on new fuels; data on changes in fuel cycles; data on new energy systems that may be developed, including hypothetical systems; and, data on energy scenarios. (Energy scenarios consist of a set of energy systems.)

b. Model Structure

TEMIS calculates emissions both upstream and downstream from the point of production. This means that all emissions produced during the fuel cycle are accounted for. The emissions are disaggregated into three areas. First, it calculates emissions at the site. These emissions consist of pollutants such as SO_x, NO_x, and CO_2, produced during the energy production stage. Second, it calculates global emissions. Global emissions are those created during the upstream production processes. Upstream production processes are activities such as fuel mining, processing, and transportation. For some fuels, emissions from upstream processes are significant. Finally, it produces estimates of emissions during materials processing. Materials processing consists of manufacture and transportation of the materials used in plant construction. The emissions are also aggregated into a total. All emissions are calculated on a user-determined per BTU or per kWh basis.

The model also calculates economic values for the emissions, although those values must not be construed as environmental cost values. Instead, the model calculates the values based on emissions avoidance costs. As discussed elsewhere in this report, emissions avoidance costs cannot be interpreted as environmental costs.

Avoidance cost information can be useful, however, for other purposes, especially when the objective is to meet emissions standards at least cost. By calculating avoidance costs it should be possible to design energy systems configured to meet environmental standards at the lowest internal cost, even if that cost bears no relation to the damage costs.

There are four main menus. In the Fuel Menu, the user specifies the fuel type and its components. Fuel data is stored in the model's data base, or can be supplied by the user. Fuel characteristics determined by the model include specific air demand, specific exhaust gas volume, maximum CO_2 content, and CO_2 emission factor. Other characteristics can also be determined at the user's option.

The Processes Menu differentiates seven categories to provide logical benchmarks for the TEMIS model. The processes are:

1) Combustion; for processes that use a fuel directly by combustion. TEMIS calculates the conversion factor between the concentration of pollutants in the exhaust gas and the corresponding emission.

2) Conversion; characterized by conversion of energy, especially from primary to secondary forms. Such processes are typically dependent on auxiliary energy. Oil refineries are conversion processes.

3) Transport; characterized by the fuel which is transported, the amount of fuel loss in transport, the amount of energy used in transport, and the distance.

4) Production; the "head" end of an energy system, delivering the primary energy. This is the "source" of the energy, examples being gas extraction or coal mining. The production process also may use auxiliary energy.

5) Dispatcher; combines several other processes into one which can then be proportioned out. For example, the dispatcher for a refinery could split the auxiliary energy to 30% delivered by an oil-fired boiler and 70% delivered by a gas-fired boiler.

6) Scenario Dispatcher; describes the dynamics of energy systems and defines up to 20 scenarios.

7) Process Chains; represents the complete upstream activity. This is used to treat the whole fuel cycle as a single activity. For example, a process-chain might be the delivery of light oil by truck to the oil tanks of residential heating systems. The environmental effects are summed and related to one unit of delivered light oil. The scenarios menu is used to aggregate processes. This menu also drives the graphics package and contains documentation on the internal data and functional relationships the analyst can print out.

The Systems menu defines parameters used by the model. The user specifies what units will be used for variables such as energy, mass, and area. Metric values and their English equivalents are available for most variables. This menu is also used to define the accuracy of the model. Because the model uses iterative processes to converge on a solution, the user must tell the model when its convergance is sufficient. Finally, the emissions avoidance costs are included in this menu. These costs can be used to determine the shadow price of reducing emissions by one unit.

By using the menus, the user can examine the emissions associated with any stage in the energy cycle. From primary energy production to secondary energy production to end use, emissions can be calculated for each stage in the process or for the entire process.

c. TEMIS as an Environmental Cost Model

TEMIS is, unfortunately, not yet ready to serve as an environmental cost model for utility resource planning. Its desirable features, particularly its ease of use, have already been noted.

Much of the model is unnecessary for the evaluation of environmental costs associated with potential new power plant additions. For example, from the point of view of the utility attempting to determine the lowest social cost energy resource, it is not necessary to compute emissions from home oil burners. Much of the data and calculations built into the model are superfluous. That is a drawback only to the extent that it reduces storage space for more pertinent data or increases run time. But the run times are short anyway, so that appears to be a minor inconvenience, at worst.

The real barrier to using TEMIS, however, is that its functional relationships apply only to the German economy and it is not available in English. Because the German economy and its energy infrastructure are not applicable to the U.S., TEMIS cannot provide an accurate depiction of emissions expected from U.S. energy plants. For example, emissions during uranium enrichment assume that, on average, a certain proportion of electric energy used during the enrichment process is produced by coal, some proportion by nuclear, and so forth. Because those proportions are not the same as those prevailing in the U.S., estimates based on the German energy system would not apply to the U.S.

As currently configured, the German basis of TEMIS is flawed. The U.S. Department of Energy, however, is developing a version of TEMIS applicable to the U.S. economy. Negotiations with the OKO Institute are now underway to accomplish that task. When completed, the model could become available to utilities around the country for use in their environmental analyses. This would obviously be the most efficient way to maximize the utility of the model and to assure consistency of analyses among its users. If this approach is followed, TEMIS could become an integral tool for conducting utility level environmental cost analyses of electric generating and conservation technologies.

3. Cornell/Carnegie-Mellon Universities Model (CCMU)

a. Background

The Cornell/Carnegie-Mellon Universities Model (CCMU) is an annual production model adapted for the New York Power Pool (NYPP). It is run at the state level (New York) but has details on specific power plants located within New York. CCMU is a linear programming model (LP) optimizing an objective function of meeting loads at the lowest utility cost. Each of the four modules of the model calculates solutions for certain variables, some of which are used in the succeeding module; that is, the output of each module serves as an input to the succeeding module. Solutions are calculated on an annual basis and the model can be run for as many years as desired by the user.

One feature in particular differentiates the CCMU model from other utility production models. That feature, a pollution control module, enables the user to estimate costs of meeting emissions targets or constraints. Rather than optimizing utility production costs without regard to pollution emissions, CCMU optimizes production costs subject to any emissions constraints the user may care to specify.

As currently configured, CCMU is not an environmental costing model. It responds to pollution avoidance costs, not to pollution damage costs. It does not now have the ability to estimate environmental costs of plant operation but such a feature could be grafted on to the model, expanding its usefulness, and obviating the need to develop, test, and disseminate a new model. This possibility is re-visited following a description of the model and how it works.

b. Demand Module

The demand module calculates electricity load for three customer classes on an annual basis. Although the model runs on an annual basis, it uses a five-part load duration curve. By using a segmented load duration curve, the model does not exclude information relevant to peaking, which it would if all information were aggregated on an annual basis. The module requires that the user provide information on projections of economic activity and on fuel prices. (In other words, this data must be supplied exogenously.) The module then calculates revenues, annual energy requirements, and loads for the three customer classes.

c. Pollution Control Module

In the pollution control module, individual generating plants are screened to ensure that they meet air quality standards. Air quality standards are specified for SO_x, NO_x, and particulates. Emissions are calculated as a function of boiler characteristics, fuel characteristics, level of generation, and control equipment. If the plant does not meet emissions standards the model has two choices. First, it can switch to a cleaner fuel. Second, it can install pollution control equipment. Because the model optimizes costs, it will select the cheaper of the two alternatives. It accounts for both the increased variable cost of production in either case, as well as for the increased capital cost of additional pollution control equipment.

d. Dispatch Module

The dispatch module is the heart of the CCMU model. It contains information on Independent Power Producers (IPP), new power sources, and existing NYPP power plants. In addition, it keeps track of imports, exports, and renewable power sources within the State of New York. The dispatch module gives the solution for the least cost generation mode subject to environmental and operating constraints. Operating constraints consist of factors such as must run plants, forced outages, scheduled maintenance, and so forth. Loads are met at least cost over the entire load duration curve. This means that no segment of that curve is necessarily met at least cost, but that the annual cost of serving loads corresponding to that curve is minimized.

As the system is dispatched, production costs and import costs are estimated. During dispatch, the model has options to fuel switch, retrofit control equipment, and to add new capacity.

e. Finance Module

The finance module is an accounting module. It accounts for all costs: production costs and capital costs. The result of the accounting is an estimate of the allowable revenues for the year. That value is fed into the demand module to be used in determining the following year's rates.

f. Deposition

CCMU uses four sites in the state for estimating deposition levels of sulfates. Based on emissions of sulfur dioxide from each plant, the model calculates the amount of wet and dry sulfates deposited at each site. Deposits are measured in pounds of sulfates per hectare.

The deposition calculation uses a transportation function to transform SO_2 emissions from specific plants into sulfate depositions at each of the four sites. This is different from models that calculate the plume dispersal from a power plant and the subsequent atmospheric concentration of particular pollutants. Gaussian Plume models and others that model the plume from power plants typically yield estimates of the dispersal of a pollutant throughout an airshed, providing estimates of the atmospheric concentration of the pollutant at different locations, usually expressed in micrograms per cubic meter (ug/m^3). Instead, CCMU uses predetermined coefficients applied to stack emissions to derive estimates of the amount of sulfates deposited at the four sites.

Gaussian Plume models are attractive for environmental cost analyses because they are capable of estimating exposures of populations almost regardless of where they live. This is done by segmenting the area surrounding a plant into individual components. The next step is calculating the average annual exposure in ug/m^3 of the pollutant for each sub-area, or component. Then, using dose-response coefficients it is possible to calculate the environmental effect or health risk faced by each individual living in the sub-area. Then, the individual risk can be aggregated over the population of the sub-area for an estimate of the total population risk in the sub-area. Finally, the risks in each sub-area are aggregated over all the sub-areas to get a total population risk.

The lack of a plume dispersal feature is a severe limitation to the use of CCMU as an environmental costing model. It can develop estimates of exposures to sulfates only for the four sites. This means that populations that may be exposed to sulfate deposition but that do not live at or near the four sites cannot be accounted for.

In principle, it would be possible to develop additional coefficients to account for both different sites as well as different pollutants. Different sites would be developed according to population centers. This may be a more daunting task then it might at first appear. As more receptor sites, or population centers, are added, coefficients must be developed for each plant whose emissions may travel to the site. Thus, the data requirements would tend to expand geometrically and could soon become overwhelming.

A better approach would be to develop the costs applicable to each plant. This would enable CCMU to account for external environmental costs in the optimization of the NYPP system. Unfortunately, it begs the question of what model can be applied to the plants themselves to estimate their environmental costs.

CCMU could be a useful model for minimizing the system costs of utility plant operation, including external costs. It does not appear to be a useful model for estimating environmental costs associated with individual energy resources. Another model or a set of models would be necessary to accomplish that task. CCMU could be used, however, to estimate the operational characteristics of a potential generating or conservation resource by running the system with the candidate resource as part of the system. This would provide an estimate of when and how often the proposed resource would be operated. That information could be used in estimating the environmental costs of the proposed plant because the environmental costs are dependent on when and how often the plant is operated.

Its most valuable use, however, could be as a system model to estimate the macro effects of alternative policies or resource development strategies. Such analyses are the primary purpose for which the model was originally designed. By augmenting the model with estimates of environmental costs associated with each plant included in the model, the social cost of energy production could be minimized. By examining social costs, including both the utility costs and the external environmental costs, CCMU could be useful in guiding policy development and assessing potential utility resource strategies.

4. Integrated Air Pollution Control System (IAPCS)

The Integrated Air Pollution Control System (IAPCS) was developed by the Air and Energy Engineering Research Laboratory of the Environmental Protection Agency. It is a PC-based simulation model used to estimate the control costs and performance of emission reduction technologies.

IAPCS is not suitable as an environmental cost model. It calculates pollution avoidance costs, only. It does not calculate environmental damage costs. Moreover, it can be applied only to coal-fired plants; other technologies and fuel types would require different models. A brief description of the model is provided because readers of this report may have other applications for which the IAPCS model would be useful.

IAPCS is capable of estimating control costs and performance for SO_2, NO_x, and particulate matter. Control technologies consist of pre-, in situ-, and post-combustion control. The technologies included in the model are:

1. Physical Control Cleaning (PCC--pre-combustion)
2. Low-NO_x combustion (LNC--in situ)
3. Limestone injection multistage burner (LIMB--in situ-combustion)
4. Electrostatic precipitator (ESP--post-combustion)
5. Fabric Filter (FF--post-combustion)
6. Spray Humidification (SH--post-combustion)
7. Dry sorbent injection (DSI--post-combustion)
8. Lime spray drying (LSD--post-combustion)
9. Flue Gas Desulfurization (FGD--post-combustion)

The model can use most combinations of these technologies except for those that are not compatible such as spray humidification and lime spray drying.

In addition to specifying the control technology the user must provide information on the boiler and fuel choices. Boiler information includes its configuration, size, whether new or retrofit, and starting date. The coal fuel choices consist of four types of bituminous coal (Pennsylvania, Ohio, West Virginia, and Illinois), Wyoming sub-bituminous coal, and North Dakota lignite.

For each control technology or combination of technologies, the model estimates the reduction in SO_2, NO_x, and particulate matter; the capital and annual costs associated with the control technologies; and, the cost effectiveness of the technologies, expressed in cost per ton of pollutant removed.

5. User's Network for Applied Modeling of Air Pollution (UNAMAP)

The User's Network for Applied Modeling of Air Pollution (UNAMAP) is actually a series of models. The models were developed by the Office of Air Quality Planning and Standards for Environmental Impact Analysis of the Environmental Protection Agency. The National Technical Information Service (NTIS) controls the distribution of the models, making them available to prospective users for a fee.

Extensive reviews of the models were not conducted for this project for two reasons. First, with respect to environmental costing the UNAMAP models do not differ significantly from the AERAM model which is reviewed here. Second, fees for obtaining models for review were not anticipated as part of this project. A brief summary of the UNAMAP models is provided for interested readers.

UNAMAP consists of 30 air quality simulation models. Each uses emission and meteorological data to project air pollutant concentrations in an airshed. Thus the models provide information necessary for calculating exposures to various substances. Those exposures could be translated into expected health risks and ultimately into health risk costs, although no such application is built into the UNAMAP models.

Collectively, the models are capable of estimating air pollutant concentrations from a variety of sources, including aluminum plants, vehicles, and industrial sources such as power plants. A wide variety of modeling options are also available to the user. Both power plant plumes and puffs can be modeled. Puffs are one-time, usually accidental, releases of pollutants. Air pollutant concentrations can be estimated for long- and short-term effects. In addition, different terrains can be handled by the models; terrains are usually categorized as flat or complex. Whatever the terrain, effects can be measured at short distances from the plant or at long distances. Finally, point, area, or line sources can be modeled as either single or multiple sources.

The primary advantage of UNAMAP is the ability to select models most suited to the problem at hand, rather than having to force a single model to fit a variety of sources and terrains. The cost of the models is relatively low, less than $1500. But the major disadvantage is that the models must be run on mainframe computers as opposed to PC-based models such as AERAM.

6. Other Models

Two other models were reviewed for this project but are not addressed at length in this report. A brief summary of each model is provided for readers who may be familiar with the existence of the models and who may have expected an evaluation of them in this report.

The Advanced Utility Simulation Model (AUSM) is a unit specific model of the U.S. electric system. It operates on either a plant specific or unit specific basis. The CCMU model evaluated previously is a scaled down version of AUSM. In effect, the CCMU model is the same model without the national level detail and without a large preprocessor which is used for new construction and dispatch on a regional level. The reason that CCMU is so close to AUSM is that it was developed from an earlier version of AUSM. The emission control, dispatch, finance, and demand modules from AUSM were used to build the CCMU model.

As currently configured, the AUSM model provides the same kind of information as does the CCMU model. It measures emissions from the stack according to fuel and boiler characteristics and according to the control technology employed. Thus, AUSM constitutes a system model that would be a candidate for using environmental costs but is not a model that would be capable of developing environmental costs for a single plant.

The Forecast Uncertainty Technique for Utility Resource Evaluation (FUTURE) model has been developed by Pacific Gas and Electric Co. (PG&E) of California. This model is used by PG&E for integrated resource planning under uncertainty. It provides estimates of the cost effectiveness of resource alternatives. It is both a simulation model and an optimizing model dependent on probability distributions for key variables such as load growth and resource supply. Those distributions are supplied by the user.

FUTURE has placeholders for environmental costs. The intent is eventually to develop environmental costs for each resource, to input those costs into the model along with traditional cost estimates for fuel, construction, O&M, etc., and to optimize all resource costs. Thus, the model would produce least social cost resource alternatives.

Again, this feature will allow PG&E to use environmental cost estimates in its planning process, but the FUTURE model does not estimate those costs. Those costs will require separate sets of analyses. Once in place, the model will provide a tool for minimizing the social cost of energy production, including environmental costs. PG&E currently has no definite timetable for estimating environmental costs to use in the FUTURE model. Whether it will do so depends, in part, on the outcome of the California Energy Commission's decisions in the ER90 case. Part of that effort is to determine how to address environmental concerns in utility resource planning processes. Until environmental costs are included in the model, no further evaluation of it for this project is warranted.

D. SUMMARY AND CONCLUSIONS

The lack of environmental costing models is disappointing. None were discovered that provide a complete estimate of the environmental costs associated with even one environmental impact of an electric power resource.

The TEMIS model and the AERAM model were the two most promising models reviewed. TEMIS is especially useful for quantifying the emissions both upstream and downstream from the point of energy production. This means that the full set of emissions associated with an entire fuel cycle can be estimated. Most other models provide estimates only of the downstream emissions; that is, estimates of the impacts of the effluents created when fuels are burned to produce electric energy. TEMIS is easy to use, resides on a PC, and has a short run time. Its disadvantages are significant, however. Although it provides estimates of emissions at all stages of the production process, it does not provide esitimates of exposures and responses to those emissions. Thus, it is impossible to determine the economic significance of those emissions. Second, TEMIS is based on the German economy. Until an American version is developed, TEMIS results are not of direct relevance to American utility systems.

AERAM is the most complete of the models reviewed. It provides estimates of emissions, transport, exposures, and responses. Except for a valuation module, this is a complete environmental costing model for health risks. Conceptually, there is no reason it could not be adapted to assess impacts on crops, materials, and forests in addition to humans. AERAM is easy to run, resides on a PC, and has a short run time. It is recommended for utilities to use as a basis for developing its own environmental costing models.

CCMU is a useful model for analyzing system impacts and for using environmental cost estimates developed elsewhere. It has a well established history of use in New York and has been used in several studies of the cost of pollution avoidance. Combining it with environmental cost estimates for each plant in the system would make it a powerful tool for macro analyses of policies and resource strategies designed to minimize social costs of energy production.

Both UNAMAP and IAPCS have good features, principally their ability to model emissions streams. The UNAMAP models appear to be similar in scope to the AERAM model. The selection of one model over the other should be based on cost, ease of running the model, and their relative accuracies. Their relative accuracies would have to be determined by air quality specialists knowledgeable about the structure of each atmospheric dispersal module. IAPCS, on the other hand, is useful only for assessing control costs because it measures only what comes out of the plant stack, not how it disperses throughout the airshed.

VIII. SPREADSHEET

VIII. SPREADSHEET

A. INTRODUCTION

The spreadsheet appearing in the following tables and contained in the enclosed disc is intended to show how environmental costs can be calculated, displayed, and modified. It is not intended to show the environmental costs of any real resource or its effects, although it could show such costs if actual data were used. It is based on a hypothetical coal plant emitting various quantities of pollutants to which people are exposed. The environmental cost of the plant consists of the economic value of the ensuing health risks.

The values used in the table are intended to be illustrative only, although they are based on modified versions of actual data from a study for the Bonneville Power Administration.[1] The formulas used to calculate the values are also displayed.

Although only one environmental effect (health risks) is calculated and valued in this spreadsheet, the same or similar procedure could be used for a variety of other environmental effects. This spreadsheet is intended to be a model; a complete accounting for all environmental costs associated with a coal plant is beyond the scope of this project.

Instructions for operating the program appear on the first page of the spreadsheet. The spreadsheet operates on the LOTUS 1-2-3 program. It is assumed that users are familiar with the operation of that program.

B. SPREADSHEET FEATURES

Based on user defined values for several variables, the spreadsheet automatically calculates the environmental cost of health risks associated with the power plant.

Values for the following variables are supplied by the user:

Unit Health Risk Value--Defined as the dollar value per statistical life. The default value is $4,000,000in 1989 dollars.

Real Discount Rate--Defined as the real discount rate at which future costs will be discounted to compute the present value and levelized cost of health risks. The value is entered as the decimal equivalent of the discount rate; e.g., 3% is entered as 0.03. The default value is 0.03.

Annual Population Growth Rate--Defined as the average annual increase in population of the region surrounding the plant. The value is entered as the percent growth rate. The default value is 1.2%.

---

[1] ECO Northwest, "Generic Coal Study," for Bonneville Power Administration, DE-AM79-86BP62884, Portland, OR, 1987.

Population Density--Defined as the number of people per square mile in the region surrounding the plant in the first year. (The program assumes that the population is uniformly distributed within a 120 mile radius of the plant.) The default value is 100.

Net Capacity of the Plant--Defined as the net installed capacity of the plant in megawatts. This value is used only to calculate the levelized health risk cost. It does not affect concentrations of pollutants; those data must be entered manually. (See below.) The default value is 603 MW.

Capacity Factor--Defined as the percent of time the plant is expected to operate over all hours of the year. The capacity factor is expressed as a proportion. The default value is 0.70.

In addition, dose-response functions for the six pollutants are provided. The user may modify these, as well.

The spreadsheet performs the following calculations. First it calculates the population in concentric rings around the plant based on the population density and the area within each ring. It then calculates population levels over time by applying the user supplied annual population growth rate.

Then it multiplies the population in each distance zone or ring by the average annual concentration of pollutants in each zone. The average annual concentration of pollutants appears in the fifth table beginning at about row 240. These data do not depend on other values in the spreadsheet: they must be enetered manually. The user can modify these vaues as desired, however. Default values are supplied. The result of that procedure is an estimate of annual exposures by pollutant by year. The pollutants included in the spreadsheet are sulfur dioxide, particulates, nitrogen oxides, sulfates, nitrates, and ozone. The total annual exposures to each pollutant are shown in the final six tables of the spreadsheet.

Next, the exposures are multiplied by the dose-response coefficients. This gives an expected value of unit health risks by pollutant by year. This information is displayed in the fourth table, beginning at about row 180.

Finally, the value per unit health risk is multiplied by the total unit health risks shown in the fourth table. This gives an annual expected value of health risk costs. These are displayed in the third table, beginning at about row 120. The table also shows the present value of health risk costs and the levelized cost of health risks at the bottom of the table. The present value is calculated using the user-specified discount rate. The levelized cost uses the present value, combined with average annual plant output based on capacity and capacity factor information supplied by the user.

The values for each of the six variables for which the user defines are displayed at the bottom of each table. This feature allows the user to conduct multiple sensitivities while the program automatically labels the output to show which values were used in each run.

The spreadsheet calculates costs for a 20-year period. This corresponds to the typical utility planning horizon. Additional years can be added to determine costs over the life of a longer lived plant. The 20-year period is sufficient to display effects over time without assaulting the viewer with too much data.

C. SAMPLE OUTPUT

Examples of the output from the spreadsheet are displayed as follows:

Brief explanatory notes and instructions for use are shown on the first page. These notes are intended to assist users of the spreadsheet who are assumed to be familiar with the workings of the LOTUS 1-2-3 Spreadsheet format.

The default values for the six variables used in the program are shown next. The dose-response coefficients are also shown. The user may modify any of these variables, press F9, and the program will automatically recalculate the tables.

The summary of the environmental costs associated with health risks are shown next. With the default values, the environmental cost of the health risks associated with the generic coal plant are $1.5 billion or a real levelized cost of 2.8 cents/kWh.

The health risks associated with each pollutant are then displayed. The table also shows the total health risks from all pollutants. As with all tables, the variable values used in that run are shown at the bottom of the table. This feature is also automatic.

The mean annual concentration of pollutants in micrograms per cubic meter appear on the next page. These values remain the same in all runs. They must be entered manually because they are not dependent on the size of the plant used in the program. This feature could be automated, if desired.

The annual population living in successive concentric rings around the plant is shown next. The program assumes that populations are uniformly dispersed around the plant according to the population density specified by the user.

The total exposures by pollutant appear on the next six pages. Total exposures are shown for sulfur dioxide, particulates, nitrogen oxides, sulfates, nitrates, and ozone. An exposure is the product of the population and the mean annual concentration of a pollutant.

Sensitivities are also shown on the following pages. Only the summary environmental cost tables and the health risks by pollutant are shown.

Changing the discount rate to 7% lowers the present value of environmental health risk costs to $1.1 billion and the real levelized costs to 1.9 cents/kWh. Increasing the annual population growth rate to 2%, on the other hand, has only a minor effect, increasing the real levelized cost to 3.0 cents/kWh. Reducing the unit health risk value to $3 million reduces the real levelized cost to 2.1 cents/kWh. Finally, increasing the population density in the initial year to 150 people per square mile increases levelized costs to 4.2 cents/kWh.

Other runs are possible. The program will automatically recalculate all tables when new data is entered and the F9 key is pressed. Any combination of variables may be entered.

The last several pages display the formulas used by the spreadsheet to perform the calculations just described. Tables for which no formulas are provided are ones that require direct data input and are used by the model to perform other calculations.

ENVIRONMENTAL COST SPREADSHEET

INTRODUCTORY NOTES AND DIRECTIONS FOR USE

1. THIS SPREADSHEET CALCULATES THE PRESENT VALUE AND LEVELIZED COST OF HEALTH RISKS ASSOCIATED WITH A GENERIC COAL PLANT.

2. IT IS INTENDED TO BE ILLUSTRATIVE: AN ATTEMPT HAS BEEN MADE TO USE REALISTIC DATA, BUT USERS MAY WISH TO USE THEIR OWN DATA.

3. THE SPREADSHEET CALCULATES UNITS OF HEALTH RISKS AS A RESULT OF EXPOSURES TO THE FOLLOWING POLLUTANTS: SULFUR DIOXIDE, PARTICULATES NITROGEN OXIDES, SULFATES, NITRATES, AND OZONE (NO DOSE RESPONSE COEFFICIENTS ARE USED FOR NOx AND NITRATES)

4. THE FIRST TABLE CONSISTS OF THE ENTRIES SUPPLIED BY THE USER. TO EXAMINE THAT TABLE OR TO MAKE CHANGES IN IT, PRESS F5A60(ENTER) MOVE THE POINTER AROUND THE TABLE TO CHANGE VALUES AS DESIRED. FOR EXAMPLE, TO ALTER THE DISCOUNT RATE, PUT THE POINTER ON CELL A68 AND ENTER YOUR NEW VALUE.

5. FOLLOW THIS PROCEDURE FOR OTHER VALUES. THE SPREADSHEET WILL AUTOMATICALLY RECALCULATE ALL TABLES AFTER YOU HAVE ENTERED THE NEW VALUES AND PRESSED F9.

6. TO VIEW THE SUMMARY TABLE OF COSTS, PRESS F5A120(ENTER). SCROLL DOWN THE TABLE TO SEE THE SUMMARY OF PRESENT VALUE OR THE LEVELIZED COST. OR YOU MAY PRESS F5A150(ENTER) TO BRING THOSE SUMMARY COSTS INTO VIEW.

7. EACH TABLE AUTOMATICALLY INCLUDES THE VALUES USED IN EACH RUN AS A LABEL AT THE BOTTOM OF THE TABLE.

8. THE PROGRAM ALLOWS USERS TO INPUT VALUES FOR: UNIT HEALTH RISKS (EXPRESSED AS A STATISTICAL LIFE), REAL DISCOUNT RATE. THE ANNUAL POPULATION GROWTH RATE IN THE REGION, THE POPULATION DENSITY (EXPRESSED AS POPULATION PER SQUARE MILE), NET CAPACITY OF THE PLANT (EXPRESSED IN MEGAWATTS), AND THE CAPACITY FACTOR. THE FINAL TWO VARIABLES ARE USED ONLY TO CALCULATE THE LEVELIZED COST. THEY DON'T AFFECT THE CONCENTRATION OF POLLUTANTS AT EACH DISTANCE FROM THE PLANT. THOSE CONCENTRATIONS MUST NOW BE ENTERED MANUALLY.

9. THE SUMMARY TABLE BEGINNING AT A120 SHOWS THE ECONOMIC VALUE OF HEALTH RISK COSTS BASED ON THE USER-SUPPLIED DATA.

10. THE NEXT TABLE DOWN PROVIDES A SUMMARY OF UNIT HEALTH RISKS BY POLLUTANT BY YEAR. VALUES ARE THE DOSE-RESPONSE COEFFICIENT MULTIPLIED BY THE MEAN ANNUAL CONCENTRATION OF POLLUTANTS IN EACH DISTANCE ZONE MULTIPLIED BY THE POPULATION IN THAT ZONE.

11. THE NEXT TABLE DOWN CONSISTS OF THE MEAN ANNUAL CONCENTRATION OF EACH POLLUTANT IN EACH DISTANCE ZONE.

12. THE NEXT TABLE DOWN GIVES THE POPULATION IN EACH ZONE.

13. THE REMAINING TABLES GIVE TOTAL EXPOSURES BY POLLUTANT

14. USERS ARE URGED TO RE-PROGRAM THE SPREADSHEET TO MEET THEIR NEEDS.

VALUES USED IN ANALYSIS

$4,000,000	VALUE PER UNIT HEALTH RISK	100.000	POPULATION DENSITY (POP/SQ.MI.)
0.030	REAL DISCOUNT RATE	603.000	MEGAWATTS
1.200	ANNUAL POPULATION GROWTH RATE (%)	0.700	CAPACITY FACTOR

DOSE-RESPONSE COEFFICIENTS

POLLUTANT	UNIT HEALTH RISKS PER ug/m3 PER YEAR
SULFUR DIOXIDE	0.00000600
PARTICULATES	0.00000300
NITROGEN OXIDES	0.00000000
SULFATES	0.00006000
NITRATES	0.00000000
OZONE	0.00000600

SUMMARY OF ENVIRONMENTAL COSTS FOR HEALTH RISKS

YEAR	UNITS OF HEALTH RISKS	VALUE OF HEALTH RISK	TOTAL COSTS ($1,000,000)	PRESENT VALUE ($1,000,000)	CUMULATIVE PRESENT VALUE ($1,000,000)
1990	23.063	$4,000,000	$92.252	$89.565	$89.565
1991	23.340	$4,000,000	$93.359	$87.999	$177.564
1992	23.620	$4,000,000	$94.479	$86.462	$264.026
1993	23.903	$4,000,000	$95.613	$84.951	$348.976
1994	24.190	$4,000,000	$96.760	$83.466	$432.443
1995	24.480	$4,000,000	$97.921	$82.007	$514.450
1996	24.774	$4,000,000	$99.096	$80.574	$595.024
1997	25.071	$4,000,000	$100.285	$79.166	$674.190
1998	25.372	$4,000,000	$101.489	$77.783	$751.973
1999	25.677	$4,000,000	$102.707	$76.423	$828.397
2000	25.985	$4,000,000	$103.939	$75.088	$903.484
2001	26.297	$4,000,000	$105.186	$73.776	$977.260
2002	26.612	$4,000,000	$106.449	$72.486	$1,049.746
2003	26.932	$4,000,000	$107.726	$71.220	$1,120.966
2004	27.255	$4,000,000	$109.019	$69.975	$1,190.941
2005	27.582	$4,000,000	$110.327	$68.752	$1,259.693
2006	27.913	$4,000,000	$111.651	$67.551	$1,327.244
2007	28.248	$4,000,000	$112.991	$66.370	$1,393.614
2008	28.587	$4,000,000	$114.347	$65.210	$1,458.824
2009	28.930	$4,000,000	$115.719	$64.071	$1,522.895

PRESENT VALUE OF HEALTH RISKS ($1000)	$1,522,895
LEVELIZED COST ($/KWH)	$0.028

4000000.000 VALUE PER UNIT HEALTH RISK	100.000 POPULATION DENSITY (POP/SQ.MI.)
0.030 REAL DISCOUNT RATE	603.000 MEGAWATTS
1.200 ANNUAL POPULATION GROWTH RATE (%)	0.700 CAPACITY FACTOR

UNIT HEALTH RISKS BY POLLUTANT PER YEAR

YEAR	SULFUR DIOXIDE	PARTIC-ULATES	NITROGEN OXIDES	SULFATES	NITRATES	OZONE	TOTAL
1990	9.030	0.244	0.000	12.100	0.000	1.689	23.063
1991	9.139	0.247	0.000	12.245	0.000	1.709	23.340
1992	9.248	0.250	0.000	12.392	0.000	1.730	23.620
1993	9.359	0.253	0.000	12.540	0.000	1.751	23.903
1994	9.472	0.256	0.000	12.691	0.000	1.772	24.190
1995	9.585	0.259	0.000	12.843	0.000	1.793	24.480
1996	9.700	0.262	0.000	12.997	0.000	1.814	24.774
1997	9.817	0.265	0.000	13.153	0.000	1.836	25.071
1998	9.934	0.268	0.000	13.311	0.000	1.858	25.372
1999	10.054	0.272	0.000	13.471	0.000	1.880	25.677
2000	10.174	0.275	0.000	13.633	0.000	1.903	25.985
2001	10.296	0.278	0.000	13.796	0.000	1.926	26.297
2002	10.420	0.282	0.000	13.962	0.000	1.949	26.612
2003	10.545	0.285	0.000	14.129	0.000	1.972	26.932
2004	10.671	0.288	0.000	14.299	0.000	1.996	27.255
2005	10.800	0.292	0.000	14.470	0.000	2.020	27.582
2006	10.929	0.295	0.000	14.644	0.000	2.044	27.913
2007	11.060	0.299	0.000	14.820	0.000	2.069	28.248
2008	11.193	0.302	0.000	14.998	0.000	2.094	28.587
2009	11.327	0.306	0.000	15.178	0.000	2.119	28.930

4000000.000 VALUE PER UNIT HEALTH RISK

0.030 REAL DISCOUNT RATE

1.200 ANNUAL POPULATION GROWTH RATE (%)

100.000 POPULATION DENSITY (POP/SQ.MI.)

603.000 MEGAWATTS

0.700 CAPACITY FACTOR

MEAN ANNUAL CONCENTRATION OF POLLUTANTS IN ug/m3

DISTANCE FROM PLANT IN MILES

POLLUTANT	0 to 5	5 to 8	8 to 11	11 to 14	14 to 23	23 to 39	39 to 55	55 to 70	70 to 85	85 to 100	100 to 120
SULFUR DIOXIDE	1.251	1.318	1.195	1.088	1.004	0.734	0.482	0.354	0.277	0.226	0.190
PARTICULATES	0.062	0.066	0.060	0.055	0.051	0.038	0.025	0.019	0.015	0.013	0.011
NITROGEN OXIDES	0.576	0.609	0.554	0.506	0.469	0.349	0.233	0.174	0.139	0.116	0.100
SULFATES	0.027	0.036	0.040	0.042	0.043	0.051	0.046	0.045	0.045	0.044	0.043
NITRATES	0.003	0.006	0.009	0.010	0.011	0.016	0.016	0.016	0.017	0.017	0.016
OZONE	0.000	0.000	0.000	0.000	0.000	0.000	0.000	0.016	0.060	0.089	0.109

4000000.000 VALUE PER UNIT HEALTH RISK

0.030 REAL DISCOUNT RATE

1.200 ANNUAL POPULATION GROWTH RATE (%)

100.000 POPULATION DENSITY (POP/SQ.MI.)

603.000 MEGAWATTS

0.700 CAPACITY FACTOR

ANNUAL POPULATION BY DISTANCE FROM PLANT

DISTANCE FROM PLANT IN MILES

YEAR	0 to 5	5 to 8	8 to 11	11 to 14	14 to 23	23 to 39	39 to 55	55 to 70	70 to 85	85 to 100	100 to 120
1990	7,850	12,250	17,900	23,560	104,620	311,650	472,500	589,050	730,420	871,790	1,382,300
1991	7,944	12,397	18,115	23,843	105,875	315,390	478,170	596,119	739,185	882,251	1,398,888
1992	8,040	12,546	18,332	24,129	107,146	319,174	483,908	603,272	748,055	892,838	1,415,674
1993	8,136	12,696	18,552	24,418	108,432	323,005	489,715	610,511	757,032	903,553	1,432,662
1994	8,234	12,849	18,775	24,711	109,733	326,881	495,592	617,837	766,116	914,395	1,449,854
1995	8,332	13,003	19,000	25,008	111,050	330,803	501,539	625,251	775,310	925,368	1,467,253
1996	8,432	13,159	19,228	25,308	112,382	334,773	507,557	632,754	784,613	936,472	1,484,860
1997	8,534	13,317	19,459	25,612	113,731	338,790	513,648	640,348	794,029	947,710	1,502,678
1998	8,636	13,477	19,692	25,919	115,096	342,856	519,812	648,032	803,557	959,083	1,520,710
1999	8,740	13,638	19,929	26,230	116,477	346,970	526,049	655,808	813,200	970,592	1,538,959
2000	8,845	13,802	20,168	26,545	117,874	351,133	532,362	663,678	822,958	982,239	1,557,426
2001	8,951	13,968	20,410	26,863	119,289	355,347	538,750	671,642	832,834	994,025	1,576,115
2002	9,058	14,135	20,655	27,186	120,720	359,611	545,215	679,702	842,828	1,005,954	1,595,029
2003	9,167	14,305	20,903	27,512	122,169	363,927	551,758	687,858	852,942	1,018,025	1,614,169
2004	9,277	14,476	21,153	27,842	123,635	368,294	558,379	696,112	863,177	1,030,242	1,633,539
2005	9,388	14,650	21,407	28,176	125,119	372,713	565,079	704,466	873,535	1,042,604	1,653,141
2006	9,501	14,826	21,664	28,514	126,620	377,186	571,860	712,919	884,017	1,055,116	1,672,979
2007	9,615	15,004	21,924	28,857	128,140	381,712	578,723	721,474	894,626	1,067,777	1,693,055
2008	9,730	15,184	22,187	29,203	129,677	386,293	585,667	730,132	905,361	1,080,590	1,713,371
2009	9,847	15,366	22,453	29,553	131,233	390,928	592,695	738,894	916,226	1,093,557	1,733,932

4000000.000 VALUE PER UNIT HEALTH RISK

100.000 POPULATION DENSITY (POP/SQ.MI.)

0.030 REAL DISCOUNT RATE

603.000 MEGAWATTS

1.200 ANNUAL POPULATION GROWTH RATE (%)

0.700 CAPACITY FACTOR

TOTAL SULFUR DIOXIDE EXPOSURES BY YEAR

(PERSON-ug/m3)

DISTANCE FROM PLANT IN MILES

YEAR	0 TO 5	5 TO 8	8 TO 11	11 TO 14	14 TO 23	23 TO 39	39 TO 55	55 TO 70	70 TO 85	85 TO 100	100 TO 120	TOTAL
1990	9820.3	16145.5	21390.5	25633.3	105038.5	228751.1	227745.0	208523.7	202326.3	197024.5	262637.0	1505035.8
1991	9938.2	16339.2	21647.2	25940.9	106298.9	231496.1	230477.9	211026.0	204754.3	199388.8	265788.6	1523096.2
1992	10057.5	16535.3	21907.0	26252.2	107574.5	234274.1	233243.7	213558.3	207211.3	201781.5	268978.1	1541373.4
1993	10178.1	16733.7	22169.8	26567.2	108865.4	237085.4	236042.6	216121.0	209697.8	204202.9	272205.8	1559869.9
1994	10300.3	16934.5	22435.9	26886.0	110171.8	239930.4	238875.1	218714.4	212214.2	206653.3	275472.3	1578588.3
1995	10423.9	17137.8	22705.1	27208.6	111493.9	242809.5	241741.6	221339.0	214760.8	209133.2	278778.0	1597531.4
1996	10549.0	17343.4	22977.6	27535.1	112831.8	245723.3	244642.5	223995.1	217337.9	211642.8	282123.3	1616701.7
1997	10675.6	17551.5	23253.3	27865.6	114185.8	248671.9	247578.2	226683.0	219946.0	214182.5	285508.8	1636102.1
1998	10803.7	17762.2	23532.3	28199.9	115556.0	251656.0	250549.2	229403.2	222585.3	216752.7	288934.9	1655735.4
1999	10933.3	17975.3	23814.7	28538.3	116942.7	254675.9	253555.7	232156.1	225256.3	219353.7	292402.1	1675604.2
2000	11064.5	18191.0	24100.5	28880.8	118346.0	257732.0	256598.4	234941.9	227959.4	221985.9	295910.9	1695711.5
2001	11197.3	18409.3	24389.7	29227.4	119766.1	260824.8	259677.6	237761.2	230694.9	224649.8	299461.9	1716060.0
2002	11331.6	18630.2	24682.4	29578.1	121203.3	263954.7	262793.7	240614.4	233463.3	227345.6	303055.4	1736652.7
2003	11467.6	18853.8	24978.6	29933.0	122657.8	267122.1	265947.3	243501.7	236264.8	230073.7	306692.1	1757492.5
2004	11605.2	19080.0	25278.3	30292.2	124129.7	270327.6	269138.6	246423.8	239100.0	232834.6	310372.4	1778582.5
2005	11744.5	19309.0	25581.7	30655.7	125619.2	273571.5	272368.3	249380.9	241969.2	235628.6	314096.9	1799925.4
2006	11885.4	19540.7	25888.6	31023.6	127126.7	276854.4	275636.7	252373.4	244872.8	238456.1	317866.0	1821524.5
2007	12028.1	19775.2	26199.3	31395.9	128652.2	280176.6	278944.3	255401.9	247811.3	241317.6	321680.4	1843382.8
2008	12172.4	20012.5	26513.7	31772.6	130196.0	283538.7	282291.7	258466.7	250785.1	244213.4	325540.6	1865503.4
2009	12318.5	20252.6	26831.9	32153.9	131758.4	286941.2	285679.2	261568.3	253794.5	247144.0	329447.1	1887889.5

4000000.000 VALUE PER UNIT HEALTH RISK   100.000 POPULATION DENSITY (POP SQ.MI.)

0.030 REAL DISCOUNT RATE   603.000 MEGAWATTS

1.200 ANNUAL POPULATION GROWTH RATE (%)   0.700 CAPACITY FACTOR

TOTAL PARTICULATE EXPOSURES BY YEAR

(PERSON-ug/m3)

DISTANCE FROM PLANT IN MILES

YEAR	0 TO 5	5 TO 8	8 TO 11	11 TO 14	14 TO 23	23 TO 39	39 TO 55	55 TO 70	70 TO 85	85 TO 100	100 TO 120	TOTAL
1990	486.7	808.5	1074.0	1295.8	5335.6	11842.7	11812.5	11191.9	10956.3	11333.3	15205.3	81342.6
1991	492.5	818.2	1086.9	1311.3	5399.6	11984.8	11954.3	11326.3	11087.8	11469.3	15387.8	82318.8
1992	498.5	828.0	1099.9	1327.1	5464.4	12128.6	12097.7	11462.2	11220.8	11606.9	15572.4	83306.6
1993	504.4	838.0	1113.1	1343.0	5530.0	12274.2	12242.9	11599.7	11355.5	11746.2	15759.3	84306.3
1994	510.5	848.0	1126.5	1359.1	5596.4	12421.5	12389.8	11738.9	11491.7	11887.1	15948.4	85317.9
1995	516.6	858.2	1140.0	1375.4	5663.5	12570.5	12538.5	11879.8	11629.6	12029.8	16139.8	86341.7
1996	522.8	868.5	1153.7	1391.9	5731.5	12721.4	12688.9	12022.3	11769.2	12174.1	16333.5	87377.8
1997	529.1	878.9	1167.5	1408.6	5800.3	12874.0	12841.2	12166.6	11910.4	12320.2	16529.5	88426.4
1998	535.4	889.5	1181.5	1425.5	5869.9	13028.5	12995.3	12312.6	12053.4	12468.1	16727.8	89487.5
1999	541.9	900.1	1195.7	1442.7	5940.3	13184.9	13151.2	12460.4	12198.0	12617.7	16928.5	90561.3
2000	548.4	910.9	1210.1	1460.0	6011.6	13343.1	13309.0	12609.9	12344.4	12769.1	17131.7	91648.1
2001	554.9	921.9	1224.6	1477.5	6083.7	13503.2	13468.8	12761.2	12492.5	12922.3	17337.3	92747.9
2002	561.6	932.9	1239.3	1495.2	6156.7	13665.2	13630.4	12914.3	12642.4	13077.4	17545.3	93860.8
2003	568.3	944.1	1254.2	1513.2	6230.6	13829.2	13793.9	13069.3	12794.1	13234.3	17755.9	94987.2
2004	575.2	955.4	1269.2	1531.3	6305.4	13995.2	13959.5	13226.1	12947.7	13393.1	17968.9	96127.0
2005	582.1	966.9	1284.4	1549.7	6381.1	14163.1	14127.0	13384.8	13103.0	13553.9	18184.6	97280.5
2006	589.0	978.5	1299.8	1568.3	6457.6	14333.1	14296.5	13545.5	13260.3	13716.5	18402.8	98447.9
2007	596.1	990.3	1315.4	1587.1	6535.1	14505.1	14468.1	13708.0	13419.4	13881.1	18623.6	99629.3
2008	603.3	1002.1	1331.2	1606.2	6613.5	14679.1	14641.7	13872.5	13580.4	14047.7	18847.1	100824.8
2009	610.5	1014.2	1347.2	1625.4	6692.9	14855.3	14817.4	14039.0	13743.4	14216.2	19073.3	102034.7

4000000.000 VALUE PER UNIT HEALTH RISK — 100.000 POPULATION DENSITY (POP/SQ.MI.)

0.030 REAL DISCOUNT RATE — 603.000 MEGAWATTS

1.200 ANNUAL POPULATION GROWTH RATE (%) — 0.700 CAPACITY FACTOR

TOTAL NITROGEN OXIDE EXPOSURES BY YEAR

(PERSON-ug/m3)

DISTANCE FROM PLANT IN MILES

YEAR	0 TO 5	5 TO 8	8 TO 11	11 TO 14	14 TO 23	23 TO 39	39 TO 55	55 TO 70	70 TO 85	85 TO 100	100 TO 120	TOTAL
1990	4521.6	7460.3	9916.6	11921.4	49066.8	108765.8	110092.5	102494.7	101528.4	101127.6	138230.0	745125.7
1991	4575.9	7549.8	10035.6	12064.4	49655.6	110071.0	111413.6	103724.6	102746.7	102341.2	139888.8	754067.2
1992	4630.8	7640.4	10156.0	12209.2	50251.4	111391.9	112750.6	104969.3	103979.7	103569.3	141567.4	763116.0
1993	4686.3	7732.1	10277.9	12355.7	50854.5	112728.6	114103.6	106229.0	105227.4	104812.1	143266.2	772273.4
1994	4742.6	7824.8	10401.2	12504.0	51464.7	114081.3	115472.8	107503.7	106490.2	106069.8	144985.4	781540.6
1995	4799.5	7918.7	10526.0	12654.0	52082.3	115450.3	116858.5	108793.8	107768.0	107342.7	146725.3	790919.1
1996	4857.1	8013.8	10652.4	12805.9	52707.3	116835.7	118260.8	110099.3	109061.3	108630.8	148486.0	800410.2
1997	4915.4	8109.9	10780.2	12959.5	53339.8	118237.7	119679.9	111420.5	110370.0	109934.4	150267.8	810015.1
1998	4974.3	8207.2	10909.6	13115.0	53979.8	119656.6	121116.1	112757.5	111694.4	111253.6	152071.0	819735.3
1999	5034.0	8305.7	11040.5	13272.4	54627.6	121092.5	122569.5	114110.6	113034.8	112588.6	153895.9	829572.1
2000	5094.4	8405.4	11173.0	13431.7	55283.1	122545.6	124040.3	115479.9	114391.2	113939.7	155742.6	839527.0
2001	5155.6	8506.3	11307.0	13592.9	55946.5	124016.1	125528.8	116865.7	115763.9	115307.0	157611.5	849601.3
2002	5217.4	8608.3	11442.7	13756.0	56617.9	125504.3	127035.1	118268.1	117153.1	116690.6	159502.9	859796.5
2003	5280.1	8711.6	11580.0	13921.1	57297.3	127010.4	128559.6	119687.3	118558.9	118090.9	161416.9	870114.1
2004	5343.4	8816.2	11719.0	14088.1	57984.9	128534.5	130102.3	121123.5	119981.6	119508.0	163353.9	880555.4
2005	5407.5	8922.0	11859.6	14257.2	58680.7	130076.9	131663.5	122577.0	121421.4	120942.1	165314.1	891122.1
2006	5472.4	9029.0	12001.9	14428.3	59384.9	131637.8	133243.5	124048.0	122878.4	122393.4	167297.9	901815.6
2007	5538.1	9137.4	12146.0	14601.4	60097.5	133217.5	134842.4	125536.5	124353.0	123862.1	169305.5	912637.3
2008	5604.6	9247.0	12291.7	14776.6	60818.7	134816.1	136460.5	127043.0	125845.2	125348.5	171337.1	923589.0
2009	5671.8	9358.0	12439.2	14953.9	61548.5	136433.9	138098.0	128567.5	127355.4	126852.7	173393.2	934672.1

TOTAL SULFATE EXPOSURES BY YEAR

(PERSON-ug/m3)

DISTANCE FROM PLANT IN MILES

YEAR	0 TO 5	5 TO 8	8 TO 11	11 TO 14	14 TO 23	23 TO 39	39 TO 55	55 TO 70	70 TO 85	85 TO 100	100 TO 120	TOTAL
1990	212.0	441.0	716.0	989.5	4498.7	15894.2	21735.0	26507.3	32868.9	38358.8	59438.9	201660.1
1991	214.5	446.3	724.6	1001.4	4552.6	16084.9	21995.8	26825.3	33263.3	38819.1	60152.2	204080.0
1992	217.1	451.6	733.3	1013.4	4607.3	16277.9	22259.8	27147.2	33662.5	39284.9	60874.0	206529.0
1993	219.7	457.1	742.1	1025.6	4662.6	16473.2	22526.9	27473.0	34066.4	39756.3	61604.5	209007.3
1994	222.3	462.6	751.0	1037.9	4718.5	16670.9	22797.2	27802.7	34475.2	40233.4	62343.7	211515.4
1995	225.0	468.1	760.0	1050.3	4775.1	16871.0	23070.8	28136.3	34888.9	40716.2	63091.9	214053.6
1996	227.7	473.7	769.1	1062.9	4832.4	17073.4	23347.6	28474.0	35307.6	41204.8	63849.0	216622.2
1997	230.4	479.4	778.4	1075.7	4890.4	17278.3	23627.8	28815.6	35731.3	41699.2	64615.1	219221.7
1998	233.2	485.2	787.7	1088.6	4949.1	17485.6	23911.3	29161.4	36160.1	42199.6	65390.5	221852.4
1999	236.0	491.0	797.1	1101.7	5008.5	17695.5	24198.3	29511.4	36594.0	42706.0	66175.2	224514.6
2000	238.8	496.9	806.7	1114.9	5068.6	17907.8	24488.6	29865.5	37033.1	43218.5	66969.3	227208.8
2001	241.7	502.8	816.4	1128.3	5129.4	18122.7	24782.5	30223.9	37477.5	43737.1	67773.0	229935.3
2002	244.6	508.9	826.2	1141.8	5191.0	18340.2	25079.9	30586.6	37927.2	44262.0	68586.2	232694.5
2003	247.5	515.0	836.1	1155.5	5253.3	18560.3	25380.9	30953.6	38382.4	44793.1	69409.3	235486.8
2004	250.5	521.2	846.1	1169.4	5316.3	18783.0	25685.4	31325.1	38843.0	45330.6	70242.2	238312.7
2005	253.5	527.4	856.3	1183.4	5380.1	19008.4	25993.7	31701.0	39309.1	45874.6	71085.1	241172.4
2006	256.5	533.7	866.6	1197.6	5444.7	19236.5	26305.6	32081.4	39780.8	46425.1	71938.1	244066.5
2007	259.6	540.1	877.0	1212.0	5510.0	19467.3	26621.2	32466.3	40258.2	46982.2	72801.4	246995.3
2008	262.7	546.6	887.5	1226.5	5576.1	19700.9	26940.7	32855.9	40741.3	47546.0	73675.0	249959.2
2009	265.9	553.2	898.1	1241.2	5643.0	19937.3	27264.0	33250.2	41230.1	48116.5	74559.1	252958.7

4000000.000 VALUE PER UNIT HEALTH RISK 100.000 POPULATION DENSITY (POP/SQ.MI.)

0.030 REAL DISCOUNT RATE 603.000 MEGAWATTS

1.200 ANNUAL POPULATION GROWTH RATE (%) 0.700 CAPACITY FACTOR

TOTAL NITRATE EXPOSURES BY YEAR

(PERSON-ug/m3)

DISTANCE FROM PLANT IN MILES

YEAR	0 TO 5	5 TO 8	8 TO 11	11 TO 14	14 TO 23	23 TO 39	39 TO 55	55 TO 70	70 TO 85	85 TO 100	100 TO 120	TOTAL
1990	23.6	73.5	161.1	235.6	1150.8	4986.4	7560.0	9424.8	12417.1	14820.4	22116.8	72970.1
1991	23.8	74.4	163.0	238.4	1164.6	5046.2	7650.7	9537.9	12566.1	14998.3	22382.2	73845.8
1992	24.1	75.3	165.0	241.3	1178.6	5106.8	7742.5	9652.4	12716.9	15178.3	22650.8	74731.9
1993	24.4	76.2	167.0	244.2	1192.7	5168.1	7835.4	9768.2	12869.5	15360.4	22922.6	75628.7
1994	24.7	77.1	169.0	247.1	1207.1	5230.1	7929.5	9885.4	13024.0	15544.7	23197.7	76536.3
1995	25.0	78.0	171.0	250.1	1221.5	5292.9	8024.6	10004.0	13180.3	15731.3	23476.0	77454.7
1996	25.3	79.0	173.1	253.1	1236.2	5356.4	8120.9	10124.1	13338.4	15920.0	23757.8	78384.2
1997	25.6	79.9	175.1	256.1	1251.0	5420.6	8218.4	10245.6	13498.5	16111.1	24042.8	79324.8
1998	25.9	80.9	177.2	259.2	1266.1	5485.7	8317.0	10368.5	13660.5	16304.4	24331.4	80276.7
1999	26.2	81.8	179.4	262.3	1281.2	5551.5	8416.8	10492.9	13824.4	16500.1	24623.3	81240.0
2000	26.5	82.8	181.5	265.4	1296.6	5618.1	8517.8	10618.8	13990.3	16698.1	24918.8	82214.9
2001	26.9	83.8	183.7	268.6	1312.2	5685.6	8620.0	10746.3	14158.2	16898.4	25217.8	83201.4
2002	27.2	84.8	185.9	271.9	1327.9	5753.8	8723.4	10875.2	14328.1	17101.2	25520.5	84199.9
2003	27.5	85.8	188.1	275.1	1343.9	5822.8	8828.1	11005.7	14500.0	17306.4	25826.7	85210.3
2004	27.8	86.9	190.4	278.4	1360.0	5892.7	8934.1	11137.8	14674.0	17514.1	26136.6	86232.8
2005	28.2	87.9	192.7	281.8	1376.3	5963.4	9041.3	11271.5	14850.1	17724.3	26450.3	87267.6
2006	28.5	89.0	195.0	285.1	1392.8	6035.0	9149.8	11406.7	15028.3	17937.0	26767.7	88314.8
2007	28.8	90.0	197.3	288.6	1409.5	6107.4	9259.6	11543.6	15208.6	18152.2	27088.9	89374.6
2008	29.2	91.1	199.7	292.0	1426.5	6180.7	9370.7	11682.1	15391.1	18370.0	27413.9	90447.0
2009	29.5	92.2	202.1	295.5	1443.6	6254.8	9483.1	11822.3	15575.8	18590.5	27742.9	91532.4

4000000.000 VALUE PER UNIT HEALTH RISK   100.000 POPULATION DENSITY (POP/SQ.MI.)

0.030 REAL DISCOUNT RATE   603.000 MEGAWATTS

1.200 ANNUAL POPULATION GROWTH RATE (%)   0.700 CAPACITY FACTOR

TOTAL OZONE EXPOSURES BY YEAR

(FERSON-ug/m3)

DISTANCE FROM PLANT IN MILES

YEAR	0 TO 5	5 TO 8	8 TO 11	11 TO 14	14 TO 23	23 TO 39	39 TO 55	55 TO 70	70 TO 85	85 TO 100	100 TO 120	TOTAL
1990	0.0	0.0	0.0	0.0	0.0	0.0	0.0	9424.8	43825.2	77589.3	150670.7	281510.0
1991	0.0	0.0	0.0	0.0	0.0	0.0	0.0	9537.9	44351.1	78520.4	152478.7	284888.1
1992	0.0	0.0	0.0	0.0	0.0	0.0	0.0	9652.4	44883.3	79462.6	154308.5	288306.8
1993	0.0	0.0	0.0	0.0	0.0	0.0	0.0	9768.2	45421.9	80416.2	156160.2	291766.5
1994	0.0	0.0	0.0	0.0	0.0	0.0	0.0	9885.4	45967.0	81381.2	158034.1	295267.7
1995	0.0	0.0	0.0	0.0	0.0	0.0	0.0	10004.0	46518.6	82357.7	159930.5	298810.9
1996	0.0	0.0	0.0	0.0	0.0	0.0	0.0	10124.1	47076.8	83346.0	161849.7	302396.6
1997	0.0	0.0	0.0	0.0	0.0	0.0	0.0	10245.6	47641.7	84346.2	163791.9	306025.4
1998	0.0	0.0	0.0	0.0	0.0	0.0	0.0	10368.5	48213.4	85358.3	165757.4	309697.7
1999	0.0	0.0	0.0	0.0	0.0	0.0	0.0	10492.9	48792.0	86382.6	167746.5	313414.0
2000	0.0	0.0	0.0	0.0	0.0	0.0	0.0	10618.8	49377.5	87419.2	169759.4	317175.0
2001	0.0	0.0	0.0	0.0	0.0	0.0	0.0	10746.3	49970.0	88468.3	171796.6	320981.1
2002	0.0	0.0	0.0	0.0	0.0	0.0	0.0	10875.2	50569.7	89529.9	173858.1	324832.9
2003	0.0	0.0	0.0	0.0	0.0	0.0	0.0	11005.7	51176.5	90604.2	175944.4	328730.9
2004	0.0	0.0	0.0	0.0	0.0	0.0	0.0	11137.8	51790.6	91691.5	178055.7	332675.7
2005	0.0	0.0	0.0	0.0	0.0	0.0	0.0	11271.5	52412.1	92791.8	180192.4	336667.8
2006	0.0	0.0	0.0	0.0	0.0	0.0	0.0	11406.7	53041.0	93905.3	182354.7	340707.8
2007	0.0	0.0	0.0	0.0	0.0	0.0	0.0	11543.6	53677.5	95032.2	184543.0	344796.3
2008	0.0	0.0	0.0	0.0	0.0	0.0	0.0	11682.1	54321.7	96172.5	186757.5	348933.8
2009	0.0	0.0	0.0	0.0	0.0	0.0	0.0	11822.3	54973.5	97326.6	188998.6	353121.0

4000000.000 VALUE PER UNIT HEALTH RISK   100.000 POPULATION DENSITY (POP/SQ.MI.)

0.030 REAL DISCOUNT RATE   603.000 MEGAWATTS

1.200 ANNUAL POPULATION GROWTH RATE (%)   0.700 CAPACITY FACTOR

IX. RESEARCH NEEDS

IX. RESEARCH NEEDS

A. INTRODUCTION

Valuation of environmental externalities is a discipline still in its infancy. For each type of electric power externality there remain significant uncertainties. In some areas there is enough data to justify use of quantified damage costs. In other areas, all that can be done at this time is to describe effects qualitatively and point to data gaps that prevent even crude estimates of cost.

This section collects recommendations from the main text of the report on research needs that deserve special attention. The recommendations follow the order of chapters and sections of this report.

B. FRONT-END COSTS

Front-end externality costs (sometimes referred to as "upstream costs") include the environmental impacts caused by manufacture and transport of materials, fuel and equipment for construction and operation of electric power generating facilities. The front-end costs of power supply options are not within the scope of this study, and need to be addressed in future research. See Chapter II, Executive Summary. This is particularly true for fossil fuel and nuclear options, the front-end costs of which may be a very significant part of total environmental externality costs.

For example, the costs discussed in this report for oil-fired electric power, do not account for the environmental damages associated with oil drilling, pipeline ruptures, tanker spills and refinery emissions, effluent and accidents. A recent news report claimed that there is an average of one oil spill a day in New York Harbor alone, including one this year that dumped 571,000 gallons.[1]

Front-end environmental damages from coal-fired power include: unreimbursed costs of mine accidents and other occupational hazards (some of them unique to coal mining, such as black lung disease); acid mine drainage; land subsidence; abandoned surface mine erosion; siltation of streams; accidents from waste impoundment failures; wildlife disturbance; explosion and noise hazards from blasting; road damage; groundwater loss and contamination; air pollution in the form of fugitive dust; transportation accidents; and water pollution, noise and solid waste burdens associated with coal preparation plants.

Nuclear power involves environmental, worker and community health damage from uranium mining and processing, including transportation and disposal of mill tailings and other wastes.

Natural gas production and transport create significant front-end environmental externality costs, including: NOx emissions from compressors; gas pipeline explosions;

---

[1] "A Spill A Day, And Hardly Anyone Has Been Checking", New York Times, Week In Review Section, February 25, 1990, p.1.

global warming effects from methane losses; land and water disturbances from well drilling, pipeline construction, and environmental damages from processing facilities.

Demand side management and renewable supply options have front end externality costs as well, but are far lower than traditional power supply options. They occur in the manufacturing of materials used in solar equipment and modern lighting components, fuel and materials used in constructing hydroelectric facilities, air pollution associated with insulation manufacturing, and, in the case of biomass, wildlife hazards, land use and other societal damages from production of crops for fuel.

All these front-end costs are important and should be researched in order to obtain complete environmental damage costs.

One of the difficulties in determining a resource's front-end environmental costs is deciding how far back in the process chain to go. The chain of events required to extract, fabricate, enrich, manufacture, and transport fuels and materials to the point of use may go almost infinitely far back into the past. For example, the manufacture of materials requires tools, fuel and factory processes. The manufacture of these elements of production also have environmental costs.

In conjunction with such an analysis, research is needed to address the extent to which front-end environmental costs are already internalized in the prices of materials and fuels. For example, workers compensation insurance internalizes at least part of the occupational health risks faced by workers in industry. Those insurance costs are passed along in the form of higher prices for goods produced by those workers. The same is true for some environmental effects. Presently, there is insufficient knowledge of what proportion of front end environmental costs are included in energy prices.

C. MEASURING ENVIRONMENTAL DAMAGES

Research is needed to improve our knowledge of ecosystem costs associated with energy resources. Not only is there a need for an improved understanding of biological and physical responses to the effects of energy resources, but there also is a need for improved economic methods for valuing ecosystem costs. See, Chapter III, Analytic Framework.

Economists typically have paid little attention to non-use, or existence, values. In an age when increasing attention is given to non-market goods, and the non-use value of such goods, greater attention must be given to determining existence values.

Researchers are in disagreement over what are the appropriate discount rates for valuing externalities. One expert working on this study advocated a 3% discount rate (used by Bonneville Power Administration to value natural resource damages), another advocated 6.5% (the carrying charge actually paid by most utilities). While other authors advocate using a zero discount rate, the discount rates in the studies reviewed generally were not stated, and no discount rate adjustment of the figures reported was made in this report. The Center for Global Change study, cited in the report, uses a 0% discount rate, asserting that damage to future generations should be of equal value as damages to today's population. The Shuman and Cavanagh study, also cited, advocates no discounting of human life and health for the same reason. The difference in the discount rate used can have a large effect on some costs and must be resolved.

Many estimates of environmental damages, whether in the energy arena or elsewhere, are based on willingness to pay. However, depending on property rights, willingness to be compensated may be the appropriate measure of value when natural resources are damaged. A great deal more work needs to be done to establish credible, defensible measures based on compensatory values. As long as willingness to pay values are the basis for the bulk of environmental cost values, those values may continue to be underpriced.

A related area requiring investigation concerns the definition of natural resource property rights. This is more than just a legal issue; it is one that depends heavily on perceptions of ethics, precedent, and equity. Currently, "ownership" of many natural resources is impossible to determine. The issue reduces most simply to the following question: Must society be compensated for degradations to natural resources, or must society pay potential degraders to refrain from doing so? The answer to this question need not be the same for all resources. Indeed, the answer may differ for the same resource beyond some threshold. For example, industry may have the "right"to pollute up to some amount; beyond that amount, society at large may have the "right" to be compensated for additional pollution. A resolution of these issues is important for future costing research.

A great deal of work needs to be done to perfect models for use in valuing environmental externality costs. A review of existing models which can be used for this purpose is included in Chapter VII of this report and indicates that none of the existing models have been adequately adapted yet for this purpose. The TEMIS model described in Chapter VII is the first model specifically designed for environmental externality costing. It was developed in Germany for valuing European energy impacts and is being adapted for U.S. data. A sample run with U.S. data is included in Appendix B of this report. More research is needed to refine modeling of environmental externality costs.

D. FOSSIL FUEL EMISSIONS

Point-of-combustion air emission factors are generally well known for most pollutants emitted by existing plants. See, Chapter IV. The primary exception to the adequacy of combustion emission knowledge is the case of nitrous oxide, a major greenhouse gas. Previous data was based on a methodological flaw detected in 1989. New data does not yet appear to be available.

The data on emissions of metals and some toxics from combustion technologies is also incomplete. Furthermore, as noted below no studies have attempted to value the human health or ecological effects of metals and other air toxic emissions from combustion of coal, solid waste and other fuels.

E. EXTERNALITY COSTS BY EMISSION

1. Global Warming

The Global Warming section of this report only considered carbon dioxide emissions. Other important greenhouse gases emitted by electric generation facilities include hydrocarbons, nitrous oxide, and methane.[2] The externalities of these gases may be valued by comparing their global warming potential to that of carbon dioxide, but research on these values is needed. Fuel-cycle emissions for methane are quite complex, especially for natural gas. Off-site methane emission issues include gas pipeline leakage, releases from coal mines, and the effect of gas use in reducing venting, flaring and leakage from oil wells.

Additional work is needed on global warming mitigation measures, including tree-planting, fuel-switching, renewable energy, conservation, and coastal protection. It is possible that the cost of the measures necessary to prevent severe damage to global climate systems will be significantly lower or higher than currently believed.

This report includes only the most cursory review of estimates of carbon-scrubber costs. Large scale carbon scrubbing is an undeveloped technology. Further review of these costs is warranted especially in the event that tree-planting, fuel-switching and conservation appear to be inadequate to achieve acceptable mitigation of climate change. It would also be useful to estimate the cost of controlling carbon emissions through a mix of control strategies.

In general, the study notes that the costs of global warming are both highly speculative and potentially enormous. In this study, global warming externality costs are based on mitigation costs involving carbon sequestration through tree planting. The cost is difficult to measure, and current estimates would benefit from additional research on the cost of reforestation, mass tree planting programs, or rain forest preservation.

Ultimately, it would be preferable to assign costs directly, based on projected global warming damages. This is needed to give a full measure of the projected catastrophic effects of global climate change. While this report did not attempt to do so, it would be possible to generate some estimates of the potential global warming costs. DOE and EPA are performing research on this topic in their global climate program. These costs could include coastal damages, reduced fishery harvests, increased energy costs, drought, famine, storm damage, and ecosystem losses, among others. The precision of these estimates is limited by changing nature of the underlying knowledge base, but such estimates would be valuable.

---

[2] Hydrocarbon and nitrogen oxides emitted from electric generation plants contribute to tropospheric ozone, which is a greenhouse gas, and in a small way to carbon monoxide, which prolongs the life of methane.

2. Other Air Pollutants: SOx, NOx, Ozone and Particulates

This report has not considered a number of air pollution environmental effects of power generation. Combustion technologies, particularly coal and waste-to-energy plants, emit substantial quantities of volatile organic compounds ("VOCs") and toxic metals. These include carcinogenic organic compounds, volatile metals (such as mercury and lead), and non-volatile heavy metals.

Further research is needed to value the risk of exposure to organics and metals released by combustion. There is a need to define the relative toxicity for VOCs emitted by various types of fuel combustion processes, especially diesel engines. Better estimates of fuel content and, controlled and uncontrolled emission levels of heavy metals are needed.

Human exposure to air-borne contaminants also occurs indirectly from dermal exposure, through plant uptake and consumption, by deposition into drinking water supply, and from bioaccumulation in fish and animal based food products. Additional research is needed to value the risk from indirect exposures.

As is clear from the Acid Rain section of this report, knowledge needed to value externalities is incomplete for many of the important aspects of acid rain, particularly for forest damage. Most studies to date measure damages on an average national or regional level, without relating them to amounts or origins of emissions. Establishing better linkage between emissions and marginal damages would be helpful.

The inventory of materials and ecosystems which are vulnerable to acid rain needs to be refined. Models for predicting "dry deposition" of sulfate and nitrate particles need to be advanced to the point of providing reliable transfer coefficients (to relate, quantitatively, emission from sources to deposition at receptors).

Many studies have estimated the human health and visibilityeffects of air pollution, but often have not related those costs to specific emission levels. Additional work in correlating existing data sources (including the recent NAPAP reports) may result in a broader base of cost estimates, without the need for further original research. For materials damage, additional research is needed on how air pollutants damage building materials and consumer products, and how to value such damage.

A special problem arises for ozone, in that few of the studies reviewed for this report explicitly consider the sensitivity of ozone levels and control costs, to varying emissions of NOx and volatile organic compounds (VOCs). The relative importance of these two ozone precursors varies with region, season, and other factors. Given the serious adverse health effects of ozone, it is important that externality costs for NO_x and VOC emissions properly account for the relationship between those emissions and ozone levels.

For all pollutants, valuation of ecosystem effects, wildlife, endangered species, and historical or cultural assets has been very limited. This is an important limitation that needs attention.

3. Land and Water Impacts

While they are very difficult to address on a generic basis, land-use issues covered in Chapter VI.E. may be important, especially for hydroelectric facilities, plant sites and transmission lines. Solar and biomass may also have external land-use costs. Additional research is needed on how to value loss of land and intrusion of these technologies.

This report only begins to assess the land use effects of power plant solid wastes. This is a particularly important issue for coal-fired plants. A full valuation of solid waste generation should include:

- classification of likely solid-waste streams: coal bottom ash, fly ash, scrubber sludge, AFBC waste, IGCC sulfur, etc.

- determination of the hazards and toxicity of each type of waste,

- estimation of leakage (leachate and runoff) risk from conventional and state-of-the-art landfills,

Very little valuation research has been carried out on the externalities of power transmission. Transmission line construction and maintenance can have significant adverse environmental effects, depending on the methods used and site conditions. The effects of electromagnetic fields created by power lines is also a concern on which the research is incomplete.

Water impacts valuation needs further investigation. Power plant operation results in chemical emissions (such as biocides), coal pile runoff, thermal emissions, and water consumption for cooling. These effects have not yet been adequately valued. Power plant use of potable water may become an important externality in areas which face future shortages of drinking water supplies. An externality cost is needed for metals, organics and other pollutants contained in waste water discharges from fossil fuel plants.

Better methodologies and research on the value of fisheries and individual species are needed to calculate entrainment and impingement costs. Other research needs include establishing a correlation between entrainment and impingement and fish population size, and between fish population size and decreased catch rate of fisheries. The effects of thermal pollution on sensitive aquatic ecosystems needs additional research.

F. EXTERNALITY COSTS BY RESOURCE

The research needs pertaining to externalities of coal, oil and natural gas plants, are described above. The following text discusses research needs for valuation of externalities of Nuclear Power, Renewables, Waste-to-Energy Plants, and Demand Side Management.

1. Nuclear Power

This report excludes the front-end of the nuclear cycle from which substantial costs are indicated by the studies reviewed. Costs from uranium mining, fuel fabrication and enrichment need to be addressed.

More detailed costing analysis is needed for all aspects of the nuclear plant operations, covered in Chapter VI.D. The most critical issues appear to be the frequency and consequences of major accidents. This is a highly controversial subject, concerning rare, and unanticipated events on which better risk assessment methodologies are needed. Insufficient data is available on component and system failure rates, human error, operator intervention and damaging external events (e.g. earthquakes). Additional studies could better define the range of plausible values.

In order to assign a cost to the human health effects of radiation, one needs to make certain assumptions about the probability of cancer induction and whether it varies in a linear fashion with increasing or decreasing doses. In section VI.D., the report notes that the linear relationship to lower dosage remains speculative and the assumption that health effects are always proportional to dose may overstate or understate effects of low doses. Additional research on this topic could increase the confidence in the values assigned to health effects due to radiation.

The report notes that much of the data underlying occupational mortality for nuclear plants is somewhat dated and does not reflect potential increases in death and injury rates due to aging plants. This is identified as an area ripe for additional research.

Additional work is needed on damages of routine low level radiation emissions of nuclear plants, for which most studies do not assign an externality cost damages. Data also should be gathered on non-routine spills of radioactive waste water and gases.

Wildlife impacts of nuclear plants (including fish impingement on water intakes) is not well established, particularly in regard to the numbers of fish affected and the costs assigned to fish losses.

Additional work is needed on the effects of thermal and chemical pollution from nuclear power plants on fauna in rivers, lakes and salt-water environments. There is currently inadequate data to assign a dollar value to these pollution discharges. This conclusion also applies to thermal and waste water pollution from coal fired power plants.

Externalities of nuclear plant decommissioning and radioactive waste disposal are difficult to measure, partly because these activities are only beginning to occur. Additional work on these activities is needed, particularly for the external costs of radioactive waste disposal, for which the studies do not estimate a damage figure.

2. Renewable Generation Resources

The literature does not assign a broadly applicable environmental externality cost for hydroelectric facilities. Additional research is needed to advance toward this goal, particularly regarding the effects of hydro facilities on fish and wildlife resources. The very useful site specific work on these subjects done in the Northwest needs to be translated for applicability to other regions of the country. For hydroelectric plants, little work was discovered on how to allocate costs among the various uses for which some hydroelectric dams are used (e.g. recreational, agricultural water supply).

For solar energy, the externality costs are almost entirely front-end costs which have been excluded from this study. Externality costs of dispersed active solar collectors are not sufficiently quantified to permit figures to be estimated. The costing literature on other solar technologies is also sparse. As solar power industries grow, there will be increasing need for accurate accounting of external costs.

Valuations of energy conserving air pollution emissions, water consumption, waste water pollution, land and agricultural effects and occupational accident potential for biomass plants have not been carried out. Biomass air pollution emission rates are also not well developed.

3. Waste-to-Energy Plants

Additional research is needed before a complete social cost figure may be assigned for waste-to-energy plants. The health effects of exposure to toxic pollutants emitted by garbage incinerators have not been adequately quantified or valued. This appears to be an important research need, since the number of these plants is growing. A proper valuation of these effects, combined with the externality costs of conventional pollutant emissions, could well influence energy supply choices in competitive bidding programs involving incinerators.

Further costing research should address the relative importance of conventional and toxic pollutant emissions of incinerators, and of the cancer and non-cancer health effects. Another import element is the risk posed by indirect exposures. The health effects of exposure of children to deposited lead and mercury requires further analysis.

There is a need for additional research in assigning a value to the positive environmental externalities of solid waste incinerators (e.g. landfill impacts and methane emissions which may be avoided by incinerator operations). This will enable the externalities associated with incinerators to be adequately apportioned between the energy and solid waste functions of incinerators.

An unresolved question concerns the risk of environmental contamination from incinerator ash. Valuation will be affected by the manner in which the combustion wastes are disposed, and will be advanced analysis regarding the effectiveness of different disposal techniques in preventing groundwater contamination and fugitive ash dust losses.

4. Demand Side Management

More analysis is needed to quantify the environmental externalities of DSM programs. Valuation of the indoor air pollution effects of weatherization programs remains elusive. Control costs are probably a reasonable surrogate, since mitigation measures can largely eliminate health risks due to conservation measures. Data on the cost of indoor air pollution mitigation measures should be collected and analyzed.

Since the technology of energy conservation is rapidly evolving, future environmental costing research should continue to assess the potential health effects from hazardous or poisonous materials used in conservation devices..

The manufacture of lighting components, insulation, and refrigeration fluids may now or in the future involve highly toxic chemicals materials. Studies should address the risk to workers who handle fluorescent bulbs and may be exposed in harmful mercury concentrations as the result of accidental breakage. Also warranting investigation is the safety of using tritium (radio-active hydrogen) in exit signs.

Efforts are needed to expand evaluation of emission impacts from load shifting programs. Air pollution increases may result from utility electric thermal storage programs and time-of-use rates. Although emissions impacts are highly variable due to differences in utility reserve capacity and dispatching, a sufficient number of case studies in this area might support a range of generally applicable externality cost figures for load shifting. Research should also address the societal benefits of load shifting on the conservation of oil and gas reserves.

Research into available CFC recycling programs for residential appliances is needed. This will assist state agencies in mitigating potential acceleration of CFC working fluid losses due to DSM programs which cause early retirement and disposal of CFC dependent residential appliances.

G. CONCLUSION

This section presents only an outline of a research program. Within most of the subjects listed, several sub-topics would have to be explored, and a range of methodological questions would have to be resolved.

If the full social costs of electric power are to be accounted for federal and state governments and utilities need to fund additional research on environmental externalities.

X. INCORPORATION OF ENVIRONMENTAL COSTS IN ELECTRIC UTILITY PLANNING AND RESOURCE SELECTION

X. INCORPORATION OF ENVIRONMENTAL COSTS IN ELECTRIC UTILITY PLANNING AND RESOURCE SELECTION

A. INTRODUCTION

Generation of electricity is pervasively regulated for economic, environmental and other governmental objectives at both the state and federal levels. A panoply of legislative and regulatory devices implicitly or explicitly influence the acquisition of generation and fuel resources seeking to achieve environmentally sound selections. Effective implementation or enforcement of these laws and policies may be impeded by the regional or global character of the environmental impacts; jurisdictional conflicts and limitations; and the division of regulatory authority between economic regulatory agencies and their environmental or energy policy counterparts.

This chapter reviews the state and federal statutory and regulatory treatment of environmental externalities and discusses alternatives for their consideration.

1. Summary

State Statutory and Regulatory Actions. First, the chapter surveys the state statutory and regulatory experience with incorporating environmental costs into utility planning and resource selection procedures. The chapter presents other incorporation mechanisms that have been proposed but not yet used. In-depth analyses are given of the incorporation procedures that have been used by selected states that have pioneered in considering environmental costs. It then outlines a suggested combination of alternatives. The Appendix to this chapter provides a state-by-state summary overview of the status of environmental costing, least-cost planning, and related legislated environmental policies for all fifty states.

Taxes and Subsidies. The chapter then reviews tax regimes and subsidies that have been used or considered for treatment of environmental costs, indicating the strengths and weaknesses of taxes and subsidies for internalizing environmental costs.

Federal Treatment. The chapter reviews relevant federal statutes with particular emphasis on the Northwest Power Planning and Conservation Act.[1]

Alternatives. Last, the chapter discusses the strengths and weaknesses of the alternative methods for incorporation reviewed.

---

[1] Pacific Northwest Electric Power Planning and Conservation Act, 16 U.S.C. 839 et. seq. (1980). The Act is implemented through the Northwest Power Planning Council (NWPPC).

2. General Issues

Regulatory and legislative options addressing environmental impacts and externality costs associated with electricity generation include: direct prospective and remedial environmental regulation and environmental impact statement requirements; general revenue driven policies including taxes and subsidies; traditionally regulated economic vehicles such as price to customer, rate of return on investment, and approval of financing; screening of resource options such as least-cost energy planning and all-source bidding programs; and system operation practices, including environmental dispatch. These options are discussed below.

a. Jurisdictional Conflicts

The power to authorize, implement, and enforce environmental costing measures may rest in different governmental entities or be divided among agencies or jurisdictions. The political dynamics of each option differ; some may not be politically feasible. These problems are discussed as they relate to environmental costing.

b. Environmental Controls

An extensive array of federal and state pollution control standards has been adopted in recent years;[2] those of most relevance to electric utility operations are those dealing with air and water pollution and nuclear power plant construction, operations, decommissioning and waste disposal. Such statutory and regulatory controls internalize environmental costs to the extent that they are successful in preventing environmental damages. They seldom eliminate environmental damages, however, except in the case of totally banned pollutants such as DDT. A residual of damages that can be substantial therefore continues after statutory and regulatory implementation of controls. These residual damages are the externalities with which this report deals.[3]

---

[2] See for example, The National Environmental Policy Act, 42 U.S.C. secs 4321 et. seq; The Clean Air Act, 42 U.S.C. secs 7401 et. seq.; The Federal Water Pollution Control Act, 42 U.S.C. secs. 1251, et.seq.; The Toxic Substances Control Act, 15 U.S.C. secs. 2601 et. seq.; The Resource Conservation and Recovery Act (RCRA), 42 U.S.C. secs 6901, et. seq.; The Safe Drinking Water Act, 42 U.S.C. secs 1401 et seq; The Comprehensive Environmental Response, Compensation and Liability Act (CERCLA), 42 U.S.C. secs 9601 et. seq.; the Atomic Energy Act of 1946 as revised, 42 U.S.C. secs 2101 et. seq. (1954); and the Nuclear Waste Policy Act of 1982, 42 U.S.C. secs 10101 et seq.

[3] The use of the costs of controls versus the cost of damages to society in valuing utility environmental externalities is discussed in Chapter III, Section H.1. ?

c. Environmental Impact Statements

For all major federal actions which affect the environment, environmental impact statements (EIS's) must be prepared.[4] Many states have their own statutory requirements for environmental assessments.[5] Many federal and state environmental impact statements (EIS's) were reviewed as well as EIS literature. No EIS's were found or referred to which value environmental damages; only unquantified impacts on human health and the environment were described. Treatment of environmental costs in EIS's is discussed at various points in the report, but particularly in Section C, dealing in depth with treatment by the states which have done most to address these costs.

B. STATE INCORPORATION METHODOLOGIES

The methodologies used by the states for incorporation of environmental externality costs include:[6] quantitative consideration, qualitative consideration, rate of return consideration, avoided cost consideration and ranking consideration. These methodologies are discussed below as well as their implementation in planning, bidding and other resource evaluations. Collaborative determination and treatment of costs are also discussed, as well as a number of innovative proposals not yet put into effect by any state.[7]

---

[4] EIS requirements are imposed by the National Environmental Policy Act (NEPA), 42 U.S.C. Secs. 4321-4370a, Pub. L. 91-190, 1969.

[5] For example, see New York's State Environmental Quality Review Act (SEQRA), New York Environmental Conservation Law, Sec. 9-107, and its implementing regulation, 6 NYCRR, Part 617.9.

[6] This section is based largely on a 50-state survey of state regulatory commissions in November, 1989, on state treatment of environmental externalities. The survey was done for the National Association of Regulatory Utility Commissioners (NARUC) by Lawrence Berkeley Laboratory (LBL), to be published shortly. Cohen, S.D., Eto, J.H., Beldock, J. and Crandall, G., A Survey of State Regulatory Commission Activities to Incorporate Environmental Externalities into Electric Utility Planning and Regulation, draft of May, 1990 [hereafter cited as LBL survey]. For other references, see "State-by-State Survey Sources" at the end of Section G of this chapter.

Discrepancies between the state participation numbers here and those in the LBL survey, are accounted for by different classifications used in the two reports. Thus, while this report uses classifications of "ordered, pending and under consideration," the LBL survey uses "operational, developing and aware." Also, more states are included here which have avoided cost and rate of return consideration. The state by state descriptions in the Appendix to this chapter and those in the LBL survey are identical in substance; the interpretations sometimes differ.

[7] Citations to the incorporation statutes and regulations in summary treatment in Section B. can be found in the State-by-State Survey of Environmental Cost Treatment in Section G of this chapter. The incorporation citations are omitted here because it would be repetitive to include them and it would detract from the text. Citations are given for references not included elsewhere. Tables 1 and 2 at the end of this section summarize graphically state-by-state actions and the treatment methodology used by each state that has acted to incorporate externalities.

1. Methodology Descriptions

Quantitative Consideration involves establishment of dollar values for environmental costs by a commission or by a utility under commission order. The values calculated are either added to the cost of resources in the selection process or used in a resource rating system. Some commissions use a proxy percentage adder to polluting resources, or a percentage credit to non-polluting resources (e.g. a non-combustion credit).

Qualitative Consideration requires utilities to incorporate or consider environmental externality costs, without specifying how these costs are to be calculated or employed.

Rate of Return Consideration involves award of an increased rate of return to utilities: 1) on particular low-polluting resource investments (usually DSM and/or renewables, sometimes resource recovery plants); or, 2) more broadly, on their total investments in low-polluting resources; or 3) on exceeding goals established by the commission for such investments.

Avoided Cost Consideration requires incorporation of environmental externality costs into utilities's calculations of their avoided cost, usually quantitatively by a percentage adder.

Ranking Consideration assigns weights to various resources or pollutants to take into account environmental externalities (e.g. givinga set number of total scoring points to environmentally benign resources or to individual pollutants) for use in resource selection. The term, as used here, applies only to ranking systems not based directly on quantified environmental costs (cost-based rankings are categorized under "quantified consideration").

Collaborative Consideration involves commission-ordered or voluntary collaboration between one or more utilities and a combination of state agencies and intervenors to establish environmental externality values and treatment.

Environmental Dispatch requires utilities or a power pool to include quantified environmental costs in dispatch on a least cost resources first basis. The term has also been used for dispatch of more environmentally benign resources ahead of more polluting resources, even though the latter may cost less (with a dollar limit).

"Environmental LCUP" is a new, as yet untried concept, requiring establishment of emission reduction targets for pollutants that utilities must meet at least cost.[8] It may readily be used only for hard-to-quantify externalities, using methods of quantified consideration for the remainder.

Set-Aside Consideration requires utilities to set aside a specified portion of their capacity needs to be filled solely by designated, more environmentally benign resources. Thus, a commission might specify that 20% of each utility's capacity needs had to be

---

[8] Proposed by Dr. Florin Krause of LBL at a Least Cost Planning Training Workshop, Lawrence Berkeley Laboratory (LBL), Berkeley, CA, February 1, 1990.

filled with DSM and/or renewable resources, in order to account for environmental externalities.

2. Methods Being Used by States

There follows a summary and brief analysis of state employment of each of these methodologies:[9]

a. Orders for Consideration

Of the remarkable number of twenty-nine state public service commissions or legislatures that have taken some action to incorporate environmental externality costs or have such action under active consideration, nineteen have issued orders or passed legislation requiring their utilities to take into account these costs in planning and/or bidding; three states have such orders pending, and seven states have them under active consideration. Twenty-three states have taken no action to incorporate environmental costs.[10]

b. Quantified Consideration

Twelve states have adopted quantified consideration of environmental costs or have quantification measures pending or under active consideration. Seven states plus Bonneville Power Administration (BPA) and the Northwest Power Planning Council (NWPPC) have acted to consider environmental externality costs quantitatively or use a proxy adder to represent these costs. Two states have quantification orders pending and three states have them under active consideration.[11]

---

[9] In the categories listed and in the following discussion of state treatment within those categories, there is overlap; thus, New York is listed as having quantitative, rate of return, avoided cost (by statute), collaborative, planning and bidding consideration. Detailed analyses of six of the states with the most extensive environmental costing treatment are contained in Section 6 of this chapter.

[10] Orders: AZ, CA, CO, ID, KA, MA, MICH, MN, NJ, NY, OH, OR, PA, TX, VA, VT, WI.
Statutes: ALSK, NV.
Pending: CT, IA, MN.
Consideration: DC*, HW, ME, MD, MONT, RI, UT.
No Consideration: ALA, ARK, DE, FL, GA, IL, IND, KY, LA, MISS, MO, NB, NH, NM, ND, NC, OK, SC, SD, TN, WA, WVA, WYO.
* The District of Columbia (DC) is considered as a state for purposes of this analysis.

[11] Quantified: CA, CO, NJ, NY, OR, WI, VT.
Pending: CT, MA, CA, (limited order: more extensive order pending)
Consideration: DC, MD, MICH.

The Northwest Power Planning Council gives a 10% bonus to energy conservation resources in its regional planning, under a statutory requirement.[12] The Council's planning is not mandatory on the region's utilities, but is persuasive with the individual commissions in the region. Bonneville Power Administration (BPA), which furnishes about half of the region's power, is guided by the plan. BPA values environmental costs and uses them itself in selecting resources and to assist its state customers in their resource selections.

The New York PSC has been the pioneer in incorporating quantified environmental externality costs, requiring its utilities to assign approximately 24% of price scoring points (about 15% of total bid evaluation scoring points) to environmental externality costs, calculated at 1.405 cents/kWh total environmental externality costs, based on a coal plant meeting Clean Air Act New Source Performance Standards.[13] The PSC has also ordered all its utilities to do a pooled study, collaboratively with intervenors to quantify the environmental externality costs of their plants' pollution.

Wisconsin has adopted a noncombustion credit (or adder, at a utility's option) for initial screening of all utility resource acquisitions, so that a non-combustion source that costs 15% more than a combustion source will be considered on a par with the latter; this screening is followed by a qualitative review for selection of resources. Also, in Wisconsin's integrated planning process, a sensitivity run to review options is required, assuming the imposition of a requirement of 20% reduction of carbon dioxide emissions by 2000 and 50% in the long run.

In Oregon, while the commission has not quantified environmental externality costs, it has ordered the utilities to do so "to the fullest extent practicable," incorporating the costs in resource selection. Where damage costs cannot be definitively quantified, the commission has ordered the utilities to indicate ranges of costs.

In New Jersey, utilities have been ordered to assign 20% of bid evaluation scoring points to "non-economic" factors, but in the first bidding evaluation to which the order was applied, only 1% of bid evaluation points were assigned to environmental externality costs and 1% to energy efficiency.

In Colorado bidding, up to 20% of official forecast demand must be reserved for "qualifyingfacilities" (QFs as defined under PURPA). For this 20% only, consideration of environmental externalities is required by fuel type, on a 100-point scoring scale: for renewables, 12 points plus 5 points at the end of the evaluation process, for a total of 17; for coal, 5 points; for natural gas, 2 points; and for oil, 1 point. Conservation is not included in the scoring.[14]

---

[12] Pacific Northwest Electric Power Planning and Conservation Act, 16 U.S.C. 839 et. seq. (1980).

[13] 42 U.S.C. sec. 7411. The New York formula is elaborated in the in-depth analysis in Section C. of this chapter, infra.

[14] The Public Utilities Regulatory Policy Act of 1978, 16 U.S.C., secs. 2601 et. seq.
The Colorado ranking does not accord with any environmental damage or control cost figures for resources reported in any of the studies reviewed. The reported ranking of environmental costs almost uniformly [with some variations for technological innovations] are, in order of least environmental cost: DSM, renewables, natural gas, oil and coal. It would seem Colorado's rankings take into account the importance of coal mining to the state and the paucity of natural gas or oil use.

The California Energy Commission (CEC) considers environmental externalities in licensing sites for all plants over 50MW. The CEC recently proposed for consideration in its next Electricity Report (ER90), quantitative valuation of environmental externalities as follows: $11,600/T for NOx, $11,500/T for SOx, $7,800/T for PM10 particulates, $3,300/T for reactive organic gases (ROG) and $7/T for CO_2. The PUC has also initiated a proceeding to consider quantified environmental costs. A collaborative DSM process, just completed, failed to come to agreement on environmental cost treatment.

The Vermont Public Service Board just recently adopted a rebuttable presumption for a 5% environmental externalities adder to all supply resource costs and a 10% risk reduction credit to all DSM resource costs in utility planning. Parties may present to the Board arguments that particular resources should get greater or lesser adders and credits.

Several state commissions have orders pending or under consideration requiring quantitative environmental externality costing determinations. The Massachusetts and Connecticut commissions have orders pending for quantitative consideration of environmental externalities and the DC, Maryland and Michigan commissions are actively considering quantification orders. The Connecticut Department of Public Utilities has developed an elaborate bidding evaluation scoring process taking environmental externalities into consideration which is pending before the commission.

c. Qualitative Consideration

Nine states presently have ordered or have under consideration orders that their utilities take into account environmental externality costs in planning and/or resource selection, without specifying how they are to be calculated or considered, seven ordered and two under consideration.[15]

The Minnesota and Texas commissions consider environmental externalities in their Certificate of Need processes and Minnesota has issued a proposed rule for doing so in resource planning. The Maine commission has adopted a rule for evaluating DSM efficiency investments that includes a societal test that is satisfied if a program's total costs to society are less than the total value of the resources saved by avoiding electricity production. Benefits include reduced environmental impacts and any other societal benefits. However, the state has not yet adopted specific measures for evaluating externalities.

d. Rate of Return Consideration

Nine states give rate of return consideration to DSM measures, stating environmental externality cost rationales, one of them for resource recovery plants

---

[15] Orders: AZ, MN, NV, OH, OR, PA, TX.
Under consideration: ME, MO.

only.[16] While only states that specifically attributed rate of return treatment to environmental costs are included here, any rate incentive for DSM or renewables could be considered a measure to take into account environmental externality costs because the incentives operate to alleviate such costs.

Washington and Montana each have statutory provisions for a 2% additional rate of return on energy conservation investments, and Connecticut 5%, citing environmental externality costs as a justification.

New York has given temporary rate of return incentives to its utilities on DSM investments, in part for environmental reasons, based on a return of net lost revenues as a result of the DSM investments plus a performance-based incentive.[17] It has ordered two incentive experiments: one of its utilities is to explore an energy revenue adjustment mechanism (similar to California's "ERAM") to separate profit from sales, plus a performance-based incentive based on achieved energy savings; another utility is to experiment with an incentive based on an index of customer bill savings attributable to DSM programs.[18]

Kansas gives a .5% to 2.0% increased rate of return on renewable and conservation resources.

The Idaho commission has announced that in future rate cases it will take into account "aggressive" utility conservation efforts in determining the allowed rate of return.

The Wisconsin Commission, as an experimental demonstration, has allowed Wisconsin Electric Co. to earn an additional 1% rate of return for each 125 MW peak reduction achieved by efficiency investments.

---

[16] Orders: ID, KA, NJ, NY, OK, WI
Statutes: CT, MONT, WA;
The Oklahoma commission gives an incentive rate of return on environmental grounds solely to resource recovery plants.

[17] The New York Supreme Court has just recently upheld the New York PSC's order to grant utility rate incentives for DSM programs; The Pace Center for Environmental Legal Studies appeared in the case in support of the PSC. Multiple Intervenors v. New York State Public Service Commission, No. 249-90 (N.Y. Sup. Ct., June 7, 1990).

[18] California's energy revenue adjustment mechanism (ERAM) is described in Section C.6. below, and New York incentives are described in detail in Section C.1.c.ii.

e. Avoided Cost Consideration

Seven state legislatures or commissions have required, or are considering requiring, valuation of avoided cost at a premium over utility-calculated avoided power plant capacity and energy costs, to help account for environmental externalities.[19]

New Jersey has established PURPA avoided cost at 10% over the regional power pool's energy billing rate to reflect the potential cost savings to society from the presumably more environmentally benign QF sources.[20]

The Virginia Commission requires addition of 15% to a utility's avoided cost submission, also based on societal costs. The Commission has stated its rationale as follows:

> "...Other factors which make cogeneration and small power production facilities beneficial and in the public interest are more intangible however, and the associated costs which can be avoided are societal and environmental in nature. Such costs are not borne directly by the utility but by the public as a whole...[and must] be addressed in fixing avoided cost rates."[21]

Similarly, the Alaska and Michigan commissions have increased avoided costs to include environmental externality cost considerations;[22] New York has a statutory 6 cents/kWh avoided cost, above most utility calculated figures, which, as noted before, FERC has challenged;[23] the Iowa commission has endorsed a consultant's report recommending a credit (e.g. 10%) to avoided cost based on environmental considerations; and the Idaho commission includes pollution control equipment in the

---

[19] Ordered: ALSK, ID, MICH, NJ, NY, VA.
Pending: IA
In New York, the State Legislature set a statutory 6 cents/kWh PURPA avoided cost rate, which is above most utility-calculated avoid costs; FERC voided application of this rate, interpreting PURPA to prohibit reimbursement in excess of avoided cost. 43 F.E.R.C..par. 61,067,1988. The FERC decision is being appealed. One of the FERC commissioners indicated that application of the decision to other situations would be decided on a generic basis.

[20] The Appropriateness and Feasibility of Various Methods of Calculating Avoided Costs, National Regulatory Research Institute, 1982, at p. 15; See, Bidding Farewell to the Social Costs of Electricity Production: Pricing Alternative Energy Under the Public Utility Regulatory Policy Act (hereinafter, Bidding Farewell), The Journal of Corporation Law, Summer 1988, 1011 at p. 1039.

[21] Virginia Electric & Power Co., 71 Pub. Util. Rept. (PUR4th 160, 168), Va. State Corp. Comm., 1985, as cited in Bidding Farewell, supra, note 20 at p. 1040.

[22] Bidding Farewell, supra note 20 at pp. 1040, 1041.

[23] Supra, note 18. It is unclear how FERC's recent Orange & Rockland decision, denying the right of state commissions to set PURPA payments above avoided costs, will affect this kind of increase in avoided costs to account for environmental externalities, since the FERC decision addressed only invalidation of New York's statutory 6 cents/kWh avoided cost law, which was not based on a calculation of environmental externality costs, but merely use environmental considerations as one of its rationales (the law's principal purpose was to promote QFs) -- and one of the FERC commissioners indicated that future decisions on payments to QF's in excess of avoided cost would be made and that they would be made generically.

capacity credit calculation on grounds that scrubbers and other pollution control devices will be required in the future and their costs should therefore be included.[24]

f. Ranking Consideration

A number of states have adopted ranking systems not calculated directly from environmental externality costs.[25]

New England Electric System (NEES) recently adopted a ranking system based on the responses to a survey of its customers as to the importance to them of specified environmental damages from operation of electric utilities.[26]

The Center for Global Change at the University of Maryland just recently has presented a ranking and weighting methodology for evaluating environmental externality costs, using data available on these costs in formulating the ranking criteria, but the rankings are not cost-specific. This was done as testimony before the Vermont Public Service Board in a proceeding to determine whether twenty-four electric utilities should make a large purchase of Hydro-Quebec hydropower from its proposed James Bay hydro facility.[27] As described in the testimony:[28]

> A standardized 100 point scale was developed for each impact category (air, water, waste, etc.) The highest impact technology in each category was assigned a scaled score of 100, and the remaining technologies assigned a relative score on the scale.
>
> Each category was then assigned a weight ranging from one to ten. The magnitude of the weight reflected staff judgment about the severity and reversibility of each impact. For each category of impact, the combined physical impact from all technologies in a given scenario was multiplied by the

---

[24] Rulemaking Proceeding for Consideration of Cogeneration & Small Power Production, 40 Pub. Util. Rept. (PUR4th) 563, 567-68, as reported in Bidding Farewell, supra note 20 at p. 1043.

[25] Ranking is defined in this report as use of a weighted scale for resources or pollutants in selection of resources, not calculated directly from environmental externality costs. Thus New York's bidding methodology is not considered here because it ranks bids for environmental costs strictly on the basis of an adder calculated from estimated costs; it is therefore included under quantified consideration.

[26] Comments by Massachusetts Electric Co. (a NEES subsidiary) at 17-21 and Attachment 2, Investigation by the Department of Public Utilities on Its Own Motion into Proposed Rules to Implement Integrated Resource Management Practices for Electric Companies in the Commonwealth, Mass. D.P.U. No. 89-239, Feb. 23, 1990.

[27] Vermont Public Service Board, Application of Twenty-four Electric Utilities...for a Certificate of Public Good Authorizing Execution and Performance of a Firm Power and Energy Contract with Hydro-Quebec and a Hydro-Quebec Participation Agreement, Docket No. 5330, testimony of Dr. Susan Hedman, Professor Alan S. Miller and Dr. Irving Mintzer, January 11, 1990.

[28] Id. at pp. 19, 20.

weighting factor for that impact. This yielded a weighted, scaled score.

For each scenario, the scaled scores are summed across all the impact categories. This sum represents the complete scaled score for that scenario across all the environmental dimensions being evaluated. By comparing these composite scaled scores among various scenarios, it is possible to rank any given set of scenarios from the least environmentally damaging to the most environmentally damaging."

This scoring system was then used to compare the various scenarios employing different resources in different combinations (coal, oil and natural gas resources, conservation, renewables, etc.). Cogeneration, efficiency and renewables scored the highest on the ranking system by a considerable margin.

g. Collaborative Consideration

Six states are involved in collaborative efforts to determine how environmental externality costs will be calculated and incorporated.[29] None of these efforts has yet come to fruition.

Collaborative design of DSM programs has been very successful, led by the Conservation Law Foundation of Boston which is working with eleven utilities, state agencies and intervenors in the New England states. So far application of the collaborative process to determine and incorporate environmental externality costs has not produced results, however. CLF has found that many of the utilities with which it works are resistant to incorporation of environmental costs. At least one utility has dropped environmental costing from its otherwise successful and continuing collaborative efforts with CLF.[30] A recent collaborative DSM effort in California, highly successful in agreeing on DSM programs, was also unable to agree on externality values or their incorporation methodologies.[31]

---

[29] CT, IA, MD, MA, NY, VT.

In New York, in addition to a voluntary collaborative between New York State Electric & Gas Co., state agencies and public intervenors, the PSC has ordered a pooled collaborative with all jurisdictional utilities, relevant state agencies and outside experts, with public participation, to determine the environmental externality costs of their plant emissions. Case 28223, Proceeding to Inquire into the Benefits to Ratepayers and Utilities from Implementation of Conservation Programs that will Reduce Electric Use. Order Concerning Long Range Demand Side Management Plans, December 23, 1988.

[30] NEES, in New England, has dropped out of the collaborative process for environmental externality cost determinations and adopted its own ranking system. Supra, Note 28.

[31] An Energy Efficiency Blueprint for California, Report of the Statewide Collaborative Process, January, 1990, at p. 68.

h. Media of Consideration

Planning Consideration. Twenty-three states, BPA and NWPPC have required or are contemplating requiring consideration of environmental externality costs in least cost planning. Twelve states have present requirements and eleven states have requirements pending or under consideration.[32]

Bid Evaluation Consideration. Seven states and BPA have considered or are considering a requirement to take into account environmental externality costs in evaluating bid scores; three have issued orders and four have orders pending or under active consideration.[33] Three state commissions have provided for specific points to be assigned in bid evaluations to account for environmental externality costs (New York, New Jersey and Colorado), but only New York's effort is substantial, assigning dollar values to be added to the prices of bid resources. Colorado authorizes QF's to participate in bidding for up to 20% of each utility's demand forecast. Its environmental externality consideration is restricted to this maximum QF share of demand and is scored by fuel type, with environmental considerations clearly a secondary consideration since no credit is given for conservation and coal is preferred over natural gas and oil; New Jersey's bidding evaluation is also minimal, with a recent decision assigning only 1% of bid evaluation points each to environmental considerations and energy efficiency.

Connecticut, Vermont and Massachusetts commissions have orders pending for consideration of environmental externalities in bid evaluations, and the Maryland commission and BPA plan such consideration.

3. Proposed Methods

a. Environmental Dispatch

No states currently are employing environmental dispatch as a means of incorporating environmental externality costs. However, Wisconsin's recently enacted acid rain statute includes environmental dispatch among the compliance options for meeting the SO_2 and NOx standards established.[34] Southern California's utilities used

---

[32] Ordered: AZ, CA, NV, NY, OH, OR, PA, TX, VT, WI.
Statute: ALSK.
Pending: CT, MA, MN.
Consideration: DC, HW, MICH, ME, MO, MONT, RI, UT.

[33] Orders: CO (by fuel type), NJ, NY.
Pending: CT, MA, VT.
Under consideration: MD.

[34] Wisc. Stats. Ann., Secs. 144.385-144.387; See also, Secs. 15.347, 16.02.

environmental dispatch based on least NOx emissions for several years, adopted to meet air quality standards, but have discontinued the practice.[35]

Environmental dispatch has the advantages of minimizing environmental damages and costs. By displacing production from existing power plants, which are universally the most heavily polluting, and thus encouraging their early closure. This methodology is by far the most effective at achieving environmental improvement. All the other methodologies presently adopted by states to incorporate environmental externality costs address only resource selection to meet new capacity or energy needs.[36]

An Ohio Consumers' Counsel study of cleaning up the state's very substantial production of acid rain precursors, found that a combination of "Least Emissions Dispatching" and aggressive investment in energy efficiency could prevent increases in SO_2, reduce cleanup costs by more than 60% and reduce cumulative costs for electric energy services by as much as $3 billion through 2005.[37]

Even though no state commission has adopted environmental dispatch, there is a great deal of interest in it. Case Western Reserve University has developed a model for analyzing environmental dispatch,[38] and BPA's production models and resources planning models are capable of analyzing environmental dispatch, but they usually are run only to determine the lowest social cost of meeting loads; the Cornell Carnegie-Mellon model developed for New York utility emission impacts could also accommodate environmental dispatch.[39]

b. "Environmental LCUP"

Wisconsin's new acid rain law[40] comes closer than any state has to use of "Environmental LCUP" (setting emission reduction targets which utilities have to meet

---

35 Conversation by Ottinger with John Wilson of Southern California Edison Co., February 22, 1990.

36 The New York PSC, however, has made some provision for some consideration of the environmental costs from existing plants by requiring inclusion of life extension of existing plants in its mandated bidding regime, which includes evaluation of environmental costs. The PSC has also stated that bid prices would be compared to costs of existing plants (not proposed for life extension) to determine the appropriateness of maintaining their operations. N.Y. PSC Case 29409, Opinion No. 88-15, Opinion and Order Concerning Bidding, Avoided Cost Pricing and Wheeling Issues, June 3, 1988.

37 Centolella, P., Clearing the Air: Using Energy Conservation to Reduce Acid Rain Compliance Costs in Ohio, Ohio Office of the Consumers' Counsel, July 1988.

38 Heslin, J. and B. Hobbs, A Multiobjective Production Costing Model for Analyzing Emissions Dispatching and Fuel Switching, IEEE Transactions on Power Systems, v. 4, No. 3, Aug. 1989, Department of Systems Engineering, Case Western Reserve University, Cleveland, Ohio.

39 Communication from Shepard Buchanan, BPA, February 22, 1990.

40 Supra, note 34.

at least cost). The statute provides that environmental externality costs must be considered in meeting the statutory So_x and No_x standards.

The advantage of "Environmental LCUP" is that it avoids the necessity for calculating environmental externality costs and is designed to achieve specific emission reduction targets. It is readily adaptable to use just for determination of hard-to-quantify resource damages, while more readily quantifiable resource damages can be incorporated using the various methodologies for quantified consideration. Thus, for hard-to-quantify climate change costs, a 20% CO_2 target could be required to be attained at least cost, while the remaining utility environmental costs were incorporated using traditional methods such as adders or credits.

The disadvantage of Environmental LCUP is that it requires calculation of the emission reduction targets, a calculation with which commissions may have difficulty. Commissions also may feel they lack legal authority to establish emission targets.

c. Set-Aside Consideration

Another method that has been suggested for consideration of environmental costs is for commissions to require that a certain part of future capacity requirements be met utilizing environmentally benign resources.[41] One could, for example, set aside a part of any given request for bid proposals for DSM and renewable or other more environmentally benign resources.

The Public Utilities Regulatory Policy Act (PURPA)[42] accomplishes some of what this methodology seeks by requiring utilities to acquire all specified small renewable generation and cogeneration electricity at the utility's avoided cost.

The advantage of set-asides is that they avoid the difficult problems of damage valuation and oversight of bidding systems for benign resources. The disadvantage is that it is difficult to correlate the set-asides in any meaningful way with environmental damages.

---

[41] Duane, T.P., Internalizing the Environmental Costs of Electricity Generation, Palo Alto, California, draft of May 7, 1990, at pp. 27, 28. To be Published by the Sierra Club.

[42] The Public Utilities Regulatory Policy Act of 1978, 16 U.S.C., secs. 2601 et. seq.

TABLE 1

STATUS OF STATE ACTIONS INCORPORATING ENVIRONMENTAL EXTERNALITY COSTS

Legend

O - Incorporation Ordered
P - Incorporation Order Pending
U - Under Consideration
N - No Action

STATE	O	P	U	N	
ALABAMA				X	
ALASKA	X				1
ARIZONA	X				
ARKANSAS				X	
CALIFORNIA	X				2
COLORADO	X				
CONNECTICUT		X			
DELAWARE				X	
DISTRICT OF COLUMBIA			X		
FLORIDA				X	
GEORGIA				X	
HAWAII			X		
IDAHO	X				
ILLINOIS				X	
INDIANA				X	
IOWA		X			
KANSAS	X				
KENTUCKY				X	
LOUISIANA				X	
MAINE			X		
MARYLAND			X		
MASSACHUSETTS	X				2
MICHIGAN	X				2
MINNESOTA	X				2
MISSISSIPPI				X	
MISSOURI				X	3
MONTANA			X		
NEBRASKA				X	
NEVADA	X				1
NEW HAMPSHIRE				X	
NEW JERSEY	X				
NEW MEXICO				X	
NEW YORK	X				
NORTH CAROLINA			X		
NORTH DAKOTA				X	
OHIO	X				
OKLAHOMA				X	
OREGON	X				
PENNSYLVANIA	X				
RHODE ISLAND			X		
SOUTH CAROLINA				X	
SOUTH DAKOTA				X	
TENNESSEE				X	
TEXAS	X				
UTAH			X		
VERMONT	X				
VIRGINIA	X				
WASHINGTON				X	
WEST VIRGINIA				X	
WISCONSIN	X				
WYOMING				X	
BPA	X				1
NWPPC	X				1

This table is derived from the references at the end of Chapter X, Section G.

1. Established by legislation.

2. Order issued to consider externalities; implementation pending.

3. Commission has stated that it may consider externalities.

TABLE 2

TYPE OF ACTION BY STATES ACTING TO INCORPORATE ENVIRONMENTAL EXTERNALITY COSTS

Legend

O - Incorp. Ordered
P - Incorp. Order Pending
U - Under Consideration
QN - Quantitative Consid.
QL - Qualitative Consid.
ROR - Rate Consideration
AC - Avoided Cost Consid.
ED - Environmental Dispatch
C - Collaborative Action
PL - Planning Consideration
B - Bidding Consideration
L - Legislative Action

State	QN	QL	ROR	AC	ED	C	PL	B	Comment
ALSK				O			L		
AZ		O					O		
CA	OP				U	C*	O		*Collab. ended
CO	O*							O*	*by fuel type
CT	P		L*			C	P	P	*5% ROR adder
DC							U		
HW							U		
ID			O	O					
IA				P		C			
KA	P		O						
ME		U					U		
MD	U					C		U	
MA	P*					C	P	P	*DSM Evaluations
MICH	U			O			U		
MN*		O					P		*Law caps SO2
MT		U	L*				U		*2% adder for DSM
NV		L					L		
NH							L*		*Law under consid.
NJ	O			O				O	
NY	O		O	L		C	O	O	
OH		O					O		
OK			O*						*ROR, trash only
OR*	O	O					O		*Law caps CO_2
PA		O*					O*		*Not implemented
RI							U		
UT							U		
TX		L					L		
VT	O*					C	O*	O*	*15% on DSM
VA				O*					*15% DSM adder to AC
WA			L*						*2% ROR law for DSM
WI	O		O		U		O		
BPA	L						L	U	
NWPPC	L						L		

This table is derived from the references at the end of Chapter X, Section G.

C. IN-DEPTH ANALYSIS OF SELECTED STATE TREATMENT

This section provides an in-depth evaluation of state utility regulatory consideration of environmental externalities to complement the above summary in Section B. It reviews the consideration of environmental externalities in the following illustrative states which have given most extensive consideration to environmental costs:

New York, has led the nation in incorporating environmental externalities into utility planning and resource acquisition decisions, adopting quantitative consideration in utility planning, bidding and DSM evaluation and the most comprehensive utility DSM incentives; Wisconsin, has also actively been a pioneer in this field, requiring quantitative and qualitative consideration, with an adder/credit for environmental costs; and Oregon, Vermont, Massachusetts and California have adopted variations on the New York and Wisconsin approaches.

1. New York

The New York Public Service Commission (PSC) has required inclusion of environmental externalities in integrated planning, all-source bidding evaluation and in demand side management (DSM) evaluation.[43] PSC has also adopted incentives proposed by each of its jurisdictional utilities to restore lost net revenues attributable to DSM programs and provide a performance-based incentive measured by energy saved, seeking to assure that a dollar invested in energy savings will be as profitable as a dollar invested in supply.

A brief review of the procedural background of these policies facilitates understanding of interlocking aspects of the PSC's environmental externality policy:

a. Overview

i. Case 29409, Planning and Bidding Background

The New York PSC has established very comprehensive environmental costing requirements for integrated resource planning and bidding. Annual and long-range supply and DSM plans must be filed with the Commission and, when approved, must be carried out by the utilities. Bidding is required for all new resources and for life extension of existing plants.

The PSC established Case 29409 on August 15, 1986, to investigate ways to meet the future electric needs of New York. In this proceeding, non-adversarial working groups investigated specific issues, gathered information, and presented analyses or

---

[43] Planning and Bidding: Case No. 29409, Proceeding on Motion of the Commission to Examine the Plans for Meeting Future Electricity Needs in New York State [hereinafter referred to as Case No. 29409];

DSM: Case No. 28223, Proceeding to Inquire into the Benefits to Ratepayers and Utilities from Implementation of Conservation Programs that will Reduce Electric Use [hereinafter referred to as Case No. 29223].

position papers. An Administrative Law Judge (ALJ) then recommended decisions involving issues addressed by different working groups to the PSC.[44] The many issues included in Case 29409 can be grouped according to the PSC orders in which the issues were initially formulated:

* Opinion No. 88-15, June, 1988, addressing bidding, avoided cost pricing and wheeling issues.[45]

* Opinion No. 88-20, July, 1988, addressing integrated planning and ratemaking issues.[46]

* Opinion 88-15A, November, 1988, in which the PSC denied utility petitions for a rehearing of the Opinion No. 88-15 order.[47]

* Order of March 24, 1989, issuing a final environmental impact statement for Orange & Rockland Utilities, Inc.'s bidding RFP, in which the PSC first required quantified environmental externality cost consideration in bidding.[48]

ii. Case 28223, DSM Programs Background

In addition to its leading role in planning and bidding, New York is also one of the most advanced states in requiring utilities to invest in DSM resources. The PSC has required each utility to invest in six specified core programs, full scale, starting January 1, 1990. It has also required DSM programs to be evaluated for cost-effectiveness using a number of different tests and incorporating environmental externality costs.

Case 28223 was established in 1982 as the result of a presentation made by the Environmental Defense Fund (EDF) in the PSC's investigation of Nine Mile Point No. 2 Nuclear Station. EDF had advocated that investment in end-use conservation was preferable to construction of the Nine Mile Point nuclear plant. As a result of the Case 28223 investigation, the PSC ordered New York utilities to use .25% of gross

---

[44] Case 29409, Recommended Decision on Bidding, Avoided Costs Pricing and Open Wheeling by A.L.J. Frank S. Robinson, December 10, 1987.

[45] Case 29409, Op. No. 88-15, Order Concerning Bidding, Avoided Cost Pricing and Wheeling Issues, issued and effective June 3, 1988 [hereafter cited as Case 29409, Op. No. 88-15].

[46] Case 29409, Op. No. 88-20, Order Concerning Integrated Planning and Ratemaking Issues, issued and effective July 7, 1988 [hereafter cited as Case 29409, Op. No. 88-20].

[47] Case 29409, Op. No. 88-15(A), Order Denying Petitions for Rehearing, issued and effective November 2, 1988, at 24 [hereafter cited as Case 29409, Op. No. 88-15(A)].

[48] Case 88-E-241 - Proceeding on Motion of the Commission (established in Opinion 88-15) as to the guidelines for bidding to meet future electric capacity needs of Orange & Rockland Utilities, Inc., Order Issuing a Final Environmental Impact Statement and Adopting Staff's Response to Agency Comments, March 24, 1989 [hereafter cited as Case 88-E-241 Costing Order].

revenues to undertake demonstration DSM projects.[49] The first order requiring the utilities to file detailed DSM plans was issued in September, 1987.[50]

The orders in this case relevant to environmental costing are as follows:

* Order of December 23, 1988, ordering each utility to engage full-scale in eight specified core DSM programs, and for the first time, requiring cost/benefit analyses to include "program benefits that are important but difficult to measure" (environmental benefits).[51]

* Opinion No. 89-15, May 23, 1989, requiring all the utilities to engage in a pooled effort to ascertain New York-specific environmental costs.[52]

* Order of December 29, 1989, concerning the utilities' 1990 DSM plan filings, establishing the first minimum requirement for DSM investments (a minimum of 0.15% of revenues for all utilities' lighting budgets), and requiring detailed cost/benefit analysis and evaluation, including environmental benefits.[53]

iii. Incentives Background

Pursuant to the Commission's order in Case 29409, Op. No. 88-20 of July 26, 1988,[54] the utilities were invited to and some did submit proposals for rate incentives to assure comparable profitability of DSM investments with supply investments. The Commission incentive orders are as follows:

* Order of April 3, 1989, issuing a Notice Soliciting Comments on rate incentive proposals of Orange & Rockland Utilities, Inc. (O&R) and Niagara Mohawk Power Corporation (NIMO), posing questions for comment on these proposals and other rate incentives, including inclusion of environmental externalities in cost/benefit analysis of incentives.[55]

---

[49] Case 28223, Op. No. 84-15, Order Requiring the Development of Conservation Programs, May 21, 1984 [hereafter cited as Case 28223, Op. No. 84-15].

[50] Case 28223, Order Directing the Submittal of Annual Demand Side Management Plans, issued September 22, 1987.

[51] Case 28223, Order Concerning Long Range Demand Side Management Plans, December 23, 1988 [hereafter cited as Case 28223, December 1988 Core DSM Order].

[52] Case 28223, Op. 89-15, Order Concerning Long Range Demand Side Management Plans, May 23, 1989 [hereafter cited as Case 28223 Op. 89-15, Pooled Costing Order].

[53] Case 28223, Order Concerning 1990 Demand Side Management Plans, December 29, 1989 [hereafter cited as Case 28223 1990 DSM Plan Order].

[54] Case 29409, Op. No. 88-20, <u>supra</u>, note 46.

[55] Case 89-E-041, <u>Proceeding on Motion of the Commission as to the rates, charges and regulations of Orange and Rockland Utilities, Inc. and Niagara Mohawk Power Corporation - Rate Incentive Proposals.</u>, Notice Soliciting Comments, April 3, 1989 [hereafter cited as Case 89-E-041 Notice Soliciting Comments].

* Order of September 12, 1989, adopting (with revisions) the incentive proposals of O&R and NIMO, basically for recovery of net lost revenues attributable to DSM programs and a performance-based incentive; and ordering two long-term incentive proposals to be submitted, from O&R to develop a revenue adjustment mechanism separating profits from sales plus a performance-based incentive, and from NIMO to develop an incentive based on utility bill indexing. The O&R proposal, including environmental costs in net resource savings, and the NIMO proposal, excluding environmental costs were both approved.[56]

iv. State Energy Plan Background

In addition the New York State Energy Office issued a State Energy Plan in September, 1989, making sweeping recommendations for inclusion of environmental externality costs in all electric utility planning and bidding.[57]

b. New York Bidding; Environmental Requirements

The PSC and New York utilities have most completely developed a framework for treating environmental externalities in all-source bidding proceedings. In Case 29409, Opinion No. 88-15,[58] the PSC required the seven major investor-owned utilities (the PSC's jurisdictional electric utilities) to file proposed guidelines for capacity bidding and draft requests for proposals (RFPs) to be used in virtually all new capacity acquisitions. The PSC established eight "guidelines for bidding."[59] The PSC instructed utilities to develop a system that would evaluate bids using an objective bid evaluation system, mandatorily including environmental costs, but indicated that exercise of subjective judgment was permissible in final selections, subject to PSC review.[60] Life extension proposals for existing plants were required to be bid, and bid prices were required to be compared to the cost of existing plants.[61] This is an important requirement because existing plants are responsible for the large majority of utility pollution.

---

[56] Case 89-E-041, Op. No. 89-29, Opinion and Order Approving Demand Side Management Rate Incentives and Establishing Further Proceedings, September 12, 1989 [hereafter cited as Case 89-E-041 Op. 89-29 Incentive Order]. The Order also establishes a new generic proceeding for considering rate incentive mechanisms, Case 89-E-176 - Proceeding on Motion of the Commission to Examine Ratemaking Practices and Incentive Mechanisms Promoting Least Cost Planning and Demand Side Management by Electric Utilities.

[57] New York State Energy Plan, jointly prepared and issued by New York State Energy Office, Department of Environmental Conservation, and Department of Public Service Commission, September, 1989.

[58] Supra, note 45.

[59] Id. at pp. 12-20, 45.

[60] Id. at p. 17 (bidding guideline 4). The PSC notes that "sole reliance on objective factors will often be impractical." Id.

[61] Id. at p. 36.

i. General Environmental Requirements for Bidding

There are three key environmental aspects to the development of the bidding system under Opinion No. 88-15. First, the PSC requires that environmental impacts be included in each utility's formula for bid evaluation.[62] The PSC notes that the environmental impacts might vary generally, for instance with fuel type, or specifically, as with respect to a particular site.[63]

Second, the PSC requires that the unit price of a bid (per-kWh or per-KW, as appropriate) include the costs of "the best available technology for all necessary environmental protection."[64] As one utility noted on exception to the PSC's order, "best available technology" is a term of art in certain federal environmental protection laws.[65] The PSC recognized, however, that bid evaluations should examine the full societal cost of environmental impacts "that could result in degradation of the environment although those impacts are permissible." By requiring that bids include estimates of the costs of best available technologies, the PSC said it was ensuring that supply options which were not required to meet "best available technology" standards under applicable environmental protection regulations, and options which must meet these regulatory control requirements, could be compared on an equal basis in the auction.[66]

Third, the PSC found that the adoption of new procedures for procuring generation capacity was an action "which may have a significant effect on the environment," thus triggering requirements under the State Environmental Quality Review Act (SEQRA)[67] an example of the effect that a state environmental review statute or "little NEPA" can have on the development of utility regulatory procedures. Similar state environmental review impacts are described for Wisconsin <u>infra</u>, Section C.2.

On exception to the PSC's interpretation of SEQRA, three of the utilities asserted that environmental effects realistically could not be attributed to the adoption of bidding procedures. Moreover, the utilities stressed, the builders of individual plants would be required to prepare any assessments because the act of construction, and

---

[62] <u>Id</u>. at pp. 18-19 (bidding guideline 5).

[63] <u>Id</u>. at p. 19 (bidding guideline 5, factor h).

[64] <u>Id</u>. at p. 18 (bidding guideline 5, factor a).

[65] Case 29409, Op. No. 88-15(A), Order Denying Petitions for Rehearing, 2 November 1988, at p. 24; see also, 33 U.S.C. § 1314(b)(2)(B) (1983) (the factors within the Clean Water Act to assess "best available technology economically achievable,"); 42 U.S.C. § 7479(3) (1986) (the section within the Clean Air Act which defines "best available control technology.")

[66] <u>Id</u>. at p. 25 (adopting staff's position as sound and rejecting one utility's exception that the "best available technology" requirement be narrowly construed).

[67] Case 29409, Op. No. 88-15, <u>supra</u> note 44 at p. 45; Environmental Conservation Law § 8-0109(2); 16 NYCRR § 7.1(a).

not the determination of price, affected the environment.[68] The PSC rejected these contentions by interpreting the term "action" in the regulations which implement SEQRA, defining the term "action" to include "adoption of agency rules, regulations, and procedures" that may affect the environment,[69] and "applicant" to include any person making a request to an agency "to grant an approval in connection with a proposed action."[70] The PSC concluded that the utilities were the prospective "applicants" contemplated under the regulations; consequently, approval of the bidding proposals was found to be an action subject to the SEQRA process.[71]

ii. Quantification Requirements for Bidding

The New York PSC has been the pioneer in incorporating quantified environmental costs into bid evaluations. The PSC has ordered it's utilities to assign approximately 24% of price scoring points in evaluation of bids or about 15% of total evaluation scoring points to environmental externalities . Total environmental costs under this formula are valued at 1.405cents/kWh, based on a coal plant meeting New Source Performance Standards under the Clean Air Act.[72] Specific values are assigned by the PSC to pollution emissions as follows:

Externality	Economic Value in cents/kWh
Suiphur oxides	0.25
Nitrogen oxides	0.55
Carbon dioxide	0.1
Particulates	0.1
	0.005
Total Air Emissions	0.905
Water discharges	0.10
Land use impacts	0.4
Total Cost of Externalities	1.405 cents/kWh[73]

The PSC has approved a different scoring mechanism, as proposed by each utility, but has required the environmental externality scoring to achieve roughly the same

[68] Case 29409,Op. No. 88-15(A), supra note 45, at pp. 44-45. Utilities stressed that an environmental impact analysis was needed only if it "can be reasonably assumed or anticipated" that generating units built under bidding would differ from units that would be otherwise constructed. The bidding process was, according to the utilities, simply a means for evaluating sales proposals, and utilities would still be obligated to purchase power from losing bidders. Id. It is worth reiterating that the bidding process contemplated under Opinion 88-15 is broader than the New York and federal PURPA requirements obligating utilities to purchase power from QFs. Consequently, utilities might not be obligated to buy power from all losing bidders.

[69] 6 NYCRR § 617.2(b)(3), as discussed in Case 29409, Op. 88-15(A), supra note 46 at p. 45.

[70] 6 NYCRR § 617.2(d), as discussed in Case 29409, Op. 88-15(A), supra note 46 at p. 45.

[71] Id.

[72] 42 U.S.C., sec. 7411 (f).

[73] Case 88-E-241 Costing Order, supra note 48.

results as described above for each utility, based on studies by the PSC and State Energy Office of control costs for the indicated utility pollution emissions.[74] The PSC has also ordered all the utilities to do a pooled study, employing outside experts and providing for participation by intervenors in the planning and bidding case, on the N.Y.-specific environmental externality damages costs of their pollution.[75]

As first developed in approval of the EIS for the bidding proceeding for Orange and Rockland Utilities, Inc. (O&R),[76] and subsequently applied to all utilities, the scoring methodology adopted in New York pioneers applying specific quantified environmental costs to all bid resources. The bid scoring methodology uses mitigation costs rather than costs of environmental damages as a "reasonable basis for the emphasis given to air emissions."[77] The PSC notes that:

> the system is based on the best information available and will provide sufficient weight, relative to other factors and appropriate weight among environmental factors to allow O&R to appropriately consider both the internal and external environmental cost of bids.[78]

Accordingly, the PSC concluded that approval of O&R's bidding plan, as revised in its Opinion and Order, would not have an adverse environmental impact and meets the requirements of SEQRA.[79]

The PSC faced three issues in developing the environmental factor for auction bids. First, the PSC had to decide what weight environmental factors should be assigned in comparison to all other factors. Second, the PSC had to choose a method of calculating the environmental scoring factor and weight the major environmental areas of air, water and land. Finally, the PSC had to decide whether the weights and methodologies should be consistent among the seven jurisdictional utilities.[80]

The PSC uses the same methodology to derive the environmental factor for the seven utilities subject to its jurisdiction. To determine the total weight assigned to environmental factors, the PSC staff first developed a total economic value for environmental externalities based primarily on mitigation costs for residual emissions

---

[74] Environmental Externality Issue Report, Division of Policy Analysis and Planning, New York State Energy Office, February 1989 (Preliminary Draft). These estimates were subsequently revised in the Draft Plan. See Staff Report, Draft NYS Energy Plan, Electricity Issues, "Issue 3a: Environmental Externalities," May, 1989, p. 7.

[75] Case 28223, Op. No. 89-15 Pooled Costing Order, supra note 51, at p. 40.

[76] Case 88-E-241 Costing Order, supra note 48.

[77] Case 88-E-241, Re Guidelines for Bidding to Meet Future Electric Capacity Needs of Orange and Rockland Utilities, Inc., Order, April 13, 1989, at p. 2 [hereafter cited as Case 88-E-241 Guidelines Order].

[78] Id.

[79] Id. at pp. 2-3.

[80] New York PSC Staff, Environmental Scoring, at p. 2 (excerpt from a March 1989 staff memorandum).

from facilities, after compliance with federal New Source Performance Standards[81] (the threshold requirement for all bids). The economic values of environmental externalities totalled 1.405 cents/kWh, as described above. This total was then adjusted to account for regional construction cost differences.[82] The methodology then assumes that the average of winning bids will be approximately 90 percent of the utility's avoided cost of electric generation. The weight to be assigned the environmental factor is equal to a fraction of the weight assigned to the price factor in a particular utility's bidding scheme (approximately 24% of the price value).

c. Planning and Rate Design

Concurrently with the development of bidding programs, the PSC has also addressed environmental externalities in its development of integrated planning policy and design of regulatory actions, such as incentives, to overcome impediments to integrated planning. For both planning and rate design the discussion of environmental considerations arises in three DSM-related issues: 1) preferences granted DSM over other resources or policies; 2) "screening" of DSM projects for inclusion in resource plans; and 3) recovery of DSM investments by utilities.

i. Planning

Since at least 1984, the New York PSC has demonstrated a commitment to consideration of conservation as one of the means for satisfying the state's power requirements and providing environmental protection.[83] Thus in 1988, the PSC concluded that "the active consideration and promotion of DSM should be part of every utility's [integrated resource] plan."[84]

In Case 29409, the PSC stressed that consideration of DSM must take account of both societal concerns and objective economic merits. The economic screening tests initially considered in the integrated planning docket did not include these societal concerns, such as "the ability of DSM to extend finite resources or curtail degradation of the environment."[85] Thus the PSC concluded that DSM programs must be evaluated with respect to a variety of factors including "the environmental benefits or

---

81 Supra Note 14.

82 For instance, in the case of Central Hudson Gas & Electric Corporation (CHG&E) the corresponding cost is 1.364 cents/kWh.

83 Case 28223, Op. No. 84-15, supra note 49.

84 Case 29409, Op. No. 88-20, supra note 46 at p. 37.

85 Id. at p. 37. The three screening tests presented by staff were: the "total resource cost test" (whether lifetime savings of the DSM program will exceed the total cost to both the utility and its participating customers); the "utility revenue requirement test" (whether lifetime savings of the DSM program will exceed the total cost to the utility); and "the unit costs test" (which evaluates the effect of the DSM on a utility's rates and is sometimes called the "no-losers test"). Id. at pp. 30-32.

costs of substituting DSM for increased generation."[86] The PSC instructed each utility to propose the combination of DSM programs best suited to meeting that utility's long term planning needs.

The utilities filed their first long range DSM plans in Case 28223 before the opinion establishing the broad economic evaluation was issued. Therefore, in Case 28223, the PSC has subsequently reiterated and strengthened the specifics of utilities' obligations to consider environmental externalities in the development of DSM programs. In developing long range DSM plan filings, utilities are to present strategic analyses which include DSM program and participation targets; program costs to the utility and program participants; revenue losses and effects on rates; and quantifiable program benefits. Analyses were also to include "any program benefits which are important but difficult to measure."[87]

In later stages of Case 28223, several parties suggested a statewide effort to develop a method to estimate environmental costs and benefits. The PSC agreed and ordered all the New York investor-owned utilities to fund and participate in a pooled effort to develop estimates of external environmental costs for all electric supply and demand options, with PSC staff, the State Energy Office (SEO), Department of Environmental Conservation (DEC), New York State Energy Research and Development Authority (NYSERDA), and outside experts, and requiring public participation to be arranged by the utilities.[88] New York utilities are currently scoping the requirements for this study.

The PSC has also directed electric utilities to develop and fully implement statewide, by January 1, 1990, a common set of eight core DSM programs called the Consumers Energy Efficiency Program (CEEP).[89] The principal objectives of CEEP are (1) to save consumers money, (2) to save energy, and (3) to achieve environmental benefits.[90] According to the PSC, the utilities' CEEP 1990 plans would reduce peak demand by 509 MW and save 552,000 mWh during 1990. Their DSM proposed budgets total $132 million.

The utility submissions were found by the PSC to be deficient, however, in that they propose inadequate energy efficiency programs and over-emphasize load shifting. Their expenditures average less than 1.5% of gross revenues and represent less than

---

[86] Id. at p. 38. Other factors included: the ability to avoid lost opportunities; enhanced competitiveness of local industry; impact on total amount paid for energy services; benefits of providing conservation to low income consumers; and increased consumer control over electricity bills. Id. at pp. 38-39.

[87] Case 28223, December 1988 Core DSM Order, supra note 51, at pp. 9, 10.

[88] Case 28223, Op. No. 89-15 Pooled Costing Order, supra, note 52 at p. 40.

[89] Case 28223, December 1988 Core DSM Order, supra note 51, at p. 19.

[90] Id. at pp. 18-19. The specific components of CEEP are: Commercial and Industrial Lighting Efficiency Incentive Programs, Commercial High Efficiency Space Conditioning Equipment Incentive Programs, Demand Management Cooperatives, Commercial and Industrial Energy Audit Programs, Consumer Energy Information Programs, and Innovative Rate Design Programs. Id. at pp. 20-26. Residential Low-Income Renter Conservation Programs, included in the December, 1988 Order, were subsequently merged into the Commission's separate Low Income Proceeding (Case 89-M-124). Not-For-Profit Organization Conservation Programs, also included in the December, 1988 Order, were dropped as a separate program requirement. Case 28223, 1990 DSM Plans Order, supra note 52, at pp. 7-8.

1% of potential economic energy savings. Accordingly, the PSC for the first time set minimum requirements for commercial and industrial lighting DSM programs, and for all DSM programs, required cost-benefit levels on accelerated DSM implementation.[91]

ii. DSM Rate Incentives

The New York PSC has also considered environmental externalities in DSM incentive proposal dockets arising from a PSC invitation to the utilities to propose DSM incentives in 1988.[92] O&R and Niagara Mohawk Power Corporation (NIMO) were the first respondents, and on April 3, 1989, the PSC issued a Notice Soliciting Comments on their incentive proposals.[93] After receiving comments, on September 12, 1989, the Commission issued an order approving the O&R and NIMO proposals, with modifications.[94]

The PSC allowed O&R to use, in its rate incentive structure for DSM investments, an externality component identical to the 1.405 cents/kWh used in its bidding proceeding. In addition to recovery of net lost revenues attributable to DSM Programs, an incentive was allowed, calculated as follows: savings attributable to DSM are multiplied by the company's avoided costs (including environmental externality costs), to produce an estimate of current resource savings. After subtracting the amortized cost of the DSM programs from the current resource savings, 20% incentive payments are calculated and recovered through the fuel adjustment clause, along with lost revenues attributable to DSM.[95]

In other words, O&R keeps 20% of its "net resource savings" as an incentive. Net resource savings are the sum of:

(1) the value of avoided capacity attributable to DSM;
(2) the value of avoided energy attributable to DSM;
(3) the value of avoided environmental impacts; and
(4) other customer and societal benefits, such as decreased land use and socioeconomic impacts, consumer surplus, and increased productivity minus
(5) DSM program expenditures, including all administrative costs and incentive payments to customers.[96]

The PSC found that the 20% incentive was "reasonable for the initial trial period." The incentive payment in any specific year is capped so that the contribution to the

---

[91] Id. at pp. 3-5; The Potential for Electricity Conservation in New York State, American Council for Energy-Efficient Economy 1064-EEED-AEP-88, Energy Authority Report 89-12 (Washington, DC September 1989).

[92] Case 29409, Op. 88-20, supra note 46.

[93] Case 89-E-041 Notice Soliciting Comments, supra, note 54.

[94] Case 89-E-041, Op. No. 89-29 Incentive Order, supra note 56, at p. 26.

[95] Id. at pp. 24-25.

[96] Id. at pp. 25-26.

company's return on common equity allocated to electric operations will not exceed 0.75%.[97]

O&R is allowed to use 1.405cents/kWh "as the cost of incremental environmental and related social benefits of programs that conserve electricity,"[98] which results in an incentive payment to the company of 0.3 cents/kWh. The PSC observed that "[i]mputed environmental benefits will account for only 10% of net resource savings during the early years of the incentive program. This estimate might be changed as more experience is gained."[99] The PSC noted, however, that this initial approval should not be viewed as a final pronouncement. Therefore, the PSC established a proceeding to examine various proposals for incentive mechanisms, with particular emphasis on treatment of savings and benefits measurement and program evaluation.[100]

Although the PSC approved the environmental benefit component of O&R's incentive, it did not require other utilities to include this component in incentive design. In Case 89-E-041, the PSC approved an incentive mechanism proposed by NIMO, which excluded environmental costs in calculating net resource savings, the base from which incentive payments are calculated.[101]

NIMO was allowed an incentive based on recovery of lost revenues and project costs through its fuel adjustment clause, plus an incentive based on 10% of net resource savings, not including environmental costs. NIMO proposed to include instead in the calculation of net resource savings, other participant benefits such as reduced consumption of non-utility fuels, productivity improvements, and consumer surplus. Although acknowledging that different environmental impacts were important in comparing resource options, NIMO believed that unresolved measurement and policy issues prevented those impacts from being estimated at present.[102]

The PSC observed that NIMO's failure to include environmental impacts in calculating net resource savings as well as its incentive proposal for 10% rather than O&R's 20% of net resource savings, would contribute to making NIMO's incentive less rewarding than O&R's incentive. The PSC noted NIMO's inclusion of fuel type in net resource savings, however, presumably as something of a proxy for environmental costs, and favored allowing utilities to experiment with different approaches.[103]

The PSC also ordered exploration of two alternative incentive programs for O&R and NIMO for possible future adoption. O&R is to develop a DSM incentive based

---

[97] Id. at pp. 27-28. The PSC notes that the first year's incentive will be small (about $109,000 in 1989, or about 5.4% return on investment) but the incentive will increase as resource savings from installed measures increase and the company's avoided costs increase.

[98] Id. at p. 26.

[99] Id.

[100] Re Ratemaking Practices and Incentive Mechanisms Promoting Least Cost Planning and Demand Side Management by Electric Utilities, Case 89-E-176.

[101] Id. at p. 35.

[102] Id. at pp. 35-36.

[103] Id. at pp. 32, 37.

on a revenue adjustment mechanism which separates profits from sales, similar to California's Electric Revenue Adjustment Mechanism (ERAM),[104] plus a performance-based incentive. NIMO is to develop a DSM incentive based on bill indexing, that would reward the utility based on the extent to which it achieved bill savings for its customers. It was not specified whether environmental costs should be included in the new proposals.[105]

d. New York State Energy Plan

The New York State Energy Office issued a State Energy Plan in September, 1989, pursuant to Governor Cuomo's Executive Order 118, which contemplates integration of "energy policy planning with environmental and economic considerations."[106] The Plan recommends adoption of a Lower Emissions Electricity Scenario and includes consideration of environmental costs, "because the scenario helps achieve air quality goals at a reasonable cost."[107] The Plan calls for utilities to implement DSM programs which achieve statewide annual electric savings of 8-10% by the year 2000, and 15% by 2008, if economically justified.[108]

The Plan's electricity recommendations are extraordinarily detailed and explicit with respect to environmental externalities, recommending quantified inclusion in all utility bidding programs.[109] It is also recommended that system reliability, fuel

---

[104] California Public Utilities Commission, Docket 87-02-030, February 11, 1987. For an explanation of California's ERAM, see Section C.6., infra.

[105] Case 89-E-041, Op. 89-29 Incentive Order, supra note 56.

[106] New York State Energy Plan, Overview at p. 1, September, 1989.

[107] Id. at pp. 9, 16.

[108] Id. at p. 2.

[109] New York State Energy Plan, September, 1989, at p. 79. The Plan recommendations are so thorough and instructive, they are deemed to be worth including here verbatim:

* Emissions of SO_2, NO_x and CO_2 should be explicitly considered in procuring future energy supplies.

* SO_2, NO_x and CO_2 emissions should be immediately incorporated in utility competitive bidding programs to allow environmentally "clean" projects to compete favorably with lower cost but less environmentally attractive proposal.

* A generally uniform methodology which measures the actual environmental impacts of a proposed facility's air emissions and gives appropriate weight to these air emission externalities should be used by all utilities.

* The methodology for evaluating and scoring air emission externalities should be based on the cost of mitigating (offsetting) the residual SO_2, NO_x and CO_2 emissions from energy supply options.

* The cost of mitigation should be added to a proposal's bid price, and the composite price should be treated as the price variable in the utility's scoring scheme. The costs of mitigating poor air quality are the costs that "good" air quality facilities avoid, and should be recognized in the price we are willing to pay for electricity from such facilities.

* Approximately 60 to 70% of the total awardable points should be for price and air emission environmental factors.

diversity and economic development be considered in bid rating.[110] The Plan further calls for review of current cost-benefit analysis methods for energy efficiency standards and financial assistance programs "to reflect the true cost of environmental emissions."[111]

While the State Energy Plan is a useful tool of persuasion to achieve its goals, especially since it has the Governor's strong backing, there is no enforcement mechanism for effectuating it. Indeed, legislation to do so failed to pass in the last two sessions of the State Legislature.

2. Wisconsin

The Wisconsin PSC has actively pursued integrated planning and incorporation of environmental concerns into the utility planning process in a series of progressively more sophisticated "Advance Plans."[112] In implementing this policy, the Wisconsin Public Service Commission has had both implicit and explicit statutory authority. The Wisconsin Power Plan Siting Law of 1975[113] and its implementing regulations require each electric utility to file with the Public Service Commission an Advance Plan which includes forecast energy and peak demand requirements over the next twenty years, generation facility construction plans over the next ten and fifteen year periods and an analysis of alternatives to the proposed facilities.[114] These plans are subject to the provisions of Wisconsin's environmental review statute.[115]

In 1986, the Wisconsin legislature enacted an aggressive acid deposition control statute.[116] The statute establishes sulfur dioxide limitations and nitrogen oxide emission goals for major utilities. After 1992, each major utility will be required to

---

* An Environmental Block for scoring externalities characterized by legal and regional environmental concerns (i.e., land use, water discharges, noise, biological impacts, aesthetics, etc.) should be included in utility competitive bidding programs. Individual utilities should provide guidance as to the types of environmental externalities of local and regional concern, and have latitude as to how these externalities should be evaluated and scored.

* The point systems for utility bidding plans should recognize favorably any decision by the Commissioner of the Department of Environmental Conservation that a particular waste-to-energy facility is a critical element of the State's Solid Waste Management Plan.

110 Id. at pp. 80, 81.

111 Id. at p. 55.

112 Re Advance Plans, Docket 05-E-5, Wisc. PUC April 6, 1989 [hereafter cited as Docket 05-E-5 Order].

113 Wisconsin Statutes Annotated, Sec. 196.491.

114 Id.

115 Id.; see also Secs. 1.11,23.11.

116 Wisconsin Statutes Annotated, Secs. 15.347,16.02.

submit annual plans for achieving mandated emission rates. Environmental dispatching is included in the compliance options.[117]

In Docket 05-E-5[118] (Wisconsin's Fifth Advanced Planning Proceeding), the Wisconsin Public Service Commission adopted a formal mechanism for crediting the cost of non-combustion options. The Commission ordered that in future Advance Plans, the technical cost of non-combustion options be reduced by 15% to account for the environmental benefits of avoiding combustion (or, at a utility's option, a 15% adder to combustion resources could be used). Under this approach a conservation option that costs $100/KW would be analyzed as if it cost $85/KW, so that a conservation option that cost $85/KW would be implemented before a combustion option that cost more than $85/KW.[119]

According to one commentator, early results from Wisconsin suggest that the non-combustion credit is augmenting the amount of demand-side programs included in utility plans, but the degree to which this is occurring will not be known until late in 1990.[120]

An advance plan chosen on the basis of the non-combustion credit might have a higher revenue requirement than a plan chosen as least-cost in a traditional revenue requirements analysis. All else being equal, the PSC concluded, however, that the plans based on the non-combustion credit would be lower in costs "to society, to future generations, and to current ratepayers in terms of quality of life."[121]

The Wisconsin PSC based the 15% level for non-combustion credit on a review of incentive levels in other states including the 10% conservation credit in the Northwest Power Planning Council (NWPPC) statute.[122] Because of environmental concerns not considered by the NWPPC, particularly global climate change and the human health effects of fine particulate emissions, the PSC felt comfortable choosing a level between the ten and 25% range that was presented in testimony. The credit/adder is applied to all non-combustion/combustion options.[123]

In an appendix, the Wisconsin commission described generally the adverse effects of air emissions on human health, materials, forest and aquatic ecosystems, and global climate. The PSC noted that those who benefit from combustion are neither those who are injured by the effects of emissions transported long distances, nor those who, in the future, will experience the effects of acid rain and global warming from current emissions. The PSC also identified the land demands posed by ash and scrubber

---

[117] Wisconsin Statutes Annotated, Sec. 144.385-144.387.

[118] Docket O5-E-5 Order, supra, note 112.

[119] Id. at pp. 11-12.

[120] Brick, S., Strategies and Methods for Incorporating Environmental Concerns Into Utility Planning and Utility Regulatory Decision-Making, MSB Energy Associates, Middleton, Wisconsin, October 2, 1989 at p. 1.

[121] Docket 05-E-5 Order, supra. note 112, at p. 12.

[122] Supra note 1.

[123] Docket 05-E-5 Order, supra. note 112 at p. 12.

wastes, in particular that new ash disposal sites in Wisconsin tend to occupy prime agricultural land, a resource highly valued in the Wisconsin economy.[124]

In the Wisconsin planning process, resource options are first ranked on the basis of technical cost per KW and per kWh. Final choice of programs depends on revenue requirements and "NEEDS" factors (costs "Not Easily Expressed in Dollars") which include external social, political and environmental costs. For each option, the choice can be made whether to include or eliminate a resource option that would slightly increase revenue requirements but has favorable NEEDS characteristics.[125]

At this point, the PSC staff and the utilities are developing various methods, both qualitative and quantitative, for using NEEDS information in the decision-making process, but no specific method of incorporation has been selected. The non-combustion credit keeps options in the running that might have been screened out based on unadjusted costs, and in the next stage the NEEDS analysis could favor selection of more environmentally benign options.[126]

Not only is Wisconsin incorporating environmental externalities in utility planning, but the PSC and legislature are imposing constraints at the beginning of the process as well. Utilities must include an explicit discussion of how consideration of NEEDS did or did not affect the plans they submit. As a sensitivity run to examine how potential global warming legislation might affect utility planning, the Wisconsin PSC directed utilities to prepare integrated plans that assume carbon dioxide emissions would have to be reduced to 80% of the 1985 level by the year 2000 and 50% in the long-run.[127] To reduce damage from acid rain, Wisconsin law also requires utilities to cut SO_2 emissions to 50% of the 1980 levels by 1993.[128]

In summary: 1) Wisconsin's long range planning law requires that environmental factors be considered in the planning process; 2) past Advance Plan orders require developing and using a method to factor externalities into the decision-making process and using a 15% credit/adder for non-combustion options; and 3) Wisconsin acid rain legislation requires utilities to cut 1980 levels of SO_2 emissions by 50% of 1980 levels by 1993.

3. Oregon

In April 1989, the Oregon Public Utility Commission (PUC) adopted least-cost planning for all Oregon utilities and required that external costs be considered in the

---

124 Docket 05-E-5, Appendix C at pp. C-1 to C-2. Not all the social costs identified by the Wisconsin PSC are environmental or health related. The PSC notes that fossil fuels may be more valuable in the future for other uses, such as chemical feedstock. In addition, as Wisconsin has no fossil fuels, using these fuels to generate electricity transfers money out of Wisconsin. Id. at C-2.

125 Docket 05-E-5 Order, supra note 112, at p. 12.

126 Communication from Anita Springer, Wisc. PSC staff.

127 Brick, supra note 120, at p. 3.

128 Wisc. Stats. Ann., Secs. 15.347,16.02.

cost-effectiveness evaluation of resource options.[129] According to the Oregon PUC, the primary criterion for determining whether a planning item is least cost is whether the item "involves the least-cost for the utility and its ratepayers consistent with the long-run public interest."[130] The PUC concluded that development of least-cost plans should include "to the fullest extent practicable and quantifiable" the costs and benefits external to any resource transaction.[131] Although recognizing that quantification of some costs might be highly uncertain, the PUC stressed that "when the certainty of costs is known, but the amount of costs is not, zero is the least desirable and least accurate cost to apply."[132]

The Oregon PUC order is not entirely clear on whether the treatment of external costs is to be based on control costs or damage costs but seems to require both. The order's language seems to allow for a "mix and match" approach. The PUC required that application of external costs be addressed both qualitatively and quantitatively. When price tags are not readily assignable to identified damages, the PUC instructed utilities to submit a range of costs and to separate those costs from conventional accounting costs.[133]

Least-cost plans must include in the cost of a resource all costs that can be internalized, including costs for pollution control or wildlife mitigation. If a utility is uncertain about the cost of environmental mitigation, the Oregon PUC requires the use of a range of damage costs and associated probabilities in evaluating resource strategies.[134] The order provides that "other external costs" might be included if inclusion of those costs were consistent with the energy policy of Oregon and the provisions of the Northwest Power Plan.[135]

The concurring opinion of Commissioner Myron Katz notes that as a practical matter, utility revenue requirements would probably not be significantly altered by the inclusion of external costs because many costs that were once external are now internalized.[136]

---

[129] In re Least-Cost Planning for Resource Acquisitions by Energy Utilities in Oregon, Docket UM 180, Order No. 89-507, Slip Op. at 10, 102 PUR (4th) 301, Ore. PUC, April 20, 1989.

[130] Id. at p. 9.

[131] Id. at p. 10.

[132] Id.

[133] Id.

[134] Id. at pp. 10-11.

[135] Id. at p. 11. The PUC excluded factors such as economic development or job creation from the determination of whether a resource was least-cost.

[136] Id. at 13 (Commissioner Katz, concurring).

> Mitigation of hydro-electric damage to fish and wildlife, installation of expensive stack scrubbers at coal-fired plants to reduce emissions, a boost in the liability ceiling for a single nuclear accident ..., and inclusion of power plant decommissioning costs in rates are all examples of internalized costs that push the price of energy to more clearly reflect social costs.[137]

Commissioner Katz identifies two benefits from the internalization of social costs: deferring development of environmentally damaging resources and making more environmentally benign power technologies compete based on more accurate costs. He concludes that incorporation of external costs furthers the goal originally found in the 10% cost differential for conservation in Oregon's Residential Energy Conservation Act and in the Northwest Power Act.[138]

An Oregon law passed in 1989 requires development of a strategy to reduce greenhouse gases 20% from 1988 levels by 2005, for implementation in 1991.[139]

4. Vermont

On April 16, 1990, the Vermont Public Service Board (PSB) issued an order substantially adopting a Hearing Examiner's report that recommended regulations for treatment of environmental externalities combining features of the Wisconsin approach and the approach of the NWPPC.[140] The PSB created a rebuttable presumption that environmental externalities and reduced risk from DSM investments be valued at 15% of avoided costs in integrated least cost planning -- a 5% supply cost adder for environmental externalities, and a 10% DSM cost credit for risk reduction.[141] The PSB also ordered recovery of lost revenues through a revenue adjustment mechanism called, "Account Correcting for Efficiency (ACE)", similar to California's Electric Revenue Adjustment Mechanism (ERAM).[142]

In another docket, the PSB is also hearing evidence quantifying environmental externality costs in long-term contracts for the purchase of Canadian power.[143]

---

137 Id.

138 Id. at p. 14. Oregon Revised Statutes; Sec 469.631.

139 An Act Relating to Global Warming, Oregon Revised Statutes, sec. 469.60,1989.

140 Investigation into Least-Cost Investments, Energy Efficiency, Conservation, and Management of Demand for Energy, Board Decision Adopting (As Modified) Hearing Officer's Report and Proposal for Decision, Vermont Public Service Board, April 16, 1990 [hereafter referred to as the PSB Decision].

141 Id. at pp. 8, 12.

142 Id. at pp. 17 et. seq.; ERAM: California Public Utilities Commission, Document 87-02-030, February 11, 1987. For a discussion of California ERAM, see Section C.6., infra.

143 Vermont Public Service Board, Docket 5330. Infra note 151.

a. Integrated Planning Docket

In February 1988, the Vermont PSB initiated an investigation into least-cost investments, energy efficiency, conservation, and management of demand for electricity. The object of this proceeding was to assess the benefits to Vermont ratepayers of enhanced demand-side management and to investigate whether current management of energy demand was consistent with long-term provision of necessary services at the least cost to Vermont ratepayers. The proceeding was later expanded to include demand-side and supply-side planning.[144] The Hearing Officer held extensive and broad evidentiary hearings and issued the report which the Commission substantially adopted.[145]

The Commission found:

> As the evidence in this docket makes clear, a simple comparison of the apparent market prices of supply and demand-side options for integrated planning purposed still produce a distorted resource plan. The prices of various resource options must be adjusted, both for differences in risks and for the significant, unpriced environmental harms associated with energy production and consumption.[146]

After adopting the 10% risk discount for DSM options and 5% adder to supply-side resources "as an initial proxy for their unpriced environmental harms," the PSB established a new, separate proceeding "for developing more accurate estimates of the unpriced environmental costs for different supply sources."[147]

The PSB included in the environmental effects supporting the 5% externalities adjustment, "acidic precipitation, carbon dioxide and other 'greenhouse gases' contributing to global warming, habitat destruction, radioactive hazards and nuclear waste disposal risks."[148] The Commission concluded:

> These effects clearly are significant, and they impose costs and risks on society that are not reflected in either the market prices or the regulated prices of energy supply sources. We may not yet have the tools to monetize these costs precisely, but that is no reason to treat them as having no value at all. We conclude that the 5% externalities adder is a reasonable proxy value for the unpriced externalities of energy supply. Based upon all of the evidence available to

---

[144] Re Least-Cost Investments, Energy Efficiency, Conservation and Load Management, Docket 5270, Hearing Officer's Report and Proposal for Decision, issued July 13, 1989, at I-9 to I-11 (Vt. PSB) [hereafter cited as Docket 5270, H.O. Report].

[145] Id.

[146] PSB Decision, supra note 140, at pp. 7,8.

[147] Id. at p. 8.

[148] Id. at p. 12.

the Board, we conclude that this is a conservative adjustment.[149]

To the utility argument that the environmental adder would constitute double-counting because of the utility obligation to meet federal New Source Performance Standards, the Board replied that the adder reflects environmental costs not remedied by the standards. "Whatever these costs may turn out to be, they will certainly not be zero."[150]

An environmental adder was applied to fuel-switching as well as supply programs. The Board invited the parties to present evidence in their compliance filings "to substantiate some credit for alternative fuels,"including natural gas advantages over oil and coal-fired resources or biomass fuels.[151]

b. Power Contract Docket

The Vermont PSB is also considering environmental externalities in proceedings requesting approval for a multi-billion dollar take-or-pay contract to purchase the largest portion of Vermont's electric power for the next twenty-five years from Hydro-Quebec,[152] the final order in the integrated planning docket will probably serve as the underlying policy for the power purchases.

In the Hydro-Quebec purchase case, utilities argued that the PSB should defer to the conclusions reached by Canadian authorities on environmental issues and dismiss the environmental contentions of the intervenors.[153]

The Vermont PSB concluded that it must consider all environmental effects of facilities within the state and the environmental and other consequences of projects beyond the state, to the extent that the consequences affected "the general good of the state".[154]

5. Massachusetts

Over the last year, Massachusetts has pursued the consideration of the environmental externalities associated with energy on several fronts. In November

---

[149] Id.

[150] Id. at p. 13.

[151] Id. at p. 15.

[152] See Re certificate of public good authorizing execution on performance of a firm power and energy contract with Hydro-Quebec, Docket No. 5330, Order re Scope Intervention, and Motion to Dismiss Slip Op. entered August 21, 1989 (Vt. PSB)[hereinafter cited as Docket No. 5330, Slip Op]. The application for approval of this purchase was filed after the integrated planning docket began, but before the Proposal for Decision was issued.

[153] Id. at pp. 1-2.

[154] Id. at p. 4.

1988, the Department of Public Utilities (DPU) issued an order requiring electric utilities to consider environmental and other social externalities in their cost-effectiveness evaluation of Conservation and Load Management (C&LM, which is the same as DSM) investments.[155] This order also initiated a process which should result in a proposed rule for integrated planning and resource acquisition that will include the issue of externalities. The DPU has discussed the appropriateness of environmental externalities in evaluating natural gas conservation investments. The Department is also required by statute to consider environmental externalities in siting decisions.[156]

As a result of the 1988 planning order, some Massachusetts electric utilities and public interest representatives led by the Conservation Law Foundation in Boston, began collaborative discussion of environmental externalities.

a. DPU Decisions

On November 30, 1988, the Massachusetts Department of Public Utilities (DPU) required that electric utilities include in the cost-effectiveness test for conservation and load management (C&LM), the cost of environmental externalities that relate to any demand or supply option.[157] The DPU found that the scope of analyses should not be limited to impacts occurring within the local vicinity of a resource option or even within Massachusetts borders. Although recognizing the difficulty involved in identifying and quantifying externalities, the DPU stated its expectation that electric companies would work with other interested persons to develop "suitable measurement methodologies over time."[158]

The DPU provided additional discussion of externalities in its discussion of a proposed regulatory structure for integrated all source planning. A utility would submit its own resource proposals and evaluate those proposals along with proposals submitted by IPPs, QFs, other electric utility suppliers, and C&LM developers (more usually called, "energy service companies" or "ESCO's"). The utility would specify how and for what price it would provide service in the absence of third party providers (e.g. its avoided cost).[159] In order to evaluate the relative prices of supply and demand side programs, the utility would propose criteria for evaluation of the costs and benefits of C&LM programs and would also indicate an evaluation method for any environmental externalities associated with each resource proposal. The DPU permitted evaluation of environmental externalities through "price and/or non-price factors."[160]

---

[155] Investigation by the Department of Public Utilities on its own motion, pursuant to Section 76 of Chapter 164 of the General Laws, into the pricing and ratemaking treatment to be afforded new electric generating facilities which are not Qualifying Facilities as defined in 220 C.M.R. 8.02, DPU 86-36-F, November 30, 1988 [hereafter referred to as DPU 86-36-F Nov. 1988 Order].

[156] Mass. Gen. Law, Ch. 40A, Sec. 3.

[157] Id. at pp. 19-20.

[158] Id. at p. 22.

[159] Id. at p. 63.

[160] Id. at p. 64.

The DPU explicitly noted that "a resource proposal that meets minimum state or federal environmental regulations may still result in environmental costs that would need to be identified in such a way that they may be evaluated according to the criteria in the electric company's resource evaluation."[161] The DPU listed several possible non-price criteria that could be considered in evaluating supply options, including quality of output, timing, risk, fuel diversity, and "external economies or diseconomies (e.g., environmental attributes)."[162]

The DPU solicited comments in response to the DPU 86-36-F order and stated that, after review of comments, it would promulgate proposed rules incorporating the provisions of the order, as modified in response to further proceedings.[163]

The DPU has also considered environmental externalities in an investigation of retail natural gas rate design.[164] In the natural gas rate case, the DPU concluded that it would include external social costs in the cost-effectiveness equation, even if this treatment did not guarantee that total ratepayer revenue would be minimized; as members of society, ratepayers would benefit by a reduction of environmental social costs, even if their direct cost of service increased.[165]

In a recent decision, the DPU issued guidelines for treatment of environmental externalities and put them out for comment. It preferred a quantified adder where feasible, or a ranking system based on quantified costs.[166] The order is under consideration, with a decision expected in the summer of 1990.

Boston Gas Company has proposed a two-step method for evaluating C&LM investments. First, C&LM benefits would be measured by the cost of avoided gas purchases; and second, they would be adjusted to account for non-price factors such as externalities. The utility proposed that this adjustment be made within the range of plus or minus 15% of avoided cost. The utility included the following environmental externalities as being capable of quantitative analysis: regional environmental costs, including air pollution and acid rain; global environmental costs; and local environmental effects, including wetlands intrusion and visual impairment.[167]

The DPU observed that recognition of external social costs for gas utilities is consistent with the standard for C&LM cost-effectiveness adopted for electric utilities; but the DPU expressed reservations about charging gas customers for external costs that might arise if conserved natural gas load were displaced by higher polluting fuel.

---

[161] Id. at p. 65.

[162] Id. at p. 67.

[163] Id. at p. 87.

[164] Re Boston Gas Co., D.P.U. 88-67 (Phase II), May 31, 1989, as discussed in Burkhart, External Social Costs as a Factor in Least-cost Planning -- An Emerging Concept, Pub. Util. Fort., August 31, 1989, at pp. 43-44 [hereafter referred to as Burkhart].

[165] Id. at p. 45.

[166] Investigation by the Department of Public Utilities on its own motion, pursuant to Section 76 of Chapter 164 of the General Laws, into the pricing and ratemaking treatment to be afforded new electric generating facilities which are not Qualifying Facilities as defined in 220 C.M.R. 8.02, DPU 86-36-G, December 6, 1989 [hereafter referred to as DPU 86-36-G Dec. 1989 Order].

[167] Burkhart, supra note 163, at p. 43. According to Burkhart, the utility also included as externalities macroeconomic effects such as employment, the cost of oil imports and direct non-gas monetary costs Id.

Externalities associated with this type of fuel substitution were found to be more appropriately internalized in the prices paid by consumers of electricity and fuel oil. The DPU encouraged industry-wide participation in a forthcoming investigation of external social costs.[168]

b. Collaborative Environmental Externality Design

In the DPU 86-36-F Nov. 1988 order,[169] the DPU stated that electric utilities and other interested persons should work together to develop suitable measurement methodologies for environmental externalities.[170] Utilities, public interest representatives and consultants met in four workshops to begin the initial scoping of environmental externalities with the aid of a consultant.[171]

The collaborative process as it pertains to calculation and incorporation of environmental externalities seems to have stalled; however, at least one utility, The New England Electric System (NEES), has adopted a rating system for incorporating environmental externality costs, based on surveys of customers of how they value such costs, a mechanism that bears little relationship to actual damage costs.[172]

6. California

Currently, determination and incorporation of environmental externalities are being considered in California by both the California Energy Commission (CEC) in licensing sites for all plants over 50MW,[173] and by the California Public Utility Commission (PUC).[174] Also, a recent DSM collaborative between utilities, state agencies and public interest groups failed to reach consensus on environmental externalities.[175]

---

[168] Id. at p. 44.

[169] DPU 86-36-F, Nov. 1988 Order, supra note 154.

[170] Id. This was reiterated in the DPU 86-36-G Dec. 1989 Order, supra note 166.

[171] Participants in these workshops include: Mary Sharpe Hayes, of Temple, Barker, Sloane (the utility sponsored consultants); Timothy M. Stout, New England Power Service (one of the utility participants); Jonathan Raab, Massachusetts DPU; Steve Burrington, Conservation Law Foundation (the primary public interest participant); Rachel Schimshak, Massachusetts Executive Office of Energy Resources; and major utility participants Boston Edison, Commonwealth Electric, and Northeast Utilities.

[172] Comments by Massachusetts Electric Co. (a NEES subsidiary), at pp. 17-21, and Attachment 2, Investigation by the Department of Public Utilities on Its Own Motion into Proposed Rules to implement Integrated Resource Management Practices for Electric Companies in the Commonwealth, Mass. D.P.U. No. 89-239, Feb. 23, 1990.

[173] See, LBL Survey, supra note 6.

[174] The following information, including cites, is derived from the LBL Survey, supra note 6.

[175] An Energy Efficiency Blueprint for California, Report of the Statewide Collaborative Process, January, 1990, at p. 68.

The CEC staff has recommended the use of quantified values in its recommendations for its 1990 Electricity Report (ER90), as follows: \$11,600/T to NO_x, \$11,500/T to SO_x, \$7,800/T to PM10 particulates, \$3,300/T to ROG and \$7/T to CO_2 to meet Southern California Air Quality Management District (SCAQMD) air quality standards. The CO_2 adder represents the lowest cost for mitigation and would add about 1.5-8 mills/kWh to the cost of a coal-fired plant.[176] The CEC recommendations are now being considered in hearings and workshops.

Simultaneously, the PUC is considering incorporating environmental externalities into its Standard Offer #4. The PUC is holding workshops to consider whether and how this should be done.[177]

California pioneered in creating a revenue adjustment mechanism, called ERAM (Electric Revenue Adjustment Mechanism)[178] for separating utility profits from sales. This mechanism operates so as to assure that both utility revenues lost from its DSM investments saving electricity for customers does not diminish its profits, and also eliminates extraneous influences on profits such as a stretch of hot weather that would increase sales and, without the mechanism, also arbitrarily increase profits.

ERAM is based on annual utility revenue projections. Each year, if revenues exceed or fall below the projections, based on DSM savings, the weather, etc., an adjustment is made to revenues to take account of these phenomena, so that the utility neither loses nor gains from them. However, while ERAM restores DSM-caused lost revenues, it does not give utilities any profit on their DSM investments such as is done in New York.

D. TAXES AND SUBSIDIES FOR INCORPORATION

Pollution taxes or fees have been much discussed of late, nationally and internationally. The OECD has recently published a review of European pollution levies, indicating a total of 85 pollution taxing regimes adopted in six countries.[179] And the U.S. House of Representatives recently held hearings on pollution taxes (March 6,7,& 14, 1990).

Federal pollution taxes would have the advantage of internalizing environmental externalities universally, not just for utilities. State pollution taxes would have the same result within the state. State taxes create interstate competitive problems, however, just as federal taxes create international competitive problems. International imposition of such taxes could solve these problems, such as the carbon dioxide taxes currently much discussed, but still far from adoption.

---

176 Roach, C., E. Kahn, and D. Modisette, Electric Resources and Environmental Impacts: Draft Phase I Report, Joint Committee on Energy Regulation and Environment, April, 1990.

177 Order Instituting Investigation on the Commission's own motion to implement the Biennial Resource Plan update following the CEC's Seventh Electricity Report, Cal. PUC, OII.89-07-004. Re the workshops, see Murley, C.,Thompson, T. and Wilsie, T., Workshop Report: Incorporating Environmental Adders into the Biennial Resource Plan Update Proceeding, Cal. PUC OII.89-04-007.

178 California Public Utilities Commission, Document 87-02-030,February 11, 1987.

179 Money from Greenery, The Enconomist, London, U.K., October 21, 1988 at p. 16.

A number of specific federal and state pollution and resource taxes tied to environmental externalities are discussed below, but the most frequently used resource taxes are limited in nature and it is found that they can inhibit technological innovation by taxing resources regardless of their polluting characteristics.

Tax subsidies are also discussed. These give tax credits or deductions for preferred resources. Fossil, wood and nuclear energy receive very heavy tax preferences in the form of depletion allowances for oil and timber, expensing of intangible drilling costs for oil, and rapid depreciation for nuclear plants.

Direct subsidies are also treated. For example, nuclear plants also receive substantial direct subsidies in the form of federal research and development programs, federal uranium enrichment and insurance protection.

The studies reviewed indicate that both tax and direct studies distort the marketplace for energy and thus inhibit the impact of consideration of environmental externality costs.

1. Taxation and Revenue Generating Measures

Taxation based on units of consumption or production may occur at all steps of the fuel cycle. Examples of tax policies which may address environmental impact costs include coal severance taxes, BTU or emission taxes, and generation fees charged for nuclear waste disposal.

a. State Severance Taxes

As of January 1, 1985, nineteen states had adopted coal severance taxes based either on the volume of coal mined or the value of coal produced.[180] In addition to revenue enhancement, legislative rationales for coal severance taxes include replacement for loss of natural heritage or compensation for depletion of limited resources; internalization of external costs; transfer of tax burdens; and growth regulation. Seventeen states specify their severance taxes to be a means of offsetting environmental and social costs, including land disruption, water and air pollution, and boomtown effects.[181]

Twelve of these states deposit all or part of severance tax revenues in restricted accounts to mitigate costs related to coal development research, land reclamation, or strain on social infrastructures such as roads and schools.[182] For example, Montana allocates 4.5 percent of its coal severance tax to its alternative energy resources

---

[180] Kaiser, R., and J. Fletcher. State Policies and Practices in Coal Severance Taxation, 27 Natural Resources Journal 591, 595, 599, 1987 (Responses to survey questionnaire of state tax commissioners).

[181] Id. at pp. 595-97.

[182] Id. at p. 601.

program.[183] Oklahoma allocates all coal tax revenues to land reclamation.[184] Deposit of tax revenues into restricted funds instead of the state's general revenue fund can help to ensure that internalization of environmental externalities actually mitigates environmental and social costs.

b. BTU Taxes

The theory of taxes based on kWh or BTU generation has been discussed for a number of years in the context of air pollution control.[185] Texas recently adopted a law requiring the Texas Air Control Board to impose a clean fuel incentive surcharge of 20 cents per MBTU on fuel oil use in industrial and utility boilers capable of using natural gas. The law applies to the use of fuel oil between April 15 and October 15 for sources located in metropolitan areas greater than 350,000 that have not met the federal ambient air quality standard for ozone.[186]

The Texas law is in part a response to Environmental Protection Agency testing in 1988 which showed the metropolitan statistical areas of Dallas-Fort Worth, Houston-Galveston, Beaumont-Port Arthur, and El Paso as failing to meet the National Ambient Air Quality Standards for ozone.[187]

As is often the case with fiscal policy mechanisms, the law may also have been intended as a way to sell more of Texas' abundant natural gas as well as to address environmental impacts.[188] Revenues from the tax are to be deposited in the state's general revenue fund.[189] Therefore, while the law may provide generators with an

---

[183] Montana Code Ann. §§ 15-35-101 to 111, 90-4-101 to 108 (1981); see Linda Steinmann, Conservation and Renewable Energy in the Four Pacific Northwest States: A Compilation of Relevant Statutes, 58 Washington L. Rev. 433, 438, Symposium on Energy Issues in the Pacific Northwest, 1983.

[184] Oklahoma Stat. Ann., Tit. 45, § 938, 1987 cum. supp. See also, Kaiser & Fletcher, supra note 180, at p. 597.

[185] Wetstone, G.S., Paying for Acid Rain Control: An Introduction to the Trust Fund Approach, Environmental Forum, August 1983, at pp. 14-20; Regens, J. and R. Rycroft, The Acid Rain Controversy at p. 104, Pitt Series in Policy and Institutional Studies, University of Pittsburgh Press, 1988.

[186] An Act relating to the adoption of certain regulations to encourage and require the use of natural gas and other alternative fuels, S.B. No. 769, sec. 3, Texas Legislative Service, Report No. 16-225 at p. 10, 1988 (Amending Vernon's Texas Civil Statutes 44 77-5) [hereinafter cited as S.B. No. 769]. The law excludes recycled waste fuel, fuel oil used during any period of natural gas curtailment or failure to deliver sufficient natural gas; certain uses of fuel oil in equipment testing or personnel training; and firms engaged in fixed price contracts with public works agencies entered into prior to the Act's effective date.

[187] Texas Air Control Board Memorandum from C. Hurd to E. Bell, Activities of the 71st Legislature, at p. 4, Austin, Texas, July 26, 1989; Legislative Budget Board Fiscal Note to Hon. Jim McWilliams, Committee on Energy, House of Representatives, from Jim Oliver, Director, re Senate Bill No. 769, Austin, Texas, May 1, 1989.

[188] See, Texas Oil-Burning Tax, IRT Newsletter, July 13, 1989, at p. 3.

[189] S.B. No. 769, supra note 186.

economic incentive to reduce air pollution, the tax revenues are not necessarily used to promote pollution reduction.

c. Use of Tax Revenues for Pollution Mitigation

A variation on the Texas approach would deposit the fee or tax in a trust fund or segregated account to be used only for specific purposes. A similar federal example is the 1 mil per kilowatt-hour surcharge on nuclear-generated power paid into the Nuclear Waste Fund. The utility-collected fees are supposed to be supplemented by Congressional appropriations and used in the construction of long-term high level waste disposal sites and related research. The fee is intended to provide a measure of intergenerational equity between current users of nuclear power (ratepayers) and ratepayers at the time of decommissioning and long-term disposal, as well as financial assurance that funds for long-term disposal facilities will be available when needed.[190]

Commentators have suggested approaches similar to the Nuclear Waste Fund as a cost-sharing mechanism to alleviate midwestern acid rain mitigation costs.[191] In one study, acid rain fees are proposed, in the range of a 1-3 mils/kWh charge, on all non-nuclear electric generation. Revenues would fund mandated pollution control equipment and could also be used to relieve the impact of rate increases on low income consumers or indirect price increases on goods and services.[192]

More sophisticated tax/fund variations would combine the generation fee with emission charges from major sources of sulfur and nitrogen oxides or use graduated kilowatt-hour fees based on emissions per MBt, which could be used to address the differences in emission levels between coal, oil, and natural gas.[193] It has been suggested that the tax/fund approach could provide a direct correlation between price and environmental consequences, as well as provide funds for mitigation or remedial actions. However, such pollution fees would also raise utility rates.[194]

Recently, David Moskovitz, a former member of the Maine Public Utilities Commission, suggested that quantified environmental externality impact costs assigned during planning or bidding might be assessed and paid into an environmental trust

---

[190] Nuclear Waste Policy Act, 42 U.S.C. Sec. 10101, et. seq.

[191] Trumble, R. and L. Parker, Acid Rain: Current Issues, Issue Brief Number IB83016, at pp. CRS-11 to CRS-12, Library of Congress, Congressional Research Service, Major Issues System, March 31, 1983, updated January 23, 1984.

[192] See, Regens & Rycroft, supra note 184, at pp. 102 - 104; Trumble & Parker, supra note 191, at p. CRS-12.

[193] Wetstone, supra note 184, at p. 16; Regens & Rycroft, supra note 184, at p. 104.

[194] One estimate places the average cost to an electric consumer of a 3 mil generation fee at about $2.25 a month based on an "average" monthly usage of 750 kWh/month. Regens & Rycroft, supra note 184, at p. 103.

fund.[195] Most public service commission treatments of externalities are phantom costs, used in the resource selection process but not actually collected from the generator.

2. Subsidies and Other Policies Related to Spending

Subsidies to alternative renewable resources or energy efficiency development programs are another method which could address externalities. These subsidies can be funded by generation fees or taxes on more polluting resources, but more commonly are in the form of tax incentives to renewable and conservation resources (as special deductions or credits) or are general revenue fund appropriations. After the energy shortages of the 1970's,federal and state governments enacted a variety of subsidy and tax benefit programs to encourage development of renewable resources, in part because of the comparative environmental impacts of conventional and renewable energy resources. The program subsidies or tax benefits were not, however, generally based on the cost of environmental impacts or the cost of controls which would reduce impacts.

At least one state is currently considering basing state energy research funding on a more careful characterization of externalities. Staff at the California Energy Commission have prepared a rough methodology to tailor the state's funding of energy research and development to comparative environmental impacts. Eventually, funding could be directly tied to the cost of environmental impacts.[196]

The Federal Republic of Germany (FRG) has decided to subsidize small locally sponsored wind generators in proportion to environmental and social externalities, based in part on a study done by Olav Hohmeyer.[197] Hohmeyer calculates the social costs for electric generation sources in the FRG, including environmental impact costs, research and development subsidies, and tax effects, and then extrapolates the amount of incentive required to rework market imperfections. The FRG wind subsidy approximates the middle range of the total social cost developed by Olav Hohmeyer for wind energy.[198]

The studies reviewed indicated that temporary subsidies for new technologies may be useful before the new technologies can make their own way into the marketplace, but temporary subsidies or tax benefits have a way of becoming permanent. If temporary subsidies are removed, furthermore, the removal can cause great harm to the development of the subsidized resource. In this way, the solar industry was seriously damaged when temporary federal tax subsidies were removed.

---

[195] Presentation of David Moskovitz, Annual Meeting of the Center for Environmental Legal Studies Advisory Board, Pace University School of Law, White Plains, New York, on November 10, 1989. A similar fund was created in New York by PSC imposition of a fee of .25% of utility net income for use as a fund for DSM demonstrations. New York PSC case et. 28233,Opinion and Order 84-15 (May 1984). The same principle is used in the nuclear waste fund.

[196] DeAngelis, M. and S. Rashkin, The Social Benefits and Costs of Electricity Generation and End-Use Technologies, California Energy Commission, Sacramento, Cal., 1989.

[197] Personal communication with Olav Hohmeyer, October 4, 1989 at Pace University School of Law.

[198] Id.

On a longer term basis, subsidies are found to distort the operation of free market determination of prices. Even if subsidies were based on environmental costs, they don't adequately internalize those costs because they prevent reflection of the true market price of the subsidized resource.

There are tremendous tax subsidies in the U.S. for all mineral extraction including coal, oil, natural gas and wood. Nuclear energy receives large tax subsidies through accelerated depreciation, and direct subsidies for research and development and insurance. If these subsidies were all removed, the true price of the resources could be reflected in the marketplace, and solar, renewable and conservation resources, which receive subsidies that are extremely smaller, would be able to compete based on their true marketplace value.[199]

E. FEDERAL ACTIONS

1. Analogous Federal Consideration of Environmental Costs

Under the Comprehensive Environmental Response, Compensation and Liability Act of 1980 (CERCLA or, popularly the Superfund Act), natural resource trustees may recover damages for injury to, destruction of, or loss of natural resources resulting from a discharge of oil or release of a hazardous substance, in addition to cost-recovery for response and cleanup actions related to the discharge.[200] All sums recovered as damages must be used only to restore, replace, or acquire the equivalent of such natural resources as were lost.[201] Regulations must identify the best available procedures to determine the damages including both direct and indirect injury, destruction, or loss, taking into consideration factors that include, but are not limited to, replacement value, use value, and the ability of the ecosystem or resource to recover.[202]

Industry petitioners in Ohio v. U.S. Department of Interior[203] challenged the DOI's use of contingent valuation (CV) methodologies. According to the industry petitioners, the use of CV by DOI was a fatal departure from common-law damage assessment principles and was considerably less than a "best available" technique. Under the DOI regulations, if a resource was not traded in the market or could not be valued using appraisal methods then non-market valuation methodologies would be available.

---

[199] See Heede, H., R. Morgan, and R. Scott, The Hidden Costs of Energy, Center for Renewable Resources, Washington, DC, October, 1985.

[200] CERCLA, 42 USC§ 9607 (Sec. 107). Damages for injury to natural resources also include the reasonable costs of assessing such injury, plus prejudgment interest.

[201] Id.

[202] Id. at § 301 (c)(2).

[203] Ohio v. U.S. Dept. of Interior, 880 F.2d 432 (D.C. Cir. 1989) [hereafter referred to as Ohio]; Colorado v. U.S. Dept. of Interior, 880 F.2d 481 (D.C. Cir. 1989) [hereafter referred to as Colorado].

Under the rules, contingent valuation includes all techniques that hypothetical markets demonstrate to elicit an individual's economic valuation of a natural resource.[204]

The DOI regulations also sanctioned the use of CV methodology to determine option values and existence values. Option values are the dollar amount an individual is willing to pay now to reserve the option to use a resource in the future even though the individual is not currently using the resource. Existence values are the dollar amount an individual is willing to pay even though not planning to use the resource, either at present or in the future.[205]

The court concluded that DOI's decision to adopt CV was made intelligently and cautiously. As an example of the DOI's intelligent and cautious decisionmaking, the court cited DOI's choice to eliminate the "willingness-to-accept" (or "willingness-to-be-compensated") feature of CV methodologies because it might have resulted in overly high assessments.[206]

2. Northwest Electric Power Planning Conservation Act

In 1980, Congress passed the Pacific Northwest Electric Power Planning and Conservation Act ("the Act");[207] a unique piece of regional energy planning legislation. The Act serves to allocate the Bonneville Power Administration's (BPA) hydroelectric power among competing customers and to provide for acquisition of new energy resources, including conservation. The NWPPC is responsible every three years for developing a twenty year regional energy plan. The NWPPC describes the Northwest Power Plan ("the Plan") as a "general scheme for implementing conservation and developing resources that will result in adequate, reliable electricity supply at the lowest cost to the region giving due consideration to environmental quality."[208] However, it also masks the costs of nuclear power plants by allowing regional consideration of their costs.

Two statutory requirements have been particularly instrumental in making the Plan a vehicle for pathbreaking consideration of the environmental impacts of energy resources. First, the Plan must include a methodology for determining quantifiable

---

[204] Ohio, supra. at 475. CV ascertains the public's willingness to pay to avoid environmental damage or willingness to be compensated for the damage. See CV discussion in Chapter III, supra.

[205] Ohio, supra note 198 at pp.475-76; 43 C.F.R. § 11.84(d)(5)(i)(1988).

[206] Id. at p. 476. For discussion of willingness to pay or to be compensated, see Chapter III.

[207] Supra note 1.

[208] Northwest Power Planning Council, Accounting for the Environmental Consequences of Electricity Resources During the Power Planning Process, Staff Issue Paper, Publication 89-7, April 17, 1989, at p. 1 [hereafter cited as NWPPC Pub. 89-7].

environmental costs and benefits.[209] The Act defines "cost-effective" as including environmental resource costs in the "system cost" used for planning purposes.[210]

Second, the Act's definition of "cost-effective" gives conservation resources a 10% advantage over traditional resources.[211] According to the Act's legislative history, the 10% advantage addresses traditional problems associated with conventional generation such as cost overruns and fuel price volatility as well as environmental and natural resource depletion concerns.[212] Subsequently the Council has recommended that Bonneville Power Administration (BPA) and the region's utilities maintain the 10% benefit, in part because "conservation results in fewer uncontrollable environmental impacts than any other source of electricity."[213]

The first Plan, issued in 1983, contains the NWPPC's most comprehensive review of methods for assessing comparative environmental costs for generating options.[214]

F. ALTERNATIVES FOR INCORPORATION OF ENVIRONMENTAL EXTERNALITY COSTS IN ELECTRIC UTILITY RESOURCE PLANNING AND SELECTION

There follows a discussion of the advantages and disadvantages of alternatives for incorporation of environmental externality costs of electricity, derived from the results of the federal and state experience set forth above.

1. Taxes and Subsidy Alternatives

National pollution taxes or fees, calculated to reflect environmental externality costs, and applying to all polluting resources, including those employed by electric utilities, appear to be the most efficient means of internalizing these costs. They put in the marketplace the costs to society of resource damages, so that, other things being equal, when any enterprise selects resources, it will be more economic to choose resources that cause less environmental damage. Taxes also eliminate the competitive

---

209 16 U.S.C. § 839b(e)(3)(c) (1980).

210 Id. at § 839a(4)(B).

211 Id. at 839a(4)(D).

212 1980 U.S. Code Cong. Adm. News 6065.

213 NWPPC Pub. 89-7, supra. note 208, at p. 5.

214 Id. at p. 2.

and fuel-switching consequences of internalizing environmental costs for utilities only.[215]

Pollution taxes are better directed at incorporating environmental damages than are the resource taxes discussed above, such as coal taxes or gasoline taxes; resource taxes do not take into account resources of the same category which may have different polluting characteristics, and they take no account of technological innovations that could permit cleaner use of the resources taxed (such as clean coal technologies).

The problems with pollution taxes are not theoretical but practical. Any taxes or fees meet public resistance. Pollution taxes or fees representing the entire environmental externality costs of resource damages would be very large. The order of magnitude is indicated by the studies reviewed in this report. With present public resistance towards taxation, such large taxes or fees seem unlikely.

Furthermore, large federal pollution taxes or fees could cause adverse international competitive effects by increasing the costs of U.S. products compared to those produced in other countries, unless other countries enacted similar taxes. Particularly with taxes that are pervasive, like carbon taxes, only treaties for internationally uniform pollution taxes could eliminate the competitive problems. Similarly, large state pollution taxes or fees could encourage state industry to move to states with lower taxes, a result that would be undesirable from both state and environmental standpoints.

Of course, from a competitive viewpoint, the other side of the coin also must be considered, namely the large costs the United States pays for energy inefficiency.[216] Dr. Arthur Rosenfeld of Lawrence Berkeley Laboratory finds that:

> In 1985, the U.S. used 11.2 % of its GNP for energy; Japan used 5%...thisdifferential of 5% of GNP means that, even if all else were equal, our products cost on average about 5% more than comparable Japanese products, thus impairing our balance of payments, the dollar/yen ration and our life-style.[217]

He finds that similar differentials in energy efficiency and resulting competitiveness exist relative to the OECD countries.[218]

---

215 The incorporation methodologies in use by utility regulatory commissions today, however, do not internalize environmental costs. They merely affect the selection of new resources to reflect some of these costs. They therefore are likely to have insignificant competitive effects and should help prevent the selection of new resources that will be rendered obsolete or require substantial and expensive retrofits in the future due to increased national, state and local environmental regulation that can be anticipated.

216 Rosenfeld, A., Conservation, Competition and National Security, Hearing on Energy Security: The Role of Conservation in the National Energy Picture, Subcommittee on Energy and Power, Committee on Energy and Commerce, U.S. House of Reps., November 4, 1987.

217 Id. at p. 10.

218 Id. at p. 3.

It therefore appears to behoove the United States competitively to adopt incentives to improve energy efficiency, and to do so with by incorporating environmental externalities would give greatest leverage for environmental improvement.

As indicated in Section D.2. above, subsidies are a far less efficient way of incorporating environmental externality costs since the subsidies are not reflected in prices and subsidies have significant distorting effects on the energy marketplace. Removal of subsidies to resources with high environmental costs would help reflect those costs more accurately in the marketplace.

2. Alternatives for State Incorporation of Environmental Costs

There has not yet been sufficient experience with incorporating environmental externality costs under any of the state commission orders described above to be able to ascertain from them what methodology will work best.

Since investor-owned utilities, those subject to state regulation, are profit-making institutions, a rate of return incentive for energy efficiency investments, so that a kWh saved is as profitable as a kWh sold, would appear essential to motivate them to invest in efficiency resources bearing among the lowest environmental costs.

The states moving most aggressively to incorporate externalities, like New York, Wisconsin, California and the New England states have all accompanied their efforts with rate revisions to return revenues lost from utility DSM investments and, in most cases, to include an incentive to make efficiency investment profits comparable to supply investment profits.

Orders requiring quantitative consideration of environmental costs are likely to be more effective than orders for qualitative consideration in motivating utilities to consider them. The experience to date has been that states like New York, the New England states and Wisconsin which have quantitative requirements have achieved much greater energy savings, and thus reductions in environmental costs, than the states having just qualitative consideration. The degree to which the results are attributable to the methodology for incorporation of environmental costs, however, is uncertain, because incorporation of externalities is so new and those states that use quantitative measures also have much stronger DSM and least cost planning provisions.

In use of quantitative consideration, the economic literature is heavily weighted in favor of the use of damage rather than control costs, because it is the damages that are sought to be eliminated. However, as this report indicates, valuation of damages for most resources still requires extensive additional research. The commissions that have ordered inclusion of environmental costs to date have all used control costs, though Oregon's recent order requires utilities to consider damage costs to the greatest extent possible, and the pooled costing effort in New York includes damage valuation. Where damage costs are not available, control costs or arbitrary adders or credits, rather than zero valuation at least captures some of the environmental externality costs.

Inclusion of environmental externality costs in calculation of avoided costs for all purposes, adopted in a number of states, also helps capture environmental externality costs, since avoided costs are used so widely as a measure of the extent to which commissions will consider economic investments in DSM and alternative resources. Of course, this is the measure mandated by PURPA for QF's.

The Moskovitz suggestion, that resource owners be required to pay into a fund for pollution mitigation the environmental externality costs attributed to the resource selected, would give incorporation of externalities much more leverage to avoid environmental damages. In bidding programs, this recommended procedure mandates that a winning bidder be required to include in its bid price, and pay into the fund, the externality costs attributed to the resource it proposes. It seems anomalous that a polluting resource that is selected in bidding, despite the environmental externality costs of its bid, should be allowed to proceed to pollute without any accounting for those costs. It must be recognized, however, that this proposal would internalize environmental costs and pose much larger competitive effects than using environmental costs merely in selection of new resources.

Such a fund does have precedent in the federal nuclear waste disposal and decommissioning funds financed by a tax on all utilities. At the state level, legislation might be required to authorize such a procedure, although there is precedent for establishment of such a fund by the New York PSC which required utilities to deposit .25% of their gross annual revenues into a fund for DSM demonstrations a number of years ago.[219]

Environmental dispatch (including environmental externality costs in least cost dispatch by utilities and power pools) would be most effective means of alleviating environmental costs because it would displace pollution from existing power plants which contribute most to environmental costs. For that very reason, commentators indicate that it would meet greatest utility resistance, since it would decrease the use and profitability of existing utility facilities. Environmental dispatch ordered by a commission might require legislative authorization in some states. While environmental dispatch has yet to be tried in any state, it is authorized as an option in Wisconsin's new acid rain legislation and is recommended in a number of the studies reviewed.

Environmental LCUP has the advantage of avoiding the difficult task of quantifying environmental externality costs and would thus be particularly useful in addressing pollutants like CO_2 where the damage costs are hard to quantify, and control costs, like the tree planting costs used in this report, are found to be speculative. The methodology is well adapted for use only to value hard-to-quantify resources, while quantified consideration could be given to resources for which damages are easier to calculate. Environmental LCUP also has the advantage of achieving emission reductions with greater certainty than other incorporation procedures, but PSC's may feel unqualified to set the emission reduction targets and some may not have the legal authority to do so.

In summary, the reported experience of the states in incorporating environmental externalities and the studies reviewed suggest the following conclusions:

* Use of quantified consideration of environmental externality costs in all planning, bidding and other resource selection;

* Use of damage costs where scientific and economic studies are adequate, otherwise control costs or an arbitrary environmental adder or credit;

* Use of rate of return incentives on acquisition of energy efficiency resources such that a kWh saved will be as profitable as a kWh sold;

---

219 New York Public Service Commission, Case No. 28233, Opinion and Order 84-15 (May 1984).

* Use of environmental externalities in setting avoided costs;

* Experimentation with assessment of environmental externality costs against resources selected, the proceeds to be placed in a Pollution Mitigation Fund; environmental dispatch; and "Environmental LCUP" for use with respect to hard-to-quantify pollution costs.

G. STATE-BY-STATE SURVEY OF ENVIRONMENTAL COST TREATMENT

This section briefly summarizes information on the status of environmental externality treatment by state legislatures and utility regulatory commissions on a state-by-state basis. Summaries of environmental externality policy appear in subsection (a) of each state entry. Integrated demand-side and supply resource acquisition, demand-side incentives and environmental externalities are closely interrelated. Therefore, subsection (b) of each state entry includes the status of least-cost planning in the states. When the information was available, subsection (b) also includes an indication of the capacity situation and fossil fuel dependence for each state's electric utilities. Subsection (c) indicates whether the state has an environmental review statute ("little NEPA") and, in some cases, acid rain control legislation or other legislation relevant to environmental impacts and associated costs for electric utilities.

The section serves as documentation for the state regulatory treatment material, supra. The paucity of thorough studies on state treatment suggests the need for future research. The state summaries below summarize material from several published articles on environmental externality policy, least cost planning and environmental review statutes in the fifty states. Abbreviated citations in the text of the entries document the source. Complete source citations appear at the end of this Appendix.[220]

The status of environmental externality policies and least cost planning at utility regulatory commissions is rapidly changing. Conversations with participants in proceedings or commission staff of a particular state may yield significantly different perspectives. Consequently, the summaries below are only a "rough cut" of state endeavors and may not entirely reflect the most current political, regulatory, or legislative climate of a particular state. When the available literature conflicts, both sides are presented unless independent verification resolved the conflict.

---

[220] The most complete state-by-state survey of treatment of environmental externality costs was done recently by Lawrence Berkeley Laboratory (LBL) for the National Association of Regulatory Utility Commissioners (NARUC). LBL generously shared with us its draft final report, S.D. Cohen, et. al., A Survey of State PUC Activities to Incorporate Environmental Externalities into Electric Utility Planning and Regulation, LBL, University of California, draft of May, 1990, Appendix A, cited as LBL/NARUC.

In addition to the state surveys cited at the end of this Appendix, the Solar Energy Research Institute (SERI) has undertaken a survey of state bidding programs which includes characterization of environmental elements. The results of this survey are not yet available. Personal communications of Susan Babb with Blair Sweezy, SERI, September 28, 1989 and January 18, 1990. See also, Barakat, Howard & Chamberlin, Inc. The Quantification of Externalities for Demand-Side and Supply-Side Resource Options: A Preliminary Study, Appendix, prepared for New England Electric Service, February 15, 1989.

Alabama

(a) No consideration of environmental externalities (LBL/NARUC at A-2).

(b) No least-cost planning; excess capacity for twenty years (EPRI at 15). Peak capacity needed in ten year period; and over 50% of electricity is generated from coal (LBL/NARUC at A-2).

(c) No environmental review statute.

Alaska

(a) According to LBL/NARUC at A-3, no consideration of environmental externalities. However, Alaska Stat. §44.83.960 (1989) requires the Department of Commerce and Economic Development to prepare and annually revise a long-term energy plan. The plan must include "an energy development component for meeting projected thermal, electrical and transportation needs in the state at the lowest reasonable cost, including environmental and social costs, consistent with acceptable standards of reliability." The plan must give "equal consideration as practicable" to all types of energy sources except nuclear fuels. The plan must also include an energyconservation component. The Alaska PUC has also relied on the social benefits of QF power to exceed a utility's calculated avoided costs. Cogeneration & Small Power Prod., U-81-35(4), at 46, Order No. 4 (1982).

(b) <u>See</u> (a). Surplus capacity for five to ten years; and generation is largely dependent on oil (EPRI at 15). No capacity anticipated (LBL/NARUC at A-3).

(c) No environmental review statute. Alaska provides for a unified permitting procedure which includes as goals, increasing coordination between state, local and federal environmental requirements and improving publicinformation and participation. Alsk. Stat. §§46.35.010to 46.35.200 (1989).

Arizona

(a Recently adopted least-cost planning process requires qualitative consideration of environmental externalities including sulfur dioxide and carbon dioxide emissions and other air quality issues (LBL/NARUC at A-4). Original draft rules required ten-year integrated resource plans that included the present value of societal costs (EPRI at 16).

(b) <u>See</u> (a). No new capacity need anticipated (LBL/NARUC at A-4). A 1989 Ariz. Corp. Commission rule requires the four major utilities to submit ten-year plans every third year, with annual data updates, subject to hearings. LBL Draft Survey Update, Appendix A at p. A-5.

(c) No environmental review statute.

Arkansas

(a) No consideration of environmental externalities (LBL/NARUC at A-5).

(b) No least-cost planning; capacity surplus. EPRI at 16; Siting decisions require EIS and consideration of environment, energy efficiency and alternative supplies. Recent PSC order urges DSM on largest utility (LBL/NARUC at A-5).

(c) Ark. Stat. Ann. §38-1-101 (1987); See Robinson at 287, 293-94.

California

(a) The California Energy Commission (CEC) considers environmental externalities in licensing sites for all plants over fifty MW. The CEC has recommended for its 1990 Electricity Report (ER90) due 9/1/90, environmental externality quantified consideration @ \$11,600/T for NO_x, \$11,500/T for SO_x, \$7,800/T for PM10, \$3,300/T for ROG to meet SCAQMD air quality standards, CEC Staff Rpt., Valuing Emission Reductions for ER90, November 21, 1989 at p. B-5; and \$7/T for CO_2 using a cost of tree-planting proxy adding about 1.5-8 mils/kWh to coal plants costs. Roach, C.R. et. al., Electric Resources and Environmental Impacts: Draft Phase 1 Report, Joint Comm. on Energy Regulation and the Environment, April 1990.

The PUC is also considering quantified consideration in its Standard Offer #4 bid pricing protocol. Cal. PUC. OII.89-07-004, Order Instituting Investigation on the Commission's own motion implement the Biennial Resource Plan update following the CEC's Seventh Electricity Report, 1989. PUC workshops are considering environmental cost inclusion in planning and resource acquisition. Murley, C., et al., Workshop Report: Incorporating Environmental Adders into the Biennial Resource Plant Update Proceeding, Cal. PUC, April 13, 1990.

California did a DSM collaborative which failed to reach consensus on environmental externalities. An Energy Efficiency Blueprint for California [Blueprint], Report of the Statewide Collaborative Process, Jan. 1990, at p. 68. Utilities filed in April, 1990 for expanded DSM approval and incentives.

For more detail on all the above, See LBL/NARUC at A-7 - A-9.

The CEC is also considering use of environmental costing in determining priorities of state energy research program budgets. See, Valuing Emission Reductions for Electricity Report 90, Staff Issue Paper #3R, Cal. Energy Resource, Conservation & Development Commission, November 21, 1989. In Re Preparation of the 1990 Electricity Report, Docket No. ER-8.

Southern California utilities formerly used environmental dispatch for NO_x emissions to meet SCAQMD air standards. The PUC has rejected environmental dispatch considerations in the calculation of avoided costs for QFs. See Re Pacific Gas and Electric, Dec. 86-07-004, 76 P.U.R. 4th 1 (Cal. PUC July 2, 1986).

(b) PUC has no formal least-cost planning process. The CEC does so, however, in its siting and Electricity Reports (LBL/NARUC at A-8). A voluntary collaborative process resulted in large DSM expansion. Blueprint (above). California electricity resources are 40% natural gas,

15-20% hydro, 10% nuclear, the rest renewables and out of state purchases.

(c) Cal. Pub. Res. Code § 21000 et seq. (West 1982); state environmental quality act guidelines at Cal. Admin. Code, tit. 1415000 et seq. See, Robinson at 256, 294. See also, Application of Environmental Impact Report Requirement of the California Environmental Quality Act to Rate Hearings of Electric Utilities, 8 U.S.F.L.Rev. 752 (1974).

Colorado

(a) Environmental externalities are considered in QF bidding approved for up to 20% of demand forecasts. Renewables are awarded seventeen points on a 100 point scale, coal five, natural gas two, and oil one. No points for DSM. No bidding yet. Amendment to Public Service Company of Colorado Request for Proposals from Qualifying Facilities, PUC, June, 1989 (LBL/NARUC at A-10).

(b) PUC least-cost planning rulemaking abandoned in 1987 (EPRI at 18). No new capacity needed before mid 1990s. (LBL/NARUC at A-10).

(c) No environmental review statute.

Connecticut

(a) A collaborative process between utilities, state agencies and intervenors is devising externality values and treatment. Utilities must submit plans for externality treatment with capacity proposals (LBL/NARUC at A-12). The Connecticut Department of Public Utility Control (DPUC) has prepared but not yet implemented rating consideration of bidding programs which includes a calculated adder for environmental externalities (Brick at 2). New England Electric System (NEES) has proposed a rating system based on customer surveys. Investigation by the Department of Public Utilities on Its Own Motion into Proposed Rules to Implement Integrated Resource Management Practices for Electric Companies in the Commonwealth, Mass. D.P.U. No 89-239, Feb. 23, 1990, Comments By Massachusetts Electric Co. (a NEES subsidiary) at 17-21 and Attachment 2. A statutory 5% rate of return bonus is given for conservation due to environmental benefits of DSM resources.

(b) A 1988 statute requires the DPUC to develop regulations incorporating least-cost supply, load management and conservation measures from private power providers into the planning process and to set rate of return incentives for cost-effective DSM measures. The rate incentive must be at least 1% percent but no more than 5% percent of the company's authorized return. Connecticut Public Act No. 88-57, 1988. EPRI at 18; Raid at 13. No capacity needs in the next five years (LBL/NARUC at A-12).

(c) Conn. Gen. Stat. Ann. §§ 22a-14 to 22a-20 (West Supp. 1974 - 1975). The Connecticut Environmental Protection Act applies only to projects which seek state funding. Generally, regulatory decisions of state agencies do not require review. See, Robinson at 258, 294-95.

Delaware

(a) No consideration of environmental externalities (LBL/NARUC at A-13).

(b) Utilities are required to submit ten year resource plans which include DSM measures and cogeneration options (EPRI at 19). Base and peak capacity will be needed; About 60% of capacity is coal-based (LBL/NARUC at A-13).

(c) No environmental review statute.

District of Columbia

(a) No present consideration of environmental externalities, but proposed PSC regulations in January, 1990, require least cost plans including non-economic screening and PSC said it is reviewing externality consideration and may require it in the future. D.C. PSC, Order No. 9417, Jan. 1990, at p. 40 (LBL/NARUC at A-14).

(b) See (a). Biennial least cost plans must be filed comparing DSM and new supply equally, the first from D.C.'s utility, PEPCO, filed in March, 1990 (LBL/NARUC at A-14).

(c) PEPCO is seeking approval for over 1100 MW of new combined cycle coal gasification, oil and natural gas-fired plants and has plans for about 230 MW more (LBL/NARUC at A-14).

Florida

(a) No consideration of environmental externalities, but Florida Power & Light has issued an 800 MW bidding RFP considering non-price factors (LBL/NARUC at A-15).

(b) 1980 Florida Energy Efficiency and Conservation Act requires utilities to adopt conservation measures to reduce peak demand and energy with five-year goal to reduce demand by 25%. Fla. Stat. Ann. § 366.80 et seq. (West Supp. 1989). Without formal least-cost planning rules, PSC is using cost-effectiveness to evaluate "utility financial projects" and conservation programs, which must be included as resource options (EPRI at 20). Florida needs both base and peak capacity in the near future (LBL/NARUC at A-16). Historically utilities have been heavily oil-based (EPRI at 20).

(c) Florida Environmental Land and Water Act of 1972, Fla. Stat. Ann. §§ 380.012 et seq. (West Supp. 1989), requires regional impact statements for certain development projects. An environmental review process is associated with the Florida Power Plan Siting Act, See, Robinson at 258-59.

Georgia

(a) No consideration of environmental externalities (LBL/NARUC at A-18).

(b) Least cost planning workshops were held in December 1988 (EPRI at 20). In 1989 the PSC appointed a task force to consider least cost planning. Base and peak capacity are needed in the near future; about 80% of electricity is from coal generation, 12% from nuclear (LBL/NARUC at A-18).

(c) No environmental review act. In 1989, the Department of Natural Resources was authorized to promulgate "minimum standards for the protection of natural resources, environment, and vital areas of the state including but not limited to watersheds and wetlands." Ga. Code Ann. § 12-2-8 (Supp. 1989).

Hawaii

(a) No present consideration of environmental externalities, but it is under active consideration. LBL/NARUC at A-19).

(b) Commission and legislature are considering least-cost planning and ways to improve consideration of DSM (EPRI at 21) and the PSC has instituted a proceeding. Docket No. 6617. The state needs both peak and base capacity. Over 90% of its electricity is from oil (LBL/NARUC at A-19).

(c) Hawaii Rev. Stat. §§ 343-1 to 343-8 (1985) applies to all projects seeking to use state or county funds which may have a significant effect on the environment. See Robinson at 259.

Idaho

(a) The Idaho PUC recently ordered rate of return consideration: "we take this opportunity to notify our regulated electric utilities that in future rate cases we will take into account the utility's commitment to energy conservation in determining allowed rate of return. A utility that aggressively addresses the issues and concerns found in this Order, conservation in particular [including environmental benefits]), all other things being equal, may expect the allowance of higher return than might otherwise be allowed." In the Matter of the Investigation by the Idaho Public Utilities Commission into Idaho Electric Conservation Standards and Practices, Idaho PUC Order No. 22299, January 1989. The order states that DSM and supply resources be given equal consideration and establishes criteria for valuing DSM (LBL/NARUC at A-17).

The Idaho PUC also includes pollution control equipment in the capacity credit calculation, stating: "The typical plant of the future will surely be one with scrubbers or other emission control devices. Elimination of these costs [a 22% reduction in capacity cost payments] is unrepresentative of the state of the art, misleads those who relied upon the figures submitted by Idaho power in these proceedings, and acts as a major disincentive to cogeneration and small power production in the state of Idaho." Rulemaking Proceeding for Consideration of Cogeneration & Small Power Prod., 40 Pub. Util. Rpt. (PUR)4th 563, 567-8 (1980)

(b) The Commission is considering role of cost-effectiveness with an order "expected in summer 1988" (EPRI at 21). PSC Order No. 22299 effectively requires least-cost planning. Electricity is about half each from hydro and coal (LBL/NARUC at A-17).

(c) No environmental review act. See Robinson at 259.

Illinois

(a) The Illinois Commerce Commission (I.C.C.) rejected a staff recommendation that environmental impacts be quantified as part of the first statewide energy planning process. Re Comprehensive Electric Energy Plan, Docket No. 89-0034 Slip Op. at 33 (October 6, 1989). According to LBL/NARUC at A-20, however, the Commission requires a discussion of environmental externalities in planning, though not providing for their incorporation.

b) 1985 Public Utilities Act requires the Ill.C.C. and the Department of Energy and Natural Resources to implement twenty-year energy plans. Ill. Rev. Stat. Ch. 111 2/3, § 8-402 (1989). An acid rain task force to analyze utility impacts has been formed as part of this process. Illinois electricity is 55% from coal and 40% from nuclear generation and no need is expected for new capacity until the late 1990s.

(c) No environmental review act. See Robinson at 259.

Indiana

(a) No consideration of environmental externalities (LBL/NARUC at A-21).

(b) Indiana certificate of need process for new plant construction requires comparison of proposed capacity with other options including DSM (EPRI at 23). Three utilities have been ordered to submit least-cost plans in 1990. Both base and peak capacity are needed; over 90% of capacity is coal-fired (LBL/NARUC at A-21).

(c) Ind. Code Ann. §§ 13-1-10-1 to 13-1-10-8 (Burns 1987 and Supp. 1989). See Robinson at 259.

Iowa

(a) The Iowa Utilities Board (IUB) endorsed a consultant's recommendations for an initial credit (e.g. 10%) to avoided supply cost to account for environmental externalities and long term quantified credits; a collaborative is designing rule changes to incorporate environmental externalities. Energy Efficiency Options Study Main Report, Morgan Systems, prepared for the IUB, October 27, 1989 (LBL/NARUC at A-23).

(b) Due to excess capacity situation, 1977 legislation required the IUB to adopt plant certification and energy conservation procedures. See Roger D. Colton, Utility Involvement in Energy Management: the Role of a State Power Certification Statute, Environmental Law 175 (1986) (discussing Iowa statute and legislative history). IUB rules require annual filings of forecasts and mandatory demand-side programs. See EPRI at 23. Peak capacity is needed. About 75% of current capacity is coal-fired and 25% nuclear (LBL/NARUC at A-23).

(c) No environmental review statute. See Robinson at 259.

Kansas

(a) The Kansas commission permits a rate of return bonus of 0.5% to 2.0% for renewable energy, conservation or higher efficiency resources (LBL/NARUC at A-25).

(b) Peak capacity is needed. Electricity is 95% from coal, 2% from nuclear (LBL/NARUC at A-25).

(c) No environmental review statute.

Kentucky

(a) No environmental externality consideration (LBL/NARUC at A-27).

(b) Under its general authority the PSC is developing statewide capacity planning (EPRI at 25). Peak capacity may be needed over the next eight years. Electricity is 96% from coal.

(c) No environmental review statute .

Louisiana

(a) No environmental externality consideration (LBL/NARUC at A-28).

(b) No least-cost planning; excess capacity (EPRI at 25); Electricity is 40% natural gas, 30% coal and 30% nuclear (LBL/NARUC at A-28).

(c) No environmental review statute.

Maine

(a) Maine recently enacted a law finding that environmental and economic costs and benefits should be taken into account in utility planning and requiring the PUC to analyze and recommend methods of determination and incorporation to the Legislature by April 1, 1991. Maine P&S Law, Chapter 110, April 6, 1990. See also, Re Demand Side Energy Management Programs by Electric Utilities, Docket 88-178, 100 P.U.R. 4th 286 (Me. PUC 22 December 1988) (proposing a 10% percent of avoided cost preference for DSM to account for environmental and social costs as part of a cost-effectiveness docket).

(b) Maine Energy Policy Act of 1988 requires consideration of all available alternatives in pursuing a least-cost energy plan for electric utilities. "When the available alternatives are otherwise equivalent, the commission shall give preference first to conservation and demand management and then to power purchased from qualifying facilities." Environmental benefits are one reason for this ranking. Me. Rev. Stat. Ann. tit. 35-A, § 3191 (West Supp. 1989). See also EPRI at 26. The Maine statute permits but does not require the PUC to ratebase cost-effective investment in DSM measures installed on customer premises; it is uncertain as to whether financial incentives can be ratebased. Raid at 16. Maine has competitive bidding for both DSM and supply resources. Its electricity is 20-25% nuclear, 25% hydro, 35% Canadian and IPP purchases, the balance from oil. Future needs are planned from DSM and Canadian purchases. (LBL/NARUC at A-29).

(c) No environmental review statute.

Maryland

(a) The PUC has initiated a collaborative process for determination and incorporation of environmental externalites in bidding as proposed by Delmarva Power and Light. The PUC is to issue a "white paper" on how to quantify environmental costs (LBL/NARUC at A-31).

(b) Least cost planning is addressed in plant certificate of need hearings and in annual utility long-range resource plans, which by law must include adequate provisions to promote energy conservation. Md. Ann. Code (Public Service Commission Law) art. 78, §§ 54A & 54B (1988) (EPRI at 26-27). Electricity is more than 50% from coal, the balance from nuclear, oil and gas. Base and peak capacity are needed. 4400 MW construction is planned and peak reductions of 1350 MW (LBL/NARUC at A-31).

(c) Md. Nat. Res. Code Ann. §§ 1-301 to 1-305 (1983 and Supp. 1987) (environmental reviews are associated with permit applications); See Robinson at 259-60, 296-97.

Massachusetts

(a) The DPU has ordered all utilities to consider environmental externalities in DSM evaluations. Investigation by the Department of Public Utilities on its own motion, pursuant to Section 76 of Chapter 164 of the General Laws, into the pricing and ratemaking treatment to be afforded new electric generating facilities which are not Qualifying Facilities as defined in 220 C.M.R. 8.02, DPU 86-36-F, November 30, 1988. The DPU recently issued proposed rules for uniform quantification of environmental externalities in planning, bidding and other resource selection, announcing its intent for adoption of rules in 1990. Id., D.P.U. 86-36-G (Dec. 6, 1989). The utilities are engaged in collaborative efforts to finalize externality rules. Massachusetts also takes environmental externalities into account in its Certificate of Need process for licensing new plants. Mass. Gen. L., Ch. 40A, Sec. 3.

(b) The DPU has proposed a regulatory structure for integrated planning and all-resource acquisition as well as policies for electric company expenditures and investments in cost effective conservation and load management. The Energy Facilities Siting Council is the lead agency for parts of the process. See (a). Collaborative DSM design has aggressively pursued conservation measures in Massachusetts (LBL/NARUC at A-33).

(c) Mass. Gen. Laws ch. 30, §§ 61 - 62H (1988) require an impact report for all proposed actions which require a state permit and have an environmental impact. See Robinson at 260, 297. By the end of 1994, utilities must comply with acid rain control regulations adopted in April 1989. The regulations allow the use of conservation measures, emissions trading, and cogeneration as measures to satisfy the emissions limitation. 310 CMR 700; Mass. Gen. Laws ch. 11, §§ 1424A-142E (1988).

Michigan

(a) Methods for including and quantifying environmental externalities in integrated resource plans are under development and expected to be used in plans submitted in December 1991 and June 1992 (LBL/NARUC at A-35). In evaluating utility conservation programs, the Michigan PSC has stated that consideration must be given to unquantifiable societal benefits. Re Michigan Residential Conservation Services Programs and Zero Interest Programs, Case U-8582, Slip Op. at 11-13 (1988). The Michigan PSC allowed higher avoid cost rates to a resource recovery plant on grounds of environmental benefits. Kent County, 81 Pub. Util. Rep. (PUR)4th 282, 286 (1987).

(b Integrated planning underway as a result of the Electricity Options Study, triggered by Consumer Power's Midland nuclear facility (EPRI at 28). Electricity is 80% from coal, 17.5% from nuclear. Baseload capacity will be needed in the mid-1990s. (LBL/NARUC at A-35).

(c) Executive Order 1974-4 requires state agencies to prepare environmental assessments for major agency activities which have a possible significant impact on the environment of human life. See Robinson at 260, 297-98.

Minnesota

(a) The Minnesota commission incorporates environmental externality cost considerations in its Certificate of Need process; acid rain and global warming externalities have been considered. In December, 1989, the PUC proposed a planning rule to incorporate environmental considerations. A 1986 law caps SO_2 emissions from the state's two main power plants to reduce acid rain (LBL/NARUC at A-36).

(b) Least-cost planning is under development (EPRI at 28). Base and peak capacity is needed; over 50% of supply is coal-based (LBL/NARUC at A-36,37).

(c) Minn. Stat. Ann. §§ 116D.01 to 07 (West 1977 and Supp. 1981) (process applies to what project is and not how it is funded and is triggered if any level of government is to be involved). See Robinson at 261, 298 - 99.

Mississippi

(a) No consideration of environmental externalities (LBL/NARUC at A-38).

(b) No least cost planning, no capacity needs (EPRI at 29).

(c) No environmental review statute.

Missouri

(a) No present consideration of environmental externalities. An Electric Strategic Resource Planning Project has been started which may consider externalities (LBL/NARUC at A-39).

(b) Least-cost planning was recommended by a staff report in 1986, but least-cost planning bills were defeated in the state legislature in 1987 and 1988 (EPRI at 29). Peaking capacity is needed; over 75% percent of supply is from coal (LBL/NARUC at A-39,40).

(c) No environmental review statute.

Montana

(a) Montana law sets a 2% rate of return bonus for conservation investment. Mont. Code Ann. §§ 69-3-701 to 69-3-713 (1989). The Montana PSC has taken a restrictive approach to its jurisdiction to incorporate quantified environmental externalitites. Re Electric Avoided Cost Rates, Docket No. 84.10.64,Order No. 5091c, 73 P.U.R. 4th 138, Mont. Dept. Pub. Serv. 5, March 1986, held that to account for externalities goes beyond the Commission's regulatory role in setting avoided costs. A task force is evaluating least cost planning and environmental externalities.

(b) No least cost planning requirement exists. The PSC is required to include eligible conservation investments in a utility's ratebase. See Raid at 11-12.

(c) Mont. Code Ann. §§ 75-1-101 to 75-1-105; 75-1-201 (1989) provides for environmental review (any major state action significantly affecting the environment). Major power plant and utility siting EIS's are coordinated under the Facility Siting Act in the Facility Siting Bureau of the Department of Natural Resources. Mont. Code Ann, §§ 75-20-101 to 75-20-1205 (1989). See also Robinson at 262, 299 - 300.

Nebraska

(a), (b) Nebraska is all public power. The largest public power district is investigating DSM planning. (EPRI at30).

(c) No environmental review statute.

Nevada

(a) By statute, qualitative consideration of environmental externalities is required in the least cost planning process. Utility's plan must adequately demonstrate "economic, environmental, and other benefits" to the state and the utility's customers associated with DSM, renewable resources, and cogeneration. PSC may give preference to measures which provide the state with the greatest environmental and economic benefits. Nevada Sen. Bill 497, approved July, 1989; See LBL/NARUC at A-42.

(b) Least-cost plans must be filed every three years under a 1983 Least-Cost Planning Act. Nev. Rev. Stat. § 704.71 to 704.751 (1987). The

PSC has allowed utilities to ratebase CL&M expenditures approved as part of a least-cost plan. Electricity is 60-65% from coal, 15% from gas, the balance from oil and imports. Capacity is needed; DSM is in plans (Raid at 15; LBL/NARUC at A-42).

(c) No environmental review statute.

New Hampshire

(a) No present consideration of environmental externalities. Proposed legislation states PUC "may consider" them in planning (LBL/NARUC at A-44).

(b) Least-cost planning order requires biennial integrated resource plans and two year implementation plans (EPRI at 31). Supply and DSM options must be evaluated consistently (LBL/NARUC at A-44).

(c) No environmental review statute.

New Jersey

(a) The New Jersey bidding system, adopted as the result of a settlement between utilities, staff and other parties, includes environmental benefits in "noneconomic factors". The category of noneconomic factors, including environmental externalities, has a minimum weight of 20% percent of the overall point ranking. Re Cogeneration and Small Power Production Standards, Docket No. 8010-687B, order (NJ Bd. Pub. Util. August 24, 1988), discussed in Michael A. Walker, New Jersey's Competitive Bidding System - An Attempt at a Balanced Energy Supply Policy, Pub. Util. Fort., February 16, 1989, at pp. 34,35 (Appeals were taken from some aspects of the settlement). In a recent bidding decision only 1% of points each was allocated to environmental factors and energy efficiency. (LBL/NARUC at A-45). A Jersey Central Power & Light RFP of June, 1989, allotted up to 2% for reduced NO_x emission and up to 4% for fuel efficiency. See, Request for Proposals to Supply Electric Capacity and Energy, Public Service Electric and Gas, August 15, 1989.

New Jersey also gives avoided cost preference to QFs, at 10% above the PNM power pool's energy billing rate, "to reflect the potential cost savings to society at the state and national levels." Bidding Farewell at 1039.

(b) Utilities must file annual long-range resource plans. Resources selected must meet a least-cost test to be included in the rate base. Biennial conservation plans are also required (LBL/NARUC at A-46). Department of Energy conservation plan regulations require analysis of conservation impacts on fifteen-year electric forecasts and the Board of Public Utilities (BPU) requires long-range resource plans. All source bidding system (see (a) above) includes conservation investments in excess of 40 KW subject to the same assessment criteria as supply bidders (EPRI at 32). Electricity is 25% from coal, 20-30% from nuclear, 10-20% from oil, gas and IPPs. New capacity is needed. The BPU is considering DSM incentives to utilities to avoid new generation (LBL/NARUC at A-45).

(c) Application for various permits may trigger preparation of an EIS. Under New Jersey Exec. Order 53 (1973), an EIS must be prepared if a project is projected to cost more than $1 million, is sited in an environmentally sensitive area, and has applied for state funding. See Robinson at 263,300.

New Mexico

(a) No consideration of environmental externalities (LBL/NARUC at A-47).

(b) No least-cost planning. New Mexico has surpluscapacity and much utility capacity investment is located out of state and not subject to PSC authorization. (EPRI at 32). Electricity is 90% from coal, 10% from gas, with a large excess capacity (LBL/NARUC at A-47).

(c) No environmental review statute.

New York

(a) The PSC has ordered its utilities to incorporate environmental externalities in planning and bidding decisions. New York PSC Case Nos. 29409 (planning and bidding) and 28223 (DSM). The PSC has also allowed consideration of environmental externalities in DSM rate incentives. See Re Orange & Rockland and Niagara Mohawk - Rate Incentive Proposals, Case 89-E-041, Opinion No. 89-29 (September 12, 1989). In bid evaluation, approximately 24% of the price score is added to bids valued at 1.405 cents/kWh for an NSPS coal plant, with specified values for criteria pollutants and land and water impacts. About 24% of price points (15% of total bid evaluation points) are assigned to environmental externalities. See Order Issuing a Final Environmental Impact Statement...in Case 88-E-241, Proceeding...as to the guidelines for bidding to meet future electric capacity needs of Orange & Rockland Utilities, Inc. (March 24, 1989). The Commission has also ordered a pooled collaborative study of New York Utility emission environmental externality costs. Order Concerning Conclusions on Long Range Demand Side Management Plans (May 23, 1989) at 40. See Chapter X, Section C.1. and LBL/NARUC at A-48,49.

(b) The PSC has mandated comprehensive annual and long-term integrated planning and requirements for DSM programs, including eight core programs which all utilities must implement. Cases 29409 (planning and bidding) and 28223 (DSM). See Chapter X, Section C.1. for detailed consideration of these requirements.

(c) N.Y. Envt'l. Conserv. Law §§ 8-0101 to 8-0117 (McKinney 1983); N.Y. Comp. Codes R. & Regs. tit. 6, Part 617(1986). SEQRA is triggered by a state action which may have a significant effect on the environment. The PSC has applied SEQRA in a variety of policy forums including all source bidding. See generally, Robinson at 263-266.

North Carolina

(a) No consideration of environmental externalities (LBL/NARUC at A-50). Pre-filed testimony in the current least cost planning docket advocates consideration of environmental externalities and quantifies these externalities for coal-fired plants at two to eight cents/kWh.

(b) Least-cost planning is in progress (EPRI at 33). Electricity is 35-40% from coal, 50-55% from nuclear. Peak capacity will be needed in five to seven years (LBL/NARUC at A-50).

(c) N.C. Gen. Stat. §§ 113A-1 to 113A-10 (1989)(EIS requirement is triggered by a request for public funding, an application for state permit, or if the project has a potential to create an environmental impact). See Robinson at 266, 301.

North Dakota

(a) No consideration of environmental externalities (LBL/NARUC at A-52).

(b) PSC has ordered least cost planning implementation. Utilities must file annual ten-year projections of loads and supply resources and a report on DSM activities (LBL/NARUC at A-52).

(c) No environmental review statute.

Ohio

(a) Review of integrated resource plans includes a category for qualitative consideration of environmental impact costs. A Power Siting Board must determine that new resources have the minimum adverse environmental impact, considering the nature and economics of alternatives (LBL/NARUC at A-53).

(b) Integrated resource plans must be filed biennially, with formal proceedings at least once every five years. Alternatives must be considered to meet a twenty-year forecast of demand. All reasonable and practical supply and demand options must be considered. Electricity is 90% from coal, 8% from nuclear (LBL/NARUC at A-53).

(c) No environmental review statute.

Oklahoma

(a) The Oklahoma Commission gives trash-burning facilities an "energy conservation incentive rate, justified to avoid the loss of energy currently being buried in landfills." Steward, The Law of Cogeneration in Oklahoma, Pub. Util. Fort. (Nov. 27, 1986) at 25; Bidding Farewell at 1041; LBL/NARUC at A-55.

(b) No least-cost planning (EPRI at 35), but an aggressive DSM program. Electricity half from coal, half from gas. No capacity needs (LBL/NARUC at A-55). One utility has been allowed to ratebase conservation financial incentives. See Raid at 15.

(c) No environmental review statute.

Oregon

(a) The Oregon PUC requires that environmental externalities be recognized in the development of each utility's plan, quantified to the greatest extent practicable," with cost ranges to be submitted where quantification is difficult. Order No. 89-507 Before the Public Utility Commission of Oregon - UM 180, Ore. PUC, April 20, 1989. Utilities are to value externalities. Pacific Power and Light plan includes a combustion adder of 10 Mils/kWh to fossil resources. State law, SB 576 (1989), requires development of a strategy to reduce greenhouse gases 20% from 1988 levels by 2005, for implementation in 1991. An Act Relating to Global Warming, Ore. Rev. Stats. §.469.60. (LBL/NARUC at A-56).

(b) In addition to the recently instituted state planning process, the Northwest Power Planning Council (NWPPC) engages in least-cost planning efforts. The NWPPC has indirect authority over 20% of Oregon's electricity (EPRI at 35-36). No capacity needs. Electricity mostly hydro, largely from Bonneville Power Authority (LBL/NARUC at A-57).

(c) No environmental review statute.

Pennsylvania

(a) No explicit incorporation. A PUC order requires DSM evaluation considering unspecified social concerns where the cost/benefit ratio is near or less than one. Pa. Bulletin, V. 14, n. 50, Pa. PSC, Dec. 15. 1984. Some utilities use externalities qualitatively in the screening process (LBL/NARUC at A-58).

(b) PUC regulations and a 1986 state law require annual integrated resource plans with only informal public review. Pa. Stat. Ann. tit. 66, § 524 (Purdon Supp. 1989); EPRI at 36. Annual plans must evaluate supply and demand options and propose least-cost plan, but PUC has no authority over them. Supply and demand bidding is under consideration. Electricity 66% from coal, 27% nuclear. No capacity is needed (LBL/NARUC at A-58,59).

(c) No environmental review statute.

Rhode Island

(a) No present consideration of environmental externalities, but PUC has announced its intent to do so in review of utility plans, and the largest utility, Narragansett Electric Co. which supplies 70% of R.I. power is planning consideration in its 1991 resource plan (LBL/NARUC at A-60).

(b) A Least-Cost Planning Committee oversees least-cost planning (EPRI at 37) and collaborative DSM design (Conservation Law Foundation). A statute requires that two-year demand forecasts include consideration of conservation and DSM measures, "but have no enforcement measure." (EPRI at 37). Plans must be filed biannually with the PUC.

R.I. imports most of its power. It has an aggressive conservation strategy for meeting future needs (LBL/NARUC at A-60).

(c) No environmental review statute.

South Carolina

(a) No consideration of environmental externalities. (LBL/NARUC at A-62).

(b) The PSC began least-cost planning proceedings in 1987. A siting law requires environmental consideration in planning and approval of resources. Electricity is 80% nuclear, 20% mainly from coal. Peaking capacity will be needed in the early 1990s (LBL/NARUC at A-60).

(c) No environmental review statute.

South Dakota

(a) No consideration of environmental externalities (LBL/NARUC at A-64).

(b) No statewide least cost planning, but some multi-jurisdictional utilities submit plans in neighboring states (EPRI at 38). Electricity is 70% from coal, the rest mostly hydro. Both base and peak capacity are needed (LBL/NARUC at A-64).

(c) S.D. Codified Laws Ann. §§ 34A-9-1 to 34A-9-13 (1986)<u>See</u> Robinson at 266.

Tennessee

(a), (b) The PSC regulates only 172 MW of power; the remainder of the state's needs are supplied through the Tennessee Valley Authority (TVA). (EPRI at 38).

(c) No environmental review statute.

Texas

(a) The Texas Public Utility Regulatory Act requires consideration of environmental externalities in granting Certificates of Convenience & Necessity, without quantification (LBL/NARUC at A-65).

(b) "Forecasting, avoided cost, and energy efficiency processes combine to approximate an integrated planning process." (EPRI at 39) Utilities are required to file biennial ten-year supply and energy efficiency plans. Filing deficiencies have resulted in rate of return penalties. Electricity is 46% gas, 43% coal. No capacity needs (LBL/NARUC at A-65,66) A 1983 statute requires that load, capacity, and energy efficiency plans be filed on a ten-year basis. Texas Civ. Stats. Ann., Art. 1446 (c), § 16 (c) (Vernon Supp. 1990).

(c) No environmental review statute.

Utah

(a) Utah Power/Pacificorp have filed a resource plan considering environmental externalities pursuant to PUC-established Least Cost Planning Docket No. 90-2035-01 (LBL/NARUC at A-67).

(b) Least-cost planning: see (a) above. The state's two largest utilities integrate their planning. (Id.)

(c) State of Utah Exec. Order (August 27, 1974) See Robinson at 267.

Vermont

(a) The Public Service Board (PSB) recently ordered as a rebuttable presumption, use of a 5% adder to supply resources to represent environmental externality costs and a 10% credit to DSM resources to represent their reduced risk. It opened a proceeding to better determine environmental costs for the adder. The PSB also ordered a revenue adjustment mechanism to separate profits from sales, an "Account Correcting for Efficiency," (ACE), similar to California's ERAM. Investigation Into Least-Cost Investments, Energy Efficiency, Conservation, and Management of Demand for Energy, Docket No. 5270, Vt. PSB. Order of April 16, 1990. Environmental externalities are also at issue in current dockets under the siting statute. Vt. Stat. Ann. tit. 30 § 248 (1986 & Supp. 1989); Re Certificate of Public Good for Contract with Hydro-Quebec, Docket No. 5330, Order entered 21 August 1989 (Vt. PSB).

(b) The Department of Public Service prepares a twenty-year electrical energy plan for the state which is reviewed every five years and, in part, annually. Development of the plan takes into account preservation of environmental quality and reduction of demand through conservation. Vt. Stat. Ann. tit. 30 § 202 (1986 & Supp. 1989). Some utilities are involved in collaborative DSM planning. See Vt. Stat. Ann. tit. 30 § 209(d)(1986 & Supp. 1989). Electricity is 40% from nuclear, 28% hydro, 20% coal, the rest oil, gas and biomass. DSM is to meet future needs (LBL/NARUC at A-69).

(c) No environmental review statute.

Virginia

(a) According to LBL/NARUC at A-71, no consideration of environmental externalities. However, the Virginia State Corporation Commission (SCC) has required a 15% increase in avoided cost payments to QFs, stating: "...theassociated costs which can be avoided are societal and environmental in nature. Such costs are not borne directly by the utility but by the public as a whole...[and must] be addressed in fixing avoided cost rates." Virginia Elec. & Power Co., 71 Pub. Util. Rep. (PUR)4th 160, 168 (1985); See also, Re Potomac Edison Co., Docket # PUE870082, 95 PUR 4th 1 (Va.S.C.C. June 14, 1988).

(b) Least cost planning includes biennially filed twenty-year plans which integrate supply and demand-side sources (EPRI at 40). Statute requires SCC to review plants over 100 MW but does not explicitly include environmental criteria. Va. Code Ann. § 56-234.4

(1986). Electricity is 65% from coal, 25-30% nuclear, the rest hydro, oil and gas. Additional capacity is needed (LBL/NARUC at A-71).

(c) Va. Code Ann. §§ 10.1-1200,10.1-1208(1989) requires environmental impact reviews for all state projects costing $100,000or more. See, Robinson at 267, 302.

Washington

(a) A Washington statute awards a 2% incentive rate of return for conservation if a utility's DSM costs are below the cost of nuclear or fossil fuels. Raid at 9-12. Bidding rules treat as a part of risk evaluation consideration of environmental externalities (LBL/NARUC at A-72). About 50% of Washington's electricity comes from the Bonneville Power Administration (BPA) which is required to consider environmental externalities under federal law (EPRI at 41).

(b) A 1987 Utilities and Transportation Commission (UTC) rule requires that utilities meet load with a least- cost mix of demand and supply and establishes a methodology for utility biennial resource plans pursuant to UTC's general authority (EPRI at 41). Bidding is required for QFs, IPPs and DSM. Electricity is primarily from hydro. No new capacity need (LBL/NARUC at A-72).

(c) Wash. Rev. Code Ann. §§ 43.21C.010- 43.21C.910(West 1983 & Supp. 1989) (applies to any project requiring state approval or any state action); Wash. Admin. Code § 197-11; See Robinson at 267, 302.

West Virginia

(a) No consideration of environmental externalities (LBL/NARUC at A-74).

(b) Least cost planning is under development. Under state statutes, ten-year supply and demand forecasts must be developed by the PSC annually (EPRI at 42). Sources conflict as to the need for capacity. Compare EPRI at 42 (surplus) with LBL/NARUC at A-74 (need). Both base and peak capacity needed. Electricity is almost 100% coal-based (LBL/NARUC at A-74).

Wisconsin

(a) Wisconsin's integrated planning process includes both qualitative consideration of environmental externalities and a 15% non-combustion credit to non-fossil resources or adder for such resources. A proceeding is exploring externalities valuation. The PSC has also ordered utilities to develop resource plans based on a sensitivity analysis that reduces CO_2 emissions to 80% of 1985 levels by 2000. Re Advance Plans, Docket 05-EP-5, 102 P.U.R. 4th 245 (Wisc. PUC April 6, 1989).

(b) Development of least-cost planning began in 1976 under 1975 plant siting legislation which required twenty-year forecasts and evaluation of alternate resources. Electricity is 60% from coal, 30% nuclear (LBL/NARUC at A-75).

(c) Wis. Stat. Ann. § 1.11 (West 1986 & Supp. 1989); Wis. Admin. Code § NR 150.01-40(Wisconsin Department of Natural Resources Rules). Each agency adopts its own implementing regulations. See also, Robinson at 268-269, 302-303. Wisconsin has one of the nation's strongest state acid rain control laws, requiring 50% reductions from 1980 levels by 1993. Wis. Stat. Ann. § 144.385 to 144.389 (West 1989).

Wyoming

(a) PSC has started to review consideration of environmental externalities including sulphur oxides and carbon dioxide (LBL/NARUC at A-77).

(b) No least cost planning (EPRI at 43). Electricity is 80% from coal, the balance from hydro. No capacity is needed. (LBL/NARUC at A-77).

(c) No environmental review statute.

H. STATE-BY-STATE SURVEY SOURCES

Barakat, Howard & Chamberlin, Inc., The Quantification of Externalities for Demand-Side and Supply-Side Resource Options: A Preliminary Study, Appendix, prepared for New England Electric Service, February 15, 1989.

Brick, S., Strategies and Methods for Incorporating Environmental Concerns Into Utility Planning and Utility Regulatory Decision-Making, MSB Energy Associates, Middleton, WI (October 2, 1989) [cited as Brick].

Cohen, S., J. Eto, C. Goldman, J. Beldock, G. Crandall, A Survey of State PUC Activities to Incorporate Environmental Externalities into Electric Utility Planning and Regulation, LBL, University of California, draft of May, 1990, Appendix A [cited as LBL/NARUC].

Electric Power Research Institute (EPRI), Status of Least-Cost Planning in the United States, prepared by Barakat, Howard, & Chamberlin, Inc. EPRI EM-6133, Palo Alto, CA (December 1988) [cited as EPRI].

Koomey, J., Comparative Analysis of Monetary Estimates of External Costs Associated with Combustion of Fossil Fuels, Lawrence Berkeley Laboratory, LBL-28313, March, 1990.

Reid, M., Ratebasing of Utility Conservation and Load Management Programs: Final Report, sponsored by Northeast Utilities, Washington, DC Alliance to Save Energy, (December 1988) [cited as Raid].

Roach, C., E. Kahn, D. Modisette, Electric Resources and Environmental Impacts: Draft Phase I Report, Joint Committee on Energy Regulation and the Environment, California, April, 1990.

Robinson, N., ed., Environmental Impact Assessment Proceedings of a Conference on the Preparation and Review of Environmental Impact Statements, held at West Point, New York on November 16-18 1987, in Albany, NY, New York State Bar Association (1989) [cited as Robinson].

Vanderlindin, B., "Bidding Farewell to the Social Costs of Electricity Production : Pricing Alternative Energy Under the Public Utility Regulatory Policies Act", The Journal of Corporation Law, Summer 1988, pp. 1011 et. seq.

XI. CONCLUSION

XI. CONCLUSION

The Executive Summary of this report contains the major findings and conclusions of this report. This section is intended merely to provide some parting thoughts on the present and future status of externality costing.

Determining the environmental externality costs of electric utility operations is a monumental task, and it is clear that a great deal more work remains to be done. This report addresses just a piece of the task, excluding front end and control costs. It is a literature review and analysis, not pretending to ascertain definitive costing figures. Nonetheless it is a start on a very important quest. It hopefully will be of value to future research to more definitively determine environmental externality cost.

In order for legislators and utility regulators to establish utility groundrules for the selection of resources at the least societal cost, including environmental costs, the external societal damage costs of their operations must be ascertained. Ignoring these costs, as is presently done in many jurisdictions, effectively sets the value of these externalities costs at zero, a clearly inaccurate value and one which leads to utility investment in resources which impose very significant human health and environmental costs upon society. This report gives the bases on which these environmental costs can be calculated and provides a beginning for ascertaining some of the values.

The most surprising and heartening information uncovered is that environmental externality costs are being addressed or are under consideration in more than half the states, with seven states having sought to quantify them for use in planning and/or bidding. In light of the difficulty of the quantification task, this is greatly encouraging. However, it also presents a challenge, since it means that there will be a rapidly growing demand for reliable externality cost figures and analyses. It is a good indication of the importance attached to the subject by state legislatures and, to a much greater extent, by utility regulatory commissions and is a call to action for researchers in this field.

In view of this considerable state interest, it is surprising that no action has been taken at the federal level, except by the Bonneville Power Administration. FERC not only has failed to address externalities, but also is still pondering whether to include DSM in its Notices of Proposed Rulemaking on bidding and avoided costs. The action of the states will hopefully spur incorporation of externality cost issues in federal energy policy.

A major omission found in current state treatment of environmental externalities is failure to address the costs of existing plants. Since existing plants, particularly older coal and oil-fired plants, not required to meet federal New Source Performance Standards, are the major source of utility-created environmental costs. Failure to include them results in incomplete accounting for the environmental costs of electricity. Inclusion of the environmental costs of existing plants could be accomplished by requiring environmental dispatch or by including existing plants in bidding and least cost planning. To make addressing these costs more acceptable to utilities, provisions could be made for the retention of appropriate costs of displaced existing power plants in the rate base, at least for some period of time.

The report finds that the most effective way to treat environmental costs is for all utilities and their regulatory commissions to address these costs quantitatively in planning, bidding and other resource selection. Damage costs are found to be most effective where adequate studies are available and use of control costs, readily available in most instances, may be used where damage cost studies are inadequate.

To adequately determine the environmental costs of electricity, priority should be given at the federal and state levels to research on these issues. The report identifies some of the principal (and very substantial) research needs in the areas addressed.

XII. GLOSSARY

XII. GLOSSARY

Average kilowatt (aKw)	Equivalent to one kilowatt-hour over all hours of the year (8760 kWh).
Average megawatt (aMw)	Equivalent to one megawatt-hour over all hours of the year (8760 mWh).
Avoided cost	Similar to opportunity cost; usually used to refer to the cost of new capacity which may be deferred as a result of some resource action.
Actual risk or Actuarial risk	The objective probability of some event determined by engineering, statistical, or other means; distinguished from perceived risk (see below).
Benefit	The value of a good or service to a consumer; the increase in welfare to an individual as a result of a good or service; a decrease in cost.
Capacity	The maximum power that a machine or system can produce or carry under specified conditions; usually expressed in kilowatts or megawatts.
Catastrophic outcome or catastrophic risk	An extremely high cost event or outcome; usually characterized by low probability; e.g., nuclear power plant accident.
Common property resource	Natural assets characterized by common ownership such that no property rights are clearly defined; e.g., the atmosphere and oceans.
Construction	The building of or installation of an energy resource such as a power plant.
Consumptive use	A consumer benefit in which the resource providing the benefits is altered or destroyed by the act of consumption; e.g., the taking of sport fish.
Contingent valuation method	A technique for measuring the benefits or costs associated with a resource or resource action; the technique relies on establishing hypothetical markets and querying respondents as to the value they place on the resource.
Control cost	The cost of avoiding or reducing an environmental effect at the source, usually applied to emissions; e.g., the cost of scrubbers to reduce SOx emissions.

CO_2 — Carbon dioxide; a greenhouse gas produced when fossil fuels are combusted.

Coping cost — The cost of adapting to new or changed circumstances; e.g., the cost of medical treatment to (attempt to) restore good health.

Cost — The foregone benefits associated with the consumption of a good or service; a reduction in benefits.

Cost effectiveness — A test of economic efficiency such that a given level of goods and services are produced or consumed at the lowest cost.

Decommissioning — The activities involved in removing a plant from service, dismantling the plant, and restoring the site to be compatible with other industrial uses.

Direct costs — The net change in value associated with production, consumption, or exchange of an economic good or service.

Discount rate — The interest rate used to convert future values to present values; a measure of the preference for receiving a benefit now rather than in the future.

Dispersal — The path taken by a pollutant emitted to the environment, from emission to final deposition.

Downstream cost — Environmental costs occurring after plant construction or plant operation; typically cost of emissions; these are the costs for which values have been derived in this report; as distinguished from "upstream costs."

Economic damage — The value of lost income or lost net economic product resulting from some activity, expressed in dollars.

Economic efficiency — Either 1) producing the maximum amount of some product at a given cost; or, 2) producing a given amount of some product at the lowest cost. Generally, economic efficiency means maximizing net benefits or minimizing net costs.

Emission — The discharge of some pollutant to the environment; e.g., smokestack emissions of sulfur dioxide.

Energy resource — An electric generating plant or demand side measure that produces or saves electric energy or capacity.

Environmental benefit — Any change in an environmental good or service that increases net benefits to society, either by increasing quantity of the good or service or quality of the good or service.

Environmental cost — Any change in an environmental good or service that decreases net benefits to society, either by decreasing quantity of the good or service or quality of the good or service.

Environmental effect — Any change in an environmental good or service or natural resource as a result of the construction, operation, or decommissioning of an energy resource.

Environmental Dispatch — The scheduling and operation of utility power plants according to their full variable cost of operation, including the variable environmental costs of plant operation.

Environmental good or service — Any natural endowment that provides social benefits; used interchangeably with natural resources.

Environmental linkage — Any stage in the process chain from environmental intrusion (or emission) to final effect, including valuation; e.g., emission, transport, exposure, or response.

Environmental risk — The set of all possible responses of the ecosystem to effects created by an energy resource, including the expected value of the response and its variability.

Equity — The concept of the fairness of the distribution of income; in contrast to efficiency.

Escalation — (See Real escalation.)

Existence benefit — The economic value to an individual from just knowing that an environmental good or service exists, even if the individual has no intent of ever using the good directly.

Expected value — A statistical measure of central tendency based on the sum of the value of all possible outcomes multiplied by their probabilities; approximately equivalent to the arithmetic mean.

Exposure — The subjection of some population (of animals, crops, vegetation, people, etc.) to a pollutant or other substance that could potentially cause a physical change in members of the population.

Exposure-response function — A mathematical relationship expressing an estimate of the number and kind of physical effects resulting from exposure to some quantity of a substance; typically expressed as the number of deaths (or some other response) resulting from an annual exposure to some pollutant (typically given in micrograms per cubic meter per year.)

Externality — A residual or side effect of an economic activity in which a benefit or cost is conferred upon a party who is not a party to the original transaction either as a producer, consumer, or agent; e.g.,air pollution from a coal-fired power plant.

Fixed costs — Costs which are incurred regardless of the variability in the level of output of an energy resource; e.g.,the construction costs of a power plant.

Fuel cycle — The sequence of activities and events associated with fuel use, including the discovery; extraction; enrichment, fabrication, conversion, refinement or other treatment; transport; storage; combustion; and disposal of the fuel.

Global effect — Any environmental effect not limited to the locality in which the effect is created; may also be called a transboundary effect; e.g.,acid rain and greenhouse effect.

Generic — Referring to a prototype or average resource or effect; as opposed to site-specific.

Health risks — The change in the probability distribution of morbidity or mortality as a result of an environmental intrusion, pollutant, or other effect.

Hedonic pricing — A technique for measuring the implicit price of resource attributes or characteristics associated with an environmental good; the price of the (non-market) good is given as a function of the quantities of various characteristics such that the coefficients on those characteristics represent implicit prices.

Indirect costs — The changes associated with ensuing rounds of production, consumption, and exchange after the primary or direct costs have been initiated; for example, increases in local retail sales as a result of an improvement in a recreation resource in the locality.

Internal costs — Costs that are included in the price of an economic good or service.

Joint products — Two or more economic goods or services produced during the same process; e.g., the simultaneous production of electricity and thermal power.

Kilowatt (kW)	An electrical unit of power, or capacity, equal to 1000 watts.
Kilowatthour (kWh)	An electrical unit of energy equal to 1000 watts of power applied for one hour.
Levelized costs	A comparative measure of resource costs derived by computing the present value of a resource's cost--including capital, financing, operating costs, and other costs--converted into a stream of equal annual payments using a discount rate and then dividing the annual payment by the average annual energy produced or saved by the resource; expressed in cents per kWh.
Local effect	An environmental change which affects local populations only; as distinguished from a global effect.
Megawatt (MW)	An electrical unit of power, or capacity, equal to one million (1,000,000) watts.
Megawatthour (MWh)	An electrical unit of energy equal to one million (1,000,000) watts of power applied for one hour.
Mill	A monetary unit equal to one one-thousandth (1/1000) of a dollar or one tenth (1/10) of a cent.
Mitigation cost	The cost of reducing or eliminating the severity of an environmental impact; may also refer to the cost of replacing the loss of an environmental good; e.g., the cost of providing additional recreational opportunities to offset the loss of another recreational opportunity.
NO_x	Nitrogen oxides emitted by fossil fuel plants as a result of combusting fuels; a pollutant.
Nominal cost	A cost expressed in current dollars from which the effect of inflation has not been removed.
Non-quantifiable	Referring to an environmental effect that cannot be measured or for which any measurement is inappropriate or meaningless; e.g., a change in the aesthetic condition of an environmental good.
Non-market goods	An economic good or service which is not traded in a market place and, therefore, has no observable price, creating the need for imputing a price through some valuation technique; e.g., wilderness recreation.
Non-consumptive use	An activity whereby an environmental good is enjoyed by a consumer, but no physical change in the good occurs; e.g., bird watching.

Occupational risk — A health risk faced by a worker associated with activities in her workplace.

Operation — The stage of an energy resource's life during which it is producing electric power.

Opportunity cost — The value of benefits or activities forgone as a result of the choice to produce, consume, or exchange an economic good or service.

Perceived risk — The environmental risk an individual believes is associated with an energy resource; a subjective assessment of the probability and magnitude of a potential environmental consequence; as distinguished from an actual or actuarial risk.

Perspective — The point of view from which environmental costs are measured; the determination of whose and what costs to include in an environmental cost analysis.

Present value — The worth today of a stream of future benefits and costs; the discounted value of a stream of benefits and costs; used to compare future costs and benefits on an equal basis.

Priced — The circumstance in which the market price associated with an environmental good is observable; e.g., crops are priced goods.

Priceable — The circumstance in which the price of an environmental good can be inferred or imputed by using non-market valuation techniques; e.g., wilderness recreation is priceable.

Private good — A good characterized by property rights which are held by an individual or firm and which can be exchanged voluntarily in the market.

Property right — The identification and assignment of ownership rights to an environmental good or service; implies the owner has a right to current circumstances and must be compensated for adverse changes in current circumstances.

Public good — An environmental good characterized by common property rights; a good for which the enjoyment obtained by one individual consuming the good does not diminish the enjoyment obtained by any other individual; e.g., clean air.

Quantifiable — Referring to the ability to measure the change in an environmental good or service or the effect on an environmental good; e.g., carbon dioxide emissions from a power plant can be measured or quantified.

Rate of time preference — The degree to which an individual or society prefers receiving a benefit today as opposed to receiving the same benefit at some time in the future; a factor in determining the appropriate discount rate for deriving present values.

Ratepayers — Utility customers who pay the utility's costs for service through electric power rates.

Real dollars — Dollar values from which the effect of inflation has been removed such that the dollars are constant with respect to a given year.

Real escalation — The rate at which the real dollar value of a benefit or cost changes over time; the cost increase of a good or service over and above the rate of inflation.

Revealed Preference — The derivation of an economic value by observing behavior from which preferences are inferred; e.g., deriving recreational site values by travel costs which reveal how much recreators are willing to pay to recreate at a site.

Resource — Any economic good or service; typically used to refer to a natural asset such as land; also used to refer to an energy producing or energy saving measure such as a coal plant or conservation measure. (See Energy resource.)

Response — How an environmental good or service changes as a result of exposure to some pollutant or other environmental intrusion.

Risk — The set of all possible responses, and their associated probabilities, to an environmental intrusion.

Site-specific — Refers to environmental effects which depend on the characteristics of the population associated with the locale of a resource and on the characteristics of the locale, itself.

SO_x — Sulfur oxides; a precursor to sulfates and acidic depositions; formed when fuel (oil or coal) containing sulfur is combusted; a regulated pollutant associated with adverse health effects.

Social cost — The full cost of an energy resource including both internalized costs such as labor and fuel as well as external costs such as environmental costs; a perspective from which all costs borne by society as a whole are accounted for.

System costs	The total costs of producing or saving energy, including capital costs, operating and maintenance costs, fuel costs, transmission and distribution costs, and external costs.
Transport	The pathway traveled by a pollutant in the environment subsequent to emission from an energy resource.
Transfers	The shifting of income from one economic agent to another without the creation of net economic costs or benefits; e.g., taxes.
Travel cost	A technique for inferring the value of an environmental good or service based on a derived demand curve as a function of the cost of traveling to a site.
Uncertainty	The inaccuracy inherent in an estimate because of errors in measurement or in statistical specification of relationships.
Upstream Costs	Costs occurring prior to plant construction or operation; typically refers to costs during materials or fuel extraction, fabrication, or transport; as distinguished from "downstream" costs.
Valuation	The monetization of changes in environmental goods and services.
Valuation method or technique	The procedure selected for monetizing changes in environmental goods and services.
Value	The net economic benefit associated with a good or service.
Variable costs	Costs that change as the level of output changes; e.g., operating and fuel costs.
WTC	Willingness to be Compensated; the amount of compensation required to induce the owner of a good or service to relinquish property rights to that good or service, or to give up part of the good or service.
WTP	Willingness to Pay; the amount that an individual would pay to acquire the property rights to a good or service or to achieve a different amount or quality of the good or service.

XIII. BIBLIOGRAPHY

XIII. BIBLIOGRAPHY

1. Introduction

This bibliography is the result of an exhaustive search for environmental costing and energy efficiency literature conducted by Professors Richard Ottinger, Susan Babb, and David Wooley, and many student assistants working for the Center for Environmental Legal Studies ("the Center") at Pace University School of Law.[1]

The central purpose of this search was to collect and review all available references pertaining to environmental costing. The search was not intended to cover the field of adverse impacts of energy production. Rather, the search was limited our efforts to studies which appeared useful in valuing environmental impacts of electric power generation. Although time and funding limitations did not allow a critique of the entire literature collection, a considerable number of the entries in the bibliography do include abstracts. For this reason, the bibliography has been divided into two parts. Part one includes all annotated references, while part two covers the remainder of the unannotated references. Approximately three-quarter of the entries in the bibliography are cited in the externalities report itself.

The student assistants used two primary methods for collecting data--university library collections and computer database searches. For the former, students conducted most of their research at the Pace University School of Law library, but also pursued research at the State University of New York (SUNY) at Purchase, Columbia University, Orange and Rockland Utilities and the New York Public Libraries.

At Pace University the students made use of law review journals, state and federal government documents, Office of Technology Assessment (OTA) reports, Electric Power Research Institute (EPRI) studies, and a large number of interlibrary loan requests. At Columbia University students were given access to the engineering library and NTIS collection. At SUNY Purchase scientific documents and periodicals were obtained using a computerized retrieval system.

The Center itself possesses an extensive collection of environmental costing materials much of which was obtained from the authors by Richard Ottinger's personal request and by the efforts of Professors Susan Babb and David Wooley, and the student assistants. Additional information was received through personal communication with the authors by telephone. Some of these communications are cited in the externalities report but have not been entered in the Procite™ bibliography.

Much of the scientific and technical materials used in the bibliography were found through online searching of data bases. Students searched LEXIS™ (produced by Mead Data Central) and Westlaw™ (produced by West Publishing Company) for legal material, and NEXIS™ (also by Mead Data Central) for some of the scientific documentation. Student assistants also had direct access to the Electric Power

---

[1] The bibliography has been created using the Procite™ computerized bibliography program, and converted to WordPerfect™ for presentation and publishing.

Database, produced by the Electric Power Research Institute (EPRI), through special arrangement with the producer.

Most of the Pace library staff online searching was performed through DIALOG™, an assembly of databases produced by Dialog Information Services.[2] The staff also used the Research Libraries Information Network (RLIN). This database provided access to bibliographic records of the holdings of most large research libraries in the United States. Unlike the DIALOG databases, RLIN contains library cataloging of books but does not contain indexes or abstracts of individual periodical articles. RLIN's subject access was used to compile lists of books on a given subject.

In the case of the DIALOG searches the results were most often merely an abstract of the actual document. In the case of RLIN, the results were even more sparse, essentially an electronic version of a library catalog card. Therefore, once a relevant document was identified, student research assistants either traveled to the library containing the document, or obtained it through an interlibrary loan. In most cases, these loan requests were processed via the Pace law library's access to the Online Cataloging Library Consortium (OCLC).

Decisions on the relevance of data retrieved from online searching and the task of digesting this material was performed by the student research assistants, not by the Law Library staff. In sum, the combined efforts of the student researchers and the Law Library staff made possible the thorough review of the pertinent environmental externalities literature.

[2] Databases accessed through in DIALOG include EnergylineTM and EnvirolineTM, by R.R. Bowker; Environmental Bibliography, by the Environmental Studies Institute; NTIS by the National Technical Information Service; DOE Energy, by the U.S. Department of Energy; Pollution Abstracts, by Cambridge Scientific Abstracts; Economic Literature Index, by the American Economic Association; Conference Papers Index, by Cambridge Scientific Abstracts; and Dissertation Abstracts Online, by University Microfilms International.

Searches were also done in such databases as ABI/InformTM, by UMI/Data Courier and PTS Prompt, by Predicasts. Such databases were most effective in identifying information of a public policy nature.

A. ANNOTATED BIBLIOGRAPHY

Ackerman, Bruce and W.T. Hassler, Clean Coal/Dirty Air: Or How the Clean Air Act Became a Multibillion-Dollar Bail Out for High-Sulfur Coal Producers and What Should Be Done About It, New Haven, Yale University Press, 1981.
Authors discuss the evolution of the Clean Air Act of 1970 and its impact on the future of coal-burning power plants. Types of coal-cleaning and coal-scrubbing are discussed in relation to the development and administration of the Clean Air Act of 1970. Discusses effect on environmental protection and practicality of installing coal-cleaning technologies.

Agriculture and Transportation Subcommittee of the Joint Economic Committee, The Chernobyl Disaster: Implications for World Food Security and the U.S. Farm Economy, 99th Cong., 2nd sess., 5 May 1986.
This Congressional hearing discusses the impact of the Chernobyl accident on the world food supply and the U.S. farm economy. The world food supply has not been endangered because of Chernobyl. The Soviet food supply has been affected slightly, but no more than it would have been affected by adverse weather conditions. Experts predict about a 10% loss in the Soviet wheat supply. The Soviet Union then has to import a portion of its wheat and other foods from other countries, including the United States. Experts predict that the U.S. has a received a marginal benefit because of the Soviet Union's need to acquire a small amount of foodstuffs from outside countries.

Aigner, Dennis J., Externalities in Electricity Production, Sierra Club Economics Committee, September 1987. An externality is created when the actions of an economic agent affect the welfare of some other agent not through the market system (that is, no cost is incurred or price paid). This paper discusses the application of externalities to the production of electricity. Discussion includes measurement of externalities, of policy implications such as taxes and subsidies, and creation of markets to deal with externalities.

Aiken, Richard and W. Taylor, An Overview of the Proposed Natural Resource Damage Assessment Regulations, RCRA Amendment Experience, Svitek, Laura L. bibliography: 353-359.
This paper describes the natural resource damage assessment regulations which were promulgated by the DOI. The regulations are to be used for assessing damages to natural resources which have been injured from a hazardous release.

Allan, R.J., A. Murdoch and A. Sudar,(1983), "An Introduction to the Niagara River/Lake Ontario Pollution Problem", Journal of Great Lakes Research, 9(2), pp. 111-117.
This is a basic overview of the pollution in the Lake Ontario region. Describes the chemical contaminants from the industrial sources. Includes a discussion of the public viewpoint on this area.

Alliance to Close Indian Point, "What is Low Level Radioactive Waste?", Counter-Point:The Newsletter of the Alliance to Close Indian Point, Ossining, New York, Spring 1989.
This article considers redefining "low-levelwaste," because many parts of a nuclear plant which are included under LLW are actually highly radioactive.

American Solar Energy Society (A.S.E.S.)Roundtable 89, Nicklas, Michael, Chairman, Spring 1989; Boulder, CO.

The A.S.E.S. Roundtable meets periodically to discuss various topics of current environmental concern. The 1989 Roundtable compilation includes: global warming, air pollution, acid rain, hydroelectric environmental impact, indoor air pollution, nuclear waste and decommissioning, military subsidies, policy directions, and solar. Of particular interest is the nuclear waste/decommissioning section.

American Council for an Energy-Efficient Economy (ACEEE), Geller, Howard S., E.L. Miller, M.R. Ledbetter and P.M. Miller, Acid Rain and Electricity Conservation, Washington, DC, ACEEE and Energy Conservation Coalition; June 1987.

This study demonstrates that cost effective, more efficient end-use technologies can reduce electricity consumption in the major acid rain emitting area of the midwest by 26% without lowering the level of energy services. The study uses an integrated analysis to review electricity conservation opportunities, electricity supply and acid rain abatement in the East Central Area Reliability Council Region. This region is very dependent on high-sulfur coal. The study proposes legislation which would give states and utilities an incentive to pursue efficiency investments as part of an acid rain abatement program.

Amos, Kenna, Hazardous Waste Cleanup: The Preliminaries, CivilEngineering/ASCE. Svitek, Laura L. bibliography; August, 1985, pp. 40-43.

Discusses the hazardous waste problem at Niagara Falls, N.Y. and the little remedial action work that has been achieved in this area. A brief action plan is discussed, consisting of survey and study programs.

Argonne National Laboratory, Energy and Environmental Systems Division, Physical Environmental Sciences Section, Argonne, IL, Emission Factor for Several Toxic Air Pollutants from Fluidized-Bed Combustion of Coal [Work sponsored by U.S. Department of Energy, Office of Fossil Energy], by Albert E. Smith.

This study compares the trace element emissions from Atmospheric Fluidized Bed Combustion (AFBC) and Pressurized Fluidized Bed Combustion (PFBC), with those from conventional combustion of coal. The trace elements considered are: Antimony, Arsenic, Beryllium, Cadmium, Chromium, Cobalt, Copper, Lead, Manganese, Mercury, Nickel, Vanadium, and Zinc. This report concludes that while AFBC offers a lower potential for these trace elements, PFBC offers a greater advantage for lowering SO2 and NOx emissions.

Argonne National Laboratory, by Albert E. Smith, Energy and Environmental Systems Division, Physical Environmental Sciences Section, Emission Factors for Several Toxic Air Pollutants from Fluidized-Bed Combustion of Coal, U.S. Department of Energy; Assistant Secretary for Fossil Energy, Office of Fossil Energy. This study compares the trace element emissions from Atmospheric Fluidized Bed Combustion (AFBC) and Pressurized Fluidized Bed Combustion (PFBC), with those from conventional combustion of coal. The trace elements considered are: Antimony, Arsenic, Beryllium, Cadmium, Chromium, Cobalt, Copper, Lead,Manganese, Mercury, Nickel, Vanadium, and Zinc. The report concludes that while AFBC offers a lower potential for these trace elements, PFBC offers a greater advantage for lowering SO2 and NOx emissions.

Bach, Wilfrid, An Effective Greenhouse Gas Emission Reduction Strategy for the Protection of the Global Climate, Munster, Germany: Center for Applied Climatology and Environmental Studies; 1989. (Energy Climate Environment v. ACE Report No. 35/1989).
A policy proposal is presented that concerns possible allocations of emissions reduction quotas among OECD countries. References.

Bach, Wilfrid, The Endangered Climate, Chapter in Research Report "Energy and Climate Change: What Can Western Europe Do?", edited by Florentin Krause and Wilfrid Bach, Munster, Germany, Center for Applied Climatology and Environmental Studies; 1988. (Energy Climate Environment v. ACE Report No.15/1988).
This study presents a model that estimates the overall climatic warming that may occur by the year 2030. It focuses on five "greenhouse gases," (carbon dioxide, water vapor, methane, nitrous oxide, ozone and the chlorofluorocarbons. It presents annual global emissions figures for NOX, SOX and CO2. It warns that the present warming due to greenhouse gases is disguised by the natural variability of climate and by the ocean which stores roughly 50% of the heat within its interior. By the time global warming is measurable, a certain amount of continued warming is inevitable making a "waitand see" approach extremely dangerous. The study concludes with policy considerations to prevent possible disaster. References.

Bach, Wilfrid, General Circulation Models as Tools in Scenario Analysis for Climatic Impact Assessment, Munster, Germany, Center for Applied Climatology and Environmental Studies, 1988. (Energy Climate Environment; v. ACE Report No. 22/1988).
In order to predict patterns of climatic change in the future, this paper presents the "general air circulation model." This method uses a system of equations that incorporate a circulation model of the atmosphere, a heat and water balance model of the continental surface, and a scheme to incorporate the ocean, glacial ice caps and the biosphere. References.

Bach, Wilfrid, Modelling the Climatic Response to Greenhouse Gases, Munster, Germany: Center for Applied Climatology and Environmental Studies; 1987. (Energy Climate Environment; v. ACE Report No.14/1987).
This report assesses "green house gases" (carbon dioxide, methane, nitric acid, ozone and chlorofluorocarbons). It identifies the burning of fossil fuels as the most important anthropogenic source of these gases. The report presents a modelling approach that facilitates prediction of global warming in discrete terms and will allow policy makers to take rational, preventative steps now rather than using a "wait and see" approach to the problem of global warming.

Bach, Wilfrid, Modelling the Climatic Effects of Trace Gases: Reduction Strategy and Options for a Low Risk Policy, Munster, Germany: Center for Applied Climatology and Environmental Studies; 1988. (Energy Climate Environment v. ACE Report No.16/1988).
This study advocates a preventative policy strategy regarding global warming. It describes the main climate-influencing trace gases, presents some modelling results using past and possible future climatic change, introduces and demonstrates a new strategy to reduce climatic and environmental threats, and ends by giving an overview of the options available for a low risk policy. References.

Bach, Wilfrid, Toward an International Convention for the Protection of the Global Climate: Reduction Strategy, Munster, Germany: Center for Applied Climatology and Environmental Studies, 1989. 29 pages plus tables. (Energy Climate Environment; v. ACE Report No.28/1989).
This paper presents a reduction strategy that would provide a scientific basis for the then upcoming climate protection convention. The individual steps proposed are: assessment of current emission rates by gas and source; assessment of future emission rates by gas and source for a range of trace gas concentrations and surface temperature based on model calculations; setting a permissible ceiling for global warming at 1-2 degrees Centigrade by the year 2100 and more. Tables.

Bach, Wilfrid and H. Scheer, Toward an International Convention for the Protection of the Global Climate: Financial Framework, Munster, Germany: Center for Applied Climatology and Environmental Studies; 1989. 9 pages. (Energy Climate Environment; v. ACE Report No.29/1989).
Note: Prepared for the Second North American Conference on
Preparing for Climatic Change, "A Cooperative Approach," Washington, D.C., December 5-8, 1988. A business deal between industrialized and developing countries is presented. To defray costs from the impacts of the greenhouse gases, the industrialized countries would pay for an emission reduction in the developing countries through a decrease in forest and soil destruction, reforestation, and the use of efficient energy technology and renewables. This plan involves a uniform 0.5 cents/kWh carbon dioxide tax on fossil fuel use in OECD or EC countries amounting to $200 billion and $50 billion, respectively. The revenues, to be put into an international fund, are earmarked for use by the developing countries.

Bates, C.F. III, C.T. Garten, Jr., F.G. Taylor and J.P. Witherspoon, (Oak Ridge National Laboratories, Environmental Sciences Division, The Long-Term Problems of Contaminated Land: Sources, Impacts and Countermeasures, Oak Ridge, Tennessee: Oak Ridge National Laboratories; November 1986; ORNL-6146.
Note: 120 pp.
This report examines the various sources of radiological land contamination and its effect on humans, agriculture, and the environment. Alternatives for decontamination, cleanup, and possible land re-use are also discussed.

Bamoul, William, (1968), "On the Social Rate of Discount", American Economic Review; 68(4): 788-802.
Note: Svitek, Laura L. bibliography.
This article examines the various aspects that must be considered when determining the social rate of discount. Aspects including taxes, externalities, uncertainty and the role of time preference are discussed.

Barnthouse, Lawrence W., R.J. Klauda, D.S. Vaughan and R. Kendall, Science, Law, and Hudson River Power Plants, Bethesda, MD, American Fisheries Society; 1988; c1988; Monograph 4.
Note: 347 pp.
This book was used for obtaining impingement and entrainment losses as a result of water intake on Hudson River power plants.

Bassel, William E., "Capital and Operating Costs of Wet Scrubbers Installed on Coal-Fired Utilities Impacting the East Coast," Journal of the Air Pollution Control Association, March 1988, 38: 327-332.
Note: 6 pp.

This paper is a description of a computer program that uses up-to-date information to determine the cost of installing wet limestone scrubbers at 83 utility sites. The capital costs of this installation for the top 50 sulfur oxide emitting plants will be about $20 billion. Installation of these control devices will result in an increased cost of electricity of an average of 0.88 cents/kwh and a reduction of sulfur oxide emissions from 1980 levels of 7.1 millon tons a year.

Baumol, William J. and W.E. Oates, The Theory of Environmental Policy, 2nd ed. ed. New York: Cambridge University Press; 1988.
Note: Svitek, Laura L. bibliography.
The main focus of this book is on the theory of externalities and government policy options to protect the environment. It explains how market imperfections lead to externalities which require government regulation through direct controls, emission permits, taxes and subsidies.

Begley, Sharon and L. Wright, 1987, "Not Your Average Terrarium," Newsweek, June 1 1988: 60-61.
Note: Svitek, Laura L. bibliography.
Begley and Wright discuss the Biosphere II Project, which is taking place in Arizona. Their main focus is the process of species selection of plants and animals. Scientists are attempting to find compatible species which will help ecosystems to be self-sustaining.

Bennett, Leonard L., "Economic Performance of Nuclear Plants: How competitive?", IAEA Bulletin; Spring 1985: 40-44.
Note: 5 pp.
A critique of the International Atomic Energy Association (IAEA) and other studies which claim that nuclear power is more economically feasible than alternative fuel cycles.

Bentover, Judith D., V. Covello, T. Vincent and J.L. Mumpower, Benefits Assessment: The State of the Art, Boston: D. Reidel Publishing Company, 1986.
Note: Svitek, Laura L. bibliography.
A compliance of well known authors contribute their analysis on the valuation of benefits assessment and general cost/benefit theories. Included is a discussion on the role of cost/benefit analysis in public policy development and environmental regulation. Valuation methods for non-market goods include an overview of CVM, TCM and HPM.

Bland, F. Paul, "Problems of Price and Transportation: Two Proposals to Encourage Competition from Alternative Energy Sources", Harvard Environmental Law Review, 1986; 10, 345-416.
Note: 72 pp.
This article discusses arguments for encouraging competition in the electricity-generating industry, focusing on the success of PURPA. The article discusses the barriers qualifying facilities face in transmitting their energy, including the need for access to wheeling services and the transmission grid. The article contains a well-detailed introduction to the importance of quantifying the external environmental costs of traditional central plant power production. The author advocates incorporating external costs into the PURPA determination of avoided costs.

Bolze, Dorene A. and M.B. Lee, Offshore Oil and Gas Development: Implications for Wildlife in Alaska, Marine Policy; June 1989.
Note: 406 pp. (In press).
This article discusses the risks to the Alaskan environment, birds, fish, and wildlife species from the activities associated with oil and gas development. Table 1 lists environmentally sensitive areas in the Bering Sea; Table 2 discusses the Gulf of Alaska; and Table 3 deals with the Alaskan Arctic. All three Tables describe the significant characteristics of each area, such as types of species, number of species, important fishery area, area where endangered species nest or migrate. The article also discusses treats from oil spills, physical habitat alteration, air and noise pollution, and toxic effluents, and their effect on birds, wetland habitat, fisheries, marine mammals, and terrestrial species.

Bolze, Dorene and M.B. Lee, Environmental Policy Analysts (National Audubon Society), Offshore Oil and Gas Development: The Ecological Effects Beyond the Offshore Platform; 11-14, July 1989.(Proceedings for COASTAL ZONE '89: The Sixth Symposium on Coastal and Ocean Management).
Note: 15 pp.
This paper presents "a comprehensive overview of the known and potential ecological effects from the various aspects of developing offshore oil and gas resources, directly and indirectly affecting wildlife." Oil and other effluents concentrations have a deleterious effect on the natural biotic community. Coastal wetlands and estuary populations are similarly effected. Environmental effects of offshore oil and gas development are assessed, by examining the whole industry as a single process.

Bonneville Power Administration (BPA), Estimating Environmental Costs and Benefits for Five Generating Resources, Final Report: Description of Generic Generating Resources, Their Likely Significant Environmental Effects, and the Economic Value of Those Effects, Prepared by ECO Northwest, Ltd., Shapiro and Associates, Inc., and Seton, Johnson, and Odell, Inc., Shepard C. Buchanan, Project Manager. Portland, OR, BPA, March 1986.
Note: Paginated by section.
This study estimates the value of significant environmental effects likely to accompany the development of cogeneration from biomass, cogeneration from municipal solid waste, geothermal, solar, and wind. The study's purpose was to develop a generic model of environmental costs for these resources which would allow BPA to estimate the future environmental costs in levelized mills per kilowatt-hour, for different facility types, sizes, and locations.

Bonneville Power Administration (BPA), Resource Analysis Documentation: 1987 Resource Strategy, DOE/BP-823, Portland, OR, BPA, May 1987.
Note: 221 pp.
This report discusses the economic effects of several resource alternatives and the impact of each alternative on the Pacific Northwest power system. Included is an examination of the environmental costs of the various types of electric power generation.

Bonneville Power Administration (BPA), Issue Backgrounder: Counting the Costs - How BPA Performs Environmental-Cost Analysis, DOE/BP-405. Portland, OR; June 1985.
Note: 11 pp.

This booklet describes the cost effectiveness analysis which BPA uses to evaluate environmental (or external) costs of power resources and the role public involvement can play in that evaluation. BPA is the first federal agency required to consider environmental costs so explicitly in its planning process.

Boyle, Kevin J. and R.C. Bishop, "Valuing Wildlife in Benefit Costs Analyses: A Case Study Involving Endangered Species", Water Resources Research (American Geophysical Union), May 1987, 23, pp. 943-950. Note: 9 pp.
This article assigns a dollar value to an endangered species. The theory and process of assigning a cost and actual estimates for the Bald Eagle and the Striped Shiner in Wisconsin are given.

Breen, Barry, "CERCLA's Natural Resource Damage Provisions: What Do We Know So Far?," Environmental Law Reporter, 14, 10304.
Note: Svitek, Laura L. bibliography.
Breen argues that CERCLA allows, at a minimum, recovery of the full cost of restoring damaged natural resources. Due to various obstacles, however, full cost recovery is rarely obtained. He believes that Congress did not clearly state its intentions in the Act, and therefore many critical questions are left unanswered.

Breen, Barry, (1983), "Natural Resource Recovery By Federal Agencies - A Roadmap to Avoid Losing Causes of Action," Environmental Law Reporter, 13, 10324-30.
Note: Svitek, Laura L. bibliography.
Breen outlines the natural resource recovery provisions of CERCLA, discussing the time limitations in the statute of limitations. He analyzes the specific costs which are recoverable for natural resource damages. Various Superfund cases are presented.

Bro, Kenneth et al., "Relative Cancer Risks of Chemical Contaminants in the Great Lakes," Environmental Management, 11(4), 495-505.
Note: Svitek, Laura L. bibliography.
This paper analyzes the lifetime cancer risks faced by consumers of sport fish from the Great Lakes. It concludes that consumption of fish from the Great Lakes threatens a higher magnitude of cancer risk than the risk of drinking Great Lakes water.

Bromley, Daniel W., Natural Resource Economics, Boston: Kluwer Nijhoff Publishing; 1986.
Note: Svitek, Laura L. bibliography.
This book examines a wide array of problems associated with natural resource economics. Valuation problems are discussed in detail, as well as externalities. Also discussed is the issue of appropriate government policy.

Brown, Gardner and R. Mendelsohn, "The Hedonic Travel Cost Method," Review of Economics and Statistics, 1984, 66(3), 427-433.
Note: Svitek, Laura L. bibliography.
This article discusses a technique that can be used to assess the amount that users are willing to pay for the individual characteristics of a recreation site. This article explains the method, and then attempts to apply it to Washington State Steelhead Fishing data.

Brown, Tommy L., 1973 New York State Statewide Angler Study, Department of Natural Resources, Cornell University.
Note: Svitek, Laura L. bibliography.
This angler survey was designed to uncover general information regarding anglers in New York. The questionnaire is designed to obtain demographic information, species desirability and angler locations. This may be of use in evaluating recreational natural resources.

Buchanan, Shepard C., Consulting Economist (Bonneville Power Administration (BPA)), Accounting for External Costs of Energy Resources in Utility Least-Cost Planning, (submitted to the Executive Office of Energy Resources) ed.; 1 March 1988.
Note: 16 pp. Plus figures.
This paper outlines the major issues to be addressed in evaluating the external costs in energy resource planning.

Buchanan, Shepard C., Project Officer (Bonneville Power Administration (BPA)), Environmental Coordinator's Office, Office of Power and Resources Management, Environmental Costs and Benefits Case Study: Nuclear Power Plants, Quantification and Economic Valuation of Selected Environmental Impacts/Effects, Portland, Oregon, Nero and Associates; 8 February 1984.
This report focuses on health costs (both as a result of routine power plant operation and accidents), socioeconomic/infrastructure effects, and consumptive use of water associated with plant #2 of the Washington Public Power Supply System. In addition, decommissioning costs are assessed, as well as environmental effects not presently quantifiable, such as stress caused by proximity to a nuclear power plant, and environmental degradation. Of particular note are the methods Buchanan uses in assessing nuclear externalities. Further, the study uses a range of value of life costs, based on several "willingness to be compensated for a loss" evaluations.

Bunyard, Peter, "The Economics of Nuclear Power," The Ecologist, 1986; 16(4/5): 192-197.
Note: 6 pp.
This article criticizes the CEGB's avoidance of the author's previous criticisms concerning his attack on the belief that nuclear power is a source of cheap electricity. (Contains some information on decommissioning).

Cairns, John, The Recovery Process in Damaged Ecosystems, Michigan: Ann Arbor Science Publishers, Inc.; 1980.
Note: Svitek, Laura L. bibliography.
Cairns examines ecosystem recovery, and the feasibility of rehabilitating small ecosystem processes to larger ones. A pertinent chapter discusses the option of rehabilitating and restoring the Great Lakes.

California Air Resources Board, The Benefits of Air Pollution Control in California, Energy and Resource Consultants, Inc., Robert D. Rowe, Project Manager, Boulder, CO, Energy and Resource Consultants; December 1986.
Note: 2 vols.
This study attempts to provide quantitative estimates of economic measures of benefits (or damage) to four air basins in California by controlling air pollution under five air pollution control scenarios. Physical and economic measures of air pollution control benefits are calculated for human health, agriculture, materials

and soiling, forests, and visibilityaesthetics. The focus of the effort was to use the best available literature, data, methods and professional judgment to estimate to the economic measures of air pollution control benefits.

Cannon, James J., The Health Costs of Air Pollution: A Survey of Studies Published 1984-1989, New York, NY, American Lung Association, January 1990. Examines 4 steps in calculating the health costs of air pollution (measuring pollution, counting the population at risk, defining dose-response functions, evaluating the health costs). Discusses various methodologies used evaluating health effects and uses percentages of reduction in air pollutants to determine the cost-savings to the U.S. for related health costs. Also examines National Ambient Air Quality Standards and the Clean Air Act, including the use of monitors.

Carlson, Cynthia, Making CERCLA Natural Resource Damage Provisions Work: The Use of the Public Trust Doctrine and Other State Remedies, Environmental Law Reporter, 18, 10299-10307.
Note: Svitek, Laura L. bibliography.
The author discusses the effect that the DOI regulations have on natural resource damage claims recovery. Carlson defends that the use of these regulations may lead to serious underestimation of damages. By supplementing these regulations with appropriate public trust and public nuisance claims, the author believes that a trustee can increase recovery.

Caukins, Peter et al., The Travel Cost Model for Lake Recreation: A Comparison of Two Methods for Incorporating Site Quality and Substitution Effects, American Journal of Argricultural Economics, May 1986, 291-297.
Note: Svitek, Laura L. bibliography.
The traditional TCM and alternative adaptions of it are discussed. A multinomial logit model allocates visits away from other sites to the improved site. The alternative TCM is a regional gravity model that addresses both the substitution and site quality effects.

Center for Clean Air Policy (Prepared by Helme, Ned and Chris Neme), Acid Rain: Road to a Middle Ground Solution, Report of the Dialogue on Acid Rain Policy, Conducted by the Center for Clean Air Policy, Washington, DC, Center for Clean Air Policy, July 1987.
Note: 107 pp. plus appendices.
This report is a result of an analytic study of the cost of various acid rain control options for two major utilities, the American Electric Power (AEP) system and the Tennessee Valley Authority (TVA). Major stockholders discuss key elements of an acid rain control program. The dialogue addressed virtually all acid rain control aspects, from implementation strategies and the value of long range transport models to the role of clean coal technologies and energy conservation.

Ceraso, Jane, C.B. Epstein, S.L. Clark and M. Oppenheimer, New York City's Water Supply: Acid Deposition, Inorganic Pollution and the Catskill Reservoirs, New York, Environmental Defense Fund, October 1986.
Note: 138 pp.
This report gives an overall view of the New York City water supply, then concentrates on the Catskill watersheds. The report describes the Catskill watersheds, analyzes the quality of the water, and discusses health effects from chemicals such as nitrate, sodium, chloride, and aluminum. The report also

includes an examination of the effects of acid deposition in soil. Predictions for the future and the importance of protecting the watersheds are discussed.

Chernick, Paul, C. Wills and A. Paulson, Economic Analysis of Vermont Yankee Retirement, Montpelier, Vermont, Vermont Public Interest Research Group, Inc., 16 February 1989.
Estimates of the cost to shut down the Vermont Yankee nuclear power station. Based on the comparison between the cost for shutting down the plant and the cost to replace the power the plant provides.

Chestnut, Lauraine G. and R.D. Rowe, Draft: Economic Measures of the Impacts of Air Pollution on Health and Visibility, World Resources Institute (WRI), Washington, D.C., 26 April 1988.
Note: 41 pp.
Examines federally set standards for total suspended particulates as well as National Ambient Air Quality Standards set by EPA and the effects on human health and visibility when these standards are exceeded.

Coaker, T.H., Applied Biology, New York, Academic Press; 1979. This text is one volume in a series of biology texts. Aspects contained in this volume are ecological perspectives for the restoration of disturbed and degraded land. Basic concepts relating to restoration are explained.

Cohen, Bernard L., "Impacts of the Nuclear Energy Industry on Human Health and Safety," American Scientist, Sept.-Oct. 1976; 64: 550-559.
Note: 10 pp..
This article estimates the effects on human health on radioactivity released into the environment by various aspects of the nuclear energy industry. It includes statistical comparisons of other human health risks that reduce life expectancy.

Commoner, Barry, Howard Boksenbaum and Michael Coors, eds. Energy and Human Welfare - A Critical Analysis, Vol. I: The Social Costs of Power Production. For Scientists' Institute for Public Information 1975, New York, MacMillan Information Press, 1975.
Note: 217 pp.
A collection of articles concerning the environmental impact of power production, which includes articles on acid rain, oil spills, nuclear reactor safety, thermal pollution, and environmental problems caused by coal mining.

Congressional Quarterly, Inc. "Energy and Environment: The Unfinished Business," Washington, DC, Congressional Quarterly, 1985.
Note: 265 pp.
Part I examines environmental policies of the Reagan administration, including energy regulation, mineral leasing, and nuclear power. Part II discusses the problems and challenges that face the federal government: clean air, contaminated water, hazardous wastes, and the management of federal lands.

"Congress Clears Superfund Legislation," Congressional Quarterly Almanac, December 1980.
Note: Svitek, Laura L. bibliography.
This summary of CERCLA discusses the legislative history of the Law. It includes both the Senate and House debates over this legislation. The provisions of the final law which passed are detailed.

Conservation & Protection, Ontario Region. An Assessment of Existing Information Regarding PCBs in the Cornwall-Massena Section of the St. Lawrence River, January 20, 1988.
Note: Svitek, Laura L. bibliography.
This report was constructed to examine the PCB contamination in the St. Lawrence River. It summarizes the contamination by using existing studies. Data on water, sediments and biota were analyzed.

Consolidated Edison Company of New York, Inc. and New York Power Authority, Final Hudson River Ecological Study in the Area of Indian Point, Middletown, New York: EA Science and Technology; July 1988. (EA Report 10156.04).
Note: Paginated by sections.
This report is the sixteenth in a series of annual reports entitled 'Hudson River Ecological Study in the Area of Indian Point'. . . This report discusses the 1987 impingement data and interprets these latest study results in conjunction with the findings of previous years. Estimates are provided for the total number of fish and blue crabs impinged at each unit and for all individual species. Seasonal impingement trends at Units 2 and 3 are also discussed.

Constanza, Robert, "Embodied Energy and Economic Valuation," Science, December, 1980; 210: 1219-1224.
Note: Svitek, Laura L. bibliography.
Input-output analysis is used to calculate energy required to produce goods and services. This method of energy analysis has recently been focused upon for the estimation of the value of natural resources.

Cox, Geraldine V. and Lindstedst-Silva, June, (1979). "Superfund--An Ecologist's Dilemma," Hearings before the Committee on Transportation and Commerce and the Committee on Interstate and Foreign Commerce; House of Representatives; Serial No. 96-114, pp. 399-416.
Note: Svitek, Laura L. bibliography.
This presentation takes a stand on the ability of ecosystems to recover naturally. The authors believe that since ecosystem dynamics are of limited understanding, many restoration procedures may increase the ecological impacts already incurred.

Critical Mass Energy Project of Public Citizen and Safe Energy Communications Council, Turning Down the Heat: Solutions to Global Warming, An Analysis of Energy Efficiency, Renewable Resources, and Other Options Versus New Nuclear Power Development, By Nancy Rader, Ken Bossong, Alex Antypas, and Scott Denman. Washington, DC; September 1988.
Note: 101 pp.
This study focuses on the generation of electricity as a contributor to the emerging global warming problem and critically evaluates the argument that nuclear power can provide a partial solution to the problem. The report concludes that other options, primarily energy efficiency, natural gas, and renewable energy technologies, are more attractive than new nuclear power development because of their lower economic and environmental costs as well as shorter lead times.

Cropper, M.L., "Measuring the Benefits from Reduced Morbidity," The American Economic Review, May 1981; 71(2), pp. 235-240.
Note: 6 pp.
Papers and Proceedings of the 93 Annual Meeting of the American Economic Association, Denver, CO, 5-7 September 1980: Measuring the Benefits from Air

Pollution Control: Where Do We Stand? This paper uses the human capital approach and tries to define what an individual would pay for a change in air quality through presentation of a model of preventative health care. This model stems from people in polluted areas who try to compensate for any decreased resistance to illness they experience by smoking less, sleeping more, and exercise.

Cummings, R.G., D.S. Brookshire and W.D. Schultz, Valuing Environmental Goods, New Jersey, Rowman & Allenheld Publishers; 1986.
Note: Svitek, Laura L. bibliography.
This book is an assessment of CVM. Various authors express their evaluation of this new method for estimating benefits attributable to environmental goods. Historical perspectives, applications and comparisons with TCM and HPM are included.

Daubert, John and Robert Young, "Recreational Demands for Maintaining Instream Flows: A Contingent Valuation Approach," American Journal of Agricultural Economics, 1981; 63(4): 666-675.
Note: Svitek, Laura L. bibliography.
Explores the demand for recreational activities using free-flowing streams. Most streamflow programs have focused on the physical and biological aspects, but neglect recreational aspects.

David, Elizabeth L., "Lakeshore Property Values: A Guide to Public Investment in Recreation," Water Resources Research; 1968; 4(4): 697-707.
Note: Svitek, Laura L. bibliography.
This paper examines lakeshore property values as a function of lake and land site characteristics and quality improvements. This study samples only one group of water users; those who own waterfront property. The model uses a property value method.

David, Isellyn Ann, Mirex, 1968.
Note: Svitek, Laura L. bibliography.
Mirex is a major source of contamination in Lake Ontario. This report details the process by which mirex entered the Lake. Hooker Chemicals and Plastics Corporation was a major contributor. Included is a discussion of the ecological and health effects of Mirex. Prepared for the NYS Department of Environmental Protection.

Decker, Daniel J. and Gary R. Goff, Valuing Wildlife, Westview Press, Colorado, 1987.
Note: Svitek, Laura L. bibliography.
This text is designed to be a guide to the methods of determining the economic and social values of wildlife. The authors examine the ecological value, the aesthetic value and the recreational values associated with wildlife. Management and planning strategies are mentioned.

Department of Energy, Office of Fossil Energy, DOE/FE-007, Washington, DC, February 1987.
The project was proposed by Coal Tech Corporation, Marion PA.

Department of Interior, Natural Resource Damage Assessments: Final Rule, Federal Register, August 1, 1986.
Note: Svitek, Laura L. bibliography.
CERCLA includes a provision that establishes regulations to aid the damage assessment process.

Department of Energy, Office of Fossil Energy, America's Clean Coal Commitment, Washington, D.C. 20585; February 1987.
This is a comprehensive report which describes in detail many of the clean coal technologies which are being developed. It discusses the national emission levels for SO2 and NOx, and lists the technologies in terms of their ability to reduce these emissions. Each technology is described in terms of, A) How Does It Work?; B) What Are Its Attributes?; and C) What Potential Does It Have For Targeted Plants? Some of the technologies discussed are: coal cleaning, flue gas scrubbing, advanced flue gas cleanup, limestone injected multistage burner, gas reburning, in-duct sorbent injection, coal slurry, Pressurized Fluidized Bed Combustion (PFBC), Atmospheric Fluidized Bed Combustion (AFBC), and Integrated Gasification Combined Cycle (IGCC).

Department of Energy, Energy Information Administration, Annual Energy Outlook, 1989.
This report focuses on U.S. energy needs and how these needs will be met. The report discusses what types of energy will be depended on to meet the present and future energy needs of this country. Looks at fossil fuel power production as a major source of energy to meet this demand.

Department of Energy, Comprehensive Report to Congress Clean Coal Technology Program, Tidd PFBC Demonstration Project, Report prepared by the DOE Office of Fossil Energy, A project proposed by American Electric Power Service Corporation on behalf of the Ohio Power Company. Washington, DC; February 1987.
This report describes a demonstration proposal of combined-cycle pressurized fluidized bed combustion (PFBC) and the PFBC joint development program by the DOE and the Ohio Power Company, a wholly powered subsidary of American Electric Power Company, Inc. PFBC permits the combustion of a wide variety of coals, including high sulfur coals, with a sorbent (limestone or dolomite) in a fluidized bed combustor at indicated pressure.

Department of Energy, Office of Civilian Radioactive Waste Management, Environmental Assessment: Yucca Mountain Site, Nevada Research and Development Area, Nevada, U.S. Dept. of Energy, Washington, D.C. 1986.
Note: 500 pp.
This is a standard environmental assessment for the Federal civilian high-level radioactive waste repository site at Yucca Mountain, Nevada.

Department of Energy, Office of Fossil Energy, Innovative Clean Coal Technology (ICCT): Programmatic Environmental Impact Analysis (PEIA), U.S. DOE, Washington, D.C., September 1988.
This report discusses need for "Clean Coal" use to reduce emissions of particulate matter, SO2 and NOx. The report details different innovative clean coal technologies and compares the environmental effects associated with each one. Some of the technologies discussed are: atmospheric fluidized bed combustion (AFBC), integrated gasification combined cycle (IGCC), fuel cells, advanced slagging combustors (ASC), and flue gas desulfurization (FGD).

Department of Energy, Report to Congress of Emerging Clean Coal Technologies, Submitted in response to section 321 of the Department of the Interior and Related Agencies Appropriations Act for Fiscal Year 1985 as enacted by House Joint Resolution 648, Public Law 98-473, 98 Stat. 1874, Washington, DC, 1 May 1985.
Note: 268 pp.
This report describes emerging clean coal technologies, including flue gas cleanup, fluidized bed combustion, surface coal gasification, coal preparation, heat engines, advanced combustors, alternative fuels, fuel cells, coal liquefaction, underground coal gasification, gas stream cleanup, magnetohydrodynamics, and non-technology specific measures. The report discusses the environmental aspects of each technology and estimated costs of each technology.

Desvousges, William H. and Richard W. Dunford, (1987), Nonmarket Valuation Methods for Measuring Natural Resource Damages, presented at the Conference on Natural Resource Damages, June 16.
Note: Svitek, Laura L. bibliography.
In this paper, four nonmarket valuation techniques were examined: the factor income method, property value method, TCM and CVM. Key assumptions, limitations, and data needs were addressed.

Desvousges, William H. and Venetia A. Skahen, Techniques to Measure Damages to Natural Resources, Final Report prepared for the DOI, June, 1987.
Note: Svitek, Laura L. bibliography.
These guidelines were written for the CERCLA 301 Task Force, in accordance to the DOI regulations for assessing damages to natural resources. Included in these guidelines were general economic theory, and various methods for valuing resources.

Dower, Roger, (1984), Superfund Sleeper Sends Signal, The Environmental Forum, March, pp. 43-6.
Note: Svitek, Laura L. bibliography.
The Act's Section 301(c) natural resource damages provision caused much controversy when the DOI failed to present the regulations in adequate time. Many States filed suit against the DOI claiming that the statute of limitations had expired.

Downing, Paul B., Environmental Economics and Policy, Little, Brown and Co., Boston, 1984.
This book explains the application of economic benefit/cost analysis to air and water pollution. Costs of pollution control as well as costs to health and the environment are discussed in a broad and theoretical manner. An extensive bibliography is included.

Ducsik, Dennis W. and Don M. Shakow, Reaching Electricity Policy Decisions with Environmental and Social Consequences: A Normative Approach for State Government. Worcester, MA: Clark University, September, 1978 (Draft only).
Note: 118pp.
This report provides a critique of the methodologies in place that govern utility planning. Topics covered include distortion in utility planning, and the inadequacy of governmental regulation. The authors then propose a normative strategy for reform, which covers methodological and institutional design. In conclusion, a research plan is outlined which consists of three "phases": baseline analysis, preparation of case studies, and synthesis and validation.

Durhan, R.W. and B.G. Oliver, History of Lake Ontario Contamination From the Niagara River by Sediment Radiodating and Chlorinated Hydrocarbon Analysis. Journal of Great Lakes Research, 1983, 9(2): 160-168.
Note: Svitek, Laura L. bibliography.
This technical article examines sediment core profiles taken 3 km from the mouth of the Niagara River. Pollution of Lake Ontario is still occurring, but the worst contamination of the Lake occurred in the 1960's. Each chemical pollutant is discussed.

ECO Northwest, Seton, Johnson & Odell, Inc., Shapiro & Associates, Inc., Economic Analysis of the Environmental Effects of the Coal-Fired Generator at Boardman, Oregon. Final Report.; 29 December 1983; BPA Agreement # DE-AC79-83BP11551.
Note: Prepared for the Bonneville Power Administration, Shepard C. Buchanan, Project Manager.
Analysis of emissions from the coal-fired power plant at Boardman, Oregon. Discusses environmental factors associated with plant from fuel extraction to plant operation. Discusses effects on humans and crops from SO2, NO2, O3, sulfates and particulates. Table III-4, p. III-15. Estimates costs of total environmental effects: Table IV-1, p. IV-2.

ECO Northwest, Economic Analysis of the Environmental Effects of a Combustion-Turbine Generating Station at Fredrickson Industrial Park, Pierce County, Washington. Final Report, Seton, Johnson & Odell, Inc., Shapiro and Associates, Inc., With technical assistance from, March 26, 1984, BPA Agreement # DE-AC79-83BP11551.
Note: Prepared for the Bonneville Power Administration; Shepard C. Buchanan, Project Manager.
Analysis of environmental costs and benefits of a combustion-turbine generator at Fredrickson Industrial Park, Pierce County, Washington. Identifies and analyzes the environmental effects of the fuel cycle associated with the plant from fuel extraction to plant operation. Compares effects of emissions from natural gas (CO, CO2, NOX, and particulates) and oil (all of above and SO2). Tables III-7 & 8, p. III-21 & 22.

ECO Northwest, Generic Coal Study: Quantification and Valuation of Environmental Impacts, Seton, Johnson, & Odell, Inc., Shapiro & Associates, Inc., with technical assistance from, 31 January 1987; BPA Contract # DE-AM79-86BP62884, Task # AT 64648.
Note: Prepared for the Bonneville Power Administration; Shepard C. Buchanan, Project Manager.

This study estimates the economic effects of emissions from a coal-fired plant. Lists primary pollutants: SOX, NOX, and particulates; and secondary pollutants (sulfates, nitrates and ozone) which occur through chemical transformation of the primaries. Tables 2-2A & 2-2B, P. 2-6 & 7. Estimates emissions of generic plants at six different sites, groundlevel concentrations, effect on human health, visibility, agriculture, materials and general ecosystem. Discusses effects to acid rain and the greenhouse effect.

ECO Northwest, Estimating Environmental Costs and Benefits for Five Generating Resources, Technical Appendices: Description of Five Generating Resources, Their Likely Significant Environmental Effects, and the Economic Value of those Effects., LTD., Shapiro & Associates, Inc., Seton, Johnson & Odell, Inc., March 1986; Contract # DE-AC79-83BP11551.
Note: Prepared for the Bonneville Power Administration.
Under a multiple-award Contract Agreement with the U.S. Department of Energy. This study quantifies and evaluates the costs and effects of five types of electricity generating resources: 1) cogeneration from biomass; 2) cogeneration from municipal solid waste; 3) geothermal; 4) solar; and 5) wind. The study characterizes the generic generating resources by type, size, and location. Calculates the present value of the expected environmental effects for each generating resource. Estimates the magnitude of the significant environmental effects, and estimates the economic value of the physical effects. Describes the potential environmental effects associated with each phase of the fuel cycle of a generating resource: extraction, transportation, construction, operation, and decommissioning.

El-Sharawi, A.H.; Esterby, S.R.; Kuntz, K.W., A Statistical Evaluation of the Trends in the Water Quality of the Niagara River, Journal of Great Lakes Research, 1983, 9(2): 234-240.
Note: Svitek, Laura L. bibliography.
Water quality data was used to examine the change in chemical concentrations over time. Examines average monthly values of pH, alkalinity, TP and Nitrate between May 1975 and December 1980.

Electric Power Research Institute (EPRI), A Compilation of Utility Sponsored Energy Efficiency Rebate Programs, prepared by Consumer Energy Council of America Research Foundation and the American Council for an Energy Efficient Economy, Final Report, December 1987.
A survey of 157 utilities found 59 companies with appliance efficiency programs. At the time of the survey 15 utilities had pilot or full scale rebate programs for refrigerators, five had programs for freezers, 22 had programs for central air conditioners and 34 had programs for heat pumps.

Electric Power Research Institute (EPRI), Benefit of Environmental Controls: Measures, Methods, and Application, prepared by Energy and Resource Consultants, Inc., Boulder, CO, EPRI #EA-6030, Palo Alto, CA, Research Reports Center, October, 1988.
Note: 99 pp.
This report is a useful introduction to the methods for assessing environmental damages and benefits of the economic costs of environmental controls. The report also reviews the use of these methods to assess air pollution damage and describes how underlying assumptions can significantly influence analysis results. Quantitative information is provided for illustrative purposes only.

Electric Power Research Institute (EPRI), Acid Precipitation and Human Health, prepared by Hoffman, S., Final Report, ed. Palo Alto, CA, EPRI, August 1989. (EN-2661-22; v. Research Project 2661-22).
Note: Paginated by section.
This report reviews literature on potential indirect human health effects of acid precipitation through ingestion of contaminated drinking water and food. The report asserts that no direct effects of acid precipitation such as skin or eye irritation have been identified. The report does not address the effect of acid precipitation precursors on human health such as effects resulting from inhalation of dry particles and acid aerosols. Types of exposure routes reviewed in this report include drinking water contamination by heavy metal and asbestos; corrosion of metals; uptake of mobilized metals in crops; and bioaccumulation of contaminants in fish and grain. Extensive reference lists and a summary of current and planned research are included.

Electric Power Research Institute (EPRI), DSM Program Monitoring, Applied Management Sciences, Inc., prepared by Battelle--Columbus Division, Final Report ed. Palo Alto, CA, EPRI, March 1988. (EPRI EM-5706; v. Research Project 2548-1).
Note: Paginated by section.
This report reviews techniques for DSM program monitoring and stresses the use of monitoring to support decision-making about future actions. The final section presents four case studies that illustrate the application of monitoring techniques and the type of results achieved. Reference list at the end of each section.

Electric Power Research Institute (EPRI), Energy Utilization Catalog: Products from R&D, prepared by the Energy Management and Utilization Division, rev. ed., Palo Alto, CA, EPRI, June 1988.
Note: 185 pp.
This catalog provides descriptions of products resulting from EPRI energy utilization (end-use) research. Products are grouped into nine categories: End-use assessment and forecasting; demand-side planning and information; marketing support; residential building systems; commercial building systems; load management; industrial electric technologies; power electronics and control systems; and electric transportation. Descriptions include the name of the EPRI technical contact and associated publications.

Electric Power Research Institute (EPRI), Potential Impacts of Climate Change on Electric Utilities, prepared by ICF Incorporated, Palo Alto, CA: EPRI; January 1989, EN-6249 (Research Project 2141-11).
Note: Paginated by section.
This report evaluates the potential impacts of greenhouse-gas climate change on electric utility planning and operations using case studies of utility systems in the southeastern United States and New York State over the period from 1986 to 2015. The report concludes that climate change could lead to increased electric generating capacity requirements, increased generation of electricity, decreased hydroelectric availability and increased production costs.

Electric Power Research Institute (EPRI), Status of Least-Cost Planning in the United States, prepared by Barakat, Howard & Chamberlin, Palo Alto, CA, EPRI, December 1988, (EM 61-613; v. Research Project 2982-2).
Note: 60 pp.

This report surveys the status of least-cost utility planning in each state, ranks each state's progress, and identifies influences contributing to least-cost planning activities. Information was primarily gathered from telephone interviews with regulatory commission contacts, who are identified in the report. The appendix analyses economic factors which might affect least-cost developments.

Electric Power Research Institute (EPRI), Utility Energy Strategies: The Role of Efficiency, Productivity, and Conservation, prepared by Energetics, Palo Alto, CA: EPRI, February 1989, EPRI CU-6272 (Project 2982-5).
Note: Paginated by section.
This study reviews the relationships between economic efficiency, energy productivity, energy efficiency, and energy conservation. Of particular interest is the study's recommendation that environmental concerns are likely to play an increasing role in national energy policy and utility regulation and that determining how to incorporate these potential costs into power production remains an important unresolved issue for utilities and regulators. Three case studies are included: the historic relationship between electricity use and economic efficiency; an overview of the relationship between building energy efficiency, the "sick building" syndrome, and economic efficiency; and the relationship between market penetration of air conditioners, economic growth, and economic efficiency in the "sunbelt" states. Reference list included.

Energy and Commerce House Committee, Safety of Aging Nuclear Power Plants, 10 November 1987; Washington, DC: U.S. Govt Printing Office, 1988, Serial No. 100-133.
Note: 119 pp.
This report was used to determine the impact of nuclear power plant aging as an external cost.

Energy & Resource Consultants, *Inc.*, Economic Assessment of Damages Related to the Eagle Mine Facility, November 27, 1985.
Note: Svitek, Laura L. bibliography.
This report was prepared for the State of Colorado for the litigation of Colorado v. Gulf & Western Inc. The study uses three methods to estimate natural resource damages. These are the recreation user day method, the property value method and the WTP survey method.

Energy & Resource Consultants, Inc., Economic Estimates of Ecological Damages from Coal-Fired Power Plants: Draft Phase 1 Report, Appendix 1. Boulder, CO. Examines methodologies used to estimate economic effects of ecological damages including local and regional impacts from coal-fired powerplants.

Environmental Protection Agency (EPA), Office of Air, Noise and Radiation, Strategies and Air Standards Division, "Benefit Analysis Estimates," Chap. 6 in: Regulatory Impact Analysis on the National Ambient Air Quality Standards for Particulate Matter, Research Triangle Park, NC, February 1984.
Note: 42 pp.
Using the county as the basic unit of analysis, this report examines benefits representing improvement in society's well-being as a result of lower particulate matter emissions and concentrations.

Environmental Protection Agency (EPA), Strategies and Air Standards Division, "Benefits Analysis Estimates", Chap. 3 in: Regulatory Impact Analysis of National Ambient Air Quality Standards for Particulate Matter: Second Addendum, Research Triangle Park, NC, U.S.E.P.A, December 1986.
Note: 10 pp.
Examines benefits of lower particulate matter emissions on society.

Environmental Protection Agency (EPA), Office of Policy Planning and Evaluation, A Model Estimating the Economic Impacts of Current Levels of Acidification on Recreational Fishing in the Adirondack Mountains, Daniel M. Violette, Boulder, Colorado: Energy and Resource Consultants, Inc.; May 1985, (EPA-230-12-86-021).
Note: paginated by sections.
The purpose of this project was to estimate the parameters of an economic model that can be combined with information on the current extent of fresh water acidification to produce economic estimates of damages in the Adirondack Mountains of New York State. Both a site characteristics based travel cost model and a simpler participation model were used to obtain estimates of the use values of recreational fishing in Adirondack lakes and the reduction in use values due to acidification were also estimated.

Environmental Protection Agency (EPA), Air Quality Management Division, Regulatory Impact Analysis on the National Ambient Air Quality Standards for Sulfur Oxides (Sulfur Dioxide), Draft; March 1988.
Note: 220 pp.
This draft examines the impacts of alternative levels standards in terms of the benefits to be derived, the cost and environmental impacts, and the economic impacts as well as other potential impacts on both the public and private sectors.

Esbasco Services Inc., Supplemental Feasibility Study Report, Marathon Battery Company Site, EPA Contract No. 68-01-7250, (1986).
Note: Svitek, Laura L. bibliography.
The USEPA authorized Ebasco Service to conduct a study at the Marathon Battery Co. Site. This report details their findings relative to the areas of Constitution and East Foundry Cove.

Ferguson, John S., Director (Deloitte Haskins & Sells, Dallas, Texas), The Impact of Decommissioning Policy on the Cost of Nuclear Power, Public Utilities Fortnightly, 1 September 1988, pp.41-44.
Note: 4 pp.
Discusses revenue requirements for decommissioning, including external (qualified and nonqualified), internal (straight-line and sinking fund) and hybrid methods. The costs of each of these is outlined as well.

Fishelson, Gideon and P. Graves, (Tel Aviv University/University of Chicago), "Air Pollution and Morbidity: SO2 Damages", Journal of the Air Pollution Control Association, August, 1978; 28(8): 785-789.
The role of SO2 and COH (coefficient of haze) as causative factors in hospital emergency room admissions for respiratory and cardiac disease is analyzed using data from Chicago's Cook County Hospital. Some of the findings are that, while COH appears not to affect morbidity, SO2 does, with most important impacts being felt by those with cardiac disease, females, and the youngest and oldest age groups. It is concluded that marginal morbidity damages, about which little had

been known, are not high relative to other damage categories. These damages are estimated to be on the order of 10 cents per microgram per cubic meter per person.

Fisher, Anthony C., Resource and Environmental Economics, Cambridge, Cambridge University Press, 1981.
This book discusses the effect of energy use of the environment. The sections on computation of the economic costs of pollution are of special interest.

Fisher, Anthony C. and V. Smith, Economic Evaluation of Energy's Environmental Costs with Special Reference to Air Pollution, Annual Review of Energy, Palo Alto, CA, 1982, 7: 1-35.
Note: 36 pp.
A technical evaluation of the impact of energy on the environment accompanied by formulas for computing energy's environmental costs.

Flavin, Christopher, and Alan B. Durning, Building on Success: The Age of Energy Efficiency, Worldwatch Paper, March 1988, 82: Washington, DC, Worldwatch Institute.
Note: 74 pp.
This paper's premise is that energy efficiency is an economic opportunity for the nineties as well as an environmental necessity. Authors use a variety of interesting statistics and examples to demonstrate that improved efficiency means less fuels burned, a reduction in urban air pollution and acid rain, and "the only means available" to reduce carbon dioxide emissions from fossil fuel combustion as well as being a key ingredient to economic success.

Ford, D., Hollocher, T., Kendall, H., MacKenzie, J., Scheinman, L., Schurgin, A., The Nuclear Fuel Cycle: A Survey of the Public Health, Environmental and National Security Effects of Nuclear Power, 2 Vols. ed. Washington, DC, Union of Concerned Scientists, 1973.
Note: 291 pp.
This report encompasses the storage and disposal of high level wastes, the health hazards of uranium, and the radiological impact on the area surrounding a nuclear reprocessing plant.

Ford Foundation, Nuclear Power Issues and Choices--Report of the Nuclear Energy Policy Study Group, Administered by the MITRE Corporation, Cambridge, Mass: Ballinger Publishing Company, 1977.
Note: 418 pp.
This report is often quoted by Ramsay, in Unpaid Costs of Electrical Energy, particularly with respect to nuclear accident probability.

Freedman, Kolker, Anne and Cohen, Jeffrey C. The Environmental Impact of Supplying Power to the Con Edison Service Territory: 1975 - 1990, New York: Citizens for Clean Air, Inc., 1975.
Note: 155 pp.
This report is divided into five major topics: (1) an examination of electrical supply and demand in the Con Edison service area including history, background information, current data and projections; (2) nuclear power, including fuel-handling, plant operations and waste storage; (3) effects on water and aquatic life by thermal pollution and toxic substances; (4) air pollution: sulfur dioxide,

particulates, oxides of nitrogen and future issues; and (5) present and future plant sites and the regulation of siting, and a discussion of transmission facilities, including environmental considerations. The report is dated but may still be useful for the New York area.

Freeman, A. Myrick, "Approaches to Measure Public Goods Demand," American Journal of Agricultural Economics, 1979; 61(5): 915-920.
Note: Svitek, Laura L. bibliography.
The author examines approaches to measuring the benefits of improved environmental quality. The article presents a review of three approaches for the estimation of demand and benefits. Included are empirical and market approaches.

Freeman III, A. Myrick, The Benefits of Environmental Improvement: Theory and Practice, Resources for the Future, Baltimore, MD, Johns Hopkins University Press, 1979.
Note: 272 pp.
This book provides guidelines for placing a dollar value on the environmental effects of pollution, including changes in property values, morbidity, values for recreational benefits, and productivity benefits. Although this work is a theoretical and instructive treatment, specific references are given for each subtopic.

Friedlaender, Anne F., Editor, Approaches to Controlling Air Pollution, Cambridge, MA: MIT Press; 1978.
This book discusses the various methods which were being developed in the late '70s to control emissions from energy production as well as other sources. Fossil fuel technologies are detailed here as a means of reducing sulfur, nitrogen and particulate emissions from power generating resource systems.

Gaines, Linda, Berry, R. Stephen, Long II, Thomas Veach, TOSCA: The Total Social Cost of Coal and Nuclear Power, Cambridge, MA, Ballinger Publishing, Inc., 1979.
Note: 126 pp.
This book explains the calculation of costs associated with coal plants and nuclear energy. The "total social cost analysis" includes damage to property, health effects, damage to human life, and other environmental effects. Formulas for determining costs and examples are given.

Gaynor, Kevin, "Stipulated Penalties and Dispute Resolution in CERCLA Consent Decrees: Practical Innovations Can Benefit Everyone," Environmental Law Reporter, 1988, 18: 10155-10157.
Note: Svitek, Laura L. bibliography.
With the pressure and deadlines EPA faces to begin cleanups on hazardous sites, EPA must negotiate on a wide scale level with potentially responsible parties. EPA has called for many stipulated penalties in CERCLA's consent decrees, which leaves PRP's weary about entering in on such an agreement.

Gerking, Shelby, and William Schulze, "What Do We Know about Benefits of Reduced Mortality from Air Pollution Control?," The American Economic Review, May 1981, 71(2): 228-234.
Note: 7 pp. Papers and Proceedings of the 93 Annual meeting of the American Economic Association, Denver, CO, 5-7 September 1980: Measuring Benefits from Air Pollution Control: Where Do We Stand? This paper examines difficulties present in statistical epidemiology and examines how these problems can effect the

estimated damage effects of air pollution on health using mortality rates, air pollution levels, and other variables for sixty U.S. cities. Includes various comments on policy implications.

Gibbons, John H., and William U. Chandler, Energy - The Conservation Revolution. New York: Plenum Press; 1981.
Note: 276 pp.
Of special interest in this thorough treatment of energy conservation is a discussion of the elements of demand analysis and a detailed examination of the environmental effects of power plants by pollutant.

Gittinger, J. Price, Economic Analysis of Agricultural Projects, John Hopkins University Press, Baltimore, Md., 1972.
Note: Svitek, Laura L. bibliography.
Gittinger includes a detailed discussion of discount rates in his book. He determines the process of choosing an appropriate rate. One section discusses cost/benefit analysis for use in determining the selection of various government project.

Glass, Norman R., ed., Environmental Effects of Increased Coal Utilization: Ecological Effects of Gaseous Emissions From Coal Combustion, Washington, DC, U.S. Environmental Protection Agency, 1978.
Note: 50 pp.
This report was written at the request of the DOE in response to a presidential environmental message. The report examines the ecological effects of oxides of sulfur complex, oxides of nitrogen complex, the particulate complex, the photochemical oxidant complex, and acid precipitation. Discusses effects on the ecosystem of such materials as metals, textiles and paper, and effects on visibility.

Goldman, Marvin, Robert Catlin and Lynn Anspaugh, (Task Group on Health and Environmental Aspects of the Soviet Nuclear Accident), Health and Environmental Consequences of the Chernobyl Nuclear Power Plant Accident, Washington, D.C., United States Department of Energy, June 1987.
Note: paginated by section.
This report attempts to estimate the worldwide radiological consequences of the Chernobyl nuclear power plant accident. The authors estimate these consequences from the information acquired from the Soviet Union and European countries. The report discusses the technical details of how the accident occurred, the immediate medical consequences, the extent to which various populations were affected, and long-term health risk projections for the entire northern hemisphere.

Gotchy, R.L., (U.S. Nuclear Regulatory Commission), Office of Nuclear Reactor Regulation, Potential Health and Environmental Impacts Attributable to the Nuclear and Coal Fuel Cycles, Washington, D.C., U.S. Government Printing Office, June 1987, NUREG-0332.
Mortality and morbidity estimates based on recent health effects data are presented. This includes effects resulting from current component designs and operations of nuclear and coal fuel cycles. Also included are fuel cycle facilities' anticipated emission rates and occupational exposure for facilities expected to go into operation during the next decade. The author's conclusion is that the coal fuel cycle alternative has greater health impacts on humans than the nuclear fuel cycle, even though there are large uncertainties in the potential health effects estimates.

Grad, Frank P., "A Legislative History of the Comprehensive Environmental Response, Compensation, & Liability Act of 1980 (CERCLA)," Columbia Journal of Environmental Law, 1982, 8(1): 1-36.
Note: Svitek, Laura L. bibliography.
Grad explained the overall history of CERCLA, including prior legislation which was deemed inadequate. Included are the House and Senate Reports and Bills which contributed to CERCLA.

Gramlich, Edward M., Benefit-Cost Analysis of Government Programs, New Jersey, Prentice-Hall, Inc., 1981.
Note: Svitek, Laura L. bibliography.
Gramlich incorporates various cost benefit assessment techniques with respect to government programs. Included are resource valuation techniques, discount rates and market pricing techniques.

Grigalunas, Thomas; Opaluch, James, The Natural Resource Damage Assessment Model for Coastal and Marine Environments, prepared for the 1987 Oil Spill Conference, 1987.
Note: Svitek, Laura L. bibliography.
This paper describes the Natural Resource Damage Assessment Model for Coastal and Marine Environments. This model is to be used for Type A, simplified assessment of damages. The model simulates biological and economic damages resulting from a release.

Grimsrud, D.T. et al., A Comparison of Indoor Air Quality in Pacific Northwest Existing and New Energy Efficient Homes, Berkeley, CA: Lawrence Berkeley Laboratory; 1986.
Indoor air pollution concentrations have a much stronger relationship with pollutant sources and source emission rates than with air infiltration rates. Most tight energy efficient homes have acceptable air quality, while leaky homes are more immune to poor air quality.

Gruhl, Schweppe, Evaluation of Health Effects of Air Pollution in the Chestnut Ridge Area,; 1980.
Note: 89 pp., 1981 NTIS abstract no. 3346, NTIS no. DOE/EV/04968 - TI (MIT, Cambridge, Mass.). Mortality and morbidity statistics for air pollution but no costing figures.

Habicht, Henry, The Expanding Role of Natural Resources Damage Claims Under Superfund, Virginia Journal of Natural Resources Law, 1987; 7(1): 1-26.
Note: Svitek, Laura L. bibliography.
Since the enactment of CERCLA, an increasing number of waste cleanup suits have included damage for natural resources. This article examines the liability found under CERCLA and the DOI assessment regulations.

Halter, Faith, Thomas, Joel, "Recovery of Damages by States for Fish and Wildlife Losses Caused by Pollution," Ecology Law Quarterly, (1980); 10(10): 5-30.
Note: Svitek, Laura L. Bibliography.
Several problems associated with the valuation process of resource damage and possible solutions. Several valuation methods are critiqued.

Halter, Faith, Thomas, Joel T., "Recovery of Damages by States for Fish and Wildlife Losses Caused by Pollution," Ecology Law Quarterly, 1982; 10: 5-35.
Note: 31 pp.
This article describes several bases for recovery of the economic value of fish and wildlife based on a survey of all state attorneys general and fish and wildlife agencies.

Hammock, Judd ; Brown Jr., Gardner M., Waterfowl and Wetlands:Towards Bioeconomic Analysis, Baltimore, Resources for the Future; 1974.
Note: Svitek, Laura L. bibliography.
This book incorporates general economic theory into a framework of valuing resources. Wetlands and waterfowl are examined. It includes an empirical test on the value of waterfowl, where a CVM questionnaire was administered to hunters.

Hazilla, Michael; Kopp, Raymond J., The Social Cost of Alternative Ambient Air Quality Standards for Total Suspended Particulates: A General Equilibrium Analysis, Washington, D.C.,Resources for the Future, Quality of the Environment Division, 1986. Discussion paper QE86-06.
Note: 57 pp.
Benefit-cost analysis examining the maximum amount of money individuals would be willing to pay to live in an area which was in compliance with pollution control standards.

Hearing Before the Committee on Military Installations and Facilities, Department of the Army's Plan to Clean Up Contamination at the Rocky Mountain Arsenal, February 25, 1985.
Note: Svitek, Laura L. bibliography.
It has been determined that the chemical contamination at the Rocky Mountain arsenal, Colorado is quite extensive. The Army and Shell Oil Co. both contribute to the contamination. These hearings contain five plans presented by the Army for cleanup of various contaminated basins.

Heising, Carolyn D., George, Varghese P. "Nuclear Financial Risk: Economy-Wide Costs of Reactor Accidents," Energy Policy, February 1986.
This report estimates both the on and off-site costs due to either a full-scale meltdown or a worst case scenario. The report also attempts to assign decommissioning costs.

Hill, Philip G., Power Generation, Resources, Hazards, Technology and Costs, Cambridge: Massachusetts Institute of Technology Press, 1977.
This book includes a chapter "Power and the Environment" which considers the hazards to the environment, which may also damage man. Human Hazards due to power generation include occupational dangers in the mining, transporting, and processing of fuel. The chapter emphasizes local effects of fuel extraction, transportation, and utilization and also includes a discussion of global problems of environmental heating.

Hirst, Eric, Electric-Utility Energy-Efficiency and Load-Management Programs: Resources for the 1990s. Oak Ridge, TN: Oak Ridge National Laboratory; June 1989. (ORNL/CON-285).
Note: 45 pp.
This report reviews the past progress and future potential of utility DSM programs. The report then makes suggestions for future utility activities, noting that utilities

must play major roles in encouraging improved energy efficiency if it is important to reduce the overall costs of energy services, reduce the environmental effects of electricity production, and to improve economic productivity (p.19). The report also discusses federal policies which would encourage utility DSM programs. This report provides a nontechnical but information packed overview of current DSM policy issues. Extensive reference list.

Hohmeyer, Olav, Social Costs of Energy Consumption: External Effects of Electricity Generation in the Federal Republic of Germany,. Berlin: Springer - Verlag; 1988.
Note: 125 pp.
This study describes the environmental impacts of electricity generation based on fossil fuel combustion or nuclear power and compares the effects of electricity generated from wind and solar energy. Wherever possible, monetary values (in Deutschemark) are assigned to external effects such as the damage done to human health, agriculture, and materials. The effects of energy generation on climate and the anticipated rate of depletion of nonrenewable resources are also discussed. The study concludes that inclusion of external effects would improve the competitive position of renewable energy sources.

Holdren, John P., "Energy and the Human Predicament," Prepared as a chapter in: Earth and the Human Future, Essays in Honor of Harrison Brown, Edited by Kirk R. Smith; Fesharaki, Fereidun; Holdren, John P. Boulder, CO: Westview Press; 1985.
Note: Reprinted as Report No. ERC-85-3. Berkeley, CA: University of California, Energy and Resources Group, May 1985. 25pp. plus tables.
This paper reviews the reasons for supposing that energy remains a fundamental problem for human society. The author concludes that the world suffers simultaneously from the consequences of having too little energy, as may be the case in developing nations, and too much energy of a costly or risky kind, the risks of which include disruption of supply, environmental consequences, and nuclear proliferation. References and statistics supporting the author's argument include a table detailing environmental liabilities of energy opinions.

Howe, Charles W., Natural Resource Economics, New York: John W. Wiley & Sons; 1979.
Note: Svitek, Laura L. bibliography.
Includes various aspects relating to natural resources. Included is a discussion of unique natural resources, outdoor recreation, TCM and CVM. Problems associated with common property resources are included.

Huber, Paul, "Electricity and the Environment: In Search of Regulatory Authority," Harvard Law Review 1987, 100:1002.
Note: Appendix.
This table lists public risks associated with energy production: coal, hydro, home insulation, nuclear, solar, and wood. The table lists incremental and catastrophic events, but provides no costing figures.

Hudson River Fishermen's Association, *On the Reconfiguration and Empirical Evaluation of a Prototype Screening Device at Indian Point Nuclear Unit 2.*, R. Ian Fletcher: Great Salt Bay Experimental Station, December 1986.
Note: 56 pages.
This report details a prototype screening device installed at Indian Point Nuclear Unit 2 which is supposed to return impinged fish back into the Hudson River water unharmed.

Huettner, David A., "Net Energy Analysis: An Economic Assessment," *Science* 1976, 192(4235): 101-104.
Note: Svitek, Laura L. Bibliography.
This article examines the limitations of net energy analysis, and its usefulness in application of public policy decisions. Many believe in the usefulness of this valuation method, and feel that it should be used to supplement traditional economic analysis.

Independent Power Corporation, *Air Quality Improvements in the Electric Power Industry: Cost or Savings to the Ratepayers?,* Oakland, CA: Independent Power Corporation; March 1989.
Note: 24 pp.
This report describes an analysis carried out by Independent Power Corporation and presented to the California Energy Commission and the South Coast Air Quality Management District. The report concludes that utilities could cost-effectively retire older, polluting, and inefficient fossil units and replacing them with new cleaner units at no additional cost to ratepayers and thus achieve or exceed the NOX emission reductions required in the proposed California Air Quality Management Plan.

Inhaber, Herbert, "Risk with Energy from Conventional and Nonconventional Sources," *Science,* 23 February 1979; 203: 718-723.
Note: 6 pp.
This article evaluates risk associated with five "conventional" energy sources (coal, oil, natural gas, nuclear, and hydroelectricity) and compare the risks to those associated with "nonconventional" sources (solar thermal, electric, solar photovoltaic, solar space heating, methanol, wind, and ocean thermal). The risk of both catastrophic and noncatastrophic events are considered in terms of risk to human health per unit of energy. The author concludes that the risk associated with nonconventional systems is as high as or higher conventional system risks because of the large amount of material and labor needed for unconventional sources as well as backup and storage requirements. Reference list.

International Atomic Energy Agency (IAEA), "Proceedings of an International Conference," Seattle, 16-20 May 1983, *Radioactive Waste Management,* Vienna: IAEA; 1984; 5.
Note: 466 pp.
The main objective of this conference was to exchange information on the various technical, environmental, regulatory, institutional, social and economic aspects of radioactive waste management, and to identify possible approaches to a solution. Of particular note for use in our nuclear report are the data for waste storage and disposal (including marine disposal), and radiation emissions figures.

Jeffery, J.W., The Real Cost of Nuclear Electricity in the U.K. Energy Policy, June 1982: 76-100.
Note: 25pp.
This discusses capital costs only (not used in report).

Jensen, Loren D., editor, Fourth National Workshop on Entrainment and Impingement. Melville, New York: EA Communications; 1977.
Note: 424 pp.
This book was used to obtain data on fish losses due to impingement and entrainment.

Jessup, Phillip, Strategies for Reducing the Cost of Acid Rain Controls Electricity Demand-site Management and Clean Coal Technologies. Washington, DC: Environmental and Energy Study Institute; January 1988. Note: 53 pp.
This report is a response to concerns that acid rain controls will have potentially adverse effects upon electricity rates and jobs, especially in the Midwest. The report explores alternatives to scrubbers and other conventional controls including clean coal technologies and electricity demand-site management strategies such as load management, conservation and cogeneration. These alternatives could present opportunities for reducing the overall cost of acid rain.

Johansson, Thomas B., Bondlund, Birgit, Williams, Robert H., eds., Electricity: Efficient End-Use and New Generation Technologies, and Their Planning Implications, Lund, Sweden: Lund University Press; 1989.
Note: 960 pp.
This book is a collection of peer reviewed presentations at the 1989 "Electricity" Congress in Gothenburg Sweden sponsored by Vattenfall, the Swedish State Power Board. The book provides an overview of energy-efficient end-use and generating technologies for electricity as well as discussions of related policy and planning implications. The majority of contributors are researchers from either the United States or Sweden. Each article is supported by extensive reference lists.

Johnson, Gary L., "Procedures, Costs and Rate Structures for Decommissioning Nuclear Reactors," Journal of Energy Law and Policy, 1983-84; 5: 245-271.
Note: 26 pp.
Discusses general decommissioning procedures and costs, including sinking fund strategy approved by the Federal Energy Regulatory Commission (FERC).

Jones, M.L.,Minns, C.K.,Marmorek, D.R.,Elder, F.C.,"Assessing the Potential Extent of Damage to Inland Lakes in Eastern Canada due to Acidic Deposition:II-Application of the Regional Model," Canadian Journal of Fisheries and Aquatic Sciences (in press).
Hydrochemical model presented in Marmorek et al. (1989) is applied on a regional scale.

Kahn, James R.; Kemp, W. Michael, "Economic Losses Associated with the Degradation of an Ecosystem: The Case of Submerged Aquatic Vegetation in Chesapeake Bay," Journal of Environmental Economics and Management, 1985; 12: 246-63.
Note: Svitek, Laura L. bibliography.
Kahn examined the ecological effects for the Chesapeake Bay Fishery, which is both commercially and recreationally exploited by the pollution of agricultural runoff of herbicides as well as soil erosion.

Kaplan, Seymour, Energy Economics: Quantitative Methods for Energy and Environmental Decisions, New York: McGraw-Hill; 1983.
Note: 352 pp.
This book explains various mathematical tools that can be used to quantify energy costs and help with decision-making. Topics covered include energy investment, risk analysis, allocation of limited energy resources, and environmental costing.

Kelso, J.R.M.; Minns, C.K.; Gray, J.E.; Jones, M.L., "Acidification of Waters in Eastern Canada and its Relationship to Aquatic Biota," Canadian Special Publication of Fisheries and Aquatic Sciences 87; 1986. A study of the effects of acid precipitation on aquatic biota using a number of predictive models on a sample of 814 lakes. Discusses the relationship of pH to fish productivity, species diversity and fish body burdens of trace metals with pH. Estimates the number of lakes currently receiving deposition considerably above background levels.

Kneese, Allen V., Measuring the Benefits of Clean Air and Water, Baltimore, MD: John Hopkins Press; 1984 for Resources for the Future.
Note: 159 pp.
This book discusses benefit/cost analysis and its application to calculating the environmental effects of air and water pollution, and placing values on clean air and water. Effects on human life, wages, agriculture, and visibility are covered. There is an extensive bibliography.

Kubo, Arthur S.; Rose, David J., "Disposal of Nuclear Wastes," Science; 21 December 1973; 182(4118): 1205-1211. Note: 7 pp.
Explores the options of disposing of wastes at an increased but still reasonable cost.

Labor and Human Resources Senate Committee, Reviewing the Causes and Consequences of the Chernobyl Nuclear Powerplant Incident, 100th Cong., 1st sess.; 1987.
Note: 42 pp.
On 20 January 1987, two prominent doctors, Yevgeny Velikhov and Robert Gale, spoke before the Senate Committee on Labor and Human Resources in the wake of the accident at Chernobyl. Dr. Velikov's testimony focused mainly upon the immediate effects on the population surrounding the Chernobyl power plant. He mentions that 31 people died, 209 suffered serious radiation injury, and 135,000 people were evacuated from an area of 18 miles around the plant. He also testifies about certain characteristics of radiation dispersal such as "hot pockets." These are areas in the vicinity of the accident site that contain higher levels of radiation than others. Dr. Gale spoke mainly about the future incidences of cancer that would result from the radiation dispersal. Of the Soviet population evacuated from the area surrounding the Chernobyl plant, there will be 1000 extra cases of cancer than would have occurred without the accident. Both doctors make recommendations on how both the United States and the Soviet Union should proceed in the use of nuclear power.

Lave, Lester B., Silverman, Lester P., "Economic Costs of Energy Related Environmental Pollution," Annual Review of Energy, Palo Alto, CA 1976, 1: 601-28.
Note: 28 pp.
This article presents the theory of benefit/cost analysis and explains its application to environmental decisions. Authors attempt to assign dollar values to the cost of

environmental damage caused by air pollution resulting from the burning of fossil fuels. The damages assessed include damage to human health, visibility, quality of life, plants and animals, and water resources.

Lawrence Berkeley Laboratory (LBL), Applied Science Division, Energy Analysis Program Annual Report FY 1988, Mark Levine, Program Leader. Berkeley, CA: LBL, Applied Science Division, March 1989. (LBL-26585).
Note: Paginated by section.
This report summarizes the research of the Energy Analysis Program at LBL in the areas of building energy analysis, building energy data, energy conservation policy, environmental policy analysis, international energy studies, and resource market mechanisms. Short summaries of specific research projects with reference lists are included. According to the introduction, appliance standards continue to be the leading energy policy analysis activity of the program.

"Legislative History and Description of Federal Superfund," Journal of Environmental Law, 2: 68-102.
Note: Svitek, Laura L. bibliography.
This paper discussed two pieces of legislation aimed at providing a remedy for the effects of improper management of hazardous substances; one is CERCLA. Included is a legislative history, and a discussion of the major provisions.

Leiter, Robert D., Friedlander, Stanley L., Economics of Resources, New York: Cycro Press, Inc., 1976.
Note: Svitek, Laura L. bibliography.
Included within this text is a description of the factors that led to the environmental state we face today. It examines private and public proposals to develop a less polluted environment and sources of cleaner energy. Topics included are conservation, energy analysis, economic growth, and resource scarcity.

Levings, S., Walfred, Reed, Scott, and Cauchois, Methodologies for Valuation of Agricultural Crop Yield Changes: A Review, Sacramento, CA: Eureka Laboratories, Inc.; August 1978.
This report considers the "physical effects of man-made and natural factors on changes in agricultural crop yields and the methodologies and models used ... to quantify the economic impacts of crop yield changes on the farm, the agricultural industry and ... the consumer."

Lewis, Ruth A., "Mars Colony Grows in Arizona," Sierra, May/June 1987.
Note: Svitek, Laura L. bibliography.
Lewis describes the Biosphere II project which should be completed in 1989. Upon completion, eight people will enter this manmade biosphere and dwell for approximately 2 years. This biosphere contains various ecosystems including a desert, a marsh and an ocean.

Library of Congress, Congressional Research Service, Library Services Division, "Selections from the: CRS Bibliographic Database," Bibliography on Social (Monetary) Costs of Energy Measures.
Note: 82 pp.
This preliminary bibliography contains 225 annotated citations to literature intended to provide an introduction to the topic of social costs of energy. References include periodical articles, pamphlets, government and congressional documents, and public policy research studies. Dates covered are 1984 through

1989. Social costs include energy security and transportation uses of energy as well as electric and natural gas policy concerns.

Library of Congress, Congressional Research Service, Environmental Factors in Benefit-Cost Analysis of Development Activities, by: Gorte, Ross W. Washington, D.C.: Library of Congress; 20 May 1986. (86-702 ENR).
A brief description of cost-benefit analysis and its limitations and how environmental impacts are included in U.S. agency project analyses. The historical background and comparison of requirements for water projects and U.S. Forest Service timber sales are particularly useful.

Lipfert, Frederick W., (Brookhaven National Laboratory, Upton, New York), "Sulfur Oxides, Particulates, and Human Mortality: Synopsis of Statistical Correlations. Journal of the Air Pollution Control Association, April, 1980, 30(4): 366-371.
Note: 6 pp.
This paper reviews the statistical evidence linking human mortality with air pollution due to sulfur oxides and particulates. Three types of analyses are discussed: episodic increases in mortality coincident with high pollution, changes in air quality, and comparisons of geographic differentials in both pollution and mortality rates. The paper concludes that there are no reliable statistical associations between SOX and mortality, but that particulates are in some cases associated with excess mortality. Establishing whether the association is in fact causal would require elimination of potential confounding effects such as occupational exposures. No costing figures.

Lochard, Jacques, Maccia, Carlo, Pages, Pierre, "Cost-Effectiveness Considerations in Reducing Occupational Radiation Exposure in Nuclear Power Plants," Nuclear Safety, November-December 1983; 24(6).
This study details how the extent of worker radiation exposure is directly proportional to both the degree to which the plant has implemented new power plant technology and the extent to which workers are instructed in the use of the technology.

Loomis, John, "Use of Travel Cost Models for Evaluating Lottery Rationed Recreation: Application to Big Game Hunting," Journal of Leisure Research, 1982; 14(2): 117-124.
Note: Svitek, Laura L. bibliography.
Modifications of the standard TCM are suggested to fulfill the assumptions necessary to use TCM in recreation benefit estimates. Using data on buffalo, sheep and antelope hunts in Utah, a TCM with and without the modifications is evaluated.

Lovins, Amory, Cost-Risk-Benefit Assessments in Energy Policy, George Washington Law Review; August 1977, 45: 911-943.
Note: 33 pp.
This article critically examines the then current methods for performing cost-risk-benefit assessments and concludes that those methods scientifically irredeemably defective, useless and dangerous. The author outlines the basis for his skepticism and examines the problems of evaluating benefits, risks, the monetary value of risks, and direct costs, the difficulty of comparing these quantities, and the use of these comparisons in decision-making.

Lovins, Amory B.; Lovins, L. Hunter, "International Project for Soft Energy Paths). Energy: What's the Problem?" Energy Policy: 302-313.
Note: 12 pp.
This article criticizes the failure of energy planners to match forms of energy with consumer requirements.

Lovins, Amory B.; Lovins, L. Hunter; Krause, Florentin; Bach, Wilfrid, Least-Cost Energy: Solving the CO2 Problem. Andover, MA, Brick House Publishing Co.,1981.
Note: 184 pp.
This work is thorough discussing of the use of energy-efficiency as a necessary means of controlling carbon dioxide pollution and thus averting global warming. The chapters explain the forecasting of energy use, the kinds of energy needed, and sustainable sources of energy. Authors also examine strategies for implementing energy-efficiency and the serious costs of failure to pursue energy efficiency.

Lum, Arnold L. "Shorebird Fauna Changes of a Small Tropical Estuary Following Habitat Alteration: Biological and Political Impacts of Environmental Restoration." Environmental Management, 1978, 2(5), 423-430.
Note: Svitek, Laura L. bibliography.
The purpose of Lum's article was to examine the effects of restoration of a lagoon located in Hawaii. He examined the biological and political impacts of the restoration project. The project was undertaken to preserve species of Hawaiian birds that dwelled in this area.

Lynne, Gary; Conroy, Patricia; Prochaska, Frederick, "Economic Valuation of Marsh Areas for Marine Production Processes," Journal of Environmental Economics and Management; 1981; 8(2): 175-186.
Note: Sviteck, L. bibliography.
This article focuses on finding an approach for quantifying and evaluating the contribution of marsha areas to the production of marine life which is marketable. The bio- economic model present in this paper attempts to emphasize the explicit role that natural ecosystems play.

MacKenzie, James J., Breathing Easier: Taking Action on Climate Change, Air Pollution, and Energy Insecurity, Washington, D.C., World Resources Institute, Undated, ISBN, circa 1988/ 1989.
Note: 23 pp.
This booklet is an accepted as a general treatment of the linkages between the energy use and the threats posed by greenhouse warming, air pollution, and oil imports. It includes illustrative charts and figures.

MacKenzie, James J.; El-Ashry, Mohamed T, Ill, Winds Airborne Pollution's Toll on Trees and Crops, Washington, DC, World Resources Institute, September 1988.
Note: 74 pp.
This report presents evidence that air pollutants are contributing to current forest and agricultural losses in the United States and explores policy options to reduce these losses. The analysis shows that multiple pollutants, including acidic compounds and ozone, are contributing to the problem. Policy recommendations are made within a broad framework for national energy planning and not in terms of regulating individual sources of pollution to meet ambient air standards.

Mackerron, Conrad, "Superfund Cleanup: The Lessons of Love Canal and Stringfellow," Chemical Week, September 2, 1987, 141, 35- 40.
Note: Svitek bibliography.
Mackerron focused on the preliminary cleanup of Love Canal. It is the author's belief that the outlook for the Stringfellow site is more hopeful than the Love Canal site.

Malcolm, Pirnie, Preliminary Value Engineering Report, Marathon Battery Company Site, 1988.
Note: Svitek, L. bibliography.
Malcolm Pirnie entered into agreement to complete a Superfund remedial action design for the Marathon Battery Company Site. The design was based on remedial investigations and feasibility studies previously conducted.

Marmorek, D.R., Jones, M.L., Minns, C.K., Elder, F.C., "Assessing the Potential Extent of Damage to Inland Lakes in Eastern Canada due to Acidic Deposition. I. Development and Evaluation of a Simple 'Site' Model." Canadian Journal of Fisheries and Aquatic Sciences, 1989.
A model is presented that uses measurements of current lake chemistry to predict lake chemistry given specified levels of acidic deposition. Model outputs are highly sensitive to estimates of pre-acidification lake sulphate levels, and less so to assumptions about the catchment's ability to neutralize incoming acidity.

Martin, Michael, [Serial No. 96-H9, pt.2, pp. 182-6]. "Statement for the Hazardous and Toxic Waste Disposal Field Hearings," March 29, 1979.
Note: Svitek, L. bibliography.
Martin discussed the quantification of ecological damage before various committees. He implied that the process is limited by sample methodologies, and the availability of time and resources. Two methods of assessing biological impacts of discharged materials are presented: direct valuation and indirect methods.

Massachusetts Department of Public Health, et al., The Greater New Bedford PCB Health Effects Study, 1984-87, [Executive Summary].
Note: Svitek, Laura L. bibliography.
This study was designed to estimate serum PCB levels in residents of the New Bedford Harbor area. The relationship between serum PCB levels, seafood consumption, age and blood pressure were examined.

McGovern, E. Carol, Summary of the Background Concentration of a Variety of Elements in Soils with Special Regard to New York State, NYSDEC, Bureau of Wildlife, 1988.
Note: Svitek, L. bibliography.
Twenty different elements were examined in this article. The background levels of these elements in soils is being determined from the literature. A summary of the current findings in included.

McMahon, John C, The Unloading of Niagara, Clearwaters, 1988, 18(1), 10-11.
Note: Svitek, L. bibliography.
This article documents important reductions in the amounts of toxic pollutants discharged to the Niagara River from industries and municipal sewage treatment plants in NYS. These reductions are seen in a comparison of two measurements of toxic loadings.

Menz, Frederick, and Wilton, Donald, "An Economic Evaluation of the St. Lawrence River-Eastern Lake Ontario Bass Fishery," Fishery Bulletin, 81(1): 168-175.
Menz and Wilton provide information on the economic importance of the bass fishery. This study uses the TCM to estimate the demand for angling in the St. Lawrence River. A description of the fishery and of the TCM are provided.

Meridian Corporation, Energy Systems Emissions and Materiel Requirements, Deputy Assistant Secretary for Renewable Energy, U.S. Department of Energy, Alexandria, VA; February 1989. (DRAFT).
Note: 34 pp.
Compares emissions from five different energy systems: a conventional coal plant with scrubbers (500 MW), an Atmospheric Fluidized Bed Combustion plant (500 MW), an Integrated Gasification Combined Cycle plant (1000 MW), a boiling water nuclear reactor (100 MW), and a central station photovoltaic plant (100 MW). This study attempts to view the environmental impacts associated with each technology.

Minns, C.K., "Acid Rain: A Preliminary Estimate of the Risk to Ontario's Inland Fisheries," Canadian Manuscript Report on Fisheries and Aquatic Sciences, 1981, No. 1622.
Quantity and geographic distribution of recreational fish species at risk from acid precipitation. Twenty fish community assemblages are presented. Some correlations are made between lake size and species present.

Minns, C.K., et al., "Large Scale Risk Assessment of Acid Rain Impacts on Fisheries: Models and Lessons," Canadian Journal of Fisheries and Aquatic Sciences, 1986, 43(4): 100-921.
A comparative analysis of two does-response models developed in the early 1980s for regional application.

Minns, C.K., Kelso, John R., "Estimates of Existing and Potential Impact of Acidification on the Freshwater Fishery Resources and their Use in Eastern Canada." Water, Air and Soil Pollution, 1986, 31: 1079-1090.
A model to predict fisheries response to lake acidification is presented. The authors estimate that 10% of economically important fisheries resources are in jeopardy. Reduction of SO4 deposition is found to greatly reduce predicted losses.

MITRE Corporation, editor, Proceedings of Quantitative Environmental Comparison of Coal and Nuclear Electrical Generation and their Associated Fuel Cycles Workshop, National Science Foundation, Office of Energy R&D Policy, McClean, Virginia, MITRE Corporation, August 1975, 1, (MTR-7010).
Note: 357 pp.
The workshop was intended to gather the available information and expert opinions on the feasibility of quantifying environmental risks associated with the coal and nuclear fuel cycles.

Morton, James Walter, Ecological Effects of Dredging and Dredge Spoil Disposal: A Literature Review, Technical Paper No. 94: U.S. Fish and Wildlife Service.
This article examines various effects that dredging and spoil disposal have on estuarine ecosystems. Included are descriptions of the types of dredging methods and the side effects accompanied with each. Chemical and biological effects are discussed.

Moskowitz, P.D., and Hamilton, L.D., Bibliography, Upton, NY: Photovoltaic Environmental, Health, and Safety Project, Biomedical and Environmental Assessment Division, Brookhaven National Laboratory, June 1989.
Note: 7 pp.
An extensive unannotated bibliography of photovoltaic environmental health and safety literature.

Mount, Timothy D., and Czerwinski, Martha E., Long Range Planning for Electricity Generation with Regional Constraints on Emissions, rev. ed., Ithaca, NY, Cornell University, 19 January 1989.
Market "Not to be quoted without permission of authors. This paper describes a model of the New York Power Pool and evaluates the effect of emissions from power plants. The scenarios discussed impose various environmental constraints and model the effect of the associated shadow prices (control costs). The paper concludes with illustrative emissions penalties for electricity generated at specific locations for any source of generation. The paper was originally presented at the seventeenth annual meeting of the Northeast Regional Science Association, Cornell University, Ithaca, NY.

Naegele, John A., Feder, William A., Brandt, Jeffrey C., Assessment of Air Pollution Damage to Vegetation in New England, July 1971 - July 1972: Final Report, US Environmental Protection Agency (EPA), Office of Research and Monitoring, Washington, DC, EPA, August 1972 (EPA-R5-72-09).
Note: 18 pp.
Assessment of losses, including grower profit losses, reduction in yield and/or quality, based on observed injury from air pollution or records of previous air pollution injury. Cultural and climatic factors were taken into account when estimating these losses. Indirect losses attributable to air pollution include costs to replace a sensitive crop with a tolerant one, aesthetic considerations, and farm abandonment. Indirect losses were either absorbed by the growers prior to this survey or could not be assessed in the time available and were therefore not included in this report. Sulfur dioxide caused losses of $43,500in agronomic crops, $3,000in commercially sold flowers and foliage and $30,000in fruit production and sales.

National Acidic Precipitation Assessmant Program (NAPAP), "Interim Assessment: The Causes and Effects of Acidic Deposition," Volume II, Emissions and Controls, 1987, 2.
This report discusses the need for alternatives to conventional fossil fuel combustion. It lists emissions associated with fossil fuel combustion and details the need for controls which can be implemented in order to reduce emissions from fossil fuel-fired generating systems.

New York Senate Committee on Environment, Conservation, and Recreation, Acid Rain: An Intergovernmental Policy Forum, Summary Report of the Proceedings, Held at Albany, NY, 7 - 8 February 1984.
Note: 94 pp.
This brief survey of the nature, sources, and environmental impact of acid rain focuses on New York and the Adirondack Mountain Region and discusses approaches to solving the acid rain problem.

New York State Energy Research and Development Authority, Indoor Air Quality, Infiltration and Ventilation in Residential Buildings, Prepared by W.S. Fleming and Associates, Inc. Syracuse, New York, March 1985.
Concludes that source strength is the dominant factor in indoor air pollutants and that the most effective general method of indoor pollution control is prevention of source emissions.

New York State Energy Office (SEO), Division of Conservation, Evaluation Unit, Program Evaluation of the New York State Energy Efficient Appliance Rebate Demonstration Program, Albany, NY, New York SEO, May 1989.
Note: 48 pp. plus appendices.
The New York State Energy Efficient Appliance Rebate Demonstration Program, a petroleum overcharge refund mechanism, was designed to determine if financial incentives influence consumers to purchase energy efficient appliances. The detailed evaluation presented in this report was based on data from two sources, consumers who received rebates and appliance dealers who participated in the program. The report concludes that cost-benefit energy savings analyses show the program as moderately successful. Among other recommendations, the evaluators suggest that if the program is to be continued the appliance eligibility criteria should be designed to insure that only models which significantly exceed the minimum federal efficiency standards are eligible for rebates and that the amount of the rebate should be lowered. Evaluators note that the avoided electricity generation resulting from the sale of appliances that received a rebate has the potential to reduce emissions levels in New York by nearly 174,000 tons (Exhibit Y, p. 39).

Nixon, Michael, "Estimating the Cost of Nuclear Decommissioning," Public Utilities Fortnightly, 15 May 1986, 47-50.
Note: 4 pp.
This article estimates the costs to decommission specific reactor, e.g. Susquehanna Units 1 & 2, Boston Edison, etc.

Nixon, Michael, "Financing of Nuclear Decommissioning Costs," Public Utilities Fortnightly, 20 March 1986, 57-60.
Note: 4 pp.
This article discusses the various ways of financing decommissioning: unsegregated funds, segregated internal funds, external funds, and income tax considerations.

Noguchi, Laura S., Bimber, David L., Tin, Heang T., Mansfield, Pamela J., Jude, David J., Field Distribution and Entrainment of Fish Larvae and Eggs at the Donald C. Cook Nuclear Power Plant, Southeastern Lake Michigan, 1980-82, Ronald Rossmann, Project Director, Ann Arbor, Michigan, Great Lakes Research Division, University of Michigan, 1985 (v. Special Report No. 116).
Note: 251 pp.
This study discusses the impact that entrainment of fish eggs and larvae and impingement of juvenile and adult fishes have on the fish population. The study mentions how these processes could significantly affect the viability of Lake Michigan fisheries.

Northeast Utilities, Marketing Services Department, A Comparison of Two Weatherization Techniques: N.U. Seal-up vs. The Air-Sealing Specialist, Northeast Utilities Service Company, Hartford, CT, March, 1988. Northeast Utilities Seal-up program is designed to save heating and cooling costs by reducing a Home's rate of air infiltration. An alternative method uses a "blower door" to depressurize the home, and special leak-detecting tools to locate air leakage sites. This study compared these two methods in terms of energy savings and economic benefits. The final section of the report discusses the effects of weatherization on indoor air quality. Radon, formaldehyde, and nitrogen dioxide were measured as representative of the chemical pollutants that can be found indoors. With all three pollutants, almost as may sites showed decreases in pollutant concentration after weatherization as showed increases. The report concludes that source strength appears to be the dominant factor as opposed to ventilation (removal) rate. Includes references to other studies of indoor air pollution.

Northwest Center for Occupational Health and Safety Department of Environmental Health and University of Washington, Sponsor, "Health Effects of Wood Smoke," NOAA Western Regional Center, Seattle, WA, 20 January 1988.
A culmination of reports and articles which provide a view of the historic evolution of concern over development of air pollution control strategies and the problems associated with environmental impacts. Deals for the most part with woodsmoke from non- commercialized and industrialized sources.

Northwest Power Planning Council (NPPC), Accounting for the Environmental Consequences of Electricity Resources During the Power Planning Process, NPPC, Portland, OR, 17 April 1989.
This paper review how the NPPC accounted for environmental costs of resources in its two previous plans and briefly discusses alternative ways of considering environmental and social impacts associated with resources used to produce electricity. The paper was prepared by staff as part of the NPPC's process to develop a new Northwest Power Plan by the early 1990s. The deadline for public comment on this paper is 16 June 1989.

Nuclear Safety Information Center (NSIC) Staff, "Comparative Risk-Cost-Benefit Study of Alternative Sources of Electrical Energy," Nuclear Safety, 17:(2), March-April 1976. pp.171-184.
This study is excerpted from what is considered "the most comprehensive assessment of the risks, costs, and benefits of coal, oil, natural gas, and nuclear fuel cycles."It quantifies conventional and societal costs of electrical energy production, focusing on routine impacts, and accidents at light water reactors (LWRs).

Nuclear Regulatory Commission, Reactor Safety Study: An Assessment of Accident Risks in U.S. Commercial Nuclear Power Plants, U.S. Nuclear Regulatory Commission, Washington, D.C., 1975.
This report was created under the direction of Norman C. Rasmussen of MIT. The study was performed to come up with an independent assessment of potential accident risks in U.S. commercial reactors. This is the first study of its kind. Later studies tend to discredit this report especially in the areas of accident probabilities and radiation effects on human beings.

Oak Ridge National Laboratory, Fusion Environmental Assessment Program, Cannon, J.B., Background Information and Technical Basis for Assessment of Environmental Implications of Magnetic Fusion Energy, Contract No. OR ENG 26 National Technical Information Service, Springfield, VA, August 1983.
This report contains background information for assessing the potential environmental implications of fusion-based central electric power stations. This

report is the principle reference upon which an environmental impact statement on magnetic fusion energy will be based. Reference list.

Oak Ridge Associated Universities, Institute for Energy Analysis, Economic and Environmental Impacts of a U.S. Nuclear Moratorium, 1985-2010, Institute for Energy Analysis and MIT Press, 1979.
This book analyzes the potential impact of a full nuclear moratorium from 1985 to 2010. Of particular note are the emissions figures for coal and nuclear.

Odum, H.T. and E.C. Odum, Energy Basis for Man and Nature, McGraw-Hill Book Co., New York, 1976. The authors introduce energy principles and discuss the flows of energy into the environment. The book includes the basic laws of energy, alternatives energy options and some possibilities for the future. Useful basic information is presented on the flows of energy in ecological systems.

OECD, Nuclear Energy Agency, "Long-Term Radiation Protection Objectives for Radioactive Waste Disposal," OECD, Paris, 1984.
This book is of use in our nuclear report for obtaining radiation emission guidelines and goals, as well as dose assessment.

Office of Technology Assessment, Acid Rain and Transported Air Pollutants: Implications for Public Policy, Washington, DC, June 1984.
This book contains a detailed exploration of air pollutants, including policy options and concerns, risks of damage and control relating to transport of air pollutants, and the regional distribution of risks. The book evaluates the legislative options available to Congress and makes some legislative proposals. Statistics and estimates of the costs of control of emissions are included, as well as outlines of major states regulatory policies. The book is summarized in a small booklet of the same title.

Office of Technology Assessment (OTA), Biological Effects of Power Frequency Electric and Magnetic Fields: Background Paper, Government Printing Office, Washington, D.C., May 1989.
This background paper was prepared as part of OTA's assessment of Electric Power Wheeling and Dealing. The report begins with a general discussion of the sources and nature of electric and magnetic fields, and then reviews studies over the last fifteen years which demonstrate that even weak low frequency electromagnetic fields can affect cell membrane biology. In addition to the cellular studies, the report reviews whole animal and human experiments examining general behavioral effects; effects on physical parameters; effects on specific biochemicals; effects on circadian rhythms; and effects in the epidemiology of cancer. The report concludes with a discussion of regulatory activity and exposure standards and policy implications. Extensive reference list.

Office of Technology Assessment (OTA), Electric Power Wheeling and Dealing: Technological Considerations for Increasing Competition, U.S. Government Printing Office, Washington, D.C., May 1989.
This report provides an overview of the electric power industry and discusses alternative scenarios for increasing competition in the electric power industry. Technological requirements, regional characteristics, siting, and environmental and health effects associated with increased competition and expanded transmission access are discussed. Policy discussion focuses on three areas of potential congressional concern: technical and institutional changes necessary to assure the reliability and economy of bulk power systems in a transition to competition; the

lack of information to support decision making about electric power industry structure and regulation; and broader issues such as state and federal jurisdiction.

Office of Technology Assessment (OTA), "Incineration," Facing America's Trash: What Next For Municipal Solid Waste?, U.S. Government Printing Office, Washington, DC, October 1989. pp.217-267.
This chapter discusses technologies and environmental characteristics of municipal waste combustion, but does not emphasize waste-to-energy facilities. Risks and control mechanisms for air emissions are included along with ash constituents and ash disposal options. Extensive reference list.

Office of Technology Assessment (OTA), Managing the Nation's Commercial High-Level Radioactive Waste, Congress of the United States, Washington, DC, 1985. This report is intended to update information concerning the Nuclear Waste Policy Act of 1982, and reviews in particular three documents that the DOE will be submitting to the 99th Congress: (a) a Mission Plan for the waste management program; (b) a monitored retrievable storage (MRS) proposal; and (c) a report on ways of financing and managing the waste program.

Ohio Office of Consumers' Counsel, Clearing the Air: Using Energy Conservation to Reduce Acid Rain Compliance Costs in Ohio, 2 vols. Ohio Office of Consumer Counsel, Columbus, Ohio, July 1988.
This study reports the potential for energy conservation and the impact if could have on sulfur emission reduction programs for Ohio electric utilities. Specific suggestions for legislation which would control acid rain through energy conservation are made. The separate volume of technical appendices includes detailed discussion of the methodology for conservation analysis and integrated electric utility planning model documentation.

Olivier, J.P., OECD Nuclear Energy Agency, "Financial provisions needed now to deal with future waste," Nuclear Engineering International, February 1978. pp.29-31.
Waste disposal could represent 50% of total waste management costs but it will be some time before waste disposal must be paid for and accurate estimation of the costs is almost impossible. An international fund set up now would overcome many of the financing problems that are likely to arise. (This discusses control costs).

Organization for Economic Co-Operation and Development (OECD), Environmental Data Compendium, OECD, Paris, 1989.
Compendium of data relating to environmental quality for OECD member nations. Data is organized into two parts: the state of the environmental and pressures on the environment.

Organization for Economic Co-operation and Development (OECD), The Costs and Benefits of Sulphur Oxide Control: A Methodological Study, OECD, Paris, 1981.

This report examines the effect of sulphur dioxide (SO2) on health, materials, crops, and ecosystems. The study computes the annual costs of emissions for each member country and also gives the dollars per ton of SO2 removed. Other costs are computed: the cost of agricultural crop damage, and the costs of damage to materials , health and ecosystems. The OECD member countries are Australia, Austria, Belgium, Canada, Denmark, Finland, France, The Federal Republic of Germany, Greece, Iceland, Ireland, Italy, Japan, Luxembourg, The Netherlands,

New Zealand, Norway, Portugal, Spain, Sweden, Switzerland, Turkey, the United Kingdom, and the United States.

Organization for Economic Co-operation and Development (OECD), Environmental Effects of Electricity Generation, OECD, Paris, 1985.
A thorough report of every aspect of the environmental effects of electricity generation that are associated with coal, gas, nuclear, and oil plants. The environmental effects of renewables such as solar, wind, hydro, geothermal, and biomass are also covered. Includes an extensive list of references.

Owens/Corning, "Energy Conservation and Indoor Air Quality," January 1981.
This paper concerns the quality of indoor air and how it relates to energy efficient homes. Indoor pollutants are discussed individually and in detail, along with explanations of their origins and effects on health.

Parker, L.B. and Robert E. Trumbule, Mitigating Acid Rain with Technology: Avoiding the Scrubbing-Switching Dilemma, Congressional Research Service; The Library of Congress, Washington, DC., July 28, 1983. This report reviews and compares various fossil fuel technologies capable of controlling SO2 and NOx emissions from electric power plants. It considers pre-combustion controls such as coal cleaning and fuel switching; in-situ techniques like fluidized bed combustion; and post-combustion controls such as flue gas desulfurization. Included are articles describing coal slurries and improved pulverized coal technology. The technologies are compared on the basis of their percent reduction of SO2 and NOx.

Pawlick, T., A Killing Rain, 1984.
This book discusses the effects of acid deposition on the world environment, from the curtailing of sport fishing in Canada to the destruction of the european forests and the contamination of well water supplies here in the United States. The book also gives a scientific overview of how acid rain is formed and discusses the alternatives for abatement through present and future technologies.

Pollock, C., Decommissioning: Nuclear Power's Missing Link, Worldwatch Institute, Washington, D.C., April 1986.
This paper discusses the costs of decommissioning and dismantlement, high level waste storage and management, reactor disposal, and waste burial. Pollock proposes that we look toward a long-term strategy in dealing with the impending costs associated with the back-end of the nuclear fuel cycle, and urges that we take steps now to avoid decommissioning problems in the near future. These measures include examining the methods in decommissioning funding employed by other countries, examining the problems encountered during recent dismantling operations, well- funded R & D programs, detailed regulations and technical guidelines, and early knowledge of decommissioning requirements, so that engineering designs can be anticipated. (Bibliography included).

Public Utilities Fortnightly Staff, "No Significant Environmental Impact for Certain Nuclear Waste Storage," Public Utilities Fortnightly, 7 July 1983. pp.53-54.
This article announces the Supreme Court's decision to uphold the NRC's regulation which states that permanent storage of nuclear wastes has no significant environmental impact under the National Environmental Policy Act, otherwise known as the "zero-release assumption".

Radar, N., K. Bossong, A. Antypas and S. Denman, Critical Mass Energy Project of Public Citizen (Radar and Bossong), and Safe Energy Communication Council (Antypas and Denman), Turning Down the Heat--Solutions to Global Warming: An Analysis of Energy Efficiency, Renewable Resources, and Other Options Versus New Nuclear Power Development, Public Citizen and the Safe Energy Communication Council, Washington, D.C., September 1988.
In the face of the global warming problem, decision makers are trying to find alternatives to the burning of fossil fuels. The authors mention that these decision makers have been continually pointing to the use of nuclear power to replace the burning of fossil fuels. The authors argue that nuclear power does not fulfill the criteria for reducing fossil fuel emissions in the shortest necessary time, with the least economic and environmental costs. Rather, the authors wish to emphasize that investments in energy efficiency, renewable energy, and selected natural gas technologies can eliminate about 68% of the carbon dioxide emissions by the year 2000.

Ragozin, D.L./Brown, Gardner, "Harvest Policies and Nonmarket Valuation in a Predator-Prey System," Journal of Environmental Economics and Management, 12:(2), 1985. pp.155-68.
Since organisms within an ecosystem have no commercial value, Ragozin and Brown attempt to show that these organisms do have economic value. Using a predator-prey model, they establish that if the predator has a market value, then the economic value of the prey can be determined.

Ramsay, W., Unpaid Costs of Electrical Energy: Health and Environmental Impacts from Coal and Nuclear Energy, Resources for the Future, Washington, D.C., 1979. The author attempts to improve the public understanding of the coal-nuclear comparison by describing the unpaid costs associated with these technologies. Ramsay asserts that these costs are uncertain because of scientific doubts (because of air pollution) and possible alterations in technologies (coal mining). In comparing the types of uncertainties associated with these technologies, he treats the concept of uncertainty as a determinant in policy decisions. Ramsay goes on to propose a three-pronged strategy for the nation despite these uncertainties: "1. to continue a coal- nuclear mix in new plant construction; 2. to push forward on research in order to advance knowledge of the true magnitude of the impacts; and 3. to place a heavy emphasis on introducing control technologies that will mitigate the impacts which are thought to be dangerous.

RCG/Hagler, Bailly, Inc., Etter, C.L., Report on Colorado Electric Power Options Study -- Phase 1, RCG/Hagler, Bailly, Inc., Boulder, CO, 1989.
This report summarizes current knowledge regarding the potential supply and demand situation in the state of Colorado. Areas of focus were: current and future supply, future demand, transmission facilities, cogeneration and small power production, conservation and demand-side management, and the overall planning process. Work was conducted under a grant from the United States Department of Energy (DE FG01- 87CE27473).

Regens, J.L. and R.W. Rycroft, "The Economic Dimension: Benefits, Costs, and Financing Options," The Acid Rain Controversy, University of Pittsburgh Press, Pittsburgh, PA, 1988. Chapter 4 of this book on acid rain policy options discusses the magnitude of environmental benefits and control costs of emissions reduction programs. The book itself has an extensive reference list of acid rain- related materials. (Other chapters discuss technological, political, and scientific aspects of acid rain policy with treatment of both state and federal approaches.).

Regulatory Impact Analysis of the National Ambient Air Quality Standards For Nitrogen Dioxide, Office of Air Quality Planning and Standards, U.S. Environmental Protection Agency, Research Triangle Park, NC., June 1985.
This report examines the tests, benefits and other economic impacts of implementing alternative primary annual nitrogen dioxide ambient air quality standards.

Renew America, Reducing the Rate of Global Warming: The States' Role, Renew America, Washington, DC, November 1988.
This report attempts to track and quantify individual state carbon dioxide emissions contributing to the greenhouse effect, as well as state policies that may help reduce matrices summarizing carbon emissions resulting from electricity production and associated policy recommendations.

Riccio, J. and S. Murphy, The Aging of Nuclear Power Plants: A Citizen's Guide to Causes and Effects, Nuclear Information and Resource Service, Washington, D.C.,
This report outlines the reasons why the aging of nuclear power plants will become an important issue in the future. For example, three-fifths of the approximately 100 operating power plants in the United States are over ten years old. Some of the hazards associated with this aging process are the corrosion of pipes and other mechanisms within the plant. The authors maintain that the N.R.C. must address this problem with greater interest than it has in the past.

Rich, P.R. and L. Joe Moffitt, "Benefits of Pollution Control on Mass. Housatonic River: A Hedonic Pricing Approach," Water Resources Research, 18:(8), 1982. pp.1033-37.
Rich and Moffitt examine one analysis for estimating the benefits of water pollution control. They use the property value technique to measure the positive benefits associated with pollution reduction The results indicate substantial benefits associated with abatement programs.

Ridker, R.G. and W.D. Watson, To Choose A Future: Resource and Environmental Consequences of Alternative Growth Paths, John Hopkins University Press, Baltimore, MD, 1980; for Resources for the Future.
This book presents scenarios of environmental problems that the United States may face during the next fifty years. One chapter covers world and domestic energy demand and supply, renewable, and nonrenewables. Other chapters survey United States energy policy, the effect of energy policy on the United States economy, costs of pollution control, and environmental problems associated with energy use.

Riely, P.L. and D. Rockland, A review of fisheries economic valuation methods, Sport Fishing Institute, June 1988.
This report analyzes the effect of chemical contaminants on sport fisheries. It discusses various methods available for valuation. They include TCM, unit day value method, and CVM.

Roach and Jaksch, Air Pollution Control Costs and Regional Impacts in the Four Corners Study Region, Report Number 3, March 1981.
Discusses control costs of air pollution.

Rosenfeld, A.H. and J.G. Koomey, "Promoting Efficiency Investments in New Buildings,"Wisconsin's Environmental Decade, 4 August 1988,Lawrence Berkeley Laboratory.
Includes avoided social costs as part of the reasons for recommended hook-up fees in the Wisconsin PSC's Advance Plan 5 docket.

Rowe, M.D., "Human Exposure to Particulate Emissions from Power Plants," Brookhaven National Laboratory, May 1981.
Health impacts of a "standard" coal-fired power plant are estimated to be 0.12 excess deaths per year from cancer caused by exposed to polycyclicorganic matter, with a range of 0.022 to 0.34 excess deaths attributable to uncertainty of the emission factor and uncertainty of same location. The health impacts were obtained from computer simulator makeup of long-range transport of fire- particle emissions from a "standard" coal- fired power plant, aggregated in frequency distributors of concentration and human exposure throughout the United States. No costing figures reported.

Rowe, R.D. and L.G. Chestnut, The Value of Visibility: Economic Theory and Applications for Air Pollution Control, Abt. Books, Cambridge, MA, 1982.
This work was undertaken to demonstrate how economic measurement of aesthetic benefits can be conducted. The authors review the theory and practice of visibility benefits assessment. A number of case studies are reviewed in detail. Includes glossary and bibliography.

Rowe, R. and L. Chestnut, "Valuing Environmental Commodities: Revisited," Land Economics, 59:(4), 1983.
This article debates a previous article by Schulze, d'Arge and Brookshire (1981), which presents a case application of contingent valuation market bidding technique. They believe that the paper strongly overstates the effectiveness of CMBT.

Schurr, S.H., Energy in America's Future: The Choices Before Us: A Study by the Staff of the RFF National Energy Strategies Project, 2 vols. John Hopkins University Press, Baltimore, MD, 1979; for Resources for the Future, Inc.
This book discusses energy conservation at length, including its relationships to energy consumption and the United States economy. Projections are made for future energy consumption and various sources of supply are examined, including renewable and synthetic fuels. Of special interest is Part IV, which concerns the health and environmental effects of electric power generation. Part IV includes references to studies that have assigned costs to the environmental and health effects of electric power generation. The impact of power generation on land use and water quality is also examined.

Scott, D.L., Pollution in the Electric Power Industry: Its Control and Costs, DC Health and Company, Lexington Books, Lexington, MA, 1973.
This book explains how economics can be used to examine the environmental effects of energy generation and of pollution control and includes an overview of the electric power industry.

Sebold, F.D., M.A. Thayer and R.K. Hageman, San Diego State University, Department of Economics and Regional Economic Research, Recognition and Valuation of Externalities in Assessing the Cost Effectiveness of Utility Conservation Programs, (undated: early 1980s).
This article discusses incorporation of external and intangible effects such as impacts on air quality, foreign fuel dependence, system reliability, participant comfort, and regional employment, assessment of conservation and load-management programs. Authors use results of a study conducted for San Diego Gas & Electric Company to illustrate the magnitude of these dollar effects. Includes a reference list.

Shenk, C.A. and W. Riley, Quantifying Environmental Impacts, U.S. Environmental Protection Agency, Seattle, WA. Region 10, May 1981.
This report was prepared to assist the Bonneville Power Administration in developing a methodology to assess the cost-effectiveness of proposed electric power projects. The report discusses difficulties in physically measuring environmental impacts and in subsequently placing dollar values on them.

Sheppard, J.D., Bureau of Fisheries New York Department of Environmental Conservation, Valuation of the Hudson River Fishery Resources: Past, Present and Future, Albany, New York, April, 1976.
The purpose of this report is to provide an overview of the Hudson River fishery resource and its related economic values- past, present and future. The accomplishment of this purpose has depended heavily upon available historical data from earlier biological survey work and commercial fishery statistics. Due to a scarcity of pertinent information, it was often necessary to employ a series of values for certain parameters to illustrate the importance (biologically, sociologically and economically) of certain environmental aspects to the fishery resources. However, this has resulted in the development of fishery valuations which fall within acceptable biological and economic ranges.

Sieving,K.W.,Consultant in energy and utility matters., "Estimating the Funding Levels for Nuclear Plant Decommissioning," Public Utilities Fortnightly, 20 August 1987. pp.17-21.
This article discusses methodology for determining an appropriate estimation method for nuclear plant decommissioning.

Sorg, C. and J. Loomis, "An Introduction to Wildlife Valuation Techniques," Wildlife Society Bulletin, 131985.pp.38-46.
Sorg and Loomis discuss a general overview of the methods for measuring value of wildlife. General demand and supply theory are analyzed as well as more specific economic valuation methods. Three methods are examined: CVM, TCM and gross expenditure method.

Spencer, D.F., S.B. Alput and H.H. Gilman, "Cool Water: Demonstration of a Clean and Efficient New Technology," Science, 2322 March 1986. pp.609-613.
"Cool Water" is the world's first commercial scale (100 mw) integrated coal gasification combined cycle power plant that has been operating in Barstow, CA since May 1984. The article shows that future baseload power plants using this technology can be built modularly and compete economically with much larger, conventional coal-fired power plants equipped for fuel gas desulfurization. An elaborate environmental monitoring program has confirmed that Cool Water

emissions are at a level comparable or superior to those of a power plant burning natural gas.

Starr, C. and C. Whipple, "Coping with Nuclear Power Risks: The Electric Utility Incentives," Nuclear Safety, 23:(1), January-February 1982.
This study first estimates the financial risks associated with nuclear power plant accidents. The study arrives at the risk estimate by considering frequency versus severity data from routine outages and the frequency versus severity estimates from the Rasmussen report for the NRC.

Starr, G. and S.B. Starr, "The True Cost of Oil (Or, What the Oil Companies Don't Want You to Know)," Earth Island Journal, Summer 1988. pp.22-23.
This short article provides a brief summary of the costs related to oil industry, including defense, federal subsidies, and environmental costs. The article includes estimates of the environmental cost to natural resources and clean-up costs associated with oil spills.

Stoloff, J., K.L. Mallory and L.R. Stearns, "Legal Issues Raised by the Environmental Impacts of Photovoltaic Energy and Wind Energy Conservation Systems," Columbia Journal of Environmental Law, November 1986. pp.379 - 416.
This article focuses on the potential environmental consequences of using the sun and wind as primary sources of energy for generation of electricity. The article is part of a special symposium issue on legal issues arising from the Audubon Energy Plan 1984.

Stopp, G.H. Jr., Acid Rain: A Bibliography of Research Annotated for Easy Access, Scarecrow Press, Inc., Metuchen, NJ, 1985.
This bibliography contains 886 annotated references for materials compiled through end-of-year 1984. Sources include materials from agronomy, atmospheric physics, biology, economics, geography, limnology, and political science. A subject index is included. Annotations attempt to evaluate relative merit and audience of sources.

Tait, G.W. C., "Cost-Benefit Analysis: Reality or Illusion?," Health Physics, 39 November 1980. pp.835-838.
This article provides a graph of collective dose commitment in man-Sieverts versus costs in nominal dollars.

Taylor, J.J., "Improved and Safer Nuclear Power," Science, 24421 April 1989. pp.318-325.
This article outlines how new and improved reactor designs will decrease the probability of future nuclear reactor accidents. The modern plant designs are simpler, have a longer lifespan, and are able to withstand more stress. New design concepts will also reduce construction and engineering costs. The authors hope that all of these savings will allow nuclear power plants to be competitive with other utilities.

Temple, Barker & Sloane, "Externalities Bibliography: Summary of Sources and Supplement," Massachusetts Department of Public Utilities Workshop, Photocopy, 1989.
Partially annotated list of externalities materials prepared as part of Massachusetts workshops discussing externalities prior to issuance of proposed rule in December 1989.

Thayer, M.A.,"Contingent Valuation Techniques for Assessing Environmental Impacts: Further Evidence," Journal of Environmental Economics and Management, 8:(1), 1981. pp.27-44.
Thayer discusses the development and application of the bidding technique as part of CVM, to assess environmental quality. Three techniques: survey technique, questionnaire development and starting point bias are examined.

Theodore, L. and A.J. Buonicore, eds., Energy and the Environment: Interactions. Volume I, Perspectives on the Environment, Part B,
This book discusses the energy cost of air pollution control devices. The impact of fossil fuel combustion on air quality is discussed as is the status of flue gas desulfurization (FGD) and the environmental considerations in the disposal of water sludge from FGD. This book also looks at the prospects of waste heat utilization.

Thibodeau, L.A., R.B. Reed, Y.M. M. Bishop and L.A. Kammerman, "Air Pollution and Human Health: A Review and Reanalysis," Environmental Health Perspectives, 34 February 1980. pp.165-183.
This report is a three part reanalysis of Lave and Seskin's book, Air Pollution and Human Health (1977) and reviews and evaluates the methodologies used by them. This report examines the strengths and/or weaknesses of their conclusions. In addition, Lave and Seskin's conclusion about the existence of an association between air pollution and mortality is accepted however, their estimates of the magnitude of this relation is less convincing in this report.

Thurber, N.J. and D.J. Jude, Impingement Losses at the D.C. Cook Nuclear Power Plant During 1975-1982 with a Discussion of Factors Responsible and Possible Impact on Local Populations, Great Lakes Research Division, Great Lakes and Marine Waters Center, University of Michigan, Ann Arbor, Michigan, 1985.
The study first details the water intake apparati of the D.C. Cook Nuclear Power Plant located on the shores of southeastern Lake Michigan. The study next details the annual impingement losses to the fish population in Lake Michigan. Tables are distributed throughout the report which illustrate fish losses both in terms of numbers and in terms of pounds.

U.S. Environmental Protection Agency (EPA) Office of Solid Waste and Emergency Response, Report to Congress: Wastes from the Combustion of Coal by Electric Utility Power Plants, reproduced by National Technical Information Service, Springfield, VA, February 1988.
This report is an extensive review of the literature related to the environmental characteristics of coal combustion wastes from electric utility plants. The report also summarizes original research undertaken to comply with RCRA requirements for EPA review of the environmental hazards of these wastes.

U.S. Department of Energy (DOE), Comprehensive report to Congress Clean Coal Technology Program; Tidd PFBC Demonstration Project, Proposed by American Electric Power Service Corporation on behalf of the Ohio Power Company, Washington, DC, February 1987.
This report describes a demonstration proposal of combined-cycle pressurized fluidized bed combustion (PFBC) and the PFBC joint development program by the DOE and the Ohio Power Company, a wholly owned subsidiary of American Electric Power Company, Inc. PFBC permits the combustion of a wide variety of

coals, including high sulfur coals, with a sorbent (limestone or dolomite) in a fluidized bed combustor at an elevated pressure.

U.S. Department of Energy (DOE), Summary Report to Congress on Emerging Clean Coal Technologies Capable of Retrofitting, Repowering, or Modernizing Existing Facilities, DOE, Washington, DC, 6 March 1987.
This summary was prepared by the DOE pursuant to Title II, Department of the Interior and Related Agencies Appropriations Act for FY 1987, Public Law No. 99-500. The summary is comprised of several public abstracts outlining demonstration proposals for several processes for reducing SO2 and NOx emissions. The summary includes demonstration proposals for circulating fluid bed flue gas desulfurization, reburning techniques, various methods of sorbent injection, the use of wet & dry scrubber technology, novel boiler injection techniques and the use of precipitators. Each abstract summarizes the predicted reductions of SOx and NOx to be accomplished by each technology. Proposals summarized include those received from the New England Power Company and the Electric Power Research Institute, Tennessee Valley Authority, Foster Wheeler Energy Corp., FMC Corporation and EMCOTEK-BTU, and the Duke Power Company.

van Lier, I.H., Acid Rain and International Law, 1981. This book is based on the author's masters thesis. It discusses the issue of transboundary air pollution, focusing on the situation in North America.
The book contains a scientific background which describes the causes of acidic deposition, and gives an economic forecast of the costs of acid rain.

van Zijl, N.A., Motor Columbus, "Technical Evaluation of Bids for Nuclear Power Stations," Nuclear Engineering International, February 1976.
The prime aspects considered during the evaluation of bids for a nuclear power station are technical, economical and financial. In some cases political and strategic considerations also have an important bearing on the final choice. In cases where financing and/or political considerations become overriding factors, a danger of technical aspects not receiving detailed attention can develop.

Vine, E. and J. Harris, Evaluating Energy and Non-Energy Impacts of Energy Conservation Programs: A Supply Curve Framework of Analysis, Lawrence Berkeley Laboratory, Applied Science Division, Berkeley, CA, June 1989.
This report extends the concept of "supply curves of conserved energy" to reflect multiple decision criteria and linkages between energy and non-energy policy decisions, such as "supply curve of reduced carbon emissions." Authors note that the proposed approach differs from other approaches used in comparing impacts such as checklist and matrices because the supply curve framework analyzes the impacts of selected projects and ranks them according to agreed upon criteria. Projects can then be chosen that meet a socially determined guideline. Authors also note that the purpose of these is to inform and structure decision making, "not replace or obscure it." The report includes a brief reference list.

Viscusi, W.K., "Toward a Diminished Role for Tort Liability: Social Insurance, Government Regulation, and Contemporary Risks to Health and Safety," Yale Journal on Regulation, 6: (65), 1989.
This article contrasts four risk-management systems: the market, tort liability, social insurance, and regulation. It analyzes the merits and problems of each of these, and suggests that regulation and insurance should play larger parts in health and safety risk assessment. Under the topic of "Adequacy of Risk-Reduction

Incentives,"a table summarizes a number of studies that estimate the implicit value of life and injuries, using a number of studies from 1967-1982.

Ware, J.H., L.A. Thibodeau, F.E. Speizer, S. Colome and B.G. Ferris Jr., "Assessment of the Health Effects of Atmospheric Sulphur Oxides and Particulate Matter: Evidence from Observational Studies," Environmental Health Perspectives, 41 October 1981. pp.255-276. This study contains human mortality and morbidity figures from exposure to SO2 and particulate matter. No costing figures.

Water Resources Council, "Economic and Environmental Principles & Guidelines for Water & Related Land Resource Implementation Studies," March 10, 1983. pp.75-87. The appendices to this report detail three methods available to value natural resource sites. They include TCM, CVM, and the unit day value method. Included are data needs, procedural steps and computational factors.

Watson, W.D. and J.A. Jaksch, "Air Pollution: Household Soiling and Consumer Welfare Losses," Journal of Environmental Economics and Management, 91982. pp.248-262.
This paper uses demand and supply functions for cleanliness to estimate household benefits from reduced particulate matter soiling. A demand curve for household cleanliness is estimated, based upon the assumption that households prefer more cleanliness to less. Empirical coefficients, related to particulate pollution levels, for shifting the cleanliness supply curve, are taken from available studies. Consumer welfare gains, aggregated across 123 SMSAs (Standard Metropolitan Statistical Area), from achieving the federal primary particulate standard, are estimated to range from $0.9 to $3.2 million per year (1971 dollars).

Westman, W.E., Economic Approaches. In, Ecology, Impact Assessment and Environmental Planning, John Wiley and Sons, New York, 1985.
Examines methods to achieve pollution emissions reductions, assesses their effectiveness and makes suggestions for future control methods and emission reduction planning.

Westman, W.E., "How Much are Nature's Services Worth?," Science, 1971977. pp.960-64.
Westman examines the social benefits associated with a functioning ecosystem. He believes that society has not placed a quantitative value on nature. The article analyzes the costs and benefits associated with restoring damaged ecosystems.

Wetstone, G.S. and A. Rosenkranz, Acid Rain in Europe and North America, 1983. This book details the nature and severity of the acid rain problem, and discusses possible national and international responses to this problem through laws, policies, and new acid rain control technologies.

Wiancko, P.M. and B.A. Green, Ontario Hydro, "Measuring Social Costs of Electrical Exports and Cost Recovery Opportunities of Environmental Pollution at Ontario Hydro," Proceedings of Technology Transfer Conference; Part E, Environmental Economics, Ministry of the Environment, pp.39-64.
The National Energy Board of Canada requires Ontario Hydroelectric to provide evidence supporting applications for electrical export licenses that the price charged would recover an appropriate share of all costs including social costs. In 1986, this social cost was established at 0.04 cents/kilowatt hour or one to two percent of the overall price for emissions due to emissions from fossil-fired

electrical export sales. This paper describes Ontario Hydro procedures for assessing potential environmental impacts and calculating social costs. Six categories were used: health; buildings; clothing; effects on the Great Lakes, vegetation and animals; and property values. Tables summarize results of related studies and the social cost estimates. Reference list included.

Williams, R.H., "Using Acid Rain Controls To Promote U.S. Competitiveness And Innovation In The Electric Utility Industry," Center for Energy and Environmental Studies, Princeton University, Princeton, New Jersey, 22 April 1988.
The author suggests that sulfur oxide emissions could be reduced by as much as 10 million tons per year nationwide at less cost than scrubbers by retiring the dirtiest coal-fired steam-electric power generating units and replacing them with advanced aeroderivative gas turbines. The turbines would be initially fired by natural gas and switched after ten years to operation on gas derived from coal. The article describes the technologies and costs in relation to SO2 reduction. Detailed cost appendix and reference list.

Yang, E.J., "Natural Resource Damages: Economics for CERCLA Lawyers," Environmental Law Reporter, 141984. pp. 10311-17.
Yang examines the alternative methods for valuing natural resources under CERCLA. He believes that damages should be valued as the value of lost services that the resource no longer supplies.

Yang, E.J., R.C. Dower and M. Menefee, The Use of Economic Analysis in Valuing Natural Resources, Environmental Law Institute, Washington, DC, June 1984.
Yang includes the general economic theory of demand in relation to the valuation of natural resources. Included is an in-depth discussion of consumer's surplus, producer's surplus and the laws of supply and demand. Economic methodologies are discussed in detail. Methods presented are CVM, net energy analysis, TCM, property value method, and replacement cost. A legislative history of CERCLA is include.

Zimmer, M.J. and J.A. Thompson Jr., eds., Acid Rain: Planning for the 80's, 1983.
This volume gives an in-depth look at research being conducted on current and future technology options and different SOx control technologies for industrial application.

B. UNANNOTATED BIBLIOGRAPHY

Abelson, P.W., V. Markandya, "The Interpretation of Capitalized Hedonic Prices in a Dynamic Environment," Journal of Environmental Economics and Management, September 1985, 12(3), pp. 195-206.

Acres Consulting Services Limited, Effects of Air Pollution on Building Materials, Prepared for Ontario Hydro, April 1980.

Adams, R. et al., "Implications for Global Climate Change for Western Agriculture," Western Journal of Agricultural Economics, 1988, 13(2), pp. 348-386.

Adams, R., J. Callaway, B. McCarl, "Pollution, Agriculture and Social Welfare: The Case of Acid Deposition," Canadian Journal of Agricultural Economics, March 1986, 34, pp. 3-19.

Adams, R., T. Crocker, N. Thanavibulchai, "An Economic Assessment of Air Pollution Damages to Selected Annual Crops in Southern California," Journal of Environmental Economics and Management, 1982, 9, pp. 42-57.

Adams, R., J. Glyer, S. Johnson, B. McCarl, "A Reassessment of the Economic Effects of Ozone to U.S. Agriculture." Journal of the Air Pollution Control Association, Vol. 39, no. 7 ed., July 1989, 39(7), pp. 960-966.

Adams, R., S. Hamilton, "An Assessment of the Economic Effects of Ozone on U.S. Agriculture," Journal of the Air Pollution Control Association, September 1983, 35(9), pp. 938-943.

Adams, R., S. Hamilton, B. McCarl, "The Benefits of Ozone Control: The Case of U.S. Agriculture." American Journal of Agricultural Economics, 1986.

Adams, R.. S. Hamilton, B. McCarl, Economic Effects of Ozone on Agriculture, Department of Agricultural and Resource Economics, Corvallis, Oregon, Oregon State University, September 1984.

Adams, R., "Issues in Assessing the Economic Benefits of Ambient Ozone Control: Some Examples from Agriculture," Environment International, 1983, 9, pp. 539-548.

Adams, R., T. Crocker, D. Thomas, Economically Relevant Response Estimation and the Value of Information: Acid Deposition, Economic Perspectives on Acid Deposition Control, Stoneham, MA, Butterworth Publishers, 1984, 8, 35-65. (editor: Teasley, J., Acid Precipitation Series).

Adams, R., B. McCarl, "Assessing the Benefits of Alternative Ozone Standards in Agriculture: The Response Information." Journal of Environmental Economics and Management, 1985.

Ahmed, J., T. Daw, Staff members in the Division of Nuclear Safety and Environmental Protection, IAEA, Cost-Benefit Analysis and Radiation Protection, [Based on a report on the same subject (in preparation by an Advisory Group of the International Atomic Energy Agency)], IAEA Bulletin, 22(5/6), 13-23.

Akbari and Rosenfeld, "Conservation Supply Curves for Reducing CO2 Emissions (Cost of CO2 Emissions Reductions), Cal. En. Comm. Hearing, 25 January 1990,

Akbari et al., "The Impact of Summer Heat Islands on Residential Cooling Energy Consumption," Miami, FL, presented at the 8th Miami International Conference on Alternate Energy Sources, 14 December 1987.

Akbari et al., "The Impact of Summer Heat Islands on Coding Energy Consumption and CO2 Emissions," Asilomar, CA, presented at ACEEE Summer Study on Energy Efficient Buildings, 12 July 1988.

Akbari et al., "Recent Development in Heat Island Studies: Technical and Policy," Berkeley, CA, presented at Heat Island Workshop, 23 February 1989.

Akbari et al., "Strategies for Reducing Urban Islands: Savings, Conflicts and City's Rite," San Jose, CA, presented at 1st National Conference on Energy Efficient Cooling, October 21, 1987.

Alchian, A., Allen, W., Exchange and Production: Theory in Use. Belmont, CA, Wadsworth, 1969.

American Council for an Energy-Efficient Economy, The Potential for Electricity Conservation in New York State: Final Report, New York State Energy Authority Report # 89-12, September 1989.

American Society of Heating, Refrigerating, and Air-Conditioning Engineers (ASHRAE), "Ventilation for Acceptable Indoor Air Quality, Standard 621981," ASHRAE Journal, Atlanta, GA, 1981.

American Society of Heating, Refrigerating, and Air-Conditioning Engineers (ASHRAE). "Ventilation and VOC's," ASHRAE Journal, Atlanta, GA, 1987, 29(7).

Anachem, Inc., and Sandia National Laboratories, Indoor Air Quality Handbook, SAND82-17773 ed. Albuquerque, N.M., Sandia National Laboratories, September 1982.

Anderson, R., T. Crocker, D. Thomas, "Air Pollution and Property Values: A Reply," Review of Economics and Statistics, November 1972, 54(4), pp. 470-473.

Argonne National Laboratory, Advanced Emission Control Technologies for Retrofit Applications: Draft Interim Report, December, 1985.

Argonne National Laboratory, Environmental Profiles of Selected Clean Coal Technologies: Draft Technical Report, 1987.

Arrow, K., R. Lind, "Uncertainty in Public Investment," American Economic Review, 1970, 60, pp. 364-378.

Arthur D. Little, Inc., Assessing the Health Risks of Airborne Carcinogens: EPRI (RP-1946-01), May 1985.

Ashlander, O., The Swedish Dioxin Memorandum, paper presented at ASCE Dioxin Symposium, New York, NY, 10 February 1987.

Association of the Bar of the City of New York, Special Committee on Electric Power and the Environment, Electricity and the Environment, St. Paul, MN, West Publishing Co., 1972.

Atkins, M.H., J. Lowe, and D. Lewis, "Air Pollution and Human Health: A Case Study of Environmental Benefit Estimation," Journal of Environmental Studies, 1980, Vol. 16, pp. 29-34.

Atkinson, S.E. and T.D. Crocker, A Bayesian Approach to Assessing the Robustness of Hedonic Property Value Studies, Journal of Applied Econometrics, 1987, 1(27), 45.

Atomic Energy Joint Committee, Environmental Effects of Producing Electric Power, 91st Congress, 1st Session, 1969.

Baboian, Robert, Materials Degradation Caused by Acid Rain, Washington, DC, American Chemical Society, State-of-the-Art Symposium, 1986.

Bailey, Martin, Reducing Risks to Life: Measurement of the Benefits, Washington, D.C., American Enterprise Institute for Public Policy Research, 1980.

Bates, D.V. and R. Sizto, "Relationship Between Air Pollutant Levels and Hospital Admissions in Southern Ontario," Canadian Journal of Public Health, March/April, 1983, 74.

Bates, D.V. and R. Sizto, A Study of Hospital Admissions and Air Pollutants in Southern Ontario, in Aerosols, Research, Risk Assessment and Control Strategies, Chelsea, Michigan, Lewis, Lee, Schneider, Grant, Verkerk, Editors, 1986.

Batie, S.S. and L. Shabman, "Valuing Non-Market Goods - Conceptual and Empirical Issues: Discussion," American Journal of Agricultural Economics, 1979, 61(5), pp. 931-932.

Bator, Francis M, "The Anatomy of Market Failure," Quarterly Journal of Economics, 1958, 72, pp. 351-379.

Bednarz, R.S, The Effect of Air Pollution on Property Value in Chicago, Chicago, University of Chicago, Research Paper No. 166, 1975.

Ben-Chieh Liu and Eden Siu-hung Yu, Physical and Economic Damage Functions for Air Pollutants by Receptors, Kansas City, MO, Midwest Research Institute, September 1976.

Benedict, H.M., C.J. Miller, and R.E. Olson, Economic Impact of Air Pollutants on Plants in the United States: Final Report, Merlo Park, CA, Stanford Research Institute, November 1971.

Benedict, Harris M., Assessment of Economic Impact of Air Pollutants on Vegetation in the United States: 1969 and 1971, Stanford Research Institute, Menlo Park, CA., July 1973.

Berkowitz, C.M. and D.S. Renne, Uncertainty Assessment for Acid Deposition, Pacific Northwest Lab., Richland, WA., January 1984.

Berner, Elizabeth Kay and Robert A. Berner, The Global Water Cycle: Geochemistry and Environment, Prentice-Hall, Inc., 1987.

Bernstein, R.S., H. Folk, D.R. Turner, J. Melius, "Nonoccupational Exposures to Indoor Air Pollutants: A Survey of State Programs and Practices," American Journal of Public Health, 74(9), September 1984, pp. 1020-1023.

Berrett, Larry B. and Thomas E. Weddell, Costs of Air Pollution Damage: A Status Report, Research Triangle Park, NC, Environmental Protection Agency, National Environmental Research Center, February, 1973.

Bhagia, G.S. and H. Stoevener, Impact of Air Pollution on the Consumption of Medical Services, Corvallis, Environmental Protection Agency, 1978.

"Bidding Farewell to the Social Costs of Electricity Production: Pricing Alternative Energy Under the Public Utility Regulatory Policy Act," The Journal of Corporation Law, Summer, 1988, p. 1011.

Bingemer, H. and Critzen. "The Production of Methane from Solid Waste," Journal of Geophysical Research, 92, p. 2189.

Birkhofer, A., Was Leisten Risikostudien? Atomwirtshaft-Atomechnik, 1986, 31, pp. 440-445.

Bishop, R.C. and T.A. Heberlein, "Measuring Values of Extramarket Goods: Are Indirect Measures Biased?" American Journal of Agricultural Economics, 1979,61, pp. 926-930.

Bishop, Richard C., Kevin J. Boyle, and Michael P. Welsh, Toward Total Economic Valuation of Great Lakes Fishery Resources, Transactions of the American Fisheries Society, 1987, 116, pp. 339-345.

Bockstael, N., K.E. McConnell, and I.E. Strand, Benefits from Improvements in Chesapeake Bay Water Quality, College Park, MD, Report for EPA under Cooperative Agreement with the University of Maryland, 1988.

Bodonsky, D. et al. Indoor Radon and Its Hazards, Seattle, WA, University of Washington Press.

Bolten, J.G., P.F. Morrison, S.A. Resetar, K.A. Wolf, Health risks of toxic emissions from a coal-fired power plant, Electric Power Research Institute, Rand Corp., 1987.

Bond, Richard G. and C.P. Straub, eds., Handbook of Environmental Control - Volume I: Air Pollution, Cleveland, OH, The Chemical Rubber Co., 1974.

Bonneville Power Administration (BPA), BPA Evaluation of Generic Environmental Costs and Benefits Studies, Portland, OR, Bonneville Power Administration, 1986.

Bonneville Power Administration (BPA), Calculation of Environmental Costs and Benefits Associated with Hydropower Development in the Pacific Northwest, prepared by P. Meyer et al.; April 1986.

Bonneville Power Administration (BPA), Cost Effectiveness Methodology, Bonneville Power Administration, December, 1986.

Bonneville Power Administration (BPA), Final Environmental Impact Statement on New Energy Efficient Home Programs, DOE EIS 0127F, August 1988, Vol. 1-3 Technical Appendices, BPA Final EIS Bonneville Exiting Homes Weatherization Program 1983-1984.

Bonneville Power Administration (BPA), Internal Review of Discount rate practices, 1986.

Bonneville Power Administration (BPA), WNP-1 and -3 Study, 1987 Resource Strategy, May, 1987.

Bonneville Power Administration (BPA), Methods for Valuation of Environmental Costs and Benefits of Hydroelectric Facilities: A Case Study of the Sultan River Project, Final Report, prepared by Biosystem Analysis, Inc., et al., June, 1984.

Bonneville Power Administration (BPA). Pacific Northwest Home Indoor Air Quality Survey and Weatherization Sensitivity Study. Berkeley, CA, prepared by Lawrence Berkeley Laboratories, February, 1988.

Bonneville Power Administration (BPA), Review of Uncertainty and Risk in BPA - Sponsored Analyses of Energy Resources: Final Report.

Booz, Allen and Hamilton Inc., Study to Determine Residential Soil Costing of Particulate Air Pollution, Raleigh, N.C., U.S. Department of Health, Education and Welfare, National Air Pollution Control Administration, October 1970.

Bower, Blair T. and Allan Kneese, Managing Water Quality, Baltimore, MD, Johns Hopkins Press, 1968.

Brick, Stephen, Strategies and Methods for Incorporating Environmental Concerns Into Utility Planning and Utility Regulatory Decision-Making, Middleton, WI, MSB Energy Associates, 2 October 1989.

Bromberg, P.A. Testimony Before the House Subcommittee on Environmental Protection, Energy and Commerce Committee Hearing on Health Effects of Air Pollution, Washington, DC, 1989.

Brookshire, D.S., Methods Development for Valuing Hazards Information, Institute for Policy Research, Univ. of Wyo., 1980.

Brookshire, David S., and D.L. Coursey, "Measuring the Value of a Public Good: An Empirical Comparison of Elicitation Procedures," The American Economic Review 77, 1987, 72(1), pp. 554-566.

Brown, Charles, "Equalizing Differences in the Labor Market," Quarterly Journal of Economics, February, 1980, 94, pp. 113-134.

Brown, G.M. et al, National Acid Precipitation Assessment Program State-of Science/Technology Report 27 Part B: Methods for Valuing Acidic Deposition and Air Pollution Effects, 1989.

Brown, L. et al, State of the World 1988, Worldwatch Institute (published by Noton), 1988.

Brown, T.C., M.T. Richards and T.C. Daniel, Scenic Beauty and Recreation Value: Assessing the Relationship, Fort Collins, CO, (unpublished manuscript, USDA Forest Service, Rocky Mountain Forest and Range Experiment Station, 1989.

Buchanan, Shepard C., Cost of Mitigating Greenhouse Effect for Generic Coal-, Oil-, and Gas-fired Plants, (unpublished report; a copy of the report is available from Buchanan at Bonneville Power Administration), 24 January 1989.

Burch, William, (ed.), Social Behavior, Natural Resources, and the Environment, Harper and Row, 1972.

Burkhart, "External Social Costs as a Factor in Least-Cost Planning-- An Emerging Concept," Public Utilities Fortnightly, 31 August 1989.

Burnell, James D., "The Effect of Air Pollution on Residential Location Decisions in Metropolitan Areas," Regional Science Perspectives, 1981, 3(18), p. 112.

Byers, Richard, Results of Energy Use: Indoor Air Quality and Ventilation Monitoring for RSDP Homes in Washington State, Proceedings of the 1988 ACEEE Summer Study on Energy Efficiency in Buildings, 1988, 1, 1.16-1.28.

Byrne, S.C. and A.C. Miller, Atmospheric Corrosion of Metals, (As reported by V. Kucera, 1986), 1982.

Cadle, J.S., The Health Costs of Air Pollution, A Survey of Studies Published 1978-1983, American Lung Association, August 1985.

Cadle, R.D., Particulate Matter in the Lower Stratosphere, in Chemistry of the Lower Stratosphere, S.I. Rassol, Plenum Press, New York, NY, 1973.

California Energy Commission, Commission Decision, Application for Certification, Lutz Engineering Corporation, SEGS IX and X Projects, Harper Lake, February 1990.

California State University Fullerton Foundation, Economic Assessment of the Health Benefits from Improvements in Air Quality in the South Coast Air Basin, prepared for the South Coast Air Quality Management District Contract No. 5685, Fullerton, CA, June 1989.

Callaway, J.M. and R.F. Darwin, Economic Valuation of Acidic Deposition Damages, Pacific Northwest Lab., Richland, WA., 13 September 1985.

Callaway, J.M., J.R.F. Darwin and R.J. Nesse, Economic Effects of Hypothetical Reductions in Tree Growth in the Northeastern and Southeastern United States, Pacific Northwest Laboratory, Richland, Washington, 1986.

Callaway, J.M., and R.F. Darwin, Economic Effects of Reduced Forest Growth on the United States and Canadian Forest Economy, Pacific Northwest Lab., Richland, WA, August 1986.

Callaway, J.M. and R.F. Darwin, Potential Economic Impacts of Air Pollution on Stumpage and Primary Wood Product Markets in the United States, Pacific Northwest Lab., Richland, WA., May 1987.

Callaway, J.M. and R.J. Nesse, Development and Application of a Framework for Assessing the Economic Impacts of Air Pollution on Forests, Pacific Northwest Lab., Richland, WA., October 1986.

Cameron, T.A. and M.D. James, The Determinants of Value for a Recreational Fishing Day: Estimates from a Contingent Valuation Survey, Canadian Technical Report of Fisheries and Aquatic Sciences 1503.

Campen, J.T., Benefit, Cost, and Beyond, Ballinger Publishing Co., Cambridge, MA, 1986.

Cannon, J.S., The Health Costs of Air Pollution: A Survey of Studies Published 1978-1983, American Lung Association, August 1985.

Canter, L.W., Acid Rain and Dry Deposition, Publishers, Chelsea, MI, 1986.

Carpenter, B.H., D.A. LeSourd, J.R. Chromy and W.D. Bach, Health Costs of Air Pollution Damages: A Study of Hospitalization Costs, Research Triangle Park; Environmental Protection Agency, 1977.

Carson, R. and P. Navarro, "Natural Resources Damage Assessment," Natural Resources Journal, Fall 1988. pp.815-836.

Catching Our Breath: Next Steps for Reducing Urban Ozone, U.S. Government Printing Office, Washington, DC, July 1989.

Cauvin, D.M., "The Valuation of Recreational Fisheries," Canadian Journal of Fisheries and Aquatic Sciences, 37 1980. pp.1321-1327.

Centolella, P., Clearing the Air: Using Energy Conservation to Reduce Acid Rain Compliance Costs in Ohio, Ohio Office of the Consumers' Counsel, July 1988.

Chapman, D. and R. Kohut, Ozone and Acid Deposition: An Economic Perspective on Agricultural and Forestry Impact, Cornell Agricultural Economics Staff Paper No. 84-28, 1984.

Charles River Associates (CRA), Benefits and Costs of Externalities and Intangibles Associated with Southern California Edison's 1985 and 1986 Conservation and Load Management Programs, CRA Report #792, 15 May 1984.

Charola, A.E. and L. Lazzarini, Deterioration of Brick Masonry Caused by Acid Rain, In R. Baboian (ed) Materials Degradation Caused by Acid Rain, American Chemical Society), 1986.

Chernick, P. and E. Caverhill, The Valuation of Externalities from Energy Production, Delivery, and Use (for Boston Gas Co., Boston, Mass), December 22, 1989.

Chestnut, L.G., Benefits of Air Pollution Control in California. Volume 2. Final Report, Energy and Resource Consultants, Inc., Boulder, CO., December 1986.

Clark, S. and D. Dudek, A Proposal for State-level Refrigerant Recycling, Environmental Defense Fund, New York, NY, 13 March 1989.

Clawson, "Forests in the Long Sweep of American History," Science, 20 1979. pp.1168-1174.

Clawson, M. and J. Knetsch, Economics of Outdoor Recreation, Johns Hopkins University Press for Resources for the Future, Baltimore, MD, 1966.

Coase, R.H., "The Problem of Social Cost," The Journal of Law and Economics, III 1960.

Cogen, D.C., Stoves in a Glass House: CFC's and Ozone Depletion, Investor Responsibility Research Center.

Cohen, A.V. and D.K. Pritchard, Comparative Risks of Electricity Production Systems: A Critical Survey of the Literature, Research Paper No. 11 of the Health & Safety Executive, Her Majesty's Stationery Office, December 1980.

Cohen, L., Economist Associate, The Rand Corporation, Santa Monica, CA, "Who Pays the Bill: Insuring Against the Risks from Low Level Nuclear Waste Disposal," Natural Resources Journal, 21 1981, p.774.

Cohen, S.D., J.H. Eto, J. Beldock and G. Crandall, A Survey of State Regulatory Commission Activities to Incorporate Environmental Externalities into Electric Utility Planning and Regulation, Lawrence Berkeley Laboratory, February 1990.

Colorado v. U.S Dept. of Interior, 8.F.2d 481 (D.C. Cir. 1989),
Competitek, State of the Art: Lighting Second Update, January 1990.

Conservation Foundation, State of the Environment: A View Toward the Nineties, 1987.

Conservation Law Foundation, Strategic Energy Efficiency Investment for the 1990s, 24 January 1989.

Conservation Foundation/World Wildlife Fund, P., The Forestry Fund: Endowment for Forest Protection, Management, and Reforestation in Cost Rica, May 1988.

Consolidated Edison Company of New York and New York Power Authority (NYPA), Hudson River Ecological Study in the Area of Indian Point, NYPA Annual Report, 1987.

Consolidated Edison Company of New York, A Study of Impinged Organisms at the Astoria Generating Station, Quirk, Lawler and Matusky Engineers, Tappan, NY, 1973.

Costs of Environmental-Related Health Effects: A Plan for Continuing Study (Final Report), Institute of Medicine, Washington, DC 1981.

Creswick, F.A., S.K. Fischer and J.R. Sand, Potential Impacts of CFC Restrictions on Refrigeration and Space-Conditioning Equipment, Oak Ridge National Laboratory, Oak Ridge, TN,

Crocker, T.D., "On the Value of the Condition of a Forest Stock," Land Economics, 61:(3), 1985. pp.244-254.

Crocker, T.D. and J.L. Regens, "Benefit-Cost Analyses of Acid Deposition Control: A Benefit-Cost Analysis: Its Prospects and Limits," Environmental Science and Technology, 19 February 1985. pp.112-16.

Crocker, T., Some Plausible Fundamental Misspecifications in Models of Preferences for Acid Deposition Control, Paper presented at the Seminar on Acid Rain Evaluation, sponsored by the Canada Department of Fisheries and Oceans, Ottawa, Ontario, 13 March 1984.

Crocker, T., Urban Air Pollution Damage Functions, University of California, Riverside, California, 1970.

Cronon, W., Changes in the Land: Indians, Colonists, and the Ecology of New England, Hill and Wang, New York, 1983.

Currie, J.W., R.J. Moe and R.J. Nesse, Economic Analysis: The National Acid Precipitation Assessment Program, Pacific Northwest Lab., Richland, WA., December 1984.

Currie, W.J. et al., "The Importance of Viewing Alternative Closed-Cycle-Cooling systems on Nuclear Power-Plant Landscapes", in Environmental Policy Formation: The Impact of Values, Ideology, and Standards, D.C. Heath and Co., Lexington, MA.

Data Resources, I., Implicit Price Deflator for GNP, Long-Term Forecast of U.S. Economy, Lexington, MA, 1990.

Davenport, J.H., Partner, Duryea, Murphy, Davenport & Van Winkle, Olympia, WA, "The Law of High-Level Nuclear Waste," Tennessee Law Review, 53 1985-86. pp.481-527.

DeAngelis, M. and Rashkin Samuel, The Social Benefits and Costs of Electricity Generation and End-Use Technologies, California energy Commission, Sacramento, CA, ca.1989.

Denver Research Institute, Assessment and Managing Socioeconomic Impacts of Power Plants, August 1984, EPRI (RP1226-04).

Denver Research Institute, Socioeconomic Impacts of Power Plant, February 1982, EPRI (RP1226-04).

Department of Energy, Energy Technology Characterization Handbook: Environmental Pollution and Control Factors, March 1983.

Department of Energy (DOE), Energy System Emissions and Materiel Requirements (Draft), prepared by Meridian Corporation, Alexandria, VA, February 1989.

Department of Energy, Energy Conservation Standards for Consumer Appliances, Refrigerators and Furnaces, November 1989.

Department of Energy (DOE), Fossil Energy, Innovative Clean Coal Technology: Programmatic Environmental Impact Analysis (PEIA), prepared by Oak Ridge National Laboratory, September 1988.

Department of Energy, Health and Environmental Consequences of the Chernobyl Nuclear Power Plant Accident, USDOE, Washington DC, 1987.

Department of Energy, "Office of Civilian Radioactive Waste Management (OCRWM) Publications Catalog," DOE/RW-0150 July 1987.

Department of Energy, The Potential of Renewable Energy: An Interlaboratory Whitepaper, March 1990.

Deyak, T.A. and V.K. Smith, "Residential Property Values and Air Pollution: Some New Evidence," The Quarterly Review of Economics and Business, 14:(4), Winter 1974. pp.93-100.

Doniger, D.D. and D.A. Wirth, Cooling the Chemical Summer: Some Policy Responses to Ozone - Destroying and Greenhouse Gases, Remarks presented to the UNEP/EPA International Conference on Health and Environmental Effects of Ozone Modification and Climate Change, Arlington, VA, 20 June 1986.

Dornbush, D.M. and S.M. Barranger, Benefit of Water Pollution Control on Property Values, U.S. Environmental Protection Agency, U.S. Government Printing Office, 1973.

Dudek, Offsetting New CO2 Emissions, New York State Energy Plan, May 1989 (revised September 1989).

Dumont, R., Building Research Note 212, National Research Council of Canada, Ottawa, Ont., 1983.

ECO Northwest, Economic Analysis of the Environmental Effects of the Coal-Fired Electric Generator at Boardman, Oregon, for Bonneville Power Administration, 29 December, 1983.

ECO Northwest et al., Economic Analysis of the Environmental Effects of a Combustion-Turbine Generating Station at Frederickson Industrial Park, Pierce County, Washington: Final Report, Bonneville Power Administration, 26 March 1984.

ECO Northwest, Estimating Environmental Costs and Benefits for Five Generating Resources, Prepared for Bonneville Power Administration, Portland, Oregon, April 1986.

ECO Northwest, Generic Coal Study: Quantification and Valuation of Environmental Impacts, for Bonneville Power Administration, Portland, OR, 1987.

Edney, E.O., S.F. Cheek, D. Stiles, E.W. Corse, J.W. Spence, F.H. Haynie and W.E. Wilson Jr., "Effects of Acid Deposition on Paints and Metals: Results of a Controlled Field Study," Atmospheric Environment, 22 1988. pp.2263-2274.

"Effects of Photochemical Oxidants or Materials," Ozone and Other Photochemical Oxidants, Washington, DC, pp.665 (Chapter 13).

Electric Power Research Institute, A Comparison of Indoor Air Quality in Pacific Northwest Existing and New Energy Efficient Homes, Lawrence Berkeley Laboratory, Berkeley, CA, 1986.

Electric Power Research Institute, "Utility Energy Strategies: The Role of Efficiency, Productivity, and Conservation," February 1989.

Electric Power Research Institute, Fuel Cells for the 1990's., Sept. 5-11, 1986.

Electric Power Research Institute, IGCC, Phased Construction for Flexible Growth., Sept. 5-11, 1986.

Electric Power Research Institute, Manual on Indoor Air Quality, Prepared by Lawrence Berkeley Laboratories, Final Report, February 1984.

Electric Power Research Institute, New Perspectives on Coal Cleaning., Nov. 14-21, 1986.

Electric Power Research Institute, Risk Assessment of Toxic Pollutants from a Fossil-Fuelled Power Plant, Electric Power Research Institute, (Prepared for EPRI by The Rand Corporation), August 1987.

Energy and Resource Consultants, Inc., The Benefits of Air Pollution Control in California, prepared for the California Air Resources Board, December 1986.

Energy and Resource Consultants, Inc., Benefits of Environmental Controls: Measures, Methods and Applications, Electric Power Research Institute, October 1988.

Energy Systems Research Group (currently Tellus Institute), The Role of Hydro-Quebec Power in a Least-Cost Energy Resource Plan for Vermont, prepared for Dept. of Public Service, State of Vermont, 19 January 1990.

Environmental Protection Agency, Air Quality Criteria for Particulate Matter and Sulphur Oxides, Environmental Criteria and Assessment Office, Research Triangle Park, NC, 1982a.

Environmental Protection Agency, A Citizens Guide to Radon, What It Is and What To Do About It, August 1986.

Environmental Protection Agency (EPA), "EPA Report to Congress on Indoor Air Quality Draft," January 27, 1989.

Environmental Protection Agency, Flexible and Rigid Foam - Technical Progress on Protecting the Ozone Layer, June 1989.

Environmental Protection Agency, How Industry is Reducing Dependence on Ozone Depleting Chemicals, A Status Report, Prepared by the Stratospheric Ozone Protection Project, Office of Air and Radiation, June 1988.

Environmental Protection Agency, Radon Reduction Risks for Detached Houses, Technical Guidelines, June 1986.

Environmental Protection Agency, Radon Reduction Methods: A Homeowners Guide, August 1986.

Environmental Protection Agency, Report to Congress on Indoor Air Quality, August 1989.

"Environmental Regulation of Biomass Facilities: A Summary of the Current System," Biologue, February/March 1989. pp.10-12.

Environmental Protection Agency, Office of Public Affairs, "Ozone and Carbon Monoxide," Environmental Backgrounder, Washington DC, June 1989.

Environmental Policy Institute, The Environmental Policy Institute Quarterly Report--Influencing Public Policy to Protect Our Future, 1989.

Environmental Protection Agency, AP-42, Compilation of Air Pollutant Emission Factors, Volume 1: Stationary Point and Area Sources, Fourth Edition, September 1985.

Environmental Protection Agency, Assessment of Health Risks Associated with Municipal Waste Combustion Emissions, EPA/530-SW-87-021G, 1987.

Environmental Protection Agency, Characterization of Municipal Waste Combuster Ashes and Leachates From Municipal Solid WAste Landfills, Monofills, and Codisposal Sites, prepared by NUS Corp, for Office of Solid Waste and Emergency Response, Washington, DC, October 1987.

Environmental Protection Agency, Characterization of the Municipal Waste Combustion Industry, EPA/530-SW-87-02H,

Environmental Protection Agency, Comprehensive Report to Congress, Clean Coal Technology Program, Advanced Cyclone Combustor with Integral Sulfur, Nitrogen and Ash Control., Washington, DC., 1987.

Environmental Protection Agency, Control Techniques for Particulate Air Pollutants, USEPA, Research Triangle Park, NC, January 1969.

Environmental Protection Agency, edited by Norman R. Glass, Environmental Effects of Increased Coal Utilization: Ecological Effects of Gaseous Emissions from Coal Combustion, 1978.

Environmental Protection Agency, Fluidized Bed Combustion: Effectiveness of an SO2 Control Technology for Industrial Boilers., Office of Air Quality Planning Standards, Research Triangle Park, NC, 1984.

Environmental Protection Agency, How Industry is Reducing Dependence on Ozone-Depleting Chemicals, 1988.

Environmental Protection Agency, Industrial Boiler SO2 Technology Update Report., Research Triangle Park, NC., 1984.

Environmental Protection Agency, Methodology for the Assessment of Health Risks Associated with Multiple Pathway Exposure to Municipal Waste Combustion Emissions, USEPA, Draft submitted for review to the Science Advisory Board, October 1986.

Environmental Protection Agency, "Municipal Waste Combustion Study," EPA/530-SW-89-012A, June 1987.

Environmental Protection Agency, Office of Solid Waste, Operating Criteria (Part C) Criteria for Municipal Solid Waste Landfills-- 40 CFR Part 258, Washington, DC, July 1988.

Environmental Protection Agency, Office of Policy, Planning and Evaluation, Policy Options for Stabilizing Global Change, Draft Report to Congress, February 1989.

Environmental Protection Agency, Report to Congress: Solid Waste Disposal in the United States, Vol.II, Washington DC, October 1988.

Environmental Protection Agency, Response to Petition for Rulemaking and Advance Notice of Proposed Rulemaking, Assessment of Municipal Waste Combustor Emission Under the Clean Air Act, 52 Fed. Reg. 25399, 25404, July 7, 1987.

Environmental Protection Agency, Second Report to Congress on Emerging Technologies Capable of Retrofitting, Repowering or Modernizing Existing Facilities., May 1987.

Erskine, H., "The Polls: Pollution and its Costs," Public Opinion Quarterly, 36:(1), Spring 1972. pp.120-135.

Eshleman, K.E., "Predicting Regional Episodic Acidification of Surface Waters Using Empirical Models," Water Resources Research, 24:(7), 1988. pp.1118-1126.

Evans, J.C., K.J. Abel, K.B. Olsen, E.A. Lepel, R.W. Sanders, C.L. Wilkerson, D.J. Hayes and N.E. Mongelson, Characterization of Trace Constituents at Canadian Coal-Fired Power Plants. Phase 1, Final Report, (Prepared for Canadian Electrical Association by Battelle Pacific Northwest Laboratories, January 1985.

Everett, J.J. and T.J. Dreher, "Institutional Aspects of Indoor Air Pollution in Energy Efficient Residences," Environment International 8, 1982. pp.525-531.

Fackelmann, K.A., "Air pollution boosts cancer spread," Science News, 137, 7 April 1990.

Falk, H.L. and W. Jurgelski Jr., "Health Effects of Coal Mining and Combustion: Carcinogens and Cofactors," Environmental Health Perspectives, 3 December 1979. pp. 203-226.

Federal Energy Regulatory Commission, Final Environmental Impact Statement, Salmon River Basin: Fifteen Hydroelectric Projects, Idaho, July 1987.

Federal Energy Regulatory Commission, Office of Hydropower Licensing, Draft Environmental Impact Statement: Milner, Twin Falls, Auger Falls, and Star Falls Hydroelectric Projects, Idaho, December 1989.

Feely, H. and D. Bogen, Contributions of Local Sources to the Acidity of Rain in an Urban Area, 23 October 1989.

Feliciano, A., 1971 Survey and Assessment of Air Pollution Damage to Vegetation in New Jersey.

Fennelly, P.F., "The Origin and Influence of Airborne Particulates," American Scientist, 64 January-February 1976. pp.46-56.

Final Environmental Impact Statement, Proposed Resource Recovery Facility at the Brooklyn Navy Yard, Technical Appendix, Vol. III, Appendix D, Air-Quality Related Issues, June 1985.

Fink, F.W., F.H. Buttner and W.K. Boyd, Battelle Memorial Institute, Technical-Economic Evaluation of Air Pollution Corrosion Costs on Metals in the U.S., February 1971.

Finn, D.P., Research Fellow, Woods Hole Oceanographic Institute, "Ocean Disposal of Radioactive Wastes: The Obligation of International Cooperation to Protect the Marine Environment," Virginia Journal of International Law, 21 1981. pp.621-692.

Fisher, A., L.G. Chestnut and D.M. Violette, "The Value of Reducing Risks of Death: A Note on New Evidence," Journal of Policy Analysis and Management, 8:(1), 1989. pp.88-100.

Fisher, A.C., "Energy and Environment in the Long Term," Energy Policy, 17:(2), April, 1989. pp.84-87.

Fisk, W.J. and Y. Turiel, Residential Air-to-Air Heat Exchangers: Performance, Energy Savings, and Economics, Lawrence Berkeley Laboratory, Berkeley, CA, February 1982.

Flescher, R.L., A. Mogro-Compero and L.G. Turner, "Indoor Radon Levels in the Northeast U.S.: Effects on Energy Efficiency in Homes," Health Phys., 45 1983. pp.407.

Fletcher, R.I., On the Reconfiguration and Empirical Evaluation of a Prototype Screening Device at Indian Point Nuclear Unit 2, Final Report to the Hudson River Fishermen's Association, Great Salt Lake Experimental Station, 1986.

Folmer, J. and E. Van Ierland, Valuation Methods and Policy Making in Environmental Economics, 1989, Elsevier, Amsterdam, Holland.

Forelaws on Board v. Johnson, 7 F.2d 677, 679-80, 682 (9th Cir. 1984).

Forster, B.A., "An Economic Assessment of the Significance of Long-Range Transported Air Pollutants for Agriculture in Eastern Canada," Canadian Journal of Agricultural Economics, 32 November 1984. pp.498-525.

Forster, B.A., Economic Impact of Acid Precipitation: A Canadian Perspective, in Economic Perspectives on Acid Deposition Control.

Franke, B., Review of the Environmental Impacts of Solid Waste Incinerators Proposed for Long Island and New York City, prepared for Newsday by Institute for Energy and Environmental Research, Tacoma Park, MD, November 1987.

Franklin, M.A., N.S. Abby, R.G. Hemp and Franklin Associates Ltd., Characterization of Municipal Solid Waste in the U.S. 1960 - 2000, Prepared for the USEPA, Washington, DC, July 11, 1986.

Freeman III, A.M., "Air Pollution and Property Values: A Methodological Comment," The Review of Economic and Statistics, November 1971. pp.415-416.

Freeman, A.M., III, Air Pollution Control: A Benefit Cost Assignment, John Wiley & Sons, New York, 1982.

Freeman, A.M., "On Estimating Air Pollution Control Benefits from Land Value Studies," Journal of Environmental Economics and Management, 1 May 1974. pp.74-83.

French, H.F., You Are What You Breathe, World Watch, May-June 1990.

Frimerman, L.A., "Key Elements of Legislative and Regulatory Framework For Using Energy Conservation to Reduce Acid Rain Compliance Costs," 1989 EPRI Demand Side Management Conference, EPRI, Palo Alto, CA, 1989.

Frishman, S., "High-Level Nuclear Waste Repository Siting: A State Perspective," Tennessee Law Review, 53 1985-86. pp.527-541.

Galster, G.C., "Nuclear Power Plants and Residential Property Values: A Comment on Short-run vs. Long-run Considerations," Journal of Regional Science, 26:(4), November 1986. pp.803-805.

Gamble, H.B. and Downing R.H., "Nuclear Power Plants and Residential Property Values: A Comment on Short-run vs. Long-run Considerations: A Reply," Journal of Regional Science, 26:(4), November 1986. pp.807-808.

Gates, D.M., Energy and Ecology, Sinauer Associates, Sunderland, MA, 1985.

Geller, H.S., Update on National and State Minimum Efficiency Standards, Proceedings of the Fourth National Conference on Utility DSM Programs, Electric Power Research Institute, Vol.1, April 1989.

Georgescu-Roegen, N., The Entropy Law and the Economic Process, Harvard University Press, Cambridge, MA, 1971.

Gibbs & Hoffman, An Approach for Generating Climate Change Hypothetical Given Limitations in Current Climate Models, in Shands and Hoffman (ed.): The Greenhouse Effect, Climate Change and United States Forests, 1987.

Gilleland and Swisher, eds., Acid Rain Control - The Costs of Compliance, Southern Illinois University Press, 1984.

Geller, H.S., Update on National and State Minimum Efficiency Standards, Proceedings of the Fourth National Conference on Utility DSM Programs, Electric Power Research Institute, Vol.1, April 1989.

Georgescu-Roegen, N., The Entropy Law and the Economic Process, Harvard University Press, Cambridge, MA, 1971.

Gibbs & Hoffman, An Approach for Generating Climate Change Hypothetical Given Limitations in Current Climate Models, in Shands and Hoffman (ed.): The Greenhouse Effect, Climate Change and United States Forests, 1987.

Gilleland and Swisher, eds., Acid Rain Control - The Costs of Compliance, Southern Illinois University Press, 1984.

Gillette, D.G., "Sulfur Dioxide and Material Damage," Journal of the Air Pollution Control Association, 25:(12), December 1975. pp.1238-1243.

Gillilang, M.W., Energy Analysis: A New Policy Tool, Westview Press Inc., Colorado, 1978.

Godar, T., Testimony before the House Subcommittee on Environmental Protection, energy and Commerce Committee hearing on Health Effects of Air Pollution, Washington, DC, 1989.

Godish, T., "Indoor Air Pollution in Offices and Other Non-residential Buildings," Journal of Environmental Health, 48:(4), pp.190-195.

Goldemberg, et. al., Energy for a Sustainable World, 1987.

Goldman, C.A. and E.P. Kahn, Comparative Assessment of the DSM Plans of Four New York Utilities, Proceedings of the Fourth National Conference on Utility DSM Programs, Electric Power Research Institute, Volume 1, April 1989.

Gordon, H.S., "The Economic Theory of a Common Property Resource: The Fishery," Journal of Political Economy, 65:(2), 1954. pp.124-142.

Gregor, J.J., Intra-Urban Mortality and Air Quality: An Economic Analysis of the Costs of Pollution Induced Mortality, Pennsylvania State University, University Park, Pennsylvania, July 1977.

Gregory, R. and T. McDaniels, "Valuing Environmental Losses: What Promise Does the Right Measure Hold?," Policy Sciences, 20 1987. pp.11-26.

Gregory, R., R. Mendelsohn and P. Slovic, Review of Uncertainty and Risk in BPA-Sponsored Analyses of Energy Resources, for Bonneville Power Administration, November 18, 1987.

Gulf South Insulation et al. v. U.S. Consumer Product Safety Commission, 7.F. 1137 (5th Cir. 1983),

Haemisegger, E., A. Jones, B. Steigerwald and V. Thomson, The Air Toxics Problem in the United States: An Analysis of Cancer Risks for Selected Pollutants, EPA Report, Contract #450/1-85-001, Washington, DC, 1985.

Hageman, R.K., Assistant Professor of Economics, University of Miami, Coral Gables, FL, "Nuclear Waste Disposal: Potential Property Value Impacts," Natural Resources Journal, 21 October 1981. pp.789-811.

Hall, J.V., Economic Assessment of the Health Benefits from Improvements in Air Quality in the South Coast Air Basin, Report to the South Coast Air Quality Management District, Contract No. 5685, California State University Fullerton Foundation, Fullerton, CA, June 1989.

Hamilton, L.D., The Health and Environmental Effects of Electricity Generation: A Preliminary Report, Brookhaven National Laboratory, July 1974.

Hanemann, W.M., Willingness to Pay and Willingness to Accept: How Much Can They Differ?, University of California, Working Paper No. 328, Berkeley, CA, March 1986.

Hansen et al, Evidence for Future Warming: How Large and When, in Shands & Hoffman (ed.), The Greenhouse Effect, Climate Change and United States Forests, 1987.

Hansen, S.J., "Indoor Air Quality: Is Increased Ventilation the Answer?," Energy Engineering, 86:(6), 1989.

Hardin, "The Tragedy of the Commons," Science, 162 1968. pp.1243-1248.

Harrington, W., Acid Rain: Science and Policy - A Primer, Resources for the Future, Washington, DC, 1989.

Harrison, D. and R. McDonald, "Willingness to Pay in Boston and Los Angeles for a Reduction in Automobile-Related Pollutants," National Academy of Science, The Costs and Benefits of Automobile Emissions Control-- Air Quality and Automobile Emission Control, 4 1974.

Harrison, D. and A.L. Nichols, Benefits of the 1989 Air Quality Management Plan for the South Coast Air Basin: A Reassessment, prepared for California Council for Environmental and Economic Balance, National Economic Research Associates, Inc., Cambridge, MA, February 1990.

Harrison, D. and D.L. Rubinfeld, "Hedonic Housing Prices and the Demand for Clean Air," Journal of Environmental Economics and Management, 5:(2), March 1978. pp.81-102.

Haymes, G.T., The Effects and Social Costs of Fossil-Fired Emissions on the Aquatic Ecosystem Due to Electrical Exports, Ontario Hydro Research Division Report, 1985.

Haynie, F.H., Atmospheric Acid Deposition Damage to Paints, U.S. Environmental Protection Agency, January 1986.

Haynie, F.H., "Derivation of Damage Functions for Atmospheric Degradation of Materials," May 1986.

Haynie, F.H., Economic Assessment of Pollution-Related Corrosion Damage, In W. H.Ailor (ed) Atmospheric Corrosion, John Wiley & Sons, 1982.

Haynie, F.H., Theoretical Air Pollution and Climate Effects on Materials Confirmed by Zinc Corrosion Data, In P. Sereda and G. Litvan (eds). Durability of Building Materials and Components, 1980.

Haynie, F.H. and J.W. Spence, "Air Pollution Damage to Exterior Household Paints," Journal of Air Pollution Control Association, 34 1984. pp.941-944.

Haynie, F.H., J.W. Spence and J.B. Upham, Atmospheric Factors Affecting the Corrosion of Engineering Metals, 1978.

Haynie, F.H. and J.B. Upham, Effects of Atmospheric Sulfur Dioxide on the Corrosion of Zinc, Materials Protection and Performance, August 1970.

Haynie, F.H., Economic Assessment of Pollution Related Corrosion Damage, Environmental Sciences Research Lab., Research Triangle Park, NC., 1983.

HDR Techserv, Health Risk Assessment for Trace Element and Organic Emissions: North County Recycling and Energy Recovery Center, San Marcos, California, (Prepared for North County Resource Recovery Associates, May 1987.

Heck, Taylor, Adams, Bingham and Miller, National Crop Loss Assessment Network, 1980 Annual Report, March 1982.

Heck, W.W., W.W. Cure, D.S. Shriner, R.J. Olson and A.S. Hegote, Ozone Impacts on the Productivity of Selected Crops, North Carolina State University, Raleigh, NC., Department of Botany, 1982.

Heck, W.W., National Crop Loss Assessment Network (NCLAN) 1982 Annual Report, Corvallis, OR, March 1984.

Heck, W.W., National Crop Loss Assessment Network (NCLAN) 1983 Annual Report, Corvallis, OR, August 1985.

Heck, W.W., National Crop Loss Assessment Network (NCLAN) 1984 Annual Report, Corvallis, OR, July 1986.

Heck, W.W., R.M. Adams, W.W. Cure, A.S. Hegote, H.E. Heggestad, R.J. Kohut, L.W. Kress, J.O. Rawlings and O.C. Taylor, "A Reassessment of Crop Loss from Ozone," Environmental Science Technology, 17:(12), 1983. pp.573A-581A.

Heck, W.W., O.C. Taylor, R. Adams, G. Bingham, J. Miller, E. Preston and L. Weinstein, "Assessment of Crop Loss from Ozone," Journal of the Air Pollution Control Association, 32:(4), April 1982. pp.353-361.

Hegote, A.S., A.J. Riordan and W.W. Heck, Field Methods to Assess the Impact of Air Pollutants on Crop Yields,

Hershaft, A., "Air Pollution and Damage Functions," Environmental Science and Technology, 10:(10), October 1976. pp.992-995.

Heslin, J.S. and B.F. Hobbs, "AMultiobjective Production Costing Model for Analyzing Emissions Dispatching and Fuel Switching, Department of Systems Engineering, Case Western Reserve University, Cleveland, OH," IEEE Transactions on Power Systems, 4:(3), August 1989.

Hill, R., The Impact of Energy on Environment and Development, prepared for the Nova Spes International Foundation Meeting, February 1990.

Hirst, E., J. Clinton, H. Geller and W. Kroner, Energy Efficiency in Buildings: Progress and Promise, ACEEE, Washington, DC, 1986.

Hodas, D.R., The Health Effects of Acid Aerosols, Widener University School of Law, 1989.

Hoehn, J.P. and A. Randall, Incentives and Performance in Contingent Valuation, mimeo, University of Kentucky, February 1983.

Hoffman, J., Responding to Global Change, University of Maryland School of Law, Baltimore, MD, 17 November 1989.

Housing and Urban Development (HUD), Mobile Home Research - An Evaluation of Formaldehyde Problems in Residential Mobile Homes, U.S. Department of Housing and Urban Development, Washington, D.C., April 1981.

"How Fast Can Trees Migrate?," Science, 243, 10 February 1989. pp.735-737.

Howard, R., "The Economic Impact," Canada-United States Law Journal, 5:(4), 1982. pp.41-46.

Howitt, R.E., T.W. Gossard and R.M. Adams, "Effects of Alternative Ozone Concentrations and Response Data on Economic Assessments: The Case of California Crops," Journal of the Air Pollution Control Association, 34:(11), November 1984. pp.1122-1127.

Huppert, D.D., Two Empirical Issues in Recreational Fisheries Economics; Mail Survey Self-Selection Bias and Divergence Between WTP and WTA, Fourth Annual Area Workshop: Marine Sport Fisheries, Economic Evaluation and Management, Seattle, WA, 23 June 1988.

ICF Resources, Economic Measurement of Environmental and Coal Market Impacts of SO2 Emissions Trading Under Alternative Acid Rain Control Proposals, ICF Resources Inc., March 1989.

ICF Resources, "Environmental Assessment and Review of Externalities Related to NYSEG's Electric Thermal Storage Program," August 1989. pp.4-7 to 4-9.

Ignelzi, P.C. and R. Ridge, The Evolution of Rebate Programs: From Conservation to Customer Service through Demand-Side Management, Proceedings of the Fourth National Conference on Utility DSM Programs, Electric Power Research Institute, April 1989.

Industrial Health Foundation, "Current Status of Health Effects of Fibrous Glass and Other Manmade Vitreous Fiber, An Annotated Bibliography," Medical Services Bulletin No. 21-82, 4th Revision, 1982.

Interior and Insular Affairs Senate Committee, New Technology of the Environment Acceptable to the Generation of Electricity, 1972.

Investigation by the Department of Public Utilities on its own Motion, P.t. Section 76 of Chapter 164 of the General Laws, into the Pricing and Ratemaking Treatment to be Afforded New Electric Generating, 30 November 1988.

Irving, P.M., Methodology for Estimating Crop Loss from Acidic Deposition, Argonne National Lab., IL., 1982.

Irving, P.M., "Acidic Precipitation Effects on Crops: A Review and Analysis of Research," Journal of Environmental Quality, 12:(4), 1983. pp.442-453.

Jacobson, B.S., "The Role of Air Pollution and Other Factors in Local Variations in General Mortality and Cancer Mortality," Archives of Environmental Health, 39:(4), July/August 1984. pp.306-313.

Jacobson, B.S., "The Role of Air Pollution and Other Factors in Local Variations in General Mortality and Cancer Mortality," Archives of Environmental Health, 39:(4), August 1984. pp.306-313.

Johansson, P.O. and B. Kristroem, "Measuring Values for Improved Air Quality from Discrete Response Data: Two Experiments," Journal of Agricultural Economics, 39:(3), September 1988. pp.439-45.

Johansson, T.B., B. Bodlund and R.H. Williams, Electricity: Efficient end-Use and New Generation Technologies and Their Planning Implications, University Press, Sweden, 1989.

Jones, et. al., "Evidence for Global Warming in the Past Decade," Nature, 332, 1988. pp.790.

Kahneman, D. and A. Tversky, "Prospect Theory: An Analysis of Decision Under Risk," Econometrics, 47:(2), March 1979.

Kaiser, R.A. and J.E. Fletcher, "State Policies and Practices in Coal Severance Taxation," Natural Resources Journal, 27 1987. pp.591.

Kalvins, A., Effects and Social Costs of Fossil-Fired Emissions Due to Electrical Exports on Structural Materials, Report No. 84-210-K, Ontario Hydro Research Division, January 1985.

Kealy, M.J., J. Dovidio and M.L. Rockel, "Willingness to Pay to Prevent Additional Damages to the Adirondacks from Acid Rain," Re. Sci. Rev., 1987.

Khalil, M.A. and R.A. Rosmussen, "The Release of Trichlorofluoromethane from Rigid Polyurethane foams," Journal of Air Pollution Control Association, 3:(2), 1986. pp.159-163.

Kimmins, J.P., Forest Ecology, Macmillan Publishing Company, New York, 1987.

Knapp and Ullman, Social Costs, Economic Development, and Environmental Disruption, University Press of America, Inc., 1983.

Kneese, A.V. and B.T. Bower, Environmental Quality and Residuals Management, Johns Hopkins University Press, Baltimore, MD, 1979.

Knetsch, J.L., Environmental and Economic Impact Assessment and the Divergence Between Willingness to Pay and the Compensation Demanded Measures of Loss, Paper presented to a workshop on Integrating Environmental and Economic Assessment: Analytical and Negotiating Approaches, Vancouver, BC, November, 1988.

Knetsch, J.L. and J.A. Sinden, "The Persistence of Evaluation Disparities," The Quarterly Journal of Economics, Harvard College.

Knetsch, J.L. and J.A. Sinden, "Willingness to pay and Compensation Demanded: Experimental Evidence of an Unexpected Disparity in Measures of Value," The Quarterly Journal of Economics, Harvard College, 1984.

Koomey, J., Comparative Analysis of Monetary Estimates of External Costs Associated with Combustion of Fossil Fuel, Energy Analysis Program, Berkeley, CA, 16 January 1990.

Kopp, R.J., W.J. Vaughan and M. Hazilla, Agricultural Sector Benefits Analysis for Ozone: Methods Evaluation and Demonstration (Final Report), Resources For the Future, Washington, DC, 15 June 1984.

Krause, F. et al., Energy Policy in the Greenhouse, International Project for Sustainable Energy Paths (IPSEP), El Cerrito, CA, September 1989.

Krawiec, F., Economic Measurement of Environmental Damages, May 1980.

Krupnick, A.J. et al., An Analysis of Selected Health Benefits from Reductions in Photochemical Oxidants in the Northeastern United States, prepared for EPA Contract No. 68-02-4323, September 1988.

Krupnick, A.J. and R.J. Kopp, The Health and Agricultural Benefits of Reductions in Ambient Ozone in the United States, Resources for the Future, Washington, DC, August 1988.

Krutilla, J.V. and A.C. Fisher, The Economics of Natural Environments, Resources for the Future, John Hopkins University Press, Baltimore, MD, 1975.

Kucera, V., Influence of Acid Deposition on Atmospheric Corrosion of Metals: A Review, In R. Baboian (ed) Materials Degradation Caused by Acid Rain, American Chemical Society, 1986.

Landefeld, J.S. and E.P. Seskin, "The Economic Value of Life: Linking Theory to Practice," American Journal of Public Health, 72 1982. pp.555-566.

Landsberg, H.H., Energy: The Next Twenty Years, Ballinger Publishing Co., Cambridge, MA, 1979.

Lashof, D.A. and D.R. Ahuja, "Relative Global Warming Potentials of Greenhouse Gas Emissions," Nature, 344 5 April 1990. pp.529-31.

Lave, L.B. and E.P. Seskin, "Air Pollution and Human Health," Science, 169 August 21, 1970. pp.723-732.

Lave, L. and E. Seskin, Air Pollution and Human Health, The John Hopkins University Press, Baltimore, 1977.

Lawrence Berkeley Laboratory, Manual on Indoor Air Quality, Electric Power Research Institute, Palo Alto, CA, February 1984.

Ledbetter, M., Preparing for the Energy Challenge of the 1990s, Energy Efficiency: An Overlooked Environmental Protection Strategy, January 1988 American Council for an Energy Efficient Economy.

Leipert, C. and U.E. Simonis, Environmental Damage-- Environmental Expenditures: Statistical Evidence on the Federal Republic of Germany, Research Professorship Environmental Policy Science Center, Berlin.

Leung, S.K., W. Reed and S. Geng, "Estimations of Ozone Damage to Selected Crops Grown in Southern California," Journal of the Air Pollution Control Association, 32:(2), February 1982. pp.160-164.

Lind, R.C., Discounting for Time and Risk in Energy Policy, Resources for the Future, Washington, DC, 1982.

Linzon, S.N., "Economic Effects of Sulfur Dioxide on Forest Growth," Journal of the Air Pollution Control Association, 21:(2), February 1971. pp.81-86.

Lipfert, F.W., Mortality and Air Pollution: Lessons From Statistics, Brookhaven National Lab., Upton, NY, 1982.

Lipfert, F.W., L.R. Dupuis, R.G. Malone, J. Schaedler and M.L. Daum, Case Study of Materials Damage Due to Air Pollution and Acid Rain in New Haven, CT, Brookhaven National Lab, Upton NY, May 1985.

Lipfert, F.W., R. Horst, S. Sherwood and T. Lareau, The 1985 Acid Precipitation Materials Damage Assessment: An Overview of Findings, In F. Mansfeld et al (ed) Proc. Symposia on Corrosion Effects of Acid Deposition and Corrosion of Electronic Materials 1985, 1985.

Lipfert, F.L., Correspondence to Richard L. Ottinger, Pace University School of Law, March 1990.

Lipfert, F.W., Effects of Acidic Deposition on the Atmospheric Deterioration of Materials, July 1987.

Lipfert, F.W., Mortality and Air Pollution: Lessons from Statistics, Brookhaven National Laboratory, Upton, NY, 1982.

Lipfert, F., "Sulphur Oxides, Particulates and Human Mortality: Synopsis of Statistical Correlations," Journal of the Air Pollution Control Association, 30:(4), April 1980. pp.366-371.

Liu, B.C., E.S. Yu (Midwest Research Institute), "Physical and Economic Damage Functions for Air Pollutants by Receptor," Corvallis Environmental Research Laboratory, Office of Development and Research, U.S. Environmental Protection Agency, September 1976.

Lomio, J.P., "International Law and Disposal of Radioactive Wastes at Sea," New England Law Review, 15 1979. pp.253-287.

Loucks, Armentano, Usher, Williams and Miller, Crop and Forest Losses Due to Current and Projected Emissions from Coal Fired Power Plants in the Ohio River Basin, March 1982.

Loucks, O.L., Crop and Forest Losses Due to Current and Projected Emission from Coal-Fired Power Plants in the Ohio River Basin, Ohio River Basin Energy Study, Urbana, Il., March 1982.

Luz International Application to the California Energy Commission for Certification of SEGS IX and X, prepared by ENSR Consulting and Engineering, February 1989.

Machado and Piltz, Reducing the Rate of Global Warming: The States' Role, Renewamerica, Washington, DC,

MacKenzie, J.J., M.T. El-Ashry and eds., Air Pollution's Toll on Forests and Crops, Yale University Press, New Haven, CT, 1989.

Macriss, R.A., "Air Infiltration and Indoor Air Quality," Proceedings of an Engineering Foundation Conference on Management of Atmospheres in Tightly Enclosed Spaces, ASHRAE, Atlanta, GA, October 1983.

Macriss, R.A. and R.H. Elkens, "Control of the Level of NOx in the Indoor Environment," Fourth International Clean Air Congress, Tokyo, May 1977.

Marcus, W.B. and J.A. Nahigan, A Quantitative Method for Valuing the Reduction of NOx Emissions, JB Energy Inc. West Sacramento CA.

Marland, The Prospect of Solving the CO2 Problem Through Global Reforestation, U.S. Department of Energy, 1988.

Massachusetts Department of Environmental Quality Engineering, Acid Rain and Related Air Pollution Damage, A National and International Call for Action.

Massachusetts Department of Environmental Quality Engineering, Development and Testimony of a Planning Approach to Acid Deposition Control.

Massachusetts Photovoltaic Center, An Overview of the External Issues of Electric Power Production, MPC Article, Boston, MA, 1988.

Mauldin, M. and P. Herman, The Quantification of Externalities for Demand-Side and Supply-Side Resources Options: A Preliminary Study.

Mazumdar, S.H. Schmmel and I.T.T.Higgins, "Relationship of Daily Mortality to Air Pollution: An Analysis of 14 London Winters," Archives of Environmental Health, 37 July/August 1982. pp.213-220.

McCarthy, E.F., Damage Cost Models for Pollution Effects on Materials, TRC Environmental Consultants, Inc., Wethersfield, CT., January 1984.

McCormich, J., Acid Earth: The Global Threat of Acid Pollution, Earthscan, London, 1985.

McCunney, R.J., "The Role of Building Construction and Ventilation in Indoor Air Pollution," New York State Journal of Medicine, April 1987. pp.203-208.

McFee, W.W., Acid Precipitation in Relation to Agriculture, Forestry and Aquatic Biology, Report No. 100, Council for Agricultural Science and Technology, Ames, Iowa, 1984.

McKean, R.N., Efficiency in Government through Systems Analysis, With Emphasis on Water Resources Development, John Hopkins Press.

McLaughlin, S.B., "Effects of Air Pollution on Forests. A Critical Review," Journal of the Air Pollution Control Association, 35(5) May 1985. pp.512-534.

McNeely, J., Economic and Biological Diversity: Developing and Using Economic Incentives to Conserve Biological Resources, Inter-Union for Conservation of Nature and National Resources, Gland, Switzerland, 1988.

McNesby, Effects of Photochemical Oxidants on Materials, 1977.

Medelsohn, R. and G. Orcutt, "An Empirical Analysis of Air Pollution Dose-Response Curves," Journal of Environmental Economics and Management, 6 1979. pp.85-106.

Medsker, L., Side Effects of Renewable Energy Sources, National Audubon Society, December 1982.

Mendelsohn, R., "An Economic Analysis of Air Pollution From Coal-Fired Power Plants," Journal of Environmental Economics and Management, 7 1980. pp.30-43.

Mendelsohn, R. and G. Orcutt, "An Empirical Analysis of Air Pollution Dose-Response Curves," Journal of Environmental Economics and Management, 6 1979. pp.85-106.

Menz, F.C. and J.K. Mullen, Acidification Impact on Fisheries, in "Economic Perspectives on Acid Deposition Control", Crocker, T.D., Ed.; Butterworth Publishers, Boston, MA.

Menz, F.C., Assessment of the Economic Magnitude of Environmental Damage from Acid Precipitation in the Adirondacks (Technical Completion Report), Clarkson College of Technology, Potsdam, NY., May 1983.

Menz, F.C. and J.K. Mullen, "Valuing the Effect of Acidification Damages in the Adirondack Fishery: Reply," American Journal of Agricultural Economics, February 1989. pp.221-222.

Meridian Corporation, Energy System Emissions and Material Requirements, Report Prepared for EPA, Washington, DC, 1989.

Meridian Corporation, Characterization of U.S. Energy Resources and Reserves, Prepared for Deputy Assistant Secretary for Renewable energy, U.S. DOE, June 1989.

Meyer, P., E. Cheslak, G. Andrews, J. Garcia and J. Hagar, Calculation of Environmental Costs and Benefits Associated with Hydropower Development in the Pacific Northwest, Bonneville Power Administration, Portland, Oregon, April 1986.

Michigan Electricity Option Study, Environmental Assessment of Electricity Resource Options, Michigan Public Service Commission, Lansing, MI, October 1987.

Miller, E.S.,editor, Economic Analysis of Environmental Problems: A Conference of the Universities, Columbia University Press, 1975.

Minnesota Pollution Control Agency, Supplemental Health Risk Assessment Technical Work Paper, Volume I: Polychlorinated Dioxins/Polychlorinated Furans, Wisconsin County Resource Recovery Facility, J.B. Stevens & Associates, April 1988.

Mintzer, "Weathering the Storms in A Warming World," Public Power, 46:(6), Nov.-Dec. 1988. pp.16.

Mintzer, I., Responding to Global Change, University of Maryland School of Law, Baltimore, MD, 17 November 1989.

Mises, L.V., Human Action, Yale University Press, New Haven, CT, 1949.

Mishan, E.J., "The Postwar Literature on Externalities: An Interpretive Essay," Journal of Economic Literature, 9 1971. pp.1-28.

Mitchell, R.C. and R.T. Carson, Using Surveys to Value Public Goods: The Contingent Valuation Method, Resources for the Future, Washington, DC, 1989.

Mjelde, J.W., R.M. Adams, B.L. Dixon and P. Garcia, "Using Farmers' Actions to Measure Crop Loss Due to Air Pollution," Journal of the Air Pollution Control Association, 31:(4), April 1984. pp.360-364.

Monson, P.C., "Radioactive Air Pollution from Uranium Mining: Regulatory Abdication in the Face of Scientific Uncertainty," Environmental Law, 13 pp.545.

Montange, C.H., Member of the Bar of the District of Columbia, "The Initial Environmental Assessments for the Nuclear Waste Repository Under Section 112 of the Nuclear Waste Policy Act," UCLA Journal of Environmental Law and Policy, 4 1984-85. pp.187-230.

Moore and W.K. Viscusi, "Doubling the Estimated Value of Life: The Implications of New Occupational Fatality Data," Journal of Policy Analysis and Management, 7 1988b.

Moore and W.K. Viscusi, "The Quantity Adjusted Value of Life," Economic Enquiry, 26:(369), 1988a.

Morey, E.R. and W.D. Shaw, An Economic Model to Assess the Impact of Acid Rain: A Characteristics Approach to Estimating the Demand for and Benefits from Recreational Fishing, in V.K. Smith and A.D. Witte, eds., Advances in Applied Microeconomic Theory, Vol 8, JAI Press Inc., Greenwich, CT.

Morey, P.R., "Microbiological Problems in Office Buildings: Recognition and Remedial Action," Energy Technology Conference XV, Government Institutes, Inc., Washington, DC, 1988. pp.445-454.

Morey, P.R. and J.E. Woods, "Indoor Air Quality in Health-Care Facilities," Occupational Medicine, July - September 1987. pp.547-563.

Moskowitz, Coveney, Medeiros and Morris, Oxidant Air Pollution: Estimating Economic Effects on U.S. Vegetation, 1981.

Moskowitz, P.D., An Environmental Source Book on the Photovoltaic Industry, Brookhaven National Laboratory, September 1986.

Moskowitz, P.D., E.A. Coveney, W.H. Medeiros and S.C. Morris, "Oxidant Air Pollution: A Model for Estimating Effects on U.S. Vegetation," Journal of the Air Pollution Control Association, 32:(2), February 1982. pp.155-160.

Moskowitz, P.D., W.H. Medeiros, S.C. Morris and E.A. Coveney, "Oxidant Air Pollution: Estimated Effects on U.S. Vegetation in 1969 and 1974," National Center for Analysis of Energy Systems Department of Energy and Environment (Brookhaven National Laboratory), November 1980.

Mount, T.D. and M.E. Czerwinski, Global Warming and Acid Rain: The Implications for Restricting Emissions from Power Plants, presented at the Workshop on Large Scale Social Science Models, Urbana-Champaign, Ill., September 1988.

Mueller, W.J. and P.B. Stickney, Final Report on a Survey and Economic Assessment of the Effects of Air Pollution on Elastomers, National Air Pollution Control Association, Battelle Memorial Institute, Columbus, OH, 1970.

Mullen, J.K. and F.C. Menz, "The Effects of Acidification Damages on the Economic Value of the Adirondack Fishery to New York Anglers," American Journal of Agricultural Economics, 1985.

Murdoch, J.C. and M.A. Thayer, "Hedonic Price Estimation of Variable Urban Air Quality," Journal of Environmental Economics and Management, 15:(2), June 1988. pp.143-46.

Murray, D.R., Assessment of Material Damage and Soiling from Air Pollution in the South Coast Air Basin (Final Report), TRC Environmental Consultants, East Hartford CT., 10 December 1985.

NARUC, Least Cost Utility Planning Handbook for Public Utility Commissioners, Washington, DC, October 1988.

National Research Council, Acid Deposition Atmospheric Processes in Eastern North America, National Academy Press, Washington, DC, 1983.

National Academy of Sciences, Biological Effects of Ionizing Radiation (BEIR), Vol. III, National Academy Press, 1989.

National Academy of Sciences, "Effects of Photochemical Oxidants on Materials", in Ozone and Other Photochemical Oxidants (Chapter 13), Washington, DC.

National Acid Precipitation Assessment Program, Interim Assessment, The Causes and Effects of Acid Deposition, Volume IV, Effects of Acid Deposition.

National Academy of Sciences, Indoor Pollutants, Committee on Indoor Pollutants, National Research Council, National Academy Press, Washington, DC, 1981.

National Acid Precipitation Assessment Program, Plan and Schedule for NAPAP Assessment Report, 1989-90, NAPAP Report, 1989.

National Air Pollution Control Administration: U.S. Public Health Service, Air Quality Criteria for Sulphur Oxides, U.S. Government Printing Office, Washington, D.C., January 1969.

National Institute for Occupational Safety and Health, Guidance for Indoor Air Quality Investigations, NIOSH Report, Cincinnati, OH, 1987.

National Research Council, Commission on Life Sciences, board on Radiation Effects Research, Committee on the Biological Effects of Ionizing Radiations, Health Effects of Exposure to Low Levels of Ionizing Radiation (BEIR V), National Academy Press, Washington, DC, 1990.

Navrud, S., "Estimating Social Benefits of Environmental Improvements from Reduced Acid Depositions: A Contingent Valuation Survey," Folmer, H. and E. van Ierland, Valuation Methods and Policy Making in Environmental Economics, Elvesier, Amsterdam, Holland, 1989.

Nazaroff, "The Use of Mechanical Ventilation with Heat Recovery for Controlling Radon and Radon-Daughter Concentrations in Houses," Atmospheric Environment, 15 1981. pp.263-270.

Nelson, J.P., The Effects of Mobile Source Air Pollution on Residential Property Value, 1975.

Nelson, J.P., "Residential Choice, Hedonic Prices and the Demand for Urban Air Quality," Journal of Urban Economics, 5 July 1978. pp.357-369.

Nero, A.V., et.al., "Radon Concentrations and Infiltration Rates Measured in Conventional and Energy Efficient Houses," Health Physics 45, August 1983. pp.401-405.

New York State Power Lines Project Scientific Advisory Panel, Biological Effects of Power Line Fields, Final Report, Prepared for the New York State Power Lines Project, New York State Department of Health, Albany, NY, 1987.

New York State Energy Office, Department of Public Service, Department of Environmental Conservation, Draft New York State Energy Plan: Electricity Supply Assessment, Nuclear Assessment, Albany, New York, May 1989.

New York State Energy Research and Development Authority, Exploration for Geothermal Resources in the Capital District of New York, prepared by Dunn Geoscience Corporation, Latham, NY, November 1982.

New York State Bureau of Fisheries, 1976-1977New York Angler Survey Final Report, 1981.

New York State Energy Research and Development Authority, Geothermal Energy Potential in the Appalachian Basin of New York State, Prepared by TAL Research and Development, New York, June 1981.

New York State Energy Research and Development Authority, Indoor Air Quality, Infiltration and Ventilation in Residential Buildings, prepared by W.S. Fleming and Associates, March 1985.

New York State Energy Office, Department of Environmental Conservation, Department of Public Service, New York State Energy Plan Draft Report, Volumes I & IV, Summary Report and Electricity Issues, May 1989.

New York State Energy Office (SEO), Dept. of Public Services (DPS), and Department of Environmental Conservation (DEC), Draft New York State Energy Plan, Prepared jointly by SEO, DPS, and DEC, May 1989.

New York Public Service Commission Case No. 28223,D.R. Benefits to Ratepayer and Utilities from Implementation of Conservation Programs that will Reduce Electric Use, Order Directing the Submittal of Annual Report, 22 September 1987.

"New York PSC Proposes to Limit Magnetic Fields for Future Transmission Lines in the State; Requests Public Comments," Issues Review and Tracking; The Energy Newsbrief, 5:(14), 21 May 1990. pp.6.

New York Public Service Commission Case No. 29409, O.N. 88-15(A) (Planning and Bidding), Order Denying Petitions for Rehearing, 2 November 1988.

Nisson, J.D. and G.S. Dutt, The Superinsulated Home Book, John Wiley and Sons, New York, February 1985.

Nitschke, I.A., et al., "A Detailed Study of Inexpensive Radon Control Techniques in New York State Houses," 3rd International Conference on Indoor Air Quality and Climate, Stockholm, August 1984.

Northwest Utilities Service Company, "A Comparison of Two Weatherization Techniques," March 1988. pp.75-77.

Nuclear Regulatory Commission, Final Generic Environmental Statement on the Use of Recycle Plutonium in Mixed Oxide fuel in Light Water Cooled Reactors: Health, Safety and Environment, Washington, DC, August 1976.

Oak Ridge National Laboratory, E.C. Fox, R.P. Krishnan and J.E. Jones Jr. C.S. Shaw, A Review of Fluidized Bed Combustion Technology in the United States,

OECD COMPASS Project, Environmental Impacts of Renewable Energy, 1988.

Office of Technology Assessment, Acid Rain and Transported Air Pollutants: Implications for Public Policy, Washington, DC, 1984.

Office of Technology Assessment, Catching Our Breath: Next Steps for Reducing Urban Ozone, Congress of the United States, August 1989.

Office of Public Affairs, EPA, CFC's and Stratospheric Ozone, EPA Report, Washington, DC, 1987.

Office of Technology Assessment, Facing America's Trash, What Next for Municipal Solid Waste?, U.S. Government Printing Office, Washington, DC, October 1989.

Office of Research and Development, Environmental Protection Agency, Indoor Air Facts No. 4: Sick Buildings, EPA Report, Washington, DC, 1988.

Office of Air and Radiation, Environmental Protection Agency, The Inside Story: A Guide to Indoor Air Quality, EPA Report 400/1-88/004, Washington, DC, 1988.

Office of Air and Radiation, Environmental Protection Agency, Regulatory Impact Analysis on the National Ambient Air Quality Standards for Sulfur Oxides (Sulfur Dioxide), EPA Report Draft, Washington, DC, 1988.

Office of Policy Analysis, Environmental Protection Agency, Unfinished Business: A Comparative Assessment of Environmental Problems, EPA Overview Report in 5 Volumes, Washington, DC, 1987.

Office of Solid Waste, Environmental Protection Agency, Wastes from the Combustion of Coal by Electric Utility Power Plants, EPA Report to Congress, Doc. #530-SW-88-002, Washington, DC, 1988.

Office of Policy, Planning and Evaluation, Environmental Protection Agency, Policy Options for Stabilizing Global Climate, EPA Draft Report to Congress, Washington, DC, 1989.

Office of Technology Assessment (OTA), New Electric Power Technologies: Problems and Prospects for the 1990s, July 1985.

Ohio v. U.S. Dept of Interior, 8.F.2d 432 (D.C. Cir. 1989),

Olsen, D., Hydroelectric Power Development on the Hamma Hamma River System: Economic and Institutional Factors Affecting the Indian, Commercial, and Sport Fisheries, Washington, DC, February 1987.

Olsen, D., Summary Report: Existence and Sport Values for Doubling the Size of the Columbia River Basin Salmon and Steelhead Runs, prepared for North Pacific Division, U.S. Army Corps of Engineers, Portland, Oregon, January 1990.

Olson, C., "An Analysis of Wage Differentials Received by Workers on Dangerous Jobs," The Journal of Human Resources, 16:(2), 1981.

Ontario Hydro, The Effect of Fossil-Fired Emissions on Property Values due to Electrical Exports, January 1985.

Order Issuing a Final Environmental Impact Statement and Adopting Staff's Response to Agency Comments, C.8. proceeding on Motion of the Commission as to the guidelines for bidding to meet the future el, 24 March 1989.

Organization for Economic Co-Operation and Development, Environmental Impacts of Renewable Energy, OECD, 1988.

Ostro, B.D., "Air Pollution, Public Health, and Inflation," Environmental Health Perspectives, 34 February 1980. pp.185-189.

An Overview of the External Issues of Electric Power Production, Massachusetts Photovoltaic Center, November 1988.

Ozkaynak, H. and G.D. Thurston, "Associations Between 1980 U.S. Mortality Rates and Alterative Measures of Airborne Particle Concentration," Risk Analysis, 7:(4), 1987.

Pacific Gas & Electric, Least Cost Planning Treatment of Externalities, Preliminary Draft, April 1990.

Page, A.L., A.A. Elseewi and I.R. Straughan, "Physical and Chemical Properties of Fly Ash from Coal Fired Power Plants with References to Environmental Impacts," Residue Reviews, 71 1979. pp.83-120.

Page, A., Fabian and Cieka, "Estimation of Economic Losses to the Agricultural Sector from Airborne Residuals in the Ohio River Basin Region," Journal of the Air Pollution Control Association, 32:(2), February 1982. pp.151.

Page, W.P., Estimating Regional Losses to Agricultural Producers from Airborne Residuals in the Ohio River Basin Energy Study Region, 1976-2000, Ohio River Basin Energy Study, Urbana, IL., October 1981.

Page, W.P., G. Arbogast, R. Fabian and J. Cieka, "Estimation of Economic Losses to the Agricultural Sector from Airborne Residuals in the Ohio River Basin Region," Journal of the Air Pollution Control Association, 32:(2), February 1982.pp.151-154.

Palmquist, R.B., Estimating the Demand for Air Quality From Property Value Studies, Prepared for the Environmental Protection Agency, November 1982.

Palmquist, R.B., Estimating the Demand for Air Quality From Property Value Studies: Further Results, Prepared for the Environmental Protection Agency, October 1983.

Pearce, D.W., editor, The Valuation of Social Costs, 1978.

Peat Marwick and Partners, Social Effects of Air Pollution Emissions from Fossil-Fired Thermal Stations: Task C6 - An Economic Appraisal, September 1974.

Peterson, D.C., et al., Improving Accuracy and Reducing Costs of Environmental benefit Assessments, Office of Policy, Planning and Evaluation, U.S. Environmental Protection Agency, Washington, DC, 1987.

Peterson, D.C. et al., Improving Accuracy and Reducing Costs of Environmental Benefit Assessments, Office of Policy Planning and Evaluation, U.S. EPA, Washington, DC, 1987.

Phalen, R.F., Testimony before the Subcommittee on Environmental Protection, hearing on Health Effects of Air Pollution, Washington, DC, 1989.

Phillips, T.P. and B.A. Forster, "Economic Impacts of Acid Rain on Forest, Aquatic, and Agricultural Ecosystems in Canada," American Journal of Agricultural Economics, December 1987. pp. 963-969.

Pierson M.D.,W.E.,Clinical Professor, "Wood Smoke: Health Effects and Legislation, Clinical Observations," Department of Pediatrics and Environmental Health, University of Washington, Seattle, WA.

Platte River Whooping Crane Critical Habitat Maintenance Trust v. Federal Energy Regulatory Commission, 8.F. 2d 109 (D.C. Cir. 1989),

Pohl, R.O., Land Use for Nuclear and Solar Energy, Environmental Conservation, Spring 1977.

Polinsky, A.M. and S. Shavell, "The Air Pollution and Property Value Debate," The Review of Economics and Statistics, 57:(1), February 1975. pp.100-107.

Pollock, C., "The Closing Act: Decommissioning Nuclear Power Plants," Environment, 28:(2), March 1986. pp.15.

Portney, P.R. and J. Mullahy, Ambient Ozone and Human Health: An Epidemiological Analysis. Volume 1 (Final Report), Resources For the Future, Washington, D.C., August 1985.

Potter, P.F. et al., Impacts of Advanced Refrigerator Insulation, Proceedings of the 1988 ACEEE Summer Study on Energy Efficiency in Buildings, Vol. 4.

Prest, A.R. and R. Turvey, "Cost-Benefit Analysis: A Survey," Surveys of Economic Theory, 1 1967.

Prest, A.R. and R. Turvey, "Market Solutions to Externality Problems: Theory and Practice," American Journal of Agricultural Economics, 54 1972. pp.175-183.

Priestly, T., Aesthetic Considerations and Electric Utilities: An Introductory Guide to the Literature, EPRI (RP2069-04), February, 1984.

Putta, S.N., New York State Department of Public Service, Competition in Electric Generation--Environmental Externalities, October 1989.

Radar, N., Power Surge: The Status and Near Term Potential of Renewable Energy Technologies, Revised., Public Citizen, Washington, DC, May 1989.

Rand Corporation, Risk Assessment of Toxic Pollutants from Fossil Fuel Power Plants, EPRI (RP-1826-05), August 1987.

Randall, A., "Market Solutions to Externality Problems: Theory and Practice," American Journal of Agricultural Economics, 54 1972. pp.175-183.

Re Benefits to Ratepayer and Utilities from Implementation of Conservation Programs that will Reduce Electric Use, C.2.,Op. No. 89-15, Order Concerning Conclusions on Long Range Demand Side Management Pl, 23 May 1989.

Re Guidelines for Bidding to Meet Future Electric Capacity Needs of Orange and Rockland Utilities, I.C. 88-E-241, Order, 13 April 1989.

Re Least-Cost Planning for Resource Acquisitions by Energy Utilities in Oregon, D.U. 180, Order No. 89-507, Slip Op. at 10, 102 PUR (4th) 301 (Ore. PUC), 20 April 1989.

Re Least-Cost INvestments, E.E., Conservation and Load Management, Docket 5270, Hearing Officer's Report and Proposal for Decision (Vt. PSB), 13 July 1989.

Re Orange and Rockland Utilities, I.A. Niagara Mohawk Power Corporation-- Rate Incentive Proposals, Case 89-E-041, Op. No. 89-29, Order Approving Demand Side Management Rate Incentives, 12 September 1989.

Reichmuth and Robison, Carbon Dioxide Offsets, available from Reichmuth at Pacific Power and Light, 2 March 1989.

Renewable Energy Institute, Annual Renewable Energy Technology Review, Washington, DC, 1989.

Repace, J.L., "Indoor Air Pollution," Environment International 8, 1982. pp.21-36.

Rescher, N., Risk: A Philosophical Introduction to the Theory of Risk Evaluation and Management, University Press of America, Lanham, MD, 1983.

Rice, D.P., "Estimating the Cost of Illness," Health Economics Series, U.S. Public Health Services:(No. 6), 1966.

Richels, R., "Climate Change and Electric Utilities," 1989 EPRI Demand Side Management Conference, EPRI, Palo Alto, CA, 1989.

Ridker, R.G. and J.A. Henning, "The Determinants of Residential Property Values with Special Reference to Air Pollution," The Review of Economics and Statistics, 49 May 1967. pp.246-257.

Rizzuto, J., "An Investigation of Infiltration and Indoor Air Quality in New York State Homes," Proceedings of the 1988 ACEEE Summer Study on Energy Efficiency in Buildings, 1 1988. pp.1.141-156.

Rodker, R.G., Economic Costs of Air Pollution, Studies and Measurement, Praeger, NY, 1967.

Rose, D.J., P.W. Walsh and L.L. Leskovjan, "Nuclear Power - Compared to What?," American Scientist, 64 May - June 1976. pp.291-299.

Rose, E.C., Environmental health and Safety Assessment of Photovoltaics, Jet Propulsion Laboratory, 1983.

Rosenfeld & Mowris, Energy Efficiency: The Best Way to Save Money and Slow Global Warming, 18-3 Physics and Society (in press), July 1989.

Rowe, R.D. and L.G. Chestnut, Visibility Benefits Assessment Guide Book - Final Report, August 1981.

Rowe, R.D. and L.G. Chestnut, "Economic Assessment of the Effects of Air Pollution on Agricultural Crops in the San Joaquin Valley," Journal of the Air Pollution Control Association, 35:(7), July 1985. pp.728-734.

Rowe, R.D. and L.G. Chestnut, Visibility Benefits Assessment Guidebook, Final Report, ABT/WEST, Denver, CO., August 1981.

Rowe, R.D., R.C. D'Arge and D.S. Brookshire, "An Experiment on the Economic Value of Visibility,"Journal of Environmental Economics and Management, 7:(1), March 1980. pp.1-19.

Ruedisili, L.C. and M.W. Firebaugh, editor, Perspectives on Energy and Environment: Issues, Ideals and Environmental Dilemmas, Oxford University Press, New York, 1982.

Rulemaking Proceeding for Consideration of Cogeneration & Small Power Production, 4.P. Util. Rept. (PUR4th) 563,

Sagan, L.A., "Human Costs of Nuclear Power," Science, 177 August 11, 1972.

Sagoff, M., "Economic Theory and Environmental Law," Michigan Law Review, 79 pp.1393-1419.

Salmon, R.L., Systems Analysis of the Effects of Air Pollution on Materials, Midwest Research Institute. Prepared for Economic Effects Research Division, National Air Pollution Control Admin., Raleigh, NC, Kansas City, Missouri, 1970.

Samuelson, P., "A Diagrammatic Exposition of a Theory of Public Expenditure," The Review of Economics and Statistics, XXXVII:(4), November 1955.

Samuelson, P., Economics, McGraw-Hill, New York, NY, 1973.

Samuelson, P. and W. Vickrey, "Discussion,"The American Economic Review, 54 1964. pp.88-96.

San Martin, R.L., Environmental Emissions from energy Technology Systems: The Total Fuel Cycle, U.S. Department of Energy, Washington, DC, April 1989.

Sandenburgh, E.A., Rising CO2, Climate Change and Forest Management: An Overview, in The Greenhouse Effect, 1987.

Schell, R.M., Estimation of the Public Health Risks Associated with Exposure to Ambient Concentrations of 87 Substances, Office of Air Quality, EPA Report, Washington, DC, 1984.

Schell, R.M., Memorandum in Response to Article Titled: Risk Assessment for Chromium Emissions from Fuel Combustion Sources, Office of Air Quality, EPA Memorandum, Washington, DC, 1984.

Schneider and Chen, "Carbon Dioxide Warming and Coastline Flooding: Physical Factors and Climatic Impact," Annual Review of Energy, 5 1980. pp.107, 135.

Schneider, "The Greenhouse Effect: Science and Policy," Science, 243, 10 February 1984. pp.771.

Schneider, K., "Scientist Who Managed to 'Shock the World' on Atomic Workers' Health," New York Times, 3 May 1990.

Schulze, W.D., R.C. d'Arge and D.S. Brookshire, "Valuing Environmental Commodities: Some Recent Experiments," Land Economics, 57 1981. pp.151-172.

Scott, "Columbia River Salmon: Benefit Cost Analysis and Mitigation," Northwest Environmental Journal, 3:(2), 1989. pp.121.

Seneca, J.J. and M.K. Taussig, Environmental Economics, Prentice-Hall, Englewood Cliffs, NJ, 1974.

Sexton, K. and J.J. Wesolowski, "Safeguarding Indoor Air Quality: Public Policy Issues and the California Response," Environmental Science and Technology 19(4), 1985. pp.305-309.

Shands, Forests-- The Momentum for a Greenhouse Effect: Physical, Economic and Political Limits to Curtailing the Magnitude of Global Warming, in Shands and Hoffman (eds.).

Sharma, K.J., Environmental Costs and Benefits Case Study: Nuclear Power Plants-- Quantification and Economic Valuation of Selected Environmental Impacts/Effects, Nero & Associates, Inc., Portland, OR.

Shaw, W.D., "Valuing the Effect of Acidification Damages on the Adirondack Fishery: Comment," American Journal of Agricultural Economics, February 1989. pp.pp. 217-220.

Shenk and Riley, Quantifying Environmental Impacts, May 1981.

Shepard, M., "The Politics of Climate," Electric Power Research Institute Journal, June 1988, EPRI, Palo Alto, CA, 1988.

Shuman, M. and R. Cavanagh, A Model Conservation and Electric Power Plan for the Pacific Northwest, for Natural Resources Defense Council (NRDC), 1981.

Shuman, M. and R. Cavanagh, A Model Electric Power and Conservation Plan for the Pacific Northwest, Bonneville Power Administration.

Siegart, R.W., Cool Water Achievements: Impressive Past for a Promising Future, presentation to Alternative Energy 1989 Conference, Tuscon, AZ, April 1989.

Slovic, P., B. Fischoff and S. Lichtenstein, Characterizing Perceived Risk, in Perilous Progress (R.W. Kates, et al., eds.) - Westview, Boulder, Colorado, 1985.

Small, K.A., "Air Pollution and Property Values: Further Comment," Review of Economics and Statistics, 57:(1), February 1975. pp.105-107.

Smart, L.E., Editor-in-Chief, Public Utilities Fortnightly, "Anticipating the Costs of Permanent Nuclear Waste Disposal," Public Utilities Fortnightly, 11 November 1982. pp.5-10.

Smith, R., The Occupational Safety and Health Act: Its Goals and Achievements, 1976.

Smith, R.I., et al., Updated Costs for Decommissioning Nuclear Power Facilities, EPRI, May 1985.

Smith, V.K., The Economic Consequences of Air Pollution, Ballinger Pub. Co., Cambridge, MA, 1976.

Smith, V.K., "The Measurement of Mortality and Air Pollution Relationships," Environment and Planning, 8 1976. pp.149-162.

Smith, V.K., "Measuring the Impact of AIr Pollution on Property Values," Journal of Regional Science, December 1975.

Smith, V.K., Nitrogen Oxides from Coal Combustion: Environmental Effects, October 1980.

Smith, V.K., W.H. Desvousges and A. Fischer, "A Comparison of Direct and Indirect Methods for Estimating Environmental Benefits," American Journal of Agricultural Economics, 86:(2), May 1986. pp.293-299.

Smith, V.K. and W.H. Desvousges, Measuring Water Quality Benefits, Kluwer-Nijhoff Publishing, 1987.

Smith & Tirpak (eds.), The Potential Effects of Global Climate Change on the United States, (Executive Summary), United States Environmental Protection Agency, October 1989.

The Social and Economic Effects of the Accident at Three Mile Island, Report to the Nuclear Regulatory Commission (U.S. Government Printing Office, January 1980.

Solholt, L.F., R.W. Vocke and et al, Handling of Combustion and Emission-Abatement Washes from Coal-Fired Power Plants: Implications for Fish and Wildlife Resources, United States Department of the Interior Fish and Wildlife Services, 1980.

South Coast Air Quality Management District, Air Quality Management Plan: South Coast Air Basin, Southern California Association of Governments, March 1989.

Spak, D.G., "The Need for a Ban on All Radioactive Waste Disposal in the Ocean," Northwestern Journal of International Law and Business, 7 1986. pp.803-833.

Spangler, M.B., "A Critique of Methods in the Quantification of Risks, Costs, and Benefits in the Societal Choice of Energy Options," Annual Nuclear Energy, 10:(3,4), 1983. pp.135.

Spence, J.W., F.H. Haynie, E.O. Edney and D.C. Stiles, The Effects of Dry and Wet Deposition on Galvanized Steel, (In Mansfeld et al (ed). Proceeding of the Symposia on corrosion Effects of Acid Deposition and Corrosion of Electronic Materials, American Chemical Society, 1985), 1985.

Spence, J.W. and F.H. Haynie, Paint Technology and Air Pollution: Survey and Economic Assessment, U.S. Environmental Protection Agency, Research Triangle Park, NC, 1972.

Spengler, J.D. and K. Sexton, "Indoor Air Pollution: A Public Health Perspective," Science, 221 1983. pp.9-17.

SRI International, Techniques and Models to Estimate the Health Benefits of Controlling Toxic Substances Emitted From Coal-Fired Power Plants, EPRI (RP-1826-01), March 1986.

Stanford, R., "The Bioeconomic Impact of Impingement and Entrainment on Yellow Perch in Lake Erie," North American Journal of Fisheries Management, 2 1982. pp.285-293.

Stankunas, A.R. and D.F. Unites, Air-Pollution Damage to Man-Made Materials: Physical and Economic Estimates, TRC Environmental Consultants, Inc., East Hartford, CT., February 1983.

Starr, C., "Social Benefit Versus Technological Risk-- What is our Science Willing to Pay for Safety?," Science, 165, 19 September 1969. pp.1232-1238.

State of New York Public Service Commission, Order Issuing a Final Environmental Impact Statement and Adopting Staff's Response to Agency Comments, Commission Case 88-E-241, New York, 1989.

Steinberg, M. and H.C. Cheng, A Systems Study for the Removal, Recovery, and Disposal of Carbon Dioxide from Fossil Fuel Power Plants in the U.S., Brookhaven National Laboratory, Department of Applied Science, Process Sciences Division, February 1985.

Steudler, P.A. et al., "Influence of Nitrogen Fertilization on Methane Uptake in Temperate Forest Soils," Nature, 341, 28 September 1989.

Strauss, C.H. and L.L. Wright, Woody Biomass Production Costs in the United States, Research sponsored by the Biofuels and Municipal Waste Technology Division, U.S. DOE, 1990.

Svitek, L.L., Department of Economics, Natural Resource Damage Assessment Under CERCLA: Economic Valuation Concept & Methodology & Survey of Restoration

Issues, Prepared for New York State Department of Environmental Conservation, SUNY at Albany, Albany, New York, March 1989.

Sykes, T. and L. Ping, Possible Health Effects of electric and Magnetic Fields from Electric Power Lines: A Summary of Scientific Studies, Washington Institute for Public Policy, The Evergreen State College, January 1990.

Taha et al., "Residential Cooling Loads and the Urban Heat Island-- the Effects of Albedo," Building and Environment, 23 1988. pp.271-283.

Techplan Associates, Assessment of Commercial and Industrial Cogeneration Potential in the Pacific Northwest, U.S. Dept. of Energy, March 1989.

Tempchin, R. and A. Makhijani, "Electric Utility Planning in Light of Global Climate Changing Concerns," 1989 EPRI Demand Side Management Conference, EPRI, Palo Alto, CA, 1989.

Tennessee Valley Authority v. Hill, 4. U.S. 153 (1978).

Texas Electric Service Co. v. Helon, 5 S.W.2d 864 (Tex. Ct. App. 1977), reh. den., March 4, 1977.

Thaler, R. and S. Rosen, The Value of Saving a Life: Evidence form the Labor Market, in Household Production and Consumption, (N. Terkeckyj, ed.), Columbia University Press, New York, 1976.

Tichler, J., K. Norden and J. Congemi, Radioactive Materials Released from Nuclear Power Plants: Annual Report, 1987, Prepared for U.S. Nuclear Regulatory Commission by Brookhaven National Laboratory, Vol. 8, October 1989.

Tingey, D.T., Impact of Ozone on Agriculture and its Consequences (Symposium Paper), Environmental Research Laboratory, Office of Research and Development, U.S. Environmental Protection Agency, Corvallis, OR, 1986.

Tomlinson, G.H., Effects of Acid Deposition on the Forests of Europe and North America, CRC Press, Boca Raton, FL, 1990.

TRC Environmental Consultants, Air Pollution Damage to Man-Made Materials: Physical and Economic Estimates, 1983.

Trexler, E.A., Forestry as a Response to Global Warming: An Analysis of the Guatemala Agroforestry and Carbon Sequestration Project, World Resources Institute, June 1989.

Trijonis, J., Air Quality Benefit Analysis for Los Angeles and San Francisco Based on Housing Values and Visibility (Final Report December 1982 - June 1984), Santa Fe Research Corp., Bloomington, MN., January 1985.

Trumble, R. and L. Parker, Acid Rain: Current Issues, Library of Congress, Congressional Research Service, 23 January 1984.

Turiel, I., Indoor Air Quality and Human Health, Stanford University Press, Stanford, CA, 1985.

Turvey, R., "On Divergences Between Social Cost and Private Cost," Economica, 30 August 1963. pp.309-313.

U.S. Department of Energy (DOE), New Technologies for Burning Coal, Washington, DC, December 1982.

Ujchara, A.M. and M. Gough, Managing Ash from Municipal Waste Incinerators, Resources for the Future, Center for Risk Management, Washington, DC, November 1989.

United States Congress, Office of Technology Assessment, Biological Effects of Power Frequency Electric & Magnetic Fields-- Background Paper, U.S. Government Printing Office, Washington, DC, 1989.

United States Department of Energy, Comprehensive Cooling Water Study, Savannah River Laboratory, Aiken, SC, 1987.

United States Department of Energy, Monthly Energy Review, National Energy Information Center, Washington, DC, February 1990.

Varner, G.E., "Do Species Have Standing," Environmental Ethics, 9:(1), Spring 1987.

Vaughan, W.J., Freshwater Recreational Fishing: The National Benefits of Water Pollution Control, Resources for the Future, Washington, DC, 1982.

Vaughan, W.J. and C.S. Russell, "Valuing a Fishing Day: An Application of a systematic Varying Parameter Model," Land Economics, 58:(4), 1982.

Versar Inc. and American Management Systems, "Hazardous Air Pollutants: A Preliminary Exposure and Risk Appraisal for 35 U.S. Counties," Washington, DC, 1984.

Veselka, Ballov and Davzvardis, Modeling Approach to Assess the Impact of Point Source Air Pollution Emission on Vegetation, September 1980.

VHB Research and Consulting Inc. and Concord Scientific Corp. Inc., A Bio-Economic Evaluation of the Effects of Fossil-Fired Generating Station Emissions on Water Quality, October 1989.

Vine, E.L. and J.P. Harris, "Evaluating Energy and Non-Energy Impacts of Energy Conservation Programs: A Supply Curve Framework of Analysis," Energy, 15:(1), 1990. pp.11-21.

Violette, D.M., A Model Estimating the Economic Impacts of Current Levels of Acidification on Recreational Fishing in the Adirondack Mountains, Environmental Protection Agency, Washington, DC, 1985.

Virginia Electric & Power Co., 7.P. Util. Rept. (PUR4th 160, 168 (Va. State Corp. Comm. 1985).

Viscusi, W.K., Employment Hazards: An Investigation of Market Performance, 1979.

Viscusi, W.K., Risk by Choice: Regulating Health and Safety in the Workplace, 1983.

Viscusi, W.K., The Valuation of Risks to Life and Health: Guidelines for Policy Analysis, Paper prepared for National Science Foundation, 1984.

Waddell, T.E., "The Economic Damages of Air Pollution," Office of Water Resources Research, U.S. Environmental Protection Agency, May 1974.

Walsh, P.J., Indoor Air Quality, CRC Press, Boca Raton, FL, 1984.
Watson Jr., W.D., "Costs and Benefits of Fly Ash Control," Journal of Economics and Business, 26 1974. Equations 7 & 14, pp.157-168.

Webster, T. and P. Connett, Critical Factors in the Assessment of Food Chain Contamination by PCDD/PCDF from Incinerators, paper presented at Dioxin '87, Las Vegas, NV, 4 October 1987.

Welburn, A., Air Pollution and Acid Rain: The Biological Impact, Longman Scientific & Technical, New York, NY, 1988.

Wellburn, A., Air Pollution and Acid Rain, 1988.

Welle, P.G., Potential Economic Impacts of Acid Rain in Minnesota: The Minnesota Acid Rain Survey, Unpublished Manuscript, Department of Economics, Bemidji State University, Bemidgi, MN, 1985.

Westman, W.E. and W.D. Conn, Quantifying Benefits of Pollution Control: Benefits of Controlling Air and Water Pollution from Energy Production and Use, 1976.

Wetstone, G.S., Paying for Acid Rain Control: An Introduction to the Trust Fund Approach, Environmental Forum, August 1983.

"Why NOX?," The Costs, Consequences and Control of Nitrogen Oxides in the Human and Natural Environment,

Wilbrich, M., "Electricity Facilities Siting," Virginia Law Review, 57 February 1972. pp.257-334.

Wilkey, M.L., R.E. Zimmerman and H.R. Isaacson, Methane from Landfills: Preliminary Assessment Workbook, Argonne National Laboratory, Department of Energy, 1982.

Willig, R.D., "Consumers' Surplus Without Apology," American Economic Review, 66:(4), September 1976. pp.589-597.

Wilson, R.a. others, Health Effects of Fossil Fuel-Burning: Assessment and Mitigation, Ballinger Publishing Co., Cambridge, MA, 1977.

Wirth, S.D. and S. Heinz (R-Pa), Project 88: Harnessing Market Forces to Protect Our Environment, Dec. 1988.

Wisconsin Public Service Commission (WPSC), "Prepared Testimony of Sarah Jenkins," Testimony from Docket 05-EP-05, before WPSC, 1988.

Woddell, T.E., "The Economic Damages of Air Pollution,":(EPA 600-5-74-012), U.S. EPA, Washington, D.C., 1974.

Wilson, R.a. others, Health Effects of Fossil Fuel-Burning: Assessment and Mitigation, Ballinger Publishing Co., Cambridge, MA, 1977.

Wirth, S.D. and S. Heinz (R-Pa), Project 88: Harnessing Market Forces to Protect Our Environment, Dec. 1988.

Wisconsin Public Service Commission (WPSC), "Prepared Testimony of Sarah Jenkins," Testimony from Docket 05-EP-05, before WPSC, 1988.

Woddell, T.E., "The Economic Damages of Air Pollution,":(EPA 600-5-74-012), U.S. EPA, Washington, D.C., 1974.

Woodin, S. and U. Skiba, "Liming fails the acid test," New Scientist, 10 March 1990.

World Resources Institute, Pollution's Toll on Trees and Crops, September 1988.

World Health Organization, PCDD and PCDF Emissions from Incinerators for Municipal Sewage Sludge and Solid Waste - Evaluation of Human Exposure,, report on World Health Organization meeting, Naples, Copenhagen: Regional Office for Europe, 1987.

Yardas, D., A.J. Krupnick, H.M. Pesking and W. Harrington, Directory of Environmental Asset Data Bases and Valuation Studies, Resources for the Future, Washington, DC, 1982.

Yocom, Stankunas and Bradow, A Review of Air Pollutant Damage to Materials, June 1982.

Yocom, J., "Air Pollution Damage to Buildings on the Acropolis," Journal of the Air Pollution Control Association, 29:(4), 1979. pp.333-338.

Yocom, J.E., A Review of Air Pollutant Damage to Materials, EPA, Research Triangle Park, NC., Environmental Criteria and Assessment Office, June 1982.

York, K.R. and R.L. Settle, "Potential Legal Facilitation or Impediment of Wind Energy Conversion system Siting," Washington Law Review, 58 1983. pp.387.

XIV. APPENDIX A

TOTAL EMISSION MODEL FOR INTEGRATED SYSTEMS (TEMIS): PRELIMINARY FINDINGS FOR THE US

UWE FRITSCHE, JUNE 1990

XIV. APPENDIX A

TOTAL EMISSION MODEL FOR INTEGRATED SYSTEMS (TEMIS): PRELIMINARY FINDINGS FOR THE US

UWE FRITSCHE[1], JUNE 1990

1. Introduction

The OKO-Institut, in co-operation with the Environmental Systems Analysis Group at the University of Kassel, developed the so-called TEMIS program (Total Emission Model for Integrated Systems).[2] TEMIS was developed to evaluate environmental effects of energy systems, i.e. air emissions (SO2, NOx, particulates, greenhouse gases), solid wastes, and land use. The TEMIS database provides prototypes for energy processes and fuels which can be used for model calculations, and was derived from a thorough review of existing literature, operation experiences, and measured data. The database describes the energy system in the Federal Republic of Germany in the early 90's.[3] Therefore, data adjustments have to be made before TEMIS computations for other countries can achieve adequate results. The major database adjustment needs for a US version are outlined in a recent paper for US DOE.[4]

Due to the cross-boundary interdependence of national energy systems[5], some parts of the TEMIS German database reflect energy processes in other countries, e.g. OPEC oil production. These data can be used in all other countries without adaption. Furthermore, some data are available for the US energy situation,

---

[1] Address: OKO-Institut Darmstadt Office, Prinz-Christians-Weg 7, 6100 Darmstadt (FRG), phone: 01149-6151-4096-24,FAX: 01149-6151-4096-33.

[2] The TEMIS data base and model development was funded by the Ministry for Economy and Technology of Hessen, Federal Republic of Germany, and by the German Federal Parliament, Bonn. The translation of the TEMIS model from the German version was funded by the US Department of Energy.

[3] Emission matrix for climate-relevant pollutants in the FRG, OKO-Institut, prepared for the German Parliament's Commission on Climate Change, Darmstadt, August 1989, translated by the US Congressional Research Service, Washington D.C., November 1989, for the US Office for Technology Assessment (OTA).

[4] Outline of Data Base Adjustment Needs for the US version of TEMIS; U.Fritsche, OKO-Institut; prepared for US DOE Office of Environmental Analysis; Darmstadt (June 1990).

[5] i.e., energy carriers are imported from other countries, and domestic energy sources are traded on an international scale.

and for other industrial countries as well[6], so that a preliminary data base adjustment for the US can be sketched roughly without further investigation.[7] The most relevant energy and emission data used in the computation are given in the last section.

2. Preliminary Results of TEMIS Runs for the US

In the following, a brief overview of the results of this rough data base adjustment are given. Please note that the results are meant only to indicate an order of magnitude, and to illustrate the need for total fuel cycle analysis in environmental costing. Results are shown for **1 kWh of electricity produced** (no transmission & distribution losses included).

TABLE 1

TOTAL ENERGY USE AND POLLUTION LOAD

Scenario	PRIMARY ENERGY [kWh/kWh]	POLLUTANT [LB/KWH PRODUCED] SO2	NOx	Partic.	CO2
oil-el-US	3.861	0.006	0.005	0.001	2.175
gas-CC-US	3.303	0.000	0.004	0.000	1.136
gas-CC-cogen	1.850	-0.002	0.004	-0.000	0.309
gasmot-cogen	1.230	-0.003	-0.000	-0.000	-0.123
coal-el	3.249	0.001	0.007	0.000	2.219
coal-cogen	0.742	-0.002	0.001	0.000	0.847
coal-IGCC	3.945	0.001	0.002	0.000	3.031
waste-cogen	3.432	0.002	0.007	0.001	0.745
biogas-cogen	1.128	-0.002	0.002	-0.000	-2.311
solar-PV loc	1.085	0.000	0.000	0.000	0.066
wind small	1.029	0.000	0.000	0.000	0.024
micro-hydro	1.005	0.000	0.000	0.000	0.005
nuclear US	3.308	0.000	0.000	0.000	0.120

Note that the "net" emissions of cogenerators are given, i.e. the amount which is associated with electricity production alone. These net emissions for electricity from cogeneration are derived from the total emissions minus the emissions of heating systems which are substituted by the cogen's waste heat utilization.

The energy and emission data base used to compute the total emissions given in Table 1 has been - as far as possible - taken from the figures of the Pace study

---

[6] e.g. for the UK see ETSU (Energy Technology Support Unit) Gaseous Emissions due to Electricity Fuel Cycles in the United Kingdom; Eyre, N.J.; Energy & Environment Paper No. 1, London 1990.

[7] A more appropriate data base adjustment for the US situation is in preparation by US DOE within the National Energy Strategy Process. We invite anybody to provide comments, critique, and additional information about the US data base.

(e.g. heat rates). In general, the TEMIS results correspond well with findings in this study.

Still, differences remain - the TEMIS model includes not only emissions stemming from the operation of energy facilities, but takes into account all "upstream" activities (i.e. the front end of fuel cycles), and the emissions due to materials acquisition, too, so that the TEMIS results are higher, indicating that neglecting "front-end" or upstream fuel cycle activities results in an underestimation of total emissions.

To illustrate this, Table 3 offers the disaggregated figures for operation ("site"), upstream activities ("global"), and system's manufacturing & construction ("material") which have been determined using TEMIS.

TABLE 2

POLLUTANT BALANCE

(site <s>, global <g>, material <m>, and total <t>)

		PRIMARY ENERGY		POLLUTANT [LB/KWH]		
Scenario		[kWh/kWh]	SO2	NOx	Partic.	CO2
oil-el-US	s		0.002	0.003	0.001	1.850
	g	3.837	0.003	0.001	0.000	0.305
	m	0.024	0.000	0.000	0.000	0.020
	t	3.861	0.006	0.005	0.001	2.175
gas-CC-US	s		0.000	0.004	0.000	0.993
	g	3.276	0.000	0.001	0.000	0.121
	m	0.027	0.000	0.000	0.000	0.022
	t	3.303	0.000	0.004	0.000	1.136
coal-el	s		0.001	0.006	0.000	2.088
	g	3.217	0.000	0.001	0.000	0.105
	m	0.032	0.000	0.000	0.000	0.026
	t	3.249	0.001	0.007	0.000	2.219
coalgas-CC	s		0.001	0.001	0.000	2.880
	g	3.915	0.000	0.001	0.000	0.128
	m	0.030	0.000	0.000	0.000	0.024
	t	3.945	0.001	0.002	0.000	3.031
solar-PV	s		0.000	0.000	0.000	0.000
	g	1.000	0.000	0.000	0.000	0.000
	m	0.085	0.000	0.000	0.000	0.066
	t	1.085	0.000	0.000	0.000	0.066
wind small	s		0.000	0.000	0.000	0.000
	g	1.000	0.000	0.000	0.000	0.000
	m	0.029	0.000	0.000	0.000	0.024
	t	1.029	0.000	0.000	0.000	0.024
micro-hydro	s		0.000	0.000	0.000	0.000
	g	1.000	0.000	0.000	0.000	0.000
	m	0.005	0.000	0.000	0.000	0.005
	t	1.005	0.000	0.000	0.000	0.005
nuclear US	s		0.000	0.000	0.000	0.000
	g	3.298	0.000	0.000	0.000	0.111
	m	0.010	0.000	0.000	0.000	0.009
	t	3.308	0.000	0.000	0.000	0.120

As it can be seen easily, the "upstream" part of fossil-fuel energy systems emissions are in the magnitude of 5 to 10 % of the total emissions - but are up to 100 % of the nuclear, and renewable (excluding biomass) electricity options.

In addition to the emissions given in Table 1 and 2, TEMIS also determines various greenhouse gas emissions, and derives from these an aggregated value (CO2 equivalent) which is based on the radiative forcing of the greenhouse gases (Table 3).

Here, the "upstream" activity part of total methane emissions is much larger than the emissions from operating fossil fuels systems.

TABLE 3

GREENHOUSE GAS EMISSIONS

Scenario	CO2	CO	CH4	NMVOC	N2O	CO2-Equiv.
	[lb/kWh]					
oil-el-US	2.175	0.000	0.008	0.002	0.000	2.261
gas-CC-US	1.136	0.001	0.001	0.000	0.000	1.148
gas-CC-cogen	0.309	0.001	-0.003	-0.001	0.000	0.288
gasmot-cogen	-0.123	0.000	-0.005	-0.001	0.000	-0.167
coal-el	2.219	0.002	0.011	0.000	0.000	2.332
coal-cogen	0.847	0.000	0.006	-0.001	0.000	0.905
coal-IGCC	3.031	0.002	0.013	0.000	0.000	3.169
waste-cogen	0.745	0.003	-0.003	0.000	0.000	0.726
biogas-cogen	-2.311	0.002	-0.010	-0.001	0.000	-2.405
solar-PV loc	0.066	0.000	0.000	0.000	0.000	0.066
wind small	0.024	0.000	0.000	0.000	0.000	0.024
micro-hydro	0.005	0.000	0.000	0.000	0.000	0.005
nuclear US	0.120	0.000	0.000	0.000	0.000	0.125

It should be noted that N2O emission data are quite uncertain, but the results show that even emissions one order of magnitude higher than assumed wouldn't change the picture.

Besides air emissions, the TEMIS data base for environmental effects also covers three categories of solid wastes, and land use impacts. Table 4 gives the results of the preliminary US data base runs for these aspects.

TABLE 4

OTHER ENVIRONMENTAL ASPECTS

Scenario	LAND USE [sqft/kWh]	FGDRESID.	ASHES [lb/kWh]	OTHER SOLIDS
oil-el-US	0.00003	0.04733	0.00508	0.00796
gas-CC-US	0.00039	0.00021	0.00030	0.00644
gas-CC-cogen	0.00030	-0.00106	-0.00059	-0.00439
gasmot-cogen	0.00026	-0.00186	-0.00112	-0.01007
coal-el	0.00971	0.02524	0.03987	0.48213
coal-cogen	0.00984	0.00073	0.00699	0.48243
coalgas-CC	0.01180	0.00022	0.00020	0.68416
waste-cogen	-0.00010	0.12607	0.94030	-0.00946
biogas-cogen	0.00038	-0.00181	-0.00598	-0.00046
solar-PV loc	0.00448	0.00000	0.00000	0.00000
wind small	0.00072	0.00000	0.00000	0.00000
micro-hydro	0.00022	0.00000	0.00000	0.00000
nuclear US	0.00100	0.00058	0.00090	0.69232

In addition to quantifiable aspects, TEMIS also points out environmental aspects which can be addressed only in a qualitative way. This aspects are meant to be assessed by the program user, not by the program itself.

To support this assessment (as far as it takes place in a comparative way), the TEMIS data base offers descriptors of the relative significance of these qualitative aspects. Because the descriptors are based on the type of primary energy used, the comparative analysis of energy systems is - at least at present - limited to a primary energy comparison.

TEMIS uses the descriptors to set up a matrix based on symbols for the relative significance of each aspect. These symbolic descriptors can be interpreted as an intensity of the qualitative aspects. The following table shows such a "qualitative effects matrix", based on the preliminary US data base adjustment.

TABLE 5

COMPARISON OF QUALITATIVE EFFECTS

Scenario	Resi-duals		Acci-dents		Micro-ecology		Land use		Special aspect
oil-el-US	-		--		--		-		tanker accidents
gas-CC-US	-		-		-		-		explosions
gas-CC-cogen	-		-	+	-	+	-		explosions
gasmot-cogen	-	+	-	++	-	++	-	+	explosions
coal-el	---		--		---		---		halogens
coal-cogen	---	+	--	++	---	++	---	+	halogens
coalgas-CC	---		--		---		---		halogens
waste-cogen	---			+		+			dioxins
biogas-cogen	-	++		+		++		++	odour
solar-PV loc					-		-		material intensity
wind small					-		-		visual intrusion
micro-hydro					-		-		multi-purpose facilities
nuclear US	----		--		---		---		core meltdown, nuclear wastes

The descriptors use the symbol for minus "-". If an energy system is neutral regarding an aspect, no symbol is used. To address the problem of cogeneration, TEMIS uses the symbol for plus "+" to describe avoided aspects due to substituted electricity or heat, showing explicitly what - and to what extent - qualitative aspects are avoided by cogen systems. So, the left part of each matrix cell (left of the delimiter symbol "|")indicates the gross impact, and the right part (left of the delimiter symbol "|") indicates the substituted impact intensity.

In addition to the symbolic descriptors, a special aspect is pointed out for each energy system. This aspect addresses an unique environmental effect which is imposed only by this type of primary energy, and is, therefore, non-comparative.

The matrices used to display qualitative environmental aspects offer a comprehensive form of information about possible environmental impacts. This figure cannot replace the interpretation and explicit valuation of the quantitative environmental aspects, but extends the available information. Note that most of the qualitative impacts addressed by the TEMIS data base are related to upstream activities (e.g. mining) which would be ignored by an "operating mode only" scope of analysis.

Finally, TEMIS offers an option to convert quantified emission figures into monetized environmental effects, using either emission control costs or specific damage costs as conversion factors. To illustrate the effect of including the total fuel cycle into the costing framework, a TEMIS run was prepared using the Pace study results as a bases for the environmental cost calculation. The emission cost factors used are given in Table 6, the results are shown in Table 7. Please note that no data for nuclear risks, and also none for land use and solid wastes, have been included in this calculation.

TABLE 6

SPECIFIC COSTING VALUES FOR MONETIZING AIR EMISSIONS
(Pace Data for the US)

Pollutant	mills/lb
CO2	6.8
SO2	2030.0
NOx	820.0
Particulates	1190.0

TABLE 7

MONETIZED ENVIRONMENTAL COSTS FOR TOTAL EMISSIONS
(Pace Data for the US)

Scenario	W/O CO2	INCL. CO2
	------[mills/kWh]-----	
oil-el-US	16.3	31.1
gas-CC-US	3.8	11.5
gas-CC-cogen	-1.1	1.0
gasmot-cogen	-7.0	-7.8
coal-el	9.1	24.2
coal-cogen	-3.0	2.8
coal IGCC	3.7	24.3
waste-cogen	9.8	14.9
biogas-cogen	-2.3	-18.0
solar-PV loc	0.2	0.6
wind small	0.1	0.3
micro-hydro	0.1	0.1
nuclear US	1.1	1.9

Note that no transmission & distribution losses have been included in the calculation - to take these into account, the values given in Table 7 would have to be multiplied by a factor of 1.1 or so, depending on the electricity grid configuration.

To contrast the results of monetizing air emissions based on the Pace study figures, a second TEMIS run was prepared using cost factors which have been derived by the OKO-Institut for the German situation. Table 8 gives the values used for this.

TABLE 8

SPECIFIC COSTING VALUES FOR MONETIZING AIR EMISSIONS
(OKO Data for FRG)

Pollutant	mills/lb
CO2 - lower value	2.3
CO2 - upper value	22.7
SO2	1134.0
NOx	907.2
Particulates	226.8

The German figures are based on real pollution abatement costs which were derived from German data sources. They represent the average costs [8] of required emission control measures for SO2, NOx and particulates emitted from stationary and automotive sources in Germany, weighted by the relative contribution of the sources. The costs to abate CO2 have been determined by means of fuel switching, strategic energy conservation (low cost value), and CO2 scrubbing (high cost value).

The cost factors used for monetizing are extremely sensitive regarding the inclusion of CO2. Therefore, the German version of TEMIS calculates three different results: monetized emissions based on avoidance costs for SO2, NOx and particulates, monetized emissions based only on the former plus "low"CO2 avoidance costs, and, finally, those based on SO2, NOx, particulates, and "high"CO2 abatement costs. The following Table 9 shows the results for all cases.

TABLE 9

MONETIZED ENVIRONMENTAL COSTS FOR TOTAL EMISSIONS
(OKO Data for FRG)

Scenario	W.O. CO2	-LOW	CO2-HIGH
	[mills/kWh]		
oil-el-US	10.6	15.6	60.0
gas-CC-US	4.1	5.4	17.5
gas-CC-cogen	1.0	0.4	-4.7
gasmot-cogen	-4.0	-5.7	-21.1
coal-el	8.1	13.2	58.5
coal-cogen	-1.3	0.7	18.0
coalgas-CC	2.8	6.5	39.3
waste-cogen	8.1	10.4	31.1
biogas-cogen	-0.5	-5.7	-52.4
solar-PV loc	0.1	0.3	1.6
wind small	0.1	0.1	0.6
micro-hydro	0.0	0.1	0.1
nuclear US	0.8	1.0	3.2

[8] There is some dispute over average vs. marginal costing in Germany, too. The KO-Institut prefers average costing, and offers to provide the rational for this on request.

The calculations show that the Pace data are in good accordance with the German figures for monetizing environmental costs.

Furthermore, the results suggest that significant environmental costs are associated with electricity generated by fossil-fuel fired condensing power plants, and that nuclear electricity offers no significant cost advantage when compared to gas-fired cogenerators, and renewables. This holds true even when neglecting any nuclear-specific environmental costs (e.g. health effects).

If nuclear risk figures in the magnitude of 10 to 100 mills/kWh electricity produced are added to nuclear generation options (as the work of Olaf Hohmeyer for Germany suggests), the disadvantage of nuclear energy in total societal costs would be even higher, and, vice versa, the benefits of renewables, and cogenerated electricity would increase still further.

BASE DATA FOR PRELIMINARYTEMIS ADAPTATIONTO THE US

Energy-related data for process: coal mining (US)

Primary energy source: hard coal

Delivered fuel: hard coal (US)

Aux. energy1: coalmine-power-US

Aux. energy1 demand [% of output]: 0.10

Aux. energy2: dieselmotor-gener-US

Aux. energy2 demand [% of output]: 0.50

Land use [sqyd]: 1.05E+08

Other solid wastes [lb/kWh]: 0.158730

CH4 [lb/MBTU]: 1.007183

Output of the process [MBTU/h]: 5118.000

Annual operation time [h/a]: 7900.00 => 1.19E+10[kWh/a]

Total operating time [a]: 25.000

Materials needed for process (total)

Steel [lb]: 5.51E+07

Energy-related data for process: coal train (US)

Upstream connection: coal mining (US)

Transport losses [%/100 mi]: 0.062137

Transport distance [mi]: 2000.000

Fuel transported: hard coal (US)

Aux. energy1: dieselmotor-US-train

Aux. eneryy1:[BTU/tn.m]: 126.1559i.e.=>0.964821[%]

Energy-related data for process: coal powerplant (US)

Upstream connection: coal train (US)

Efficiency for the main output [%]: 34.10

Land use [sqft]: 2.15E+06

Emission data for process: coal powerplant (US)

Fuel: hard coal (US)

Flue gas @ 6.00 Vol%-O2 13.0 Vol%-CO2

Specific flue gas rate: 0.013 [scfd/BTU HHV]

POLLUTANT	RAW GAS [mg/m^3]	ABATEMENT [%]	CLEAN GAS [mg/m^3]	[ppm]	[lb/MBTU]
SO2:	1319.2	90.00	131.916	45.014	0.107
NOx:	1000.0	25.50	745.000	362.948	0.604
HCl:	194.01	90.00	19.401	11.813	0.016
HF:	9.933	90.00	0.993	1.113	0.001
Partic.:	10000	99.60	40.000		0.032
CO:	150.00		150.000	119.955	0.122
CH4:	30.000		30.000	41.813	0.024
NMVOC:	50.000		50.000	42.687	0.041
CO2:					208.722

Energy-related data for process: coal-cogen-el/oil-US

Upstream connection: coal train (US)

Efficiency for the main output [%]: 33.00

couple product: oil-heating US

coupling ratio: 1.667

Emission data for process: coal-cogen-el/oil-US

Fuel: hard coal (US)

Flue gas @ 6.00 Vol%-O2 13.0 Vol%-CO2

Specific flue gas rate: 0.013 [scfd/BTU HHV]

POLLUTANT	RAW GAS [mg/m^3]	ABATEMENT [%]	CLEAN GAS [mg/m^3]	[ppm]	[lb/MBTU]
SO2:	1319.2	90.00	131.916	45.014	0.107
NOx:	900.00	80.00	180.000	87.692	0.146
HCl:	194.01	90.00	19.401	11.813	0.016
HF:	9.933	95.00	0.497	0.556	0.000
Partic.:	10000	99.75	25.000		0.020
CO:	50.000		50.000	39.985	0.041
CH4:	5.0000		5.000	6.969	0.004
NMVOC:	10.000		10.000	8.537	0.008
N2O:	0.5000		0.500	0.253	0.000
CO2:					208.722

Data set for dispatcher: el-baseload-grid US

no.	upstream connection	percentual share
1	coal powerplant (US)	40.0000
2	nuclear power US	25.0000
3	hydro big ROR plant	20.0000
4	gas CC plant (US)	15.0000

Data set for dispatcher: el-grid US

no.	upstream connection	percentual share
1	coal powerplant (US)	45.0000
2	nuclear power US	15.0000
3	hydro big ROR plant	20.0000
4	gas CC plant (US)	10.0000
5	res-oil-powerpl-US	10.0000

Energy-related data for process: gas processing (US)

Upstream connection: gas extrac/onsh (US)

Efficiency for the main output [%]: 90.00

Aux. energy1: el-baseload-grid US

Aux. energy1 demand [% of output]: 0.50

Aux. energy2: gas-boiler US

Aux. energy2 demand [% of output]: 0.425

Land use [sqft]: 1.61E+06

CH4 [lb/MBTU]: 0.011630

Energy-related data for process: gas pipeline (US)

Upstream connection: gas processing (US)

Transport losses [%/100 mi]: 5.59E-05

Transport distance [mi]: 2500.000

Fuel transported: natural gas (US)

Aux. energy 1: compressor GT (US)

Aux. energy 1:[BTU/tn.m]: 379.0822i.e.=>2.161593[%]

Land use [sqyd]: 2.14E+07

CH4 [lb/MBTU]: 1.07E-03

Output of the process [MBTU/h]: 34094.56

Annual operation time [h/a]: 6000.00 =>6.00E+10[kWh/a]

Total operating time [a]: 40.000

Materials needed for process (total)

Steel [lb]: 3.31E+09

Energy-related data for process: gas loc.distrib.(US)

Upstream connection: gas-US/CAN-split

Transport losses [%/100 mi]: 4.349582

Transport distance [mi]: 10.00

Fuel transported: natural gas (US)

Aux. energy 1: compr.motor (US)

Aux. energy1:[BTU/tn.m]: 766.4504i.e.=>0.017482[%]

CH4 [lb/MBTU]: 0.332920

Energy-related data for process: gas CC plant (US)

Upstream connection: gas pipeline (US)

Efficiency for the main output [%]: 37.90

Land use [sqft]: 10763.91

Emission data for process: gas CC plant (US)

Fuel: natural gas (US)

Flue gas @ 15.0 Vol%-O2 3.28 Vol%-CO2

Specific flue gas rate: 0.028 [scfd/BTU HHV]

POLLUTANT	RAW GAS [mg/m^3]	ABATEMENT [%]	CLEAN GAS [mg/m^3]	[ppm]	[lb/MBTU]
SO2:	4.165		4.165	1.421	0.007
NOx:	240.00		240.000	116.923	0.420
Partic.:	1.0000		1.000		0.002
CO:	60.000		60.000	47.982	0.105
CH4:	6.0000		6.000	8.363	0.011
NMVOC:	2.5000		2.500	2.134	0.004
N2O:	1.5000		1.500	0.758	0.003
CO2:		3.000			110.063

Emission data for process: gas-CC-cog-el/oil-US

Fuel: natural gas (US)

Flue gas @ 15.0 Vol%-O2 3.28 Vol%-CO2

Specific flue gas rate: 0.028 [scfd/BTU HHV]

POLLUTANT	RAW GAS [mg/m^3]	ABATEMENT [%]	CLEAN GAS [mg/m^3]	[ppm]	[lb/MBTU]
SO2:	4.165		4.165	1.421	0.007
NOx:	240.00		240.000	116.923	0.420
Partic.:	1.0000		1.000		0.002
CO:	60.000		60.000	47.982	0.105
CH4:	6.0000		6.000	8.363	0.011
NMVOC:	2.5000		2.500	2.134	0.004
N2O:	1.5000		1.500	0.758	0.003
CO2:		3.000			110.063

Energy-related data for process: gasmot-cog-el/oil-US

Upstream connection: gas-US/CAN-split

Efficiency for the main output [%]: 32.00

couple product: oil-heating US

coupling ratio: 1.667

Emission data for process: gasmot-cog-el/oil-US

Fuel: natural gas (US)

Flue gas @ 5.00 Vol%-O2 8.74 Vol%-CO2

Specific flue gas rate: 0.011 [scfd/BTU HHV]

POLLUTANT	RAW GAS [mg/m^3]	ABATEMENT [%]	CLEAN GAS [mg/m^3]	[ppm]	[lb/MBTU]
SO2:	11.107		11.107	3.790	0.007
NOx:	2000.0	95.00	100.000	48.718	0.066
Partic.:	5.0000		5.000		0.003
CO:	800.00	90.00	80.000	63.976	0.053
CH4:	50.000	80.00	10.000	13.938	0.007
NMVOC:	100.00	75.00	25.000	21.344	0.016
N2O:	5.0000	50.00	2.500	1.264	0.002
CO2:		3.000			110.063

Emission data for process: gas-boiler US

Fuel: natural gas (US)

Flue gas @ 3.00 Vol%-O2 9.84 Vol%-CO2

Specific flue gas rate: 0.009 [scfd/BTU HHV]

POLLUTANT	RAW GAS [mg/m^3]	ABATEMENT [%]	CLEAN GAS [mg/m^3]	[ppm]	[lb/MBTU]
SO2:	12.496		12.496	4.264	0.007
NOx:	400.00	50.00	200.000	97.436	0.117
Partic.:	0.5000		0.500		0.000
CO:	72.000		72.000	57.578	0.042
CH4:	13.650		13.650	19.025	0.008
NMVOC:	4.6750		4.675	3.991	0.003
CO2:					113.467

Energy-related data for process: oil-extr-US-prim

Primary energy source: oil

Delivered fuel: crude oil

Aux. energy1: res-oil-powerpl-US

Aux. energy1 demand [% of output]: 0.10

Aux. energy2: resid-oil-boil-US

Aux. energy2 demand [% of output]: 0.255

NMVOC [lb/MBTU]: 0.018608

CH4 [lb/MBTU]: 0.146542

Energy-related data for process: oil-extr-US-second

Primary energy source: oil

Delivered fuel: crude oil

Aux. energy1: res-oil-powerpl-US

Aux. energy1 demand [% of output]: 0.25

Aux. energy2: res-oil-powerpl-US

Aux. energy2 demand [% of output]: 1.00

NMVOC [lb/MBTU]: 0.018608

CH4 [lb/MBTU]: 0.146542

Energy-related data for process: oil-EOR-US

Primary energy source: oil

Delivered fuel: crude oil

Aux. energy1: res-oil-powerpl-US

Aux. energy1 demand [% of output]: 0.30

Aux. energy2: resid-oil-boil-US

Aux. energy2 demand [% of output]: 25.50

Land use [sqft]: 2.15E+06

NMVOC [lb/MBTU]: 0.018608

CH4 [lb/MBTU]: 0.146542

Data set for dispatcher: oil-source-US

no.	upstream connection	percentual share
1	oil-extr-US-prim	25.0000
2	oil-extr-US-second	25.0000
3	oil-EOR-US	10.0000
4	oil-tanker	40.0000

Energy-related data for process: oil-refinery-US

Upstream connection: oil-source-US

Efficiency for the main output [%]: 98.00

Aux. energy1: res-oil-powerpl-US

Aux. energy1 demand [% of output]: 1.00

Aux. energy2: resid-oil-boil-US

Aux. energy2 demand [% of output]: 7.00

NMVOC [lb/MBTU]: 0.10

CH4 [lb/MBTU]: 0.50

Energy-related data for process: oil/diesel-truck US

Upstream connection: oil-refinery-US

Transport losses [%/100 mi]: 0.062137

Transport distance [mi]: 100.00

Fuel transported: premium light oil

Aux. energy1: dieselmotor-gener-US

Aux. eneryy1:[BTU/tn.m]: 720.9131i.e.=>0.188008[%]

Energy-related data for process: res-oil-powerpl-US

Upstream connection: res-oil-truck-US

Efficiency for the main output [%]: 32.80

couple product: none

Emission data for process: res-oil-powerpl-US

Fuel: residual oil

Flue gas @ 3.00 Vol%-O2 13.6 Vol%-CO2

Specific flue gas rate: 0.010 [scfd/BTU HHV]

POLLUTANT	RAW GAS [mg/m^3]	ABATEMENT [%]	CLEAN GAS [mg/m^3]	[ppm]	[lb/MBTU]
SO2:	3145.9	90.00	314.589	107.346	0.205
NOx:	900.00	50.00	450.000	219.230	0.293
Partic.:	500.00	72.50	137.500		0.090
CO:	17.500		17.500	13.995	0.011
CH4:	1.7500		1.750	2.439	0.001
NMVOC:	3.5000		3.500	2.988	0.002
N2O:	0.5000		0.500	0.253	0.000
CO2:		3.500			169.121

Emission data for process: resid-oil-boil-US

Fuel: residual oil

Flue gas @ 3.00 Vol%-O2 13.6 Vol%-CO2

Specific flue gas rate: 0.010 [scfd/BTU HHV]

POLLUTANT	RAW GAS [mg/m^3]	ABATEMENT [%]	CLEAN GAS [mg/m^3]	[ppm]	[lb/MBTU]
SO2:	3145.9		3145.889	1073.465	2.048
NOx:	900.00	20.00	720.000	350.769	0.469
Partic.:	500.00	70.00	150.000		0.098
CO:	35.000		35.000	27.989	0.023
CH4:	5.0000		5.000	6.969	0.003
NMVOC:	10.000		10.000	8.537	0.007
N2O:	0.5000		0.500	0.253	0.000
CO2:		3.500			169.121

Emission data for process: oil-heating US

Fuel: premium light oil

Flue gas @ 3.00 Vol%-O2 12.9 Vol%-CO2

Specific flue gas rate: 0.010 [scfd/BTU HHV]

POLLUTANT	RAW GAS [mg/m^3]	ABATEMENT [%]	CLEAN GAS [mg/m^3]	[ppm]	[lb/MBTU]
SO2:	260.56		260.559	88.910	0.167
NOx:	139.55		139.550	67.986	0.089
Partic.:	3.5000		3.500		0.002
CO:	104.65		104.650	83.688	0.067
CH4:	3.5000		3.500	4.878	0.002
NMVOC:	14.000		14.000	11.952	0.009
CO2:					162.793

Energy-related data for process: coalgas CC-el (IGCC)

Upstream connection: coal gasification

Efficiency for the main output [%]: 37.50

Emission data for process: coalgas CC-el (IGCC)

Fuel: coalgas

Flue gas @ 15.0 Vol%-O2 8.12 Vol%-CO2

Specific flue gas rate: 0.029 [scfd/BTU HHV]

POLLUTANT	RAW GAS [mg/m^3]	ABATEMENT [%]	CLEAN GAS [mg/m^3]	[ppm]	[lb/MBTU]
SO2:	331.95	90.00	33.195	11.327	0.061
NOx:	100.00	67.00	33.000	16.077	0.061
Partic.:	5.0000		5.000		0.009
CO:	60.000		60.000	47.982	0.110
CH4:	6.0000		6.000	8.363	0.011
NMVOC:	2.5000		2.500	2.134	0.005
N2O:	1.5000		1.500	0.758	0.003
CO2:					295.394

Energy-related data for process: waste/incinerator US

Upstream connection: waste source

Efficiency for the main output [%]: 20.00

couple product: oil-heating US

coupling ratio: 1.00

Emission data for process: waste/incinerator US

Fuel: municip.waste (US)

Flue gas @ 11.0 Vol%-O2 8.54 Vol%-CO2

Specific flue gas rate: 0.018 [scfd/BTU HHV]

POLLUTANT	RAW GAS [mg/m^3]	ABATEMENT [%]	CLEAN GAS [mg/m^3]	[ppm]	[lb/MBTU]
SO2:	1918.0	90.00	191.801	65.448	0.215
NOx:	400.00		400.000	194.871	0.447
HCl:	592.36	95.00	29.618	18.034	0.033
HF:	20.218	95.00	1.011	1.133	0.001
Partic.:	10000	99.50	.000		0.056
CO:	150.00		150.000	119.955	0.168
CH4:	5.0000		5.000	6.969	0.006
NMVOC:	50.000		50.000	42.687	0.056
N2O:	5.0000		5.000	2.528	0.006
CO2:		50.00			94.418

Energy-related data for process: wind turbine small

Primary energy source: wind

Land use [sqft]: 1076.391

Output of the process [MBTU/h]: 0.085300

Annual operation time [h/a]: 3000.00 => 75000.00[kWh/a]

Total operating time [a]: 20.000

Materials needed for process (total)

Steel [lb]: 9921

Concrete [lb]: 2646

Plastics [lb]: 44

Copper [lb]: 378

Energy-related data for process: solar cell panel

Primary energy source: solar energy

Land use [sqft]: 2691

Output of the process [MBTU/h]: 0.085300

Annual operation time [h/a]: 1200.00 = > 30000.00[kWh/a]

Total operating time [a]: 20.000

Materials needed for process (total)

Glass [lb]: 1

Steel [lb]: 4078

Plastics [lb]: 231

Aluminium [lb]: 794

Copper [lb]: 728

Energy-related data for process: hydro small-scale

Primary energy source: hydro power

Land use [sqft]: 5380.571

Output of the process [MBTU/h]: 0.341200

Annual operation time [h/a]: 5000.00 = > 5.00E+05[kWh/a]

Total operating time [a]: 50.000

Materials needed for process (total)

Steel [lb]: 24250

Concrete [lb]: 44092

Copper [lb]: 220

Energy-related data for process: uranium-extract-US

Primary energy source: uranium

Aux. energy1: el-grid US

Aux. energy1 demand [% of output]: 0.01

Aux. energy2: dieselmotor-gener-US

Aux. energy2 demand [% of output]: 0.08

Land use [sqft]: 4.79E+08

Other solid wastes [lb/kWh]: 0.22

Output of the process [MBTU/h]: 47085.60

Annual operation time [h/a]: 7000 => 9.66E+10 [kWh/a]

Total operating time [a]: 20

Materials needed for process (total)

Steel [lb]: 1.10E+07

Concrete [lb]: 2.20E+06

Energy-related data for process: U-conversion US

Upstream connection: uranium-extract-US

Efficiency for the main output [%]: 100.0

Aux. energy1: el-grid US

Aux. energy1 demand [% of output]: 0.03

Aux. energy2: resid-oil-boil-US

Aux. energy2 demand [% of output]: 1.00

Land use [sqft]: 5.38E+06

Other solid wastes [lb/kWh]: 5.51E-05

Output of the process [MBTU/h]: 27296.00

Annual operation time [h/a]: 7000 => 5.60E+10 [kWh/a]

Total operating time [a]: 20

Materials needed for process (total)

Steel [lb]: 1.76E+07

Concrete [lb]: 4.41E+08

Energy-related data for process: u-enrichment diff US

Upstream connection: u-conversion US

Efficiency for the main output [%]: 100.0

couple product: none

coupling ratio:

Aux. energy1: el-baseload-grid US

Aux. energy1 demand [% of output]: 1.60

Aux. energy2: gas-boiler US

Aux. energy2 demand [% of output]: 1.00

Land use [sqft]: 1.08E+06

Output of the process [MBTU/h]: 34120.00

Annual operation time [h/a]: 7000 => 7.00E+10 [kWh/a]

Total operating time [a]: 20

Materials needed for process (total)

Steel [lb]: 1.54E+06

Concrete [lb]: 3.31E+06

Energy-related data for process: u-fuel-fabric US

Upstream connection: u-enrichment diff US

Efficiency for the main output [%]: 100.0

Aux. energy1: el-grid US

Aux. energy1 demand [% of output]: 0.01

Aux. energy2: gas-boiler US

Aux. energy2 demand [% of output]: 0.50

Land use [sqft]: 5.38E+05

Output of the process [MBTU/h]: 68240.00

Annual operation time [h/a]: 7000 => 1.40E+11 [kWh/a]

Total operating time [a]: 20

Materials needed for process (total)

Steel [lb]: 2.20E+06

Concrete [lb]: 2.20E+07

Energy-related data for process: nuclear power US

Upstream connection: u-fuel-fabric US

Efficiency for the main output [%]: 33.00

Aux. energy1: dieselmotor-gener-US

Aux. energy1 demand [% of output]: 1.00E-04

Land use [sqft]: 1.94E+06

Other solid wastes [lb/kWh]: 7.94E-08

Output of the process [MBTU/h]: 4435.600

Annual operation time [h/a]: 6000.00 => 7.80E+09 [kWh/a]

Total operating time [a]: 25.000

Materials needed for process (total)

Steel [lb]: 2.58E+08

Concrete [lb]: 3.79E+08

Material Emission Factors used in Computation

	GLAS	STEEL	CONCRETE	PLASTIC	ALUMINIUM	COPPER	
Energy	0.0344	0.0516	0.0069	0.1118	0.4300	0.1634	[BTU/lb]
CO2	3800	6000	1800	12000	50000	17600	[lb/tn]
SO2	4	6	10	10	50	8	[lb/tn]
NOx	30	10	30	10	40	10	[lb/tn]
Partic.	2	1	2	2	10	2	[lb/tn]

(Note: Material data refer to the German situation. No adaptation to the US is available.)

XV. APPENDIX B

BIBLIOGRAPHY FOR CHAPTERS V. B, C, AND E

XV. APPENDIX B

5. Bibliography for Chapters V. B, C, AND E

Berrett, L. and T. Weddell, Costs of Air Pollution Damage: A Status Report, Environmental Protection Agency, National Environmental Research Center, Research Triangle Park, North Carolina, February 1973, p. 59.

Birkhofer, A., Was Leisten Risikostudien?, atomwirtshaft-atomechnik, vol. 31, 1986.

Bromberg, P., Testimony before the House Subcommittee on Environmental Protection, Energy and Commerce Committee hearing on Health Effects of Air Pollution, Washington D.C., 1989.

Brookshire, D., Methods Development for Valuing Hazards Information, Institute for Policy Research, 1980.

Bureau of National Affairs, "DOE Releases State, Regional Guidance on Compliance with Low Level Waste Act," vol. 10., no. 24, October 8, 1987, p. 1516.

Cadle, R., "Particulate Matter in the Lower Stratosphere," Chemistry of the Lower Stratosphere, NY, Plenum Press, 1973.

California State University Fullerton Foundation, Economic Assessment of the Health Benefits from Improvements in Air Quality in the South Coast Air Basin, Prepared for the South Coast Air Quality Management District Contract No. 5685, Fullerton, Calif., June 1989.

Cannon, J., The Health Costs of Air Pollution: A Survey of Studies Published 1978-1983, American Lung Association, August 1985, pp. 12-14.

_____, The Health Costs of Air Pollution: A Survey of Studies Published 1984-1989, American Lung Association, 1990.

Charles River Associates (CRA), Benefits and costs of Externalities and Intangibles Associated with Southern California Edison's 1985 and 1986 Conservation and Load Management Programs, CRA Report #792, May 15, 1984.

Chernick, P. and Caverhill, E., The Valuation of Externalities from Energy Production, Delivery, and Use, Boston, MA, PLC, Inc., December, 1989.

______, The Valuation of Externalities from Energy Production, PLC, Inc., Boston, MA, December 1989.

Chernick, P., W. Fairley, M. Meyer, and L. Scharff, Design, Costs and Acceptability of an Electric Utility Self-Insurance Pool for Assuring the Adequacy of Funds for Nuclear Power Plant Decommissioning Expense, (NUREG/CR-2370), U.S. Nuclear Regulatory Commission, December, 1981.

Chernick, P., and J. Wallach, Testimony on Behalf of the Massachusetts Executive Office of Energy Resources, MDPU 89-100, June 30, 1989.

"Nevada Sues Energy Chief Over Nuclear Dump Efforts," Chicago Tribune, December 29, 1989, p. 14.

Consolidated Edison Company of New York and New York Power Authority (NYPA), Hudson River Ecological Study in the Area of Indian Point, NYPA 1987 Annual Report.

Currie, William J. et al., "The Importance of Viewing Alternative Closed-Cycle-Cooling Systems on Nuclear Power-Plant Landscapes," Environmental Policy Formation: The Impact of Values, Ideology, and Standards, D.C. Heath and Co., Lexington, Mass.

ECO Northwest et al., Final Report: Economic Analysis of the Environmental Effects of the Coal-Fired Electric Generator at Boardman, Oregon, Report commissioned by Bonneville Power Administration, December 29, 1983.

_____, Economic Analysis of the Environmental Effects of a Combustion-Turbine Generating Station at Frederickson Industrial Park, Pierce County, Washington: Final Report, Report commissioned by Bonneville Power Administration, March 26, 1984.

_____, Generic Coal Study: Quantification and Valuation of Environmental Impacts, Report commissioned by Bonneville Power Administration, January 31, 1987.

Electric Power Research Institute Journal, Decommissioning Nuclear Power Plants, July/August, 1985.

Energy Research and Development Administration, Cleaning Up the Remains of Nuclear Facilities -- A Multibillion Dollar Problem, June, 1977.

Energy and Resource Consultants, Inc., The Benefits of Air Pollution Control in California, Prepared for the California Air Resources Board, December 1986.

Energy Systems Research Group, Inc. (currently Tellus Institute), The Role of Hydro-Quebec Power in a Least-Cost Energy Resource Plan for Vermont, Vermont Department of Public Service, Boston, December 1989.

Evans, J., T. Tosteson, P. Kinney, "Cross Sectional Mortality Studies and Air Pollution Assessment," Environmental International, vol. 10, pp. 55-83.

_____, "Ozone and Carbon Monoxide", Environmental Backgrounder, Office of Public Affairs, Washington, D.C., June 1989, p. 4.

Fackelmann, K., "Air pollution boosts cancer spread," Science News, Vol. 137, April 7, 1990.

Federal Register, v. 50, no. 28, 1985.

Federal Register, v. 53, no. 123, 1988.

Fisher, A., and V. Smith, "Economic Evaluation of Energy's Environmental Costs with Special Reference to Air Pollution," Annual Reviews of Energy, 7:1-35, 1982.

Fletcher, R. Ian, On the Reconfiguration and Empirical Evaluation of a Prototype Screening Device at Indian Point Nuclear Unit 2, Final Report to the Hudson River Fisherman's Association, 1986.

Freeman, A., Air Pollution Control: A Benefit-Cost Assignment, John Wiley and Sons, NY 1982.

French, H., "You Are What You Breathe," Worldwatch, May-June 1990.

Gillette, "Sulfur Dioxide and Material Damage," Air Pollution Control Association Journal, December 1975, p. 1239.

Godar, T., Testimony on behalf of the American Lung Association before the House Subcommittee on Environmental Protection, Energy and Commerce Committee hearing on Health Effects of Air Pollution, Washington D.C., 1989.

Graham, J., L. Grant, J. Folinskie, D. Gardner, R. Schlesinger, J. Overton, S. Lounsburry, T. McCurdy, V. Hasselblad, D. McKee, H. Richmond, B. Polkosky, and A. Marcus, Direct Health Effects of Air Pollutants Associated with Acidic Precursor Emissions, National Acidic Precipitation Program (NAPAP), State-of-Science Technology Report 22, Vol. II, Secs. 4, 5, 6, and Appendix A, U.S.E.P.A., NC, December 1989.

Hall, J., Economic Assessment of the Health Benefits from Improvements in Air Quality in the South Coast Air Basin, Report to the South Coast Air Quality Management District, Contract No. 5685, California State University Fullerton Foundation, Fullerton, Calif., June 1989.

Hamilton, L., The Health and Environmental Effects of Electricity Generation: A Preliminary Report, Brookhaven National Laboratory, July, 1974.

Harrison, D., and A. Nichols, Benefits of the 1989 Air Quality Management Plan for the South Coast Air Basin: A Reassessment, Prepared for California Council for Environmental and Economic Balance, National Economic Research Associates, Inc., Cambridge, Mass., February 1990.

Hearing before the Committee on Labor and Human Resources, U.S. Senate, 100th Congress, 1st Session, on Reviewing the Causes and Consequences of the Chernobyl Nuclear Plant Accident, January 20, 1987.

Hearing before the U.S. Congress, Subcommittee on Agriculture and Transportation and Joint Economic Committee, The Chernobyl Disaster: Implications for World Food Security and the U.S. Farm Economy, May 5, 1986.

Hearing before the U.S. House of Representatives, Subcommittee on Oversight and Investigations, Calculation of Reactor Accident Consequences for U.S. Nuclear Power Plants (Health Effects and Costs), November 1, 1982.

Hill, R., The Impact of Energy on Environment and Development, IVth Nobel Prize Winners Meeting, December, 1990.

Hodas, D., The Health Effects of Acid Aerosols, unpublished paper prepared for LL.M. in Environmental Law, Pace University School of Law, 1989.

Hohmeyer, O., Social Costs of Energy Consumption, Springer-Verlag, New York, 1988.

ICF Resources, Economic, Environmental, and Coal Market Impacts of SO_2 Emissions Trading Under Alternative Acid Rain Control Proposals, March 1989.

IRT Publications, Nuclear Waste: Yucca Mountain, December, 1989.

Jacobson, B. "The Role of Air Pollution and Other Factors in Local Variations in General Mortality and Cancer Mortality," Archives of Environmental Health, Vol. 39, No. 4, August 1984, pp. 306-313.

Koomey, J., Comparative Analysis of Monetary Estimates of External Environmental Costs Associated with Combustion of Fossil Fuels, Berkeley, Calif., April 1990.

Krawiec, F., Economic Measurement of Environmental Damages, Golden, Colorado, Solar Energy Research Institute, May 1980.

Krupnick, A., et al., An Analysis of Selected Health Benefits from Reductions in Photochemical Oxidants in the Northeastern United States, Prepared for EPA Contract No. 68-02-4323, September 1988.

Krupnick, A., and R. Kopp, The Health and Agricultural Benefits of Reductions in Ambient Ozone in the United States, Prepared for OTA Contract No. H3-6820.0, June 1988.

Lashof, D., and D. Ahuja, "Relative Global Warming Potentials of Greenhouse Gas Emissions," Nature, Vol. 344, April 5, 1990, pp. 529-31.

Lave, L., and E. Seskin, Air Pollution and Human Health, Johns Hopkins Press, Baltimore, 1978.

Leipert, C. and U. Simonis, Environmental Damage-Environmental Expenditures: Statistical Evidence on the Federal Republic of Germany, Research Professorship Environmental Policy Science Center, Berlin.

Lipfert, F., Correspondence to Richard L. Ottinger, Pace University School of Law, March 1990.

Mackenzie, J. and E. Mohamed, Ill Winds: Airborne Pollution's Toll on Trees and Crops, World Resources Institute, September 1988, p. 35.

Mazumdar, S., H. Schmmel, and I. Higgins, "Relationship of Daily Mortality to Air Pollution: An Analysis of 14 London Winters, 1958/59-1971/72," Archives of Environmental Health, Vol. 37, (July/August): 213-220, 1982.

Mendelsohn, R., "An Economic Analysis of Air Pollution from Coal-Fired Power Plant," Journal of Environmental Economics and Management, 7:30-43, 1980.

Mendelsohn, R. and G. Orcutt, "An Empirical Analysis of Air Pollution Dose-Response Curves," Journal of Environmental Economics and Management, Vol. 6, pp. 85-106, 1979.

Mitchell, R. and R. Carson, Using Surveys to Value Public Goods: The Contingent Caluation Method, Resources for the Future, Washington D.C., September 1986.

Mount, T., and M. Czerwinski, Global Warming and Acid Rain: The Implications for Restricting Emissions from Power Plants, presented at the Workshop on Large Scale Social Science Models, Urbana-Champaign, IL, September 1988.

Mueller, W., and P. Stickney, Final Report on a Survey and Economic Assessment of the Effects of Air Pollution on Elastomers. National Air Pollution Control Association, Contract CPA-22-69-146, Battelle Memorial Institute, Columbus, Ohio, 1970.

National Academy of Sciences, Biological Effects of Ionizing Radiation, (BEIR), vol. III, National Academy Press, Washington, DC, 1989.

_____, "Effects of Photochemical Oxidants on Materials," Ozone and Other Photochemical Oxidants, Washington, D.C., Chapter 13, p. 665.

New York Times, September 10, 1989, p. 40.

Northwest Power Planning Council, New Resources: Supply Curves and Environmental Effects, Staff Issue Paper, Portland, Oregon, February 1990.

NSIC, "Comparative Risk-Cost-Benefit Study of Alternative Sources of Electric Energy," Nuclear Safety, no. 2, March-April, 1976.

Nucleonics Week, April 25, 1985.

Office of Technology Assessment, Catching Our Breath: Next Steps for Reducing Urban Ozone, Congress of the United States, Washington, DC, August 1989.

Ozkaynak, H., and G. Thurston, "Associations Between 1980 U.S. Mortality Rates and Alternative Measures of Airborne Particle Concentration," Risk Analysis, Vol. 7, No. 4, 1987.

Pacific Gas & Electric, Least Cost Planning Treatment of Externalities, Preliminary Draft, April 1990.

Page, Arbogast, Fabian and Cieka, "Estimation of Economic Losses to the Agricultural Sector from Airborne Residuals in the Ohio River Basin Region," Journal of the Air Pollution Control Association, 32: No.2, February, 1982, p. 151.

Phalen, R., Testimony before the Subcommittee on Environmental Protection, Hearing on Health Effects of Air Pollution, Washington, D.C., 1989.

_____, Decommissioning Nuclear Power's Missing Link, Worldwatch Institute, 1986.

Radar, N. et al., "Turning Down the Heat -- Solutions to Global Warming: An Analysis of Energy Efficiency, Renewable Resources, and Other Options Versus New Nuclear Power Development," Public Citizen, Washington, D.C., September, 1988.

Rowe, R. and L. Chestnut, The Value of Visibility: Economic Theory for Air Pollution Control, Cambridge, Mass., Abt. Books, 1982.

Schneider, K., "Scientist Who Managed to 'Shock the World' on Atomic Workers' Health," New York Times, May 3, 1990.

Sharma, K., Environmental Costs and Benefits Case Study: Nuclear Power Plants -- Quantification and Economic Valuation of Selected Environmental Impacts/Effects, Nero & Associates, Inc., Portland, Ore., 1984.

Spence, J. and F. Haynie, Paint Technology and Air Pollution: Survey and Economic Assessment, EPA-AP-103, U.S.E.P.A., Research Triangle Park, N.C., 1972.

Statistical Abstract of the United States, 1989, Table 744.

Steudler, P., R. Bowden, J. Mellilo, and J. Aber, "Influence of Nitrogen Fertilization on Methane Uptake in Temperate Forest Soils," Nature, Vol. 341, September 28, 1989.

Telitsky, A., Chairperson, New York Power Pool Task Force on Environmental Externalities, letter to David R. Wolcott, May 15, 1990.

Tellus Institute (formerly Energy Systems Research Group), The Role of Hydro-Quebec Power in a Least-Cost Energy Plan for Vermont, E.S.R.G. #89-078, An analysis on behalf of the Vermont Department of Public Service for Docket #5330 before the Vermont Public Service Board, December 29, 1989.

Texas Electric Service Co. v. Helon, 546 S.W.2d 864 (Tex. Ct. App. 1977), reh.den., March 4, 1977.

Tomlinson, G., Effects of Acid Deposition on the Forests of Europe and North America, CRC Press, Boca Raton, Florida, 1990.

U.S. Department of Energy, Health and Environmental Consequences of the Chernobyl Nuclear Power Plant Accident, Washington, D.C., 1987.

U.S.E.P.A., Air Quality Criteria for Particulate Matter and Sulphur Oxides, EPA 600-8-82-029, Environmental Criteria and Assessment Office, Research Triangle Park, North Carolina, 1982.

U.S.E.P.A., Clean Air Scientific Advisory Committee, Acid Aerosol Subcommittee, minutes of public meeting, Washington, DC, June 14-15, 1988.

U.S.E.P.A., Clean Air Scientific Advisory Committee, transcript of public meeting, October 6, 1988.

Vine, E. and J. Harris, "Evaluating Energy and Non-Energy Impacts of Energy Conservation Programs: A Supply Curve Framework of Analysis," Energy, vol. 15, No. 1, 1990, pp. 11-21.

Violette, D., and L. Chestnut, Valuing Reductions in Risk: A Review of the Empirical Estimates, EPA-230-05-83-003, 1983.

Waddell, T., The Economic Damages of Air Pollution, EPA, 1974.

Wellburn, A., Air Pollution and Acid Rain, 1988.

Westman, W., and W. Conn, Quantifying Benefits of Controlling Air and Water Pollution from Energy Production and Use, Energy Resources Conservation and Development Commission, Sacramento, Calif., 1976.

Woodin, S. and U. Skiba, "Liming fails the acid test," New Scientist, March 10, 1990.

World Resources Institute, Pollution's Toll on Trees and Crops, September 1988, p. 35.

Yocom, J. "Air Pollution Damage to Buildings on the Acropolis," Journal of the Air Pollution Control Association, vol. 29, No. 4, 1979, pp. 333-338.

